From
the
Margin

Writings
in
Italian
Americana

Edited by

Anthony Julian Tamburri
Paolo A. Giordano
Fred L. Gardaphé

Purdue University Press
West Lafayette, Indiana

Printed in the United States of America

Second printing, May 1994

Design by Anita Noble

Jacket and cover painting, *Family Supper,* by Ralph Fasanella.
Reproduced by permission of the artist.

Library of Congress Cataloging-in-Publication Data
From the margin: writings in Italian Americana / edited by Anthony Julian Tamburri, Paolo A.
    Giordano, Fred L. Gardaphé.
        p. cm.
            Includes bibliographical references.
            ISBN 1-55753-007-6 (alk. paper) — ISBN 1-55753-008-4 (pbk. : alk. paper)
            1. American literature—Italian-American authors. 2. Italian Americans—Literary
    collections. I. Tamburri, Anthony Julian. II. Giordano, Paolo A. III. Gardaphé, Fred L.
    PS508.I73F76 1990
    810.8'0851073—dc20
                                                                        90-8116
                                                                        CIP

*This book is dedicated
to the memory of*

**Robert S. Pastena
(1949–1975)**

friend and colleague

Contents

Creative Works

Critical Essays

Preface

The idea for this book grew out of a few informal conversations among the three editors after the annual Twentieth-Century Literature Conference at the University of Louisville in February 1987. At that conference, we three participated in a session dedicated to Italian/American literature.[1] During the question-and-answer period, an interesting discussion developed.

At first it seemed that everyone present, the vast majority of whom were Italian Americans, were delighted with what we had done. Their numerous questions and comments stimulated further thought and analysis. Soon it became apparent, however, that not everyone appreciated our enterprise, and what followed was a discussion of a totally different tone.

This time the questions were provocative and accusatory, alleging that our exploration into the field of Italian/American literature was not at all a service to the writers we had just discussed. Indeed one individual accused us of ghettoizing these and other American writers of Italian descent. (In retrospect, we recognize a somewhat humorous irony to that situation.) In part, this volume is our response to that accusation.

Our initial idea was that we would develop further our own essays and eventually publish them in a modest-sized book. Our enthusiasm for the project, however, propelled us to seek essays other than our own as well as to include creative pieces.[2] Our primary goal was to disseminate works by and information about Italian Americans in North America. To this end, we decided at the outset to divide the anthology into two major parts: Creative Works and Critical Essays. In so doing, however, we did not intend to coordinate tightly the second part with the first. The reader will note that the theme of Italian Americana is the basic common denominator of the two parts; only two of the nine essays in the second part deal with works by authors in the first part.

The reader will note also our treatment of the phrase *Italian American*. Because of its sociocultural meaning, we three editors decided to replace the hyphen in this Preface and our Introduction with a slash when the phrase is used as an adjective. This is our way of eliminating, from an ideological standpoint, the hyphen of the "hyphenate writer."[3]

With some trepidation—that we might not find a sufficient number of interested accomplished writers—we immediately embarked upon a campaign to recruit creative writers first. To our surprise, the response to our invitation was overwhelming. We found ourselves turning away many poems and short stories of high quality because of lack of space.

Less successful was our search for essays. A quick glance at the Select Bibliography of critical studies in our volume will show that fewer than a hundred entries were published from 1980 to 1990. In one sense, such figures tell a good story: that literary and cultural scholars have begun to recognize the significance of the ethnic component in American literature, whether implicit or explicit. However, the reader will notice also that the number of scholars who have sustained a program of study in Italian Americana is indeed small. Consequently, we did experience some difficulty in acquiring never-before-published essays for our anthology.

What we subsequently decided was to dedicate the critical part of our book to three different types of essays: one type deals with notions and/or characteristics of Italian/American literature in a general sense (Robert Viscusi, Lucia Chiavola Birnbaum, and Fred L. Gardaphé); the second type is dedicated to specific writers (Franco Mulas, John Paul Russo, Anthony Julian Tamburri, Samuel J. Patti, and Paolo A. Giordano); and a third type treats film (Robert Casillo and Ben Lawton). Our decision to include essays on film stems from the fact that directors such as Francis Ford Coppola, Martin Scorsese, and Michael Cimino, to name three, have brought to the fore, each in his own way, a sense of what it means to capture artistically, and thus recapture from within, a sense of *italianità*.[4]

Our goal for both parts of the anthology has been to collect as many never-before-published pieces as possible. In fact, in the first part, approximately ninety percent of the creative works appear here for the first time; and in the second part, all of the essays appear here for the first time in their present form. We feel we have achieved our goal and are pleased.

Notes

1. We would add at this point that this session was offered under the general rubric of Italian literature. Except for a journal such as *MELUS,* it is rather difficult to find an outlet for scholarship dedicated to literature with a strong Italian/American bent. In the last two years, however, *la bella figura* appeared in 1988 and *Italian Americana* has resumed publication. Finally, until recently, it has been extremely difficult to find an advanced graduate program in Anglo-American literature that would allow candidates to dedicate their doctoral dissertation research to Italian/American literature.

2. We were already aware of Helen Barolini's then recently published *Dream Book* (1985), the nature of which (i.e., devoted to women only) left ample room for other endeavors such as ours. Barolini's book proves to be indeed historical. It is the first extensive anthology of its kind (i.e., containing both creative and critical pieces) with regard to Italian/American writers. That she dedicated her book to women only, surely places it in a category of its own. What is significant here from the perspective of gender (lest we lose the irony also) is that while Barolini's book had already gone to a paperback edition, we, approximately one and a half years later, were engaged in a discussion with Italian/Amerian males who, in their own way, were engaging in ethnic denial by refusing to recognize the presence of *italianità* in the writers we discussed that day at the conference in Louisville.

3. See Daniel Aaron, "The Hyphenate Writer and American Letters," *Smith Alumnae Quarterly* (July 1964): 213–17. For more on the replacement of the hyphen, see Anthony Julian Tamburri, "To Hyphenate or Not to Hyphenate: The Italian/American Writer and *Italianità,*" *Italian Journal* 3, no. 5:37–42.

4. We refer the reader to that part of our Introduction to this volume in which we deal briefly with the notion of *italianità*.

Acknowledgments

In putting together any book, one incurs numerous debts to others. We have incurred our share, to say the least, in compiling this anthology. We had initially decided on doing this project because of our participation in the Twentieth-Century Literature Conference in Louisville, Kentucky; therefore, to Professor Augustus Mastri and other members of the selection committee we owe a debt for their having accepted what was considered at that time an unusual session. Rosa Bellino-Giordano and Susan Gardaphé demonstrated great enthusiasm, confidence, and encouragement, as well as unlimited patience throughout the various stages of development of this project. Our respective departments at Purdue University, Rosary College, and Columbia College provided generous support in the form of secretarial help, photocopies, mailing, and telephone calls, all of which eased the burden of organizing and putting together the manuscript. Our thanks also go to the many friends and colleagues, too numerous to mention here, all over the United States, Canada, and Italy, who lent an unrelenting ear and provided much encouragement along the way. We also owe our thanks to Professor Djelal Kadir, chairman, and other members of the editorial board of Purdue University Press, as well as their anonymous readers, for having graciously accepted this manuscript. To Verna Emery, Margaret Hunt, and Anita Noble goes our appreciation for their relentless dedication to the production of this volume. Finally, we should also thank those who demonstrated skepticism at the early stages, for this, too, served us well in our venture.

Jonathan Galassi: "Conscience," "Montale's Grave," "San Francesco," and "Morning Run." Reprinted from *Morning Run* by Jonathan Galassi. Paris Review Editions, 1988. Reprinted by permission of the author.

Kenneth Gangemi: "Easter Week in Rome," "Winter Afternoon at the Museum," "Bruno the Magnificent," and "In Praise of Radio." Copyright © 1990 by Kenneth Gangemi.

Sandra M. Gilbert: "The Summer Kitchen," first published in the *Massachusetts Review* and reprinted in *Summer Kitchen* by Sandra M. Gilbert (Heyeck Press, 1983) and in *Blood Pressure* by Sandra M. Gilbert (W. W. Norton and Co., 1988); "In the Golden *Sala*," first published in *Poetry* and reprinted in *Blood Pressure* by Sandra M. Gilbert (W. W. Norton and Co., 1988).

Maria Mazziotti Gillan: "Dark on Dark," first published in *Negative Capability*; "The Young Men in Black Leather Jackets" and "Arturo," first published in *Lips*; "Betrayals," first published in *Flowers from the Tree of Night* (Chantry Press, 1980).

Dana Gioia: "Photograph of My Mother as a Young Girl," "The Garden on the *Campagna*," "The Journey, the Arrival, and the Dream," and "An Emigré in Autumn," reprinted from *Daily Horoscope* (Graywolf Press, 1986).

Daniela Gioseffi: Short Stories—"Marital Bliss." Copyright © 1988 by Daniela Gioseffi. "Rosa in Television Land." Copyright © 1989 by Daniela Gioseffi. Poems—"The Exotic Enemy." Copyright © 1988 (revised) by Daniela Gioseffi. "Cento At Dawn," "Ants and Worms," "Returning from Paradise We Stop at a Carnival," "Aperture," "The Lily Shivers." The following copyright notice refers to the five immediately preceding poems: Copyright © 1988 by Daniela Gioseffi. "As When Some Long Silenced Singer Hears Her Aria," first published in *Confrontation* (spring 1988). Copyright © 1989 (revised) by Daniela Gioseffi.

Jerry Mangione: "David on Trial." Copyright © 1989 by Jerre Mangione. All rights reserved.

Ben Morreale: *Ava Gardner's Brother-in-Law: A Word Play in Sicily.* Copyright © 1986 by Ben Morreale.

Giose Rimanelli: "Memory of Two Tuesdays." From the unpublished novel *The Trestle*. Copyright © 1987 Giose Rimanelli.

Felix Stefanile: "The Americanization of the Immigrant," first published in *Kayah*; "How I Changed My Name, Felice," first published in *A Fig Tree in America* (Elizabeth Press, 1970).

Introduction

Very few people have truly pondered the notion of Italian/American art, be it literature, film, painting or any other art form to which Americans of Italian descent have contributed. Nor have many people specifically asked, What is Italian Americana and does it exist in America? While we do not pretend to answer this question within the parameters of this Introduction, we will consider it, as well as a second question that is related, What role does the mysterious concept of *italianità* play in the creation of Italian/American art?

We would like these questions to reverberate in the ears and minds of those who read the stories, poems, plays, and essays included in this anthology. Only then, after a consideration of these and other works, and further intertextual recall, will readers be able to formulate for themselves answers to the questions.

Italian Americana: From Sideshow to Center Stage

We developed the Creative Works part of this anthology with two major goals in mind. First of all, we wanted to gather current never-before-published works by living, active writers. Then, secondly, we very consciously included a broad range of writers, from both the perspective of literary style and generation, in order to offer our readers a vast and variegated view of the Italian/American literary scene.

Except for the three writers that open and close the prose and poetry sections, we do not privilege one writer over the other in the order of appearance. Our readers will notice, however, that a short story by Jerre Mangione opens the creative prose section and a Lawrence Ferlinghetti work leads into the poetry collection. Similarly, we decided to close these two sections with works by Joseph Tusiani. (In recognition of Tusiani's distinguished career as a writer in English, Italian, and Latin, we have included works he has composed in all three languages.) These three writers, we believe, are deserving of this modest acknowledgment for their indispensable contributions to Italian, Italian/American, and American studies. Otherwise, we leave to our readers the granting of privilege or preference.

From a literary perspective, the reader will notice that the short-story writers run the gamut from the traditionally grounded artist to the divergent type of writer whose works may actually fall into the category of the noncanonical. Significantly, we do not necessarily divide the different types of writers by generation. The poignant realism of Lisa Ruffolo and Tony Ardizzone, two writers of the newer generation, can be juxtaposed with the step away from the center taken by Giose Rimanelli and Joseph Papaleo, two writers we respectfully place in the category of the elders.

1

We continue our intention to represent a vast and varied collection by our choice of poets. We believe that poetry in this anthology demonstrates how truly powerful that art is as a communicative act. The poets assembled here speak loudly and they do so in many forms and styles. Thus, our readers will notice that popular verse forms and rhythms may be followed by radical ones: Jay Parini's, Diane Raptosh's, and Felix Stefanile's verse remains formalistically tied to the canon, whereas Phyllis Capello's reveals how language can be brought to a point well beyond the expected while still exhibiting its communicative potentiality.

The theatre section in this anthology also spans the spectrum of its genre. The humor and parody in Ben Morreale's *Ava Gardner's Brother-in-Law* is well juxtaposed with Peter Carravetta's esoteric *Scoring the Digest.* Unfortunately, theatre seems to remain a hidden genre vis-à-vis Italian Americana. Only after compiling and completing our anthology did we come to know of other playwrights. Indeed meritorious, they will become the subject of our future investigation in another forum.

Our readers will doubtless enjoy the creative works in this anthology precisely for what they are: high quality literary pieces worthy of dissemination regardless of any subgenre into which we might decide to place them. For us, however, they are excellent representative works of American writers whose work is informed by *italianità.*

When we began to compile the Critical Essays part of this anthology, we realized how little critical work had been done on Italian/American literature prior to or early in the 1980s. One of the few scholars who had given critical thought to Italian/Americana with regard to literature is Rose Basile Green. In her *The Italian-American Novel: A Document of the Interaction of Two Cultures,* she bridges an initial major gap between Italian/American narrative and the dominant group's notion of American literature.[1] Basile Green engages in a chronological analysis of Italian/American narrative indicating the aesthetic and social values inherent in the novels she includes in her study.

William Boelhower is another scholar who made an early major critical contribution to the study of Italian/American literature. In his 1981 essay, "Immigrant Novel as Genre," Boelhower focuses on the literature from the perspective of sign production.[2] In 1984, he published his *Through a Glass Darkly: Ethnic Semiosis in American Literature.* In this book, Boelhower establishes the ethnic signs as "above all an interpretation relation, a putting into relation, and not a series of semantic correspondences."[3]

Robert Viscusi is also one of the few who had previously explored such a notion.[4] His contribution to our volume furthers such theoretical discussion. For Viscusi, allegory, as the "method that literature offers to deal with the cultural dissonance produced by historical process," is a "communal work of art" through which a literature will eventually "define its own history." Surely, this is the case with the American writer of Italian descent, who for many decades in this country spoke "in *other* terms" (emphasis added), that is, *allegorically.*[5] Surely, the American writer of Italian descent, as well as other ethnics who created art, did so from the perspective of *other.* This notion of *other* is indeed the point of departure for Viscusi's discourse.

In a similiar vein, Lucia Chiavola Birnbaum offers a provocative view of the origins of an eventual Italian canon for Italian/American culture. She sees the culture of most Italians and Americans of Italian descent in this country steeped in the folklore literature of the Italian peasants, especially those from the south. Here, too, one must speak in terms of *other*. For Birnbaum, such folklore looks through the lens of the emarginated: namely, the poor, the politically oppressed, the woman.[6]

Dealing more specifically with the theme of orality and Italian/American writing, Fred L. Gardaphé's essay ties in well with both Viscusi's and Birnbaum's. In viewing "Italian/American literature as an extension of [the] oral tradition," in seeing its roots (or a good amount thereof) in the tradition of the *cantastorie,* he too considers the new culture steeped in the southern Italian folklore. According to Gardaphé, the autobiographical bent of early Italian/American writing especially represents the energy and early forms of the *allegory* that such a literature and/or culture, in Viscusi's terms, would develop in its quest for self-preservation.

Each of the remaining essays on literature deals with a specific author and, in some cases, a specific work. While approaches to the subject matter may differ, these essays individually treat to one degree or another the notions and ideas presented in the essays just mentioned. Franco Mulas, Samuel Patti, and Paolo A. Giordano deal with three figures—two fiction writers (John Fante and Pietro Di Donato) and a poet (Joseph Tusiani)—whose work in one form or another may now be considered *classics* of Italian/American writing. The works of these three writers are heavily imbued with their Italian heritage. Their works celebrate their ethnicity and cultural origin as they weave tales and create verses which tell of the trials and tribulations of the Italian immigrants and their children.

In their respective essays, Patti and Mulas show how Fante and Di Donato confronted both the ethnic dilemma and the writer's task of communicating this dilemma in narrative form. Taking another perspective, as Giordano points out, Tusiani invites his reader through the medium of poetry to understand better the "cynical and somber awareness of what it means to be an immigrant" and to experience the "alienation and realization that the new world is not the 'land of hospitality' he/she believed it was." So that, be it the novelist Di Donato or the short-story writer Fante, Tusiani's "riddle of [his] day" figures indeed as the riddle of many of his generation. It continues to sound a familiar chord for those of subsequent generations: "Two languages, two lands, perhaps two souls... / Am I a man or two strange halves of one?" ("Song of the Bicentennial (V)," *Gente Mia*).

In a cultural-literary sense, it is clear that these and other writers of their generation belong to what Daniel Aaron considers stage one of the *hyphenate writer.*[7] This writer not only questions his/her origins, but is indeed bent on disproving the suspicions and prejudices of the dominant culture. Fante, Di Donato, and Tusiani, as also their confreres, all examined their status in the New World and, insofar as possible, presented a positive image of the Italian in America.[8]

John Paul Russo and Anthony Julian Tamburri, on the other hand, discuss writers who have securely passed from the first to the second stage of hyphenation. While it is true that both writers, Gilbert Sorrentino and Helen Barolini, have dealt with their cultural heritage in their work, each has done so differently from the other as well as from those who had preceded them. No longer feeling the urge to please the dominant culture, both writers adopted the thematics of *italianità* insofar as it coincided with their personal development as writers. As we shall see in Russo's essay, Sorrentino does attempt to fuse his inherited immigrant culture with his artistic concern. Yet, references to Italian/American culture are infrequent throughout his *opus*. In his own works, Sorrentino surely "knew the reality of [his] generation that had to be written,"[9] as he too contributed to this cultural and literary chronicle. He took one step further, however, and dropped the hyphen. While he was keenly aware of the American literary tradition behind him, Sorrentino appropriated yet another form of emargination; with the likes of Jack Kerouac and Lawrence Ferlinghetti as immediate predecessors, Sorrentino chose the poetics of late Modernism over mainstream literary America.[10]

To be sure, Barolini's *Umbertina* could not be more Italian/American. The author of a novel which spans four generations of an Italian/American family, she is undoubtedly acutely aware of her ethnicity and hyphenation. In Tamburri's essay, however, it becomes clear that Barolini has gone one step further than her sister writers who preceded her. She combines her historical awareness of the Italian's and Italian American's plight with her own strong sense of feminism, and ultimately the reader becomes aware of what it meant to be not just an Italian American but indeed an Italian/American woman.[11]

Finally, the two essays on film deal with notions and concepts of the Italian American similar to what one finds in the literary field. Indeed, it is the close intertextual rapport between these two media, the written word and the silver screen, that prompted us to include essays on film in the second part of our anthology. Robert Casillo approaches the topic of Italian/American cinema from two different perspectives. From a historical viewpoint, he examines the popular image of Italy and the Italian American in films from the 1930s to the 1960s. In the second half of his essay, with this conventional Hollywood—that is, not necessarily Italian/American—image as a point of comparison, Casillo goes on to discuss the Italian/American director and his representation of the image of the Italian American.

Ben Lawton's essay examines the notion of the American dream and how it is depicted by Italian/American filmmakers. Lawton states that Italian/American directors ultimately consider the notion of the American dream as a "lie, a trick, and a deception." While he articulates his discourse at the outset in general terms and with multiple references, he soon moves to the films of Michael Cimino as an example of his central idea. Lawton also brings to the fore another important point: the Italian American's familiarity with his cultural heritage. In this essay, it becomes clear that Cimino, like many second-, third-, and fourth-generation Italian Americans, knows well his immediate Italian/American milieu. What he does not seem to know well is his ancestors' Italian heritage: their rural and parochial culture of southern Italy.

Italianità in American Letters: A Manifesto

Some of us come from Italy. Many of us come from Little Italys. All of us have made a voyage from a known to an unknown world. We have moved from an explicit to implicit ethnicity, and the works of the writers in this volume present variations of a worldview colored by *italianità*. Their work deals with generational differences, the conflicts of expectations and realizations, and the movement from alienation to assimilation, from the margin to the mainstream.

The Writer as Cultural Immigrant. When our immigrant ancestors left Italy, they founded Little Italys. When we leave our families and our Little Italys, we embark on a journey into American culture, the dominant culture.[12] The first thing we must do is explain ourselves to others because it is we, the *other,* who have lived on the margin. "Where do you come from?" "What kind of name is yours?" "What do you eat?" "Where do you live?" These are only some of the questions we are expected to answer. And, indeed, when we begin to respond to these questions, we take on characteristics of the *cantastorie,* the history singers who explain the quality of our life that includes the past of our people.

The first generation traveled to find work and to create a better life. The second and third generations travel to establish their place in the American culture and to share their notions and ideas with the American mind. Many of the writers in this anthology believe enough in their heritage to strengthen it by learning the language, culture, and history that their ancestors have carried to the cemetery. They share the same goal: to find a life on earth for the dead who have given life to us. As Tusiani put it, "For this, my life, their deaths made ample room" ("Song of the Bicentennial").

It is up to the writers to carry those immigrants where they have not been and where they could not enter and to enable them to see what they had not seen. We write the story the illiterate told and lived but was never able to write. To paraphrase Ferlinghetti's poem, old Italians are dying, and what their lives meant we can find in this antholgy: voices of the past, the present, and the future. Through our writing, we enable the past to live, to breathe, and to contribute its life experiences to this thing we call culture. Indeed, the past speaks through the writer.

The writers here are just a sampling of the rich and variegated Italian/American experience. Some weave *italianità* into their work with obvious connections to their ethnicity. Others create their work with only the most subtle hints of their ethnic background. In either case, they speak of an experience that is common to all, that of being cultural immigrants.

The Recovery of *italianità*. In an interview with *Fra Noi* (April 1987), poet and novelist Jay Parini revealed that his second fictional effort, *The Patch Boys,* was a novel of recovery. In it he has been able to use the Italian elements of his upbringing to tell a story, and in so doing, he was able to regain aspects of his heritage that, for the most part, had been previously ignored or untapped. Parini's recovery of *italianità* is indeed indicative of the sentiment and spirit of today's younger Italian/American writers such as

Tony Ardizzone, Kenny Marotta, Lisa Ruffolo, Diane Raptosh, and Dana Gioia, to mention a few.

What is this *italianità* that these and other writers are interested in recovering? What lies at the base of their need or desire for such a recovery? *Italianità* is indeed a term expressive of many notions, ideas, feelings, and sentiments. To be sure, it is any and all of these things that lead young Italian Americans back to their real and mythical images of the land, the way of life, the values, and the cultural trappings of their ancestors. It could be language, food, a way of determining life values, a familial structure, a sense of religion; it could be all of these and certainly much more. Undoubtedly, a polysemic term such as *italianità* evades a precise definition. We believe, however, that such a cultural concept is possible to perceive and ultimately interpret through the evidence found in the creative writings included in the first part of our volume.

Many of the Italians who immigrated to the United States did so soon after the geopolitical unification of Italy. Thus, they left—many indeed coming from an economically depressed southern Italy—during a period in which the notion of *italianità* was just beginning to develop as a national identity. In fact, most of what we know about those early immigrants leads us to believe that they identified themselves more with their hometown or region rather than with Italy as a country. Thus, what we refer to today as *italianità* would have been called, only a few generations earlier, *abruzzese*, *calabrese*, or *molisano*. Through assimilation, such regional association has given way to national identification.

Though regional identification is still possible even in third- and fourth-generation Italian Americans, the tendency is to relate to each other first as Italian Americans. This established Italian/American identity is composed of the qualities which separate us from Americans of other ethnic backgrounds. If we can isolate these characteristics, then we can identify the ingredients of *italianità*, and ultimately we can construct a basis for establishing a distinct Italian/American culture.

The Trouble with *italianità*. American writers of Italian descent have contributed greatly to the establishment of an Italian identity in America, yet few have been able to avoid being relegated to the category of *ethnic* writers as opposed to being considered part of the larger, dominant group we call American writers. Many have even avoided direct association with their ethnic heritage. This avoidance is sometimes preferred precisely because too often the literary contribution of American writers of Italian descent has been channeled onto an ethnic side street of American literature. Such *ghettoizing* is characterized by an incident recounted by the late John Ciardi. He once published a poem in the *Atlantic Monthly* about Italy and Mussolini. The late poet and critic Robert Lowell acknowledged the poem as, according to Ciardi,

> the best Italian American poem he had ever seen. And I thought, "Does this son of a bitch think he is more American than I am." Where does he think I was brought up? Because my name is Ciardi, he decided to hyphenate the poem. Had it been a Yankee name, he would have thought,

"Ah, a scholar who knows about Italy." Sure he made assumptions, but I can't grant for a minute that Lowell is any more American than I am.[13]

To be sure, Ciardi's complaint is one which echoes throughout the careers of most American writers of Italian descent. Perhaps what Lowell and other critics found in the writings of many Italian Americans such as Ciardi was their feeling of *italianità*—the writer's notion of self which earlier critics had trouble perceiving or accepting as something which could be American.

Italianità **Demands Identity.** Because they were identified as foreigners, be it due to their dress, food, native language, or accented English, first- and second-generation Italian Americans suffered misinterpretation and prejudice. These early generations, the ones from which our first writers emerged, had a closer connection to and thus a stronger identification with *italianità*. The results of such a bond were not always constructive; for instance, those who did not possess the emotional strength to defend their cultural heritage disguised it with new names, new fashions, or other assimilative techniques.

Very often, one's *italianità* became something that prohibited entrance into the American cultural mainstream. Early in their American education, many Italian Americans were taught that their ethnicity was worthless. Leonard Covello, an educator and early promoter of Italian culture in the United States (who with the help of novelist Guido D'Agostino wrote his memoirs *The Heart Is the Teacher*), recalls this experience in the American school:

> During this period [1900s], the Italian language was completely ignored. In fact, throughout my whole elementary school career, I do not recall one mention of Italy or the Italian language or what famous Italians had done in the world with the possible exception of Columbus, who was pretty popular in America. We soon got the idea that Italian meant something inferior, and a barrier was erected between children of Italian origin and their parents. This was the accepted process of Americanization. We were becoming Americans by learning how to be ashamed of our parents.[14]

In part, Covello's words explain why so many first- and second-generation Italian Americans found economic paths and the more popular cultural avenues (sports and entertainment) easier to travel on their journey to becoming American. These choices afforded them success without strong identification with what was considered a non-American way of life. Very few of these immigrants or their children ventured into the field of letters; and those who did were treated as cultural immigrants, just as their parents had become immigrants of economy.

Pioneers of *italianità*. The earliest American writers of Italian descent became, in essence, pioneers of Italian/American self-discovery, -definition, and -declamation. Their writing depicted the struggles, the dreams, the nightmares, and the reality of what it meant to be an American of Italian descent. Not by choice, most of them were restricted to life in Little Italys, and, thus, their writing began with anecdotal accounts of the joys and sorrows—the reality of life—in these immigrant enclaves. These experiences created a number of obstacles that challenged the writing abilities of early Italian/American authors. First, there was the need to establish enough economic security to enable the development of a writing discipline: though not impossible, it was indeed difficult for them to concentrate on their writing when they had to struggle to secure life's necessities. Second, there was the need to acquire the requisite tools of the writer. Those whose first language was Italian needed to master English before they could even consider the possibility of contributing to American literature. This meant attending American schools, reading American literature, and developing an American identity.

Those writers who managed to overcome these first two obstacles still faced a third and more difficult one: the need to enter the publishing world in order to gain access to the American audience. The writers who were able to meet all three of these requirements were few in number, and, yet, their efforts have given us a body of writing we may now consider classic of *italianità* in America. Some of the writers of Italian descent whose works have endured the test of time are John Fante, Pietro Di Donato, Jerre Mangione, and Joseph Tusiani.[15] And while it is true that these and others were earlier singled out because of their peculiarities, they are writers whose works, according to Giose Rimanelli, "endure the reflex of time or impose themselves on new generations."[16] Evidence to Rimanelli's statement is that their works not only remain in print but indeed are also the subjects of scholarly inquiries.

Only in retrospect can we identify the works of these authors as classics. And it is precisely upon this recently established classical basis that a great body of American literature, imbued to a significant degree with *italianità*, has begun to take form and also distinguish itself as a literature which can no longer be relegated to the side streets of American literature.

In an interview with *Fra Noi* (September 1986), Helen Barolini offered the following explanation as to why Italian/American literature has not fared better in this country:

> The greatest Italian American literary piece is still *Christ in Concrete*. And perhaps as a female counterpart, the illiterate Rosa Cassettari's story which was written down as oral history by Marie Hall Ets. Both these narratives are autobiographical, although Di Donato's is couched in fictional form. But both leave the brute strength of experience, and it is this experiential mode that denotes both our richness and our burden. It is as though style and linguistic daring are still being sacrificed to the white heat of telling our story...only when our history—our story, if you will—has been transcended will we come into our own stylistically and be open to some greater experimentation of theme and style.

Transcending the history in order to present the story is an approach that has been practiced and realized by the third generation of Italian/American writers, the best of whom have met the challenge of experimenting with technique and style and in so doing have carried *italianità* to new heights.

As a writer whose education came more from the streets of America than its schools, Di Donato is aware both of his generation's limitations and of the potential for future generations of Italian Americans to create masterpieces of American art. In a 1978 lecture at the University of Illinois at Chicago, Di Donato spoke of this difference:

> The Tony Macaroni writers are shot. This new breed of writers must know the highest standards. They must become aristocrats of the soul. It is coming now, the renaissance. Our time is now. I see it because you are no longer "figli dei muratori." You go to school and you are children with brains. The true artist is a true seeker, a person with a mind of his own, and you must remember that real education is truth.

For the most part, the early Italian/American writers were dealing with contemporary subjects and themes which were based on autobiographical reflections of life in America. As we examine the later writers, the children and grandchildren of immigrants, we enter a period in which the immigrant past is examined, not through self-reflection but through a more distant, historical perspective resulting in the re-creation of the immigrant experience in America through more distant and often more mythical, fictional forms.

As Italian Americans have assimilated via educational institutions, intermarriages, and other adaptive paths, there has been a shift in the focus of their work, a tilt in their angle of reflection, so that their fiction becomes less a vehicle for presenting what it means to be Italian in America and more of what it means to carry the cultural trappings of *italianità* into their everyday American lives. This recovery of *italianità* has become a theme addressed by many of today's American writers of Italian descent. For these writers, *italianità* is an inheritance—one that is better invested than squandered. From John Fante to Jay Parini, from Rosa Cassettari to Diane di Prima, *italianità* has set strong roots in American literature. Though the nature of its presence has changed, as has the Italian experience in America, *italianità* has established itself as an essential element in American storytelling and verse writing.

Only now can we look back and recognize the existence of a tradition of Italian/American writing within American literature. In dealing with *italianità*, each writer picks up something different as she/he may perceive and interpret his/her cultural heritage filtered through personal experiences. Yet, there resounds a familiar ring, an echo that connects them all.

Indeed, today more than ever before, a collective consciousness of *italianità* is well formed and maintained. Italian/American authors, especially with the onset of the newer generation, now meet, come to know, and support each other's literary and cultural endeavors.[17] Even Italian/American organizations, once established for "*mutuo soccorso*" and economic survival of *paesani* and their families, are shifting their focus from life insurance to artistic support. The Sons of Italy and the National Italian American Foundation are just two of the many organizations offering college scholarships. Amerital UNICO has paved the way for recognition of the artistic achievement of Italian American writers by sponsoring annual national literary contests that have enabled young Italian/American writers to find both acceptance from and support in an audience of their people.

Italian/American writers have slowly but surely built their niche in the body of American literature. Collectively their work can be viewed as a written expression par excellence of Italian/American culture; individually they have enabled American literature to ring with *italianità*, thus bringing to the fore another voice of the great sociocultural mosaic that we may call Americana. We can rightfully expect, as Birnbaum would agree in her provocative essay in the second part of our anthology, that as long as there is an Italy, as long as there is a memory flavored with *italianità*, there will be the American writer of Italian descent whose contribution to American letters adds new dimensions to what it means to be American.

Finally, with what is found in the following pages, we respond to our initial question, What is Italian Americana and does it exist in America? It is our readers' task to reconcile the textual offerings in this book with their cultural reservoir of knowledge. In this manner, they should succeed, we believe, in bringing closer together, as Viscusi states, "that large intersection of scripture and interpretation which goes by the name *allegoresis*." Thus, in this manner, they are ultimately one step closer to perceiving the "cultural dissonance produced by historical process."

Notes

1. Madison, N.J.: Fairleigh Dickinson University Press, 1974.

2. *MELUS* 8:1 (1981); 3-14.

3. Venice, Italy: Edizioni Helvitia, 1984; Oxford: Oxford University Press, 1987.

4. We refer the reader to our bibliography.

5. In an etymological sense, *allegory* means, in fact, to "speak in *other* terms" (emphasis added). (See *Webster's Ninth New Collegiate Dictionary*.)

6. Both Viscusi and Birnbaum speak to the plight of the southern Italian at one point in their respective essays. Surely, one would be hard-pressed to find another more emarginated and oppressed group that emigrated from Italy.

7. Referring to the writer, Aaron says, "...the dropping of the hyphen does not completely eliminate his marginal perspective. He has detached himself, to be sure, from one cultural environment without becoming a completely naturalized member of the official environment. It is not so much that he retains a divided allegiance but that as a writer, if not necessarily as a private citizen, he has transcended a mere parochial allegiance and can now operate freely in the republic of the spirit" ("The Hyphenate Writer and American Letters, *Smith Alumnae Quarterly* [July 1964]: 213-17).

8. Ten years later Rose Basile Green spoke to a similar phenomenon with specific regard to the history of Italian/American narrative when she discussed her four stages of development. She classified them in the following manner: (1) "the need for assimilation," (2) "revulsion," (3) "counterrevulsion," and (4) "rooting." See *The Italian-American Novel: A Document of the Interaction of Two Cultures*, especially chapts. 4-7.

9. *Vort* 2 (1974): 19. We owe this quote to John Paul Russo, "The Poetics of Gilbert Sorrentino," *Rivista di studi anglo-americani* 3 (1984-85): 281-303.

10. For more on Sorrentino's poetics, see Russo's "The Poetics of Gilbert Sorrentino."

11. In a later novel, *Love in the Middle Ages*, the subject matter is much more universal insofar as ethnicity and cultural origin are backdrops to a love story involving a middle-aged couple.

12. This notion of *cultural immigrant* was conceived by Fred L. Gardaphé and presented in the paper "The Recovery of *italianità*" at the June 1987 conference, Molise-America: Emigration and Southern Italy. Publication of this paper is forthcoming in 1990.

13. See Linda Caetura, ed., *Growing Up Italian* (New York: Morrow and Co., 1986), 150.

14. Leonard Covello with Guido D'Agostino, *The Heart Is the Teacher* (New York: McGraw-Hill, 1958), 43.

15. We would point out that in these early years there were very few women who engaged in creative writing. As opposed to the figure of the woman writer of the dominant culture, work on the figure of the female Italian/American writer has yet to be greatly explored. To date, to name a few, one may consult Betty Boyd Caroli, Robert F. Harney, and Lydio F. Tomasi, eds. *The Italian Immigrant Woman in North America* (Toronto: The Multicultural History Society in Ontario, 1978) and Helen Barolini, ed., "Introduction," *The Dream Book: An Anthology of Writings by Italian American Women* (New York: Schocken, 1985).

16. "Introduction," *Modern Canadian Studies* (Toronto: Reyerson Press, 1966): xiii.

17. While our project is limited to literature and film, one should not forget the accomplishments of the painters, sculptors, and musicians. Ralph Fasanella, for example, has been actively painting for decades. Robert Buono, on the other hand, a younger painter from Chicago, recently gained nationwide prominence for his *Murphy's Dream Vision*, an autobiographical portrait of three Vietnam soldiers.

Creative Works

David On Trial

After several days of storming, the sea was calm again. Puffy white clouds lounged against an innocent sky, and a triumphant sun glared down on the *Vandalla*, Philadelphia bound with some four hundred men, women, and children from the displaced persons camps of Europe.

The children were the first to recover from the storm. Breakfast was hardly over when they began to congregate on the top deck of the ship. After being confined so long, they rose to the occasion with enthusiasm, releasing their pent-up energy in a happy torrent of play. Now and then one of the adults would climb the stairs to investigate the noise and laughter but would soon come down again, overwhelmed by the contrast between his world and the children's.

Despite the differences in their languages and ages, the children played together as a group. Their leader was Artur Mikorska, a gangling thirteen-year-old Pole, who knew several languages and could converse with any of the children. Nearly always it was Artur who decided what game would be played and what rules would be followed. Attracted by his greater size, his zest, and his adventurous past, none of the children ever disputed his leadership. Some of the boys his age may have resented his arrogance, but they feared Artur's fists, which he did not hesitate to use to emphasize his wishes. A few of the younger children, like David Springer, who was only nine, admired Artur unreservedly and enjoyed being led by him.

To David, who was an orphan, the Polish boy was like a cinema hero. He knew by heart the stories Artur had told him of his experiences as a member of the Polish underground, his capture by the enemy, and his subsequent escape from a labor camp through territory thick with soldiers. Artur's life seemed much more exciting than his own; he wished he could grow up to be as big and strong and have as many adventures.

The children were playing hide-and-go-seek when Artur called a halt to the game and announced that he had thought up a better one. He described it as a "drama." Did they know what it was? Some said it was like a cinema, others said it was something acted out by marionettes, and a few children who had attended performances at legitimate theatres knew exactly what was meant. Artur said that his "drama" was better than anything they had ever seen because it was based on something he had actually witnessed when he was a member of the Polish underground: the trial of a German spy.

Artur's suggestion met with loud approval. Although some of the children were too young to know what a trial was, they all understood the connotation of "German spy."

"May I be the judge?" one of the older boys asked.

"No, I shall be the judge," Artur said. He then proceeded to choose the other members of the court: two lawyers, "one to prosecute and the other to defend"; six guards; and one clerk. The rest of the children were made members of the jury and told that they would be the ones to decide on the prisoner's fate.

"Now I must choose someone to be the German spy," Artur said.

No one seemed willing to play the part. Afraid that Artur might select him, David Springer tried to hide behind a larger boy. But Arthur noticed him anyway.

"You will be the spy," he announced. "You will be the German spy who is captured by the underground."

David feebly protested that he didn't want the role: he hated all German spies. To this Artur replied that if he didn't take the part, he would never be allowed to play with them again. "Besides," he added, "you are German and a German should play the part...what's the matter? Are you afraid?"

David's foster sister, Herta, sensing his fright, suggested they abandon the game. Ashamed of her intervention, he pushed her away. "No," he said, "I am not afraid."

"Very well," Artur said. "Come forward, prisoner. And face the judge."

"What is your name, prisoner?" asked Artur, affecting a deep voice.

"David Springer."

"That doesn't sound right," Artur said. "We'll have to give you another name." He thought for a moment, then told the clerk that the prisoner's name would be Captain Goering.

"Tell us your name again, prisoner."

"David—I mean Captain Goering."

Artur regarded him severely. "Captain Goering, you are accused of the crime of being in the pay of the Gestapo. Are you guilty or not guilty?"

"I don't know," David answered meekly.

Artur was disgusted. "You are guilty. Do you understand?"

"Yes."

"Don't just say 'yes.' Say 'yes, your honor'—now say it." The children snickered.

"Quiet in the courtroom," Artur shouted. He turned to David again. "Speak up, Captain Goering. What did I tell you to say?"

"I forget," David whimpered.

"This will teach you not to forget," Artur said fiercely, and he slapped the boy on the face. "Now say it—'Yes, your honor.'" David began to cry instead.

"If you don't say it," Artur threatened, "I am going to slap you again."

"Yes, your honor," David mumbled through his tears.

The questioning went on in this fashion, with Artur continuing to force answers out of David. He slapped the boy again when he thought he was too slow. David cringed in fear and bewilderment, trembling under the impact of the sobs he was trying hard to suppress. Only Herta screamed out in protest when he was slapped the second time, but it did no good. At Artur's command, one of the guards warned her that if she interrupted the trial once more they would put her out of the courtroom.

The rest of the children, incited by the dramatic inflections in Artur's voice and even more by David's discomfort, found the game engrossing. The more abusive Artur became the keener was their pleasure. In their imaginations David and the German Gestapo became interchangeable villains. Every sign of fear that David showed meant one more victory for their side.

Artur continued to monopolize the game. At one point the boy who had been appointed prosecutor came forward and said it was his turn to play, but the judge informed him that if he did not keep still someone else would be chosen to take his place, and two or three of the children applauded the decision.

Following this interruption, Artur turned to the jury and announced that he was now ready to summarize all the "terrible crimes" the prisoner had committed. David, taking advantage of this brief respite, made a dash for the stairs but was quicky seized by some of the guards and returned to Artur.

"This is for trying to escape..." and Artur slapped David's face again.

"Ladies and gentleman," Artur began exultantly, "you yourselves can see how guilty the prisoner is. If he were innocent, he would not try to run away..."

In his summary to the jury, he accused the prisoner of delivering them into the hands of the Gestapo, of torturing allied prisoners, and, finally, "of murdering that courageous member of the Polish underground, Wladyslaw Mikorska, my father."

The more David wilted and wept under his abuse, the fiercer Artur became in his denunciation, at one point becoming so carried away by his sense of drama that he spat into the prisoner's face. It was difficult to tell whom he hated more, David or the Nazis. But the children, fascinated by his eloquence and his gestures, and excited by the destructive effect his harangue was having on David, were in no mood to think of such distinctions. They were having a fine time; that is, all but Herta, who was now crying as openly as David.

Artur wound up his speech by declaring that death was the only penalty fit for enemies. "Shall we throw the prisoner into the ocean or shall we hang him?" he shouted to the jury, and he uttered the word "hang" with such relish that the children knew which he preferred. "Hang him!" they yelled. "Seize the prisoner," Artur commanded, and the guards and lawyers enthusiastically fell on David and pinned his arms behind his back. David offered no resistance; the ordeal of being abused in public by the hero he had worshipped was too much for him; in his numbness he could only cry and wonder what criminal thing he had done that made Artur and everyone else turn against him. Was he, perhaps, a German spy, without realizing it? He had stopped believing it was all a game; there was nothing make-believe about this. They had pretended it was all going to be a game, but all along they must have known what they intended to do with him: he must be a German spy; otherwise, why would they be treating him this way? He looked about him desperately searching for friendly faces. He saw only one: Herta's, and hers was also covered with tears. All the other faces were dry and bright.

When he saw a boy approaching with a rope, David cried out, "Please, I do not wish to hang..." The words were hardly out of his mouth when one of the guards struck him across the mouth, another pinched him on the arm, and he heard Artur roaring, "Shut up!"

The boy handed the rope to Artur. Two or three of the children became frightened at this point and quietly left. The rest clustered around Artur to see what he would do with the rope. Grinning at the eager faces around him, he borrowed a jackknife from one of the boys and cut the rope in two. With one piece he carefully bound David's wrists behind his back. He made a noose with the other piece and looped it over David's neck.

"This is what we do with all the traitors in Poland," he explained to his audience.

Herta could stand no more. With a wild cry, she tore away from the children and dashed downstairs to the lower deck. Blinded with tears, she tripped and fell on the last step. Before any of the passengers could reach her, she picked herself up and ran down the deck until she came to the chairs on which her parents were stretched out. Sobbing violently, she threw herself into her father's arms and burrowed her head into his shoulder.

For a few moments, they could get no word out of her. "Something terrible must have happened. She never cries like this," her mother said.

"What is it Herta?" Stefan asked, brushing away her tears. "Tell your father what is wrong." But she kept on crying, louder than before.

"Did David hurt you, Herta?"

"No," she wailed. "They...they are choking David."

"Who, Herta? Who is choking him?"

"Artur and the others. Artur says David is a German spy."

Stefan held her face between his hands and smiled at her. "Don't cry, *Liebling*. Artur wouldn't hurt David...you mustn't believe everything he says."

"It's true, Papa. It's true," she shouted, breaking into tears again.

"Stefan, there must be something wrong," his wife insisted.

Stefan got out of his chair and took hold of Herta's hand. "Let's go find David. Show me where he is."

As he climbed the stairway with Herta in his arms, Stefan began to worry; he heard none of the noises and laughter of the children playing together.

"Are you certain they were playing up here, Herta?"

Herta nodded and wound her arms around him more tightly.

Just before he reached the top of the stairway, he heard the voice of a young boy shout, "It is Herta's father!" The next instant there was the sound of running toward the opposite end of the deck.

There were no children in sight when he reached the top. He called David's name several times but got no response.

"Exactly where were you playing, Herta?"

She pointed to an area around the middle of the deck. There he found David behind a parapet. The boy was seated on the deck with his bound ankles stuck out in front of him. There was a gag around his mouth; from his neck dangled a rope. While he was removing the rope, David's eyes opened slowly. They were like the eyes of a dog that has just been beaten.

"Oh, God, please God, let him be all right," Stefan prayed while he removed the gag and bindings. There were raw bruises on his ankles and wrists, and the rope had left a pink welt around his neck. In a hasty examination Stefan could find nothing else that was physically wrong with him.

He took the boy up in his arms and gently kissed him. "David, are you hurt?" he asked anxiously.

The boy said nothing.

"Is your neck all right, David? Bend it so that I can see."

He did not seem to be listening; Stefan had the impression he did not recognize him.

"Look, David, here is Herta."

When he saw her, the muscles in his face twitched as if he were about to cry but no tears came.

"Cry, David, cry," Stefan wanted to say. "Your hurt is like a poison; let it out of your heart...cry now, David, or you may never be able to trust anyone again, not even those you love and want to trust."

Instead he said, "David, Herta, listen to me. What happened was bad, but it was intended as a game. Artur forgot himself and should be punished, but, remember, it was only a game. Artur did not realize what he was doing. Do you understand?"

The children looked at him but said nothing.

"Go ahead and cry, David, if you wish," he urged. "Herta and I won't mind. Will we, Herta?"

"No, Papa."

But David did not cry.

Rosa in Television Land

Rosa, a pear-shaped woman who faintly resembles an aging Sophia Loren, limps peacefully through Brooklyn's Red Hook section past the groceries or fruit stands of her usual route along Smith Street. She has no idea of the peculiar events that await her. Trucks are unloaded by denim-clad workers as wooden crates filled with fruits and boxes of canned goods roll noisily down unloading ramps, aluminum wheels purring in the morning bustle. Groggy-faced children gambol toward a red brick public school which Rosa Della Rosa passes precisely at eight o'clock every weekday morning of her life. Rosa holds her head a little higher as she walks past the school, knowing that she was never able to attend it.

A schoolboy, just ahead of Rosa, stops to pick up a delinquent grapefruit which has rolled from a broken crate onto the sidewalk. He aims it at the seat of his schoolmate's pants. As the boys scurry into the schoolyard, Rosa bends down into the gutter to rescue the fruit and deposit it in her string shopping bag. "Only trees should throw fruit to the ground!" she exclaims softly, repeating an adage her mother learned long ago in southern Italy, where the wasting of food was considered a sin against the earth. Rosa, by her act of salvage, hopes to redeem the schoolboy's soul from his naive prank, as well as have a nice piece of citrus for her breakfast.

As she stands, Rosa pats the bun at the back of her neck, which is held with a large Florentine hairpin her mother brought long ago from the Old Country. She winds her long grey hair in the same way every morning and secures it exactly as her mother did her own. Not a strand is out of place. Her sturdy black oxford heels serve her well as she boards the bus at the corner of Atlantic Avenue. She smooths her black dress and coat into place as she slides her seventy-eight-year-old body into the seat behind the driver— just as she has for over twenty-five years. Retirement has never once occurred to her. Her birth certificate was lost long ago in Italy. She simply pretends with the help of a worn baptismal certificate, that she's under retirement age. Since she works efficiently enough, the factory manager has never bothered to check into it. To the few faint hairs that grow on her chin, she pays no mind. Girlish vanities and dreams of romance have long ago faded with her fading irises.

"Rosa, you look beautiful and happy today! What's the spark in your eyes?" asks the bus driver who's seen Rosa board his bus every work day for the past ten years, from 1966, when he began working his morning route, to 1976.

"*Niente*. Nothing at all. I looka da same as yesterday. Dis dress is just like de other one. I wash one; wear one. Wash one; wear the other! Why do you joke? I found a good grapefruit for breakfast, so I smile more. But, it's a nice day, *sì*?

"*Sì*. Sunny as Italy!" The driver, an African-American, agrees.

"No, nowhere is sunny as Italia!" Rosa smiles and laughs, "except Africa. *Sì?* But almosta!"

Rosa disembarks from the crowded bus full of screaming high school students and enters a small factory where she takes the elevator to the third floor, removes her coat, and sits as she always does, every weekday morning of her life, at the end of a long conveyor belt which carries tiny boxes, row upon row, past her inspection. It's Rosa's job to make sure that each box contains exactly eight pieces of candy-coated laxative gum. Then, she takes lid after lid in her right hand, clamps it down with her left, and transfers the closed box to another conveyor beside her where it passes along to be automatically sealed in cellophane.

Rosa Della Rosa has worked in the chocolate laxative factory on Atlantic Avenue since her husband died thirty years ago. She never considers staying home and collecting social security, as it would be shameful to take government funds. Financial help can only be accepted from *la famiglia*, and the only family Rosa has left is her ailing older sister, Helena, for whom she cares. She was unable to have children with her husband, and now, all her family is dead except for Helena, feeble and bedridden, with whom she lives in an old Red Hook tenement apartment. Rosa's father declared long ago that any man who would have so little pride as to accept welfare is "a lazy bum." Rosa never managed to make the distinctions between hard-earned social security and welfare or charity.

She lives in a world of simple infinitives where the answer to the mystery of life is: to wake to work to sleep to see to say to drink to eat to walk to go and to come, to be born and to die. She speaks only the minimum of English needed to get her through her evenly patterned days. As a girl, she remembers nearly starving to death when crops failed after World War I, creating a severe famine throughout southern Italy. Her father, after the First World War, sick of watching his family's agony, worked and bartered his way to the New World. A few months later, he sent steerage passage tickets from New York so that Rosa, her mother, and her older sister, Helena, could follow. Later, her brothers were brought, too, and finally the whole family was reunited on Mulberry Street in New York. From that tearful reunion, they lived in a small, crowded apartment, huddling around a coal stove in freezing winter and fanning themselves for relief on the fire escape in sweltering summer.

The mid-morning factory whistle sounds, and Rosa gladly goes down to the basement for her coffeebreak. She meets with her fellow women workers there, around an aluminum percolator, to rest and talk of husbands, children, family crises, and the price of food. Rosa, considered indomitably cheerful, always sits in a corner of the room, nibbling her daily piece of anisette toast, now and then offering a bit of wisdom to the conversation. "Children, dey gotta have da rules, butta da rules musta be putta widda love from *la famiglia*." When the other women complain of their husbands' behavior, she always states, as if for the first time, "A man, he no can cry too mucha; is a woman's work to cry, to worry, to make a nice housa, cooka da food and lova da bambinos. Da man, he pusha here and he pusha dere, but he no can afford to cry!"

Since Rosa seldom says anything that can be debated, the younger women nod their head in affirmation and continue with their chatter. This morning, the conversation goes differently than ever before. Domenica, a petite curly-haired brunette of forty-three, sits beside Rosa and speaks animatedly:

"Listen, Rosa, I figured out how you can earn the money for Helena's hospital bed—the one I showed you in the catalog—so you don't have to hurt your back no more helping her to sit up! My nephew, Don, is casting director for a commercial television studio—ya know? Where they make commercials to sell things on TV? Well, he was over for dinner last night and he's looking for a nice elderly lady to do a false denture adhesive commercial, and I told him about you. He wants her to have a cheerful smile and a foreign accent and look like everybody's sweet old grandmother. 'I wish you'd give Rosa, where I work, the job,' I says to him! Because of your sister's hospital bed. He says, okay, he would use you if he could. I showed him your picture that I took with the other women—at Christmas— when my kids gave me that new polaroid camera. Don says you look just like his grandmother—my mother, Lisa, who passed away not long ago. I hadn't really thought about it until he said it, but it's true, you do. And Rosa, guess what? He's coming by this afternoon to meet you and maybe take you for a screen test. He says he'll make sure they pay you good, if he can use you!"

Domenica's dark eyes sparkle with cheerful enthusiasm. "Just think, Rosa, you'll be on *television*!" Domenica is proud to have something so exciting to tell everybody, but Rosa feels embarrassed by the public admission of her need for money.

"Holy Mary, Domenica! Um no needa money. Uma save lidda by lidda. But, uma be so glad to meet you nephew!" Rosa feels that to introduce one to a member of one's family is to bestow a great honor of friendship.

When the workday ends, she rushes to the lavatory to wash her hands and recomb her hair into a fresh knot. As she carefully smooths down her black skirt and picks a few pieces of lint from it, Domenica enters excitedly. "He's here. Don's here! I saw him from the window!" She quickly hurries Rosa to the elevator and out onto busy Atlantic Avenue. A bright yellow taxi stands at the curb and a young, dark-haired, fair-skinned man alights from it. Domenica, short and olive-skinned, gives her tall blue-eyed nephew a warm hug and proudly introduces him to Rosa.

"*Mi piace! Piacere!*" Rosa beams.

"My pleasure, too, Mrs. Della Rosa. I think you might do fine for our spot, but I want to take you to the studio with me now for a quick test, to see how you come out on camera. I can take you right there in this cab and get you back home in a couple of hours."

Rosa instantly fills Don with nostalgic memories of his grandmother who died several weeks earlier. Don's grandmother was his staunch defender from the wrath of his parents all through his youth. When things were difficult during his teen years at home, he went to live with his grandmother, who indulged him greatly with food, affection, and approval. The smell of Rosa, a mixture of garlic and rose water, fills Don with a pleasant sensation of remembered solace. He immediately treats Rosa with gentle respect, despite her limited command of English. He decides to personally escort her through the entire job to make things easier for her.

"Me, get in a taxi?" Rosa shys away hardly capable of being persuaded to break the regular pattern of her day. "*Mama mia!* It's very nice, but uma go home to my sister and cooka da minestrone for her supper!"

"Oh, for heaven's sakes, Rosa, I'll stop by and look in on Helena and explain. I have the extra keys you gave me to keep safe for you. I'll get her anything she needs until you get home. You'll be home soon, anyway! You can use the money you make from the commercial for the bed to make Helena more comfortable. She'll understand. Don came all this way just to meet you!"

She lowers her eyes. She doesn't mean to insult Domenica or her nephew's efforts. She's seen just enough television to know what a commercial is, but she can't believe what's happening. The idea of a taxi ride fills her with trepidation. At last, she consents to embark with Don. The cab speeds quickly up the avenue toward the Brooklyn Bridge. As it buzzes over the metal groundwork of the big bridge, Rosa sits stiffly upright hanging onto the backrest in front of her. Accustomed to subways and buses, she's never driven over the Brooklyn Bridge in all her years in the city. Her dark pupils dart about as the huge cables of the bridge and its lofty granite arches loom over her. The sudden change in her routine puts her in a state of shock as Don escorts her into the television studio with its bright lights, chrome, cameras, wires, and bustling personnel. She can do nothing but stare, listen, smell, sense what's happening. Her heart throbs, but she smiles and murmurs, "*Piacere!*" assuring everyone that meeting them is her pleasure. She holds her worn black leather purse to her bosom to keep her hands from trembling. Still, they shake a little as they caress the familiar leather.

Rosa is placed before the camera at different angles and asked to smile and say her name. She complies humbly with Don's every wish.

"Well, Mrs. Della Rosa, the producer agrees. You'll do just fine. You'll be on camera for about half a minute and you'll only need to say one sentence.

"...Which we'll teach you. Don't worry about a thing!" Don adds reassuringly. "We're taping on Monday at an old Victorian farmhouse in Morristown, New Jersey. I'll bring you there in a studio limousine."

Rosa's not at all sure about what the producer or Don is describing, but she understands she'll go in a car with Don next Monday to a place somewhere outside the city. What concerns her most is having to take a day off from work at the factory—something she's done so rarely that the thought fills her with dread.

"Rosa, you'll make more on Monday than you make in a month at the factory!" Domenica is proud to exclaim aloud at Friday morning's coffee break. "Don says so!" Domenica stretches her small frame to its full four-foot eleven-inch height and smooths her curly brown hair as she stands beside the perking percolator.

"*Madre di Dio!*" Rosa crosses herself, though she rarely goes to church. She believes what her father told her: "Most priests are thieves who want to take from a hardworking man and his family, so they can have nice dinners with plenty of wine!" Her father, like his father before him, had wearied of paying indulgences to the local churchmen who ran his village in southern Italy—while the North and the Vatican seemed to grow richer on the back of the starving South. "Faith in God is infinite, but the Church is infinitely corrupt!" Her father often declared with passionate conviction. "Hail Mary!"

Monday morning dawns and Rosa in wonder sits nervously by her kitchen window, peering diligently out into the street for Don's arrival. She sips coffee and nibbles a piece of anisette toast. She has never ventured from the Red Hook ghetto of immigrant Italians, with its rapidly arriving and integrating Hispanic community, since her husband died thirty years ago. She asks little from life. Ordinary daily bread is good enough and anisette toast to her is a great luxury. When she can't, out of agitation, finish the piece she's begun, she carefully wraps it in wax paper and puts it back in the bread box.

Around her, Rosa has watched soul after soul writhe in the agonies of ambition. Though she's full of empathy for their miseries and longings, she's content to care for Helena and feed an occasional neglected child of the neighborhood or a stray animal. She knows every family on her block, and all the local storekeepers. Sometimes she tries to comfort a widow with soup or herb teas, home remedies learned long ago from her mother. Rosa wrings an old lace and linen handkerchief and clutches her purse to her bosom as she peers nervously out the window through the fire escape to the street, watching for Don's car to appear.

The bun at the back of her neck has been more painstakingly arranged than usual. Rosa remembers the last time she left Brooklyn was to go to her parents' funeral in Manhattan's Little Italy. In their late eighties, they had died twenty years ago, within two days of each other, half frozen in the bad winter weather when their apartment house furnace failed. Rosa is ashamed that she wasn't able to relieve their poverty beyond taking the burden of Helena from them. Her three brothers were better able to make money for the family, but they'd all been killed—one in World War II, another in the Korean War, and her eldest in a construction accident when he was sixty-three, a few years before their elderly parents died. As she sits vigilantly awaiting Don, she recalls that her food-bearing visits to her parents meant much in their old age, when they retired from factory work but neglected to collect social security.

Rosa's husband was a mason, a bricklayer like her brothers. One of her brothers introduced him to her, and when they were married, her husband brought her to live near his family in Brooklyn. Rosa's father was able to offer no dowry, as in the Old Country, so she felt fortunate to find a husband at all. Though Rosa earned money for the family table from her factory work, her father was always worried about her virginity and honor, and sorrowful over Helena's aging maidenhood, in a city whose customs he never really understood. He was greatly relieved when Rosa married, but Rosa's mother was heartbroken to have her daughter move away from their neighborhood village.

As the studio limousine speeds through the Lincoln Tunnel, Don remarks to Rosa how they are riding through a tube under the water. Frightened, Rosa holds her breath from the carbon monoxide fumes and fears she will drown under the Hudson River. To all Don offers, Rosa nods her head in constant awe, exclaiming, *"Madre di Dio!"*

With Don's help, Rosa finally alights from the studio car which brings them to a plush green lawn in the back of a huge white Victorian mansion in Morristown. Rosa sighs in wide-eyed wonder. Voluptuous sunlit shrubs, trees, flowers of every bright springtime color, sweet smells of pine and fresh mown grass surround her. This, she decides, at last must be the America my family was promised by the ticket salesman who came to our village—who sold us steerage passage aboard a steamship to the New World. This is the America bathed in golden light that lit our dreams as we rocked across the sea on our sickening voyage. This is the America my family never saw! Here the trees are as green as *Apulia's* olive groves! "Blue sky, sunlight like *patria mia!*" Rosa sighs.

"Che belleza! Madre mia!" She gasps breathlessly to Don: "Um no can believa dis! Brooklyn *è brutto*, butta dis? *Simulare la Provincia d'Apulia! Bellisima!* Dis isa America uma dream when um holda my Mamma's skirt ona da cold oceana! Uma wisha Helena coulda see disa! Uma wisha Mamma and Papa coulda see dis bella America! *Madre mia!*" Rosa crosses herself at the thought of her parents sharing the sight with her.

Don leads Rosa to the edge of a giant picnic table where she is greeted by a makeup artist who begins staring at her face, but not her eyes still wide with amazement. She's made to sit in a folding chair while she's powdered and rouged and lined with mascara. "Ina my ola village, only a *putana* putsa paint ona *la faccia!* she jokes with the makeup artist who pays her no mind as he doesn't understand what she's saying. "Don't talk, it ruins the lips!" he commands. Rosa humbly stilled, thinks to herself how in Puglese villages along the Adriatic coast across from the Greek Islands, the women wear black dresses after their husbands die and go to church every day to say the rosary. They keep their hair in a bun and work in the fields until they are too old to. Her mother never wore any powder or rouge, saying it was only for bad women.

As the makeup man continues to fuss over Rosa's face, she takes in more of the scene around them. A long redwood picnic table is spread on the sprawling, manicured lawn around which tremendous pine trees loom in dark green splendor, accented against a clear blue sky. No factory stacks or noises rise in the distance. On the seemingly infinite table, Rosa stares in wonder at the plentiful food. Great roasted hams with glistening pineapple slices shining in silver trays and glowing with glazed red cherries. Platters of roasted turkeys, crisp and brown, stand beside bowls of cooked yellow corn dripping with butter. Great mounds of shiny fruit spill forth from gleaming porcelain bowls beside sparkling crystal goblets from which electric blue linen napkins are puffed. Sumptuous loaves of bread, rolls, pies, cakes, cookies of every description and bright ripe vegetables in abundant variety, radiant with the cool sunshine of early spring. The air fresh and crisp, the tranquil countryside mesmerizes Rosa. "At lasta, uma see America ina my family's dreams,'' she remarks as the makeup man, who pays no attention to her words, finishes.

A cicada, singing in a nearby tree makes the sound man curse aloud to break her spell. "If that goddamned bug doesn't quit singing loud enough to be taken for a frigging buzz saw or a jet stream,'' he shouts to the director, "we'll have to end up doing a voice-over back at the studio!''

Shocked out of her reveries by the coarse language, her visage prepared for the camera, Rosa is abruptly greeted by the director who immediately begins drumming a sentence into her head while the costume mistress wraps and ties a crisply starched, magnificently flowered blue and red apron over Rosa's plain black dress. The director makes her smile broadly and repeat the sentence over and over again, until she thinks her head will burst from the strain of stress and gesture. Don stands by and helps her drill until, finally, after several minutes, the crew breaks for a rest before the rolling of the cameras. When at last they pause, the powdered, smiling Rosa in her brightly colored apron can grin perfectly into the big red light on the camera, hold a lacquered cob of yellow corn beside her face, and say "Uma always use *Ultragrip* ona my dentures to enjoy my family pic-a-nicks!''

During the break, while the prop girls scurry about putting finishing touches on the set and the director gives commands to the several extras who will be used to represent Rosa's family, Don explains to her: "There's a child psychiatrist and pediatrician on the set to supervise the children. They get paid $150 per hour!'' Don points to a man and a woman beside several children and toddlers dressed in gingham country frocks and suits. There are two babies sitting in highchairs and several pseudo-relatives of every age now gathering around the huge picnic table. Don explains that they will pretend to be picnicking merrily behind her as she stands before the table to recite her line, smiling into the camera. "Considering the prop girls, director, sound and camera men, studio personnel, commercial script writers, our salaries at the ad agency, yours and the other actors' fees, remote control rig, trucks and transportation, this commercial will probably cost close to three-quarters of a million dollars to produce!''

"Holy Mother of God!'' Rosa sighs in disbelief. "Um betcha da food alone costa alot a money! Did you ever see such a bigga table, such a bigga turkey ina you life?''

"Yeah, and not one 'spicy meatball' anywhere!'' Don teases, smiling. "This is an All-American feast!'' He enjoys Rosa's wide-eyed wonder at the incredible world of television into which he has benevolently brought her.

"Okay, Mrs. Della Rosa. Ready on the set!'' calls the director.

"*Si signore*. Uma ready!'' Rosa answers, practicing her smile at him. "Uma ready.'' She remarks to Don as he leads her to her spot on the set, "Uma lika to smile. You can take da smile from you face and put ina you heart, widda a feast likka dis in you eyes!''

All becomes hushed; then, at the director's cue, the pseudo-relatives behind Rosa, on camera, begin to gesture and laugh as if at a picnic. Rosa, as she was bid, holds up her lacquered cob of corn, smiles broadly into the red light on the camera, and repeats her line: "Uma *always* use *Ultragrip* ona my dentures to *enjoy* my family pic-a-nicks!''

"Cut!" shouts the director, "Mrs. Della Rosa, the corn was hiding your face too much. Hold it away to the side of your face, with your pinky out more!"

Don explains from the sidelines in Italian. He murmurs reassuringly.

Si signore!" Rosa nods obediently and moves the corn away from her face. She sticks out her pinky in a delicate gesture.

"Ready, cut two, take two!" the stage manager claps his board. "Roll um!" and so the process is repeated through several takes until the director is satisfied with the results.

"Okay! Cut and print!" He finally shouts and perfunctorily adds, "Thanks everybody. You can go home. Dismissed!"

Rosa can hardly take the smile from her face. It seems frozen there from repetition. The muscles of her cheeks ache.

"Well, Rosa," exclaims Don. "You're a star! You'll be watching yourself on television before you know it!"

"Helena will no believe when she sees me! Holy Mother of God!"

While Don tends to business, Rosa sits exhausted on a bench at the edge of the picnic table. She watches the prop girls begin to dismantle the set. Too excited to eat breakfast or lunch, her ordeal now over, Rosa's mouth waters at the glorious repast. Before she can even think of tasting a morsel, the prop and set workers begin shoveling the platters of food into huge, black plastic garbage bags. Rosa's eyes gape in silent horror as breads, rolls, pies, cakes, corn, vegetables, fruits, and amazingly glazed hams are swept from sight, bagged as garbage. In utter disbelief, Rosa sees the feast of her dreams unceremoniously destroyed, shoveled into garbage bags, thrown to the ground.

Finally, unable to contain herself, she asks quietly, "Whadda you gonna do widda dat bigga turkey? Uma know a nice orphanage ina Brooklyn..."

The prop mistress is used to being asked such scavaging questions by perpetually starving actors dismissed from sets. Without giving Rosa even a sidelong glance, she answers contemptuously, "Throw it away with the rest of the perishable props, of course! Salvaging perishables from sets complicates tax matters. Excuse me." She reaches over Rosa, grabs the turkey platter, and slides the sumptuous roasted bird into a black plastic sack full of cracked and crumbling pies, cookies, and squashed fruit. It lands with a sloppy thud, spraying soggy crumbs over Rosa's flowered apron.

Don reappears as a costume girl bids Rosa to stand while she removes the apron. As Don escorts her home through the Lincoln Tunnel again, she does not speak or exclaim anything in Holy-Mother-of-God phrases. In her mind she sees the food of her dreams behind the house of her dreams shoveled into a huge black plastic mouth of hell as her starving parents, Helena, her brothers, and herself, as a child, look on with saddened faces, somber with shadows of death.

"Well, Rosa, what do you think of Television Land?" Don questions cheerfully.

"*Non capisco nulla di niente. Non capisco, Signore. Non capisco,*" Rosa utters softly. Don decides she is weary from her exciting day, as she rests back against the cushions of the limousine, her eyes half-closed. When they arrive in front of her tenement home in Red Hook, Don helps Rosa out of the car and to the door, thinking that she is tired just as his grandmother would be after such a long and eventful day. "Will you be all right, Mrs. Della Rosa?"

"Sì, molte grazie, Signore. Grazie mille." Rosa puts her hand on Don's arm as if in sympathy and nods weakly. She enters her hallway without turning back. "Buona notte!"

"Good night, to you, too." Don watches her grey hair disappear into the darkness.

She slowly climbs the stairs to her apartment and, in the dim light of the landing, opens the door, depositing her keys in her worn black purse which she leaves, as always, on the old hall table. She peers into the dusky bedroom, where Helena wheezes quietly in her sleep. Without turning on any lights to brighten the twilight kitchen, she goes to the sink and washes her hands with soap and cold water—because the hot water tap hasn't worked for years like the one in the bathroom does, but it's too close to the bedroom and sound of hissing pipes might wake Helena out of her pain-filled respite from slow dying.

Rosa goes to the bread box and extracts from its near empty depths the waxed-paper-wrapped, half-eaten piece of anisette toast left over from her vigilant breakfast at the window. She sits again by the window and peers into the coming night, as slowly she chews the dry bread with her quite good, very old, real teeth, crushing it crumb by crumb, morsel by precious morsel.

Marital Bliss

The secret of life sang in Pete's pants to be misunderstood and forgotten. He was a womanizer whose ethnos no one knew—not even himself—because he was entirely American. Mary Alice, his wife, had never touched with the dumb fury of tongues or drawn a moan of ecstasy from the bent world's insanity. If Mary Alice and Pete could have spoken to each other with their thighs and thought with their hands, they might have made sweet music against the belly of eternity or sung the algebra of glands to the wet mathematics of creation, as if God lived in our bodies and we prayed to them with the dreams of our fingers. Pete had big blue eyes and muscles and a huge double-barreled shotgun, easily unzipped and fired anywhere. He went all around the town aiming it at every woman he could, then carving commemorative notches on his leather belt with his sleek and steely penknife. He walked down the street flashing his groin, hips, and chest, his elbows moving in the fresh air. His animal nature billowed along with him, so that even those angered by it were charmed, as had been Mary Alice long ago. She was pretty, but plain compared to Pete.

"I am a man," Pete thought.

"No, you're not," whispered his wife, Mary Alice, who stayed home caring for all the children he'd fathered in the house and on the lawn and in the garage, and in the back seat of his old souped-up Plymouth, and all around the neighborhood and the city. She kept them all tucked up under her tattered skirts, safe from the cold and want which was their lot. She even started a day-care center to give them friends to play with and to earn money for all the rare hamburgers and cold beers Pete thrived on to consummate his consuming.

But, the mayor and city hall closed Mary Alice's day-care center, because she naively didn't have a degree or a license. So, she started a home laundry, and all the kids pitched in, hanging out the clothes, because she made a cheery game of it—singing nursery rhymes while they worked—about a maid in the garden hanging out the clothes, a snippy blackbird, and a king with a lot of birds baked into his fat pie.

She managed pretty well and kept handsome Pete in hamburgers, too.

"This is a good life," Pete said, until he grew older and his shotgun rusted and became bent from so much firing—as bent as the famous one in the limerick about the young man from Kent who instead of coming, went.

So Mary Alice, who had a pleasant matronly face, to save his male pride, since she'd become by feverish work the most important laundress in the whole town, set him to work driving her laundry truck to keep his mind off his problem and keep him going.

"We don't talk much, Pete," she pointed out one day.

"Huh?" asked Pete, watching the final playoff of the World Serious on TV. "Talk? About what?"

"Well, maybe our children, for example."

"Oh, them? They're kinda cute—especially the little girls—the way they hop and skip and call me 'Daddy' and look up to me."

"Well," said Mary Alice. "You are a lot taller."

One Friday, as Pete was driving Mary Alice along in the truck on their way to deposit a month's laundry earnings in the bank, they were held up at a red light by a guy with a little tiny revolver which he pointed stiffly at Alice's breast. Alice, clutching her purse full of money to her chest with her reddened knuckles, pretended to faint, and that gave Pete, who had a lot of confidence from all the notches in his leather belt, time to rip it off and lash the hairy wrist holding the tiny revolver with it—using it like a lion tamer's whip.

Then, Pete knocked the robber down, as the robber dropped his gun and Pete his pants. Pete sat on the robber while Mary Alice ran for the police.

Later, that evening, Mary Alice and Pete drove home together and shut out the lights—after all the children were tucked in—and Pete made love for the first time in his life to anyone, to Mary Alice, his wife, because he thought how scared he'd be without her when the robber pointed his revolver at her breast and threatened to shoot her dead. He thought of her as a small furry animal, warm and soft with a dark hold of worry in the center of her—wet and inviting—a place he could fill with himself. She felt like the object of his need pressed between her thighs waiting to be opened by touch. His fingers willed the thrill of her desire and a warm light exploded a sunburst in their dark minds. Her face shed the winter of its worry over all the murdered roses torn from flesh with tortured shrieks. Her skin bloomed like spring petals, pitying and pink—yellow, purple veined buds of beneficent being filled her dreams. Pete's red heart burned him with her life and she understood for the first time all the life, like an indigestible summer of merciless heat, she had pushed out of herself. She heard Pete's sweet murmurs in the night and thought of how hard and selfish he could be and pulled herself closed and he rubbed her back and neck, and she felt him become the father of all things waiting to be spilled into and out of her, to make her bloom like a round melon. She understood why the roses must die to be beautiful like the sea from which she smelled her own body, throbbing and rolling as he thrust need into her. She felt as necessary as earth planted in spring so that grass grows for eating, vibrant in the green summer sun, festering with insects, birds, sticky-throated flowers. Syllables spilled prattling to the small round animals that came seeing out of her, breathing her belly—laughing, weeping, seeping, yelping, dancing. She nearly felt totally content to bleed in and out of the mystery that only skies can know, only mountains touch, only stars breathe.

Mary Alice, after that, almost acquired the habit of happiness. For two years her skin sang songs to her bones as she worked, but in any case, she died three years later, tired from too much work, but triumphant.

Memory of Two Tuesdays

Today we made love in the afternoon. It is Tuesday.

It was on a Tuesday afternoon that I came upon them together, him and Roseanne. The memory of the scene is so alive that today, while we were making love, I got to thinking that he was comparing me to her.

We made love in the little room on the battered mattress which we had used during the first years of our marriage. It had become flaccid and lumpy with the passage of time and uncomfortable nights. No matter how much I beat it in the garden and spray it with special detergents it still smells, and the effect is suffocating. It's like dried-out leather and horse manure in stables. Once during the afternoons of dizziness, I passed my tongue over it before beating it, while he was away at school. I licked the dry roses of stains which today are rusty like decalcomanias and thus gave vent to my venery.

But today, after Roseanne, it no longer attracts me.

He bought it at a sale in Scarsdale, Westchester County, New York, when Cress, my mother, bought us our first house in 1963. I didn't sleep much in it because at that time I was pregnant with Daniel and I spent a great deal of my time in New Canaan where my mother insisted I should give birth.

With Daniel's birth, which coincided with Simon's first clamorous break with my mother, Cress evicted him from that house. And she at the same time insisted that I should divorce him, reminding me that she had two savings bank books for me: the first, containing a modest sum, was for my studies; the second, containing lots of money ($95,000!), was for my adulthood—when I would have found the man that she, too, would have approved as a groom, that is to say when she would have made the choice for me. But since I had made an insane choice by marrying Simon, she now wanted me to divorce him. She adduced two reasons: first, she was afraid of Simon's independence, considered as important as her own independence; and second, I and the baby, by living with her in the same house, would serve as a shield against the flaccid presence of her husband, whose wretched existence had been reduced to correcting homework assignments in elementary French and to walking our dog in the garden.

She had never taught me to call him dad.

Like everybody else, in fact, I called him Trick, which was his name, a diminutive for Patrick. And he said nothing, never a word. He was totally aware of and offended by his situation, but he could not escape; he had never wanted to escape. I believe that Cress, jealous and displeased, must have been wracked for many nights and days by the crazy notion that the stranger Simon was none other than her Venetian lover who had died at sea at the outbreak of World War II. And that now, transformed, he had come back to her in the guise of Simon in order to retrieve his daughter by marrying her and thus relegate Cress to an unsmiling old age and to her weirdish widowhood.

Desperate, my mother had even attempted to have Simon arrested in connection with the disappearance of some jewelry from the house in New Canaan, one Sunday when he had remained alone at home while we had gone to a wedding.

Simon told the police that he had spent his time on the porch, reading, And he declared that he had never set foot in the house, not even to fetch himself a glass of water. My mother had hidden the jewels in some drawer, but I don't believe that she had done so purposely. In fact she found them years later when to her resigned eyes we began to appear as a well-matched, compatible couple.

When she evicted him from Scarsdale, Simon realized that he had his back to the wall. The world continued to be against him. He had always said that the world was against him. But he did not want to be saved. He did not want to end up like Trick, the man who would have been so happy if I had called him "Pa," even if only once and for all time. So Simon sold everything he had bought for our house, keeping only his books and his mattress. He rented a U-Haul and dragged that mattress back to his old studio in New York on East Ninety-fourth Street.

I didn't want to divorce him, but in this situation it was not even possible to live together, especially because of the hemorrhages that afflicted me after the baby's birth. They were of great help to my mother in her plan to superprotect me and keep me for herself. I had already recovered, I wanted and desired him, so I went to New York once a week—even though Cress's approval contained a tacit reproach—and I became his weekend prostitute. I carefully checked that mattress for signs of other occupants, but all I could detect were the cat's prints. I could not reproach him because he waited for me and I for him. I really wanted to stay with him and start all over again with him, so I urged him to take me away but now, as quickly as possible, because I too wanted to escape from my mother's overbearingness. He understood and made a further sacrifice, giving up his teaching career at Yale. He accepted a teaching job in Vancouver, Canada, which paid less but which, at least, had a fine supply of monkeys.

And I didn't even know where Vancouver was!

"It is located on the northern Pacific Coast. It is beautiful, sunny, hygienic. Our son will grow up there and become a fisherman," he said.

That was fine. But I had already decided to leave Daniel with my mother, since I had no desire to play the mother role, and she would be pleased to learn how to be a grandmother. But Simon insisted that I should return to fetch Daniel once we were settled down. I agreed and we loaded all our belongings—including the mattress, of course—on the Imperial 63, the automobile which my mother had given us as a gift.

From the East we set out for the Northwest, using the mattress in the orchards, on the edges of roads in the South, on the beaches in California, and in the woods of Oregon. We would stop and he would pull it out of the car. Once on the ground, that mattress was already home, the encampment, canned foods, laughter, and our future.

We called the mattress Byron and Milly Bloom, Molly's daughter. He was Byron, I was Milly.

One morning, as we were making love on that mattress in our house in Vancouver, an earthquake tremor paralyzed us. Crouched, he remained inside me, especially since the crash of the TV set when it fell from the stool was accompanied by the noise of shattered window panes.

Shuddering, he said, "I've impaled you, sorry!"

I panicked, forgetting all about the earthquake. I had read about cases of priapism in medical pocketbooks and about how it required medical intervention. But if, on the one hand, I did not want the doctor or the ambulance to take us to the hospital fastened together, on the other, I did want to get out of the house.

It had been a light quake. In order to calm me down, he said, "You'll see, there'll be no further quakes. We should phone First Aid."

We lived in a two-story house on the edge of the campus, and the telephone was on the lower floor. He lifted me up by my bottom and I suddenly realized that I was soaking wet, and it was blood. I figured that my menstrual period had begun one week in advance of schedule precisely because of my panic. I dripped as he carried me in that peculiar position across the room and down the stairs to the kitchen where the phone was located. I was still dripping all over his legs.

"There's only one way to do it," he said, laughing. "Origen's cut!"

Upon finally reaching the room below, Simon freed himself with a sudden backward thrust and placed me on the couch in a sitting posture.

In between brief and nervous outbursts of laughter, licking the blood off his legs, I wept silently.

"Why did you want to scare me?"

"So as to make you forget the real scare, the earthquake."

And, in fact, I had already forgotten everything. The scattered pieces of the shattered TV set were all that remained of the earthquake's arrival, and a puddle of blood on the mattress was all that remained of Simon's priapism.

He gathered up the splinters of glass, while I washed the mattress with a duster.

I wanted to free myself of that mattress. I wanted a king-size one, but he feigned deafness. And for awhile I did not insist. I knew that he was fond of that mattress because it symbolized home, family. To change mattresses for him signified a breaking-up of the home, like wife-swapping. And people with a tradition like his, stemming from European middle-class intellectuals, change mattresses only when one of the spouses dies. Even divorce, or carnal separation, is like death for them.

His face contorted when I told him a couple of years later that I was fed up with life in Vancouver and that he should find a new job in the States. "For me America is where I am well off," he said. Later, nevertheless, he accepted an offer from California, so we transferred to Oakland with the mattress duly loaded in our Imperial 63.

We set up house in Berkeley on Keeler Avenue with flowers and fountains and a swimming pool. Daniel continued to remain with his grandmother in New Canaan because I felt no particular affection for him, whereas he was a consolation for my mother, poor woman. Simon protested, but I told him quite clearly: "If you insist, you will have neither me nor Daniel, because I'll divorce you."

It was like a slap in the face, but in the end he resignedly bowed to my threat. We made many trips together to the East, but he always avoided going to New Canaan to meet his son. He was thinking of his mother-in-law, not of his son. And when in 1968 I wanted to return to the East, he almost hit me. "According to your lights," he said, "am I always to begin all over again from scratch? Leave a job and find another one the moment we're acclimatized to it?" He stormed out of the house in a fury and went fishing on the Grand River in the Rocky Mountains. When he came back, he was in a totally different state of mind. He said he had met a doctor and a chemist from Anaconda, New York, and they had suggested he transfer and go to work with them.

Even this move turned out to be easy. In Anaconda we bought a house and other furniture and, at long last, also a king-sized bed. But we had also brought the old mattress along with us, and it now found its proper place in the small room. I had the presentiment that the transfer of that mattress signified not only a slight alienation from him but also from ourselves. Such turned out to be the case, in fact. When Simon's relatives came for a visit, they slept on that mattress in the small room. When Daniel came from New Canaan, he slept on that mattress. And when his two sons came from Italy or when his friends came for a visit, they also slept on that mattress. It had become a place of arrival for everybody, but no longer for us. And one day Simon was to bring also Roseanne onto that mattress. Today he brought me there too, a Tuesday afternoon.

We have made love in the afternoon so many times. The reason for this is that we did not have daily office hours or fixed days of rest for extravagances. A professor is always free, even when he is working, for whether in the office or at home, he is always working. Sex is the logical sublimation of this continuous work. On the other hand, today's American academic life encourages constant production and not research work that requires years; it does not wait for the masterpiece of the historian, the philosopher, or the man of letters, the great books. Rather, it demands specialized works, something quickly put together, like textbooks. Simon is aware of this, so with a monotonous regularity, he produces studies and monographs with which he himself, often, is not content but which permit him to remain on the uppermost rung of the ladder. Economic restrictions ever weigh on private and state universities alike and are the underlying causes of dismembering departments, for firings which lead to court suits and litigation lasting for years. Indeed, department heads often must turn to private persons for funds and donations which allow some programs to be kept alive. Simon himself is almost always involved in campaigns for the collection of hundreds of thousands of dollars so as to assure the survival of his monkeys and his experiments. And in order to do so, he not only immerses himself in conferences and embarks on trips of all kinds but also produces, together with Andrew, a series of scientific films with a sexual base, inasmuch as he is of the opinion that sex should be taught in schools at all levels because it lies at the base of every human and social activity.

After the laboratory and the seminars, he comes back home if he so wishes, and he often brings friends and students along: they talk, write, study labyrinthine maps, or just listen to music. With Simon one is always in the classroom. He writes, paints, plays the organ, rides a motorcycle, works in the garden, cooks, visits his monkeys. He knows a little of everything (in gloomy moments he is known to repeat, "I was born dead because I belong to the times of Leon Battista Alberti and those times have gone forever!"), but above all he is a consummate conversationalist.

Often we give parties which he does not deduct from his income tax as professional expenses, despite my insistence. They involve cultural activities linked to his professional work, but he prefers to deduct his trips having to do with his professional researches rather than fiscally exploit his social encounters and friendships, which often are the prime impulse and the financial backing of his journeys on behalf of his scholarly pursuits. We have a lot of friends, but Cara and Bart and Peter and Punks are the ones closest to us, and it is only rarely that we get a visit from Matthias and his wife, Sue. Nevertheless we enjoy a perfect harmony with them. We are never in agreement on everything with Simon, instinctively realizing that each one of us would have done exactly what he or she planned to do, sharing the woe or the weal ensuing from the action. But in the matter of love, we have always been in agreement, and like him, I prefer it in the afternoon, the siesta hours in which I melt away and swoon. In the spring I change my panties twice a day, and I don't wear any at all in the summertime. Often in the spring, desire suddenly comes over me in the car or the library or watching the bulge in the pants of someone walking alongside me. (I never raise my eyes when I walk, but I do keep them half-raised, thereby checking the point of my sandals and whatever appears to me at medium level, that is, legs, bodies, then the face and then the trunk, the legs and, again, the point of my sandals.) If my need arises when I am at home and Simon is not, I vent my frustration by getting down to work on my Ph.D. thesis which, given the market, is worth nothing. *And I am no scholar!* Yet, recently, we had not made love in the afternoon for several weeks. And it is for this reason, I suspected, he was comparing me to Roseanne.

The use of the little three-quarter bed, the mattress of our first years of marriage and now of his affair with Roseanne, was a premeditated choice on his part. "This is the bed of sex," he told me once, "whereas the other, the king-size, is the bed of love." I understood what he meant, but now I also know that I am very jealous of this mattress in the small room. Is love jealous? I had seen myself as brought up in a system that views jealousy as a crime against the independent person, and now I know I was mistaken. Instead, jealously gnaws away at me, and at times it makes me see things through dark, tragic, movie-like tones. I see that everything is crumbling and I'm afraid of dying under the ruins.

So while he was caressing me, I was thinking of Roseanne, then of Roseanne with us two, she in my skin and in his, I with her and with him, and she with me and with him. I became so ecstatic over these thoughts that, as a result of persistently pursuing them, I came, suddenly, but my whole body was suffused by a supreme, sinking feeling of utter sweetness. Alas, I came too soon because he was still pulsating inside me and this time—strangely—like a miner: seeking, whirling around, beating, caressing, biting, riveting me, slavering. I came again and this time the Van Goghian suns reappeared to my eyes, those I had seen the first time as an adolescent. They were in my eyes and on my face, I was tattooed with sunflowers. But soon the mind resumed dominion over the senses and the torturing analyses continued. Did Roseanne ever enjoy a moment like this? Had she ever taken a shower together with him?

I reasoned in this way, being now sexually passive because actually Roseanne was not with us and I was not she, even if for a certain period of time I had not given myself to him but to her in the anxiety of a stupid emulation, which after all was wholly in my mind. But my pleasure had been succeeded by the anxiety that he may love her more than me, and this gave the afternoon a touch of sadness. Also, I wanted to believe that my thoughts were inconsistent, because, after all Simon did love me well and very effectively in the extended, oriental manner marked by rapid and sinuous movements inside and outside my flesh. My second orgasm was devastated by the way he brought it to a conclusion in an absolutely new way. He withdrew, and that was exceedingly strange since I was taking the pill.

"Why did you do that?" I asked him, flabbergasted.

"You can eat it, if you like."

I suddenly felt most unwell. Now I was certain that he had been thinking about her while making love to me since coming outside was his contraceptive method. He was against abortion in principle. But he quickly drew me to himself again, adjusted his body to mine, and said, "Let's sleep now. It was very beautiful!"

He slept like a baby, sucking a nipple while I caressed his hair. I didn't know whether I loved him. But he had given me comfort, he had given me pleasure. Nevertheless, perhaps stupidly, I asked, "Has Roseanne ever had an orgasm?"

He gave a start.

"Why do you bring her up?"

"I would have liked her to have been with us this afternoon."

"It's a thing of the past, over and done with. Does it still bother you?"

"Not any more. But I would like to be her friend."

"It's dangerous. Are you looking for trouble?" he said.

I took his hand and placed it on my breast. I wanted to be adored. He understood. His kisses gave me a sudden yen to eat cheese. And in fact we ate some together, in a big hurry, suddenly realizing that we both had to get back to work. As we were getting into the car, curiosity overcame me again and I asked, "What kind of orgasms does Roseanne have?"

He did not answer, looking suddenly sad. We parted company in the parking lot, he walking toward his office, I toward the library. It seemed like a real separation. In fact both of us forgot to make the customary appointment to meet later so that we could go back home in the only car we had. But that had happened many times before and we always waited for each other in the parking lot.

Determined to continue my work on the *Amoretti*, I went to my cubicle in the library. A message Scotch-taped on the door made me change my mind. "If you'd like a coffee, you'll find me at Catt's." It was from Slingerlink, my thesis adviser, who was an affable and distinguished Renaissance scholar. I went. By a strange coincidence Matthias was having a cup of coffee with him. Both of them looked at me, guessing that I had just been making love. I half-shut my eyes and again felt normal.

You came to look for me in the library to my utter surprise, and you smiled at me and caressingly rested a hand. I find that very strange, you know.

What of me and you remains with you and me is not this particular minute but yesterday afternoon. The night following the afternoon, which we also spent together in the usual room and in the usual bed, has been so canceled out now that you are beside me that I cannot manage even to recall the many other nights of our life spent together in a state of remorse or weariness. If you were to ask me, as you always do, to write down what we did last night—even what we ate, the phone calls received—I could write down nothing because I have no memory of last night. And now you come and, with your strange smile, you ask, "Are you feeling better?"

When you noticed my diary open on the table, I understood your curiosity, and without the slightest hesitation I said, "You can read it, if you wish." But as I was telling you to read it, you had already done so because I saw you flip through the pages at a rate of 500 words per minute thanks to your speed-reading skills. This horrifies me. Usually you read a book in a half hour, and you annotate it in two hours after a rereading. You read thirty to forty books a week while I require three days to read one, five for a James novel, and spend two weeks in rereading it and making notes. What horrifies me is your racing around in a thousand directions which disorients me and leaves me behind.

You said, "I've the impression that you have invented 90 percent of your feeling by committing them to writing, and now that they are down on paper they serve you as an alibi every time you feel like accusing me of something."

"It's only my point of view of the situation," I retorted. Then you picked up the diary and said, "I'll now write my point of view right above this, OK?" You went out and came back in fifteen minutes. "It's all here. Now I'm going back to my office. As for tonight...if you'd like, come pick me up and we'll go home together."

I paid no attention to what he had said, but I began to read what he had written:

It began this way, Lisa, a few minutes ago in your cubicle where, full of love, I dropped for a visit. You wanted to ask me why I had a strange smile on my face, but you did not do so. You sat back in your seat the better to determine whether a relationship between you and me still existed. Your diary is more intelligent than accurate and now you are using it to erect walls. Instead of making the revelations in the diary, you begin to hide things and to hide yourself in it. The diary of your life in New England, that I asked you to write at the beginning of our relationship in New York, had a greater "purity."

I compare you? I didn't even remember that yesterday was Tuesday. And the other Tuesday, the one you cite involving Roseanne, had been canceled from my memory for a long time. I simply don't understand why you should insist upon bringing it up. Actually, I know why: that Tuesday serves your purposes more than mine. This is so because you want to run away, you are at a turn in the road and are looking for a big excuse. I compare you? Roseanne wasn't at all in my consciousness yesterday afternoon when I was making love with you. And yesterday, as many, many times before, it was beautiful to make love to you. Would you like to know what two professors of mathematics were saying today as they were eating the sandwiches prepared for them by their wives the night before? "Do you do it regularly?" They confessed to each other that it was no longer regular, perhaps once a month. And one of them admitted with an appalling metaphor, "We are like two blocks of marble in the graveyard of our bed."

Oh Lisa, if our love dies it will not be because of Roseanne.

It's convenient to play the injured party, now. The difficult thing to learn, if we want to continue to be together, is merely to rediscover ourselves with absolute probity. Shall we try it?

I bend over these pages and I feel the hollowness of my life. Try it? I would like to, but I am more disenchanted than ever. One gets used to love the way one gets used to the suffering of love. Why not try it? In fact the sufferance of love is something that could be overcome by other commitments, indeed by other loves. But what I don't want now is to be left alone with myself. I want to be "me" and no longer me with "you" or in terms of you. My confessions began from the moment that you asked them of me, Father Confessor. So that you could nourish yourself on me. Now I'm going to throw everything topsy-turvy, and all alone with myself I shall set out towards that great experience because what in reality urges me on beckoningly, at age thirty-three, is precisely the great experience. And at this point I avail myself of your beloved Jung. He writes: "the *One* does not wish to choose the *Other* because he is afraid of losing his character, and the *Other* breaks off from the *One* in order to exist."

I am the *Other*, Simon.

Greener Grass

When, in school during World War II, I first heard the acronym WASP, it stood for the Women's Airforce Service Pilots. Later, in a brilliant encapsulation, it came to stand for the particular ethnic group whose sting I had felt regularly during my growing up. Marianne Moore who wrote poems to strange creatures, never wrote one to a wasp. But coming of age when I did, child of Italian surnames, I might well have thought, in a Browning cadence, "Oh, to be a WASP, now that teen-age is here..."

By seventh or eighth grade I was enviously aware of classmates with names like Sallie Shipton, Howard Wareham, Graham Fuller, Grace Goldfarb. They weren't asked, as I was in each new class, to stand up, pronounce my name, spell it, and then hear it given back, carelessly mangled, by my teachers.

"Pietrofesso," I would repeat to Miss Fiske or Miss Conan or Mr. Wright. "P-i-e-t-r-o-f-e-s-s-o," I would spell out, mortified, "Stefana, with an f, Pietrofesso."

Staff is what they called me. And my last name slurred into Peterface-oh. Later, in college I was known as Petrify. My feelings could be shared only by the other non-American names in my class—those like Sophie Filarski, the skinny, pale, and pimply girl whose father was an apartment building janitor, or Gennaro Cacciacavallo, a dark-skinned, dark-eyed son of Neopolitans. Gennaro was fast-thinking without even trying, and cocky, too—he didn't give a damn about grades, as did the good, plodding WASP boys who were already talking about colleges. Sometimes I wonder what happened to Gennaro and if, in middle age, he ever had second thoughts about how the Warehams and Fullers became lawyers and executives while he, mercurial, quick, a brilliant flame of intelligence in our math and science classes, never had a chance for college and was out of school and working by age seventeen.

We were recognizably alien—Sophie, Gennaro, and I—with names that made the teachers grimace and strain when the roll was called. In those days, every so often at school or at the Y or on camp applications, we would be asked to fill in information forms. One blank was always for "Nationality." I never knew what to put down. I had been born in Schenectady, New York, and so had my parents, yet I didn't recognize myself as American. Should I just write "foreigner"?

After all, those foreign-type people who talked funny and looked wrong, and whom I saw at weddings or at Christmas—*they* were my relatives. Their faces were grim, lined with old worries and a sense of perpetual bewilderment. They were not the jolly comely Americans of *Saturday Evening Post* covers. In fifty years of living in America, my grandparents never put together enough English to speak to my brothers and me. It was hard to think of myself as American, and though it seemed not correct to write

"Italian" in the blank (for I had never been to Italy and didn't speak or understand Italian), yet that is what I wrote as my nationality. No teacher ever corrected me.

I had to *become* American. And the first step I took came at the time of my Catholic confirmation when I had to choose a name to add to the one I was baptized with—supposedly, the name of the saint who would thereafter be my guide and protector and to whom I could turn for inspiration and steadfastness in my faith.

I didn't even consider the saints; I wanted an American name. I chose Nancy. For Nancy Drew. And Lincoln's mother, Nancy Hanks. When I was twelve years old, my dream was to get away from Schenectady and start life as a real American named Nancy Peters.

As it worked out, instead, I took what my mother called a giant step backwards. I went to study in Italy, and there I met and married an Italian with another flamboyant name. It was while living in Italy that I realized how American I had been right along, and how unimportant it really all was.

Except that nothing is unimportant during adolescence, as my story will tell.

I went to a dreary public school in Schenectady, and there was no teacher along the way who illumined any bit of life or learning for me. From what I could see, success was with the WASPS. They had the correct traditions and attitudes and the social prominence. All I had was my library card. Each Saturday I'd walk twenty blocks to the public library and twenty blocks back lugging home piles of books written by men and women with good, regular names. I wormed my way into Anglo-Saxon life: Trollope's cathedral closes, Huxley's London smart set, Jane Austen's country life. They were my idealized habitats.

In those days, Sophie, Gennaro, and I were always at the top of the class. But grades meant nothing; my real aspiration was to sit at the same cafeteria table where Sallie Shipton and her friends had staked out their territory. One day—a miraculous day!—it happened that the others were absent and Sallie was sitting alone. I got up my courage and asked if I could sit with her. I hoped she wouldn't notice my sandwich made with Italian bread; I left the crusts uneaten as a sign of gentility.

Sallie was wearing a Shetland sweater monogrammed *SWS* and, to make conversation, I asked, "What is the *W* for?"

"My middle name is Willson. With two *l*'s. That's very rare and it's a great honor because it means our ancestors were with William the Conqueror."

William the Conqueror! I was silenced with awe. My family was unknown beyond the goatherd in Calabria and the fisherman in Sicily who had both immigrated to America and become my grandfathers. Once, in a fit of romanticism, I set myself to draw our family tree only to find that no one knew any names for the branches; we came from faceless and nameless people, like windblown weeds, and three generations were all we had.

I started sitting at Sallie's table from then on and there my real education began. She talked about her Willson cousins and about her brother in college who before that had been an Eagle Scout. (My brothers, who loved cars and sports, scorned scouting.) Just before Christmas, Sallie talked a lot about the Junior Assembly holiday dances which she and her crowd would be going to. The Junior Assembly was sponsored by the Junior League for sons and daughters of socially prominent families. Sallie wondered a lot about what to wear. I sat there, like Cinderella, glad to have gotten, if not to the dance, at least to the table where I could hear about it.

Perhaps my loyal listening was what paid off. The day came when Sallie told me I could call for her at her house so that we could go to the school play together. It was my greatest school triumph.

"We've never had a Catholic in our house," she mentioned in the same way she once proudly told me they had no ashtrays at her house because they were Methodists and didn't smoke.

Torn between my social ambition and the discomfort I sensed I would feel as the first Catholic (and Italian!) in that heretofore perfect household, I of course let ambition win. Yet, when I actually stood on the Shipton porch and rang the doorbell, I was shaky and nervous. Wonder if they wouldn't let me in? Would just call out "Sallie will be there!" and keep me standing outside.

I had dressed in my navy blue Easter suit and felt very circumspect. It was neat and simple with a white collar, for I wanted to reassure the Shiptons that I wasn't one of those garish, gangland or clown types that were associated with Italians. I also didn't want to look as if I were wearing a parochial school uniform, thus reminding them of my unfortunate religion. I decided to offset the sobriety of my navy blue suit by pushing the sleeves up in a contrived but nonchalant way and wearing a wide silver-link bracelet on my right wrist.

Someone *did* let me in the front door—maybe it was the mother, I don't remember because I was immediately left alone in the living room to wait. I could see for myself that there were no ashtrays, no popular magazines, no glass rings on end tables, no saints' pictures in the Shipton home. Everything was so tidy and spare that I felt acutely how my name alone created disorder in that setting. I pulled my sleeves down quickly over my suddenly too-large bracelet. I sat on the edge of a chair and waited for Sallie. The WASPness of America has never again been so formidable to me as the few minutes I sat in that parlor.

Sallie and I parted company after our graduation from junior high. I went on to an all-girls' Catholic high school where I immediately and irredeemably lost my faith and became secularized, which was the radicalism of my day, but also won a scholarship to college. The college I chose was small but select, the second oldest women's college in the country. Kimball College was named for the nineteenth-century inventor who founded and endowed it, believing ardently in higher (but separate) education for the future wives of upper-class American men. There I struggled to keep up with the girls who had come from prep schools and from families where current events were discussed at the dinner table.

The girls at Kimball all arrived with stuffed animals, quoting lines from Winnie-the-Pooh, which they had been brought up on, while I hastily went to the library and read it for the first time. I wasn't the only outsider; there were a special student from the Philippines and two Japanese-American girls who embodied the college notion of liberalism since we were at war with Japan at the time. The dozen or so Jewish girls at Kimball had their big-city backgrounds, their extroverted ways, and sound educations to help them in that WASP world. Though I no longer had the kind of adulation that had incited my schoolgirl crush on Sallie Shipton, I still regarded my college classmates as beings of a favored world. And above all, M'Lou Kimball, who was a direct descendant of the college founder and a great spouter of her family lore.

Now M'Lou Kimball was one of the glories of Kimball College. Small, pretty enough, witty, intelligent, full of charm and spirit, she had great big blue eyes and a deep laugh and was everything there was to be in that small college. Short as she was, she made the basketball team; then judicial committee; then editor of *Jottings*, the literary magazine; and in her sophomore year, she had as her prom date the grandson of a Supreme Court justice. She came from a Philadelphia suburb where everyone had acres and a colored maid, and children had trust accounts.

Her full name was Mary Louise Long Kimball, and both her Kimball and Long forebears had settled raw America. They had built towns in Pennsylvania and Ohio that still bear the family names. They had gone West. Seth Kimball had founded our college. A great-aunt of M'Lou's was a dean at Vassar; another relative, against society's disapproval, had been the first practicing woman doctor in Kimballton, Pennyslvania. And then there was the ancestor who had gone to Montana at age sixteen to get cured of brain fever, had built himself a ranch there, and advertised in the Eastern papers for a woman to come out and marry him. He drove a herd of cattle a thousand miles with only one cowhand to help him. M'Lou belonged to the race of those tall, silent, steely pioneers of Scots-Irish-English blood who had settled the wild lands and made a country; they were grave, steady-looking men and brave, diary-writing women. I revered them all.

I left Kimball after two years and finished college and graduate work at a large university. I won a Fulbright to Italy. Time passed as I met and married my Italian husband and took up life in Rome. I never lost track of my Kimball classmates for I always, out of some respect from my days at Kimball, contributed news to its *Alumnae Bulletin* while completely ignoring the *University Alumni News*. I wrote periodically to tell of my husband's books and literary awards, the birth of our children, my own publications. Was I still trying to catch up, to draw abreast of girls who were now women with den packs, charities, and civic committees, while I, bemused, wondered if I'd ever establish contact with their America?

One day, a short female stranger with a wide grin showed up at our Rome apartment exclaiming, "Petrify! Old Petrify, *how are you?*" I stared at the smiling woman in sneakers and grubby raincoat and tried to connect her with someone who would know that old nickname. ("Hi, old Petrify, how are the bananas?" the Kimball girls would call, passing me in the dorm, for my parents had often driven down from Schenectady with such woppy things as bananas and grapes for me.) Then, I recognized M'Lou Kimball.

She looked, to eyes now educated on Italian elegance, terrible. She looked, in fact, typically American.

As I knew from the *Alumnae Bulletin*, M'Lou Kimball was now Louise Rivkin. She had married Irving Rivkin while they both worked in publishing in New York, and they had gone off to Europe in a free-spirited quest of their destinies as writers. She had been the bright star of the college literary magazine, and Irv had grown up in the Chicago of James Farrell, also aspiring to write proletarian novels.

So far they had produced nothing except their annual Christmas letter; their free-spiritedness seemed to have given way to organization life and four children. Irving worked for an international committee that sent them to a new base every four or five years and gave them home-leave to the States every other year, so that though they kept up their air as struggling expatriates, they had actually ended up like foreign service personnel. They seemed to have given their creativity to a complicated lifestyle which involved dwellings in several countries and constant traveling between them all. Still I admired her courage in being so bizarre.

"It's been twenty years!" I exclaimed.

"Can't be," she said, with that old peremptory air that said she was right, I was wrong. She lit a cigarette, looked around the living room and said, "Look at you—you're married to a well-known author, you know everybody in Rome, and Irving who tracked you down and saw you on your balcony says you're prettier now than in our graduation picture." I might have been pleased at her admiration, but something rang false.

She went over to the window and looked at the apartment buildings across the way. "Looks like Hollywood," she snickered. I found what bothered me: she had referred to our graduation picture.

"Irving couldn't have seen a graduation picture with me in it," I told her, "because I didn't graduate from Kimball."

"Oh, I thought you did," she said smoothly, unruffled.

We had been a small class of only seventy-six. M'Lou and I and only one other girl had made up the entire advanced Latin class for two years—and she hadn't even noticed that I wasn't there after sophomore year to call out, "Hi, Petrify" to?

"But I had to leave!" I told her excitedly. My Rome life receded on the spot and I was old Petrify again. "I didn't belong at Kimball. You WASPS were all like one big family and I was an outsider."

"Why I never thought of that," she said, opening wide her big blue eyes. "Actually I was the one who felt different from everyone. Besides," she laughed, "I haven't been a WASP since I married Irv." Only a true one could have declined the honor with such ease, I thought.

I showed her around the apartment and asked "How did you find me?"

"You're one of the few people who kept track of our moves and answered our Christmas letter," she told me. In the kitchen she stood in mock wonder exclaiming, "Look at all your American applicances. We couldn't possibly afford such a display. You're so organized, Staff, with your washing machine and everything." And I understood what she meant: she was still the bohemian who didn't know about machines and I was the middle-class housewife.

But why should it bother me? I was amused. How could I have imagined during my two lonely years at Kimball College that I'd ever have M'Lou Kimball at my place drinking scotch, looking to me for company and advice, and asking about the literary life in Rome.

I asked about her children.

"Betty Jean, Nigel, and George—the oldest—are at school in England, and Addie, our youngest, is going to the French lycée here."

"Why don't they go to the American schools here?" I asked, since mine did.

"No point in that," Louise answered. "They won't be going to American colleges—far too expensive."

"But you've said your parents and a great-aunt left inheritances. And doesn't Irving's organization contribute to their education? *We're* the ones who have to worry about expenses!"

"Oh, Staff," Louise remonstrated with exasperation, "our kids aren't American! They don't even think about being American. They've lived all over and frankly I think it's just as well. Who cares about nationality?"

I silently remembered who had. Then I said, "But that makes no sense. Don't you tell them they're Jewish?"

"Because they are!" she said emphatically.

"Well, you and Irving are still American—you spend every other summer at your place in Vermont. So doesn't that make the kids American, too? Mine have always felt both American and Italian." I was trying to make some sense out of her statements, trying to muffle the shock I felt at her disclaimer, but she waved her hand in dismissal at my probing and went on to a literary conversation.

"Nothing in American writing is as good as an Angus Wilson novel," Louise said. "John Cheever can only be regarded as a craftsman, comparable, say, to Ford Madox Ford."

I listened to this odd stuff until she finally declared, "Irv and I gave up on Stephen Spender way back in 1948. He can't be considered a poet anymore—hasn't written a poem in years."

"How can you say that?" I quickly reacted. "Isn't Rimbaud a poet even though he never wrote anything after he was nineteen?"

But then I closed my ears to her talk with its somehow touching overtones of old-fashionedness and squareness, and freshened our drinks. She was living and talking in another age, in another place which I had once thought I wanted to inhabit. I felt kindly and somehow protective towards her. She seemed fragile despite her tennis shoes and hearty air. More, she didn't seem real. Sallie Shipton's strict Methodist parlor had been real; and the Montana ranch of the Kimball great-uncle; and the *shtetl* in eastern Europe from which Irving's grandfather had peddled his way to Chicago. But it was as if Louise and Irving hadn't held on to themselves, had drifted lazily into...what? that funny term *cosmopolitans*?

I asked Louise if she had looked up any of our other Kimball classmates who were living in Europe?

"No," she said, adding (unbelievably when I thought how she came unannounced to my door), "I guess I'm shy. But I am going to look up a friend of mine from home who now lives in Florence. She's married to a Polish painter."

"Where did she meet a Polish painter?"

"In evening art clases in Philadelphia."

I frowned and mulled over her words. "You mean, he's an American painter of Polish background?" I felt as if I were back in school with Sophie Filarski on one side of the room and Gennaro Cacciocavallo over towards the windows, and Miss Fiske was passing out some form we had to fill in and we didn't know what to put in the blank after Nationality. "Why do you call him Polish?" I asked Louise, intrigued, waiting finally for the answer.

"Because that's what he is."

I smiled and relaxed; Louise was still M'Lou Kimball.

I asked her about returning to the States at her father's death and whether she had found among his papers the preserved journals and momentoes of that Kimball forebear who had trekked west to Montana. What had happened to all those documents?

"I threw it all away," she said.

"My God!" I exclaimed. "Why didn't you give it to a library or a museum?"

"Because libraries and museums are for beautiful things," she answered.

And I wanted to ask her: What is Beauty? And, like Pilate, what is Truth? But I knew that she no longer had those answers for me.

Nonna

She has seen it all change.

Follow her now as she slowly walks down Loomis toward Taylor, her heavy black purse dangling at her side. Though it is the middle of summer she wears her black overcoat. The air conditioning is too cold inside the stores, she thinks. But the woman is not sure she is outside today to do her shopping. It is afternoon, and on summer afternoons she walks to escape the stifling heat of her tiny apartment, the thick drapes drawn shut to shade her two rooms from the sun, the air flat and silent, except for the ticking of her clock. Walking is good for her blood, she believes. Like eating the cloves of *aglio*.

She hesitates, the taste of *aglio* on her tongue. Perhaps she is outside this afternoon to shop. She cannot decide. The children of the old neighborhood call out to her as she passes them. *Na-na!* The sound used to call in goats from feeding. Or, sometimes, to tease. Or is it *Nonna*, grandmother, that they call? It makes no difference, the woman thinks. The thin-ribbed city dogs sniff the hem of her long black dress, wagging their dark tails against her legs. Birds fly above her head.

Around her is the bustle of the street corner, the steady rumble and jounce of cars and delivery trucks, the sharply honking horns, the long screeching hiss of a braking CTA bus. The young men from the Taylor Street Social and Athletic Club seem to ignore her as she passes. They lean against streetlight poles and parking meters in the afternoon sun. One chews a cigar; another, a toothpick. One walks in front of her, then turns to the gutter and spits. The woman looks into their faces but she does not recognize any of them, though she knows they are the sons of the sons of the neighborhood men she and her Vincenzo once knew. Grandsons of *compari*. Do they speak the old language? she wonders. Like a young girl, she is too shy to ask them.

One boy wears a *cornicelli* and a thin cross around his neck. The gold sparkles in the light. Nonna squints. Well, at least they are still Catholics, she thinks, and her lips move as she says to herself *They are still Catholics*, and her hand begins to form the sign of the Cross. Then she remembers she is out on the street, so she stops herself. Some things are better done privately. The boy's muscled arms are dark, tanned, folded gracefully over his sleeveless T-shirt. The boy has a strong chin. Nonna smiles and wets her lips in anticipation of greeting him, but his eyes stare past her, vacantly, at the rutted potholes and assorted litter lying next to the curb in the street.

She looks at what he stares at. He grunts to himself and joins his friends. On the shaded side of Loomis is the new store, a bookstore. The letters above the front window read T SWANKS. Could the *T* stand for Tonio? she wonders. She crosses the street. Then it should properly be an *A*. For Antonio. Anthony. Named for any one of the holy Antonios, maybe even the gentle Francescano from Padova. Nonna always preferred the Francescano but never told anyone. He had helped her to find many lost things. She believes that if she were to speak her preference aloud she would give offense to all the others, and what does she know of them—Heaven is full of marvelous saints. Her lips whisper Padova.

The sound is light. Nonna enjoys it and smiles. She pictures Padova on the worn, tired boot. Vincenzo called Italy that. Nonna remembers that Padova sits far up in the north, west of Venezia. She looks down at her black shoes. Italia. She was from the south, from Napoli, and Vincenzo, her husband, may he rest, came from the town of Altofonte, near Palermo, in Sicilia. The good strong second son of *contadini*.

A placard in the bookstore window reads FREE TEA OR COFFEE—BROWSERS WELCOME. Nonna is tempted to enter. She draws together the flaps of her black overcoat. She could look at a map of Italia if the store had one, and then maybe she could ask Mr. Swanks for which of the Antonios was he named. And what part of the boot his family came from, and does he still speak the old language. She does not realize that T Swanks might not be the name of the store's proprietor. She assumes that, like many, Swanks is an Italian who has shortened his name.

Beneath the sign in the window is a chess set. Its pieces are made of ivory. The woman stares at the tiny white horse. It resembles bone. She remembers the evening she and Vincenzo were out walking in the fields and came across a skeleton. That was in New Jersey, where they had met, before they came to Chicago. She thought the skeleton was a young child's—she flailed her arms and screamed—but then Vincenzo held her hands and assured her it was only an animal. Eh, a dog or a lamb, he had said, his thin face smiling. Digging with his shoe, Vincenzo then uncovered the carcass. It indeed had looked like a dog or a lamb. That was a night she would never forget, the woman thinks. And that smell. *Dio!* It had made her young husband turn away and vomit. But Nonna is certain now that what she saw in that field that dusky autumn evening had been a child, a newborn *bambino*, clothed only by a damp blanket of leaves. The Devil had made it look like a dog! New Jersey was never the same after that. She made Vincenzo quit his good job at the foundry. They had to go away from that terrible place. Nonna openly makes the sign of the Cross.

She knows what she has seen. And she knows what kind of woman did it. Not a Catholic, she thinks, for that would have been the very worst of sins. It had been someone without religious training. Maybe a Mexican. But there hadn't been any Mexicans in New Jersey. Nonna is puzzled again. And all Mexicans are Catholics, she thinks. Each Sunday now the church is full of them. They sit to the one side, the Virgin's side, in the back pews. Afterward they all go to their Mexican grocery store. And what do they buy? Nonna had wondered about that all during Mass one bright morning, and then from church she had followed them. The Mexicans came out of their strange store talking their quick Mexican and carrying bananas and bags of little flat breads. Great bunches of long bananas. So green—

Maybe Mexicans don't know how to bake with yeast. Nonna realizes her lips are moving again, so she covers her mouth with her hand. If that is true, she thinks, then maybe she should go inside Mr. Antonio Swanks's new bookstore and see if he has a book on how to use yeast. Then she could bring it to the Mexicans. It might make them happy. When they kneel in the rear pews, the Mexicans never look happy. Nonna shifts her weight from foot to foot, staring at the little white horse.

But the book would have to be in Mexican. And it would cost money, she thinks. She does not have much money. Barely enough for necessities, for neckbones and the beans of coffee and *formaggio* and *aglio* and salt. And of course for bread. What was she thinking about? she asks herself. Did she have to go to the store to buy something? Or is she just outside for her walk?

She looks inside the bookstore window and sees a long-haired girl behind the counter. Her head is bent. She is reading. Nonna smiles. It is what a young girl should do when she is in a bookstore. She should study books. When she is in church, she should pray for a good husband, someone young, with a job, who will not hit her. Then when she is older, married, she should pray to the Madonna for some children. To have one. To have enough. Nonna nods and begins counting on her fingers. For a moment she stops, wondering where she placed her rosary.

No, she says aloud. She is counting children, not saying the rosary.

Nonna is pleased she has remembered. It is a pleasant thought. Five children for the girl—one for each finger—and one special child for her to hold tightly in her palm. That would be enough. They would keep the girl busy until she became an old woman, and then, if she has been a good mother, she could live with one of her sons. The girl behind the counter turns a page of her book. Nonna wonders what happened to her own children. Where were Nonna's sons?

She hears a shout from the street. She turns. A carload of boys has driven up, and now, from the long red automobile, the boys are spilling out. Are they her sons? Nonna stares at them. The boys gather around the car's hood. One thumps his hand on the shining metal on his way to the others. One boy is laughing. She sees his white teeth. He embraces the other boy, then throws a mock punch.

They are not her sons.

She turns back. It is clear to her now that the girl has no childen. So that is why she is praying there behind the counter! Nonna wants to go inside so she can tell the unfortunate Mrs. Swanks not to give up her hopes yet, that she is still young and healthy, that there is still time, that regardless of how it appears the holy saints are always listening, always testing, always waiting for you to throw up your hands and say *basta* and give up so that they can say, heh, we would have given you a house full of *bambini* if only you had said one more novena. Recited one more rosary. Lit one more candle. But you gave up hope. The saints and the Madonna were like that. Time to them does not mean very much. And even God knows that each woman deserves her own baby. Didn't He even give the Virgin a son?

Poor Mrs. Swanks, Nonna thinks. Her Antonio must not be good for her. It is often the fault of the man. The doctors in New Jersey had told her that. Not once, but many times. That was so long ago. But do you think I listened? Nonna says to herself. For one moment? For all those years? My ears were deaf! Nonna is gesturing angrily with her hands. She strikes the store's glass window. It was part of Heaven's test, she is saying, to see if I would stop believing. She pulls her arms to her breasts as she notices the black horses. They stare at her with hollow eyes. Inside the bookstore the manager closes his book and comes toward the window. Nonna watches her close her book and stand, then raise her head. She wears a mustache. It is a boy.

Nonna shuts her eyes and turns. She was thinking of something— But now she has forgotten again. She breathes through her open mouth. It was the boys, she thinks. They did something to upset her. She walks slowly now to slow her racing heart. Did they throw snowballs at me? No, it is not winter again. Nonna looks around at the street and the sidewalk. No, there is no snow. But she feels cold.

Then they must have said something again, she thinks. What was it? Something cruel. She stops on the street. Something about—

The word returns. Bread.

So she is outside to go to the bakery. Nonna smiles. It is a very good idea, she thinks, because she has no bread. She begins walking again, wondering why she had trekked all the way to Taylor Street if she was out only for bread. The Speranza Bakery is on Flournoy Street, she says aloud. Still, it is pleasant today and walking is good for her heart. She thinks of what she might buy. A small roll to soak in her evening coffee?

The afternoon is bright, and Nonna walks up the shaded side of Loomis, looking ahead like an excited child at the statue of Christopher Columbus in the park. She likes the statue. Furry white clouds float behind the statue's head. Jets of water splash at its feet. She remembers the day the workers uncovered it. There had been a big parade and many important speeches. Was there a parade now? Nonna faces the street. There is only a garbage truck.

So it must not be Columbus Day. Unless the garbage truck is leading the parade. But it is the mayor who leads the parade, Nonna says, and he is not a garbage truck. She laughs at her joke. She is enjoying herself, and she looks again at the green leaves on the trees and at the pure clean clouds in the blue sky.

The mayor, she hears herself saying, is Irish. Nonna wonders why Irish is green. Italia too is green, but it is also red and white. The garbage truck clattering by her now is blue. So many colors.

She thinks of something but cannot place it. It is something about Italians and the Irish. The mayor. His name. He cannot be *paesano* because he is not from Italy. But she knows it is something to do with that. At the curb alongside her a pigeon pecks a crushed can.

It is Judas. Nonna remembers everything now. How the mayor unveiled the statue and then switched on the water in the fountain, how all of the neighborhood people cheered him when he waved to them from the street. All the police. Then the people were very angry, and the police held them back. Where did they want to go? Nonna thinks, then remembers. To the university, she says, to the new school of Illinois that the Irish Judas had decided to build in their neighborhood. The mayor's Judas shovel broke the dirt. And then, one by one, the old Italian stores closed, and the *compari* and *amici* boxed their belongings and moved, and the Judas trucks and bulldozers drove in and knocked down their stores and houses. The people watched from the broken sidewalk. Nonna remembers the woman who had tapped on her door, asking if she would sign the petition paper. The paper asked the mayor to leave the university where it was, out on a pier on the lake. Was that any place for a school? Nonna asked the woman. The woman then spoke to her in the old language, but in the Sicilian dialect, saying that Navy Pier was a perfectly good place. Then why build the school here? Nonna said. Daley, the woman said. Because of Mayor Daley. Because he betrayed us. Because he wants to destroy all that the Italians have built. First on the North Side, with the Cabrini Green projects, he drove us out. Now he wants to do it again here. He wants to drive us entirely from his city, even though we have always voted for him and supported his political machine. Sign the paper. If you understand me and agree, please sign the paper. For a moment Nonna thinks she is the woman. She looks down to see the paper in her hands.

There is no paper. The paper had not been any good. The men in the street had told Nonna that. Shouting up to her windows, waving at her with their angry fists. She had yelled from her windows for them not to make so much noise. Two men tried to explain. Then what is good? Nonna had asked them. You tell me. I want to know. What is good? She is shouting. A car on Loomis slows, then passes her by and speeds up.

These, the men had answered. Rocks. Nonna is afraid again as she remembers. She had pulled her drapes tightly shut. But still from behind her open windows she had been able to hear all through the long night the shouts of the men who kept her awake and the rocks, rocks, rocks, thrown at the squad cars patrolling the streets and through the windows of the alderman's office.

She hears the water. Splashing up to the feet of Christopher Columbus, the boy who stood at the sea's edge thinking the world was round like a shiny new apple. Nonna knows history. She memorized it to pass the citizen test. Columbus asked himself why he first saw the tall sails of approaching ships, and then the apple fell from the tree and hit him on the head and he discovered it. Nonna is smiling. She is proud that Columbus is *paesano*. Sometimes when she studied and could not remember an answer, she would hit herself on the head. That knocks the answer out of sleeping, she says. Though sometimes it does not, and Nonna thinks of her own head, how once it had been full of answers, but now many answers are no longer there. She must have lost them when she wasn't looking. Should she pray to Saint Antonio? But he helps only with things, with objects. Maybe, Nonna thinks, when she puts something new inside her head, something old must then fall out. And then it is lost forever. That makes sense, she says. She laughs to herself. It is the way it is with everything. The new pushes out the old. And then— She puts her hands to her head.

There is only so much here, she says. Only so many places to put the answers. Nonna thinks of the inside of her head. She pictures brain and bone and blood. Like in the round white cartons in the butcher's shop, she

says. The same. She makes a face. All those answers in all those little
cartons. Suddenly Nonna is hungry. She wants a red apple.

A group of girls sits at the fountain's edge. Nonna hears their talk. She
looks at them, cocking her head. Did they just ask her for an apple? Someone
had been asking her a question. I don't have any, she says to the girls. She
pats the pockets of her black coat. See? she says. No apples. She wonders
what kind of girls they are, to be laughing like that on the street.

They must be common, Nonna thinks. Their laughter bounces up and
down the sunny street. Like Lucia, the girl who lives downstairs, who
sometimes sits out on the steps on summer nights playing her radio. Nonna
often watches the girl from her windows; how can she help it, the music is
always so loud. A polite girl, Nonna thinks, but always with that radio. And
once, one night when Nonna was kneeling in her front room before her
statue of the Madonna, she heard Lucia with somebody below on the stairs.
She stopped praying and listened. She could not understand any of the
words, but she recognized the tone, and, oh, she knew what the girl and the
boy were doing. The night was hot, and that brought back to her the thin
face of her Vincenzo, and she was suddenly young again and back in terrible
New Jersey, in her parents' house, with young Vincenzo in the stuffed chair
opposite her and around them the soft sound of her mother's tranquil
snoring. Nonna shakes her head. She knows what she must feel about that
night. She was trusting, and Vincenzo was so handsome—his black curls lay
so delicately across his forehead, and his smile was so wet and so white,
bright—and she allowed the young boy to sit next to her on the sofa, and
she did not protest when he took her hand, and then, when he kissed her,
she even opened her mouth and let his wet tongue touch hers. Oh, she was
so frightened. Her mouth had been so dry. On the street now she is trembling.
She is too terrified to remember the rest. But the memory spills across her
mind with the sound of the girls' easy laughter, and she moves back on the
pink sofa and does not put up her hands as Vincenzo strokes her cheek and
then touches her, gently, on the front of her green dress. And then she turns
to the boy and quickly kisses him. The light from the oil lamp flickers. The
snoring stops. She looks at Vincenzo, and then she blushes with the shame
of her mortal sin, and now if Vincenzo does not say they will marry she
knows she will have to kill herself, and that in God's eyes she has already
died.

Nonna is still, silent, standing in her guilt on the street, afraid even now
to cross herself for fear she will be struck down. She feels the stifling weight
of her sin. Vincenzo then moved back to the stuffed chair, coughing. Neither
spoke. She began to cry. The next morning, Vincenzo spoke to her father.

There are boys at the fountain now, talking. Nonna looks up from the
crack in the sidewalk she was staring at. The girls sit like bananas, all in a
bunch. One of the boys flexes his arm muscles, like a real *malandrino*. The
girls look at him and laugh. Nonna recognizes Lucia. She wears a tight pink
top and short pants. Why doesn't she hear Lucia's radio? Nonna wonders.
A voice inside her head answers her question. Because the girl is with the
boys. And when you are with them, Nonna says out loud, you do not need
the radio.

They look up. Nonna knows she must avoid them. They heard me, she whispers to herself, and now they will throw apples at me. *Santa Maria, madre di Dio.* She feels awkward as her feet strike the pavement. From behind she hears them calling.

Nonna! Hey Nonna! Who were you talking to? Hey, Nonna!

Nonna begins to run, and as she does her heavy purse bangs her side, up and down, again and again. Then the sound of their laughter fades away, and Nonna slows, feeling the banging inside her chest. Now they heard, she thinks, now they know my sin, and they will tell everyone. And then everyone, even the old priests here in Chicago, will know. I'll have to move to another neighborhood, she tells a fire hydrant. I'll pack my pans and the Madonnina and flee. But I have done that already two times. First, from New Jersey, and then when I was punished by the machines who flattened my house down. Nonna does not count the move from Naples, when her family fled poverty and the coming war, nor the move from her parents' house when she married Vincenzo.

He would not have wanted her to be so lonely, she thinks. She is lucid, then confused. Vincenzo understood why she could bear no children; it was because of their sin. Perhaps now that everybody knows, she thinks, she would not have to move any more. Maybe since the whole world knows, I can finally rest where I am now and be finished with my punishment. And then I'll die, Nonna says. And then, if I have been punished enough, I will be once again with my Vincenzo.

Her legs turn the corner for her. They are familiar with the streets. Nonna is on Flournoy, across from the church of Our Lady of Pompeii. At first the building looks strange to her, as if she were dreaming. The heavy wooden doors hang before her inside a golden cloud. She walks into the cloud. It is the blood in her head, the bone and the brain, she thinks. She pictures the fat butcher. The church's stone steps are hollowed, like spoons. Again she feels hungry. As she walks into the sunlight she wonders why she is wearing such a heavy coat. Nonna asks the door her question. The doors stand high before her, silent. She pulls on their metal handles. The doors are locked.

She could go to the rectory and ask the priest for the keys. But they never give them to me, Nonna tells the doors. The priests tell me to come back for the Mass that evening, and I ask them if they don't think the saints and the Madonna are lonely with no one praying to them in the afternoon, and they say there are people all over the world who are praying, every moment of the day, but I don't believe it. If it was true, it would be a different world, don't you think? She presses her cheek against the wood. Don't you think? she says. Don't you understand me?

Then she hears something behind her and she turns. A dog. Panting before the first of the stone steps. Its ears are cocked. It is listening. Nonna laughs. The dog gives her a bark, and then from the middle of the park across the street comes the sound of a boy calling. He jumps in the sun, waving a dark stick. Nonna points to him. The boy is dark, like the stick. A Mexican. So it is a Mexican dog. And Nonna says, I would tell you that boy wants you, but I don't know Mexican, and if I spoke to you in my tongue from Napoli you would just be confused. The dog turns and runs, as if understanding. Again Nonna laughs. What is she doing at the top of the stairs? She knows the church is kept locked in the afternoon because of the vandals. Haven't the priests often told her that?

Her hand grasps the iron railing. She must be careful because of her legs. They get too tired from all the time holding her up. When she reaches the sidewalk she stops and faces the church and kneels, making the sign of the Cross. Then she walks again down Flournoy Street.

Why was I at the church? she thinks. She makes the sign of the Cross and then smiles as she walks past the rectory, and now she remembers the church-basement meeting she attended because of the paper she signed. It is good to sit with *paesani*, she thinks, and she pictures the faces of the neighborhood people, then the resolute eyes and mouth of the woman who gave the big speech. How much intelligence the woman has! Nonna notices that her hands are moving together, clapping. It is good to clap, good for the blood. She stops. But only in the meetings. The woman had said once and for all that it was the mayor's fault.

Vincenzo, Nonna whispers. She sees his still face sleeping on a soft pillow. His mouth is turned down into a frown. Vincenzo, I tell you, it was not your fault.

Nonna closes her eyes. She feels dizzy. It was the meeting, all the talk, the smoke. Then she realizes that was years ago, but she feels she had just been talking with her Vincenzo. Had he been at the meeting? No. Vincenzo died before the neighborhood changed. Before the students came. The *stranieri*. Before the Mexicans crept into the holes left by the *compari*. Then she must be walking home from Vincenzo's funeral. It was held at Our Lady of Pompeii. No, she had been driven to the cemetery in a long black car. Where is home? she thinks. Where am I walking to? And she pictures the faces of her parents, the rooms in the house in Napoli, the house in New Jersey, Vincenzo's house, the house in Chicago and the dust and the machines. Then—

Two rooms.

Nonna remembers where she lives.

So. She must go there. She worries that she has left something burning on the stove. Was it neckbones? Was that what she had taken out for her supper? Or was it meat in the white cartons? Had she bought brains? She cannot think. Her legs are very tired. She will eat, if it is time, when she gets home.

The color of the sky is changing, and the traffic grows more heavy in the streets. It must be time, Nonna says to herself. She wishes to hurry so she won't be late. She does not like to eat when it is dark out. When it is dark she prays, then goes to bed. That is why there is the night, so people have a time for that.

Nonna approaches the street corner, and when she sees a woman coming out of a doorway with a bag full of groceries she remembers that she is out shopping. So that is why she has worn her heavy coat! But first she took a walk. The afternoon had been very nice, very pleasant. Did I enjoy myself? she thinks. It is difficult to decide. Finally she says yes, but only if I can remember what I am outside shopping for. What is it? It was on the tip of her tongue. What was it that she needed?

She turns at the door, and as she opens it she realizes that this is no longer the Speranza Bakery. It is now the Mexican food store. She is frightened. Her legs carry her into the store. The dark man behind the counter looks up at her and nods. Now she cannot turn around and leave, she thinks. She hopes the Mexican will not ask her what she wants. What would she say? Her feet move slowly down the first aisle. Her hands draw together the flaps of her coat.

Well, she thinks, I must need something. She does not want a can of vegetables, nor any of the juices in heavy bottles. She sees the butcher's case and tries to remember if she needs meat. Then she pictures neckbones in a pan atop her stove. She must hurry, she thinks, before they burn.

Cereal, vinegar, *biscotti* in paper boxes. Cottage cheese or eggs? Nonna's heart beats loudly when she sees the red apples, but she remembers how difficult apples are to chew, and she is too impatient now to cut them first into tiny pieces. Nonna smiles. Vincenzo had always said she was a patient woman. But not any longer. Not with hard red apples and a sharp knife.

Then she sees the bananas and, excited, she remembers.

What she needs is next to the counter. In plastic bags. Nonna is so happy that tears come to her eyes. So this is why she was outside, she thinks, why she is now inside this strange store. She had wanted to try the freckled Mexican flat breads. Hadn't someone before been telling her about them? Nonna holds the package in her hands and thinks. She cannot remember, but she is sure it had been someone. The woman with the petition paper, or maybe the girl who prayed for babies in the bookstore. Someone who explained that her punishment was nearly over, that soon she would be with her Vincenzo. That there were the breads that were too simple to have been baked with yeast, that these did not rise, round and golden, like other breads, like women fortunate enough to feel their bellies swell, their breasts grow heavy with the promise of milk, but instead these stayed in one shape, simple, flat.

The dark man behind the counter nods and smiles.

Perhaps, Nonna thinks as her fingers unclasp her purse and search for the coins her eyes no longer clearly see, perhaps bread is just as good this way.

Juniper Street Sketches

Excerpts from a Novel-in-Progress

1

Juniper Street was many things but most of all a boundary. It closed us in and did so with the briefest of fences: a neat black oblong on a tall black pole, JUNIPER STREET, written in squat white letters in a metal frame to certify enclosure. It was a tidy frontier, thrust like a stake in the concrete belly of the earth, a proletarian flag befitting the city-scale and row-house elegance it served. It might have seemed a neat obituary to some, but black and white on sidewalk gray, they were our city colors and standard, telegraphing our totem to the encroaching world, so that on entering and departing all who passed there might know our clan.

Unflappable, JUNIPER STREET looked coolly, crisply out, establishing sovereignty, stipulating turf. Never mind there was no juniper tree in sight; it might not have fared half so well as that barren stake of New World manufacture with concrete roots and painted trunk, spreading invisible branches and conspiring with pavement, porch-rail, and front stoop to supplant the family tree.

Granted, it was a "family" larger than most, extending a street long and a street wide, registered in three dozen names that stood, in turn, for over a hundred souls—its numbers nowhere impaled upon a page and never static. Few souls left except for the ultimate irreversible frontier, though children were forever being born into it. But that didn't mean "the family" was limitless either, for the kin-zone was rigorously confined to just those who were a part—street-end to dead-end, front stoop to alley—the immediate neighborhood. One street over, one street down—Camac, Montrose, Hicks—made no difference: they were equally another order, each as distinguishable from us as Jesuits and Franciscans, Bostonians and Atlantans are from one another.... *They*, after all, required no loyalty, no partisanship right-or-wrong from us, for which we might have to sacrifice a bloody nose, a badge of honor that we *did*, in fact, belong. The essential bond was *address*, and it was every bit as firm a fracture as San Pietro and Rebibia were in the Old Country, where—as we had heard countless times in reminiscences about "back there"—the presence of the next hilltown was signaled by a sign no one knew how old, four times as tall and deep as that embossed JUNIPER STREET was for us, holding equally strange power: black words impaled an ochre ground.

For, more than what one was or did, it was common—back there "on the other side"—to be identified by place. Physical, mental traits might be acknowledged in person but they were assigned by town. It made no difference the age or sex, whether a member left or strayed or had established residence elsewhere: all shared the village character. If town members did not presently conform, there was no hurry; they would in time *become* so. It was just this widespread, credulous terrain Pasquale built on in the telling of a tale, that interfacing of people with their places. Thus, no one wondered that "the women in San Pietro are vain, the men short on imagination." He might just as easily have proposed other places, other traits and achieved an equally undisputed, acquiesced-to profile: in Arsino they had wide foreheads and long noses; San Martino was the home of the short chin; in Inna they were prone to warts; in Genina one would do well to count the change; and in Orla people were so contentious they fought even in their sleep.

Our village profiles were hardly different. On Sundays the arbor seethed with certain knowledge. The characterizing phrase, the instant analysis helped to illuminate the night. . . . Beware of Montrose, they nursed a nasty grudge; Hicks, good company and good wine but watch out for "the easy touch"; Camac, fists first, talk later, the men were insanely jealous of their wives. And Juniper Street? . . . It may have been many things in the argot of the adjoining "hilltowns," but perhaps it was said most often that people there had little cunning and were remarkably foolish in matters of the heart. . . .

Don't think such capsule profiles were merely fanciful, just randomly or spitefully arrived at. Quite the contrary. They were fully documented— part family album, part oral history, a psychic log peculiar to each village, destined in our urban hilltowns to become the folklore of each block. "The block" was final arbiter of nicknames and reputations, a huge repository of even the small detail, and in its vast stores were preserved places of origin, occupations, striking or identifying hallmarks, peccadilloes, family skeletons even, all condensed and codified in the brief explanatory coda often appended to a name—Mary from Aquila, Pete the Fruitman, Eleanor the Redhead, Tony the Hunchback, Frankie Next-Door, Hookey George, Carla the Tramp—and those might be still remembered after surnames, circumstances, nature's endowments and proclivities were long altered and forgotten. It was convenient shorthand, too, for the much larger dramas, the culled episodes that had galvanized and impressed "the block," stirring not only gossip but that lingering group imagination that fed the street totem and fortified the clan. There was Old Man Joseph on Hicks Street and his two wives—one we knew nagged him relentlessly though he couldn't hear, and she was toothless, while the other, left long ago in Orla, still waited for his long-promised, prosperous return and still wrote letters of recrimination with the aid of the village priest, which alternated with curious amorous notes that appeared in a different, suddenly passionate and flowing hand, reputedly penned—in the mysterious ways of knowing of the block—by a philandering notary public who was having his fun with her. There was Henrietta from Montrose, who had buried her only son twelve years before and never ceased ironing and setting out his clothes for school each day, a familiar figure going back and forth to church in a fruitless, candle-burning search for the peace of his soul and her own, her skin taking on the look and smell of redemptive tallow, and she was only thirty-eight. There were the Old Maid De Zio sisters, twins who had never married and who sat in summer in identical sundresses and straw hats at the open window, fanning one another and finishing each other's sentences, and, as long as anyone could remember, sharing with a deep sigh of mutual comprehension the exact affliction—a rare and incurable inflammation of the heart.

These brief lives—and endless capsule histories more—were served up with fruit and conversation in the arbor, each reinforced with brandy and unadulterated through the years. These vintage tales, scattered with ease and malice upon the night, reduced an infinitely complicated world to finite scale, to known, less ominous frontiers, much as the wicked stepmother, the good fairy, the simpleton and wiseman compress a universe too large to habitable contours in the imagination of a child. Only, tales of the block were grown-up stepping-stones, where adults, like children moving story by story, boundary by boundary through other lives, could find temporary refuge, and where they, too, might effect a crossing.

But Juniper Street was only partly barrier-frontier. It was protection, too, a safety net beyond which it could prove hazardous to venture. Children knew this instinctively and went to school, to church, on errands, to the corner store in groups, learning to trust and distrust the street pack as they grew, clustering on corners, choosing hangouts and front stoops in little enclaves, rarely doing or thinking anything alone. Even "the friends" from the equally tight-knit world of parents were like that, as though hanging laundry, sipping tea, playing cards in common were documentary proof and welcome confirmation of their non-aloneness in an alien world beset with danger. All we, the children of the block, could hope for was cautious escape from the encroaching cover, and, after each hazardous foray out-of-bounds, safe landing in a benign Juniper Street of adults.

2

The night was long and languid, one of those unending peaks of summer, the best time for "the old friends" and full enjoyment of the arbor—that grapevine and morning glory splendor Uncle Sandro had planted, tended, and trimmed to the perfect sanctuary stillness of that moment. My cousin Paul and I were expectantly tucked away in our trellis corner instead of the beds assigned to us upstairs, suddenly living out the fantasy—lush, perfumed, and well-hidden—we had already discussed before, of being both *with* and spying *on* the grown-ups, who were happily reminiscing amid abundant wine and cherries, capping the day's outing with one, and then another, and still "one more for the road."

The night-light had been turned on, a muted but not too gentle glow, vying with spots of color from two oil lamps my mother and Aunt Louisa had set out along with the earthenware pitchers, the decanter of homemade brandy, and small plump glasses that went with it. There was an afterglow about the evening, like the churchlight in Our Lady's Grotto, where votive candles played light-and-dark, sin-and-forgiveness games on our faces as we said penance on Saturday afternoons and "returned to grace." In fact, it seemed a giant halo, a golden crown of leaves, had slipped onto the arbor. A hush settled, the way it did a moment before an actor took the stage, and

Pasquale, not looking half so paunchy and neighborly as he did every day, drew all eyes and attention to the lampglow and his voice.

"You want a story. Well, this is a true one. . .you may not think so, but I swear it happened. In fact, it made San Pietro, the next village from my own—over there, 'on the other side'—famous in our parts. The women ever since are considered vain there and the men short on imagination." Pasquale paused as his voice made a slight descent from conversation that gave the women time to glance slyly at one another while the men nodded.

"Well, I don't have to tell you funerals are taken very seriously in such places. Why, a man's reputation is measured by the size of his funeral, the type of procession, the kind of wreaths, and, of course, the ribbons." The last word was pronounced deliberately and was meant to become the focus of all thoughts.

"In San Pietro these are kept in the sexton's shed at the entrance of the graveyard. It's the perfect place to check on what goes on among the living and to take care of the needs of the dead. The sexton keeps his shovels and shears there, and for one night—the one imediately following the funeral— the ribbons are kept there, too. The ribbons are removed from the wreaths and flowers right after the funeral party has gone home and are stored in the shed until the next morning when someone from the family is sent out to collect them. Then and thereafter, they are set in a special place—the best spot in the parlor—along with the photographs of the dead."

"This is going to be a long one," someone interrupted to the accompaniment of dark looks and many irritated "shhhhs."

"Well, I mention it so you can appreciate how the people of San Pietro felt when the funeral ribbons were stolen the first time. Yes, *stolen*. In the dead of night—the funeral night—when the sexton was home sleeping and the ribbons were unguarded. But you can imagine the excitement after the *next* funeral when the sexton ran to the village priest and announced those ribbons had been stolen too. They tried to keep the matter quiet but already there was talk. A meeting—a secret one—was held of the most important men in town: the mayor, the priest, the chief of police, and in San Pietro, very likely, the 'friend of a friend.'" The men all smiled at this age-old reference to a Mafia presence, and the women nodded.

"They decided, in strictest confidence of course, to keep an all-night vigil the evening of the next funeral. They reasoned—and they were right— that such criminals go unreformed, and the culprit, having struck twice, would rob again. They hid by the sexton's shed, waiting past three to almost four in the morning. It's dark and cold in the graveyard then, and San Pietro's is eerier and draftier than most. . . ."

"Get on with it, Pasquale. . ."

"Give me another brandy, quick, before the next part. . ."

"It was pitch dark in the cemetery when. . .at that hour. . .ready to give up, they heard a branch snap. They heard heavy breathing, as though someone had been running. Someone was now almost upon the spot. They jumped out. They struggled as she tried to get away. . . ."

"*She*?" The women looked more horrified than the men.

"She! They brought her within the hour before the judge, who had been summoned excitedly from his bed. Because of the unusual features of the case, a few important people in the town were present, which is how *I* heard about it...."

"Pasquale, please!"

"The court stenographer was there, very pale and shaken, barely able to take notes...but then, she was his cousin."

There was absolute silence as Pasquale sipped his wine.

"The judge was wide awake and solemn and brought matters immediately to the point.'What can you say for yourself? How can you have done this terrible, terrible thing?' The woman almost whispered. 'I did it...for the satin. There is none so fine.'

"Scandal had spread from face to face and the woman looked contrite. 'For the satin!' The judge seemed truly stupefied at that. 'But what did you do with it?...with such fine satin...as you put it?'

"'I...I use it. I make things....' She said this so modestly she might have passed for the victim and not the criminal apprehended at the scene. "'You *use* it? You *make* things! Next you will tell me you *sell* it...and to the next village at that!' The judge was bellowing by then, more and more aware that his select audience had never been so riveted before. 'Well, if you make things, perhaps you have a example of your handiwork to show the court. You do, don't you?'

"She hesitated. 'Yes, sir, I do.'

"'And do you have it with you?'

"'Yes, sir, I do.' The woman seemed resigned to being before the court, and while her voice was still not firm, she answered without pausing.

"'Well, then,'—and here the judge made a dramatic gesture to underscore the moment—'show the court then...right now...what it is you do with floral ribbons robbed from the dead, poached from a family's honor.'

"The woman froze. The judge gave her a truly fierce, even a menacing look. He could hardly afford to get the worst of the encounter before such distinguished witnesses who, by daybreak, would report to the entire village how seriously—or not—he took San Pietro's reputation and good name."

Pasquale paused, taking another sip of wine in a silence so startling the crickets crowed.

"The woman, more desperate than contrite, looked from the judge, who never ceased his glaring, to her cousin, paler than ever now and slowly shrinking, intent, as both court stenographer and as kin, on every word. She closed her eyes. She took a step closer to the bench. She pulled up her skirt...lifting it up, up, high enough to hide her face behind and block her shame. There were ripples of shock. For there, exposed to the judge's and, of course, the general view, glossy and white above her immense thighs, were her fine satin bloomers. In front, in banner letters across her navel and pointing down to the regions below, embossed like a judgment from beyond the grave, was proclaimed, *Sempre Amata* (Always Loved). While in the rear, etched in delicate blue script, in appreciation and in solemn memory of the deceased, *Resquiescat in Pace* (Rest in Peace) was stamped lovingly on her behind."

There was a burst of laughter, like the cannonfire of audience applause—the growing hilarity that always marked the end of Pasquale's tales.

These, long and complicated, with all the turns and touches of the practiced raconteur, were eagerly awaited among "the friends," for he was their neighborhood bard, annointed by laughter wherever he went, their beloved mimic who slipped in a pinch of malice to enliven the brew. The arbor was his surrogate village square and he the lone commedia dell'arte player, bowing and occasionally bellowing on a green-fringed, tile-walk stage to rival any in Rebibia, his hometown, or in San Pietro, or a thousand Old Country places that could command a loyal following and, despite the occasional "get-on-with-it" grumble, an affectionate audience of old friends. Even now the men still hugged themselves, clutching and thumping their sides as they guffawed uproariously. The women smiled in spite of themselves; some were even fully laughing, lifting the cloak of modesty usually put on for the occasion. As the renewed hilarity spread, some—men and women alike—were almost in tears from the accumulated tension that had finally exploded in the peculiar finale of Pasquale's tale.

Paul and I struggled to keep silent, suppressing the outburst that had begun to build the moment the woman picked up her skirt to show the floral ribbons—a picture that remained morbidly fixed in the imagination, and which was, for all that was lost on us, the punchline. Never mind that any titillated giggle from our corner would have been devoured like the proverbial snowball in hell in the insatiable swells of grown-up laughter. At the moment we felt morally superior to a titter and admirably restrained all sound in favor of two or three meaningful looks with accompanying jab of elbow. Each of us prayed the other had fully understood the Latin or, at least, remembered individual words well enough for a search of the school library the next day. For, although bloomers alone were more than enough to enthrall *us*, it was clear something in the peculiar foreign phrases whipped the grown-ups to a strange and raucous pitch of laughter. Someone would shout *Sempre Amata*, someone else *Requiescat in Pace*, and a new round would immediately be set off, with lamplight throwing hectic light upon their faces. Fortunately, the renewed slapping of sides with repeated catchword helped us to commit the strange words very solidly to memory for the next day.

Still, we were unhappy about missing some important secret part; it disturbed us that with all our straining, our attention to every word and detail in their looks, there was a more-than-we-could fathom in the way the grown-ups chortled, in how they rolled their eyes and exchanged those playful, sidelong glances. We were afraid—as in our trellis watch in spring—that seeing and hearing were not all, that other layers camouflaged their secret. What they knew was like the illustrations in our textbook *Ages of the Earth:* there were deep understrata where trapped life abounded, a stilled record of habitats and migrations, matings and moltings, an exacting log of incursions and invasions by ice, lava, and water armies—all the unwritten confessions of the natural world. Who would have suspected they were there had not our textbook cross-sectioned and diagrammed the message? And now, we, too, were armed with a fossil clue. From a low of feeling still-left-out, it generated new excitement for our watching, requiring of us not the slow painstaking research of an earth science but a sense of instant retrieval and discovery. It was the type of "find" that accompanied those unplanned adventures that perpetually overtook our favorite hero and heroine on holiday in the mystery books we loved. We felt in our heady expectation every bit as they did—those relentless explorers and over-curious sleuths not much older than ourselves, excavating untold human lives and relations, digging for motives, uncovering old passions, restoring lost children, exposing frauds, and matchmaking with an impunity that made their adolescence a golden and safe retreat. Now we, too, were armed with the key word, the lost map, the soon-to-be-deciphered code by which a Nancy Drew or a Hardy Boy resolved the mystery. In the same way, we counted on those foreign phrases, the school library, and "tomorrow" to crack the code and provide us with a solid point of entry into the elusive world of the adults.

But the evening had not yet relinquished all its puzzles, and the most important revelation was still to be offered up by lamplight to our trellis watch. The general laughter had already subsided when Paul suddenly gave my hand three rapid squeezes—our pre-arranged signal to mean DANGER, WATCH OUT, or else LOOK QUICK, LOOK CLOSE—a sign to take precedence over any other communication. This mute alarm in the direction of his father placed Uncle Sandro under instant and intense scrutiny.

He was sitting, back to us, at the marble table, his huge salt-and-pepper, electrically alive head more charged than ever in the lamplight. It was shaking comfortably just then in a happy mix of animated talk, listening, and laughter. Invisible to "the friends" who sat in various arrangements of filigree chairs to one or the other side of the marble table, but very clear to us, his hand was moving. It roamed, in fact, up and down, over and around a soft object. There, close by his own, was an exposed and softly shining knee. It belonged to Pasquale's wife, Jenny, as did the summer-bare and half-uncovered upper leg Uncle Sandro—to our surprise and fascination—reached for. We watched him stroke the inner thigh. We observed this maneuver with great attention. Uncle Sandro never missed a single syllable or inflection and continued his animated conversation above the stroking. Jenny never moved. She made no attempt to take away his hand, cry out, murmur a protest, utter a sigh, or whisper. She simply sat much as she always did, slightly nodding in agreement, as though listening was not an imposed but quite genuine pleasure, showing a quiet smile in profile that seemed more than ever full of wifely pride and lingering merriment at yet another Pasquale tale.

I, for one, looked instinctively about for Aunt Louisa. She had for some moments absented herself and only now returned in tandem with my mother, each brandishing a platter of fig-centered cookies and a replenished pitcher of wine. She seemed more serene than usual, the tight line around her mouth soft in the lamplight. Uncle Sandro, seeing her framed in the votive light at the head of the tile-stone walk, shifted in his seat, and his hand became suddenly visible and sprightly on the table. Under it, we saw his thigh move ever so slightly, freeing Jenny's.

With the passing of platters and refilling of glasses, all returned to the typical Sunday evening among "the friends," each detail recurring, alternately, exactly as a hundred times before. The intimate moment vanished, had ceased to be so thoroughly that we felt disoriented and deceived, as though we had dreamed company, half-light, meandering tale, volleys of laughter, that brief incursion beneath the table, in a queer montage through the trellis slats.

Her Sister

"And why didn't we hear about these fits before?"

That was Enzo's mother's question when she heard the news.

"First a dowry a beggar would turn up his nose at—and now this!" The old lady flung out her hands, as if it were to spite her that her son's betrothed had died mere days before the wedding.

Enzo himself, however, could think of nothing but some hasty words the girl had once spoken. Although the courtship had been brief—he had seen Assunta no more than a half dozen times and always in the presence of her family—it had not been entirely smooth. One day, when he was telling her his plans, she had suddenly opened her black eyes wide and said, "Then we're not going to America?"

Her surprise was understandable. The young men of Pianosanto had been going to America for over ten years, and the girls liked to follow them. For the single girls, there was a larger field of marriageable men. Girls both single and married could find jobs there, at which they could earn their own money.

Enzo explained himself to Assunta in the same terms he had several times offered to his mother. ("Is it to make sure your sisters die old maids?" Ma had demanded. "Is that why you want to stay in this pen that even the pigs have left behind?") In the low murmur that provided their only privacy, Enzo reminded the girl that most men went to America simply so they could come back and buy a house of their own. But Enzo was hampered by no such necessity. His childless Uncle Tonio, the lawyer, had promised him a house at the birth of his first son. Not just any house, either, but the noblest house on the piazza. A baron had once lived there, although, like so many houses in Pianosanto, it had been empty for years. It had fallen into Zio Tonio's hands, the barons having been distant connections of the family; but the lawyer preferred to live frugally, in the back of his office. The upright man, who wore a clean shirt and collar every day of his life, could think of no more fitting end for the house than once more to shelter baronial blood.

Why go to America, Enzo asked his betrothed, to live among men who didn't know his name, when an abode suitable to his family's dignity already awaited him here? He and his wife would live with his mother until the moment came.

Ma had had an answer ready, of course; when had she ever had to go begging for words? Assunta, however, was properly silent for a moment after he finished. And when she looked up from the hands folded in her lap, she smiled sweetly, as at an innocent child. Her teeth were small and perfect as factory-made *acini di pepe*. Nor was there any effrontery in the words she spoke at last, despite the disappointment they showed. "You know," she said, "I've always planned to go to America. My cousin Mafalda has a job waiting for me."

"Ah, no," Enzo gently replied, making free to touch her wrist since her mother was engaged in conversation with Zio Tonio.

The girl seized back her arm and stood up so quickly her chair scraped on the brick floor. "I'm going to America," she said, not loudly but with an iron firmness that drew the attention of all. Her teeth were now bared in a less ingratiating expression. "If it's the last thing I do!" she added, and walked out of the room.

There had been nothing for Enzo but to leave as well. In choosing Assunta, he had followed his uncle's counsel, as always: he had taken a girl without much money and, therefore, sure to be deferential. Pa's mistake, Zio Tonio frequently observed, was marrying a woman with a little land of her own. Enzo began to wonder if he too had erred, perhaps in allowing himself a girl of Assunta's striking beauty. He had thought that single gift could make little difference, given her limited means. But this show of pride!

Her sin had been quickly atoned for. The next day her mother had come to apologize and assured him he would find Assunta changed if he returned. When he did the family this honor, though the girl was a little tight-lipped—and though her mother's eyes never left her, as if Assunta were a pot that might at any moment boil over and douse the flame—she made no further objections. As the day approached, Enzo almost forgot about the baron's house in his wonder that this fine creature was about to be his.

But when the day had finally come, that creature belonged to death alone. Enzo could not help remembering her bold words: "The last thing I'll do!" It was as if she had thoughtlessly called her death upon her.

Two months passed before he could think of marriage again. When he did, it was only natural his thoughts should turn to the same family. They had grown no richer in the meantime, and the brother himself had come to remind Enzo there was another sister remaining.

The day Enzo went to meet Rosaria—she had always been there, but how could he see her with Assunta in the room?—he knew at once that she, at least, was unlikely to become guilty of even a moment's pride. Although not repulsive, she had none of Assunta's beauty. Her eyebrows grew together, as if permanently knitted in anxiety. Her face was drawn, possibly because, when not called upon to speak, she was always gnawing the insides of her lips, with a preoccupied look as if she were trying to remember the flavor she had once found there.

That wasn't all. Her family's manner with the girl revealed to Enzo, by contrast, how warily they had always treated Assunta. Indeed, Enzo felt it wouldn't have been improper if they had addressed Rosaria (or Saredda, as they called her) with a little more delicacy. The mother spoke quite frankly of Saredda's luck in winning Enzo's interest and did not endeavor to conceal her inferiority to Assunta in every respect. Nor did the praise of Assunta's greater piety, cleverness, and dignity seem to be only the poignant expression of so fresh a loss. Saredda appeared long practiced in acknowledging her sister's higher virtues.

Could a girl be too deferential? When Enzo first spoke of their wedding as a definite prospect, Saredda let out an inarticulate sound, like a gasp. And when he asked her thought, she replied, "Are you—are you sure you want to marry me, signore?"

"Don't talk foolishness!" her mother scolded, while Enzo reassured her as he could. Still, throughout the courting, Saredda, for all her efforts, could never sustain a smile longer than she could have walked on her hands. On the wedding day itself, still dressed in black, she looked more inconsolable than ever.

The secret came out at last, when the bride and groom sat receiving guests in her mother's house, the trousseau hung up on strings for all to admire.

"Signore," she began. She had not yet spoken his name to his face. She was trembling and had evidently waited to speak until the view of the guests was cut off by one of her camisoles. "I must tell you. I'm afraid I have no right to—what should have been my sister's."

"What an idea!" Enzo replied with a smile. Her feelings must be strained by the sight of the linens and underthings; much of the trousseau was originally her sister's.

"It's Assunta, not me, you should be taking to America."

Enzo had been about to offer more reassurances when that word threw him off. "America? But we're not going to America," he reminded her. Each time he spoke the name, she closed her eyes as a reformed voluptuary might at the glimpse of a naked limb. "I wasn't going to take your sister either. Did you forget?"

Saredda looked puzzled in her turn but then said, with sad understanding, "Ah, that's right. It wasn't until after you were gone that she said it to my mother: how she didn't want to live in a house where people would say she didn't belong, to live even in a palace where, though she might be the king's wife, everyone would remind her she deserved no better than to be his servant. And she asked why Mafalda should get to wear a hat every day, and not her. My mother said she must not think about America but about keeping from starving—at least until she had the ring."

From her first sentence, Enzo had begun to stiffen and draw back in his chair. At her last, he positively froze. But Saredda didn't seem to notice.

"When you could no longer escape, my mother said, then she could surely have her way, for no man could ever deny her. And surely she would have. All the relatives, and my own godmother, too, used to kiss her and say that, even with her fits, she deserved to have been born a queen!"

"A queen in America?" Enzo said after a moment's silence. "And is that what you plan to be, too?"

If he had expected defiance, he was disappointed. Saredda only moaned, "As if just to think of it weren't crime enough!"

She had given him much to think of as well. Indeed, for a moment he had turned blood red, as if the color of his thoughts had dyed his face. But he was called to himself by the place, his *comare* just then walking in. Besides, Saredda's distress was evidently sincere. Her revelations might have come, after all, in quite another tone than her penitent one. Does the priest turn away even the blackest sinner when he's coming for confession?

He glanced at the girl again. Her eyes were downcast with shame. "Rosaria," he whispered, so his approaching godmother wouldn't hear. He used the girl's formal name, as it had been used in the ceremony, to remind her of his pledge to her. "We won't speak more of this." He was beginning to think, after all, that he might have won the saintlier of the two sisters.

Certainly no saint could have accepted more humbly his mother's graceless welcome. The girl had hardly walked in the door before Ma was handing her the empty jug, so that the world might be granted the spectacle of a bride fetching water on her own wedding day. Enzo attempted to intervene. Didn't he have sisters who could go in her place? But Saredda insisted on taking the jug, like those virgin martyrs who didn't let their stigmata interfere with their lowly duties.

More than one of those martyrs, too, would doubtless have given Enzo the same answer he received from Saredda that night.

"Forgive me," Saredda said when he asked for an explanantion. "Not—not yet."

He let her have her way, but he lost some sleep over it—among other reasons because he wasn't entirely sure that his mother, with her penchant for the indecorous, might not insist upon displaying the sheet.

As it turned out, however, Ma had had no time to think of that, so busy had she been in devising chores for Saredda. She could begin with the dusting and sweeping; then she could take out the slops. Saredda did it all without complaint. Indeed, there seemed to be only one thing she objected to, and she made her objection three nights in a row.

On the fourth night, Enzo could no longer contain himself. "It will have to be some time. Your fear will be the same until it's done. Must we wait until we're dead?" He whispered, for his sisters were no further than the loft above, but his voice cracked on the last word.

"It isn't fear," Saredda replied, looking at the yoke of his nightshirt but doubtless not seeing even that. "It's—it's Assunta."

"Assunta?" She had spoken with such conviction Enzo couldn't help glancing behind him.

"I know you said we couldn't speak of it," the girl began, shaking her head in regret at her own misdeed. "But when I put the pad on my head to carry the water, I always think of Assunta!"

It wasn't that Assunta had done it so often—as the younger sister, such chores ordinarily fell to Saredda—but Assunta never spilled a drop, never broke the jug, like her imperfect sister. Assunta's occasional stitching, too, it seemed, won universal praise; her once-a-year cooking had a taste as popular. What else could Saredda think of when Enzo's mother sent her to the stove or gave her some mending, but how much greater was Assunta's claim to the privileges Enzo offered—even if Assunta hadn't been his first choice as well?

"No one, no one would tell you different!" Saredda's whisper became a soft hiss. "It was for her my cousin Mafalda got a job, she never wrote a word about me. Mafalda's only been there a few years, you know," Saredda could not help interjecting, "and she already has three different pairs of shoes, ah!" She caught her breath as if she had swallowed a fly.

"Let Mafalda keep all the jobs, let her be cut in two by the machine that would have done for your sister. As for you," Enzo added, reaching tenderly toward her, "what is your job but to be my wife? Would the priest have married us otherwise?"

She rolled away, making the straw in the mattress swish. "Do you think he'll be punished for it, too?" she asked, bringing a hand to her cheek as if she had a toothache.

Enzo heaved onto his back and said to the beams above, through which his sisters' snoring filtered down, "Maybe time will help."

The next morning he took his mother aside and asked that Saredda be excused from household tasks for the present.

The old lady didn't fly into a rage. She simply held out her hand and answered, "Three *lire* a week."

Enzo couldn't believe it. But all his mother would say was that if the girl wouldn't work for her board, then Enzo must pay. She reminded him that she had not yet seen a penny of what he earned from Zio Tonio; that she had fed, clothed, and sheltered him for ten years since he was old enough to make money; that she had daughters still to marry off and a son who refused to make a home for them where that end might most naturally be achieved—that is, in America.

"Excuse me," Enzo replied solemnly, "I thought there was a matter of some blood between you and me. As for your daughters, I would have thought you'd rather have them wait, perhaps in a proper home, for husbands who are suited to them, rather than to run after those who are not."

His mother looked up at him; like his father he was a head taller than she. "So you're still thinking of that house your uncle holds in front of your nose, as he did with your cousin Luca before you?"

Enzo was shocked by the comparison, even coming from his mother. Luca had forfeited Zio Tonio's interest by marrying a woman so disreputable there was no telling what the origin of her children might be. "In this case," Enzo observed with a slight nod, "Zio Tonio doesn't have to fear any spot coming to his name."

"And if your uncle is so concerned about his name," the old lady replied, "why doesn't he give it to the child poor Mariuzza, the peddler's daughter, bore him?"

This question always reminded Enzo that there was no use talking to her. It was a Saturday, and that night he turned over every bit of pay, leaving nothing even for a cup of coffee. Three *lire* was all he got for making himself available for Zio Tonio's extra copying. Then he looked at his wife. She sat just where he had left her that morning, in a position by which she evidently strove to take up as little room as possible. "I hope you've been enjoying your leisure," he observed. "I'm paying enough for it." When the time came, he couldn't even make his usual request, his stomach was tied up in such knots.

Nor, when his powers returned to him with the passing days, did Saredda's leisure appear to have produced all the effects he had hoped for. After a week, happening to pass through the piazza with his uncle, Enzo was conscious of some awkward feelings when the old man pointed to the wrought-iron balcony of the empty baronial house.

"In a year," Zio Tonio said, nodding gravely, "you'll be sitting up there—if you've done what's right."

Enzo responded only by clearing his throat. There was to need to trouble his benefactor with the information that it might be rather more than a year before either of those events came to pass.

"I've been thinking," Zio Tonio went on; these deceptively modest words were always the preface to his advice. "Shame though it is to say, you may have had a lucky escape. A girl who looked like that Assunta, may she rest in peace, who can say what she might have led you to?" He clucked to himself. As a lawyer, there was no crime he hadn't heard of, yet familiarity hadn't affected his principles. Whatever rumors were passed about his private life, it was well-known that he wouldn't stay in a room where disgraceful jokes were being told.

"Your Rosaria," he concluded, "may have been the better bargain."

Again Ezno feigned assent. Tonio knew nothing of the weekly board, of course. Even if he'd considered Saredda a bargain at the price, however, Enzo might have observed that there was such a thing as false economy. As soon as she had been excused from chores—a release in which she took no pleasure—Saredda began to be plagued by dreams.

Dressed in her wedding clothes, the same that had served for her burial, Assunta rose up in the dreams to accuse Saredda of unpardonable presumption. Wasn't she ashamed to be waited on in her husband's house, as if his family were her servants? Didn't she know the world was appalled by her? Why, Assunta demanded, didn't Saredda start for America at once? She had as much right there, after all, to parade in a feathered hat and be bowed to the same as if she'd been somebody in Pianosanto, instead of the nobody she was.

"But no one thinks that of you!" Enzo assured his wife.

"If they don't, they should! My sister's right!" Saredda began to chew her knuckles.

Enzo took her hand from her mouth and held it between his own two. It turned cold at his touch, but this only added ardor to his words. "How can you listen to that creature, a girl who wanted to defy her husband, to drag him where his name meant nothing? Besides," he added, as the haunted girl showed no sign of hearing anything but the terrible words of the dream, "what kind of woman could wish to cause such pain to a sister? How must she have been to you in life, to bring you such terror in death?"

This question succeeded in waking her; the look of fear was gone. But it was replaced by a gloomy wonder he recognized too well, as she took up one of her old explanations. "But it couldn't have been wrong for Assunta to go there. Mafalda wrote us that they use only silk sheets in that country, and Zio Turiddu always said Assunta should sleep on nothing else. And she never did anything to me, even"—Saredda lowered her eyes a little in addressing this second point—"even when she pinched me or pulled my hair, she never did anything I didn't deserve."

Enzo couldn't speak, so far did these words go beyond his suspicion. When Saredda sought to withdraw her hand, he let it go lest she be reminded of her sister's torments. He looked at her hair, lying limply on the pillow. It was thin, not thick like Assunta's, who would probably not even have felt a yank.

As Saredda lay breathing beside him, in a world he was unable to rescue her from, Enzo could not help thinking of watching at his father's deathbed. But in body, at least, Saredda seemed healthy.

"Should we go to the priest?" he asked after a time. He had heard, in church, of possession by demons, the closest thing he knew of to Saredda's case.

The idea embarrassed her and, if truth be told, Enzo was relieved she shrank from exposing their private trouble. But it gave her a thought. Perhaps she could give a gift to San Rocco on his feast day, seeking forgiveness for her presumption—or, if that were too much, seeking only freedom. What she meant by freedom Enzo didn't ask, nor did he let himself think of how his father, in pain, had made the same prayer. Besides, Saredda's voice had brightened a little, as the sky does when the black clouds give place to gray ones.

Even so small a change was enough to make Enzo feel generous. "We could afford five *lire*, or six," he said; for he wasn't entirely without savings.

"Ah, you'd call six *lire* a gift, then," Saedda bleakly replied.

So the gift amounted to something more. When the *festa* came, not long after Enzo's talk with his uncle, the sum was enough not only to elate the priest but also to cause the band, who stopped at the houses of donors, to make its longest pause outside Enzo's mother's house. The stop was so long that no one could fail to notice. Certainly Ma herself didn't.

That evening, when the supper was through, she stepped into their corner and said to her son, "Well, then, what crime have you committed that required so great a gift? What crime that you'll confess to, that is, for I know how hardened you are about offenses to your flesh and blood." As Enzo did not choose to reply, his mother went on. "I'll admit, I was surprised to see this payment. I thought it was for that house you were saving the money you've stolen from my daughters."

"Ma—" Enzo began, tired already.

"But after all, I have only one thing to say to you. Since I see how rich you are, what I took three of before, I'll take five of now."

"Five!"

"Yes. Five, or the street." She gestured to the dirt path that unquestionably lay outside the door.

Enzo strode out and took that path, but only for the moment. He walked to the torchlit piazza where the explosions of the fireworks would seem like peace compared to the sound of women's voices. How could he pay? If he met her price, he'd soon enough have nothing, and as it was, Saredda's dowry would hardly suffice to furnish a single room of the new house. He couldn't ask more of Zio Tonio. Whenever his father had admitted not standing up to Ma, Tonio would shake his head disgustedly, as at the confession of a murder or other impropriety.

Among the shadowy crowd he made out his uncle. Like everyone else, Zio Tonio had noted the band's serenade and the generosity it signified.

"Enzo," he said, fixing his nephew with a curious gaze. "I hope it's no problem about the little ones?"

"No, *zio*," Enzo replied, trying to keep all his thoughts from his face. "It was only to ask for holiness."

"Ah, I should have guessed." Then his uncle motioned him on his way. Enzo walked on, listening to those words over and over. Was there a new formality, a new distance in the old man's tone?

Back home, he didn't trust himself to look at Saredda, who sat as motionless in her best dress as if she were the decorated statue of San Rocco. He didn't speak to her until they were alone in bed. Then, although his turmoil would have made him useless for much, he turned to her and put his proposition once again. Had San Rocco heard her prayer?

"But—but it's so soon!" she stuttered, as if there were something to fear from him.

Certainly the look in his eyes would have given her reason. "Is it? Then we'll wait. And in the meantime you can take up this family's slops once more. My mother won't get five, she'll get none. And we'll stay in this house until my beard is gray!" From that night on, he slept at his wife's side as little responsive to her presence as if she were a statue in fact. If she were anything else, if she knew a burning like her husband's, she was welcome to enjoy as he did the sensation of being eaten alive.

But after all, Enzo couldn't stay angry at Saredda, as the nights passed with no proof of San Rocco's intercession. She took up her burden of housework again with eager dutifulness, though it meant a return to still more burdensome thoughts. Enzo knew what she was feeling when, on hands and knees to scrub the bricks, she would suddenly pause, looking as if she'd found her doom inscribed there. Nor did her nights provide the rest she needed after her days of labor. Her dreams, now that they had begun, refused to stop. How could he nurture bitterness when he saw her losing flesh? Her bedclothes were open to the collarbone, and he saw the strings of her neck grow more prominent by the week.

Nor did Enzo dwell on his mother's crimes. What should have surprised him in her behavior? He knew where the greatest blame lay. He knew who had deluded him, lured him to his ruin. One day, returning from an errand to the next town in his uncle's cart, he stopped at the graveyard.

He hadn't visited since his wedding, four months before. The grapes had been harvested, and smoke rose from the fires in the picked-over fields. Wild wheat and asphodel now covered her grave the same as the others. Only the sharp edges of the stone distinguished it. The years of her life were pathetically brief; but they had proven long enough to do who knows what harm to him, to Saredda.

"Do you think to hide from me?" he demanded in his thoughts, looking at the stone. "Do you think from the protection of that earth you'll destroy us?"

His heart beat as if he had shouted out the words. And with the blood roaring in his ears, he solemnly resolved that, no matter how, he'd get a son and cheat the fate that seemed in store for him. "And may you be cursed!" he concluded, letting these last words find passage into the open air.

That night, by coincidence, Saredda spoke of a new idea. She told it as they lay in bed. This had come to be the place for conversation: free of his mother's commentary, Saredda would tell, in her hesitant, unassuming way, the little tales of her day; and he would repeat those happenings in the greater world he touched in his visits to Zio Tonio's office. It was as if they were old people together in the piazza, beyond everything but chatter, whose bodies are no more than blocks to drape the clothes on, whose flesh is as emptied of all promise as the chairs on which they sit. The couple never even spoke of her dreams any more. He knew she continued to have them only by her restlessness at night—and by this news of her plan.

"You know the Feast of the Rosary is next week—my name day, you know."

He saw her thought at once. She had spoken with such modesty, however, that he tried not to scold as he informed her he could afford no more for the saints.

"No," she replied, "I think perhaps it was wrong to believe money was the answer. It might be something else the Virgin wants."

A meaner man, or one less given over to despair, might have turned these last words to blasphemy. Enzo only asked, with some weariness, what Saredda meant. But it was a vow, and she could not tell him. She turned away, adding this to the other secrets she kept from him. Her mention of the subject, however, brought back all those thoughts of the impossible, and cost him another night's sleep.

When the town's autumn *festa* arrived, Saredda was gone from the conjugal bed before anyone else was awake. Enzo's mother didn't remark on it, for no one could be expected to work on a feast day. When Enzo's sisters went out to watch the procession, he accompanied them. Saredda was sure to be following behind it.

They stood in the piazza looking east, where the Madonna of the Rosary was being carried from the shrine outside town to the church. All looked that way, as if they were the summer's wheat bending to the wind. Why should anyone have cast an eye the other way? True, processions had once included the western path as well, starting from the far edge of Cataldo's field which lay like an apron on the side of a high hill, almost as straight up and down as if the apron were indeed hanging from a woman's waist. At the top of that hill, an old stone crucifix was planted, worn with rain and kisses. But some years since, this walk had been found too tiring. It wasn't easy, especially if you wore pebbles in your shoes for penance, as the gravest sinners used to do, wearing hoods as well to hide their faces. It must have been in turning to slap a fly or gossip with a neighbor that someone happened to glimpse the western path and cried out, "Look there!"

Like the others, Enzo turned, saw nothing—then, yes, a spot. It moved slowly and was strangely short. Was it a child? No, a woman on her hands and knees, her skirts bunched above. Had she really gone up the mountain and back again? Who could it be, they asked, though they would know soon enough, for she wore no hood. But Enzo was already running in the direction of the creeping penitent.

When he came close enough definitely to recognize her shape, he saw also that she was coated with dust, even her face, like a creature of mud. The coating was thicker on her forearms and her calves and feet, so thick that any cuts upon them, any blood, did not show, even when he was at her side.

"Saredda!" he cried. "What are you doing?" She didn't reply, but went on, in a trance. Presumably silence was part of the pledge.

"But no one does this, Saredda! God Himself doesn't ask it!" Still she crept on; he could see her lungs heave.

"Saredda, come home!" he pleaded, kneeling to lift her up in his arms if necessary. But she resisted, moving on as relentlessly as Cataldo's threshing machine. Enzo walked beside her a little way, but it was like sitting at his father's bedside when he no longer recognized them or even knew anyone was in the room. At last he began to walk at a normal pace back towards town, and then, uncontrollably, to run.

He stopped on the outskirts, however—stopped at the graveyard. Since his last visit, a sunflower had grown out of Assunta, a gaudy, heartless flower. He could have torn it from the ground, had he not had some last remnant of respect for what it touched. To prevent himself, he held his hands tightly in fists until the white showed.

He opened his mouth, but there was nothing to say. He had already cursed her, and he couldn't expect her to answer his question, which was this: was it his life she held against him?

After all, however, he could answer this himself. It couldn't be his survival she begrudged him, for her enmity had begun before her death. If she had married him, it would have been only to thwart him. In choosing her, what was his crime that should have made her want to blight his life for all eternity, and the life of a sister, too, the blood of her blood? Ought not one sister to seek the other's good? And if she chanced to sin against it, ought she not be willing to give as much as her own life in atonement?

No response came to his unasked questions, not even a wind to disarrange the petals of the flower. He stood looking at it for a while, then returned to town.

His uncle was the first person he encountered. He was standing just outside the piazza. By now, everyone knew who was so slowly and painfully making her pilgrimage. "Well!" Zio Tonio said, with no prefatory greeting. He had that flinty look Enzo had seen him wear only when debtors came into the office—and once, the peddler, poor Mariuzza's father. "No wonder God has refused to bless you!"

Enzo was puzzled, but quickly answered, "Uncle, it's been only a matter of months!"

"Then pray that it's forever, as I do! To think of your shamelessness, bringing such a girl among us!"

"But what do you mean?" His uncle stepped back when Enzo put out a hand in appeal.

"I don't know what her crime may be, but the sight of that"—Zio Tonio pointed in the direction of Cataldo's field—"makes me afraid to ask."

He wouldn't listen to reason. Lest Enzo hadn't sufficiently understood, he stated explicitly that no penny of his would go to feed the offspring of a creature already guilty of such vice at so young an age.

"My God, Uncle, what shall I do?" Enzo cried. "Must I live forever in my mother's house?"

"Don't you have enough to take you to America with the other *cafoni*? Don't fear that you'll be missed!"

After that Enzo didn't know what he did. He bumped into the people crowded in the piazza without knowing who they were or what they said to him. For a time he carried a piece of fried dough a child had put into his hand. At last he was home and Saredda was there, the Saredda of mud. She and his mother stood outside the doorway, Saredda in tears, mumbling to herself. When his mother spied him she said, "Now I see why you paid so much to bribe San Rocco! You thought you'd escape a disgrace like this!"

"But Ma!"

She didn't listen. "All I know," she said, "is that you have to get out. I have daughters to marry. You've taken enough from them without robbing their house of its reputation as well!"

A few weeks later, Enzo and his bride lay on a bed in a hotel near the docks of Palermo. It was still light, but they were tired from their journey, by cart, train, and streetcar. Above the stand with the ewer and basin hung tinted images of the king and queen, bidding a personal farewell. The hotel was full, and you could hear the sounds of many different families through the walls. All the same, it was more privacy than the couple had ever had. They might speak as loudly as they liked.

Yet they had said little. Saredda only repeated that he shouldn't have married her, she had no right to go where he was taking her. Enzo, when he could work up the strength, assured her it wasn't her fault, and besides—it was the coldest thing he was ever to say to her—there was nothing to be done about it now.

At the moment, Enzo was freed from the obligation of making any reply at all, for Saredda had been dozing since the dinner downstairs. He had noticed that she stirred in her sleep, as she did when she was dreaming. Indeed, when she suddenly woke, the first thing she said was, "Enzo, I've had another dream."

She placed her hand on his, no doubt frightened by the strangeness of the place. Enzo closed his hand around hers but answered, "Please. It's time for sleep." Then he shut his eyes.

She heeded him and said no more. But then he felt her other hand on his shoulder. When he opened his eyes, she was looking straight at him. She blushed, but she looked, like an animal who has never seen a man before and doesn't know whether to be afraid. Unlikely as it was, and with his own heart beating as in fear, Enzo guessed what she meant and took her into his arms.

When they lay still once more, Enzo could not take his eyes off her. At last, when he could speak, he said, "But what did you dream?"

"I dreamed how—how I could rightly be your wife."

She was looking at him again, and the sight lifted Enzo to a kind of grave playfulness. "Do you think San Rocco will be waiting for you in America, then? Do you think you'll find the Madonna of your *paese* there?"

Saredda shook her head, then spoke in that familiar tone of sober explanation. "No, signore. But do you remember how they spoke at dinner of the new names people are given in America?"

Enzo nodded and couldn't restrain a sigh. The couple across the table had told of it. Enzo had been readying himself for a land where no one knew him but he hadn't expected it to be so bad as that.

"Well," Saredda went on, "in my dream you called me by another name. And I don't know how it was, but when you called me that, I felt there could be nothing wrong in whatever you asked of me—even going to America, though I once was certain the gates would stay closed against me."

Enzo smiled with a lighter heart than might have been expected in one who'd been through so much to find so simple an answer. "And what shall I tell the man your name is, then? Dearest Heart? Queen of the Sea?"

He whispered the words into her ear, and in the same manner, she replied with that name evidently powerful to open any door of iron, flesh, or stone.

"Tell him: Assunta."

My Grandfather's Suit

I never met my grandfather; he died on the day I was born. That was almost all I knew about him until the other day when my father caught me mugging in front of the mirror in our foyer. I was trying on a new collection of hats and scarves, hoping that my summer tan would make me look more like my beautiful mother. But I still didn't look like her or anyone else in the family. The family joke is that I really was found on my parents' doorstep, delivered not by a stork but by a chicken, which somehow accounts for my short legs.

My father opened the screen door and found me staring intently at myself in the mirror. I was imagining that my brown eyes were flecked with gold, like my mother's. "Now I know who you look like," he said. He pulled the rubber band from the evening newspaper. "There's a picture of my father with that same expression on his face." Then he picked up his car keys from a candy dish and headed for the garage.

After I heard his car back down the driveway, I snuck upstairs to my father's bureau, where he keeps his college ring and our birth announcements and other things from the past. Underneath a pile of handkerchiefs, I found a photograph with my grandfather's name, Gianfranco Cavallo, written in a shaky script on the back. The photo is fuzzy and yellowed, and it looks like my grandfather's image had been cut out, touched up, and glued onto an aristocratic background of marble steps and chandeliers. He's seated on a wooden chair with ornate arms and wears a dark double-breasted suit, probably custom-made. His brother was a tailor in Calabria. My grandfather looks composed, dapper, but though I see the shadow of my father's lips and hairline, he also looks undeniably foreign, fresh from Italy. The expression on his face is fierce—not quite a scowl, but tougher than a frown. Seventeen and not pretty at all, I practice that expression in front of the bathroom mirror, flexing my jaw, flaring my nostrils, trying to look like him.

Except for me, everyone in my family plays a distinct role in the family drama. My mother is the Beautiful One. She teaches fourth grade and makes extra money modeling misses clothes at the malls. Her students send her love letters all summer long. My brother Mark is the Jock. No one ever expects him to contribute more than scores and statistics to our dinner conversations. He seems to have a new nickname every week. Right now, everyone is calling him Quark, even my father, because he managed to pass freshman chemistry. My brother Michael is the Klutz. He wore casts and splints even as a baby and knows the names of all the nurses in the emergency room of St. Mary's Hospital. My father is the Sentimental One. He has a whole library of films and videotapes he's taken of us through the years, and some nights I find him in the basement rec room, sitting in the dark and watching us on a screen as we head off to kindergarten or swing at baseballs on the school playground. But I am simply Anna. Not Ann or Annie, or even Anna Marie when my mother gets exasperated with me. I've tried for a role of my own, jockeying for the Smart One or the Talented One. Then I flunk a quiz or get kicked out of choir, and I'm back to simply Anna.

I imagine that my grandfather had talents. He could bring people to their windows when he sang. He could pick up a fiddle and play a tune he'd heard only once. He could keep people rapt with his complicated tales in which the hero was cunning and handsome. Or he could listen to a roomful of complaints and dilemmas, and pronounce a solution in a sentence.

I try this last trick out with my brothers when they are arguing in the family room about raking leaves. Michael can't rake because he twisted his ankle in wrestling practice. Quark won't because it was his turn last week. I sit in my father's La-Z-Boy, clutch its arms, and scowl. "What you should do is fill two pots of water for spaghetti, and if your water boils first, you rake the front because it's smaller, and if your water boils last, you have to make the spaghetti and rake the back." They stare at me for a moment, ears perked up like dogs, then pull me off the chair and bury me under a sofa cushion.

My father clears out the back of my mother's paneled Wagoneer, and I climb in for the drive down to Petrifying Springs Park where he can fill his empty gallon jugs with spring water. He won't drink tap, says it tastes like formaldehyde, and I imagine him grimacing and pursing his lips when he washes his face. These are my favorite moments with him—alone in the car, remarking on the shifting seasons. If my grandfather were alive, I suppose we'd talk about the same things, but in Italian, which I don't speak. I had a dream the other night: my grandfather in his chair looked stern until I walked into the room, my wavy hair done up in a bun. Then his face relaxed and opened. He put his hands on my cheeks and kissed my forehead, then traced a circle on it with his thumb. After that, the Italian rolled out of me like a song, and my skin grew dark, my eyes dreamy.

"How did your father get over to America?" I ask. I am sure we have never spoken of this before. My father drives on, looking neither happy nor sad, glancing at the speedometer.

"Well, that's quite a story." He cracks his window and we smell the musk of a recent rain and the sharpness of wet plowed fields, fragrant as coffee. "Your grandfather was a rich man, rich for his village. He had sheep and oxen and the best land. But he fell in love with a poor beautiful woman from another village. His people forbid him to marry her, so he went up the mountain and killed his two best oxen, sold them for a good price. Then he came to America and sent the money back for the beautiful woman, your grandmother, and married her."

The rest of the day in the park, I collect berries, yellow wildflowers, and leaves with red veins. Tomorrow, back home, I will follow a recipe I found in a woman's magazine and mix these with my shampoo to wash my hair. Then I'll dry it in the sun until it is as soft and burnished as my grandmother's.

After dinner, I find my mother alone in the kitchen, making bologna sandwiches for tomorrow's lunches. A couple years ago, when I was fifteen, I loved to sit in the kitchen with my mother and her visiting sisters. The women would tie aprons over their dark skirts, set their wedding rings on a windowsill, and roll pasta out for ravioli or slice the tops from peppers and stuff them. I would drink coffee with condensed milk until they forgot about me and started talking about their cousins and the other women at church. That's where I first heard that my grandfather had died on my birthday.

Apparently he had been working out in his garden all morning, then came in and complained of a headache. He lay down in the back bedroom, the one reserved for visiting family. My grandmother and the others went off to the hospital, where I would soon be born. He rose to fry a sausage with peppers, and as he held the skillet over the flame, a vein burst in his head, and he fell to the floor. They found the sausage and peppers under the overturned skillet on the speckled linoleum.

I watch my mother fold plastic wrap around the bologna sandwiches then say, "Mom, do you remember when Grampa Cavallo died?" I tear a piece of lettuce from its head and chew it.

"Oh, Anna, I don't know. It was a long time ago." Dressed in pumps and a navy blue suit, she has just come home from a school-board meeting and is wiping mustard from her lacquered fingernails.

"Did you ever get to know him? Were you close?"

My mother pushes her hair off her face with the back of her hand and throws her head back. "All I really remember is that your grandmother was often exasperated with him. Everyone said that he was such a good man, a saint, and your grandmother complained that it was hard to live with a saint. He was very poor in Italy, and any extra money he made here in America he wanted to give away, send back. Your grandmother took his weekly pay, and she'd dole it out, a few dollars for groceries, some for gas. Once a month she'd give him a little extra so he could have anisette in his coffee with his friends at the Italian American."

Later, I find the gold cross my parents gave me for confirmation and iron all my white blouses. The next morning I scrub my cheeks then head off to school, face shining like a madonna, my cross hanging on a gold chain under my collar. I spend all of my allowance on thin mints and doughnuts, give them away to classmates I hardly know in study hall. At night, I sneak anisette from the dining room cabinet and sip it from a coffee mug, savoring it like a nectar.

I take Dad's Oldsmobile to pick up Quark and Michael from school. I am wearing a fedora I found at a rummage sale—it looks like something my grandfather would wear on an outing.

"Cut this," Quark says, and tips the hat over my eyes.

"I am trying to drive," I say, and make a show of checking the rearview mirror. I am the only full-fledged driver among us. Quark is fourteen and Michael has his temps.

"Did you guys know that Grampa Cavallo was a great singer in Italy? And when he came over here he went down to Chicago and sang there? He had to give it up during the Depression." We had just begun our Depression unit in American history.

"Oh, yeah?" Michael rips off a piece of white adhesive tape from his hockey stick and presses it on the toe of his tennis shoe. "Is that why you've been bellowing in the bathroom in the morning? La lala la." He sings the opening notes to Beethoven's Ninth, voice full of vibrato.

"And did you know, Mr. Pavaroti, that Grampa was one of the first people in America to taste Coca-Cola and he wanted to buy stock, but Gramma wouldn't let him?"

"Oh, right," Quark says, twirling his hockey stick. "Then we'd all be rich and wouldn't have to go to college."

"And that once at a bus stop in Cicero he met Al Capone and told him no one really needed or deserved solid gold bath fixtures, and that living like a king was a state of mind?"

Quark and Michael poke at each other with their sports equipment. They are American through and through.

My cousin Giuseppa, daughter of my father's sister, is having a wedding shower. All of us—my mother, my aunts, their daughters—are crowded into a damp basement where pink ribbons have been taped on the painted concrete blocks. I hear the heater in the utility part of the room clunk and hum as it starts up. Everyone seems stylish in new boots and patterned stockings.

Giuseppa sits on a backless chair, the kind you'd find in front of a vanity mirror, and opens gifts. She is thin, but busty, and receives five lacy negligees. I have given her a wedding photo album, and I slump down in my chair.

Afterwards, we eat beef sandwiches and pasta salad. Giuseppa's fiance arrives, a moody guy named Sam, and eats almost all the leftovers. Finally, I help my aunt and her friends pick up the paper plates.

"Did they have showers when Grampa was alive?" I ask my aunt. She pulls a hanky out of her blouse sleeve and daubs at her nose. She is small-boned and thin, and likes to seem delicate. She often wears pink or baby blue and can't stand on her feet too long before her veins "act up."

"Gee, Anna, I don't think so," she says, wrapping the cheeses. "I think they had proper dowries in those days."

Her friends Mary and Lil, old high school chums, whisk into the kitchen, bearing trays of disheveled antipasto. They sigh as they set the trays on the sink—they are both the kind of women who sigh as they work—then Mary covers a box of Perugina chocolates and slips it in a shopping bag in the dining room.

"My father was telling me that Grampa Cavallo could have been an actor in the movies. That he looked just like that guy who played in *Lost Horizon*."

Mary turns to look at me, her glasses slipping down her nose. "Your grandfather was a quiet man. He'd never have made it in the movies. You never heard one peep out of him."

"Oh, I don't know," says Lil. She's the prettier of the two with her big brown eyes and face softened by a halo of blonde down. "He was quite a ladies' man, really. Your grandmother had her hands full, keeping him happy at home."

My aunt swats Lil with a towel. "Lil, really. Where did you get such an idea?" She busies herself by stacking cookies in a tin. "My father was a very pious man. He had no interest in the ladies at all, except for my mother, even though she was nothing much to look at, just a slip of a thing." Ten years after my grandfather, my grandmother died, quietly, in the hospital. I remember her as a big-armed woman with coppery hair who wore shawls and carried bushels of tomatoes down into her cellar.

"He walked to church every morning before work," my aunt continues, "then prayed as he worked on the assembly line. Poor man. He just didn't know what he wanted." She turns to Lil and Mary, who have poured themselves fresh cups of coffee. "Did you know that when he was in Calabria, he couldn't wait to come over? And then when he got here, all he wanted to do was return? We'd be in Italy today if my brother hadn't got the measles that time he wanted us to all go back together."

"When? When was that?" I ask. My aunt seems all wound up, ready to tell me something big.

She dismisses me with a wave. "Oh, Anna, that was so long ago. I don't even like to think about these things since my mother died." She closes the cookie tin with a snap and places it in the cupboard.

My father decides to finally sell the house he grew up in. He's been renting it to family friends since my grandmother died, but now they want a bigger place, and the apartment owner next door wants to expand. "All that stuff," my father says as we pile into the Wagoneer. "We've got to get rid of all of it." On the way to the old place, even Quark and Michael are quiet. We haven't been there in ten years.

We gather in the kitchen first and pull green trash bags from a roll. "We're making a clean sweep," my mother reminds us. "The trick is to work fast." Everyone disperses, but I can hardly move from the kitchen. My father rented the place as my grandmother left it, and as I recognize most of the furniture, appliances, and even knickknacks from my childhood, I feel dizzy. Everything seems so small and cramped, as if it were shrinking in from the walls. I remember the stove as huge, heating squat enameled pots of tomato sauce and minestrone that fed every cousin and uninvited guest. And I remember cleaning mounds of purplish pole beans, flat as thumbs, in the vast double porcelain sink where my grandmother used to bathe me. And the enormous varnished table under which I hid, scooping frozen custard out of a waxed tub to feed the backyard cat. Now everything is shrunken, almost miniaturized. I sit at the varnished table and bump my knees against its carved legs.

The faint, familiar smell of the kitchen—like onions and soap—conjures up things I haven't thought of in years: the loopy green bric-a-brac on the apron my grandmother wore when she made Christmas pastries, the bowls of milky coffee she used to serve us in the morning so we could dunk our dry toast, the collection of ceramic cats on the kitchen windowsill. I try to imagine my grandfather in this kitchen, praying over a plate full of food, his elbows reaching past the corners of the table, but he seems too big for this small room.

I look around, scrounging for memories, and notice a funny little cabinet in the corner of the kitchen—it looks like it could contain a sewing machine—where my grandmother used to store homemade wine. I remember once she poured some into a shot glass etched with a gold spiral and let me sip it. I must have had a sore throat or stomachache, because she never drank wine herself. Then I realize my grandfather must have been the one to make and drink the wine. I rush across the speckled linoleum floor to inspect the cabinet. In it I find only empty plastic containers and pickle jars.

I open the door to the oven, where my grandmother stored her pots and pans. I look for my grandfather's skillet—I imagine it as blackened and shallow—but all I find is a greasy broiler pan.

Then I go to the back bedroom, where my grandfather must have rested moments before he died. The previous tenants used their own furniture in here, and the room is bare except for my father's old record player, a folding chair, and an old shoe-shining kit propping open the door to the closet.

Stepping onto the creaking linoleum on the closet floor, I duck my head to avoid crocheted sachets hanging from a brass hook, then push wooden hangers along the rod to get at something dark in the back of the closet, a clothesbag. I unzip the clothesbag to find what must be my grandfather's suit, the one he wore in the photograph—it's double-breasted, blue, with darker blue pin stripes and darts at the waist. I slip it out of the bag and hold the jacket to my nose—it smells of shoe polish and talc and something sharper than sweat, maybe cigar smoke. I pull the jacket on over my T-shirt. Then I step into the pants and button its fly.

I stretch out my arms and turn on my tiptoes in front of the mirror that hangs on the closet door. The suit is, surprisingly, too small for me: my forearms jut out of its sleeves, my shoulders pull its lapels. But it is a well-made suit, and the fabric still feels springy, full of nap; the lining is a rich blue satin. I put my hands on my hips and pose, wait to see the grandfather in me appear. But the blue wool can't hide my second generation bones, my American health. Still, I can see that this is not the suit of a ladies' man or a poor man.

I set the folding chair in front of the mirror, sit, and hold my elbows as if they are resting on the arms of an ornate chair. I push my brow and cheeks into their practiced scowl. Now the suit settles into place—its blueness and padding make me look darker, smaller, its tailored lines make me elegant. I lean back and compose my hands with easy grace. I am someone who knows who she is.

I open my mouth and begin to sing made up words to the tune of "Arrivederci Roma." My voice, echoing on the bare walls, sounds mature, full of color and vibrato. Suddenly I remember the Italian lyrics and understand how to sing a line in a breath, to phrase the song, to pull back on a note, then give it my all. And my voice has soul—it is the voice of a rich man, a saint, a quiet man, a singer.

Cakes

That summer he sweated first from the humidity which in 1940 everyone in Brooklyn sweated from; then he sweated from the hot ovens at Carlo Amato's pastry shop in Bensonhurst four or five nights a week; then he sweated from the hot ovens at a pastry shop Downtown every day of the week except on Sunday, when he usually slept until noon. From Downtown, Giovanni Vitale came home at the end of a workday on the BMT subway to his wife, Lisa, to their three kids, Anna, Steve, and Johnny. After dinner they would all listen to the Philco. Then Giovanni and the eldest kid, Johnny, eleven, walked three long blocks and two short blocks, past the old people who fanned themselves on the stoops, to Carlo's shop on Seventeenth Avenue.

For five dollars extra, that August night's work began with a batch of cannoli. The burned lard once again was ladled from a tall can into a large copper pot which was put on the ring stove with its lone, very big and very hot burner. When the cannoli wrapped on short broomsticks were fried to a crisp, they bobbed up to the surface of the steamy and boiling lard and he scooped them out with a strainer.

"You want some coffee I could give you, or a sandwich?" the shop owner's wife, Martina Amato, asked Giovanni. "How about you, Johnny? You want some ice cream, some soda?" Johnny watched his father as his father watched the woman get the coffee. Carlo Amato, who usually baked the goods sold in his own shop, had nodded from a small marble table without moving from his chair when Giovanni and Johnny came in. Giovanni had nodded back. Carlo wasn't too strong, Giovanni had said to his son, so he helped Carlo out at night, as Johnny helped him out. With Johnny's help, father and son would finish up by eleven instead of after midnight for the father alone. The next morning Johnny would still be sleepy, and his mother would tickle his toes until he climbed out of bed for breakfast with his sister and brother. By then his father would already be on the subway headed again for the pastry shop Downtown.

"Hey, Dad, in the flour here, moving around, are some brown things, you ought to see this." Johnny was at the mixer where he put in a scoop of flour after his previous scoop was worked in by the blade that rotated. "I put in two scoops, but you ought to see this, Dad. I don't think I should put in any more. I see what they are. Bugs. The flour is crawling with bugs. Wow! Look at those bugs."

A Chesterfield was attached to Giovanni's lower lip when he came over with his hands covered with tufts of yellow butter cream which he whipped by hand in another copper pot and his cigarette would be ruined if he touched it. "In the flour after a while the eggs hatch," he said. "Insects lay them in the wheat in the field. When we bake the cookies, it won't matter; the bugs will melt. In some countries, they eat things like ants and grasshoppers." The movement of his lip as he spoke caused the long ash at the end of his cigarette to drop into the dough with the insects. Johnny reached in for the ash but he was quickly yanked back by his father. "Never, never do that." The risky things a son could do worried him even though Giovanni was too tired to worry about bugs and cigarette ash in the dough. After Johnny hesitated a moment over his father's easy acceptance of the bugs, he too decided that it was no big deal. Even the cigarette ash in the dough that turned with the blade was forgotten after Johnny covered the ash with another scoop of flour.

Back at the marble-top worktable big enough for two pastrymen, Giovanni would make next a batch of *sfudelle*. Ghostly white, his face and arms covered with flour, he rolled out a sheet of dough until it was thin as cloth and then rolled it up like a thick window shade. With a broad blade, he sliced it like bread, and using his quick and calloused fingers, he then fanned out the slices until half the rings were on top and half were on bottom. Between the dough-hinged halves, he stuffed the yellow butter cream.

The physical work, the heat from the ovens with their wide mouths and black iron doors one above the other in two rows from about the level of his knees to above his head, the long hours for little pay in those times when most other Sicilians too didn't earn enough to buy many cakes—when almost no one was well off—all these conditions left Giovanni little time for anything else but more work; maybe one joke for his own kids, maybe two tender words for Lisa. To keep doing his work, he found pleasure from the batches that looked good and tasted good with nothing wasted or burned or flushed down the toilet where a failed batch was sent. Another pleasure he had was when he told stories about his bachelor days when he ice-skated in Central Park with the rich girls who lived in brownstones off Fifth Avenue nearby and how they brought him presents and behind the bushes he kissed them—but they wouldn't take him home.

"I don't believe you, Giovanni, that you kissed so many girls that you said you kissed," said Martina, at the small table with her husband where they both sipped black coffee with anisette. Her husband's face turned to her and then to Giovanni, but Carlo really looked elsewhere, inside himself or out past the shop to a distant place. Giovanni understood, but there was nothing he could do for Carlo, aside from the cakes he made for his old friend. Martina said, "You should go to bed now, Carlo. It's better you don't stay up so late. I close up the shop myself."

"I'm not so tired," Carlo said. "About Giovanni, for myself, I believe him. I believe he kissed all the girls he said, because he gave them his *biscotti,* from the recipe from his father. Not because he is so handsome. Tell me, who is more handsome, me or Giovanni?"

"You are more handsome, Carlo," his wife said, as she touched his wavy white hair.

"He is," agreed Giovanni. "He still has all his hair while mine is half gone."

Into the center of stars and half moons that would be baked as cookies, Johnny pressed pieces of red or green maraschino cherries. He looked over at his father and then looked at Carlo and thought that his father was more handsome. There was no doubt about it. When Johnny had placed the cookies in the pans, his father shuffled the pans like oversized playing cards into the ovens. The anise biscuits that his father had just taken out of the ovens Johnny carried to the front shop where he would stack them up. While out there he also had a slice of spumoni and soda-jerked a soda for himself that was mostly chocolate syrup. At that late hour no customers had come into the front shop, which had white walls and white floor tiles and white fluorescents. All that white helped Johnny to keep his eyes open.

Quietly the boy sat behind the counter and worked there, and when Carlo later came by and suggested that Johnny also sample the tortoni which were in the freezer, Johnny took a tortoni too. Carlo went out the door and up to the apartment over the shop. In the ceiling Johnny could hear Carlo's footsteps and wondered if Carlo would be all right. Then he went to the back shop to ask his father if he would like to have a tortoni.

With the ricotta cream, his father stuffed the fresh cannoli skins he had just made. At the small table with her forehead on her arm, Martina cried softly to herself: at this late hour she could no longer pretend that Carlo's illness was just a bad dream; if she could drain her tears, then she too could go upstairs and hold Carlo as if her arms could keep him here.

"Sure, bring me a tortoni, please," his father said. "And bring me a glass of soda water, plain."

Then Johnny carried the pans of baked stars and half-moons out to the front shop where he dusted them with a large shaker of powdered sugar, and also now and then dusted his own tongue. Between yawns, he built the cookies up in trays decorated with doilies. To stay awake he tried to think about the Harley he intended to have someday, but when he put his head down for two seconds, he dropped off. The old couple who came in minutes later for lemon ice startled him. He went to get Martina who came out to serve them, and after they left she stayed there while Johnny tried again to build up the cookies. His head nodded more than once and he had to jerk himself awake. So Martina seated herself beside him, put her arms around him, and before he knew what happened his eyes closed and his face went down on her breast where he was held like that. For half an hour he slept there until his father finished up and came out to the front shop where he half filled a sack with cookies and biscuits to take home to the family.

"You have to wake up now," Giovanni said as he shook the boy.

As his eyes snapped open, Johnny said, "I'm wide awake."

Angelina

In the room bathed with the peculiar, ghost-like darkness of 3 A.M., my eyes spring open, wide-eyed, incapable of closing. This sort of thing happened to dolls occasionally when I was a child. The eyes would spring open and stare; they refused to close. When you made a crack in the head to look inside, the wires holding the lids would be snapped beyond repair. I wonder if someone with a hacksaw were to cut a neat line down the middle of my head like a part in the hair, only longer, and were to look inside, would my wires, too, be rusted away?

Tonight, although I want to sleep, my eyes won't close. I feel as though hundreds of voices from the past have come to join me in my bed, with my husband sleeping next to me, his face indistinct in the darkness, his body pumping heat into the sheets like an old wood stove. His body temperature is higher than mine so that on cold nights, when my skin gets icy and shiny with chill, I gravitate toward him and his radiating warmth. He says, "You make me feel too warm," and pushes me away. Our bed is strange looking, too, for he sleeps under a sheet even on the iciest nights, while I, all winter, pile on doubled-over blankets, three and four high, sleeping under a blanket of loose woolen loops crocheted by my mother, the regular blankets warm and heavy on top of me.

I try to will myself to sleep, to ignore those voices, to count backward from one hundred. By eighty-nine I am bored and forget to count. I listen instead to those people from the past who will not be still. "Speak for us," they cry, "Speak." And those people who are dead or have fallen out of my life like old dreams press around me. I can see them all as clearly as if they were in the room with me, remember their names, hear them speak. Sometimes they are clearer to me than the people I know today or the ones I knew last year; although it takes time for me to remember them, they come back to me in turn.

Tonight it is Angie who is loudest—Angelina Mazzarro, the blonde Italian with golden curls, her large eyes as deeply shaded as violets, and her body, unfashionably full-figured, giving off the musky aroma of sensuality, strangely like the odor of votive candles burning in a church, that permeated any place through which she walked.

I was young when I first saw her. She is clear to me in her beauty and in my envy of her body, her face; I, who had only my large dark eyes and my slimness, viewed her as a goddess. I was eighteen then and in my first year of college, trying to convince myself that brains were all that mattered, knowing inside that wasn't true, at least not for me, not then anyway.

When I saw her first, she was standing in Aunt Nina's kitchen—Aunt Nina, chunky and fun loving, a mole on her cheek, hair under her nose (a dark moustache of it), with three husbands dead, looking for the fourth, and bleaching her hair an artificial red like rusty tin. She had buried three husbands, driven them to their graves with her shrewdness and her nagging, pinching pennies, crying poverty, when all the while she was a usurer, lending money at 5 percent interest, payable every three months, to those who came to her kitchen begging for help. She charged 20 percent a year and called it five and got richer and richer, though she continued to work sewing coats at Ferraro's factory. Her money was stolen by her nephew, Bill, whom she came to consider her son, for she was childless. She loved him like a child and like a demon lover; jealous in fits, she guarded him cruelly until he ran away home to Italy when he was thirty-seven.

But that was later.

Angie was beautiful when she first arrived in Riverside. They all agreed, the old ladies who slashed at her with their tongues like two-edged razor blades, slashed at her until there was no meat left. At first they said, *"Quando e bella."* Yes. And she was lovely in a way that was unusual in Italians, at least in the Italians I knew in the Riverside section of Paterson. Her blonde curls hugged her head like a bathing cap. This was no blonde rinse from a bottle, but a true honey-blonde color that gleamed so that even the women felt compelled to touch her head. As if that hair alone were not enough, her magnificent violet eyes were ringed with dark lashes that reflected themselves on honey-colored skin.

She was not thin in the American fashion; instead she was rounded and curved, her bust full, her waist narrow, her hips wide and flaring. When she walked, it was almost as though a veil of sensuality fell over her. It seemed to be bursting from her, shouting life and affirmation to anyone who cared to notice.

When she first arrived in Riverside, people were enchanted by those northern Italian looks. She grew up in a little town near Stressa, in northern Italy, close to the Swiss border, and she met Joe when he was a soldier in the Italian army. Though she was only sixteen, they married quickly and had two sons—who were about two and four when they came to Riverside. For a few weeks the tongues of the old ladies wagged ferociously over her beauty. But soon they tired of talking of her over the shelves of *Ronzoni* boxes in Maztalia's Grocery. Soon they found other topics which interested them more.

For a long time, then, I forgot her. I graduated from high school and fought ferociously to be allowed to go to college. My parents insisted that girls should be secretaries while they waited to get married, like my sister and my cousins. "If girls had to go to college," my father said, "they should be grammar school teachers." When I announced that I wanted to be a writer, my mother threw her hands in the air; my father shouted and raged. My cousin Joey, the accountant, told me I was being impractical. I should teach first grade. Against their resistance, I pushed with all my strength, and when I won a full four-year scholarship, they had to let me go, though in the kitchen, my mother muttered dark prophecies of doom. So I was involved with myself, then, not interested in anyone else. Angie fell into some half-remembered place in my brain.

One day, though, I went to visit Aunt Nina. I enjoyed her admiration of my brains since she certainly could not have admired my beauty. Bill was there with his sixteen-year-old wife, heavy with late pregnancy. When he ran away from Aunt Nina, he had found this fresh-faced woman-child; her brothers complained that he was too old for her until he paid them off with Aunt Nina's money, and then he came back with his wife to live with Aunt Nina in her little tenement apartment. But Bill was growing restless waiting for Aunt Nina to die; finally, he walked the streets after work and paced the house prowling in and out of the small rooms, testing the bars.

Anyway, Bill was there in Aunt Nina's yellow kitchen; he stood with his back to the room, his shoulders hunched, chain-smoking Camels and glaring out of the window. His young wife was there also looking solid and bovine in her pregnancy. She sat, along with Antoinette from next door, at Aunt Nina's metal kitchen table, drinking black coffee from tiny cups. Old Philomena, eighty if she was a day, skinny and sharp as a hook, sat with them; her voracious old eyes took everything in.

Finally, after I had been there a few minutes, Angie walked in. The room got still as a box before an explosion. She was lovely. Though five years had passed since I had seen her, the impression of bursting sensuality was still there. I felt a pang of jealousy at her face and figure, at her possession of something I could never have no matter how many degrees I accumulated.

But the women had stopped speaking, and although she tried to start a conversation, they barely answered her. Afterward she left, and I felt everyone in the room exhale as though she had pulled their breaths out the door with her into the winter day. They began speaking of trivalities. No one mentioned what was wrong. It was only later, when I asked my mother, that she said there were rumors flying around about Angie, the way they do in any small, insular place, rumors that she had lovers and that, in fact, she had slept with Aunt Nina's nephew.

I became angry, defending her. In my fantasies I imagined myself looking like that and having boys follow me around, panting, but I knew, in reality, that would never happen to me. "They're just jealous," I cried, slamming my way into the cubicle I shared with my sister, Laura, throwing myself across our bed and sobbing.

Gradually, the whispering voices of the women gained momentum. They become so loud, so insistent, like crickets in summer, that finally Joe heard the rumors, too. He had always been tall, thin, with knobby elbows and knees like a young boy, but now, he shrank to the size of a skeleton, so that his clothes draped over his body. He was an odd-looking man anyway, with bushy brown hair, curly and tight on his head except for a bald path down the middle, and a thin elongated face with tormented eyes which slanted down at the corners like the ones in Modigliani's paintings.

The rumors, of course, covered him, too, with mud thick as that on the bottom of a river. Some said he was impotent. Others that he only liked men. Others that they slept in separate beds ever since he found out about her first lover. Whatever the truth was, none of us knew, but Joe denied all; flagrantly, stubbornly, in the face of all proof, he insisted the rumors were not true.

Obviously relishing the story, my cousin told me Angie's nine-year-old came home one day and found the house empty. He went to the garage to see if his mother's car was there, and saw instead his mother and her lover, the little Italian tailor with the flashing dark eyes from the small dusty tailor shop on Main Street. The son was so shocked at the sight of his mother, lying on the greasy garage floor, her skirt flung practically over her head, and the tailor, his behind in the air, pumping away, that at first he kept trying to call out to her, but no sound came. Then she saw him. Her eyes widened with horror, and she began to try to push the tailor off her.

The son opened the garage door and began to scream, "Ma, Ma, Ma!" He ran down the street like someone who has just been beaten, ran holding his stomach and moving back and forth in a rocking motion while he moaned and moaned, a high-pitched sound like the keening of grief at old Italian funerals. The neighbors all came out to stare; goggle-eyed, they watched his crazed progress down the street, unsure whether the boy had gone mad.

Still, the marriage continued, though the story spread throughout Riverside in a matter of hours. People stopped speaking to her, except when they could not avoid a direct confrontation as when Joe was with her. My cousin laughed at her, and I kept asking, "Why the garage? Why?" But suddenly, as though I had walked into her mind, I felt the violent need that had driven her out of the house to that greasy garage floor.

The years pass. One day I meet Angie on the street; she is distraught and crying. She tells me that she has breast cancer; she needs surgery.

Several months later I see Angie in church. She kneels through the entire mass, her eyes lowered, fingering her beads. She is subdued; her body seems to have lost some of its vibrating energy. She has grown paler than I remembered. When we pass each other in the aisle, she looks at me for a moment; in her eyes, dark as pansies, something retreats into hiding. I reach out toward her, instinctively, in recognition of a connection between us. Slowly, shyly, she lifts her lowered lashes, stares directly at me, her eyes wide open. At first I am reminded of a china doll, but the illusion of a doll's eyes dissipates as her eyes darken with feeling. *"Buona fortuna, buona fortuna."* She reaches up, touches my face. "You're a smart girl. Get right away. Don't wait." For a moment, she stands straighter, some of the old Angie back in her stance.

Even now, with my own life unravelling in my hands and my loneliness grown to fit me like a second skin, I look back at Angie, carved like a cameo in memory, and feel again the quickened pulse of hope as I watch her standing in the dimness of the church. A beam of sunlight through stained glass ignites her face and hair to burnished gold. She burns with a deep fire, the years erased, and her face radiant.

Shrinks

"Let me just tell you what happened yesterday." His sister Grace was angry. "We took the car out to go to the doctor's. And he went and disappeared. We had to go looking all over the streets for him. You know where we found him?"

"I think it means he doesn't want to see this kind of doctor. What can a man like that talk about with a psychiatrist?"

"John, he told us he ran away because we were taking him to the doctor for his infected toes. And they would make him cry. Does that sound like your father?"

"Gianni!" Their father's voice came from downstairs. He had reached the front porch after going for cigars and seen the big car. Grace looked frightened. She stopped still at his footsteps on the stairs coming up.

John was staring at her. "What's the matter? You scared of him?" Grace nodded but did not speak.

The door opened. The old craggy face was smiling out of control. *"Ey? When you came?"* He used loudness to hide feelings but walked quickly to his son, embraced him, and held on too long.

"I'm here no more than five minutes," John said, and held him until he was solid on his feet again. "Pop, I came to ask you why you're trying to escape this doctor."

The old man sat down slowly in a kitchen chair and, seeing Grace, waved a hand that meant he wanted coffee. Grace went for the pot. He looked at his son, "This doctor has money. He don't need me."

As his daughter poured the coffee before him, he stood up, waiting silently for the completion. Then he took his cup and led John towards the parlor, saying nothing to Grace, who called after him, "Momma got the car out again, you know. You going this time?"

"Let me speak to my son first," the old man said.

John could see something different, but it was only a rearrangement of the old irritations. His father was still being *padrone* of the mind.

Grace walked to her room after the slight by her father. The old man entered the parlor and sat in the green armchair, looking up, "Johnny, I didn't know you was coming. I took a walk."

John stood watching him and the doilies on the chairs, now like the color of the old white walls. John remembered that the doilies had been crocheted when the porch was enclosed to make another room and his mother bought new furniture.

As he sat on the couch across from his father, John said, "Where did we ever get this fabric that pricks the skin?"

"From the Americans. Ask your mother."

"You never liked this stuff, did you, Pop?"

The old man coughed deep in his throat, then made a sound as if to spit but did not. "This is fake junk. Is white pine they cover with stain and nails. They tell her good enough for the *contessa*. The *contessa di merda*. You understand that?"

"Yes, Maestro, I understand that much. Listen, where's the old Atwater Kent?"

The old man leaned forward and looked at the corner of the room as John added, "The big radio."

"Look in the cellar," the old man answered, and looked around the room. "They put it all down the cellar."

"They're back in style again," John said. "Put a new finish on them— even the old radio shows—"

He saw that his father was following him—but perhaps not listening. John asked, "Remember when I used to sit under the radio and listen?"

"And your mother telling me, get him to eat. Get him to *eat*!"

The old man was smiling in recognition. John said, "Do you remember a lot these days?"

The old man smiled a different way. "That you asked me every question. You was the special son. I said, this one will *be* something."

"I checked it out, Pop. They said *no*, Consoli is not a famous name."

"You shouldn't talk like that. You with the senator now. You go with the Washington people. Don't bury yourself because the Americans invite you into the grave."

John shook his head. The old man always had his one or two Brechtian lines. John should have taken the old man for coffee every week. Fridays at the *caffe*. They would have smoked a Tuscan cigar and talked their lines. "Pop, when exactly are you moving?"

"A few weeks. We go live with the millionaire. And eat American bread. And get full with cotton. But I save you money. When I go, you don't call the undertaker. You just drop me in the hole, and I am nice soft cotton."

"I can't understand *why* don't you want to leave here? The burning houses are a block away. Nobody's cleaning it up. And the senator even tried. They just don't want to do it yet."

"Your sister tells me. So I go to the world of the priests, the shower. I take a shower every day and put butter on my bread and spray under my arms to smell like a *puttana*."

John began pacing the room in front of his father, trying to turn the tone to joking. "Then I take it you are really very excited about making the big move to Florida."

"Yes, I will make a party and give cigars and then I go into the ground, six feet down, frac frac, cover the hole. This man is over. Forget this *chidrool*."

"I hope they get you a Jewish one," John said softly.

"What's that?"

"That doctor, the doctor you will go talk to."

"You mean *psichologo*—"

"Therapist, psychiatrist, whatever you want to call him—*shrink*."

"Shrink. What? Shrinks the head?"

"You got it, Pop. Now why do you think they made up that word?"

His father looked at him intently for a moment, then folded his right leg over his left to bring his toes closer for examination. Then he looked for a cigar in his shirt pockets as he spoke, "It means—it means the head gets full. From living in this house, all what happened. Your life."

"And what is your head full of?" John asked. "Is it Calabria when you were a kid?"

The old man stopped smiling. "My head is full of things you don't know." His thoughts were passing too fast. He would lose them if he had to talk.

John interrupted him, "Which is why I'm asking you."

"Which is why I don't tell you. You can't understand. The shrink can't understand. And nobody in here can understand."

"You mean nobody who wasn't a stonecutter and then sold produce at Bronx Terminal market."

The old man nodded.

"You remember in high school when I tried to work in the early morning with you and couldn't stay awake?"

The old man nodded but did not remember more than irritation. John could not forget the shame of it when his father had said at the table that each of his children got weaker and without energy or stamina and that eventually the ideal American child would not be able to walk and would only watch things with its eyes but would be able to watch TV forever, even in its sleep.

The old man asked, "Why wasn't you a doctor?"

"I hated the sight of blood," John said.

"You loved the blood. You cried for me to take you the poultry market in Ely Avenue. And you loved to watch the chicken heads come off. You love it."

"I thought you told me I was a sweet, gentle kid," John said.

"But what kid don't like to see the chicken head chop off?"

"The guilty ones," John said, and saw his father's smile of confusion. John added, "The ones who want to chop somebody else off." John felt his face flush. It was not a joke. It was not a thought he intended. His face got hotter.

His father was lost in his own thoughts. "They don't kill a father anymore," he said. "Now they send him to Florida. Give his money to Merrow Lynch." The old man stood up suddenly to exercise his toes. "You like these shoes? This is your mother's shoes."

"They look all right."

"They look all right? You, too, crazy, *Giowan*. They making me into a woman around here, and you say all right. You should help me. Let me come live with you, and then your mother and sister can go have a nice time together."

The old man sat down and lit his cigar. Mrs. Consoli came in with a tray of coffee and pine nuts and sat after pouring around. Then she explained that John would stay over and take his father to the doctor tomorrow.

Then she asked John about the new job, his trips on the plane to Washington every week. She was pleased with the names. But the old man was fighting to keep awake. His head would drop, and he would rush to bring it back up. John stopped talking and promised he would tell them the rest tomorrow. The old man got up silently and went to his room. Mrs. Consoli waited for his door to slam before talking to her son. "What do you say?"

"I don't know."

"What do you mean, you don't know? You see your father?"

John collected the coffee cups onto the tray and swept up crumbs. "Tell me something," his mother said loud. "I have to go with this man to live in Florida."

"I see a man who wants to die," John said, and walked to the kitchen with the tray.

His mother followed him. "Tell me what I should do. He forgets my name."

"He's not that bad."

"Then live with him."

"His mind is perfectly lucid."

Mrs. Consoli looked at her son as if he were speaking in another language. "Go take him to the doctor," she said, and went to the bedroom. John saw she did not use another room.

He went in and slept after listening to the house and identifying its odors. To him the Bronx was always smells, night and day, from stuffy rooms to cookies baking on the wind.

In the morning he heard a knock; it was still dark. "You want to come walk now?" his father asked.

John got up and dressed quickly. In the kitchen he found a small cup of black coffee and drank it rather than look for anybody. Downstairs his father was waiting on the stoop.

They walked towards Arthur Avenue as the red light of day came up. John looked at his watch when his father went in for cigars. It was later than he thought, almost eight.

The old man came out lining his cigars in his shirt pocket like pens. Then he set out fast to the edge of Bronx Park where the river was isolated beyond the thruway lanes cut through the green of the park. Between the highway and the river was an inaccessible place for walking, but car doors and innersprings and truck tires sliced in half were piled around.

They turned away from it and were quickly at the high school. John spoke as they passed the concrete yard, "I burned a lot of sneakers on that ground."

"You burned sneakers? Maybe you better come with me to see this doctor?"

It was the first time the old man had shown he knew what kind of behavior was required for this new doctor.

John stopped. "Pop. You shouldn't be afraid of this kind of doctor. I went to one myself for three years. They listen to you. They think about what you say. They take it seriously."

The old man looked at his son with what John thought was fear. Then he led John back to Arthur Avenue. "What is it?" John said. "Something I said scared you?"

The old man stopped and turned to John. Moved by his son's care, he embraced John but took his arms back quickly.

John said, gently, "Now tell me what's the matter?"

"Every morning you go to the store, you get me a *mozzarella*, fresh, in the water, no salt, and you go pack it up and mail to Florida."

"And how about Terranova's bread? I can send you two big loaves a day air freight."

"And don't forget *sageesh,* one pound, sweet."

His father walked again, down Arthur Avenue. As they passed the restaurant, John said, "I could even try to bottle the smell from Dominic's and send it down every week."

The old man walked to his house and stood at the car door. John let him in, then went to the driver's seat, started the engine, drove off.

After some minutes, the old man looked around. "This is the city?"

"This doctor is in Purchase. Near White Plains."

"You know him?" Consoli said.

"I heard he's a very good man."

"John, he won't put me away?"

"Pop, cut that out. Nobody does anything to you, not while I'm around."

The old man sat back in the car seat and looked for a cigar. When they arrived in front of the house, John opened the door but did not get out. The old man went up to the office and John slowly followed, watching his father shake hands with the short, balding doctor and hand him a cigar.

When it was over and father and son were driving home, John asked, "Did it go all right?"

"All right, all right," the old man said. "This one is crazy like me."

"So you liked him, then?" John said.

The old man smiled but did not speak for the rest of the trip home. At the door to the house, John helped his father out and then got back in his car. "I have got to get the plane by noon."

The old man went to the porch alone and waved his son off. John drove downtown, put the car away, and took a cab to the airport. He had enough time for a few calls and called home. Grace answered. "It's amazing," she said. "Like a miracle happened. Let's hope this sticks. What do you think this guy did?"

"I don't know," John said. "He only said he and the doctor are crazy in the same way."

"That's got to be true," Grace said. "If he could talk to him that long. But thank God for it."

Twenty-Nine Steps towards Re-adhesion

1. Florence. 1982. The broom (Ezio calls it *ginestre*) is brilliant yellow against the green hills of Chianti. Leaves of the wine grapes overhead. We are going to Greve for lunch. Ezio swears he will take me to a different town in Chianti every day; we will have a *pranzo*, taste the local wine all afternoon. By the time I leave, we will have tried all the Chiantis. This is also to distract me gastronomically and aesthetically, he says. Yesterday I found a book in Via Tornaboni, the shop just up from Piazza Trinità. A history of all the Chianti wine farms. One hundred sixty-four pages, and each page a different label with a minihistory of the farm. My liver will go before we drink them all.

2. Ginny liked broom. She went to sit in the fields of it the first day she saw it. And cried. We had rented a car in Florence and were on the way to Siena. We never made it. We sat drinking Chianti we had bought on the road, and she remembered her mother. Something about the two of them and the fields of broom on the Cape: the only year she was ever happy.

3. I was saying nothing when Ezio stopped for the broom. Atypical for him to ever stop. And the way he turned to look at me. With what? A compassionate stare? A pitying grin? Did he know Ginny liked it, the broom? I thought he was about to mention her, but he looked at me with that look. He catches my emanations perhaps. He often says that Ginny was blind. "On her magic carpet ride, like those women of Henry James. What does she do? She falls in love with her picture of an Italian, and he isn't even an authentic one." I nod at his certainty, the dogma that haunts Italian men. He says, "You must know by now that the woman falls in love with her construction of love." My silence gets him eventually, and his voice goes up. "Let it go, let it go. It happened only inside her head. You had yours. Now let it end."

4. He is a Florentine. They have been business men since God knows when. They hold the scales of trade always in hand. Everything can be weighed out. Proper measuring makes logic, makes conclusions. For instance, he sees me tainted with bad blood from my father's side, Naples, the South. We see love as a candy heart. We want only to suck on the sugar—then we get sick. He attacks me for that when he gets a bit drunk (something he learned living in the States): "You don't know what is over is over. You want to feast on your wound. *Senti*? If you can say to yourself, *Over*, then it is gone." I stand up and salute him: *"Sì, Commandante."* "Sit down, *stronzo*," he shouts, and laughs at his word.

5. Lillies, red poppies, blue wild flowers I can't name in Italian. Did I know them as a child? I am fluent but for the fishes and the flowers. Ezio was looking up at the broom and said the yellow makes the green greener this time of year. Like Ireland. He tells me Ireland has the greenest grass in the world.

6. As we drove through the Tuscan hills, the cypresses going brown in clumps along the way, I thought of what a great place this would be for Paul to come and paint. But his last letter said it was getting too hard: getting a one man show, making it in that world of cliques; if you didn't toady up, you faced a century of hunger. So he was thinking of med school again, without illusion, as he put it, that there are doctors who paint on weekends. I mentioned it to Ezio, who said that paintings were no longer necessary— nor books—except for old dogs like us. The young have the Tee Voo, which does everything for them. It provides for their aesthetic needs. I said to him, "Do you really believe that?" And he paused, pursing his lips to show the heavy thought, adding slow slight nods. "Michael, I think we are dead," he said. "*You*, especially. Because at least I can keep the past here a little. You threw out the Victorian furniture of your mother when you moved out of the Village. What did you get? You inherited Yonkers. And now you live like a man on the back of a truck. Downtown the young gays buy and sell your living room as antiques and make a new world." I said to him, "This must be your new cyclical theory of history." And he shot off one more tight Medici minismile: *Deny it as I wish, it was still true,* his face said. Like Galileo.

7. "Good friends and friendship, *caro mio*," I said, "means being pissed off and eating it all the time." And Galileo spake again: "I can only tell you the truth," he said. "A friend is to speak the truth you can't see."

8. I am silent, sullen—whether from his lectures or the returning I don't know. I can't remember anything Ginny and I did or said. I can't remember *her*. I experience brief bits—like a toothache—of memory, feel something and then am very quiet and down. It happens fast. And just as I have tried to probe it, Ezio starts as Galileo again. "Michael, *senti*. Everything comes round again. People change hands. The haughty German countess who was caught by the Russian army and raped by a platoon of peasants is in power again—did you read it?—and shot one of the Russians thirty years later. Did you see it? He was on business in Berlin." I looked up at his disturbing story, and he was nodding. "Yes, only books and paintings do not change."

9. He must think I'm drunk most of the time. Each morning he leaves for work as I am getting up to go to the john. He returns at one-thirty, and I'm just shaving. I tell him I've been revising my book, and he looks down at the pages which look exactly as yesterday and nods. "Is it on Caravaggio?" he asks. "Caravaggio and a few others," I say. Then we go out to Chianti for another lunch.

10. Yesterday we had lunch in San Casciano; first a restaurant and then, after, a walk to a *pizzicheria* that made coffee. Ezio and the proprietor started talking. Ezio told him I was an American. The man explained he had four hundred different types of prosciutto. I said that that was difficult to believe. Ezio said, "How about the French and four hundred cheeses?" I nodded to Galileo, then watched the owner, who wanted me to do a tasting. The best was thinly sliced *finocchioncino*. I watched an old man squeezing lemons into his wine. Ezio said the farmers believe it cools them off in heat. Like the Chinese putting warm rags on their faces. Ezio says, "The lemons really work." Galilean truths abound. I offer no questions.

11. Ezio's apartment is his monument-in-the-making. Two great rooms and a kitchen, a foyer larger than a Manhattan studio apartment. It faces the piazza the Medicis built for a fish market. Now it's a flea market for imitation furniture and imitation armor and what tourists seem to like. Ezio found old craftsmen who knew the ancient techniques of stucco and the waxing of beams with beeswax. The men chopped out the modern ceiling that was built in the sixteen hundreds, found the beams from the eleven hundreds, and restored them. You look up at incredibly long hand-cut wooden beams. And Ezio has filled the rooms with his objects bought on business trips. In Jugoslavia he found an old man who made church wall hangings in plaster and wood, painted in bright tempera. Stations of the Cross. Christ being soothed by Mary. Treasures. Ezio found a tile man who redid the floors with old red tiles he found in a barn out in Chianti. He has a carved wooden table, bits of the ivory inlays fallen out, on which he places the Etruscan stuff he bought from grave robbers he knows in the hills. Gold pins—the Etruscans knew how to work pure gold—and vases and dancing figures. In the corner is his pride, an old wood carving made from a tree trunk. A monk in habit, cappucino, I think. It reminds Ezio of his first employer, Brother Clementino, the miracle monk who lived in Fiesole and received thousands of letters a day from all over the world (Ezio delivered them up the hill). "I can't believe you never heard of him," Ezio says to me with irritation. "Even people in Russia used to write to him for a miracle."

12. Ezio gets excited about a little *gita* up to Fiesole. He wants to show me the monastery where Clementino worked, built over the Etruscan ruins, and where Ezio played as a boy. He is the most eager tourist. Anywhere we go he searches down all the narrow streets, more curious than any foreigners he has shown the town. He calls me inauthentic but not yet a foreigner. He says of me, "Born of Italians and away from Italy by mistake, an accident of history." This historical accident has come to Florence to commune with fragments that might be left. He wishes to complete his puzzle. I told Ezio I really had no Italian personna—unless I make it up. Ezio says I am obscured from myself running from the wounds of Ginny. I tell him a broken love affair has nothing to do with remembering my first two years in Italy here. And he says, ending it, "But you were born here."

13. One day after lunch—always after a meal—Ezio said, "Why don't you just try living here permanently?" I said to him, "I would miss bagels and Katz's deli too much." His face turned into a false smiling, nodding at me. He doesn't believe what I say. He says, "It's time you found out where your home is. I was ten years in Chicago; they offered me a vice presidency. But then I knew I had to come back here. Because this is home inside me. When I thought, vice president means Chicago forever, I left." I said, "But New York has made me Jewish." "Bullshit on toast," he said quickly. "You're about as Jewish as I am. Listen. Home is the place that stays inside you wherever you go. Now what is that for you? Find it."

14. Maybe I could do it here with somebody who loved it with me. Ginny used to say she wanted to live here. And I believed her. And started to consider it. But she was back here by herself in May. Maybe she was thinking of it. I mention this to Ezio.

15. He nods and seems about to answer, then stops himself. He does not speak about her anymore. If I bring her up, he will be about to say something, then think better of it.

16. Now and then he busts out, usually late at night after we have sat for some hours drinking and talking. (His own drinking seems desperate to me.) He has not mentioned Marianna, his ex-wife, who lives nearby, somewhere in town. (She told me his screaming frightened her when they argued.) One night Ezio started on me: "You must stop moping around. Ginny was a woman trying to escape. She met you, she used you a while to get out of prison. Then she wanted to go back inside." He wanted a rise out of me, but I was silent. "The woman didn't like you!" He had begun to scream. "She could not even *see* you! Her eyes were on the locks of her door, and that's all she could see. Be thankful she came out a while for you. And stop thinking she needed you. She told me she didn't even like you. Now don't get hot. It was in May. She said you were spoiled, always stuck in yourself—"

17. I walked out of the room to my bedroom on the second floor and heard him shouting up the steps. "Don't get mad at the truth. Come down. Listen, I'm worse than you; ask Marianna. Nobody can bear to live with me, either. *Stronzo!* Come down again."

18. Last days. I wanted to go to Greve again. We ate at a restaurant in the main piazza. There were geranium flowers in pots blooming along the cement wall. The statue in the center of the piazza was Verrazzano. I asked Ezio what the ocean navigators were doing deep inside Chianti. "A mystery I often think about," Ezio said. "How did these inland towns produce all those amazing explorers who opened up the world for Europe? They never even *saw* the water. You know about Verrazzano?" "Yes," I said. "He's a bridge, and he comes from Staten Island."

19. The restaurant was a long, shallow room, high back chairs in dark brown, simple Tuscan decor. The melon and prosciutti—we have at least three or four each time now—were optimum, the veal chop like a T-bone steak before the invention of muscles, the stuffed zucchini beefy in the Tuscan style, the artichokes tender enough to eat raw. And the local wine better than other days. I tell Ezio I can't remember which wine was best after all these months. "Then we'll have to start again," he says, and shakes my hand.

20. We drove to an eighth-century town above Greve—Monteferallo—and walked the very narrow streets to get the feel of the past. Ezio wanted a *digestivo*, and we found the town bar. It had three rows of scotches, and Ezio had one. He reminded me of the day ten years before in Milano when he ordered me a large glass of Fernet Branca for my birthday. "I thought it was rat poison," I said. Ezio slaps my back and laughs, invites me to have a Fernet now. He has another scotch. Then we drove to the Enoteca shop in Greve where the growers keep a small museum at the site of ancient wine cellars. The two men in charge looked like Amherst profs in their tweed and leather patches, both pipe-smoking, lean. But then again, Tuscany looks like Vermont.

21. Ezio worries about my inaction. "Why don't you get out and go around Florence when I'm working? We are so near the Bargello. You always liked Santa Croce. It's just down the street." He believes that true therapy is getting off the butt, never sitting down, doing something fast.

22. In the mornings here, I have remembered my mother. The voices and the silences here are different and let me daydream. There is no hum of surrounding thruways that makes you feel as if the phone is about to ring and you're due somewhere soon. I walked the street where my mother lived as a girl and tried to imagine something I didn't remember or know. I could only see her in exile, in a New York kitchen. Three young women went by, and I followed them, listening. But nothing happened. I walked downtown and stopped for coffee in Piazza Duomo and began to feel guilty for making the trip alone. But everyone had said, *go, go, you need it*. I responded like their favorite patient. But something has changed. I enjoyed Greve the second time. To the depths of me. I can't recall a place that sank deeper than Greve. Leaving me feeling a lightness I thought I could never have again.

23. Ezio is snoring. He has had seven scotches since we came back to the apartment, each in a small liqueur glass. The Florentines have really fallen for scotch, but they drink it in little glasses, warm, with their after-dinner espresso. Ezio goes for the scotch every night when he gets home. He says it comes from living alone. I asked him if it takes the place of a fight with your woman. He didn't want to talk and said tomorrow we would visit old Fantini in the morning and then drive to Pisa for my plane.

24. We saw Fantini in the Siena hospital. Seven hundred or so friends in his room. Hospital rooms and halls full of families all day. Nobody stops them. All the sick with squads holding their hands and milling around the bed. Like worship. Italians think affection can actually cure. At least, it is the medicine of choice for them. A great argument now begins. Workers, unions. You cannot fire even the worst *stronzo* of a worker anymore. In fact, you must keep money in escrow to pay him a few years should you go bankrupt. Imagine! Ezio is screaming. Horrible! Fantini had to start fixing his own trucks at night because the workers walked off at four. And that's how the big back door crushed his right hip. Sabotage! Ezio began shouting about the disappearance of craftsmen, what I call his what-ever-happened-to-the-Renaissance speech. I am kissed goodbye with tears of regret, a poor fool who is leaving Florence. Leaving! Oh *Dio*! Embraces. Expressions of grief for me rather than Fantini. Then Ezio drove me to Pisa.

25. I checked my baggage and went outside to the gate where Ezio was looking at the plane on the apron. "What is it?" I said. I thought he had been crying, but there was more in his look. "Don't you think I'm ever coming back?" I said, and even as I did I caught on. I don't know how things come together, expressions, tones, the eyes. I said, "It's all right. We were totally split when she came here in May. Whatever you did between you was your business. I have no connection to her anymore." He kept crying softly and turned his head away from me, striking his cheek on the fence. I put down my plastic carry-on and embraced him. "Stop it now," I said, but he could not speak.

26. In Milano the 747 was not crowded. People walk out to the plane. Alitalia and its blessed vagueness. All right to board? *Sì, signore*, why not?

I am leaving a country where the size of things does not shrink me. The 747 is my first reminder of grandeur in three months. I am reluctant to be at the leading edge of the hi-tech future.

27. The movie begins quickly: shut curtains; no sky watching here. The film is an English actor sweating out a silly love story that ends in joy and confusion. He is one of a group today I call the pooches. They appeal like small terriers or poodles—brisk, light, huggable, shallow. Americans love to watch those pooch men in the movies today. They tell us we are gentle and would never press the button.

28. I think I see snow along the runway, but it is summer in Washington and Virginia. Eddie and my sister Blanche pick me up and invite me to stay at their house in Falls Church a few days. They want to check me out before releasing me. I am OK, I tell Blanche, but she sulks. I tell them to take me to my apartment. As we ride I say, "Did you know there's a blight that's killing the cypresses in Tuscany?" Blanche nods and comes back at me. Did I know that Momma has more friends in Florida than she ever had up here? And she is waiting for my call.

29. I am left off. I watch them drive away, and I go up to my rooms on the third floor. Inside, I feel the eight hours in my muscles. I want to sleep. But as I take my clothes off, I smell the airplane stinks, and I must shower. I come out with my robe on and tour the apartment. I feel as if I've landed in a pleasant new country. I want to call somebody to say I'm back. I shall stop myself from calling anybody. I will admit to jet lag. I will try to sleep Florence away. Work starts tomorrow.

Our Lady's Field

First Chapter of a Novel-in-Progress

Outside my window: a too-hot August day. A skinny Puerto Rican kid sitting on the front fender of a parked car is chanting, "that fuckin' bitch, that fuckin' bitch, that fuckin' bitch..." He's wearing just pants and sneakers. Though only a boy, his bare chest is the miniature of a man's. (If Caravaggio painted him you'd think he was a fine-looking boy, thin but muscled—proportioned like a satyr.) He has dark, curly hair and arched, almost feminine, eyebrows. When he snarls to this street where every other word is *fuckin'*—and bangs his heels hard against the fender, wop, wop, wop—his anger makes him ugly.

Again, like a bitter electricity, his anger surfaces. Turning his head, he yells up the block to someone just out of my sight, "Come ovah here!"

A reedy, high-pitched voice answers, "No!"

If I switch windows, I can see her standing about twenty feet away. She's thin as a pole. A plastic headband keeps her dyed, yellow-orange hair from falling into her eyes. She's standing by another parked car with her girlfriend and a little girl. The girlfriend wears shorts; she has heavy legs. The little girl, about three and a half, has a long, dark ponytail. A bright-yellow plastic bucket with a red shovel in it swings from her arm.

At this moment the boy springs from the car and runs at them. They cannot run away because of the child. The skinny girl cowers behind the thick one. Rushing at them wildly he pushes them both off the curb into the street.

He pulls at her shirt. She wails. I hear a loud slap and see the headband go flying. She is crying, still trying to stay behind her friend. The child, silent and patient, watches from the sidewalk. She does not seem surprised.

Then he really starts hitting her. I hear the horrible thuds on her chest, on her back, and yell, "Hey! Hey!" but he keeps hitting her.

I try to think of some way to stop him—then bellow in my best Brooklyn voice: 'I'm not gonna let anybody get beat up in front of my house!" Holding the phone to my ear, I stand right up against the screen where they can see me. Who would I call? The cops wouldn't come.

They wrangle, but less vigorously now, then separate warily. He bends down to retrieve the fallen headband—which he offers her. She grabs it from him mumbling something.

He says, "Why did you just walk away from me when I called ya, like I was fuckin' nobody?"

Ah, I think, this was her transgression: he was hanging out with some buddies on a nearby streetcorner and called out to her. She passed by, but she did not acknowledge him. They are fourteen years old, but they have slept together so she must answer to him.

She's hurt his pride, but somehow she has also managed to put a hole in his lip—it's bleeding—with what? Her fist, a ring, her nail. . .?

He walks away from them and leans against the same fender. She follows meekly, knowing now she is not allowed to walk away. She nurses a sore hand and cheek; he wipes away blood from his mouth with a ragged T-shirt he pulls from his back jeans pocket.

I hear him call her Titi. I can't understand her when she speaks—her voice is still shaky from the crying. Then I realize they're speaking Spanish. On this white, mostly Irish block, they have their own kind of privacy.

He slides towards her, arm extended, his brown hand seeking her thin shoulder. She shakes him off.

His voice is calm now, childlike: "Ya know, all I wanted ta do was talk ta ya, Titi, that's all, I only wanted to fuckin' talk ta ya. Why'd you walk away from me, like I was fuckin' nobody?"

Titi still whimpers a bit. She looks up the block where her girlfriend catches the child's hand and starts to walk away. The little ponytail swings and the sturdy brown legs move doll-like under her red skirt.

This time when he tries to put his arm around her again she slides farther down the car, out of reach.

"Ya know, you done a lot of things to me, Titi."

She looks him in the eye. She is not crying anymore. "I done a lot of things for you," she says.

"Yeah, to me and for me."

They speak easily in two languages, not even knowing when they switch. Intimate now, they walk away side by side. The rest of the afternoon lies before them.

When they catch up to the little girl, she pulls her hand away from the girlfriend and stops walking. Looking up at Titi she says, "Show me where he hit you, Titi. I want to see."

Mora Amore

"Cheen-kway!"

"Sayeee!"

Frankie heard the Italian numbers and ran toward the yelling.

"Do-ayeee!"

"Boom-mah!"

After dinner he had carried two cannolo away from the old people's table and walked to the field of stiff prairie grass that his Uncle Vince had mowed the day before the picnic. He sat down under one of the oak trees that separated the new lawn from the prairie and ate the cannolo while watching the children play.

Frankie Benet was the oldest of Mario and Carmella Ranellos' grand-children and felt that he was too old to be playing baseball with those who still wore shorts. Angela had just given his summer shorts, the tight tan pair that made his legs bulge like two of Grandpa's freshly stuffed sausages, to his younger brother, Mario. Mario was rounding the stained paper plate that was second base and stretching his thin legs toward third when Frankie heard the yelling. Frankie saw the baggy shorts that hung to his brother's shins and was happy that they were no longer his. The hair on his legs had sprouted into black wires and he swore he would only bare those legs to swim.

Growing up in the Ranello family was marked in two ways. There were the formal stages, which were usually religious: Baptism, First Holy Com-munion, and Confirmation. There were the informal stages, marked by table placement during family meals: the high chairs in the living room, the children's table in the bedroom adjacent to the large dining room, and the grown-ups' table. Frankie was between Communion and Confirmation, between the children's table and the grown-ups' table, so he endured the association of his younger relatives. Last year he had heard the same yelling, but he had been too involved with the baseball game to pay attention to the bunch of wine-drinking men who threw their hands at each other and yelled numbers loudly into each other's face. But this year he was bored enough by the ball game that the yelling was able to pull him away from the shade of the oak leaves and lure him toward the newly built concrete patio.

From the open space of the prairie he ran through a narrow tunnel of neatly trimmed evergreens into a smaller lawned yard that led to the patio. He ran between two rows of picnic tables still cluttered with oil-stained paper plates, speckled with glistening leaves of barbed endive and *cicoria,* olive pits, grape seeds, drips of cannoli filling that had escaped the last licks of sticky fingers, and bits of garlic that lay in tiny puddles of browned olive oil. He passed half-filled, paper coffee cups that had lost their steam, oil-stained paper napkins that held stems from the peppers that had been fried with eggs, smeared with lipstick, and wrapped around chicken bones, licked clean by the adults and half eaten by the children. He rushed by the old men sitting in lawn chairs that encircled a plastic TV tray where a green, labelless, almost empty gallon of Mario's wine sat next to an uncorked gallon of the same waiting its turn.

He passed high chairs, where lay tiny chopped pieces of sausage and peppers, oranged spaghetti that was drying out in the sun, and dixie cups turned upside down in small pools of watered-down wine. He slowed at the table in the shade where the women had gathered to talk before they would clean up the remains of the meal. He stopped at the large galvanized tub that was filled with chunks of ice sweating onto the tops of beer cans and soda pop.

"KWAAAH-TRO!"

He looked up at the sound of the number *four* to see a clenched fist raised in the air that then swung down throwing four fingers against another open palm that shot out four fingers at the same time.

"AAH-TOE," "SAYEEE," followed by a victorious, "AH, HA!"

He looked from the meeting of the fingers to the face of Uncle Carlo. His young uncle flashed a grin and reached for his paper cup of wine. He gulped more than he could swallow, and dark purple drops dribbled down his stubbled chin to rest permanently on his sweat-stained white shirt. He looked to his Uncle Vince, who was standing face to face with his younger brother, Carlo. Vince looked angry. The tanned skin of his forehead tightened and tugged the black curls on his head. He filled his lungs and lengthened the ash on his cigarette without removing it from his mouth. Four fingers met in the space between his uncles' stomachs.

"Dee-ay-chay!"

"Sayee!"

The uncles studied each other's eyes in silence. Two fists flew into the air and swooped down, casting fingers accompanied by the loud, "Doo-ayee!"

"Kwaah-tro!" Two fingers, then two more fingers, and then a laugh from Uncle Vince as he flashed the forefinger of his left hand straight up; the same hand dropped down to grab his cup of wine.

Uncle Johnnie then called out, "Doo-ayee al Oono."

Frankie still had no idea what it was the men were doing. He knew, from listening to Uncle Johnnie, that Uncle Carlo's team was winning two to one, but he still wasn't sure how the points were scored.

He looked to his grandmother. She had a small knife in her right hand and was paring a peach. Her eyes focused on her youngest daughter; her fingers spun the fruit against the knife and the peel slid off the fruit in one piece. She could tell that her grandson was in a hurry to ask her something, but she ignored him and began slicing the pared peach. She lifted a crescent to her lips with the knife, her eyes still on her daughter. Frankie thought he had heard the word *divorce,* but the talk of the women was so loud and chaotic that he couldn't tell who had said the word. He searched the faces at the table and returned to his grandmother. All eyes were on her. The juice from the sliced peach dripped from the blade of her knife, down the rosewood handle, and onto her thin wrist, where it pooled and dripped to the flabby white underside of her forearm. She wiped her arm on the table and resumed the conversation.

"I doan like it. Isa wrong. This thing was not possible years ago. Once a woman an' a man is marry is too late to worry for the past. They 'ave the family an' that is what to worry for." Her youngest daughter interrupted her.

"But mamma, these are not once upon a times. These are new times and . . ."

Frankie couldn't tell who they were talking about and he didn't care. He wanted to know about this game the men were playing. He turned his attention back to the uncles.

Fists shot up, flexed, and dropped down flashing fingers. He watched for a while, keeping an ear on the women, waiting for a break to ask his grandmother about this game. Carmella was getting riled. He could tell by the twitching that nudged him and by the fury with which she ate the peach; the knife grating the peach stone made him shiver. He turned to ask her and saw her plop the peach pit into her wrinkled mouth. She looked into his face. Her cheeks puffed and the peach pit poked out. Her wide eyes and wet lips told him that he shouldn't be here listening to the women talk. He blurted out, "Nonna, what is the game they are playing?"

Her hand rose to her lips, and after she passed the pit from her mouth to her palm, she splurted out, "That's ah more-ah. Ay . . ." And before he could get an explanation, she turned to her daughter and angrily hollered out, "How can you know. I no care what you say. Is a sin. Not joosta sin against God, ma the worst of all sins, is a sin 'gainst the family." She shouted something else in Italian. Then, as if by some prearranged cue, the entire conversation shifted into Italian. The older aunts were on his grandma's side. He could tell from their loud yelling that they were cheering what she had just said.

The yelling of Italian numbers, of Italian words, the laughing and wine guzzling by the men, the arguing of the women—all combined to spin his head. He decided to get away from these crazy adults, even if it meant going back to play ball with his young cousins. As he walked away from the table, he saw his older uncles and his grandfather sitting around the newly opened, green gallon of red wine. He walked up to his Uncle Giacomo, the old man with the thick white moustache (and the even thicker white hair that was always stuffed under a grey flannel cap with the purple-stained brim that came from years of adjusting the cap unconsciously with fingers still wet with wine). Frankie knew he could get a quick answer from Uncle Jock.

"Hey, Uncle Jock," he yelled.

"Ay Unca Jock w'at," mimicked the old man. "*Vieni qua* Franco. What'sa bodder you?"

Frankie walked over to the circle of old men who were telling stories of the old days. He had heard the stories so many times that they all sounded the same. He couldn't understand how they could listen to the same old stories over and over again. He thought they changed the details from time to time, not because they no longer remembered accurately, not because they were liars, but because the facts no longer mattered.

"Uncle Jockie, what's ah-more-ay?"

Giacomo blinked his wine-reddened eyes and laughed so loud it took the attention away from the story that his brother was telling of the wine-making business they had operated during Prohibition. The faces of Tony's listeners turned together toward Giacomo for an explanation of the outburst. Giacomo sputtered, "Ay, goombah. You boy wan' know what is ah-more-ay, ahahahah."

A voice shouted out, "He does? Well then, you should give 'im to Lucky Luisa. She tell 'im evertingah! Ah, haha!"

Frankie couldn't tell what the old men were talking about and he was lost in all their laughing. Uncle Giacomo caught his breath and asked, "Why you wan' know what is ah-more-ay? You too young. Oh, do you 'ava the girla fr'en' already?"

By now Frankie was lost and his frustration couldn't be masked. He yelled out, "Tell me what the game ah-more-ay is!"

The old men howled. He tried to yell out his question again, but before he could, his Uncle Guido hobbled up to him and put his arm around the boy's shoulder. Guido's breath smelled like the inside of the store he had closed to come to the picnic today. It reeked a combination of salami, peppermint smelling anisette, and various secret spices he kept inside wooden barrels. "*Caro* Franco, ah-more-ay is some-a-ting you too young for an' a some-a-ting we too old for."

"Speak fo' youself," laughed Tony and the old men joined his laughter. Guido shook Frankie teasingly, grabbed his cheeks with his thumbs and forefingers, gave them a strong twist, and returned to his lawn chair. On his way he grabbed the wine bottle, swiped a swig, and wiped his mouth with his shirt sleeve.

Frankie cursed to himself and yelled, "I know I'm too young to play ah-more-ay, but why can't you tell me what it is so that when I get old enough I will know how to play it!"

Their laughter chased him off to the trees to sit, think, and decide if he really wasn't too old to play with his cousins after all. He closed his eyes, and when he turned them toward the sun, against the orange of his eyelids he saw flying fists, toothless laughing faces, and dripping peach slices. The sounds of the family behind him and of his cousins playing in front of him blended into a hum. A tune came from inside his head and moved from behind his ear, words were added to the melody to create: "When the moon hits your eye like a big pizza pie, that's ah-more-ay." *That's it!* he thought and leapt from his crosslegged position beneath the tree.

He ran back through the rows of picnic tables to the circle of old men, whose roars of laughter had settled as they listened to the retelling of another story. He slowed down as he neared his grandfather, who now was almost asleep in a green and white, braided-plastic lawn chair. In his grandfather's lap was a paper cup filled with his own wine. Frankie stopped at his grandfather's side, and the old man looked into Frankie's eyes, lifted his cup to his lips, and blinked.

"*Caro* Franco, w'at-sah bodder you?"

"Nonno, what's that game that Uncle Carlo and Vince are playing. Nonna told me that it was ah-more-ay." And before his grandfather could reply, the young boy inhaled quickly and continued. "Is it something to do with that song?" He then sang: "When the moon hits your eye like a big pizza pie," and before he could finish his grandfather laughed and said, "That's *amore*. You know, when you fall ina love an' get marry. The game you uncles play is calla more-ah, eh?"

And before it hit, Frankie thought, *But the word is the same.* "Oh, Nonno, what do you mean? What is the game with the fingers and the yelling of the numbers!" The old man grabbed his grandson's chubby arm and pulled him toward his mouth. "*Vieni qua,* I tell you. Is old game. A game we play inah Italy. Is call ah-more-ah, because when you put out all you fingers they's all the fingers you got. Is-ah no more, ay? I show you." Frankie took a seat on his grandfather's knee.

"W'at you gotta do is guess w'at the total number fingers will be. Like this. I t'ro down a t'ree fingers an' you t'row down two. But before the fingers show, you shout out what you think the total will be. If you right, then you get the point. You mark point with you left hand. When you get five points, then you play the next player. Whoever team wins, the' get the vino. *Capisci*?"

"But, Nonno, how do you know what the total will be?"

"Oh, w'ennah you firs' play, you doan know, you guess. But after you play years an' years with the same people, you know. You look deep in they eyes, an' you can see the number right there, inside they head, big as a bocce ball," he pointed into Frankie's eyes. "I never tell you about Joey Lawyer an' Sammie Parenti?"

Of course, thought Frankie, *everyone heard about those winos.* They were the two who stood all day outside the closed store on Twenty-third and Lake Streets in Dago Corners. Sammie was the ex-baseball player. People said he used to be a pro until he got thrown out for betting on the games, or drinking, or something. And Joey Lawyer, he was the old wino who used to be a lawyer for some big shot, and the rumor was that he once was a sharp, powerful attorney until he took a fall for one of his clients. He was the man with the missing forefinger and pinky on his left hand. And Sammie was the man with the fingerless left hand, who always wore a black glove.

The thing to do with both of them was to get them to wave at you and then wave back to them holding a few fingers down. Frankie let his grandfather continue.

"Listen a me, Franco. These two guys wasa best-ah more-ah players in town. No one could a beat them. They know jus' how everone play. One ver' cold day in Jan-wary back when wasa no work for us, we was all sittin' in a saloon over Twenty-Third an' Lake an' someone, I doan remember who was, ask them who wasa the best. Now, they never play each other, only was on same team, so no one really know. This day they wasa both full of vino an' wasa braggin' how they wasa best team. So Mister Rotelli he put a bottle of vino in between them an' say, 'The best of youse two win this bottle.' Now, ol' Joe he wasa so drunk he say he was not 'fraid to play fo' fingers."

"For fingers!" exclaimed Frankie. "What?"

"Yeah. They say whoever win the point the other would cut off a finger to keepa the score."

The other men were now turning to listen to the old white-haired Mario tell the story that they themselves had told so often. They knew it because Mario had told it to them. He had actually been there and told the story better than anyone else. Frankie sat still, mystified by his grandfather's telling. The old man lifted Frankie off his lap and took a stance next to his chair when he saw that he had everyone's attention. Frankie sat in the chair that had been kept warm by Grandpa. He tilted his head up and listened.

Mario's arms were still muscular. His thick wrists lay on each pocket. His forehead oozed sweat that slowly dripped down to his wine blushed cheeks. His glasses, faded from years of absorbing sweat, dipped when his head bobbed; and when they slipped to the end of his nose, they revealed a pale strip of skin. He threw his hands into the air and began.

"'Doo-ayee, trray-ee,' they yell but didn't show those numbers. 'Cheenkway, kwaah-tro,' they yell again, but nothin'. Then they stare deep in the eyes."

Mario opened his wrinkled eyelids wide and stared right into the brown eyes of his grandson. In a raspy whisper, he said, "An' there wasa no soun' in the whole bar. They hans fly up," and so did the tightened fists of the old man, slowly they dropped, flashing four fingers from each hand into Frankie's face. "They both yello 'Ah-toe!' an' they t'row four fingers. Everone wasa ona they toes. An' after seein' this they all move back to they heels. Then, they stop to sip a lil' vino and look back to Joe an' Sammie. These guys they play fo' t'ree 'ours an' no one score a point."

The white shirt was now transparent with sweat, revealing the old man's beige T-shirt and cloth scapular. He stopped here, took off his glasses with his right hand, and with his left reached into his back pocket to pull out a large, wrinkled red bandanna.

"And then what happened, Nonno? What happened next?" Frankie begged.

"*Aspetta*, Franco. You nonno is thirsty. Go bring to me some vino, eh," Mario said swabbing his face with the handkerchief.

Frankie jumped from his seat and ran to the TV tray where the opened wine bottle lay in the shade. With both hands, he lifted the heavy bottle and lumbered back to his chair. He shook the bottle until the wine reached the top of the withered, purple-lipped cup. Mario took it and without spilling a drop, swallowed off the top fourth of the liquid. He wiped his lips with the back of his hand, shook the drops off his thumb, cleared his throat, and continued.

"Well they play fo' t'ree 'ours, and Joey's wife she sen' his boy to tell him wasa time to eat. He say he wasa no hungry. I tella you they play an' they play for a night an' a day. They just stop to drink more vino. This go on for one, two, t'ree days. The whole town 'ear 'bout this game an' everone who was livin' back then stop by to see them play. They no eat o' sleep fo' those t'ree days. Ona t'ird day, they was people sleepin on a bar, an' lil' Midget Mikey, he sleep right up on a juke-ah-box. Ol' Nino, he was the bartennor, an' he was worry for where to get more vino. He sold everting in a place. All was left wasa Coke Cola. They was no more vino for poor Joe, an' maybe that'sa why he lose the first finger. They was a yellin' 'setta-ah' for seven-ah times. Everone know Sammie would a change his t'row the next time. Everone but ol' Joe.

"Some say his brain she dry up without that vino an' he not wasa t'inkin' right. Others say wasa no eatin' his wife's *pastafagioli* fo' t'ree days that make him mistake. But no one, not even Joe his self, can tell you why he t'row that four for the eight time. But he did. An' Sammie catch him."

Mario flashed the index finger of his left had into the air and yelled, "The first point wasa win by Sammie, an' Joe had to cut offa finger!"

With his right had waving an invisible knife, he continued.

"Well, Joe, he reach ina pocket, and without takin' his eyes off-ah Sammie, he pull out his curve knife, and he reach over an' slice off the little finger of his left hand. The finger fall to the ground like a dead bird. Boom. An' the blood was drippin down, like was a broke faucet or someatin."

Mario wiggled the fingers of his right hand down under the stump he made of the little finger on his left hand and dropped the wiggling fingers almost to the green lawn at his feet. With this motion, his white shirt left the tight hold of his waistband and flapped a white flag against his blue flannel pants. He inhaled and the breath sounded like a piece of old Parmesan cheese rubbing against a metal grater. He looked into Frankie's eyes.

"He tell Midget Mikey to go fine him some more vino. Then he say, 'Sammie, the game she stop at five. Eat'sah joosta begin.' The whole crowd move in to see Joe's finger, and he wave it across they faces and the blood was aflyin' all over the place. He shot, 'Come on! Le's play!' The score was Sammie uno an' Joe nuttin.'"

Mario was tiring. His wide chest heaved and he began gulping air. But there was more to the story. Mario reached down, grabbed the tilting paper cup of wine, and swallowed it all. He held out the empty cup. Frankie poured the wine without taking his eyes off Grandpa's hands. The wedding band on his grandfather's hand seemed to be choking his finger. Mario swiped the cup away from Frankie. He slurped then smacked his lips three times before he continued.

"They play fo' four more days, an' when was all finish Joe lose a forefinger an' his li'l finger. Sammie had alla his. The game she probably still go to today if Sammie din't have to take a piss and had leave for to go to buckhouse. Sammie, he walk out the door, an' maybe he think all the white snow was a bed. After old man Rotelli say, 'Ay, I know Sammie drink a lot of vino, but can he still be apissin! Is been an hour. Go see to find him.' Well, they fine Sammie lyin down ina snow. He was all purple, but that old rooster wasa still breedin'. The doctor he say Sammie was a luck to be pre-ser-ved with alcohol 'cause he get the frosta bite all over an' loose all-ah finger on his lef' hand. His right hand was o-kay, because wasa still innah pants. But he could no play ah-more-ah no more. They say that was the end of ah-more-ah in town. No one wanna try an' beat that game. Sometime you see someone play ona street, but is not like used to be. We still play in a family, but for vino, no for fingers! So maybe someday, my boy, you play. Us old men can play no more, but maybe soon you play with you uncles."

With a deep breath and a sigh, Mario reached for his wine and finished the cup in one swallow. When the last dropped circled the rim of the cup and was lifted from the paper rim by his purple tongue, he tapped his shirt pocket, pulled out his cigarettes, and lit one looking into Frankie's eyes.

"An' so my boy that's what is-ah more-ah."

The crowd of men dispersed. Mario picked up Frankie and took his place on the lawn chair. Frankie sat on the ground next to the old man, who soon fell asleep with the smoking, unfiltered cigarette in his fingers. He pushed the burning butt from his grandfather's yellowed fingers and decided that it was time to go back to the ball game and hit some home runs.

Somewhere in My Past

Musing
Memory
Mnemosyne
Music to dream by
Memoria.
Memories gleaming
Memories meaning
Memories mending
Memoria.
Memories are made of . . .
Musical, magical
Remembering embers
Memorials.
Remembrances rendering
Past never ending
Unto mementoes
Memento mei.
Memorabilia
Mori remember
Meandering filigree
Tracery untangling
Dangling, ambling
Remember me
Ay!

An immigrant sits here before you to tell a tale, or a series of tales. Stories, anecdotes, sorties into the past. Poems. Burst forth from his memory. Recollections, recalling, calling again, bringing into the present motes of time he has lived through. So that in the end, you may perhaps say, that something of me has been made known to you. So that you may, perhaps, relate that you heard an immigrant, here, today unfold events that tried to reveal, make manifest, wherein his life, a life among millions, a life like any other life, wherein his life, I say, can be perceived as unique because he can remember what only he can remember.

And so each of you, reading at your leisure, could be cataloguing the smells, the noises, the sights which have made your existence (though one among an infinitude) an unrepeatable and inimitable entity.

"Cataloguing" is perhaps the apt word, for it conjures up lists, sterile, unbiased, unjudgemental. Let us try an example of a story from the past, call it for the sake of argument, a memory.

When I was a boy, not much happened to me. Later, as a man, I met a woman. I fell in love. We fell in love. Then out of love. Then she met another man. They had children. Four children to be precise. One of them bears my name, though her husband does not know this.

End of short story. Facts. Just the facts, ma'am. Like Sergeant Friday. As though the facts could speak for themselves. As though, once the sequence of occurrences has been laid down end to end, there is nothing to be done but to draw a logical conclusion, mathematical, ineluctable, beyond dispute.

But what conclusion? The antiseptic nature of the above minitale seems satisfactory. It appears to leave out only the interpretation. But is its surface simplicity a ploy? Is there a deception, purposely or otherwise, perpetrated? And if so, who or what is the perpetrator? Is it that the past is unknowable? Is it that I (the writer) am trying to conceal?

It is not necessary to interject, though of course I will, that it is not a true tale. Or rather that since it gives you nothing that would allow you to break into its truth, the truth of it at this point is not an issue. There is nothing to decode. There are no details that would allow positive identification. The only thing certain is that "I" am the teller, the person to whom the above has happened, if indeed it did happen to me.

It tells my side of the story. It seems to leave out any attempt at giving ambiguity to these "facts." Nothing in it serves to localize it. There is a paucity of detail. Nothing fleshed in. No description of the woman. No emotional outburst about the pain of leaving, the hurt of real or perceived betrayal. It calmly gives the "precise" number of children. It states the apparently simple truth that one of the children was named after me.

It is clearly a tale that could have come from my past. If it did come from my past, it was brought to you out of my memory. If I tell you that it is true (and I am not saying it is), you have the perfect right, perhaps the obligation, to counter: So what? I could tell you that about me, too. Only the children are three, and none bears my name. Why bother telling it if you don't elaborate? What is its meaning?

And yet, had I provided an abundance of details—the colour of her eyes, the sweater I wore when we walked along Bloor Street (pick your own street name), the number of clouds that were in the sky, the tears shed— would any of this and more have added anything towards convincing you of the veracity or otherwise of the tale?

Aha, someone may think at this point. Wait a minute. That particular tidbit about the child's name is interesting. Is the writer/storyteller/recollector vaguely or not-so-vaguely alluding to the fact that the child bears his name for some reason? Is it his child? Is the woman still in love with him, and if so, why did he say: "We fell out of love"? A process has begun in the listener/reader which could, in theory, lead down many a path, each with its own ending. Each perfectly "true." Each a conclusion with its defenders. And so the interpretations multiply and bear forth fruit. And so I/we/you, the critics, proliferate papers on the meaning of this and that. So are the *interpretations du texte* churned out without end.

If the piece of writing is taken as "fiction," then it must stand on its own and be subjected to the scrutiny of the interpreter without flinching.

Whatever is read into it is as "valid" as are the reasons that can be adduced for such a reading. But if, as in the case of "biographical" material, one wants to get at the "historicity," the "what-did-really-happen?," then matters become more complex and the "truth" may become elusive indeed.

Let me point out that the above story was typed as fast as the words could come. No particular memory was attached to it a priori, no woman and no children. I "made it up" as an example as I went along. I did not premeditate it. Nor did I do any editing. It was born in the fifteen or so seconds it took to type. It is a piece of fiction, if you like, "created" on the spot as an example of no forethought.

And yet, as I think about it, or rather thought about it while writing this, every one of these details belongs in some way or another to my life, to my past, to my experiences. To my memory, in short. Indeed I did fall in love. Who hasn't? We did fall in love. Madly! Not so common. A woman has four children somewhere. But not the same woman, perhaps. None of the children bears my name. But a child of another couple was named after a friend of mine. That was somewhere in my head when I did that short piece of automatic writing. So even though I set out to compose a little piece of fictional writing for the mere purpose of illustration, on going back over it, nothing in it was not out of my memory. Even though I had no intention of purposely telling you somethng specific about me with the story, somehow all the details concern me or something I had heard about. But how much of it is true?

De Iuliis, I hear some readers muttering, What's the point of this? Get on with some details from your past as an immigrant. I know all about fact and fiction mingling in literature. Fact being the stranger of the two. Pirandello (let us by all means drop names) was only one among myriad writers, philosophers, and critics who have pointed that out. But get to the facts of your own life. Tell us the things that happened to you. Never mind fiction.

Yes, yes. Alright! Let me tell you a story which is "true" to me. Or is it? You judge and then perhaps you can tell me if I (or anyone for that matter) can ever tell the truth again. I say this, of course, slightly with tongue in cheek. But only slightly. Listen. And tell me if you can, how much of my past, so real to me, is fiction.

I went to high school in Toronto, Canada. I attended Bloor Collegiate Institute ("good old B.C.I.," as we used to sing in the school song) from 1960 to 1965; the records will verify that. I was a pretty ordinary teenager. Got fairly good grades. Suffered from acne, was shy with girls, played pool, told dirty jokes, was awkward at dances—the full gamut. I had the usual number of crushes on girls who couldn't stand me and was repelled by the girls who had crushes on me. (There's an allusion there to Shaw, it seems to me, but I was not aware of it at the time of typing, although I don't think that has any significance.) Of all the high school memories, and there are many I have cherished through the years, one stands out. And the ramifications of it have gone very far indeed insofar as my emotional and psychological existence are concerned. I cannot do justice to those ramifications here. I wonder how many hours would be required to deal with that in any meaningful way.

In the Year of our Lord 1964, just after the Christmas break, a blonde, blue-eyed girl named Kris came up behind me as I was getting my books out of my school locker. She was in grade thirteen and I in twelve. She had been a cheerleader. I had eyed her from afar. We had had some casual encounters, exchanged a word here and there, waved to each other in a friendly manner at football games, and so on. What she had felt for me, if anything, I do not know. I, needless to say, had an enormous crush on her. But to all intents and purposes it was an unrequited emotion, one of those things you carry around with you until time or another more urgent object of desire erases it or makes it recede into the subconscious, there to remain largely untouchable, and yet destined to perish only with death.

There were additions and renovations being made to the school. Many of the grade thirteens had had their lockers torn down because of construction and so had to make do for the rest of the year. Naturally, most of them asked their friends if they could share a locker with them.

And so it was that on that day, for me, a miracle happened. It was during the lunch break. I was at my locker, my smelly running shoes at the bottom (a detail which has stood out in my mind, as though it had happened yesterday, as the expression goes). I was busy with my books. Kris came up behind me and, somewhat embarrassed, asked me if she could share my locker for the rest of the year. A fairly inane request. She needed a place to put her things. Nothing to get excited about.

Well, I almost lost consciousness! Could she share my locker! She could have it, if she wanted it. I would do without, I would...I would...Well, you get the picture. I was ecstatic. We would be seeing each other at the locker for the rest of the year. We would both be privy to the same secret, the combination of the lock! I couldn't believe my good fortune.

And for the rest of the year it was so. We often walked home together since we took the same route, though I had farther to go. We were constantly, in my recollection, at the same lunch table, along with my friend, Geza. I even remember going to her house and helping her with her Latin homework (she was terrible at languages).

During this period of bliss for me, nothing occurred, of course. No kiss, no holding hands, no exchanged words of affection. But I kept nurturing those feelings of intense emotion towards her. The year ended. She was off to the university. I had another year of high school to go. I found someone to go steady with. She was put, or so I thought, out of my mind. But as I went through the university, as I began writing more and more, I discovered that she kept surfacing. I carried her memory with me, an icon to venerate and revel in. Precious beyond understanding.

Sometime in 1970 I wrote a poem about Kris. I hadn't seen her in over four years. The poem was impossibly sentimental and romantic. But it evoked that time at high school when for almost six months we had spent so much of our time together, a time in which I felt privileged to share her company, and also, of course, unworthy. Still that time was real. It had happened. For six months—not for a day or two. Daily, repeatedly meeting at the locker, having lunch, walking home, being invited in.

Over a dozen years later, both of us married (not to each other), those memories continued to instill warmth and pleasure. Nothing physical had ever happened, but, I felt sure, there was the spiritual to be treasured. Surely she must also have felt that, at least!

In 1978, I discovered she was teaching physical education at Oakwood Collegiate—one of Bloor's old rivals. I chanced to pass by there one day in early spring, at around three thirty. School was out but I thought she might be in the gym supervising. So on a whim I decided to stop and try to see if she was still there. Even after such a long time, surely, I felt, she would be pleased to see me, to say hello, to go over old times, to smile again one of her smiles.

I found the gym. I stood at the door and looked around for her. Some girls were practicing with basketballs, running about in their pale blue bloomers, the same uniforms girls wore during gym when Kris and I had spent part of our youth in each other's presence. I felt very apprehensive. The same churning in my stomach that had tormented me in those long-gone days. Kris was nowhere in sight. I stood around, doggedly determined to see her but not knowing how to go about it. I didn't know her married name, so I couldn't ask for her. I thought she might be in the teacher's office across the gym, but I didn't have the courage to walk across with all those young girls looking at me. I felt weak-kneed, embarrassed, adolescent all over again.

When I was about to leave, Kris poked her head out of the office. I think one of the girls must have mentioned that a stranger was standing near the door eyeing them. She looked at me. A smile of recognition lit her face. She ambled across the gym, almost in slow motion, like in the movies. She came up to me, her smile growing as she got nearer, and called: "Geza!"

"No. No," I muttered. "Celestino. How are you?"

She was ever so slightly taken aback but recovered immediately. We talked of various things. I brought up (what else?) the locker episode, the lunches, etc. She didn't remember a thing. "Surely," I protested, trying to turn it into a joke, though my insides had been wrenched, "Surely, you remember sharing the locker. You came up to me. You asked me if you could use it. Remember?" It was to no avail. She remembered nothing, not the locker, not the lunches, not the walks home. Not the fact that she had tried to teach me an Estonian folk song during one of those walks home.

For days afterward I was in a state of semishock. How could I have invented it, how could she not remember? It was during a six-month period, after all. Yet, nothing! Not even an attempt at: "Oh, yes. I seem to recall now! Why that's right! I hadn't thought of that for so long!" Not even that small consolation.

I went about for some time doubting my recollection. Could I have dreamt it up? Had I invented the whole thing in order to fill some deep, psychological need I was not aware of? Or could I have been so insignificant to her that she would have forgotten all those encounters which lasted for almost half a year? Where was the truth? I interrogated a number of former high school friends. None of them remembered the fact that I shared that locker with Kris. It was startling to have given such significance to a person, to have carried her memory about for so long, to have felt such tenderness at the thought of her, and then to discover that she had erased me completely from her mind. It was a jolt from which to some extent I am still reeling.

In an article on the second volume of Alaine Robbe-Grillet's fantasied autobiography, Michel Contat states:

> Novelists are free to use, or not, as the case may be, their own lives as material for fiction. Biographers have less freedom: an aspect of a person's life is biographical only when it has been attested by a third party. Things are more complicated for autobiographers, who are often the sole witnesses of the private events they describe: are they to be believed?

Are they to be believed?

I was not the sole witness to the Kris episode. And yet the other major player denied the episode's existence. Had I written an autobiography, and had a subsequent biographer sought the corroboration of Kris, she would, as she did with me, have denied everything. Unless by some miracle she did an about face. Would that time in my life be relegated by the historian/biographer to fact or fancy?

In this particular case, there is an answer which is provided by a written document. In *The Banner*, the school yearbook, the last two pages were always blank so you could get your friends to sign their names, usually accompanied by some silly but deeply felt message. "Rots of Ruck" or "Be careful!! Because accidents cause people!" were two very popular standard ones. They were useful. Gawky and unpractised as we were, these codifed messages helped us through the embarrassment of expressing, seemingly without commitment, some of the emerging emotions we were beginning to experience. In my 1964 *Banner,* the following entry appears.

> Thanks for my yo-yo!
> Kris
> P.S. Now that I've thought of something to say you'll be sorry!! I must thank you for the use of your locker for all these months, for putting up with Bro. & I, for those wonderful and stimulating lunches, for the use of this paper—for EVERYTHING!
> Love Kris.

Well, my memory was vindicated when I discovered that documentary evidence some months later, even though my ego remained unconsoled.

Yet, because of the Kris episode, I do not think I will ever be quite comfortable in using what is deposited in my memory as totally factual and reliable evidence of what happened in the past. Something has been lost. I have been infused with a sense that not only are the present and future uncertain and precarious, but the very fabric of what we are convinced has come to pass in our own lives, and which ought therefore to be unalterable, may begin to crumble under scrutiny. This is somewhat disconcerting.

Still, somewhere in my past lie the sources of what I write. And I can take solace in this uncertainty: I do not know whether it is the historian's "facts" or the creative writer's "fiction" that better reveals the truth or more clearly examines what our lives mean or have meant.

Piacere Conoscerla: On Being an Italian-American

What is it like to be an "Italian-American"? What does such a hybrid self-definition mean? To me, the whole concept is a mystery (_misterioso_, as they say in the opera).

Just the other day I had the good fortune (_Buona fortuna_, they put it, in a language that is not my own) to be at a dinner table with my ninety-three-year-old Aunt Frances (_Zia Francesca_) who told me the wonderful story of how she met her husband. Her _Zia Seraphina_ was working, she said, in a "shop" (a "sweat shop!" my mother, her Americanized younger sister, interjected) where she met two "lovely girls"—Mary and Rose, I believe—and they felt that Seraphina's niece, a beautiful twenty-four-year-old woman who knew how to cook "essence of tomatoes" ("like sun-dried tomatoes," one cousin explained), must meet their brother. So they brought her to their house for coffee and cake, and there my Uncle Frank (to be), a thirty-year-old architect from Sicily, was waiting—waiting with his mustache, his socialism, his hairy arms, his models (that I remember from my childhood) of Mayan temples.

"_Piacere conoscerla_, _signorina_," he said, and "It was so romantic," sighed my aunt seventy years later. So romantic, so courtly, I agreed, turning to her son and asking, "Would you spell that _conoscerla_ or _cognoscerla_?" I was in favor of the _g_ in "knowing you" ("It pleases me to know you, dear miss"), while my cousin, a little more Italian than I, insisted I was wrong.

We made a bet: a bottle of Haig and Haig Pinch to a bottle of Jack Daniels. Of course, I was wrong. I owe him a bottle of Jack Daniels. That is what it is like, that is what it means, to be an "Italian-American."

In other words, to be an Italian-American is to live in a world of perpetual mystery. Almost always to be wrong—and then, worse still, to drown your troubles in American booze. _Omertà?_ The silence? Not just _omertà_—the silence—about, as I will tell you, the life and lives of ancestors, but for some of us—second and third generation, whatever we are (and that's itself debatable)—a silence about our language, our food, our selves.

They don't tell you, those people who come from the Old Country, a lot about what it meant to be not an Italian-American but an Italian in America. You get it in bits and pieces, like the recipes for _arancini_, those amazing Sicilian rice balls meant to mimic, I suppose, the oranges that glowed on trees back there in Palermo, Messina, Siracusa.

"_Piacere conoscerla, signorina!_" Uncle Frank, the proto-Marxist, not yet modeler of Mayan temples, bending over the hand of Aunt Frances, good Italian girl that she was, and declaiming "It pleases me to make your acquaintance, signorina." A gesture opaque to me. _Misterioso:_ mysterious and misty!

When I was a little girl, we used to go to Williamsburg, in Brooklyn, to visit my mother's Sicilian family—especially Aunt Frances, Uncle Frank, and their three children—with some regularity. My mother herself, the Americanized "flapper," had moved to a "genteel" part of Queens with great alacrity, soon after her marriage. What was I? I was an only child, an "American girl," with clean hair, clean nails, and movie-induced fantasies of living in a small town where newspaper boys bicycled down shady streets in a sentimental dawn, the milkman's bottles clinked on an old-fashioned porch, and the postman never had to knock twice because he met you all the time in the general store anyway. Never mind that we lived on the fourth floor of a zombie-like brick apartment house whose elevator I obsessively decorated with carvings of kites and balloons!

But those places in the Italian-American ghetto of Williamsburg were different. Close, hot flats above drugstores, some of them—for several of my many Sicilian uncles were *farmacisti*—where we ate *arancini* and spaghetti, and people babbled in a dialect I couldn't understand about relatives in Palermo that I didn't know. But, most important, there was my Aunt Frances's narrow brownstone on Arion Place, just across the street from the Arion Ballroom and down the street from the Bushwick Avenue El. Here there was a gigantic Old-Country kitchen on the second floor, where the whole family gathered to eat *pasta infornata* (which I now understand was what we in the United States call lasagna) and *salsiccia* (spicy sausages) on New Year's Eve and other holidays.

Just behind the kitchen, in the floor-through brownstone fashion, there was a narrow windowless "parlor" with a small upright piano. In this room, my aunt, who saw herself as a frustrated soprano, would bang away on the piano and sing Verdi or Puccini operas while we children danced or shrieked along with her. As I recall, I hated that. Pragmatically enough, I loved the good food, strange though it was, but I hated what seemed to me the alien "organ-grinder" music I felt myself forced to intone—and to love. *Che gelida manina! Vissi d'arte!* Such phrases filled me with loathing at least until I went to college and had several Jewish boyfriends who persuaded me that these rantings might be defined, by some connoisseurs, as "culture."

But what could seem like culture, seem *valuable*, in a world where you knew nothing, *nothing*, about anyone? There were, in fact, seven Sicilian uncles—not counting uncles by marriage—a few of whom came and went in mysterious ways, the splashings of their speech incomprehensible to me. One at least (I know this now) was deported to Rome, where, as I understand it, he lived on gloomily with a somewhat shady woman (I can't be more specific about her, alas) until he recently died. People used to send him care packages of castoff American suits. Another died in California of unknown causes, though something about alcoholism was darkly hinted in hushed tones. A third—the most brilliant of my mother's brothers, I believe—was sent to an asylum at an early age, for enigmatic reasons. Immigration takes its toll in this land of shady streets, newspaper boys, milkmen, postmen, "colonial" porches.

Through all this, however, or so I have also been told, my Sicilian grandmother endured, continuing to practice midwifery (in Palermo, a cousin lately boasted, she had been the only woman licensed "to perform the episiotomy," just like a real doctor). In pictures, she is a lean, hawklike woman, mother of nine (plus several miscarriages and stillbirths), religious, dazzlingly brilliant (according to the family mythology), and ferociously aggressive.

Her husband, a socialist and skeptic, refused to let her send her children to parochial schools. Like so many Mediterranean anticlerics, he hated the Church. He longed for the Revolution. He prayed, if at all, to Vittorio Emanuele, Re D'Italia—who turned, eventually, into VERDI. But she worshipped in private, visited her patients, scolded her children, fed them (so my mother says) such delicacies as octopus and eel and escarole with garlic—and made my mother, the youngest, the oppressed American flapper, wash dishes in a white wool sailor dress at the age of ten.

That my mother could never forgive: the dishes, the itchy white wool dress, the humiliation before "the boys," who were being trained as *farmacisti* while she, an ambitious girl, was told that it was pointless to send her to school. Perhaps that is why I hated arias, why those places in Williamsburg became so alien to me, that language so strange, that food so bizarre?

In Queens, where I grew up imagining myself a squeaky clean denizen of smalltown America, we ate lamb chops and baked potatoes. The six-story brick apartment buildings anchored us to some sort of WASP "reality." We were grounded; we were real; we were really American. I went to camp, to college, learned to eat tuna casserole with crushed potato chips on top (although even my mother thought that sounded loathsome).

What was the glamour, then, of the house on Arion Place? Besides the big upstairs kitchen, where the family squabbled and sang and gossiped and drank strong red wine and ate fierce sausages, there was *another* kitchen, a downstairs room called "the summer kitchen," to which all of us descended when the heat rose in Brooklyn. The El thundered by. A tiny, intricately detailed garden bloomed just outside, religiously tended by my operatic aunt. Basil (although I didn't know it was that, at the time) perfumed the paths; a quasi-American glider hung under a grape arbor; pink and orange geraniums, roses, petunias bloodied the air.

Grandma the midwife, whom in any case I never knew, had long since passed to her righteous rest. The various blacksheep uncles were scattered to their graves and asylums. The successful ones wore white coats and presided over American drugstores. Maybe they drew long drafts of soda water for thirsting customers; I don't know what they did. Somewhere older cousins named "Jojo" and "Petrina" tried to be American but kept on (hopelessly, I thought) being Italians. In the meantime, we all sat in the summer kitchen, watching Aunt Frances perform magical prestidigitations over pots of pasta and escarole. She remembered what her mother had taught her—for between bouts of midwifery and performances of "the episiotomy," the Sicilian matriarch had taught at least one daughter to cook something beyond lamb chops.

Why were we all in that odd underground room? I never understood it, never imagined that there might have been a sensible reason (like "beating the heat") for Sicilians to have such a place. No, to me this place was the *ur* enigma (notice my use of another language), the Italian "heart of darkness." Yet here the straw was turned to gold, the pasta to precious gems, the cornucopia of herbs and vegetables—basil, escarole, zucchini, garlic, all un-American growths—to some sort of fairy-tale money. The walls of the kitchen were white but the room was dark and cool. The noise of the El was far away, an insect scratching. The creak of the swing and the scrape of the branches of the grapevine were close and comforting. Even my mother spoke Sicilian here: like everyone else, she said *beddu* instead of *bella*, she said *ricodda* instead of *ricotta*.

And the ghosts of lost uncles kissed the windows, stooped among the roses, and asked to be let in. *Piacere conoscerla!* Did they want to know us, to know what had happened to us as we became not Italians in America, but Italian-Americans? My cousins were going to Brooklyn College, to City College, to Boston University. I was going to Cornell. We wore cashmere sweaters, we *were* Americans, we said, as we devoured Aunt Frances's *pasta infornata* and creamy *cannoli*. We would live on shady streets, have front porches, chat with milkmen, never again eat escarole.

My aunt's life has led her to Framingham, Massachusetts, where she lives with her oldest daughter, her son-in-law, and her grandson, in a "colonial" ranch house, though she still cooks her *pasta* for us on special occasions. All the *farmacisti* uncles are dead and so are most of their wives. No one remembers much about grandma except for "the episiotomy." No one will tell me and my cousins about the deportations, the asylums, the humiliations. We are Americans, we are *professori*.

But when my aunt and her daughter sold the house on Arion Place, they took away a cutting from the grapevine, so that a slender twig from that garden still struggles for life, twenty years later, in New England. And when I stood in my aunt's kitchen the other day (her daughter's, nominally, but it is really my aunt's), she worked hard to instruct me in the mysteries of artichokes *alla Siciliana*, mysteries she had learned from her mother, the midwife. And my cousin, her son, is planning to write a cookbook that will include *all* the recipes ("at least a hundred") for *arancini*. He is the one who won the bottle of Jack Daniels from me because I couldn't spell *conoscerla*.

Still, how long do we preserve them—the recipes, the grape arbor, the summer kitchen, the midwife, the *farmacisti*, the Mayan temples of my uncle, and the *arancini*? My children are Americans—that is, they are Jewish-American/Italian-Americans and my cousins' children all have equally hybrid inheritances. What is *misterioso* to me is simply lost in the mists of time to them: the journey here from Palermo (or was it Siracusa?), the first sight of the cold northern harbor, the move to Brooklyn, the arias that were not "culture" but (as they saw it) "nature," the day they planted the basil and the grapevine in the garden, the day grandma first (illegally) performed an episiotomy in America, the day she bought the vexing white wool dress for her youngest daughter.

All the past is always lost, of course; our Italian-American history is not terribly special that way. Yet to someone who has lived on the cusp of that culture—in the hyphen between Italian and American, so to speak—the world that mediated between the Old World and the New World seems especially fragile. My Aunt Frances told, just the other day, that story about her first meeting with Uncle Frank because her son said "Mama, you've never really explained how you met papa." There ensued the anecdote of *Zia Seraphina* and the two "lovely girls," the coffee and cake, the suitor with his socialism and his models of Mayan temples. None of us knew it. Few could imagine the world in which it happened.

Piacere conoscerla, my ancestors, my relatives, my friends! I would like to revisit your kitchens. I hope you will keep the grapevine going somewhere—in New England, in Brooklyn, in California. And may the *arancini* glow, not just in cookbooks, but on your trees, your stoves. *Piacere conscerla*. It would please me to know you.

La Velatura del Fico

Arrivò il treno che ci avrebbe portati nel Bronx, la contea dell'accidia, e ci sedemmo l'uno a fianco dell'altro.

Avevo in mano libri preziosi, ma a mio zio quelle cose non importavano.

"Ma tua madre, che s'è messa in testa?" mi chiese, a bruciapelo, non appena il treno cominciò a filare verso la Quarantaduesima Strada. "Tuo padre mi ha detto che lo sta facendo martire con tutti i suoi discorsi di tornarsene in Italia. Ma che ci va a fare, in Italia? Vuole andare a morire di fame come una volta? Ci sono ancora le macerie di guerra lì. Ma che? È impazzita quella donna? Ma io la conosco bene, mia sorella. Questa stessa sera le dico una cosa che le farà passar di mente tutte le sue fantasie. Ma, prima, tu devi passare per casa mia perché devo farti vedere una cosa molto importante."

"Ma, zio, non ho tempo," dissi con tono implorante, "mi aspettano."

"Farai una telefonata da casa mia," rispose lui, felice di aver risolto il problema. "Devo farti vedere una cosa che, son sicuro, non hai mai visto."

"Cosa?"

"Eh no, non te lo dico. Vedrai."

"Ma dimmi almeno di che si tratta, zio."

"Si tratta di una. . . .una velatura."

"Una velatura? Non capisco. . ."

"Capirai. . .capirai quando la vedi. È una cosa che, se non riesce, ne va di sotto la nostra Italia."

Sotto il placido anacoluto dello Zio Giuseppe si celava qualcosa di grande o di semplice—il che, a veder quell'uomo, era poi la stessa cosa.

Feci la mia telefonata per spiegare il ritardo, e, sentendomi ormai in regola come figlio e fratello maggiore, mi diedi tutto alla misteriosa operazione dello zio.

"Vieni," mi disse Zio Giuseppe, dopo che si fu liberato dei suoi arnesi di manovale e imbianchino. "È una cosa che dovevo far ieri; ma il tempo non era buono. Oggi, invece, è una bella giornata asciutta. Vieni!"

Scendemmo nella *iarda*, cioè nei sette o otto metri quadrati d'orticello attaccato alla casa.

"Devo velare il mio fico," annunziò finalmente lo zio, come se rivelasse il maggiore dei misteri eleusini. Si avvicinò all'albero—un tronco d'alberello malaticcio che il primo gelo dell'inverno americano avrebbe indubbiamente ucciso—lo toccò più d'una volta delicatamente con quella sua mano ruvida come se volesse dirgli di non aver paura, e, voltosi poi a me, "debbo velarlo prima che arrivi il freddo di dicembre," disse con una tenerezza che era già parte del suo solenne rito annuale.

"Se non lo velo," continuò, "muore, e se. . .muore questo mio fico, muore l'Italia." Insisteva a dire "velare," non "fasciare." L'alberello che con le sue mani aveva piantato nella sua *iarda* e, a dispetto del clima immite, era riuscito a far vivere, non voleva pensarlo come cosa ferita e sanguinante; lo vedeva, invece, come una bella statua da tener velata finché non si riaprisse il museo col sole della nuova primavera. E, naturalmente, quello stesso alberello ricordava, anzi rappresentava l'Italia, il bel Tavoliere di Puglia col suo clima balsamico e coi suoi lunghi filari di fichi dolcissimi: era, dunque, il miracolo che univa due mondi, due amori, due fedi. No! Quell'albero non poteva, non doveva morire.

"Ed ora ti mostro come si fa," disse lo zio. "Per prima cosa, io ci metto degli stracci puliti—ecco, così." Prese, infatti, due o tre camicie vecchie e bucherellate, ma pulite, e cominciò con esse a fasciare, voglio dire, a velare il povero smilzo fico, ch'era tutto il suo orgoglio d'emigrato.

"Molti italiani incominciano la velatura con strisce di carta incatramata," continuò senza voltarsi; "ma io non sono d'accordo. La carta incatramata è ruvida e nessuno la vorrebbe a carni nude. Anima sei, anima credi—dice il nostro proverbio sammarchese. E così, per non fargli male, io lo velo prima con questi stracci puliti e soffici, e poi lo avvolgo di carta incatramata. Ecco qua. . . ."

Prese allora un enorme rotolo di carta, appunto incatramata, e da basso in alto, lentamente, delicatamente, ma allo stesso tempo con una forza che equivaleva a pietà, cominciò a svolgerlo intorno al tronco già rivestito di morbidi panni. Mi accorsi, però, che, con gesto furtivo e rapido, in cima all'albero, fra stracci e catrame, egli mise una cosa—mi sembrò un pezzettino di carta ordinaria—che s'era tolta da una tasca dei pantaloni.

"Cos'è quello, zio?" domandai.

"Niente, niente," rispose lui, sorpreso che io me ne fossi accorto.

"Ci hai messo un pezzo di carta," insistetti io: "cos'è? Che significa?"

"E va bene: te lo dico," fece lui, rassegnato. "Ci ho messo. . .ci ho messo. . .l'immaginetta di San Michele Arcangelo, il protettore del Gargano. Lui che ha sconfitto il diavolo può sconfiggere l'inverno con tutto il suo gelo, non ti pare?"

"Ma certo, zio," risposi, ammirando la bontà naturale di quell'uomo che in chiesa non ci andava ma che, con ingenuità di bimbo, credeva ancora nella forza dell'arcangelo protettore della sua terra lontana.

"E adesso," proseguì, "ci metto altri stracci puliti come un secondo cuscino e poi, per ultimo, faccio l'ultima velatura con altre strisce di carta incatramata. Te l'assicuro io, caro nipote, che neppure dieci gradi sotto zero potranno far male a questa povera creatura."

Osservai il resto dell'operazione di salvataggio arboreo come se io stesso ne fossi l'autore. Stavo scoprendo un'America nuova, quell'America che non scoprì Cristoforo Colombo ma che ogni emigrato scopre in sé ogni giorno, ogni momento della vita.

"Ed ora," concluse Zio Giuseppe, "ci mettiamo su un bel telone di plastica, lo leghiamo ben bene, e la velatura è bell'e finita. Caro fico, sogni d'oro per sei mesi!"

Dopo che ebbe legato ben bene il telone di plastica, dall'altra tasca dei pantaloni tirò fuori un bel ferro di cavallo e, come una bella corona regale, lo inchiodò in cima al tronco completamente coperto, anzi corazzato contro l'inverno imminente.

"Ma, zio," chiesi io, sorpreso e divertito, "non basta San Michele?"

"Sì che basta," rispose il buon uomo, "ma la prudenza non è mai troppa. Sai perché ce lo metto tutti gli anni, questo ferro di cavallo? Contro il malocchio di Benedettino qui a fianco, che ha un fico più grande del mio e ci mette sotto non una ma due immaginette della Madonna Addolorata. Io, invece, come hai visto, ci metto San Michele Arcangelo: un uomo contro una donna. E chi è più potente: un bel giovane con la spada in mano o una povera femmina che piange il figlio morto?"

Caro zio Giuseppe! Per amore del suo alberello, era perfino capace di spropositare.

"Questo ferro di cavallo," aggiunse, "è buono non solo contro il malocchio di Benedettino, che è un mio caro amico, ma anche contro quello di tutti i *sanamabbì*...." ma non finì la sua parola preferita, che, da quando la zia gli aveva ricordato l'episodio del battesimo del figlio, egli usava meno frequentemente, almeno in pubblico.

Ben Morreale

Ava Gardner's Brother-in-Law

A Word Play in Sicily

Over the years I often had the occasion to return to the town of Racalmuto in Sicily. There I walked in the piazza with Turidru Sinatra, and we talked as if our conversation had not been interrupted by an absence, on my part, of now a year, now two, at times as much as five.

Turidru Sinatra is a wiry man now in his late fifties who still has the hungry look I first saw in him soon after the war. He speaks French, some English, and sarcastically calls himself *the pique-assiette* of the Western World. He has always lived with his mother, who put him through three years of law school, which he never finished, after he had given up on a teaching certificate within a year of obtaining it. For a while he was called, with some Sicilian irony, the lawyer Sinatra, until he wrote to Frank Sinatra, that is, who he was convinced was a cousin. Frank Sinatra did not answer, but he did send Turidru packages which arrived regularly every three months for two years. It was the sort of thing a relative from America would do. It was understandable then, if when Frank Sinatra married Ava Gardner, he became known as *Lu Cugnatu di* Ava Gardner, Ava Gardner's brother-in-law.

I never knew how he discovered I had arrived in town, but two days into my stay, Turidru would be at my door hungry for conversation.

Turidru Ah, Mr. *L'Americanu*, once again among the shrewd and the crazy. What brings you here this time?

    I I've come to settle the affairs of my aunt who's old and has retired to the convent of the Sisters of Mercy; and I like to be here, to walk these old streets, to listen. I find it restful after America.

Turidru Restful! With all these gossips, all the eyes of the town on you, so that half the time you live looking over your shoulder, and not for yourself? But let us speak of things that matter. Do you think Frank Sinatra likes Mary McCarthy?

    I I really don't know if Sinatra reads anything.

Turidru He must. You don't become a singer of genius unless you are well read. I once read he liked Erskine Caldwell. Do you think he likes Mary McCarthy?

    I What a strange pair. But it makes me think; now if Mary McCarthy made half the money Sinatra did or had his renown...

Turidru What do you mean?

I   Well it's what America thinks important. Sinatra, who's just a singer after all, is overwhelmed with money and attention—even honors. Mary McCarthy, a writer—well, if she makes one hundredth of the money—and you don't even know who she is married to.

Turidru   But there is a harmony in all that. Sinatra brings sweetness and pleasure to millions. Speaks of a haunting yearning in all of us. McCarthy writes as if she has a burr up her, if you will excuse the expression, *cher ami, culo,* if not somewhere else.

I   It is a question of fairness. Sinatra is just a singer.

Turidru   Eeh! First, if there were justice in the world, we'd all have voices like Sinatra, and then where would we be. There will always be injustice, if we are to have geniuses. Or let me put it another way—as long as there are geniuses in the world, there will be injustices in the world.

I   Then Sinatra is not a just man?

Turidru   What makes you say that?

I   You say he is a genius and genius produces injustice, which confirms then what many have said of him: that he hurts people, hurts many people with his arrogance and tyranny.

Turidru   Genius can hurt and it can soothe. It can destroy and comfort. When Frank sings "Old Black Magic," there is the echo of yearning as old as Magna Grecia itself. Or when he sings [*here, in the middle of the piazza, Turidru begins to sing softly to himself, his eyes half closed*], "You are the dearest things I know—are what you are." I'd give anything to hear Frank sing that at the Sands in Las Vegas. You know, I am just a bit younger than Frank. If my parents had gone to America, who knows. It would be nice to have people point to you and say, "There goes Turidru Sinatra." But you need an audience, and here everyone believes himself a genius, and there is no audience. All men see themselves to be the best lovers—in competition with anyone, we will outlast anyone—we believe it so much, it is a reality. Sicilian men will die to prove it. Men are competitive and women are possessive. This is our apple of discord.

But that Frank—all those girls of the chorus line, eeh, Old Blue Eyes, eeh!

I   There you are, Turi—that's the evil of genius then, eeh? to treat women like meat. Here at least that is avoided. A woman has a role and look how furiously she plays the role. My distant cousin, a woman of eighty-seven, she cooks, she shops, she walks loaded with vegetables, meat, and cheese up the long stony hill and will not let me lift a finger to help. She washed my underwear the other day, and in a huff says, "I see you have been washing your own underwear."

With pride, she lets me know only women know how to wash clothes. And my aunt, she begs a ride to come all the way from Grotte, ten kilometers, to make my bed.

They fight for this right, to serve, not us, just to serve. It gives meaning to their lives. The greatest joy my cousin had these past few days was to discover I like artichokes. "He likes artichokes," she said to a friend. She called another, and I heard her shouting to the neighbors, while I napped, "My nephew from America, he likes artichokes."

Turidru Eeh! You're right. You've put your finger on the blight of Sicily. I was served by women since childhood. The first and only son of a hero of the First Great War, killed on the field of honor at Caporetto. I was caressed, coddled, taken to bed with many girls as a child. I still feel their warm mouths on my chubby cold feet, the smell of bread on their breath. And how I was told I was beautiful, that with my blue eyes and fair skin, I'd be a prince. It was the education of a rooster. How could I ever find all that love once I went out into the world? Only Frank Sinatra could achieve it, find all that adulation in the real world. It is his true genius. He found an audience to serve, one which sends back rivers of love. He found harmony.

Our difficulty, we men of Sicily, is we have a great need and talent to serve, but no one to give it to; and we are forced into a role by women, because of their needs, into the role of roosters. We can marry, sire children, even have mistresses, imagine ourselves the world's best lovers. But our poor women are forced into a role by the way of the world. Here we men are forced to live too much in our heads, because reality is not livable. But we must permit women to serve us.

I A fine excuse for a system that serves you well.

Turidru Sure, I am the example of a man well served. I'd rather belong to Sinatra's happy America, where women don't serve men, where love is made freely. If we made love here more freely, there would be less warfare, less violence, let me tell you. As it is, the only way we can show affection, that we care for one another, is by killing each other.

I You speak of America like a priest speaks to a child about heaven. Turi, America too is in your head.

Turidru Excuse me, in many ways I am a fool, if not I wouldn't be in my present condition—approaching sixty—my life a long complaining desire, but I know of no one who has died, gone to heaven, and returned to tell me about its wonders. You, on the contrary, go to America and return, many times. That is reality. And there are books. I read them. America has a language; it speaks to me. Heaven has no language. America speaks to me in John O'Hara, Melville, in Hemingway, Mary McCarthy. America is a reality, my friend.

I It is your America, Turi. American women do serve men, you know. I've seen ardent feminists fight over men, take men away from women they call sisters. And then never mention women's rights again.

Turidru Feudal vestiges. The nunneries play the same role as feminism here. Vestiges, nothing but vestiges, of a dying way of life.

I And you really believe American women freer, that they make love more freely, and according to you, then, we should be happier, less violent?

Turidru Where could there be more violence, less happiness, more emotional misery than here?

I [*Irritated*] There is more rape in Los Angeles than in all of Sicily. More murder in Phoenix or Dallas than in Palermo. More women battered, not to speak of the violence we perpetrate on others—the Indian, the Asian, the Latin American. We have our need to be roosters. And it makes for a great deal of violence and not much happiness. God, look at our alcoholism, our rate of divorce. In America you wake up at forty with two houses, two cars, two children, and one wife; and you start wondering if there is something wrong with you. And you start using women...for...

Turidru And why not the Blacks? You left out the Blacks, the buffalo, and the very air you breathe. You have the sense of the Christian martyr. These are the difficulties of a society in transition, the mixing of races, the turmoil of the emerging new way of life. Frank and his friends don't have a problem of violence.

I Sure, their violence is against women. You don't think the use they make of the chorus line at Las Vegas is violence against those women? The violence of men using their position, their power to dominate, humiliate, by forcing women to perform sexually? If you went there, do you think you'd have your choice of the chorus line women? It would be the powerless meeting the powerless.

Turidru The girls of the chorus don't have to go if they don't want to. They are free to choose.

I No they are not. They must choose the men with power. They would not choose you; you are powerless. The violence of Frank Sinatra is institutionalized violence—power telling women to dance *culo di fora*, to jump through sexual hoops. It is a subtle violence but nonetheless violence. It is not fair.

Turidru Life is not fair.

I How comfortable. The lazy and the rich always say, "Life is unfair." How comfortable, how comfortable for those who, after a good meal and good wine, look out at the beggars of the world and say, "Life is unfair." It is not enough to say life is unfair. What are you going to do about the unfairness?

Turidru Just being born is unfair. And we can't do anything about that, except to lead a full life as Frank does, the life most of us would lead if we had the power and the money Frank has. There are no new vices you know. What is wonderful about America is that vices which once were considered aristocratic are open to all.

I And what would you do if you had the power and the money of Frank Sinatra?

Turidru Ah! I would eat well, have my person taken care of, baths, coiffure. And I would have many women—see what are the possibilities of my sexual appetite. I'd permit myself to fall in love and marry and divorce and marry. Until I found my true love. And I'd tell people what songs to write, what films to make, who was to play in them. I would tell this one, "You can be published," to the other, "You cannot be published." I'd make careers and unmake them. In a word, the same old vices, but they would be American. That is, the wealth and the women/men relationships would be in circulation. Not as it is here where the wealth and women are just held onto and nothing grows. But most of all, I would like to come home to an elegant apartment filled with white furniture, and a phone would ring as soon as I came home. I would like that.

I I don't think you understand, Turi. We pay and have paid a high price for what you call growth. My aunt, whose affairs I've come to settle, has seen all her brothers and sisters go to America. Her life had been devoted to caring for them. They went and lived in dank buildings that smelled of urine. Three died of tuberculosis; one was killed in a steel mill accident; one died in the Great War. The women lived among the insults of immigrants who had preceded them by a few decades. My father, who worked as a mason, had to admit that America was better, not that where he had come from was inferior, mind you, but simply that America was better. Do you understand that subtlety?

Turidru Of course, it is very Pirandellian. But all that suffering has made it possible for you to be what you are: an American. I remember you the first time you came from Paris in an automobile. We were living on wind and smoke here. It was a thing Frank Sinatra would have done, coming from Paris in a car as an American. All your relatives worked and suffered, so that you didn't have to live as I live. Here the suffering simply goes on and on.

I You have your dignity.

Turidru Bah! Dignity without power or money is humiliation.

I Power without dignity is brutality. And we are not any happier for it, you know. Look, I've seen men reach the age of forty, fifty, even sixty, and look around at their two cars, two houses, and one wife, and they soon begin to think they must consume women. We are not happier for our growth as you say.

Turidru I know. You keep saying that. But better to consume than to be consumed by these abstract furies.

I Consuming others leads to bad conscience.

Turidru Only when you are not in harmony with your true nature. And it is a question of liberty, too.

I But liberty without conscience is to put no limits on liberty. Where do you draw the line?

Turidru I don't draw lines; lines appear. The wonder of America is that freedom of enterprise is translated to everything: commerce, religion, education, marriage, and divorce. And you are right; we all want to consume, and what greater logic than to enjoy people, in the free exchange of human commerce. What greater logic than to enjoy people. I would prefer to say, enjoy people, not to consume them.

I As you would enjoy a TV set, a new car. These are objects, Turi. We are talking about human beings. And once you abstract people, then you can do anything you want to them. What do you think Hitler was all about?

Turidru Now, don't you abstract? Of course. A TV, a new car, I would enjoy as an object. A woman, I enjoy as a relationship to a human being who has the ability to love me, to hate me. She has the freedom to choose, to develop, to grow because of the joy or suffering of knowing me.

I Sure, grow, discover. And how could you with your Sicilian jealousy accommodate to having a woman who has been another man's. Who has been with another man? After all, Ava Gardner had been married to Mickey Rooney before she married Frank Sinatra, and here in Sicily if a man looks at another man's woman, she is compromised in the spasm of a glance. You know as well as I do the word for widow in Sicilian is *cattiva*—evil.

Turidru Oh, this much touted Sicilian jealousy! First of all, the word *cattiva* might refer to the condition of widowhood, of being alone, the evil of being alone. Look, I was captured in North Africa, and I did a sort of war tourism. I was sent to Yorkshire, Hull, and Darlington, in England. I've lived in Paris for a year, not under the best of conditions, but I've lived there just the same. I've seen other ways of living. And I can tell you, our jealousy here comes from our insecurities, our *paura storica*—from our historical fear.

In summer, have you ever seen those playful sails rise out of the horizon and grow larger and larger. Imagine what it must have been like for centuries on this island, crossroads of the Mediterranean World. Pirates, marauders, conquerors, men—insane men—storming our villages and mounting our women. Racalmuto came into existence because people fled the coastal towns, such as Agrigento, which were constantly sacked by the insane of the world. Centuries of insecurities have been hoarded in the image of women. *Roba*, wealth, stable wealth, land, houses, and women, these are the two things which comfort the insecure; you save, you hoard, never take risks with money or women. So, if you touch the only thing giving a sense of security to men, you touch his vitals. And that is why the Sicilian is a great lover; his insecurities make him imagine all kinds of images, producing jealousy—and what is more flattering than a jealous lover?

I Turi, you would be mincemeat within a year in America.

Turidru No. Jealousy is a great aphrodisiac. It is. And a form of violence, a self-inflicted wound, and a murderous feeling that often leads to suicide or murder. Here it is most often murder.

I And in America it . . .

Turidru No, let me finish. Jealousy here is not real. It's just a way of controlling our women. Who would think of betraying even the most insupportable man when he is insanely jealous? So women find subtle ways of dominating.

I And in America jealousy leads to suicide. Look at Sinatra. They'd make mincemeat of you in America. In no time, mincemeat.

Turidru Sinatra learned to accommodate. I would too.

I Look at Sinatra. At what price. He must have gone through his own season in hell with Ava Gardner.

Turidru Sure. But what an experience, eeh! Only a Sicilian can understand what he went through. It's consuming pride—a wound without healing. But I've fallen into the Sicilian abyss—abstraction. As if *I* am Sicily. Can't you see the consuming pride in all this?

I You exaggerate.

Turidru Sicily is an exaggeration . . . has been for two thousand years. But we exaggerate because we abstract. I am incapable of talking, in all my suffering, about a relationship between *a* man and *a* woman, a man and a man, a woman and a priest, a child and a mother, without abstracting and turning it into an absolute. I knew a writer, Bonaviri, and in the morning I'd call him. "What are you doing Giuseppe?" I'd ask. And without hesitating he'd answer, "I'm thinking of death." And you know why? Because we all aspire to be gods, and when we look around us, we see that we live like failed humans. We are, as the French say, *ambitieux ratés*. Worse, we are *des dieux ratés*—failed gods. Here too I'm abstracting. What I can't say in my own tongue is that *I* am an *ambitieux raté*.

I It's the fault of the language, Turi.

Turidru What do you mean?

I Italian sounds lovely. People like to hear it. It's melodious, limpid, and you say things just for the beauty of hearing it. The language makes you think you're important. It turned a fop like D'Annuzio into a hero. And listeners into sheep. I once heard Sara Ferratti, the actress, read the telephone book in Rome. She moved me, us to tears.

Turidru That may be so. It's the banality of our lives. But we have to live with it. Let me be more specific then. For years I wrote songs and sang as a young man without success. I followed the Pepi Boda show around Sicily—nothing. I wrote stories of my adventures around Sicily—a novel too. I took it with my own hands to an editor in Caltanissetta. "It is well done," I was told, "but this has been done so often, it will not sell." And I saw the greatest of stupidities being published. And my songs—I couldn't get a shepherd to sing them on Christmas eve, songs which I tore my heart out to write. I was left braying like a jackass. So I started painting, the *metier* of the solitary and the independent, of those with pride and no power. But even that is frozen here. Guttuso and Bruno Caruso, great painters, but they are traditionalists, fine craftsmen of the line drawing, depth of perception, intelligent, committed, but the kind of talent needing years of study and practice, as old as Leonardo, the art of the elite and talented, *quoi*. In America art is open to everyone. A bucket of paint sprinkled on a canvas—*voilà* Jackson Pollack, Hans Hoffman. Even art has been opened to all in America. Oh beatific America!

I But how limiting. No boundaries. No boundaries in this school of bucket and sprinkle painting.

Turidru Not to the artist.

I I can't even call it a school of painting. In that painting there is no tie to the audience, who loves a story, loves to see faces and gestures. The abstract loses all that. It becomes like you; talk only a few can listen to and everyone else is bored.

Turidru But the artist finds himself in his art with the hope others will find him in his work. If the artist has lost his audience or if the audience has shrunk, so what. What is important is that now every man is capable of being an artist. Oh beatific America, where every man is capable of becoming a Frank Sinatra.

I Turi, how can you see so clearly about Sicily and yet be so muddled about America and yourself. You love America because you hate your country.

Turidru I see myself too clearly. There lies my difficulty. And you might like Sicily because you dislike America.

I That's not so. To think of an America that does not exist is no solution. Why have you given up on your writing? And don't tell me it's your Sicilian pride. Have you tried other editors, other pleasures, satisfactions?

Turidru That, no! I won't grovel before editors and journalists, because in this country if you are not taken to a publisher by a friend, only the wife of the concierge will read you, and it ends there. Everything here begins and ends with a friend, *l'amici*. Now I have no friends at court. No, let me be honest. If my work isn't startling enough to seized by the first editor, then it is not good enough. Pleasures? Now I can only revel in the pleasures I find in other men's sorrows. I read only the bad reviews of films, of books, of tenors who were booed off the stage.

I Turi?

Turidru Yes.

I Can I tell you something?

Turidru Certainly.

I You won't be offended?

Turidru I am beyond offense.

I I am simply wanting to understand.

Turidru If I can contribute to human understanding, I am at your service.

I People here seem pigheaded, and some are obsessed and call it pride. Why beat your head against the wall, as they say at home. There are so many pleasures in life, things to give yourself to. Why didn't you marry. If I may speak clearly...why didn't you? For most of us, the family is a comfort—a good wife, the pleasures of raising a son, a daughter, the ability to love and be loved. We find our satisfactions where we can. I'm sorry if this sounds like a banality, but even banalities must be confronted as possibilities helping us to live. If you took away childbearing and all that surrounds it—courtship, lovemaking, birth, raising the child— most people would have little reason to live. You've missed out...

Turidru You've missed the point, *cher ami*. Let me put it this way, because I don't want to be abstract.

In Rome, many years ago, soon after the war, I met a young and beautiful woman who came with me to Sicily. She was from Finland, a headmistress of a kindergarten. Every summer she came to Italy to be wicked. I fluttered around her like a bird, puffing up my chest, sticking out my bottom: I did a fandango. I bought her flowers, scarves, and small blue earrings. I dined her; I wined her; I nearly bankrupted my mother. We stayed in Mondello, and one night while the lights of the automobiles descending from Mount Pellegrino stared down at us, I made furious love to her. I was insane. The things I did were maddening, a pleasure as old and hysterical as life itself—all in telling her, "I love you," almost as a shield against the desire I had to kill her.

I   Good god! What for?

Turidru   What for! I resented, I hated her freedom, her freedom as a woman capable of inexhaustible desire. I pummeled her with love. She mistook it for ardor. I left her in the early morning. The next day I met her in the piazza. She looked so common and ordinary to me.

I   Poor woman.

Turidru   She smelled slightly of decay. What was all the fuss about, I asked myself. I turned and walked away without saying a word as if I had never known her.

I   The poor woman.

Turidru   Far from that. And I tell you this because it is not an abstraction. But how could I tell her I felt disabused. The pleasure she had provoked in me had turned to the hatred of one who realized he had been dominated, subjugated to another will. What we call here being cuckold. I was ashamed and could not look her in the eye. Then too how could any woman come up to the images of Woman I had been tediously weaving for ten years as I watched a rooster proudly mount hens in the streets or Lana Turner come walking towards me in her soft sweater in the darkness of our sweat-smelling cinema.

Is it true that Sinara made it for himself with Lana Turner? [*And here Turidru puts his two forefingers together as if joining a seam.*]

I   I don't know. But it was a lot to lay on her.

Turidru   What do you mean. All I laid on her was myself.

I   I mean abstractly. It's a way we have of speaking at home. To lay your troubles on to someone else. She made use of you, too. Abstractly or otherwise.

Turidru   The abstractions certainly laid on to me over the years. I just had it with women. It was not time and is not time to be living with them. There is a great divorce between men and women just now.

I Hasn't there always been. I once met a woman whose father had mol...

Turidru Maybe in time we can find a better arrangement, but right now we can only make each other sick. All the accoutrements of childbearing you speak of: love is sick, companionship is sick, friendship between men and women is sick, and those who live *ensemble* are just pretending. The world is being Sicilianized.

I Come on now. Quit bragging. Let me tell you I once knew...

Turidru No, for us men here there is something else. There is the inability to give ourselves to someone else. We can't even give ourselves to God. Look how few men are truly Christian in this cuckold country. The churches in Sicily are filled with women, but you'll find only a few frightened and defeated men there. How can Sicilian men believe in a religion whose founder is a cuckold, cuckold for having himself killed that way, for being made a fool. Because in Sicily death is the ultimate cuckoldry. It is the ultimate subjugation and why our pleasures come from other men's sorrows. And we grieve for other men's successes.

I Goddamn it, Turi, if you understand, why don't you do something about it! What a waste of human intelligence.

Turidru About what? Excuse me. I don't mean to be dull. Do you mean my relationship to women? That is not determined by me. For all our roosterism, we men of Sicily are led by our noses by women. Let me tell you, with the woman from Finland I learned something. She made me feel a responsibility to play the role of the ardent Sicilian. What a responsibility! Thank God my organs were functioning *à merveille*. I learned then the role of ardent Sicilian did not suit me. I was a hypocrite—that is, I was not in harmony with the world. I was playing the role she wanted me to play.

I So she turned *you* into an abstraction and you didn't like it. But why the desire to kill?

Turidru Because she made me aware of how much I needed a woman—that kind of woman—the eternal slut of inexhaustible desire who serves innumerable men and their desires. I learned that the source of that great and sad Sicilian jealousy at heart came from the realization that a woman is always calculating, controlled but capable of inexhaustible lust, and I thought I could overwhelm that lust. And because of the primeval stupidity, how much of life, men's lives, really was a failure. I wanted to kill her because she made me see what I would become in twenty years. Because I saw myself as I am now.

I Turi. Turi.

Turidru What?

I Why didn't you kill her?

Turidru Because Frank Sinatra would never do a thing like that. And I am a sensitive soul, which is a way of saying I am crazy in a different way. In any case, we rarely kill women here. Our insanity comes from other men. Our pleasure comes from seeing other men suffer, and we are pleased that women can make us rage so we can go out and kill men. Why destroy the source of our pleasure.

[*He points*] See that girl passing, going to church of the Madonna of the Mount, wearing tight jeans like that? You would say something has changed; nothing has changed. We used to be controlled by the black skirt draped over the curve of a buttock— now it is the tight blue jeans in the shape of a mandolin. And I feel a great sorrow for that girl. It is the only way she can survive.

I But Turi, what is it that you want now?

Turidru Ohfff. I would like to have an apartment of my own with a phone and have it ring the moment I came home.

I You ought to think of the things you really need.

Turidru Harmony with the world the way it really is and with my nature. As Frank Sinatra has found. He would be as crazy as I am if he had not found harmony. Harmony! Harmony is a way of saying a state of grace, and then I will be ready to die, to leave.

We have the gift of time—an *impasto* of life and death—time in which to find harmony, a state of grace. My state of grace would be to come home to my apartment and have my phone ring as soon as the door was closed behind me, not before or after but as soon as I closed the door behind me. That would be nice.

I Turi, you sound like a character out of a Pirandello play.

Turidru Where do you think Pirandello found his characters? Right here in the piazza, listening to the likes of me. Men who could not live their meager lives without imagining they were gods in search of believers.

Let me tell you, in the face of all this imposing talk, do you know how I spend my days? In the morning I have a bowl of milk with a spot of coffee. My head is thick with reading I did the night before. I pick up the few lira my mother has left me on the table, and I walk, avoiding the twenty-four imbeciles I must meet before I encounter one intelligent man. At noon I return to my mother's house, and there I have a plate of escarole and bread and cheese. In winter, lentils and chicory. In the evening a bowl of milk and leftover bread, after which I walk in the piazza hoping once again to find an intelligent man. Around ten o'clock I'm back in my room to read and wait for a song or a poem to come to me. In the morning my mother silently shuffles in the kitchen, which smells of ancient decay. I rise to find the bowl of milk with a spot of coffee waiting for me and a few lira in the table.

How else could one lead such a life without imagining oneself a god, especially when I know I am related to Ava Gardner. So I sit and wait, knowing that Time is a gentleman and forgives us everything.

The next day I went to the house on Cavour Street which had been my grandfather's house and from which all his children, except the daughter Pina, had left for America. The house was empty, picked clean of all the cane-bottomed chairs that once lined the room, the beds in the alcove, the armoire. The house had been pillaged by the neighbors and a priest who would never have touched a wet rag in the house while Pina lived there. Once it was known that she had "put herself away" in the convent, the house was stripped clean. There were no relatives living in the town and only one daughter was left in Brooklyn.

In the second floor, where I once slept as a boy, there still was the reproduction of Christ tearing his chest apart to expose his bleeding heart, now speckled with fly droppings. By the window was the trunk I used to stand on in order to see the Norman castle down by La Baruna. Inside the trunk I found pictures of marriages, confirmations, graduations, of men and women on the roofs of New York, in gardens in the suburbs of Argentina, one before a restaurant in Houston, Texas. One large picture was of an uncle in front of his grocery store in Brooklyn, and in the foreground I recognized Ezra Lapidus, a childhood friend of mine who was killed in the Philippines in 1945. In the picture he is a boy of ten or so and he is holding a pineapple. Underneath the pictures, scattered about, were letters of the son Dominick, killed in France in 1917. All his letters began "Beloved parents."

Peter Carravetta

Scoring the Digest

A Drama Poem Written upon Rereading Some Poems from My College Days

For Robert Viscusi

And why, when mirth unseals all tongues,
Should mine alone be dumb?
Ah! late I spoke to silent throngs,
And now their hour is come.
           —R. W. Emerson

    Batteva l'ora su estrema
riva d'Europa, insistente, smaniosa
d'innocenza.
          —S. Quasimodo

With the exception of God *and* Homereid *whose voices will be heard coming from behind the curtain (one from somewhere above, the other from either side of the stage), all characters will stand relatively motionless in a semicircle, dressed as director sees fit, with only a one-color spotlight on each as the character recites his or her lines. The color of the lights varies with each voice and is never twice the same for a given character. Light background music should be matched to pieces but with a variety of styles and moods, not excluding acoustic guitar and the sound of raindrops on a window pane or a howling wind. Chorus is made up of three female and two male voices of different timbres and forms a second half-circle not too far behind the other characters. Props and stands of a simple geometric design may be used for identification and to support the text, provided they are not illuminated by the spotlights. The stage is otherwise empty and darkened, with a predawn pallor at one end. The lineup of the characters from left to right is:* Author, Helios, Gaea, Humanus, Sophia.

Chorus The seasons will return, no fear,
        but stay the moods
        and the ringing of the voices...
        it's really more than amusing to hear

Helios days on end without money to spend
        and many a dank corner to piss at
                —thousands of colleagues, peers, friends
                  mothering the universities
                  and the proliferation of analysts—

Author Some have stopped demonstrating—and Finley Hall is
        now a greening mount of rubble, sad—so as to consider

who is worse off, to tend the sting of squelched prides
drives and dreams by burrowing into the labyrinths
of the past listening for echoes
for tablets for recordings of vague calls for justice
for respect for your loved other's profile and tension
refusing to play the lottery

Chorus: Then they caressed the endings of their words
the accounts were clogs and smelled pollen
stirrings of mortal frame here and there:
the parabola of the gesturing spirit
dawdles away untranslatable ideals
transfixed on the lofts of the hands

Humanus: The institutions, their heads—capoccioni, jefes—
and much printed matter praise and fan such so-called
humanitarianism
— matter printed mostly by Authorities and Co.,
needs people to dispel to defuse any alarming
uncomplicated questioning
with quiescent smiles
with a ready-made myth down your throat—

Helios true: you have seen and read about depravity
tamed furors and stereotyping

Humanus Yes in deed if there's a life or a story
or a study of those of you who felt compunction and
now unsheath hyperboles on social incomprehensibility

Helios but we must be silent—how dare you
to appeal?—the authorities
really do know
what's good for us
and then we ought to concede
they are trained specifically
to maintain each organism dangling
on a string (reflected a million ways)
in its externally induced equilibrium
its proper course

Humanus Some did not wish to depend on others
did not forage pieties or harvest lies
from eight on to eighteen and since
nixed platitudes and prayers
gave room tips encouragement
and one was in love with astrophysics and chemistry
and a Puerto Rican Venus from 122nd St. who played piano
(her name was Norma,
and I remember
she told me once

I should start reading
Italian poetry)

Chorus   Author you must, o Helios, o Voices feeble and
quick, another occurrence
another time o so tense
is knocking at the gates

Gaea   perhaps you're aware
of the ages
I trampled through
to finally travel
the velvety snows to your hut
and taste the sorrow
of your lyrics
        to feel the unsaid
of our expendable condition
constantly murdered
by the very life we cherish
have
        (or maybe had)
in the celestial harmony
of a reassuring history

Helios   some heard Howl beyond the visceral
and braced electric bodies real
again finally resolving
to be
licking their wounds

Author   Some got B.A.'s wop or not
washing dishes and snorting flour
without the blessed precincts of the Shepherd
without the frontier brawn of the Miller

Humanus   But then neither did they feign tears
for the victims of Managua:
some'd believe nature angry and
like a God
punishing with resentment
        wronged people twice wronged

Sophia   Nighttime
it is raining
silently and weary to the window I draw
        I see you staring at the hills
                introsume glyphs lenticular and
                cloudy crescents

Gaea but today
majakovskij is safe
ly sold at five ninety-five
and a pack of insatiables
still sing him melancholy voice
—even parody his uselessness
next to a bazooka—
elegies and odes
(you'd never believe it!)
are real only to sophomores
writing papers

Humanus And yet were enraged by Lee Ying and Sacco and
a decade of sublime obtuseness against Ulysses
(much, very much unlike the scores of students
who are bolted into tractable tetrahedra)

Helios some have seen have been the working force
from disparate lands uglified gloomy accents askew
reinventing their trades and wrestling with facades
welding trestles for the Essences to redouble
    long were the hours and humility debauched
tracking humiliations extolling toughness pursuing
the self, the life, the miracle, the uncertain
dream, one's dream, that is: The Dream

Humanus (Often defined as the freedom to continue to
be able to breathe and to shit unhindered)

Helios of course no one would want the Capitol to un
do history or to neglect its uniform priorities
(there's more than Watergate at stake here...

Author [*Typescript dated: substitute* "Irangate..."]

Sophia Mighty is the night
swirling spark-like drops against
and off the shivering lamppost
on the pane my numbed flesh
wailing the branches the ghosts
and too quivering are the flected
vines the grass my predisposition

Helios or stop reminding We the people—il popolo
el pueblo la razza and so on and so off—
of how sorry we are for starving people
for the victims of—I swear it
I heard it—a "disease called poverty!"
    —doesn't that make you cringe and
    wanna kick your television screen in the face—

those same people whose legal moral function
is to pay their taxes stay in lane
and whose supernal pact
is to continue to breathe and to shit "accordingly"

Chorus   Do not believe it for a second
the antennae of a society theory
the force is in the guts
desire an unseen lava
o power no longer the objects the investments
that ludicrous cosmic imbecility
that bursts unpredictably like a summer storm

Sophia   I listen
I see you staring at the hills
it is dark
and darkness knows no names

Gaea   and writing and reading
about your life your poems...it
is pure chance a fluke—come now—
except to bleary-eyes linguists who
          however
in the dusty recesses of our res public
patiently recompose your face

Chorus   As if the Pilgrim the Runaway were my sole ancestor
as if Hamlet were only
your own exclusive private imperial patricide
and pain could not subsist
below our syntax

Gaea   no room or realm
for somber flights no
tundras decamped
of individual really global
despiteful undespumated countenances
or video updated flashes
of fairness equity

Humanus   You heard the song and dearly you loved them all
at times dreaming Aurora no Hesperides
and did you not hear Minerva humming
all through and tender the spring thaw?

Helios   working to stretch the evenings
sweat and all, smoking the pavement
our lungs our minds devoted and in ambush;
specimens, ultimately: your own kind unkind
dejected vilifying orphan mentors of
stability assimilation clock hours—

abide, you were told, grab a few bucks and
harpoon rip the flanks of them zombies out there
recycling goods and needs and pray, no, prey

Gaea these are not read
are not indicative
of a well-thought out
pattern
     it points inevitably to
     not being down-to-earth

Author A grim laugh and a brow gripping the eye
let these saprophytes evoke
the practice of the in-between
earthy earthly earthness earthbound earthhood...terrone!
the perverse grin of necromancers, no: hyenas

Homereid "Eldest of things, Great Earth, I sing of thee
All shapes that have their dwelling in the sea,
All things that fly, or on the ground divine
Live, move, and there are nourished: these are thine;
These from thy wealth thou dost sustain..."

Sophia O I have watched you
listened to the strumming of the echoes
recumbent sinners gasping
pelagic vistas or even
dromedary haven
until
drenched memories wade knee-deep
and unperturbed is the soul
     defying thunderous fathers

Humanus Who demand we study and write to convince tout le monde
we all feel bad, truly, for those vermin refugees and
immigrants and wetbacks and the proverbial bowery bum
and also indians and other even microscopic holocausts
expatriated sons and daughters unemployed students
malpensioned old folks we all knew and touched and

Gaea yet
the bronx is not
I's sure un
like dingy but telestic moscow alleys
officialdom a paper circus
an eyesore here a suasive pharmakos there
symbols of affluence
billboards statistics net works
glamorizing to sell
the rut the banner the trenches
death itself

—as if it were a mere word, a coffin—
and then again we were made aware
beware they spell our
daily diet
as if slaughterhouse bovines or
picture this
     mandel'stam
huskies hauling firearms
on the ghastly siberian plains

God AND SO THE END IS TO LET THINGS BE (AS THEY ARE)

Helios which means we ought to cultivate an ear
a philanthropistemological Amore causa sui
a pathological mise en scene
a sociophatic defensive mechanism
    for instance
racism laced syllables from family my
friends and, voilà, the prof's also
and, 'tween the lines, the prez said so

Humanus And that implies being careful
secretively trepanning
those idea lists who dream and stubbornly
traum denkt of other realizable
visions amidst the thicket
the hollows of systems
yet untried

Sophia I garded the siliceous teardrops on your hand
I savored the procession of your unspoken fables
I have seen you compose alarmingly an alibi
a thought vexed Alas mired in the gutter
Save your freedom before the season takes us

Gaea all that i can say
is that
it is too bad
    i cannot collage your poems
    over and through
    the retinas of my peers
       they too
       like the marble busts
       of our noble ancestors
       a sigh will elicit
       or maybe a quaint yet timed nod
       or most likely be left
       ignored to comrades unknown
       like an ancient roman fascio
       in the lybian deserts
       rotting to nothingness

Author And it must follow that there's but one believable
complacent mythography of manageable heroes
lurching towards depthless frontiers
but actually anxious often shoeless
city monsters wrenching hoi polloi
the malcapitati behind in search of
    Hesperia

Gaea if I only could believe
in immortality

Helios so the runes will seep by taxed onomas
identities reshuffled post mortem
a crater to gather the trickle
of blood bile earthly scripts
when terra infirma vanishes
and entropy rules supreme
unmatched alone aloof
mocking the past our selves
the human condition

Sophia The view the rain
the euphonic stillness
appease avert the spurious
comets rivulets
a tremulous call
to timeless sleep
    I recede
squinting diamonds
lull me to further
shores
alone
    it is nighttime
        raining

Author [*Silentium altum*]

Carrara, Looking Seaward

Saw Carrara's marble mountains
    their great white faces
      open to the sea
Somewhere a voice was singing
          in sea caves off Saranza
   somewhere
        upon the white wind echoing
    far off
       in white stone sky
    Again...
        again...
           still echoing
      voce delirante
          figlia di mare
    Breasts of white marble
         Hair blown back
     aie
      aie
        che tanta bella luce
        della carne umana

The Old Italians Dying

For years the old Italians have been dying
all over America
For years the old Italians in faded felt hats
have been sunning themselves and dying
You have seen them on the benches
in the park in Washington Square
the old Italians in their black high button shoes
the old men in their old felt fedoras
         with stained hatbands
have been dying and dying
       day by day

You have seen them
every day in Washington Square San Francisco
the slow bell
tolls in the morning
in the Church of Peter & Paul
in the marzipan church on the plaza
toward ten in the morning the slow bell tolls
in the towers of Peter & Paul
and the old men who are still alive
sit sunning themselves in a row
on the wood benches in the park
and watch the processions in an out
funerals in the morning
weddings in the afternoon
slow bell in the morning Fast bell at noon
In one door out the other
the old men sit there in their hats
and watch the coming & going
You have seen them
the ones who feed the pigeons
                cutting the stale bread
                    with their thumbs & penknives
the ones with old pocketwatches
the old ones with gnarled hands
                            and wild eyebrows
the ones with the baggy pants
                    with both belt & suspenders
the grappa drinkers with teeth like corn
the Piemontesi the Genovesi the Siciliani
                smelling of garlic & pepperonis
the ones who loved Mussolini
the old fascists
the ones who loved Garibaldi
the old anarchists reading *L'Umanita Nova*
the ones who loved Sacco & Vanzetti
They are almost all gone now
They are sitting and waiting their turn
and sunning themselves in front of the church
over the doors of which is inscribed
a phrase which would seem to be unfinished
from Dante's *Paradiso*
about the glory of the One
                who moves everything...

The old men are waiting
for it to be finished
for their glorious sentence on earth
                          to be finished
the slow bell tolls & tolls
the pigeons strut about
not even thinking of flying
the air too heavy with heavy tolling
The black hired hearses draw up
the black limousines with black windowshades
shielding the widows
the widows with the long black veils
who will outlive them all
You have seen them
madre di terra, madre di mare
The widows climb out of the limousines
The family mourners step out in stiff suits
The widows walk so slowly
up the steps of the cathedral
fishnet veils drawn down
leaning hard on darkcloth arms
Their faces do not fall apart
They are merely drawn apart
They are still the matriarchs
outliving everyone
the old dagos dying out
in Little Italys all over America
the old dead dagos
hauled out in the morning sun
that does not mourn for anyone
One by one Year by year
they are carried out
The bell
never stops tolling

The old Italians with lapstrake faces
are hauled out of the hearses
by the paid pallbearers
in mafioso mourning coats & dark glasses
The old dead men are hauled out
in their black coffins like small skiffs
They enter the true church
for the first time in many years
in these carved black boats
                    ready to be ferried over
The priests scurry about
                as if to cast off the lines
The other old men
                        still alive on the benches
watch it all with their hats on
You have seen them sitting there
waiting for the bocci ball to stop rolling
waiting for the bell
                    to stop tolling & tolling
for the slow bell
                to be finished tolling
telling the unfinished *Paradiso* story
as seen in an unfinished phrase
                    on the face of a church
as seen in a fisherman's face
in a black boat without sails
making his final haul

Backyard

where angels turned into honeysuckle & poured nectar into my mouth
where I french-kissed the roses in the rain
where demons tossed me a knife to kill my father in the stark
    simplicity of the sky
where I never cried
where all the roofs were black
where no one opened the venetian blinds
O Brooklyn! Brooklyn!
where fences crumbled under the weight of rambling roses
and naked plaster women bent eternally white over birdbaths
the icicles on the chains of the swings tore my fingers
& the creaking tomato plants tore my heart as they wrapped their
    roots around fish heads rotting beneath them
& the phonograph too creaked Caruso come down from the skies;
    Titi Gobbi in gondola; Gigli ridiculous in soldier uniform;
    Lanza frenetic
& the needle tore at the records & my fingers
tore poems into little pieces & watched the sky
where clouds torn into pieces & livid w/neon or rain
scudded away from Red Hook, away from Gowanus Canal, away
from Brooklyn Navy Yard where everybody worked, to fall to pieces
    over Clinton Street
and the plaster saints in the yard never looked at the naked women
    in the birdbaths
and the folks coming home from work in pizza parlor or furniture store,
    slamming wrought iron gates to come upon brownstone houses,
never looked at either; they saw that the lawns were dry
were eternally parched beneath red gloomy sunsets we viewed from
    a thousand brownstone stoops
leaning together by thousands on the same
wrought-iron bannister, watching the sun impaled
on black St. Stephen's steeple

April Fool Birthday Poem for Grandpa

Today is your
birthday and I have tried
writing these things before,
but now
in the gathering madness, I want to
thank you
for telling me what to expect
for pulling
no punches, back there in that scrubbed Bronx parlor
thank you
for honestly weeping in time to
innumerable heartbreaking
italian operas for
pulling my hair when I
pulled the leaves off the trees so I'd
know how it feels, we are
involved in it now, revolution, up to our
knees and the tide is rising, I embrace
strangers on the street, filled with their love and
mine, the love you told us had to come or we
die, told them all in that Bronx park, me listening in
spring Bronx dusk, breathing stars, so glorious
to me your white hair, your height your fierce
blue eyes, rare among italians, I stood
a ways off, looking up at you, my grandpa
people listened to, I stand
a ways off listening as I pour out soup
young men with light in their faces
at my table, talking love, talking revolution
which is love, spelled backwards, how
you would love us all, would thunder your anarchist wisdom
at us, would thunder Dante, and Giordano Bruno, orderly men
bent to your ends, well I want you to know
we do it for you, and your ilk, for Carlo Tresca,
for Sacco and Vanzetti, without knowing
it, or thinking about it, as we do it for Aubrey Beardsley
Oscar Wilde (all street lights
shall be purple), do it
for Trotsky and Shelley and big/dumb
Kropotkin
Eisenstein's Strike people, Jean Cocteau's ennui, we do it for
the stars over the Bronx
that they may look on earth
and not be ashamed.

To My Father—2

You were dying of grief from the moment I saw you
Or fear, tho there *was* a slight chink
thru which we cd signal each other.
How many nights w/a pillow over my face
did I struggle w/rage   /   or desire
exhaustion. There are no fat gods
I thought then. Tho yr tears bloated
you & yr anger puffed you out.
There is Bes, the dwarf, but
I didn't know it then. I will not die
yr death. I will mourn but will not
join you in that house
you build away from the others.
I will know
the tower inside & out, the goddess
in the lingam. Orchards
which do not grow
on city roofs.   If only you'd lie down
to die in an orchard.   Amaranth,
almond, even the feckless
acacia. You are dying of grief
on the rooftops   /   of yr mind, but things
grow in the ground.

The Spirit of Romance

....in Gaelic *rūn* means both
"mystery" & "the beloved"
                    —Ezra Pound

& we say "casting the Runes"
as if we cd talk
                    to the Mystery
as if the Word
                    were mystery
& the cast/
          of Divination
archaic & direct as
love

    Oracle where we
are present to the Word
& cast of Light:
                    Beloved. Mystery.

Rant

You cannot write a single line w/out a cosmology
a cosmogony
laid out, before all eyes

there is no part of yourself you can separate out
saying, this is memory, this is sensation
this is the work I care about, this is how I
make a living

it is whole, it is a whole, it always was whole
you do not "make" it so
there is nothing to integrate, you are a presence
you are an appendage of the work, the work stems from
hangs from the heaven you create

every man / every woman carries a firmament inside
& the stars in it are not the stars in the sky

w/out imagination there is no memory
w/out imagination there is no sensation
w/out imagination there is no will, desire

history is a living weapon in yr hand
& you have imagined it, it is thus that you
"find out for yourself"
history is the dream of what can be, it is
the relation between things in a continuum

of imagination
what you find out for yourself is what you select
out of an infinite sea of possibility
no one can inhabit yr world

yet it is not lonely,
the ground of imagination is fearlessness
discourse is video tape of a movie of a shadow play
but the puppets are in yr hand
your counters in a multidimensional chess
which is divination
         & strategy

the war that matters is the war against the imagination
all other wars are subsumed in it.

the ultimate famine is the starvation
of the imagination

it is death to be sure, but the undead
seek to inhabit someone else's world

the ultimate claustrophobia is the syllogism
the ultimate claustrophobia is "it all adds up"
nothing adds up & nothing stands in for
anything else

THE ONLY WAR THAT MATTERS IS THE WAR AGAINST THE IMAGINATION
THE ONLY WAR THAT MATTERS IS THE WAR AGAINST THE IMAGINATION
THE ONLY WAR THAT MATTERS IS THE WAR AGAINST THE IMAGINATION

ALL OTHER WARS ARE SUBSUMED IN IT

There is no way out of the spiritual battle
There is no way you can avoid taking sides
There is no way you can *not* have a poetics
no matter what you do: plumber, baker, teacher

you do it in the consciousness of making
or not making yr world
you have a poetics: you step into the world
like a suit of ready-made clothes

or you etch in light
your firmament spills into the shape of your room
the shape of the poem, of yr body, of yr loves

A man's life / a woman's life is an allegory

Dig it

There is no way out of the spiritual battle
the war is the war against the imagination
you can't sign up as a conscientious objector

the war of the worlds hangs here, right now, in the balance
it is a war for this world, to keep it
a vale of soul-making

the taste in all our mouths is the taste of our power
and it is bitter as death

bring yr self home to yrself, enter the garden
the guy at the gate w/the flaming sword is yrself

the war is the war for the human imagination
and no one can fight it but you / & no one can fight it for you

The imagination is not only holy, it is precise
it is not only fierce, it is practical
men die everyday for the lack of it,
it is vast & elegant

intellectus means "light of the mind"
it is not discourse it is not even language
the inner sun

the *polis* is constellated around the sun
the fire is central

Prayer to the Mothers

they say you lurk here still, perhaps
in the depths of the earth or on
some sacred mountain, they say
you walk (still) among men, writing signs
in the air, in the sand, warning warning weaving
the crooked shape of our deliverance, anxious
not hasty. Careful. You step among cups, step out of
crystal, heal with the holy glow of your
dark eyes, they say you unveil
a green face in the jungle, wear blue
in the snows, attend on
births, dance on our dead, croon, fuck, embrace
our weariness, you lurk here still, mutter
in caves, warn warn & weave
warp of our hope, link hands against
the evil in the stars, O rain
poison upon us, acid which eats clean
wake us like children from a nightmare, give the slip
to the devourers whom I cannot name
the metal men who walk
on all our substance, crushing flesh
to swamp

Poem in Praise of My Husband (Taos)

I suppose it hasn't been easy living with me either,
with my piques, and ups and downs, my need for privacy
leo pride and weeping in bed when you're trying to sleep
and you, interrupting me in the middle of a thousand poems
did I call the insurance people? the time you stopped a poem
in the middle of our drive over the nebraska hills and
into colorado, odetta singing, the whole world singing in me
the triumph of our revolution in the air
me about to get that down, and you
you saying something about the carburetor
so that it all went away

but we cling to each other
as if each thought the other was the raft
and he adrift alone, as in this mud house
not big enough, the walls dusting down around us, a fine dust rain
counteracting the good, high air, and stuffing our nostrils
we hang our pictures of the several worlds:
new york collage, and san francisco posters,
set out our japanese dishes, chinese knives
hammer small indian marriage cloths in the adobe
we stumble through silence into each other's gut

blundering thru from one wrong place to the next
like kids who snuck out to play on a boat at night
and the boat slipped from its moorings, and they look at the stars
about which they know nothing, to find out
where they are going

The Dance at Saint Gabriel's

For Louis Otto, 1943

We were the smart kids of the neighborhood
where, after high school, no one went to school,
you NYU, and I CCNY.
We eyed each other at Saint Gabriel's
on Friday nights, and eyed each other's girls.
You were the cute, proverbial good catch,
just think of it—nineteen, and so was I,
but all we had was moonlight on our minds.
This made us cagey; we would meet outside
to figure how to dump our dates, go cruising.
In those hag-ridden and race-conscious times
we wanted to be known as anti-fascists,
and thus get over our Italian names.
The war came, and you volunteered, while I
backed in by not applying for deferment,
for which my loving family named me Fool.
Once, furloughs overlapping, we met up,
the Flight Lieutenant and the PFC;
we joked about the pair we made, and sauntered.
That Father Murray took one look at us,
and said our Air Force wings were the only wings
we'd ever earn. We lofted up our beers.
Ah, Louis, what good times we two have missed.
Your first time up and out the Germans had you,
and for your golden wings, they blew you down.

The Wedding Photograph, 1915

They are stunned into poise. Their fixed eyes stare
at something strange. The studious camera,
the photographer in his mantle of black
command their attention. They are used to waiting.
In her wedding gown my mother's face shows pale
beneath her blazing veil, the flying fillets.
My father glares. Confined in a gaudy peace,
he seems to be thinking this is serious business.

The seconds pass, and then they move away;
they will never be so still again until
they stop forever. I remember them now,
heads nodding, pondering, or with gesturing hands
one or the other exclaiming, "Life is work."
They never saw that picture but they laughed out loud.

Tony

Tall,
smiling-faced immigrant,
at school your handsome snickering
obsessed the rest of us.
The windows,
barred, as in prison,
looked down and gleamed at you,
which made us mad to follow
in the wake of your little scandals.
Our kind teacher
talked over our heads to you.

I remember
bouts of snobbery
when I schemed like a gambler
over my homework,
and rolled my eyes in class
at your inexorable ignorance.
Alert as a mouse
I used to loiter in the hallway
to hear
the useless reprimands
you received after class.
I scampered home,
thrilled with your shame.

Across the aisle
I ogled you like a girl.
I envied you your wild curls,
hair, that like you,
refused to stay in place.
I think I pitied you,
the holes in your shoes.

How brave,
how uselessly brave, Tony,
to dare your banishment.
What a scene at thirteen years,
you, chiding the Cyclops
to find you out.
Recalling that
plagues me now
like something choked down—
we laughed, we stamped our feet,
we hooted the principal
at her harangue,
the teacher, tears in his eyes,
who escorted you down the hall
like a jail-house priest.

Destiny, Destiny,
why were you so pretty,
so sure to die?

Before the summer was out,
and the grass dead,
you were struck down
as by a thunderbolt.

You were caught in a stolen car,
yourself the darting child you didn't see,
and iron rang in your ears.

Years later I saw you on Tenth Street,
pushing your wagon-load of fruit.
The sun seized you
like a searchlight
in our little square,
where you peddled your wares
in a brutal tremolo,
hoarse, out of breath.
Smiling-faced,
I stood before you,
blocking your way.
But you pushed around,
you stared right through me,
like a prisoner at Auschwitz,
seeing nothing but his death.

The Americanization of the Immigrant

Your words, Genoveffa,
through the open window,
telling me once again
what to buy at the store:
don't forget, don't forget—
aroma of fresh bread,
almost a halo.

That was a long time ago.
I never forgot.
Like Dante
I have pondered and pondered
the speech I was born with,
lost now, mother gone,
the whole neighborhood bulldozed,
and no one to say it on the TV,
that words are dreams.

Antonio Stefanile

Nola, Italy, 1873-1959

You were a peaceful king, with many spies.
I think of all the slow and careful strangers
walking through the streets of foreign towns
who wore on their watch-chains the gift you sent,
the little coral horn that fought bad luck.
Now you are dead, the lurching continents
seem even less safe than they were before,
so scattered are we—like the Jews, surprised
to our identity this seventh year.
In Argentina children call your name;
who is there left now, old and queer enough
to write, and give advice, and pray for us?
New York and Canada send telegrams,
but where's the Elder now of all our tribe,
the shaman, pipe and proverb, we left home?
Your strength was stubbornness, not luxury:
Anchises turned about, you carried us.
Beyond the sea's walls we remembered Troy,
and you, old shade, who stalked that abandoned rubble
like a good shepherd, among sheep of stone.
In Boston an Irish priest trips on your name
to welcome to a world you had not walked
your late reality, your myth that bloomed

like mist beneath that moon of memories,
our banishment. O gentle, antique king,
of spirit large enough for large farewells,
the wind is but a roster of our names
that blow like seeds cast from your ancient earth.

How I Changed My Name, Felice

In Italy a man's name, here a woman's,
transliterated so I went to school
for seven years, and no one told me different.
The teachers hardly cared, and in the class
Italian boys who knew me said Felice,
although outside they called me feh-LEE-tchay.

I might have lived, my noun so neutralized,
another seven years, except one day
I broke a window like nobody's girl,
and the old lady called a cop, whose sass
was wonderful when all the neighbors smiled
and said that there was no boy named Felice.
And then it was it came on me, my shame,
and I stepped up, and told him, and he grinned.

My father paid a quarter for my sin,
called me inside to look up in a book
that Felix was American for me.
A Roman name, I read. And what he said
was that no Roman broke a widow's glass,
and fanned my little Neapolitan ass.

The Exotic Enemy

Deep in us this fascination with the exotic other—
no sentiment about it—this passion
with the blood of the other
stains our hands and tongues—
to poke at the fruit until its juices run on the ground,
to tear the rose from its stem, scatter petals to the wind,
to pluck the butterfly's wings for the microscope's lens,
to plunge a fist
into a teetering tower of bricks,
watch the debris sail, explode fireworks
until all crumbles to dust and is undone, open
to the curious eye.

Does this or that creature die as I die,
cry as I cry, writhe as I if my guts were ripped
from the walls of my flesh,
my ripe heart eaten alive.

The probing questions of sacred exploration,
as if science can
progress without
empathy.

Does a penis feel as a clitoris feels?
Do slanted eyes see as I see? Is a white or black skin
or sin the same as a red one;
is it like me? Does it burn, does it peel, does it boil
in oil or reel in pain?

The obsession to possess the other so completely that his blood
fills the mouth and you eat of her flesh from its bone,
and then know if she, if he, feels as you feel,
if your world
is
real.

Cento at Dawn

The wind blows out of the gates of the day.
Let the night keep what the night takes away,
dreamt in a dream the heavy soul, somewhere
struck suddenly and dark down to its knees,
sighs as a griffin sighs off in the orphic air—
awakes as morning at the brown brink eastward springs
and the whole landscape flushes on a sudden at a sound—
the clang of waking life; the streets are stirred,
    birds fly to the glistening roofs and sing;
an omnibus across the bridge
    crawls like a yellow butterfly,
while I stand on the roadway and on the pavement grey
and dream that beauty passes like a dream
    fastened to a dying animal.

The *cento* is an Italian form in which the poet deliberately uses lines and refrains from poets of the past, combining them into a new poem.

Ants and Worms

Because of the great press of earth upon earth
and living things on each other, I can't
hear music, hunched under the hill of muddy moods today—
only munches and grinds of teeth, ants and worms work.
Instead of Baroque emotions, civilized control, spiritual aspirations,
I play a record of animal sounds magnified:
boars snort and crunch bones, pitcher plants smother insects,
ants scurry and chew crumbs, lizards leap, snakes slither or hiss,
worms burrow and defecate slime,
as they run in tunnels under and all over the carnivorous earth;
natural sounds: farts or burps, dolphins cry, birds scream,
ocean waves, rain, bears grunt, llamas copulate, lions snore,
panthers breathe, water drips or flows, and finally—

a loud clock ticks
its mechanical monotony in silent mind.

Always, as we tick with mechanical time
they are there beneath the surface of our lives,
working, eating, burrowing,
making music of shit, food and slime,
as we do, as we rhyme love lyrics
or sing wails, laughter or death sighs
here in the wet green valley which trembles terribly
                    with aching egos
so that we think the universe feels love
by which we believe the world
is often converted to chaos,
but it's not love
that makes the thunder or lightening,
the pyromania, xenophobia,
                    the war machines grind,
or the stupid innocent music
of ants and worms.

Returning from Paradise We Stop at a Carnival

and view the usual freaks
watching us, and offer a smile
to the snake charmer. She nods at us
        knowing we are lovers returning from paradise.

At night, just before dawn of the last day
of an old year, we have a common nightmare.
Each falls asleep and wakes alone
in a dream on a cold shore
far from home, without shelter from wind, sun,
                    dark, cold, heat.
I feel like a tiny breathing thing alone in a vast night
no hand anywhere to hold mine. I call to you, friend,
brother, lover, husband, but you cannot answer
out of your body, alone in your dream crying for friend,
sister, lover, wife!

We wake into life
sure of dying under the frozen sky
and mute stars, glistening with winter light.
We have returned from paradise and visited a carnival
many times again, to view the freaks watching us and
smile at the knowing snake charmer.
Sometimes as we look at each other, the pain in our eyes
recalls the nightmare each has had separately,
but we do not speak of it. We hold hands into new years,
knowing all new years turn old, and listen to the night,
snow creaking in mounds, and the air iced from the northwind.

For the sake of the other
we do not say
how each together
is alone
returning from paradise.

Aperture

    I attempt to rearrange the past in Venetian palaces
built by blood thirsts or delicate lusts,
full of plaintive strains of Monteverdi
trilled in Gothic arches,
Through a camera's eye,
I look backward on hope,
every lost stroke between us
mesmerizes mind
into something fair and kind—
as here, in the present, dying drones
drone in autumn sun,
leaves rot, purple asters turn to grey seed—
like tiny mushroom clouds dotting umber and siena land-
    scapes of late autumn, muddled earth
  with garbage of greed
everywhere, crushed cans, poisons, wasted paper,
but in my mind, dusk pours in slanted light of high windows,
twilight motes dance amid red velvet curtains
in Venetian palaces above shimmering waters, narrow streets,
we lie embracing, intertwined forever
until darkness erases us,
the woods here in dark.

The stamina of memory opens an aperture,
a window on forever, before
the nuclear age
when only a burnt out
floating of Earth toward Vega,
after the sun was done,
was an end so far off
it couldn't be imagined.

The Lily Shivers

on the autumn pond afloat with shriveled leaves.
Nothing stays.

Feelings in the blood drain
from the corpse as seeds fall
beneath dead leaves.
Love is half of longing.

When we are together,
longing goes
as a sunset sinks behind a mountain top
leaving a halo glow.
Seeds root beneath rotting leaves.

I must be careful
not to long for the ache
of wanting you, to lick the sweetness
which is gone from me, to miss
the wish
which is unfulfilled
more than savor its repose,
here, now,
the sun on the autumn pond,
an iridescent duck with his mallard brown mate
amidst the dying leaves,
lilies still bright with beauty shiver as they go
into winter,
thrilling with the cold that will
come when it will come,
as necessary as the setting of the sun.

As When Some Silenced Singer Hears Her Aria

For Vittoria Colonna
Naples, Ischia, 1492–1547

or creatures crawl riding foam to hurry back to salty home,
as oceans pound fruit to pecking pipers,
or shells keep tunes in earlike chambers,
filled with sand and sea to roam
like songs rejoicing feathered nest and comb
as warm eggs crack chirping hunger, and a child slithers
forth to touch, smell, see, hear earthly cries and laughters
pushed suckling free from nurturing womb—

my tongue is loosed beyond a private caroling, my pen prances
urged by mysterious love as if it had no part in what is sighed
as Earth Herself sings Her praises through me,
my eyes are green sea, red skies, wildflowers, a child who dances
well when loved beyond the pain of men's tribal wars, pride,
threatened suicide, and bloody rivalry.

Vittoria Colonna is emulated in the Petrarchan style of sonnet. Daughter of the Grand
Constable of Naples and born in Rome, she was married to the Marquis of Pescara and had
two happy youthful years on the island of Ischia with her husband before constant invasions
by Spain, France, and Germany resulted in his imprisonment and involvement in wars of
resistance. She carried on a long correspondence in prose and verse with her absent husband
who was wounded and died in battle in 1525. She retired to Ischia where her grief and love
for her husband found expression in her sonnets. She never remarried but had many
admirers, among them Michelangelo, who dedicated some of his finest sonnets to her. Her
collection of poems, which appeared in 1538, was the first volume of poetry by a European
woman to be published and widely read.

In the Golden *Sala*

Sun of Sicilian hillsides,
heat of poppies opening like fierce
boutonnieres of Apollo,
light of Agrigento, fretting the sea and the seaside cliffs—
light of the golden *sala*,
the great *sala* of the ruined *palazzo*
where my Sicilian grandmother and her nine children
camped outside Palermo.

Gold leaf, gold moldings,
shredding tapestries with gold threads.
"Once it belonged to a prince.
Mama kept chickens on the terrace
but they came in sometimes, and the donkey too."
Gold chairs, gilt around the windows,
angels with shining hair and empty eyes
staring from the ceiling.

"Mama made our beds in the corners:
the big room scared us, we thought
the prince's ghost was there."
Gold railings where her laundry hung,
gold curtains, new eggs under them.
Her cooking fire in a corner,
the center of the *sala* a cave of gold
for spankings and scoldings.

"Mama was a midwife, knew
everything about herbs and births.
The peasant women came from farms around Palermo
so she could help them."
On floors still streaked with gold
she made them spaces
in the dazzling spaces where the prince once walked.
Gold of forgotten dances, tattered rugs.

When a new baby slid out in a splash of water
he must have looked up, dazed,
toward the prince's Apollonian light,
and the black eyes of the midwife
and the black eyes of the midwife's nine blackhaired children
would have looked quizzically down,
as if from a high cliff by the sea
hot and yellow with new poppies.

The Summer Kitchen

In June when the Brooklyn garden
boiled with blossom,
when leaflets of basil lined the paths
and new green fruitless fingers of vine
climbed the airy arbor roof,

my Sicilian aunts withdrew
to the summer kitchen,
the white bare secret room
at the bottom of the house.
Outside, in the upper world,

sun blistered the bricks of the tiny
imitation Taormina terrace where fierce
socialisti uncles
chainsmoked Camels and plotted politics;
nieces and nephew tusseled

among thorny bloodcolored
American roses;
a pimply concrete
birdbath-fountain dribbled ineffectual
water warm as olive oil.

Cool and below it all,
my aunts labored among great cauldrons
in the spicy air
of the summer kitchen: in one kettle
tomatoes bloomed into sauce;

in another, ivory *pasta*
leaped and swam
on the clean white table
at the center of the room
heads of lettuce flung themselves open,

and black-green poles of zucchini
fell into slices of yellow
like fairytale money.
Skidding around the white
sink in one corner

the trout that Uncle Christopher brought back
from the Adirondacks gave up
the glitter of its fins
to the glitter of *Zia* Francesca's
powerful knife.

Every August day *Zia* Petrina
rose at four to tend the morning:
smoky Green chignon
drawn sleek,
she stood at the sink.

Her quick shears
flashed in the silence,
separating day from night, trunk
from branch, leaf
from shadow.

As the damp
New World sunrays struggled to rise
past sooty housetops,
she'd look suddenly up
with eyes black as the grapes

that fattened in the arbor:
through one dirt-streaked window
high above her
she could see the ledge of soil
where her pansies and geraniums anchored.

Higher still,
in tangles of heat,
my uncles' simmering garden grew,
like green steam swelling from the cool
root of her kitchen.

Piazza

Life circulates here, watched
only by the random few:
the tourist with her blank regard
or a conqueror passing through.

It's a square, sometimes a circle
or a wobbly tetrahedron,
channeling the cars, the kindly
chatter going on and on.

All know one truth, that nothing
appertains beyond
this circus, and the human
commerce it depends on.

All love the hubbub, which connotes
success in multiples
of children, vespas, coins,
the slick materials

the young must wear to track
the eyes of other young,
young men and women
who will loll their tongue

and live on wheels, a Honda
or a Fiat, maybe just
a bike; the point's in wheeling it—
it's move or bust.

Life seems so easy if one lets
the fountain's water-spouting
breasts become a focus,
if one lets the shouting

fill the ears with operatic
tones of bull or barter,
the pervasive tease, the snub,
the genially senseless banter

of the balding lad who cuts
a brutish figure in the crowd
but nonetheless is loved
by Mamma, who's serenely proud

he keeps a wife and wears
silk shirts. Who cares,
they seem to say, if politics
are local, or if pairs

of lovers are the only sight
worth dreaming when, at last,
one goes to bed? Tomorrow,
what-has-been becomes the Past

and therefore boring. Life
is what comes next, and how
one meets it, preferably poised,
applauding every bow.

Grandmother in Heaven

In a plume-field, white above the blue,
she's pulling up a hoard of rootcrops
planted in a former life and left to ripen:
soft gold carrots, beets, bright gourds.
There's coffee in the wind, tobacco smoke
and garlic, olive oil and lemon.
Fires burn coolly through the day,
the water boils at zero heat.
It's always almost time for Sunday dinner,
with the boys all home: dark Nello,
who became his cancer and refused to breathe;
her little Gino, who went down the mines
and whom they had to dig all week to find;
that willow, Tony, who became so thin
he blew away; then Julius and Leo,
who survived the others by their wits alone
but found no reason, after all was said,
for hanging on. They'll take their places
in the sun today at her high table,
as the antique beams light up the plates,
the faces that have lately come to shine.

At the Ruined Monastery in Amalfi

For Charles Wright

On a hill, approaching Easter,
well above the sea's bland repetitions
of the same old story
and the town's impenitent composure,
I survey old grounds.

The fire-winged gulls engulf the tower.
Lesser grackles, nuns and tourists,
scatter on the grass.

The brandy-colored light of afternoon
seeps through the stonework;
creeping flowers buzz and flutter
in the limestone cracks.

Wisteria-choked loggias drip with sun.

A honeycomb of cells absorbs the absence
it has learned to savor;
court and cloister close on silence,
the auroral prayers long since burned off
like morning fog.

The business of eternity goes on behind our backs.

In the chapel dark,
I'm trying to make out a worn inscription
on a wind-smudged altar,
but the Latin hieroglyphs have lost their edge.

Remember me, *Signore*,
who has not yet learned to read your hand,
its alphabet of buzz and drip and flutter.

Syrinx

A summer glebe
at zero noon.
Syrinx—the sound
of pipes across
a weedy pond
unrustles trees.
I wonder if
the sound I think
I heard was real
or not, as in
that wet glade
where Pan discerned
a wilder note
and waded into
water thick
with reeds. That day
he lay as if
unmade against
a mossbank, trying
to recall a note
more overheard
than heard, a sleight
of wind, a sudden
rightness passing.

Crops

And there is sadness in the way they grow—
bell peppers at full gong in mid-July,
the corn breast-high
where mudprints followed me uphill in May,
loud snapping fingers, peas or beans,
the feathery and light-engorging dill,
the long-haired chives or rough-tongued mint,
engaging basil,
my fair son,
his tendril body climbing through the air.

Coda for Salvation

1

For months this feeling
has been coming closer
like a shy guest
till now he stands before me,
openly, twirling
has hat in his hand.

2

I welcome him in,
knowing he carries
truth in his hatband
and stuffed in his pockets.
Here are the words
I've been running from,
I who have grown deliberately
blind.

3

I look at the jumble
of my desk; the papers spill
in all directions. The phone
almost seems to leap
as it rings
and rings. I say the same words
over and over,
until I am nearly screaming.

4

The office moves forward
in stops and starts
like an old, defective motor.
I write grants and memos
even in my sleep; make lists
of things to be done, words
I should have said. Despair
with its fine gray dust, coats
my hair.

5

I dream of winning the lottery.
of escape. In my office,
the window doesn't open
and there is no door. By 10 A.M.
my voice has broken edges
sharper than teeth. "The better
to eat you with," cries the wolf,
and another day vanishes.

6

I pray for salvation, looking
for the one who will save me.
I stare at the space
between two tall shelves
that serves as a door. The man,
in a suit two sizes too small,
stands just inside the space
and grins.

7

At night, I dream of a billboard.
The message, in large orange letters,
reads "Save yourself."
In the morning, patient
as a spider, I begin.

After Seeing Pierre Bonnard's *The Breakfast Room*

In the painting the room floats
in clear afternoon light.
I imagine how the room
changes as the sun climbs
across the day,
till finally, at dusk,
the woman returns alone.
The house resonates emptiness,
and with the light
leaking out of the room,
the woman looks over her shoulder,
feeling for an alien presence
in the shadows.
She sits in the hard
wooden chair, and watches
the mountains disappear.
Half asleep, she dreams
of a different life,
and imagines the room
as it looks at high noon,
that quality of light
that allows no hidden corners,
remembering afternoons
passed in this room
of polished fruit and ordinary pleasures.

White Lies

In Washington, D.C., you are watching
"St. Elsewhere" on television; in the program,
the mother dies. You call me, your voice heavy
with tears, needing to know that I am still there.
I remember watching Paul Gallico's "Snow Goose"
on television with you when you were only four,
and at the end of the program, your face
crumpled with anguish and you sobbed
as though you had lost the world.

Tonight, reminded of that evening
by the terror in your voice, I see how our roots
have mingled, how the thread winds backward
on the spool of love, how the ground shifts under us.
I lie to comfort you, tell you I will dance
at my grandchildren's weddings
even as I feel the hot breath
of that brooding shadow,
that dark bear,
on my neck.

Poem to Monica Ochtrap

This morning, unable to sleep, I open
your book and read, confronted by darkness
outside my own small circle of light.
At first, I think: "What can I have in common
with this woman and her sparse poems
written in the shadow of Minnesota winters
and the stubble of cornfields I can only imagine?
But each poem pushes me deeper into a life,
stark and seething as my own.

I see you sitting in your kitchen. Outside, darkness
pushes against the window and in the house,
your children sleep. In the picture at the back
of your book, you are sitting at a small table,
the daylit windows behind you. Your chin is cupped

In your hand; in the double exposure,
your eyes seem blind and your mouth, the bones
of the hand, vulnerable. My children
are in college; the time when their breath
steamed the nightglass is gone.
Your children are a presence, milky
and giving breath to the house of your life.

Under the ordered lines of your poems, I hear
the words you will come to recognize
as the road unrolls like a wedding carpet
or a thick rope. Monica Ochtrap, you cannot know
I hold your book in my hand; though we spring
from different soil, we have explored the same country
and in the night, we hear the same cry.

Dark on Dark

The veal sputters on the stove;
the aroma of wine sauce fills the kitchen.
The moon, white and clear as a plate,
pokes through dark winter branches.
From one window, I see only patterns of dark on dark.
and the lights of this small kitchen
reflected in glass.
I wait for you, listening
for the sound of your car.
I cannot know where you have traveled
this day. You cannot know
where I have been, though I try
to explain, the waiting
for test results and calls from doctors,
the fear that lies under my breast
bone, my own death,
real to me as it has not been before.

Reunion at Berkeley

1

Kay, I carry you with me like an icon,
a tinted photograph of you as a young woman
in your suburban Kansas kitchen.
You always seem to be cooking
or bearing steaming bowls to the table.
The summer before your youngest child entered school,
you and Jack took a trip to Colorado.
You slept in your friends' four-poster bed.
A few weeks after you returned, you told me
you were pregnant.
I remember your call to suicide prevention
Hotline, your frantic, tearful confessions.

Now fifteen years later, in the Ladies' Room
of the bar we go to after my reading,
we slip back into our old roles,
you, honest with me in person,
me, honest only in my poems.

Earlier, sitting across from you at dinner,
I ask you both: "Are you happy with your lives?"
The question seems to fall for miles.
Finally, Jack answers,
tells us how he gave up his career
so you could stay in a town
green and safe for children.
Now, one by one, they leave you behind.
You wonder: "Was it worth it?"

Kay, as always, you have more courage than I.
I do not say that only last night,
a few hours before our 23rd anniversary,
I tell my husband I want a separation
"We have nothing in common anymore," I shout.
"We did once," he says, his face still
as though I had slapped him.
He goes out for a walk, I cry.
When he returns, we do not speak,
the stillness thick with anger.
I fall asleep first, but in the morning,
I wake up to his hands. After we make love,
neither of us mentions the night before,
and we go on. Something that had seemed irreparably
broken is mended and we don't know why.
During the day, we touch gently
as though we must lose each other,
over and over,
to rediscover our need.

2

At your house, the tree
in the front yard is weighted down
with huge lemons.
Six jars of canned apricots
glow gold and amber on your kitchen counter.
In the still July night, I walk with your daughter
through the streets of the quiet town.
In the gathering darkness. I feel as close to her
as if she were my own. She promises
to send me poems, tells me that you
put up those apricots together.
"That's the first thing we've done together
in years," she says.

At home again, my own daughter turns
from me, and my son tells me to stop interfering.
All this rage directed at us
who only want their lives
to be better than our own.
How young we were in Kansas City!
We thought our skin would remain firm forever
and there was no death.

After my reading, Jack hugs me,
tells me he likes my poems
and he'll be at my San Francisco reading.
Kay shows me pictures
of their three grown-up daughters.
I marvel that while they grew,
we lost our youth.
"I bought three pairs of earrings," she says.
"I want something for myself now."
I do not say that I am ashamed
of my rage, that I bury it, like a campfire,
to keep it from burning down my life.
I sense that once again we are
in the same place in our lives.
"Where do we go next?" we ask
"Is this all there is?"

Betrayals

At thirteen, I screamed,
"You're disgusting,"
drinking your coffee from a saucer.
Your startled eyes darkened with shame.

You, one dead leg dragging,
counting your night-shift hours,
You, smiling past yellowed, gaping teeth,
You, mixing the eggnog for me yourself
in a fat dime store cup,

How I betrayed you,
over and over, ashamed of your broken tongue,
how I laughed, savage and innocent,
at your mutilations.

Today, my son shouts,
"Don't tell anyone you're my mother,"
hunching down in the car
so the other boys won't see us together.

Daddy, are you laughing?
Oh, how things turn full circle,
My own words coming back
to slap my face.

I was sixteen when you called one night from your work.
I called you dear,
loving you in that moment
past all the barriers of the heart.
You called again every night for a week.
I never said it again.
I wish I could say it now.

Dear, my Dear
with your twisted tongue
I did not understand you
dragging your burden of love.

The Eyes of Women

The eyes of women over forty
are smudged with shadows;
even the blonde woman,
slender and tall,
bears the deep thumb print
of sorrow.

I notice, suddenly, in men over forty
an absence of shadow. Men seem younger,
less frayed at the edges as though women
carry the full weight.

Sisters, our smudged eyes
are the chain that links us
as we bend to fit our men,
learn early to smile and please,
to smooth surfaces with our calm hands.

Midnight Incantations

Tonight dim moonlight outlines
a snow-covered roof,
a street haunting in its silvery radiance.
I imagine you asleep
in your room in New South,
your teal blue quilt
tucked up to your chin.
This gray light illuminates
your baskets of drying rose petals,
your plants and bouquets of flowers,
the stuffed animals lined up
on the shelf,
the I LOVE NY posters on the walls,
the books by Flannery O'Connor
and Zora Neale Hurston
neat in the corner, the pictures
of your friends from high school,
of me. I cannot sleep tonight
thinking of you and how Washington
opens before you
like a secret flower.
I see your boyfriend's eyes on you,
mesmerized by the life
that spits and crackles
from your face, the radiance
of it, and his eyes yearning.
I watch him in memory, those
dark eyes that burn.

Miles away from you,
in our Hawthorne kitchen,
I mumble incantations
against the darkness
that always encroaches,
the darkness I know will come,
though you have not yet learned
this lesson, this litany of
sorrow.

The Young Men in Black Leather Jackets

Today I am reminded
of the young men
who stood for hours
in front of the candy store
on 19th Street and 2nd Avenue
in Paterson, New Jersey,
the young men in black leather
jackets and tough faces,
their ducktail haircuts identical,
the young men who stared with their hard
bright eyes at the girls passing by
and made comments like "Here chickie, chickie,
C'mere, Chickie," their laughter following us
down the street.

For years I remember their song,
the look of terrible mockery in their eyes,
their hatred of women and their need of them.

One day, when I am dreaming my way through
one of the long novels I love,
their footsteps sound on the pavement,
three of them, walking in perfect step,
their long legs scissoring as they sing
in their loudest voices:

> "My Bonnie lies over the ocean.
> My Bonnie lies over the sea.
> My mother lies over my father's knee
> And that's how they got little me."

It is August. Late. Almost time
for school again. They are 17 or 18; I am 13.
I do not understand their song; I only know
I am ashamed as though I, and not they,
have done wrong.

Arturo

I told everyone
your name was Arthur,
tried to turn you
into the imaginary father
in the three-piece suit
that I wanted instead of my own.
I changed my name to Marie,
hoping no one would notice
my face with its dark Italian eyes.

Arturo, I send you this message
from my younger self, that fool
who needed to deny
the words
(Wop! Guinea! Greaseball!)
slung like curved spears,
the anguish of sandwiches
made from spinach and oil,
the roasted peppers on homemade bread,
the rice pies of Easter.

Today, I watch you,
clean as a cherub,
your ruddy face shining,
closed by your growing deafness
in a world where my words
cannot touch you.

At 80, you still worship
Roosevelt and JFK,
read the newspaper carefully,
know with a quick shrewdness
the details of revolutions and dictators,
the cause and effect of all wars,
no matter how small.
Only your legs betray you
as you limp from pillar to pillar,
yet your convictions remain
as strong now as they were at 20.
For the children, you carry chocolates
wrapped in goldfoil
and find for them always
your crooked grin and a $5 bill.

I smile when I think of you.
Listen, America,
this is my father, Arturo,
and I am his daughter, Maria.
Do not call me Marie.

Conscience

After Natalia Ginzburg

Then we start to grow away from our old friends.
Their pretensions and refinements have become annoying.
Their mania for distinction is bourgeois.
Now we want to be poor. We make poor friends,
visit them with pride in their unheated houses.
We take pride in our beat-up raincoat.
We're still waiting for the right person
but she will have to love our old raincoat,
our beat-up shoes and cheap cigarettes and bare red hands.

Evenings we walk alone in our raincoat
past the houses at the edge of town.
We have discovered the periphery,
the signs of snack bars along the river.
We stand entranced in front of store windows
hung with workshirts, overalls and long underwear.
We're enthralled with old cards and hairpins.

Everything old and poor and dusty calls to us.
We stalk the city, hunting the authentic.
It's pouring but we stand bareheaded,
soaking in our leaking raincoat.
We'd rather die than carry an umbrella.
We have no umbrella,
no hat, no gloves, no money for the streetcar.
All we have in our pockets is a dirty handkerchief,
crushed cigarettes and kitchen matches.

Montale's Grave

Now that the ticket to eternity
has your name on it, we are here to pay
the awkward tribute post-modernity
allows to those who think they think your way

but hear you only faintly, filtered through
a gauze of echoes, sounding in a voice
that could be counterfeit; and yet the noise
seems to expand our notion of the true.

An ivory forehead, landscape drunk on light,
mother-of-pearl that flashes in the night:
intimations of the miracle
when the null steps forward as the all—

these were signals, sparks that spattered from
the anvil of illusions where you learned
the music of a generation burned
by an old myth: the end that will not come.

There is no other myth. This sun-drenched yard
proves it, freighted with the waiting dead,
where votive plastic hyacinths relay
the promise of one more technicolor day

—the promise that is vouchsafed to you, scribe,
and your dictator, while your names get blurred
with all the others, like your hardest word
dissolving in the language of the tribe.

San Francesco

Here where the figs are falling from the trees
here in midsummer where immortal flowers
pepper fields that yesterday were green
and ten varieties of vine
threaten to engulf the old garden
and what you thought was silence gives
into patterns of humming: flies, mosquitoes, bees—
here where the steam is rising off the hills
to hide the mountains in a mystic haze
(not to mention all the scales of bells)
you start to see that years are days.

I won't say the litany the trees
give off with their names, varieties of sun
and sunset that the broken wall gives back
or the fluidities the landscape makes
into motion. I can't imitate
the narrow line of cypress going up
the hill in the dark, or how the glade below
seems to offer its fruit like a bowl,
still and whole,
pale and full,
or the dark tower above or the saint in the window.
I know it's all imprinted on you too
and you can bring it back with just the name:
what the memory of a place can save,
how it reflects another part of us
without a warning, when we least expect it.

Morning Run

Villa Doria Pamphili, Rome

Often you start the day here, when the sun
is softest, having only just begun
climbing, and the lowest foliage steams,
clearing itself of nightsweat and the dreams
of the old city waking into heat,
crowdedness, poverty, terror, human dirt.
You dodge the lines of traffic where you can
and jog up to a neoclassic span
of russet stucco crowned with limestone lords,
arms, and abbreviated Latin words
memorializing Innocent,
who "pamphilized" Rome; then past his monument
and under shade along an aqueduct
through which St. Peter's cupola—the top
alone—gleams like a gazebo or a teahouse
adrift in farmland, eloquent and senseless,
and veer left at a second, smaller gate
through undergrowth and past the headless late-
Imperial boy in an embarrassed pose
to come out on a scraggly field where rose,
bluebell and poppy manage to be seen
amid tall grass, no longer really green.

The orangery that brackets the Casino
is eerie, sun-dazed, bleached and empty now,
its maze of formal gardens gone to seed,
the terracotta tubs profuse with weed,
the walkways overrun, the statues down,
like the old town of tombs the house was built on
—and the facade, all filleting and frieze,
peeling and opulent in the thin haze.
Belrespiro, where the favored came
for respite from the heat and stench of Rome
to breathe free in a nature they could mold,
symmetrical, humane, rich and controlled,
all disappearing now in ripe confusion,
waste and disparity, the baroque tension
of topiary, marble, sky and trees
lost to corruption, disarray and ease.
Eight o'clock and there is just a breeze
stirring the tallest ilex, papal bees
are working in the flowers and the birds
are filling up the silence with their words.
The emptiness reverberates as air,
light, heat, scent, color, timelessness: desire.
You gather energy and take the stairs—
leftover heads and bodies everywhere—
three at a time to reach the fields the boys
will pepper later with their games and noise
and shirts and hair, as lover paired with lover
will lie down in the grove beyond and hover
between decorum and abandon, spread-
eagled together on the needle bed,
while down the hill the pensioners complain
over their *bocce* in the shady lane.
In a low wall you find another gate.
The fields beyond are wild, unmown, and yet
water is running in the knee-high straw,
fountains are playing somewhere, someone saw
an order here, too...and you make it out:
the lake below, its curve that swings about
halfway through the vista like a scythe
and finds its echo in the twining, lithe
limbs of Bernini's several mingled writhing
nymphs, who mock your fervor to embrace
the weather and the moment and the place.

You are alone here, yet you seem
verging on some encounter, some deep dream
surfacing in which the body tries
to become nature and the world complies—
a fusing with the air, a loss of self
into an energy that could be life,
a surging forward to become the wind,
hunger no experience can end
half satisfied in being body, sweat,
speed, color, an equivalence of heat,
while the repeating rhythm of your feet
synchs with your breathing till it is your heartbeat
and the land you're running on is ocean,
rising and falling, fluent with your motion
until you can believe you are the day,
you are the sun that brings life and decay,
that warms and soothes and in a moment turns
merciless and withers, burns.
You keep on running, closed inside your breath's
spondaic trance of oneness, power and health,
follow the ragged trees, as overgrown
as your own eagerness for the unknown
which threatens to spill forth at every turn
until you rise once more to a new plain,
another level, a new rush of pain,
and spring down an aisle of poplars to a barn,
which was the goal.

                    And now you must return.
You round the mottled walls, the moment shifts,
the sunlight broadens and the last cloud lifts
over Monteverde, where the day
is gathering its errands. The caffes
are crowding and the gates are going up
over the shopfronts. Time to call a stop
to your exuberance, time to be tame and calm.
The morning's work is waiting in your room.
You leave the park to other runners now.
Trapped in their heavy clothes or else extreme
in their expertise, their search for form,
they seem to need to work against the heat,
but you for once luxuriate in sweat
as you lope halfway down the hill to home
and bath and coffee, and one look at Rome
from the window, laid out like a brain,
its crenelations steaming: your demesne—
or so it looks this morning, from this height—
who knows the colors it will wear tonight?
You gaze again, then shut away its din
and face the table, ready to begin.

Tina DeRosa

Psalm of the Eucharist

The extraordinary stars led us to You.
We were confused.
You called to us,
a high gleam over Jerusalem,
over Bethlehem.
We thought
You were a fixed point
in the sky.
Someone unreachable.
We imagined You with
angelic bearing,
the stunning blue
You would cast:
the universe's shadow,
Your eyes like mystery
and Your strong, white feet.
You dictated to us;
we wrote it all down.
We fell before the Law
that Your words wrought;
the books
were locked.

Then: We longed for You.
We wept for You.
Then, oh Lord, we cried out
into the solemn sky
into the blue Your presence carved:
When will you let us
see Your face?

We kept the law,
observed the rules.
The sheep were silent
on the hillsides: as white
as we could make them.

Then called the star.
Palms shot high
as fountains.
Our very flesh
was stilled.

Then called the star
—or so we thought it—
the light gathered,
and You leapt down.

This is the straw. Here are our lambs. We notice, now,
how their coats curl, rise upward, how everything about them
rests, and grows.

Once, You asked us to slaughter them:
Then paint,
You said,
the doorways of your houses with their blood:
The Lord passes over.

Now, they bleat
at the star,
pure silences.
This time, they cry *with* us.

From all nations, we gather.
Here: Take our jewels.

When she was pregnant,
When she carried You:

>   Ah! Then!
>   That was
>   the simplest beginning.
>   There, in her flesh,
>   You rested.
>   There, in her flesh,
>   You dreamed of us.
>   It would be only
>   a matter of days, now,
>   for You.

You were
drawing nearer.

You watched us,
from her womb.
Already, You sang.
Already, You saw us the way we really are.
Already, You forgave us.

You understood us, now—
All of it:
The Eden tree, and why we did it:
why we reached out for You.
Now, You reached back for us—

And in her,
where You hovered in her privacy,
finally, we touched each other.

She walked with You.
She carried You, and You
were like a wound,
You were a promise.
The blood began.
The body began.
All flesh mended.

Later, when You said:
This is *mine*
—My body
—My blood
Some of us understood:

She was the *new* tabernacle,
where You grew Yourself like a tree.
Always, You had moved among us:
You were fire.
You were voice, and flame.

Now, You began to understand us—
those You have created.
You grew hands.

She became
the new center of Your dwelling places.
Angels knelt before her,
gathered around her.
Angels grew like curtains
near this,
Your holiest place.

All the membranes
split dead center.
You were here.

We tasted Your mercy.
Then we knew we were starving.
Oh, Gentle God!
The placenta of the universe moved,
It bled You into us.
Into our skin.
Into our flesh.

You stunned us.
Blind men groped towards You.
The deaf heard something move, grow:
It was the bread, rising.
It was the wheat calling out to You.
Vineyards groaned.

A Spirit passionate as fruit,
bright as fire,
rested upon us.
Mercy, we cried:
This love
bears down on us,
Forces us out into
    new air,
    new skin.

We cannot bear this birthing process.
Our skin is starved.

Fish leapt at Your voice, and multiplied themselves.
Like beads of rain,
universal atoms split:
The world intensified.

    You called, and the wind stopped.
    You spoke, and the molecules of water flexed, breathed,
        became wine.

In a boy's hand,
loaves grow.

This is only the beginning of Your blessings.

We were starving.
We were homeless, there, where we stood
    in the dust of Your shattered law.

So: You had succeeded.
    You had made us perfect:
    a pure people, a chosen race.

We never knew why:
We never knew it had all led up
to this: a virgin.
One so pure,
You could *enter* by her,
as through an open door.

And now, You walk on water.
You claim
extraordinary allegiance.

You are here, again.
Among us, as first You were
in the garden. Again:
This is the voice of the Lord
who entered
not by the garden's gate,
but through a virgin's womb.

Forgive us.
But again, we are jealous.
We want more.

You forgot Yourself.
You walked upon the water.
Again: You gave Yourself away.
          Such power, such Godliness. Perfection.

Some of us cannot bear it.

Here: On this clear hillside,
          where bread remembers its original seed, and grows again,
          we are famished, and confused.

     You expect this of *us*:
          this transformation,
          this purity of being.

     You expect this of *us*:
          this presence in Your universe
          like the high beam of light
          that announced You.

The women understand.
Already, they are scouring the pots.
Always, they anticipated this: Your presence in the simplest places.
The children understand, and are frightened.
At night, they bleat like lambs.

You move among us like a wedding veil.
All the facades are falling.

This water, for example,
blushes in Your presence
becomes wine at the feast.

And Your blood,
 stunned by the purity of the virgin who led You home.

 You take the blood she gave to You,
 and give her wine, in return.

 You take the flesh she gave to You,
 the flesh of Your own body—
 as freely given to You as Eve gave rib to Adam—
 and transform her flesh
 to eternal bread.

 She, the mother, is a simple woman.
 She followed You
 through Spirit, through flesh, through birth.

 A pillar of fire is no longer adequate.

 Only the flesh and blood of her body,
 blessed and broken open by Yours,
 will fix Your presence among us.

 It is finished. You are here forever.

Children fall on their knees, gather wheat and grapes.
They came the same way. They remember.

In the darkness, lambs bleat.
Under the straightened blue of *this* sky,
they lift up their eyes towards the mountains:

 They are the pure retina.
 Theirs too was once the purest flesh.

 The skin of their bodies curls upwards in memory.

 Like flame, like desire,
 the Christ sky folds down on this,
 Your people.

In Your eyes, Oh Christ,
 fixed as a lamp on the exemplary universe,
 fixed as a vigil over our paltry history,
 the moments will not pass.

 Now do You truly descend among us—
 Your hands reach *down* for the hammers You used as a child.
 Your hands reach down for the nails Joseph laid with a whisper
  into Your palms,
 and You call out, Oh Christ,
 for the Father.

Now, in the garden, Your feet still as trees,
Your hands, folded like fruit into pleading,
You breathe Your own fate, and cry out:
>   The child Jacob was spared, his bones are bleached
>   like birds where they rest in the ground.
>   Noah was spared, and all the sweet fruit of the earth with him:
>   children, animals.

In Your eyes, Oh Christ, high and clear as the shadow of forgiven sin,
>   the past meets the future,
>   and forms a cross.

In this garden, Oh High Christ, which in Your eyes You have guarded
>   like a prayer from the beginning, when You hovered with the Father
>   from all beginnings and said:
>   Let this prayer be said.
>   Let these words be spoken.

In this garden, Oh Immaculate Christ,
>   beneath the sweet sky of Israel,
>   beneath the anonymous stars
>   next to the grapes which bleed for You,
>   where the bread of the Father's will is broken before Your eyes,
>   and spoken to You like a word,
>   You faint beneath the weight of it:
>   and the world like a fruit
>   opens and bleeds,
>   spills into the chalice
>   of Your being.

Then:
>   Palms shoot high as fountains,
>   high as the miracles in Tyre,
>   high as the unforgivable sins of Sodom and Gomorrah,
>   of David and Bathsheba,
>   high as the pain of tortured and blinded Samson,
>   high as the faith of Simeon,
>   higher than the wisdom of stone-white Solomon,
>   Higher.
>   We
>   led You to this hill,
>   pinned You to wood,
>   where You could never leave us again, Oh Gentle God,
>   worker of miracles,
>   with Your tendencies
>   towards the blind,
>   towards the deaf,
>   always *towards*.

You came so close, You touched us.

We nailed You there,
held Your flesh bound to us.
We only wanted to *be*, with You.

There,
at the top of a hill,
in the shadow of a tree.
We lost Eden, but we have Calvary.
Somehow, we will keep You with us:
Here, in the shadow of Your own blood,
marked by the only crown we know how to *give* You—Oh Gentle God—
Here, in the shadow of our grief,
where we rend our imperfect flesh, so pale in comparison.
Even as we *do* this, we pray: *Change* us.
We want to *be* like You.
We are so fixed at the sight of Your flesh—
pure as a fish, clean as bread, where now You are broken,
In our grief we cry: Do You love us enough to *change* us?
Oh Son of God, can You undo what we have done?
We cannot help ourselves.
Without You, we are crucifiers, we are malignant thieves,
bombers of frail cities, marauders of innocence,
destroyers of children.

Without You, we are nothing.

Love us enough, Oh Christ of the Father,
to break us.
Love us enough to let us fail in this,
our newest enterprise:
   gluttons for the flesh of this,
   our God.

Certainly You love us this much: You won't *let* us kill You.

Then:
   On this still evening,
   in this clean space of time,
   into this purity of world and stopped history,
   into this newly carved tomb:
   we seed the flesh of God
   we seed the flesh of miracles,
   we place You oh so reverently into the ground
   and hope, once more,
   that You will multiply.

Oh Christ, innocent as bread,
bless us even as You remember this,
our slaughter.
Dress our skulls with the blood of Your newest passover.
Blanch our minds with purity so that,
like the virgin's womb,
our very thoughts may bid You:
Enter, and grow.

We remain here,
our faces fixed on the emptied stars,
our faces white as the stones at Your sepulchre,
brightened white at the sight of Your blood which now drips
from *our* hands,
and we remember Cain, and are afraid to judge him.

We pray:
Be our bodies: these simple prayers, seeds, loaves.
Be our blood, the fruit of Your passing.
Never let us do this again.
Wake us, Oh Bright Christ!
We want to *see* the sudden light that has fallen.

Be our bearings.
Be our pale, astonished face.
Pour Yourself through this mild day.
Emerge pure.

Your face forms itself
around our dumb tongues.
Silent. Elusive. Like snow.

Easter Week in Rome

Katie was eighteen, from Chicago,
bright and cheerful. We met
in the Galleria Borghese,
then sat outside on the steps,
where she read to me from her journal.
It was her last day in Rome.
Like other American students she
had jeans, a backpack, hitchhiked
everywhere, stayed in youth
hostels. We talked of Lollypop
panties, Babar and Celeste,
the Ngorongoro Crater. That night
we walked to my hotel near the
Campo dei Fiori. She had warm eyes
after the second glass of wine,
and a yes-no-maybe smile.
In the morning I lay in bed,
watching her dress and brush her
hair. The white straps of her bra
indented the baby fat of her shoulders.
Katie was talking of Florence
and Venice. Then she kissed
me goodbye, tasting of toothpaste.

Winter Afternoon at the Museum

From the Italian aristocracy
of the sixteenth century comes
the massive Farnese table,
marvelous to look at, inlaid
with marble and precious stones,
now under the hands of democratic
America. The Greek and Roman
sculpture of athletes and warriors
shows the perfect bodies of men,
with veined biceps, prominent
deltoids, lean and muscular bellies.

In *The Rape of Persephone*,
a sculpture by Bernini, we see a
bearded and powerful man carrying
a protesting girl in his arms,
the marble fingers of the man
indenting forever the marble thigh
of the girl. In the section of
European paintings are Dutch
landscapes, *Girl Eating an Apple*,
a satyr pursuing a nymph.
Some portraits are like old
friends: a Flemish girl with pink
cheeks, and a Florentine youth,
both smiling through the centuries.

Bruno the Magnificent

There was a time in San Francisco
when I ate alone at counters. One
restaurant in North Beach was my
favorite, with an ambience I needed.
Warm with Italians, it was filled
with people, and had a waitress
who called me Honey. At the time
this superficial human contact
was better than none at all.
Bruno worked most nights in this
restaurant. He was a combination
griddle man, short-order cook,
sandwich maker, and broiler chef,
one of the best. I enjoyed sitting
at the counter and watching him,
only a few feet away, expertly
grilling steaks and lamb chops.
Bruno knew he was good, and had
pride in himself and his trade.
He did honest work, socially
valuable. I loved to watch him
slice tomatoes and chop onions
with lightning movements. When
orders flew in from the waitresses,
I was amazed at his composure
and grace under pressure. Bruno
made sandwiches rapidly, but with
flair: patty melt, turkey club,

Monte Cristo, fried ham and egg,
grilled cheese and bacon. He
was a master of skillet cookery.
When he made an omelet, breaking
eggs with one hand, it was like
watching a ballet. Bruno was
friendly to me, knowing I was one
of his fans. On special nights
I ordered sautéed chicken livers
or shrimp scampi or veal scallopini
and mushrooms. With flames leaping
high around his skillet, Bruno
would pour in some oil, and once
again begin his superb performance.

In Praise of Radio

The golden age of radio flourished
from 1925 to 1950. It was a time
of exciting dramas, great comedians,
tense newscasts during World War
II. Whole families gathered
around streamlined wooden radios
with yellow dials. Now the
audience is composed of solitary
listeners, appropriate to our time.

I was a boy during the end of the
golden age of radio. With my
friends I saved cereal boxtops
and sent away for secret rings.
Every afternoon we came in to
listen to programs. Entranced by
the music, voice casting, and sound
effects, we made our own pictures,
developing our imaginations. We
listened to Superman, Gangbusters,
Tom Mix, Buck Rogers, Jack Armstrong,
Boston Blackie, Inner Sanctum, The
Shadow, The Lone Ranger, The Green
Hornet, and The House of Mystery.

A few words in praise of radio.
This intimate medium, a vital means
of communication, is free, in
the comfort of our homes. The
turning of a dial brings surprises,
random learning, endless discoveries.
Radio is efficient: we can listen
and be active at the same time.
It is our lecture room and concert
hall, an extension of the library,
our companion on winter nights.

The miracle of radio brings a wealth
of spoken words: *The Glass Menagerie*,
Orson Welles reading Walt Whitman,
a BBC portrait of George Orwell,
the soundtrack of *A Man for All Seasons*,
Ed Begley reading Mark Twain, the
rich Welsh voice of Dylan Thomas.

From abroad come a Congolese
mass, traditional Irish melodies,
songs and marches of the French
Foreign Legion. I love the
variety: German dances, then a
mystery serial, then jazz
introduced by a deep black voice.
On a Sunday morning I listen to
a medley of church hymns, the
old favorites, sung by a good
chorus. At other times, perhaps
during heavy rain or bitter cold,
I listen to folk songs from
the sixties, the voices of Paul
Robeson and Marian Anderson,
a choir of French schoolgirls
singing carols on Christmas Eve.

On Lincoln's Birthday we hear songs
of the Civil War, the voices of
the women contrasting marvelously
with the voices of the men.
Americana on the Fourth of July
brings melodies of Stephen Foster,
piano rags by Scott Joplin, ballet
suites of Aaron Copland, film scores
by Virgil Thomson. On Columbus
Day the Italian composers are
featured: Corelli, Tartini, Vivaldi,
Gabrieli, Respighi, Pergolesi,
Scarlatti, Monteverdi, Boccherini.

Alone, late at night, I listen to
Gregorian chants, but am not lonely.
Like a time machine, the radio
brings medieval music, highlights
from the *Messiah*, French dances
of the sixteenth century, ceremonial
music of the Renaissance. My
notebook of favorite compositions,
the record of an autodidact, now
runs to forty pages. Music is
first: I will put aside Shakespeare
to listen to Mozart. Schubert
is for poets, Haydn is like an
old friend, Bach and his sons
are the first family of music.
But the greatest of them all is
Beethoven. There is more feeling
in one of his sonatas than in
the symphonies of lesser composers.

The concert on New Year's Day in
Vienna is beamed by satellite all
over the world. The same woman
announces the selections in German,
French, English and Italian, a feat
in itself. I like to think of all
the people, children and adults,
who are listening to the music
of Johann Strauss: the different
countries, types of radios, rooms
and settings all over the globe.
It is a world holiday, something
to share and celebrate: we and the
planet have survived another year.

Letters from Concetta's Palmist

1

To those of you mostly left-
or right-hemisphere ruled,
these notes may waft of their own
will. They might, though, lie
unread, like scads of rich terrain
I may never read
north of the third wristlet,
that chain denoting will to endure. It might
occur to you to doubt my being
fit for what amounts to big time
slinging of ink. Let me
say I've a lengthy index
and the pinky's its match
in terms of flex-
ibility and pointedness. Plus
my kind of palm grid counts
for a lot: My islanded heart
line's deeply set and drooping
well nigh that of the head,
itself twice forked
and offset at an obtuse
angle at the line
of fate. Each of these bespeaks
a missive smith's trait.
You'll want to trust me on this.

2

How intermittent absenthandedness
sometimes gets the best
of me: I could swear
these mitts have ids
of their own! My aim mustn't
swerve from Concetta's
prime clay, which comes in
second only to the stratum above
seventh heaven itself. What
with her well-rounded Mount
of Venus—that pith
with hints of pink and blue
below the thumb—well hers has
yet to hollow out: A sign
she's lost no youth-
ful lust nor a jot of moxie. Not a bad
Venusian bulge for someone
56! And I've yet to touch
on dermaglyphs (like hieroglyphs,
behind which lie penchants rather than words).

3

"Say, fella, care to see my etchings? I've worlds
of those collectibles above
my wrists. You say you'd like
a print of one? Take *this*!"

I laugh to think of lines
she must have used to fend
off gallants. Yet hers
could be a tactful
sensibility. This was clear
in her faintest of glyphs, what
look like strands of scant
hair sweeping across the palm:
The finer each "hair," the more fine-grained
that person is. Her strands
swirled like diminutive
sylphs, until they merged
in a triad under Saturn,
beneath the middle finger.
Each pattern then began
to deepen: Those three lines
gathered into one
marked how self-will took
the upper hand at times. This held
true in both her deep-tracking,
feathered line of fate and heart-
line that lacked clear
beginning and end and arced
like a horizon inching its way around the sun.

4

I'd still like to slipstitch her hands into one
circular relief map of flesh,
palms turned up. That sphere
shape means she'll skirt
getting burned most times.
She has something coming to her—
that I know. And I don't
doubt she can be pure
left hand, subtle as a napping
dove. But like a bat
from you-know-where, her hand
could shoot off and I might be just
clipping right along,
doing my work, and she'd be flipping me
the bird for something I'd just said!
You see, the right hand likes to
leap headlong
in the objective world; the left
relies on innuendo. This fact
brings me to the gist
of her palms' score: If she played
her hands just so, she could
have it *made*—should it happen that
she doesn't have it now,
as both coasts teeter on each palm.

Gloss on Uncle Louie's Fingernails

"Okay, here," you say, hands splayed and sure
as a mime's. "Now get on with the gloss,
and don't give me lip." (I start to shake
the bottle of clear polish, my one prop;
the table quakes too as if an expert
Ouija player willed it.) "My son's taking the vow.

Can't look slack for the paisans," you vow.
Coating your thumbnails with shine, I nod: "Sure."
Such fingers on a GM factory hand! Expert
tapering, shapely waning moons: I gloss
a future where you're not the kids' fiscal prop....
Three clouds rising through this nail foretell a shake-

up. Cars might do you in. You got a fair shake
in that trade still; took the union vow
while your brother Sam, wheelchair his prop,
played violin, lullabied the clan. I'm sure
Sam wouldn't want you to grow lax, to gloss
over lumps such as these. All's *not* well; no expert

mind, Sam knew this before his expert
hands failed to tendonitis and the shake.
So, Unc, what to make of you? I'll spread gloss,
shellac both hands so they'll keep, like a vow.
Or you could paint your own nails, that's for sure.
Shine them every day, show them off, prop

ghosts of dead kin, as conjuror. Or prop
a string section, become expert
at churning wand and song and air. Cocksure
hands gesticulating full-time—in a shake,
you'd be a smash! You flail arms best, I vow.
Let them follow whims, these hands tipped with gloss.

The kids'll get by, your son beam like gloss
on his big day. Your lead will be his prop:
Just throw your arms toward his embrace and vow
there's beauty in all motion, as in expert
ballet. Then with an almost stifled shake
in your voice, wish them well. They're blessed, you're sure.

If you vow your way of blessing's not expert,
then gloss your wave's calligraphy, its shake,
and toss your hands, prop ghosts, the sky, what's sure.

Casting Hand Shadows

The Box Turtle.
You can stay in bed
and do this. Raise both hands like fists
of smoke rising from a bedmate's
cigarettes. The left behind
the right hand forms the bony
shell. Cold blood pulses
in your suspended hands,
but the reptile's in its favorite
habitat, head and limbs
withdrawn. It rests below
a calendar insisting days and nights.
October, the relentless awning.

Toby, the Dog.

Stay in bed. Ease up
your fists, allow
right hand to ascend slowly.
Cross two fingers of this hand
into a snout; thumb and index
finger of the left form a "V"
along the wrist. Your thumb-tail
does not wag. You're convinced
of two facts: It's November now;
dogs have visionary powers
to see ghosts.

Grandpa.

Old Italian men are easy. Leave
a space between middle and ring
finger of left hand for his
eye. You can achieve
93 years of Roman
nose in the curve
of an index finger joint.
You enjoy looking up
at him—more animated
than he ever was, he looks
down at your life.

The Goose.

Your two palms must face you.
Right hand passes in front
of left until thumbs
intersect. Here's a goose
fleeing its reflection
in the water,
your two hands. January,
and the bed is a stencil
of your body.

The Bactrian Camel.

Here your arms come into play.
Right arm falls into a lean
throat while fingers act
as head and mouth.
Left arm undulates
two humps: One to store
rancor; the other,
longing. You've convinced
yourself you're living
on the largest continent. The beast
and you share the weight of February.

The Man.
You take pride in your agile
fingers. Here's the dexterity
test: Both hands must appear
to be holding on
to something. Right
hand on top of left
curves slowly,
as on the frog of a violin
bow. Left hand forms
a bottomless cup
below, as if
to catch
a sound.
You became a violinist
once. You turned
to ventriloquism
for yourself,
throwing unheard
sounds and words
you wanted.

Get out of bed for this.
Stand up, face
the wall, move
positioned hands
away from it. The man grows
on you. The two of you decide
to throw
a party in honor
of his birthday
this twenty-ninth
day of March.

Astonishment.
You're an expert
as you stand now, hands
poised like a conductor's.
You can orchestrate the abstract
into shadow; give astonishment
any shape: Let go of the violin
bow and it's a mouth
agape. The new
curve of this
hand might be
him. But let it
be Grandpa on the wall again, seeing
himself a youth in April.

Emanuela in the New World Garden

finds Arizona, Vegas, Idaho pretty
much one place, one promise: One palm tree
in every other pot stands an off-chance
of bearing flesh
only ripest
pineapples can boast.
     If she's not
found bowing among flora, try the wilderness of green on green, where flocks
play 21, placing low bets—
a couple of bucks or so.
She'll be the one whose hand's just
indicated "hit" once more. One flick
of the wrist and she's off.
      Watch her
watch the dealer shuffling the deck so
fast the cards are blurred
waves not even the Mediterranean
she's memorized
could match.

And what that dealer,
Rich (from New Jersey—they all wear name
tags here) lets her get away
with! Once all bets are placed
she reaches past the chalked-in sphere
to touch her chips, unreal
to her as shrunken jets
enclosed in lighted circles
on test pilots' screens.

There's no doubt
she was raised to play this card
game in which each query and response calls
for gesture, plus a tweak
or two of luck.
And faith, which she pronounces
"fate." One word
she credits with having coaxed her to this
part of the world.
                    "Fate" and the few
things she gathered from her whatnot:
The Mary statuette, Lotto
card tucked at her chest. Plus
a suitcase of provolone
and a change of clothes   .
for casino nights
when she pulls up a stool at Rich's place,
places her bet—fifty cents
more than the last, then closes her eyes,
blazing a bird's trail
with her hand
across the green
felt, meaning "I'm good.
This time I'll stay."

Pullover

For Emanuela Cardinale, my grandmother

You've heard that grandmother jive:
"Homemade just for you, darling!"
But the good deed seemed better on
her lap—skein of handspun

corkscrewing its way into a sleeve.
Still, you forgave her well-meant
effort, as she held forth what
you hoped was fact: A bona fide

ideal, the promise all would be OK,
even in the worst cold snap.
Think of the first chance
you had to try it on. Arms thrown up

in wishbone halves, you waited
as she cajoled the sweater
on. "Bend your elbows,
kiddo!" You agreed to, right

then left. She insisted "Wear this
or you'll catch your death of—" What?
The neckhole stuck; a vise clamped
on your head. With your pleas

of "Grandma, help, it's dark!"
the goosebumps formed. Tough luck:
She meant to get the sweater on.
In one last tug there was a vague

lull, "*There.*" Your ears returned.
She spoke: "It fits! Go on.
Have fun. You'll keep
much warmer than the rest."

Lullaby

Softly, so softly, the snow falls.
A child is being sung to sleep.
Softly, so softly, the voice sings.
It tells him of the falling snow.
Softly, so softly, she gets up,
afraid she may awaken him.
Softly, so softly, he drifts on,
amid the blankets' high snow banks.
His mother's man, he settles there,
oblivious to cold outside.
Softly, so softly, the snow falls.
Softly, so softly, the song ends.

Early Afternoon, Chautauqua

Out on the lake, an outbound boatman calls
        to a small boat headed back. In the square,
the bang of workmen drowning out the yells
        corrects more damage of a winter's wear.

We park our Cherokee along the street
        and walk, reacting to the morning's word.
We vow to give that cancer one good fight.
        Meanwhile, in Miller Park the clipped shrubs nod.

Knolls of its Palestine are clean again,
        and ghosts of the once-fat orators lurk
in the dimmed, everchanging pavilion,
        where occasionally, too, there's Bible talk.

America's "most American thing,"
        this melding of strong will and miracle.
At home, polled Indians promise uprising
        in courts to regain townlands once tribal.

We claim our own damaged years together,
        having by craft prolonged their run of luck,
knowing they could never last forever.
        We give the boatman a departing look

217

and head back to the car, ready to face
    the upbeat nods that neither of us needs.
Two men are setting marigolds in place
    to dress the park's still budless flowerbeds.

Collegially weaving brief, quiet lanes
    of shops and grand hotels toward revival
and shaded homes are hale, young denizens,
    drawn by a hope of honing some lapsed skill.

They homestead like the land's first pioneers,
    trusting a providence to see them through,
as we will do through your brief treatment's course,
    hopeful to build back with what we have to.

Drawn mainly by the shock or old romance
    to this lakefront's cool, woodsy reminder
to shed all past urban deprivations,
    we leave, thankful to still have each other.

The Caves of Love

Lodged in the early morning, in dark pews,
away from the main aisle, each week they wind
sniffling and wheezing closer to life's end,
grey faces grown as doubtful as church dues,
where just their clothes, grown shabbier and odd,
and their own body smells increase each week,
as lighted, perfumed candles stall the reek
and incense curves man's worldly thoughts to God.

Listless and nasal, seeping as some mist,
the stale air grows more stagnant with their drone,
invading both my thinking and their own,
like some marred surface giving way to rust
as their own homes give way each year to rot,
the ruin offset, they hope, by stronger love
or obligation to brute force above.
They draw to trappings like an opiate.

Hobbled or humpbacked, bobbing as they move,
they seem as trolls or victims of long wars,
their outer forms betraying inner scars.
And winter does make this place seem a cave.
Light barely breaks in through the speckled air,
and echoes hollow in their each response.
A cave remembered from a legend once—
a Venusberg or hill or dragon's lair.

I try to think on them as they were young—
their parents beaming in a Sunday best—
bright children at a first communion feast
eager to taste God with each pushing tongue,
cowed by the sisters as they must have been;
and how the aging sisters struggle hard,
failing to keep quick children on their guard
who follow them each year in one communion.

They pray for their own soul's recovery,
the hardy independence of the old,
and for lapsed children, missing from the fold,
cut off as lambs by gorse along the way,
knowing how all youth go to meet the world,
fresh with illusion, eager to begin,
and how a world's indifference shuts them in.
Each meek adjustment spots an inner mold.

It is a club for which I seem the priest,
where just the dying gain full membership
and only death can free one from its grip—
a horror club, whose restless coughs persist
and camphor makes one wish he'd never come.
But who can face a world devoid of love?
Quiet and anxious, keeping hopes alive,
I feel the dwindling number bulk like doom.

After Spring Storms

Checking the olive groves after a storm,
seeing among the gnarled limbs
which lightning struck, which must be grafted,
and which, come Palm Sunday, must be watched
from the theft of town boys,
I begin to understand something of farming.
I think of Noah's dove,
Claudius dipping lobster at Capri,
the smooth, rich, buttery taste of the oil,
my own mortality,
and the immemorial stones imbedded in the land.

Flowers

One could almost taste the straw red onions
hanging there in the stall above
the fake straw flowers one would almost swear were real,
and which even in winter one could buy
for only a few pennies.
Or if real flowers were what one wanted
to bring spring to one corner of a room,
they were there in another stall,
more expensive,
wafting their sweet aromas for passers-by,
fooling no one with their fragrances,
not even the small, disinterested flies.

Library Tapestry

That threaded brilliance, Hannibal in silk
gaping the elephants and fat as grouse,
his faded flesh the color of whole milk
against an armor's faded, silvery blues,
preserves the man as he was pictured once:
He stands among six well-groomed elephants,
plotting a final march on frightened Rome,
perfect except for stains left by the years,
which even careful cleanings cannot dim,
weaving a second tale upon his first.
One stain, the faded yellow of beef broth,
suspends his middle. I watch the tapestry,
my mother reading Invernizio
aloud, and think the stain some blood, for she
has told me bloodstains fade a yellow.
Perhaps some prince was knifed against the cloth
as in her books? Savonarola waged
his war with Rome and pillaged Florence both
its art and men after the weaver staged
this scene; his heresy might cause such stains.
Or old Lorenzo, vomiting his pains,
dying, refusing finally to give in
to that disloyal monk he'd valued once,
deprived at last of his last absolution,
resting where his sleep's sweeter than a stone's.
Her voice absorbs. Caught in its dulling rounds
of family feuds and deadly treacheries,
I fight my boyish mind for English sounds,

staring beyond our arbor at the trees
that weave the borders of her Roman world
until I'm drowsed like Florence going mad,
or Hannibal among his milling herd,
waging a future, harmless, reckless raid
like Charles against a Vatican Swiss Guard,
staining my war with drops of lemonade.

Blue Haze

Those early spring mornings
when air is so green with foliage
that haze strikes everything
eventually give way
to summer's burning sun.
So, too, those darkened rooms,
clouded by an eye's blue haze
after bright sun, turn clear:
table edges, lamps, chairs.

I wait as each familiar shape
comes into line again,
gaining a freshness lost
in familiarity
to glory finally
like rainstruck leaves.

You say, "It's like those poems
that blur until a phrase or word
puts everything in place,"
and offer me a beer,
then check the barbecue.

Inside the smoke, flames sear and dim.

But this blue haze is more
a smoke of burning leaves
tearing the eye.
It warns of excess.
"Like fires," you say,
"burning a troubled and infected air."

Buffalo/Stasis

Another heavy snowstorm. The air
crackles with sounds of closings—
city offices, banks, schools.
Red Jacket's monument in the
cemetery disappears in
blowing snow and sculpted drifts.

Bidding the day to stop is like
King Canute commanding waves.
Snowplows become futile acts
of will as much as poets' naive
promises of timelessness:
Children keep being born; stomachs
ache for food; and thoughts go
racing to tomorrow.

A Paris velodrome gets my own thought,
the cyclists spinning breezes with
their wheels in the patterned commotion
of an event marred only by accidents.
You look up from your growing afghan
and ask if I would like some tea.

Outside are hearty welcomes, handshakes,
bought drinks and, soon to be seen,
green grass blades eating at the snow.

Cairo

Cairo,
murmuring.
Morning dust cloud
rising.
Tissued garlic
high on creaking carts.
Swish of calabeya.

I seek you in the Kahn
mid crimson phials
of perfumes from Khartoum.

I seek you mid the spices,
the red hibiscus,
devil's eye and camomile,
the searing ginger root.

I think I catch a glimpse of you,
a hand
beating orange copper,
twisting sultry silver,
melting luscious gold.

But you are fleeting
as the boy, the child,
the twinkle in his eye,
the would-be lust
I hope for
as he looks at me.

Veiled feluka
glide upstream to Luxor
with needle mast
to pierce my sleep
to stain my bed

Egyptian red.

Person to Person

Somewhere in the Adriatic
between Ancona and Split
the shipboard radio operator
Fabrizio (Milanese)
tried to pick me up.

He had naval experience:
20 years on the open seas
brass buttons with tiny anchors
blue striped epaulettes.

He repeatedly repeated my name
brushed my knee
looked me straight in the eye
"Separata?"
"Ma come lo sapevi?"

Then your secretary answered
my "person to person"
I choked, sighed,
gave myself away.

She too is part of our legend
and Fabrizio awaits my second crossing.

Gelosia

Women like that
always bothered me
with breasts protruding,
bouncing breasts
taxing flimsy bras
stretching stringy straps
with their
excessive
weight.

Women in tight jeans
forever caressing buttocks
writhing, shifting
twisting, rubbing
glancing,
winning glances
tossing wetted wisps,
nipping, sucking
puckered, heaving.

Women with parted lips
called Deborah.

May I Dance for You

May I dance for you
my puppeteer?
The slightest tug
upon my strings
results desired response,
wild gesticulations
with the minimum
of effort
debt-equity conversion
brought to the nth degree,
leveraging perfected.

Only a small request
my handsome puppeteer:
in your loving
exercise of power—please—
direct in harmony
the movement
of my parts
lest
in your quest
to have me dance
a perfect role
you tear me
limb from limb.

Fossalto

Ventun'ora
tolling
over the bandaged town,
blazened church steps
pocked and polished
drip
unanswered
prayers:
"Che Dio ti bendica"
"Che la Madonna ti aiuti"
fall on wooden ears.

Sunday morning
climbing cobbles
on the way to Mass
eyes avert
from Angelina's wrought iron railing
unfurled there
red star on candid field
bludgeoned ensign
of her call to rank.

Bouche de la Seine

Bouche de la Seine
welcoming with wanton lips
the full Atlantic's
crystal flow
while we above
discuss propriety
morality
normality
and sex.

A fleeting glance your way
might well correct
our clouded sight
redress
our errant ways

An open ear
poised close to hear—

Speak truth to us
where error reigns
where hatred gains
sigh—love.

Victor

Church bells sing in jubilation
proclaiming to the world
my friend
is dead

The learned bishop tells me
he sees clearly now
where once he needed glasses.
He has scaled the wall
crossed the threshold,
enjoys eternal peace.

I
hear
only the silence,
the pause,
before he called me
sweetheart.

Triptych, Outside of Siena

Ancient man on the other hand, neither awake nor in dreams,
knew of that primal cosmic loneliness...
　　　　　—Ludwig Binswanger

1. Hilary

Spinning and turning,
the fire clotting still,
the ring stretching out

without frame, without grace,
now rejoining the train
come to gather dry claims

outside time, without space.
And the tribe takes us in
where the flame circles light

till the cock crows the day
and the words disappear
with the sun—outside Siena.

2. Noreen

"Dig in!"—she yells—"Be silent.
Be still. Fail your self.
Touch the well through the hole.

"Don't shatter. Grasp hands.
Let me dare you within, far outside this dragnetting despair.

"Father drank mostly tears;
let me hide the crabbed stars
where his cigarette flared.

"Let me draw you the pledge
that will clown in delight,
how to drink mandrake root.

"I seek redemption.
Don't falter. Don't fret.
Drive this nail through my foot

"and the blood will pool out
and my skin will rub thin
as we climb our stone hill..."

3. Maria

And soon Mary's tears disappeared
in the folds of her lace: "He
left me but oh, how I do love
him still. My children, at home,

"scrape alone with their plays
that won't chill to the bone
while I clasp all my will,

"spilled somewhere, far within
this long crouch of the night
on my bed—outside Siena."

Imaginary Slides besides Inside, upon Revere's Mare

grazie, Italo Svevo/Calvino

astride some chair, cigarette lit, wishing to slide *medias res*
off the typewriter like Saul of Tarsus unsaddled by shadows, yet
nothing but smoke rings ascending to darken my streetlamp (but O,
for just one rind as my lonely trope for salvation. Keep up
your delusions. Light up another: *in nomine nomini, res*: the truth
could arrive well denounced by commercials delighting to please
all our riddles departing Eraclitan shores, & better this merry-go-
rounding besides inside upon Revere's mare than attending on
walled streets some mooning ascendant/descendant from horse.
Such *mal de mer* could clear out puckings & suckings & drippings
from gangrenous sores as mucus from pipelines & eros from scores
of our dearly departed ejected from 7-11 family stores: the 60's
my friend, come home to score as the sink's faucet next to my bedroom dribbles dark fragrances well measured out with more patience
than most coffeespoons) & poor mr. eliot your proofrocks, your
wastelands converted to whiskey rebellions & scabrous slums
eradicated in search of new heights: Chicago skyline, your trojan
praxes patrolling hyde parks, & still & always: the poets, they're
coming! The poets are coming with shovels clenched / mikes at
their throats / wands in their hands would deliver mankind
from salvation; dearprecious amphor, how carry
my smokings with such coffeespoons?

NOTES

1. "grazie": The prefactory "thanks," besides serving an ancient "prefacing" function, is also a "gifting back" to the two sources (*La conscienza di Zeno* & *Mr. Palomar* especially) who generated/guided my own. See also John Barth's *The Friday Book*, in particular "Tales within Tales within Tales."

2. "the 60's / my friend..." At least one ought to be aware of the current revivalism(s), as the labour(s) of tunneling through from the outside to the inside, back & forth, keeps going on...

3. "proofrocks...whiskey rebellions": The free association(s) made between "proofs" of TSL's origin and connotative/denotative resonances to whiskeyproof a/o rebellion are simply that; the reader might derive what most pleases...

4. "dearprecious amphor": The *vas* containing magical unguents that are poured upon one's ears/body/spirit are not translatable via the *logos*. Words are only signs that attempt paradoxically to carry across reality. But only smoke remains of life lived (or, even better, ashes). Yet we always desperately try to deny our ultimate fear(s) by, among other means, the art of graphology—of scratching signs & senhals in the sands of eternity, of which of course we can know absolutely nothing.

1.1 "Such *mal de mer*": See Georges Bataille, *Erotism: Death & Sensuality* (City Lights Books, 1986) for contrast(s) & comparison(s). Eros is still (& always?) a frighteningly repugnant/attracting *daimon* for us all...so is it's counterpart sister, Thana...

The Journeys Back Home

sola resurgit vita...

Because now the walls standing fall & seas dry at will,
because my gate now swings wide & light simmers in
just keep on walking, you must keep on walking; how
narrow the Word & the Song matters still...
& what kind of man makes me turn,
makes me sense who / where i am? Please
tell me who, please tell me when; wherefore
Dear Cat, near old window-sills i sit & listen
to mornings breaking
& keep on re-reading dead Merton
& oh how so cleanly the same
your two trips
& how so deep, & how so sweet both
your claims to the heart: such
infinite gracings your brotherloves
pulling my snailfooted pace to the core...
How else one give love simple thanks
if not by sharing it back? Therefore the truth
of your paths that uncloud through moonvalleys
& milkwoods to mirrors & snares of the sun
until most fat camels come slouching through needles
within the shut eyes of the Son...And yet
let some days be not far
when Lord of the Dance
you take me homeward to weave
the same song for i, too,
my brother my sister
am strung on the road to find out
& yes, this i know: sitting with Buddhas
& chanting with wild bulls at four
while sailing long boats to the shore
as, one hosanna, your stillness comes in
where i finally stand at the start
again & again & again...

So just keep on pushing where spaces become
the One Light: & then the child-loves
& and man-loves & all woman-loves
we wanted so hard to take in
could tell us earthlove is all
bitterroot from seawaves...
Oh, would you remember
the One
neither number nor icon,
not monosyllable
& neither sunlight nor the moonshadows
but
the Still Center becoming
if / when our gates
would gape open
& calm swam the fishes
& tall played the grasses
with this one song
of woman & man
forever splitting the stillness of noon.

The Language of Bed

Your hands creep
    like little verbs,
      up the trellis of my ribcage.

My fingers tickle tiny
    adjectives
    on the "V"
    of your thighs.

My bones lay on your bones
    like a compound word
    body to body:
    unhyphenated.

Your mouth leaves
    poems on my lips,
    vowels in my ears.

Your penis: sweet as French,
    classy as Latin,
    rhythmic as Shakespeare;
    dipping in, dipping in;

My hips rhyme and rhyme!
Come slide your slippery noun
    into mine

And we will twist, and slip
    and whisper in:
The vocabulary
    of the skin.

The Lioness Lullabye

The crickets squeak in the Baobab tree,
The leopard's across the Serengeti,
The hyena's not hungry for lion today—
So sleep, little cub, and dream of your prey
As we lie on our pillows of grass
And the moonrise is just like a dance!
      The zebra are hidden in stripes
        Just a flicker of black and a murmur of white
The night is all ringing with stars
I can feel the wind pound in our hearts
Dream of the hunt and the leap!
Dream of the throat in your teeth,
Dream of your belly all swollen with meat
And sleep, little lion cub, sleep.

Heat

95 at 11 PM
window fan whirs
lamp clicked off,
like snakes
our bones swallow
the warm dark

no words, no wit tonight
no pecking, or pawing—
just slow/slow
touch-for-touch
(streetlamp makes ghost-silver cheekbone
hollow eye)

aware only of the me
you inhabit,
hips so drenched in heat
we use it
like a dark-red clay
and mold it to
the shape that sings!

The Unborn Child as Poem

I push you / out of me
syllable by syllable
a long piece of typing paper
from this clicking place of birth
trailing your baggage of placenta

    your eyes will rhyme
    your hands will rhyme
    your feet will rhyme

I have written your hair to curl
I have written your fingers to clutch at mine
I have written your verbs into feet

I open my legs to push you into the room
be born!

be born!
I open my legs to push you into the room

I have written your verbs into feet
I have written your fingers to clutch at mine
I have written your hair to curl

Your feet will rhyme
your hands will rhyme
your eyes will rhyme

trailing your baggage of placenta
from this clicking place of birth
a long piece of typing paper
syllable by syllable
I push you / out of me

Rotting Fruit

my little babe is dead
milk drips from my red-silk nipples,
twin rivers.
I need his little lips to suck me dry.
    Put the honey back into the bee—
    My little babe is dead!
And I am Mama-no-more
Mama-No-More.

Concentration Camp

children's bodies
thrown like litter
pipecleaner legs bent

the maimed, the hollow-eyed
the starved, the molested
the burned, the blinded
the frozen, the slashed, the raped
the ripped-sewn-together-freaks
the ashes...

     who threw the babies in
     to burn alive?
     they scream in my belly
     the babies torn from mothers
     like flesh from bone

layers of men in graves
blood and mud and men
blood and mud and men
wives open-legged before the officers

     meat hooks, crosses, ovens
     the maimed, the slashed, the frozen
     who threw the babies in?
     (flesh from bone/
     layers of men)
     they burned alive!

the wives, the gas, the ashes, the graves
who threw the babies in?
they scream in my belly
and burn in my heart

Our Lady's Field—Vignettes

1

Unshaven old man
sits early in the morning
on a folding chair
in the doorway of his tiny tailor's shop,
knees crossed and locked at the ankles
like a circus contortionist,
the silver needle hems and mends
hems and mends

2

Old woman, potato-shaped, cigarette dangling,
pulls an empty shopping cart with one hand
her middle-aged retarded daughter
with the other
they walk, old-lady-pace
down Sixteenth Street to the Avenue.
The daughter looks at me with recognition
I attempt a smile,
the mother—suspicious heart shrunk by her life's work,
stares and demands my apathy

3

Leaning on her daughter
the old, old black lady
walks tiny-child-steps,
her cheekbones shine like brown polished stones
white sweaters pad her bony shoulders
on this fair autumn day
and one little white cornrow braid
swings side to side across her forehead
a slowing pendulum,
she smiles at me
she is already an angel

Who Threw the Stone?

Dark curls bounced
where the blanket fell away
from the girl's still face;
I closed my eyes—
as if the medics
were carrying her
through my living room.

Was the stone
(round and heavy)
just a stoop away
on the rocky ground,
or carried all day
like a black promise
in a dark pocket?

Was it from the village wall
a stretch away—
rough and hard
in the other child's palm
            there
and then gone.

Drive to the Country

up ahead
a rounded mountain rises
like a sigh in the darkness

car rumbles and purrs
down the curve of black

in the backseat
my little boy dreams

three pearls of light
in darkness
each angle—
point of brightness:

the ghost-faced moon
   my sleeping son
         and I.

In Memory of Jenny and Evelyn
Who Were Playing When the Stoop Collapsed

Your stoop is where you dream your life.
It is your homebase
 there your bestfriend's whispered secrets
 (warm puffs of breath behind cupped brown hands)
 are delivered like separate beads of understanding.

From there you assemble the mysteries:
 the drunk staggers,
 the addict steals from his sister,
 the deliveryman leers,
 the baby's mother smiles,
 father comes home after work, to swing you
 way up to the blue sky
 laughing for joy.

It's where your first boyfriend finds you
when he rides over on his bike from around the corner
to smile at you
 waiting your turn for jump rope.

It's your seat on the hot summer night
 as your older brother points out the constellations
 he studied in science—
 all shimmering shapes and magic names
 suspended dizzyingly up, up
 over the illuminated buildings that eclipse the moon
 and erase the horizon.
It's where the season's first snowflake
 falls on your own unique tongue.

Where life is as endlessly repeated
 as the drunk's midnight patter
 the baby's first word
 the gossip's last tidbit;
 and reinvented by every child
 who dreams her life
 spinning out
 from the stone center of the shining web.

It is where as Chinese-school graduates
you move up,
step at a time,
with each correct guess,
until you sit in the doorway;
of what should have been,
the beginning of your lives.

"Chinese school" is a stoop game played in Brooklyn.

Dream of Flying

No other nonhuman creatures but the birds utter human words and phrases.
                    —*The Life and Lore of the Bird*

This dream of flying
has no sex in it
but is all a flight of language.
She said do you like my candy,
plot, stanza, sense, villanelle?
I replied
if on Monday, ripeness is all
I am Tuesday,
like a mobius strip
the convolutions of the brain
will fly you into another dimension.
She flew into me
saying
lagniappe, zygodactyl,
take a plane to desert moon.
I replied
as we grow older the world grows
stranger,
time, like sparks from a flint,
suddenly flares
into revelation,
lights our way
then plunges us
into the deep and dazzling darkness
in which we fly
or fall.
She said
in luminous, empyrean cadenzas of light,
when all time is eternity and a perpetual sabbath,
my body is echo chamber to the world,
resounding the voices of a thousand small birds.

A Modern Odyssey

Since I don't cut the grass any more
than I have to,
wind turns it to waves,
making a ghostly and grounded galleon
of our rented old gray house,

staggered brick chimney the sagging mast
above the widow's walk
where, after cleaning, cooking, writing,
weaving and re-weaving the same and varied patterns,
waiting for me, you look out
for my return, my head,
bobbing above high weeds,
filled with tales of siren and cyclops
but no Calypso nor princess Nausicaa,
anchored by a briefcase stuffed
with student papers that wander
after wanderings
(and will too soon set me straying again from you)
"I'm home," I shout,
sailing past the jetty of the front porch
into the harbor of your encircling arms.

Appomattox

1

We begin at the Confederate Cemetery,
where eighteen Rebels, ten unnamed,
and an unknown Union soldier are buried,
killed on April 9, 1865,
the day Lee surrendered to Grant.
A warm spring day in Virginia,
trees and bushes beginning to bud,
crocuses and hyacinths already blooming,
my wife and I walk single file
between the red dirt ruts
of the Old Richmond-Lynchburg Stage Road,
where soldiers of North and South
marched and fought
during the last days of the War.
We feel the strong spirit of this place,
feel we are among the remaining Rebels,
remnants of Lee's once vast Army of Northern Virginia,
heads high, marching to Surrender Triangle,
measured tread a requiem for a fallen cause,
weapons in one hand, paroles in the other,
Union troops silently lining both sides of the road,
their rifles shifted to present arms,
while General Gordon, observing the honor
accorded to his exhausted men,
rears up his black horse
and points his sword to his boot toe
in a gesture of recognition and surrender.

2

To escape the carnage
Wilmer McLean moved his family
from their Manassas plantation,
where the Civil War's first major battle was fought,
to the village of Appomattox Court House,
where, as if in fated rendezvous,
the War's last battles were fought,
the Surrender signed in McLean's parlor
because April 9 fell on Palm Sunday
and the courthouse was closed.

3

When Lee, on his horse, head bowed, returns
from the McLean house,
great, gray masses of soldiers
break ranks to surround
and hail and cheer him,
tossing hats, haversacks, weapons in the air.
Without a word, realizing
he has surrendered,
saving certainly doomed lives,
they hold their silence.
Many finally break down
and weep.

4

From the back of countless covered wagons
Union soldiers hand out food
to Confederates, who haven't eaten for three days,
their supplies cut off,
the Rebel Army trapped by Yankees,
over seven thousand men lost and eight generals,
including Lee's son Custis, captured
in the single battle of Sayler's Creek.
"My God," Lee says,
"has the Army of Northern Virginia dissolved?"

5

On the fourth anniversary of the firing on Fort Sumter,
at Surrender Triangle
in front of the Widow Kelley's cabin
long lines of Confederates give up
their munitions and weapons,
rifles stacked in the shape of small tepees,
and furl their battle flags,
while, from dawn to afternoon, the Yankees
stand by the road at silent attention.
One Rebel says he now has neither home nor country.
Some speak to their weapons,
say farewell before parting with them.
Another addresses his rifle as his wife
and kisses her.

6

From Surrender Triangle,
hand in hand, we walk back
down this quiet country road
and stop again at the graveyard,
where crocuses and hyacinths bloom.
The names of the identified soldiers
are followed by their rank, regiment, and
home state.
This land
they and their unkown
Union and Confederate comrades
fought upon
is now their home,
as it is ours.

Why I Don't Speak Italian

God knows, teaching the Renaissance I could use it.

Every Sunday and national holiday
during World War II
my Italian grandfather raised the American flag
up the pole planted in our front lawn.

My Aunt Clara told childhood stories
about being called *dago* and *guinea*,
hurt by friends' juvenile jokes:
"When Italian tires become flat
dago wop, wop, wop, wop."
Once, when I was four,
to console my swarthy Aunt I told her
she was almost as beautiful
                        as a blonde.

In wartime movies my buddies and I saw
white-skinned Germans stand firm and doomed
while a tan Italian surrendered in the Sahara to Bogart,
sang *Aida* and fixed the stalled American tank.

The teenaged girls who flourished on Bay Ridge Avenue
passing by our whistles and wisecracks
giggled and flashed back in English only.

To visit Rome, Venice, and Florence,
where I could identify Da Vinci's drawings
by their left-handed strokes,
I bought a recorded language course.
The first disk was cracked, skipped and repeated.

Oh I know enough, when teaching sonnets,
to explain why Teutonic English is rime-poor
compared to vowel-rich, mellifluous Italian.
I even recite Dante's Ulysses:
       Considerate la vostra semenza
fatti non foste a viver come bruti
ma per sequir virtute e canoscenza.

Too old to gape on corners any more,
at times, when I see a stunning
fair-skinned and magnificent blonde,
I also know how my dark, civilized
Roman ancestors felt
when they crossed the Rhine
and gazed,
speechless,
upon the giant, golden-haloed barbarians.

Elegy

1

Eyes shining like wetted sapphires
my sanguine grandfather
pealed out against the night
"let there be light, let there be more light"
quoting poets and madmen he went down
to turn with friends the winding press
expressing grape's blood, carmine,
heady, fragrant juice in great wooden barrels
and touched singing glasses
to toast the first bottle
in their Redman's "freedom, friendship, charity"
Salud!

2

He journeyed past Liberty and the Island
to a dark wine cellar in this new world
journeyed to light overwhelming hills and fields
a fertile land more bright than haloes
where he moved amid the blaze of noon
through cloisters of vine trellises
rows of tomato plants, viburnum shrubs
gnarled apple trees, smooth silver trees
of figs fleshed purple scarlet
figs swelling among susurrant leaves
he moved blessing with fruitful gifts
in the garden green I followed.

3

Wine glass at hand
ear turned toward radio
listening to his native opera
ruddy face lifted in the hymn of eating
wine-dipped bread
peaches from his trees floating in the ruby glass
face intent downward in the labor of cutting
gold cane swinging, spats white under striped pants
taking us to the far cemetery to honor our dead
on lambent Sundays
he dealt the cards
so I won.

4

Gentle man, groaning, from the dying bed
rose on your last day out of our room
not to disturb my dreams
went gently down to that dark wine cellar
let the bright sun wake to realms of light
in this body and blood
dark fire wine still flows
I followed, seeing face to face
found you fallen on that last day
(not to disturb my dreams you rose!)
and trying to rise again
your shining eyes closed.

Photograph of My Mother as a Young Girl

She wasn't looking
when they took this picture:
sitting on the grass
in her bare feet
wearing a cotton dress,
she stares off to the side
watching something on the lawn
the camera didn't catch.
What was it?
A ladybug? A flower?
Judging from her expression,
possibly nothing at all,
or else
the lawn was like a mirror,
and she sat watching herself,
wondering who she was
and how she came to be there
sitting in this backyard,
wearing a cheap, white dress,
imagining that tomorrow would be like all her yesterdays,
while her parents chatted
and watched, as I do
years later,
too distantly to interfere.

The Garden on the *Campagna*

Noon—and the shadows of the trees
have fallen from the branches. The frail
blue butterflies still flutter hungrily
among the weeds, and a few pale flowers
climb up the yellow hill and fade away.
The scarred brown lizards lie immobile
in the dust. A line of ants
picks clean the carcass of a frog.

Only the smallest things survive
in this exhausted land the gods
so long ago abandoned. Time
and rain have washed the hero's face
from off the statue. The sundial
stands perpetually in shade.

The bankrupt palace still remains
beyond the wall that summer builds,
doors bolted shut, the roof caved in,
the ancient family without heirs,
and one half-blind old man who sits
each day beside the empty pond
mumbling to himself in dialect.
The village boys throw stones at him,
but he will never leave, and there
is no one left who knows if he
was once the servant or the sire.

The Journey, the Arrival, and the Dream

1

You're here. Finally. After hours in a hot compartment
on the slow train coming through the mountains.
And everywhere the same crowd of brown-toothed men
and fools in uniform stood smoking in the shade,
waiting on the platform as if each train
might bring the fortune missing from their lives.

As the local dragged
from one such dusty station to another,
did it cross your mind that this same village
lost in the dry mountains was all
there ever would be, that your life was bound
by the four walls of your compartment, and the women,
their brats, and blank-eyed daughters were freer
than you would ever be again? That the pale clerk
behind the counter at the last connection,
looking at his watch, nodding at everything you said,
had not understood a word?
                              No matter. You are here:
a woman still young enough to feel pain
as undeserved. And no time left for bitterness.
The car is waiting. One short drive and then
your final destination,
an ancient house on a yellow hill. Reality
more sinister than any clerk's revenge.

2

It is late afternoon,
and you are standing in a room where the servant
has already left and shut the door. The wood-framed windows
look down a sloping valley somewhat bleached in haze,
and you lean against the windowpanes amazed
that these mountains and the mountains there beyond them,
dark green blurring into blue, then into grey and black,
could have been the obstacles you passed.
Journeys are the despair before discovery,
you hope, wondering if this one ends.

Emptying your pockets on the dresser, notice
how carefully you put down all the useless keys
and currency you've brought from home, so terrified
of scratching the patina of the varnished wood
that innocently reflects the lamp, your hand, the curtains,
and the badly painted cherubs on the ceiling
who ignore you. Light a cigarette and watch
the lazy smoke creep up and tickle them
to no effect and realize you don't
belong here in their world where everything
is much too good for you, and though the angels
will say nothing, they watch everything you do.

3

But you are also in another room
finishing a letter in a language
you don't understand, your dark hair pulled
back loosely in a bun, and the crucifix
you bring everywhere set upon the desk
like a photograph from home.
                              Long ago,
had someone told you this would happen,
you would have thought then only of escape,
of returning to yourself. Instead you feel calm,
relaxing in this dying body
like a swimmer on a sunlit beach, and death,
the light you cannot look directly into, seems
as illuminating and warm.
                              Now the hand, your hand,
is sealing up the envelope, and you turn to face
an old man in a dark-red uniform.
He nods. You speak affectionately.
And word by word the language too becomes
familiar. But still you wonder,
who is he? Husband? Servant? Ancient friend?
Too late. He takes the envelope and leaves.

The door has closed and from outside you hear
his footsteps fade into the murmuring
of swallows in the eaves.
                        Where do they come from?
Why can't you see them from the window?
No use to look. There's only this blue patch
of sky and endlessly empty afternoon,
where the light is fading.
                        Close your eyes. Accept
that some things must remain invisible.
Somewhere in the valley a grey fox
is moving through the underbrush. Old men
are harvesting the grapes. And the dark swallows
you cannot see are circling in the sunlight
slowly gliding downward in the valley
as if the light would last forever.

An Emigré in Autumn

Walking down the garden path
From the house you do not own,
Once again you think of how
Cool the autumns were at home.
Dressed as if you had just left
The courtyard of the summer palace,
Walk the boundaries of the park,
Count the steps you take each day—
Miles that span no distances,
Journeys in sunlight toward the dark.

Sit and watch the daylight play
Idly on the tops of leaves
Glistening overhead in autumn's
Absolute dominion.
Nothing lost by you excels
These empires of sunlight.
But even here the subtle breeze
Plots with underlying shadows.
One gust of wind and suddenly
The sun is falling from the trees.

Old Woman Being Interviewed

You think I'm just an old lady.
You don't know nothing,
nothing,
young man,
with your little machine there
whirring around,
telling me,

"Forget it's there,
just forget it's there
and tell me how you feel,
how you feel.
Were you ashamed to work as a
maid?
Were you humiliated to scrub toilets?
Do you have low self-esteem
because you ironed the
boxer shorts of rich men?"

You don't know nothing,
nothing,
young man.

You're bored with me.
And I'm bored with you.
Why don't we end
this thing right now
so you can find someone who really
interests you,
and I can go about my business.

You want me to tell you
my secrets
but you think I don't have any.
You think I'm just an
old lady
with red hands.

Wait till you're ninety years old and
we'll have a stranger with a machine
ask you a lot of questions,
ask you to sum it all up
in forty-five minutes.
You don't know the half of it,
young man.

"It's best you go now, I think,
Yes.
Nice to meet you, too,
young man."

But you didn't find out
nothing,
nothing,
young man.
You don't know that
I was young once
with full lips
and two lovers.

A Joke on the Souls of Two Women

I am going to give my *zia*,
Teresa,
my grandmother's name
in stories and poems.
And to my grandmother,
Mariuccia, I will give
my aunt's name
so they will think each other's thoughts
and drink each other's fires
and will bicker for eternity,
extend in perpetuity,
a battle that began
in nineteen twenty-nine
when Mariuccia married Teresa's baby brother.
Why should Death dissolve dissention?
How presumptuous of Death
to end
their feud.
And when I arrive at the Door,
(for I'll be wherever they are)
they'll push away others with more claim,
shove aside Saint Peter,
to be the first to greet me,
to be the first to cry,
"Why did you give me the voice of
that woman?"
"*Per dispetto!*"
I will say,
because I wanted to give you something to do
in retirement.

Coffee Poems

Cup O'Courage
Some knock back a shot of white lightning
before the big meeting
but me,
give me one cup o'java
and I'm set,
gives me chutzpah
and courage,
makes me crazy in the middle of the night
when the kick o'caffeine knocks me
awake
like an
errant knee
in the back.

***Vischio* in My Coffee**
I take *vischio* in my coffee.
And lots of sugar.
I like my coffee strong.
Forte. Forte.
Forza. Forza.
Dammi un po' di vischio—
un guccin'.
American coffee is
weak.
I like my coffee
bitter.

Maria with the Purple Earrings

Maria with the purple earrings
swooped down
in ruby slippers
and emerald skirt,
clicked open a satchel
to free
parrots, canaries
and hummingbirds.
She distributed neon butterflies
to members of the board
who folded them up
and tapped them into breast
coat pockets.
She fanned folders and
shook out pinwheels.
She danced over exasperated balloons,
dropped to the floor like shamed heads,
and replaced them with
dirigibles of competing colors,
inflated with melody
and tied together with a string of words.
She sang off key
but her notes were confetti.

The Wrong Voice

When they laughed, not
at my punch line,
but at me,
I shrank,
defiantly,
waiting for another chance
to offer asymmetry.
When I thrust my hand
to the doctor,
it was an affront,
me, being a hand-shaking lady
who beat him to the punch.
My voice was decibels too loud,
my tone dissonant.
I laid irreverent asides at the
front door
instead of using the servants' entrance.
I spoke with a Midwestern edge,
my voice, a metal nail file,
instead of a muffled buff,
so that when I said,
"Bless her heart,"
it sounded, not like a
graceful cradle,
but a Northerner's mockery,
a bastardized cadence,
a poor performance
by a Yankee actress
imitating a Mississippi sister.
Surely, I intended no insult.
It was just the
wrong voice.

Joseph Tusiani

The Soliloquy of Francis Vigo

If God himself has now forsaken me,
should I expect a man to know me still?
Only the mountains of my native land
remember me (farewell, my Mondovì!)
whereas the country that I call my home
has now no home for me. It is too late—
even for bitterness. If I recall,
in this cold season, the reviving sun,
I neither curse the winter that is mine
nor the warm springtime that is not. Too long
deprived of sunshine, a small bird complains,
and does not know why. But not even you,
friends of my yesterdays, can take away
(does Heaven ever cancel its own light?)
the beauty of your company from me.
You are all here around my dying bed—
so I'm not really lonesome. Loneliness
is never to have had a hand to shake,
a gift to give, a service to perform.
But I remember when for the first time
(what does first mean when last is also first?)
there, in the Wabash Valley, Colonel Clark,
I shook your hand, in which I gladly laid
the savings of my lifetime—a small sum
for the great glory that still lay ahead.
It does not matter, Sir; your *IOU*
your honorable word makes valid still,
and what is this my indigence compared
to all the riches of our Liberty?
For I am dying in America
and for America... can one ask more?
While in Kaskaskia your time you bided
(how does one bide one's time when there's no time?)
five hundred miles I paddled, counting each
stroke of the oar as liberating song,
till, as I reached you from the wilderness,
just like a child relating his last dream
all I had learned I said to you that day.

And soon Fort Sackvill fell, and your "Surrender
or die" is still resounding in my ears.
O happy morning! Washington is here
to bid me do what I've already done?
Did I not follow you before? I knew
the Indians well, and me they knew as well,
and all that knowledge was my gift to you.
So, when you asked me once again to go
(maybe to go is all we know of life)
there, where the British desperately hoped
to save what they could not, how could my faith
have possibly refused my eager love?
Battle of Fallen Timbers! If my deed
hastened its most astounding brightness, then
maybe I do deserve your presence here.
Where are you, General? I see you not...
I only wished to tell you someone tried
to sadden my last day on this our earth
by making me believe I've nothing left—
no business and no mansion and no wife.
But I am even richer, and feel warm
as if the warmest fur I ever sold
were large enough to cover the whole world...
What month is this? Still March?... I thought it was
July the Fourth... I even heard (did you?)
the country courthouse bell joyously ring
over my grave... but I'm Grand Marshall still...

Ad Patrem

Longinqua in terra crevi sine sole et amore,
  care pater, pater a Sorte remote fera.

Me non vidisti laeto sub lumine nasci
  nec gressus movi, te vigili, timidos.

Cum genitorem alii tranquilla voce vocabant
  solus eram et trepidus languidulusque puer.

Numquam te vidi redeuntem in vespere lento
  ad tristem casulam quae mihi nidus erat,

nec nota audivi resonantia in aëre verba,
  care pater, pater a Sorte remote fera!

Nos diruperunt radicitus aspera Fata,
  a sponsa sponsum, meque ab amore tuo.

Quam facile est hodie tam festum dicere verbum
  teque vocare *patrem*! Quam facile et tenerum!

Sed tu, mortuus, hoc non audis nomen amatum
  quod tibi viventi dicere non potui.

Heu, dilecte pater, remanet migratio nostra—
  mortis ferrea lex imperiumque tenax.

Iter ad Garganum

Curre, mens, ad olentia
prata, curre ad amabile
culmen, omne ubi lumen est
   veris imperiosi.

Curre ad intima murmura
rivuli et zephyri levis,
murmura omnibus arbutis
   nota nocte dieque.

Cur gemis procul a domo?
Cur manes ubi nox manet?
Curre, mens mea torpida:
   te vocant avis alae.

Voce te viridi vocat
herba; visere te cupit
mons nova iride splendidus,
   montis arx veneranda.

Iam venusta oculis meis
terra cernitur inclita,
iam patet mihi gratia
   gloriosa iuventae.

Quid loquor tibi, mens mea?
Vana verba ego profero.
Non tibi est faciendum iter:
   iam celerrima es illic.

Forsan unica veritas
somnium est mihi candidum:
numquam ab aëre limpido
   fata me rapuere.

Ethnic Quartet

1. Nonno Giuseppe

Should a small burgeon question its own tree?
Yet I was only seven years of age
when, proud of my grandfather who had built
skyscrapers in America as tall
as seven hundred giants all in one,
I wondered why a hero such as he
could not have learned the day of his own birth.
"Nonno, when were you born?" and he would say,
fondling his big moustache as if to find
a way to make me understand a truth
too regal for my mind to penetrate,
"The year our King Emmanuel was born."
But, unaware of courts and purple cloaks,
I wanted to know more—the day and month
of his appearance on our common earth.
"But, Nonno," I insisted, "tell me when."
Once again stroking his moustache with pride,
he would reply to me, "See, I was born
together with the Virgin Mary." What?
"But how can this be, Nonno? You are old,
but not so old as our Madonna is,
who lived so many centuries ago."
At this, Grandfather with a childish glee,
as if desirous to confound the clerks
of City Hall and City Hall itself,
said, "I, unlike your dad and you, was born
during the great Novena of the great
Immaculate Conception." In his words
the revelation of the great event
sounded so truly great it made the birth
of other people just a worthless day.
I felt so cheated in that radiance
I hated those who made my birth a date
and not the mystery a birth should be.

2. Nonna Carolina

Come, Nonna Carolina, come, you too,
to this reunion of roots tonight.
You burned the longest candle on this earth,
which simply means you knew how to protect
your little flame against the blowing wind
or maybe that no cruel wind at all
for some odd reasons ever came your way.

At ninety-six you wanted still to live,
and rightly so; they had not asked you yet
which boy or girl (check first the family!)
deserved your grandson's or granddaughter's hand.
Therefore you wondered, when the priest appeared
to give you last Communion (not yet!),
how a thin wafer could replace true bread.
So you recovered, and were shocked to hear
that, without asking your permission first,
they had already paid someone to sew
the dress you were to wear on your last day.
You tried it on and found it much too short
(what would Nonno Giuseppe think of you
after so many years of widowhood?)
When alterations were completed (two
more inches, please!), you liked the thing you saw.
"Now put it carefully away," you said,
"and when I need it I will let you know."
Meanwhile far more important, urgent things
were there for you to see and comment on—
your great-granddaughter's lipstick (wash it off!),
your great-grandson's first secret cigarette
(what did he try to do—burn down the house?),
and who was talking in the street and why—
solemn events you witnessed from your chair
for one more year. And then the day arrived
when, feeling suddenly so warm and cold,
with your own eyes you wanted to make sure
your special dress had not one wrinkle on it
(what would Nonno Giuseppe think of you—
that you had turned into a sloppy wife?).
You looked so lovely in your lovely dress
I'm sure Nonno Giuseppe once again,
that very evening, fell in love with you.

3. Nonno Michelarcangelo

You, second Grandpa that I never knew,
maybe you are the one I should know best.
Dead when your daughter was just one day old,
you do not know I have, because of you,
all of these years mistaken until now
meaning of birth for mystery of death.
I have been told that, as you lifeless lay
next to the cradle of that baby girl
who was to be the source of this my day,
over that cradle a black ribbon hung
as the sole emblem of both love and loss.

Somebody even spoke (the mountain's rules
were merciless) of choking that first stir
which in its smallness mimicked your last breath
therefore insulting your enormous end.
There, Grandpa, I was there, in that one room
where women did not know whether to mourn
a sturdy man pneumonia had killed
or to rejoice in life, which once again,
despite your final immobility,
reminded them that loss and love are one.
Out of that sorrow this my heart began,
beating the days that bring me back to you,
Grandfather, whom my mother never knew
and I for this one reason know quite well,
so very well I now can even guess
why we so loved each other instantly,
who did not even meet beneath this sun.

4. Nonna Lucia

Nonna Lucia, is it really true
you scrubbed the floors of Don Saverio's home,
and washed his priestly cassocks and his shirts
and all his sisters' and his nieces' gowns
because you could not pay for the one truth
you needed most—your *Buon Passaggio* Mass?
Your *Buon Passaggio!* If you did not *pass*
from earth to heaven in the grace of God,
who ever will? Not I, who, were I Christ,
would have but told you from the depth of life,
"Woman, thy faith has saved thee: go in peace!,"
but, being only man, would now consign
good Don Saverio to hell and worse.
Nonna, forgive me... Too much aching love
has made me blasphemous. I will therefore
only remember I should praise the Lord
for the great joy that made you always shun
the operation that would have restored
your failing sight so that your savings (almost
eight hundred lire, all your lifetime's sweat)
could buy me suits and shoes and books to read.
Then lead me, blind Grandmother (here's my hand),
into the world of your eternal light
where Jesus preaches His beatitudes
and, no more weeping, people such as you
around Him reign—bright rubies on His ring.

Critical Essays

Robert Viscusi `

A Literature Considering Itself:
The Allegory of Italian America

E la poesia si costituisce come esercizio
      di fronte alla morte.
          —Luigi Ballerini

A literature may be defined as a combination of what it is and what it thinks it is. Persons interested in Italian American writing have largely concerned themselves with the first half of this definition. Bibliographers, archivists, linguists, chroniclers, and anthologists have been successfully at work, often against very formidable obstacles, for two generations and have at least laid down the secure foundations of a literary history.[1] But we have had very little contribution to the theoretical debate implied by the second half of my equation. What does Italian American literature think that it is?

A Few Preliminary Problems

Readers experienced in this kind of inquiry will recognize the difficulties in the question as I have posed it here. Can a literature think? is the first problem, and Can *this* one think? is the second. A literature *can* think. The way a literature thinks is called its *intertext*, its weaving, from generation to generation, new fabrics that contain what everyone will recognize to be bits of old familiar patterns. The number of tales in the *Decameron* calls delicately to mind the number of cantos in the *Commedia*. The conversation of Vergil in the *Commedia* is a reminiscence of prophecies long-since superseded. This weaving, despite its random appearance, actually does constitute real thinking about real situations. Dante's appropriation of Vergilian voices has notoriously served purposes of authority and of political vision, or, to put it differently, has given to the Italian foreground a shape that we can still recognize. This revising of the past points to the particular value of the ways that a literature can think. A literature can harmonize sharp historical dissonances—in the manner, for example, that the long baptism of Vergil and Statius in Italian literature recuperates the heritage of paganism for the purposes of Christianity. In a similar fashion, American literature, constantly reviving the contractual metaphors of the Old Testament, finds new means to think of the American continent as a Promised Land, and this tightly woven intertext serves to soften the pain of old doubts about whether or not the White European has any right to appropriate these territories at all. Not only can a literature think, but it can think to considerable purpose.

    But can Italian American literature think? Some critics, to be sure, have argued that what it can do is think its way into the American tradition, so that there certainly is an open question whether this literature possesses a distinct and effective intertext of its own.[2] Then, one might pause for a long time over the relations between Italian and American literary traditions within the Italian American intertext. It has forcefully been argued, for example, that Italian American writing is a document of the interaction between two cultures.³ Indeed, there is no reason to stop at just two. It might be difficult to decide precisely how many ethnic, regional, prenational, and national encyclopedias contribute to the stock of motives and figures available to a literature that could call itself both Italian and American. It would be interesting to catalog these. It could be endlessly amusing to follow the predictable confrontations among cultures so diverse and even antipathetic as these might be painted. Nonetheless, though I would be the last to deny the possibilities of pleasure in a contrapuntal ethnography, it seems to me that such an approach would evade the burden of literary work, which is precisely to discover how to answer those needs that only literature can meet, by providing both ontological orientation and historical authority.

These *are* needs, though only a cultural cataclysm like a mass migration can allow them to be felt as such by a whole people. It may often be forgotten, but great literatures do flourish in answering actual social appetites. Perhaps it is a lingering heritage of the Arcadians that we still tend to separate the intertexuality of a piece of writing from its direct social utility. But it is always a mistake to do this. No area of literary history more suffers from such separation than does that large intersection of scripture and interpretation that goes by the name *allegoresis*. Even to pronounce the word is to call up the names of such schoolroom divinities as Macrobius and Origen, or such pedagogical gems as the famous distich of Nicholas of Lyra: "Littera gesta docet, quid credas allegoria, / Moralis quid agas, quo tendas anagogia."⁴ But allegory belongs neither to its historical heroes nor to its heroic pedants. Before all else, allegory is the method that literature offers to deal with the cultural dissonance produced by historical process.

No one has ever understood this capacity better than the two great virtuosi of the method, Saint Augustine and Dante Alighieri. Augustine needed allegory to resolve the violent disharmony of the Old Testament with the New, and Dante employed it in order to reconcile Christianity with the Roman antiquity that Augustine had done so much to reject. Neither of these projects was an idle academic amusement. Both represented what the enterpriser in question saw as a pressing historical necessity. Nor could it have been otherwise. For allegory, when employed thus with the fullness of its power, exacts enormous mental and emotional effort. It also requires the commitment of long generations of such effort. The virtuosi represent, as it were, peaks along a continuous range. Allegory, if it successfully answers a historical requirement, calls into play a long and collective literary enterprise. A great allegory is no less a communal work of art than a great cathedral.

Further, in producing a great allegory, a literature defines its own history. This effect, though often overlooked, is fundamental. It explains the striking exhaustiveness we seem to find in the works of our virtuosi—the sense that subsequent Christian literature never quite managed to subsume Augustine, or the recurrent fear that Dante, in inventing Italian literature, had somehow used up most of its possibilities in advance. Neither suspicion is justified, but both reflect the enormous historiographical force of allegory, which seems to develop an energy of its own, beyond that belonging to other kinds of textual power. It has a way of continuing to grow and to explain things that had not even begun to exist when the allegory assumed its canonical form. Thus, at the end of Rousseau's confessions, there seems to stand the figure of the Bishop of Hippo, and it was always easy to imagine Dante lingering in the doorway of the opera house where they were singing *Nabucco*.

Italian American writing is still discovering the shape and strength of its allegory. The gradual appearance of this textual complex gives to this young tradition the excitement that belongs to great explanatory power when it is still discovering its own capacities. Through it, we begin to comprehend a future whose projectors mean to generate a literary history no less corrosive, no less definitive, than what Augustine and Dante represent for us now. How will they do this? *Littera gesta docet:* let us begin with what the letter of this text teaches.

Gesta italoamericana

After Columbus and Vespucci, the continents of the Western Hemisphere acquired a European identity: they were called *Americas*, and an Italian was the reason for that. Thus we begin by remarking that the Italian presence in America shares all of the contradictions built into the project from the outset. To understand these, one must recognize that, from the start, it was a literary enterprise. Columbus, forging ahead with the unwavering conviction of the consummate autodidact that he was, had misread his maps and was convinced he had found Japan. Vespucci realized that there was a continental mass between him and East Asia, and he, as he says, "lightly" called this the "New World,"[5] correcting the misconstruction of Columbus with a new and powerful interpretation. This bold metaphor invented a theoretical space into which Europeans, among others, have been pouring ever since. It has been argued that Vespucci's figure of speech would revolutionize the conception of the cosmos. Even more than that, the expression *Novus Mundus* suggested that a human universe could be created as the double of the one Europeans had left behind.

This is just what happened. The New World quickly was subjected to the hard hand of the Old: within a few years of Columbus's discovery, Rodrigo Borgia, Pope Alexander VI, would take part in the dismantling of the Americas as if they had been Italy herself. It was a touching irony that eventually these same Americas would teach the art of colonial resistance to Garibaldi, who would return to march across Italy as if it were a slender Brazil. Italian American writing begins, then, in a theoretically divided space, a space divided by the theory of the explorers and doubly divided by the worldly powers that sustained their enterprise. It should come as no surprise to find that Italian American writing recognizes the total disconnection that such a space imposes.

> Dal nuovo mondo, la remota sponda
> Da un Italo Navarca a noi concessa;
> La nostalgia profonda,

Che nel laco del cuor geme repressa,
A te trasmetto quale
Figlio devoto; terra mia natale.

I miei vagiti primi, il Coccigliano
Castello s'ebbe, in umile dimora:
Nel bel suolo toscano
Che della tua bellezza il serto infiora.
Con le altre doti incluse
Che natura, o mia Italia in te profuse.

E bambinello ancor, sempre correndo
Da fiore a fiore come farfalletta
Che i petali suggendo
Felice va; sovra la molle erbetta
Giocarellavo lieto
Quale agnelletto vispo e mansueto.

Ma, volgendo l'età, speme sicura
Non dava il pane al morso quotidiano;
Per la coscienza dura
Della tua prole, un manipolo insano
D'ingordi: i suoi diritti
Di padroni, imponendo ai derelitti.

E misero e negletto, ahimé imbarcarmi
Per altri lidi, fu forza maggiore;
Per non assoggettarmi
Ai sanguisuga del proprio sudore:
Ai torvi pescicani
Che su le tue ricchezze hanno le mani.

Così, fintanto che da quei sinistri
Nemici, non avrai le polve scossa;
Famelici ministri
Ti roderanno oltre la pelle, le ossa.
Lasciandoti disfatta
Quale carogna, marcia e putrefatta.

Deh! Italia salva tu se pur ti preme
L'immensa schiera dei reietti figli;
L'umil falange geme
Lontan da te in incogniti perigli.
Soccorrila e imparziale
Concedi a norma il bene tuo sociale.

From the New World, the remote shores
given to us by an Italian navigator;
the deep nostalgia
which repressed sighs in the depth of the heart,
this I pass on to you
as a devout son, O my native land.

In a humble house, Coccigliano
Castello knew my first cries:
in the beautiful Tuscan land

which is considered the crown of your beauty.
Along with the other gifts
which nature lavished on you, O my Italy.

When still a child, always running
from flower to flower like a butterfly
which goes happily sucking the petals,
I used to play merrily on the soft grass
just like a lively and docile lamb.

But, with the passing years,
there was no longer certain hope
of carning daily bread for daily hunger
due to the insensitive conscience of an insane
and greedy bunch of your own progeny
who has chosen to impose master's privileges
on those weaker and poorer wretches.

Poor and neglected, alas, I was forced
to leave for other shores
in order not to subject myself
to the bloodsuckers of my own sweat,
to the cruel sharks
who control all your riches.

So, until you have eliminated
those sinister enemies
hungry ministers
will devour not only your skin but even your bones,
leaving you destroyed
just like a carcass, rotten and purified.

For pity's sake, O Italy, if you really care,
save this immense group of rejected children,
this humble army cries
far from you in unknown perils.
Help it and impartial
grant it just social conditions.

(Alfonsi 1985, 304–37)

This poem, let us admit, is not in full command of its own tradition. The blunt invocation of Leopardi in the title is scarcely sustained by the awkward use of anticlerical pastoral in stanzas three through six.[6] Why read it, then? one may inquire. To which the reply is that its very weaknesses exhibit with considerable force the painful complexity of the Italian American literary situation, where the loftiest ambitions are forever smashing against the walls of a reality altogether of a humbler kind. This complexity grows directly from the fact that America is an Italian inscription and from the implied requirement that, in order to attain the almost divine status implied in this inscriptional identity, the poet must assume as his own an *italianità* that, precisely for him, is impossible to claim without a certain appearance of (at best) bravado.[7]

At the same time that Nardi plainly attributes to Italy the responsibility for the social disaster of migration, he reveals, almost as if by accident, the pure emotional force that, for me at least, saves the poem from its own shortcomings: "l'immensa schiera dei reietti figli." This image of a vast wave of abandoned and rejected children explains the recurrence in the poem of the sad verb *concedere*. That is, Nardi's hobbled ode reduces and concentrates all Italian history, the Renaissance discovery of America no less than the long chronicle of exploitation of the poor, into this one simple memory of rejection. The poet Emanuel Carnevali, with a similar notion, if a better sense of humor, after returning from his difficult years in America, writes, "O Italia, o grande stivale / non buttarmi ancora via a calci!" ("O Italy, o great boot, don't kick me out again!") (Carnevali 1978, 239).

That recollection has a long half-life, like the bitter aftertaste of burnt coffee, and it characterizes much of Italian American chronicle, narrative, poetry, and song. The theoretical prospect laid out by Vespucci is the name of a great hope, certainly, a great opportunity, but at the same time it remains the memory, held consciously and at almost every instant, of a sharp and inconsolable loss. Only one who recognizes the central mythological role that the memory of this loss has assumed can understand the characterizing bent of Italian American discourse. The Blacks were transported to America as slaves; the Anglo-Saxons remember coming in search of religious freedom. These are their founding myths, even if some Anglo-Saxons came as prisoners in chains or others as the transporters of Africans. The founding myth for the Italians is this memory of how the rich expelled the poor into the world invented for them by the great Amerigo.

That is, this New World has turned out to replicate some of the more unlovely features of the Old. The Milanesi will tell you, "Da Roma in giù comincia l'Africa." Northern Italians fear the South, regarding it as the source of various ills and weaknesses that racial myth associates with Africans and Semitic tribes. The stigma associated with southern Italians has followed them to the United States, where we shall see that it has become, by a striking and improbable paradox, the source of deep historical strength.

But, before we look at the nature of this strength, it is worth pausing to consider the difficulties Italian immigrants needed to face in developing a discourse of their own entitlement in America. There was no chance that these new arrivals could identify themselves with the ruling peoples. The Anglo-Saxons had resisted the entry of the Irish Catholics. Now these groups began to cooperate, as a way of insuring the definitive marginalizing of the Italians, who found themselves forming, as they still do, a part of the vivid and highly decorated frame of American society, along with the Blacks, the Hispanics, and the East European Jews. Naturally, in a society as mobile as that of the United States, there is always room to absorb some members of these border tribes into the operating centers, but much larger proportions remain, as before, to a greater or lesser degree visibly tattooed with their ethnic or racial otherness. For Italians, this exclusion has been less rigid than for Blacks or Hispanics, but more rigid than for Jews and Irish Catholics.[8] In short, to the regional and class divisions of Italy has been added in the

United States the machinery of ethnic boundary markers. The borders are such that Italians who cross them must do so at the cost of their own historical identity.

Allegoria divina

Not surprisingly, most Italians have refused to pay this price. What have they done instead?

It is at this point that one may observe the cognitive engine of allegory industriously at work—almost, as it seems, on every street corner. That is, one might expect that a device with so noble a literary lineage would live best in academies. But this has not been the case. Italian Americans have found the answer to their dilemma within the models that their own tradition provided. Garibaldi La Polla understood this when he made the hero of his novel *The Grand Gennaro* an immigrant who had left nothing behind him in Italy but bad debts and bad memories. Gennaro Accuci became in Italian Harlem not merely a successful businessman but, more consequentially, a builder of churches and a leader of processions. La Polla's vision of the meaning of life in Italian Harlem has been successfully adapted by the historian Robert Orsi in *The Madonna of 115th Street: Faith and Community in Italian Harlem, 1880–1950*. What both of these mythographers outline is a habit of thinking that one may call *processional*, a habit that produces a visible event in which the contradictions of the communal life become the materials of a public ritual. Orsi, quite as intent upon the Madonna as his theme requires him to be, might with profit have more plainly emphasized that the object of this ritual is not the Madonna but the adaptation to America. For an appraisal of the full weight of this enterprise one must return to La Polla, whose narrative understands precisely what is at stake for his hero in the melée of Italian Harlem, 1880:

> Gennaro Accuci actually found a place in this confusion, and sent for his family. But he did not send for his family before he had succeeded in what he called, and all his fellow immigrants called, "making America." "Making good" is an approximation, but without body and expression. Something both finer and coarser clings to the expression. There is the suggestion of envy on the part of the user and also of contempt. For it means that a nobody, a mere clodhopper, a good-for-nothing on the other side, had contrived by hook or crook in this new, strange country, with its queer ways and its lack of distinctions, to amass enough money to strut about and proclaim himself the equal of those who had been his superiors in the Old Country. And if one said of himself that he had made America, he said it with an air of rough boasting, implying "I told you so" or "Look at me." Although he knew that his spectators would be inclined to despise him for the word, he threw out his chest. And yet there were comfort and solidity, the double fruit of egotism, in its use, and he used it, even roared it out, and laughed. (La Polla 1935, 4–5)

The innumerable parades that Gennaro leads, like the annual feasts of the Madonna that Orsi describes, do not serve merely to communicate secret feelings or to consolidate community. They also serve, quite literally, to "make America." Gennaro, as bluntly as any conquistador, intends to invent both himself and this continent along the lines of a European ambition. That is, like every consequential European, this hero comes to America not merely to escape something but also to demonstrate a hypothesis. He has a theory of America; and his career is, in effect, a series of experiments designed to test and to apply that theory. Gennaro is willing to do anything, to labor as hard as imaginable, to commit whatever treason, in order to give life to his imaginary self in its imaginary America. This projected place has a precise architecture and social structure, replicating the pyramid of nobles and *galantuomini* that Gennaro recalls from Italy—all just as it was, except, of course, that now he is installed at its apex. He succeeds in his ambition, but the machinery of the plot insists also that he shall die as the price of this flawed triumph.

It is not surprising that he must die. For what Gennaro has accomplished in "making America" is to become a god. This is the allegorical destiny of Italian American heroes, to endure ritual death and processional reidentification in the process of becoming divinities. Emanuel Carnevali wrote that, during the crisis provoked by the very bitter life of an immigrant, he believed himself to be the One God: "Ora credevo fermamente di essere l'unico Dio" (Carnevali 1978, 129). His autobiographical allegory *Il primo dio* lays out the emotional problematic of the Italian immigrant with a clarity that only makes one wish that more readers had ever examined it. Nonetheless, it is also true that the only two Italian American novels to enter the syllabus of American literature advertise in their titles exactly the same impulse to divinity: *Christ in Concrete* and *The Godfather*. In their diverse ways, these two works demonstrate that the force of Italian American writing has sprung from its adaptation of the collective allegorizing engaged in by Italian migrants in America. In Di Donato's *Christ In Concrete*, the immigrant bricklayer Geremio falls from a scaffolding and is buried in concrete. It takes two days to recover his body. Because the day of his death is Good Friday and the day on which his body is exhumed is Easter Sunday, the migrant community weaves a long funeral discourse in which Geremio is first compared with and then *becomes* the risen Christ. Twenty years after *Christ in Concrete*, Di Donato published *Three Circles of Light*, in which he attempted to come to terms with other, less presentable, facts about Geremio's death. The scaffolding collapsed because the contractor had skimped on materials. Geremio, the foreman, it turns out, had known of this and so had been complicit in his own death. But the eloquent honesty of *Three Circles of Light* has gone unnoticed. What attracts readers is the divinity of *Christ in Concrete*.

This is, I think, as it must be. A similar logic has led most readers to prefer *The Godfather* and its film version, *The Godfather, Part I*, to the moralizing sequel, *The Godfather, Part II*. In Puzo's novel, the identification of Don Corleone with the myth of God the Father is all but complete and carries only a light dusting of irony, often mistaken for satire. While there is a good deal of ironic, even bitter and sarcastic, social commentary in *The Godfather*'s attitude towards American hypocrisy, there is little of actual satire in this novel. We are expected to take its heroes very seriously indeed. Don Vito Corleone's divine stature comes directly from the sufferings and loyalties that he sustains. His one true son, Michael, himself becomes a godfather in the moment he avenges his father's losses. All this is perfectly well portrayed in their various ways by both the novel and the film. The film sequel, which aims to portray a spiritual emptiness and hollowness in the Corleone family's victory, has relatively little resonance in anyone's imagination. For what gives *The Godfather* its power as myth is not the morality of the Mafia, but the stature of the immigrant who has "made America"— who has, in effect, paid the price of making real the theoretical continent. Michael's wife sees him as the reader is meant to, at the end of the novel; she does not believe, even yet, what his sister Connie says he has done; but at this moment, going to the kitchen to get ice for a drink, she turns and sees him in what is presented as the fullness of his destined nature:

> She went into the kitchen for ice and while there heard the front door open. She went out of the kitchen and saw Clemenza, Neri and Rocco Lampone come in with the bodyguards. Michael had his back to her, but she moved so that she could see him in profile. At that moment Clemenza addressed her husband, greeting him formally.
> "Don Michael," Clemenza said.
> Kay could see how Michael stood to receive their homage. He reminded her of statues in Rome, statues of those Roman emperors of antiquity, who, by divine right, held the power of life and death over their fellow men. One hand was on his hip, the profile of his face showed a cold proud power, his body was carelessly, arrogantly at ease, weight resting on one foot slightly behind the other. The *caporegimes* stood before him. In that moment Kay knew that everything Connie had accused Michael of was true. She went back into the kitchen and wept. (Puzo 1969, 437)

The temptation, of course, is to read this divinization as a straightforward *embourgeoisement* of the poor migrants.[9] This is a narrow interpretation, however, and altogether insensitive to the persistence of religious feeling that allows Italian American literary tradition to assign this status almost reflexively to its dead heroes. Here, for example, on the other end of the political spectrum, is the conclusion of Daniel Gabriel's "narrative longpoem" on Sacco and Vanzetti:

> but who could say
> their death was not
> a kind of defeat?
> defeat of this tyranny?
> who could say
> they were not killed
> definitively?
> their bodies
> burned magnificently,
> their spirits
> quenched by
> another fire,
> their language

scalded?
....
so the victory
of the Commonwealth
became
through the transformation
of the act
over time
a victory for the two
and their following.

simply: act, memory,
eternity.
not so simply,
but through the
persistence of the two,
the case, the trial,
passion and memory
they are
like singing birds
forever singing
over the landscape.
they are a metaphor
of something bolder,
of an unknown—
and are sending,
even as we breathe,
a stitch of light
to generations
not yet born.

(Gabriel 1983, 74–76)

It is worth adding that Gabriel is a younger poet, who displays a thorough awareness of all the devices of distancing and irony that a well-trained contemporary is likely to find stained in his marrow, and so the straightforward monumentality of this ending is, accordingly, all the more striking. Gabriel calls this part of the text "Metapoem (9)," though at first its more obvious filiation does not seem to indicate an articulable metapoetics but rather to echo a simple elegiac line. In fact, the crucial point, towards which the poet carefully labors, is the statement "they are metaphor," since the metapoet recognizes that it is precisely a figure of which we have need, not in order to celebrate a simple passage, but rather to make sense of a violent confrontation.

Tropologia olimpica

To die into theory is to become a divinity. This is something that Italian American narrative has recognized *before* its metapoetics did—recognized it not just as efficacious but as essential. It was clear to the discourse, if not to its explicators, that no other role was open to Italians in the American imagination *except* that of divinities. The Puritans had preempted the role of moralists, and the Blacks the place of the victim. The imaginary economy of America seems to have allowed Italians specifically the divine space that had been opened for them by Columbus and Vespucci, Verrazzano and Caboto, that of the primeval progenitors or projectors of the very ontology of the New World.

Thus it has been that the cultural implications of Italian American myth have been more than a little constricting. The martyred bricklayer and the omniscient gangster entered directly into American myth. Demiurges of sexuality like John Travolta and Madonna Ciccone have no difficulty of access. But who is the archetype of the Italian American intellectual?[10] Is there a Saul Bellow or an Irving Howe? This figure is going to take time to develop. In the meantime, it would appear that the most successful strategy is to capitalize on achievements of accomplished divinity. Thus, to protest the foreign religion that masqueraded as Catholicism, the poet Elaine Romaine can now write the following:

> You were always irish, god
> in a church where I confessed
> to being Italian.
>
> But then St. Anthony
> had a feast and lights ringed
> the street as sausage and peppers
> steamed in booths, gambling wheels spun
> as the tenor held his stomach, pushing
> a note higher. Behind a booth my brother
> pitched pennies with a priest, rolling
> deep fried bread sprinkled with sugar
> in his mouth. The processions began.
> My father and his brothers shoulder
> the statue through the crowd, hymns
> and feast bless the air.
>
> And all the sights of you, god,
> were wine-filled.
> For these sins we took communion
> the next morning, sleeping on each other
> in the pews until the altar bell rang
> and we filed up to the railing,
> opening our mouths, for your blood
> and flesh. O god,
> god, I confess nothing.
>
> (In Barolini 1985, 306)

This is religious warfare on an Olympian field—no intervention of priests or even theologians, but simply one god against another, hegemony established in the jumbled demotic *ecclesia* of the streets where the procession and the feast fill the sensorium.

We confront here an extraordinary morality, if it is a morality at all. Italian American writing has only begun to learn the capacities of its mythogenic power. Thus, though the allegory is everywhere present, its tropology is difficult to detect. It would be easy to mistake these new divinities for the familiar stereotypes of the Nietzschean Italian who can do anything and feel no remorse. For indeed there is a similarity between these gods and those older caricatures. The difference is that these gods have suffered, have died, and have awakened, as who should say, in possession. In possession of their names and powers, and in possession, too, of their theoretical selves, made real by death.

Anagogia cartografica

It has been something of a puzzle what to make of this peculiar security, and Italian Americans have watched bemused as their food, their manners, and their families, transfigured with celestial light, have become the playthings of advertising and the poetry of political speeches. Bemused but untouched. There is no question that theirs has appeared at times to be an unnatural calm. Social scientists and journalists have not seen in it any reason to rejoice; such persons have always approached Italian American reality with the nervous apprehension that their training teaches them to mistake for close attention. Uneasy and (it seems) unloved, they are great seekers after noise and pretense; they want definitive action, they look for solutions with riddles attached. But there is every reason to think that poets and novelists among the Italians in America are passing through a period of energetic assimilation. Understanding that the crisis of great strife associated with the migration has finally drawn to a conclusion, these writers have recognized the vast access of grace and power that the dying migrants have left as their nimbus.

Thus it is that contemporary Italian American writers often seem to display a meditative and glistening front at exactly the moment that their predecessors would have been hauling out the stakes and spikes and tommy guns. The novels and poems these days often include visions of transfigured grandmothers:

> "We used to eat these," she said, bending over and plucking a dandelion from the green lawn. "We used to like these very much. A simple weed. We cooked it with garlic and olive oil and a few flakes of red pepper. We ate weeds and we were happy."
>
> My grandmother waved her arms above her head in some private choreography now, bending over and brushing her ankles in a wide, delicate sweep, a graceful rhythmic gesture.
>
> She was humming the tarantella again, she separated from us and whirled and whirled, moving one hand to her eyes as if shading them from some brutal Italian sun. (Maso 1986, 224)

This whimsical Shakespearean goddess inhabits a nursing home in Carole Maso's poetic narrative *Ghost Dance*. Nor is this antique presence really unusual in her almost unbearable enclosure of a distant divinity. The heroine of Helen Barolini's *Umbertina* is a Calabrian grandmother whose life the narrator very fully imagines, all the while making it clear that the grandmother spoke no English and the narrator no Italian, so that the entire recollection is a charged imagining rather than a history, not a record but self-consciously a myth.

Quo tendas anagogia.   Our analysis ought to tell us what this literature sees in its prospect, floating somewhere, it may be, just a step ahead of its vanishing point. This has to be a question of realizing possibilities that were written into the paper continent at the opening of its career as a utopia for Europeans who wanted to try again. Thus it is that the aspect of Italian American life least understood by its many students and critics is its sense of time. For its inhabitants, Italian America *is* America, exactly as old as Vespucci's figure of speech. There is a sense of common purpose extending over not years but generations, not decades but centuries. "Our grandfathers built these buildings," an Italian American college administrator said to me, pointing to the campus of a great American university. "Now we want to work in them."[11] Such bone-bred wisdoms of possession persist without needing any clearer case to put. Not only do they persist, but specifically in their lack of an articulated argument, they retain the power to rest like gods upon their own peculiar abstract authority. Their having as yet no settled hierarchy reflects merely the slow revolution of calendars, they feel. The burden of their theoretical inheritance, their chart of primeval lustre, has become as well the privilege of a starry equanimity. It almost seems the name of a permanent disappointment, you might say, all these clouds of prestige that so rarely seem to alight upon the actual lawn. The temptation, to which I am in the act of not yielding any longer, would be to outline a history of the future of this name, *America,* knowing that, however it differs from its past, it will carry something of the same impossible removal, will remain a sacrament of loss so pure as to give to each remaining thing, each stone and every flowering vine, its own shimmering position in the general and expanding edifice of divinities impaled upon a theory, persistently imprinted in the map.

Notes

1. Important archives: Center for Migration Studies, Staten Island; Immigration History Research Center, University of Minnesota; Balch Institute for Ethnic Studies, Philadelphia. Important analytic and historical essays: Alba, Amfitheatrof, Barzini, Cammett, Caporale, Caroli, Child, Cinel, Covello, Crispino, DeConde, di Leonardo, Foerster, Fucilla, Gallo, Gambino, Gans, Glazer, Juliani, Mangione, Pane, and Tomasi. Anthologies: Alfonsi and Barolini. It is useful, as well, to reconsider the whole history of the effort to establish an Italian American studies in the context of the image of America among Italian intellectuals; see Blengino, Massara, Rubeo, and Soldati.

2. The theses of Boelhower (1982, 1987) stand firmly upon this article of faith in American literary historiography.

3. The subtitle of Green's study points precisely to this sort of interaction. In fact, we should not speak of relations between two (or three or thirty) cultures, but rather between two groups of languages, anglophone and italophone, whose interweaving produces the Italian American intertext. This encounter will take place at various levels; I have attempted a methodologically articulated approach that distinguishes clearly between treatments that are linguistic (cf. Viscusi, 1981), ecological (1983a), cognitive (1985), mythographic (1982), or, as in the present essay, figurative.

4. *Cit.* Lynch, 229.

5. See Amfitheatrof (1973), Arciniegas, Benzoni, O'Gorman, and Todorov for informed historical and theoretical discussion of the implications of these literary events.

6. For example, consider Dante: "In vesta di pastor lupi rapaci / si veggon di qua sù per tutti paschi: / difesa di Dio, perché pur giaci?" *Paradiso,* 27, 56–58. "Rapacious wolves, in shepherd's garb, are seen from here above in all the pastures. O defense of God, wherefore dost thou yet lie still?" (Singleton)

7. The Coalition of Italo-American Associations of New York prints on its stationery the slogan "'America'—A Beautiful Italian Name."

8. See Gambino, Glazer and Moynihan, and Kessner for informed comparative discussion of the social necessities confronted by these various groups in the United States.

9. So argues Torgovnik, implicitly reviving Basile Green's argument, both as it reads *The Godfather* and as it interprets the whole tradition.

10. Of, that is, not merely the intellectual who happens to be well-known and of Italian descent—John Ciardi, A. Bartlett Giamatti, Frank Lentricchia—but who is known, in the way that Irving Howe or Saul Bellow is known, as an interpreter of the minority culture to which he belongs by birth.

11. Joseph Capobianco, registrar, Queens College, City University of New York.

Works Cited

Alba, R. D. 1985. *Italian Americans: Into the Twilight of Ethnicity.* Englewood Cliffs, N.J.: Prentice-Hall.

Alfonsi, Ferdinardo, ed. 1985. *Poeti italo-americani / Italo-American Poets.* Catanzaro: Antonio Carello Editori.

Amfitheatrof, Eric. 1973. *The Children of Columbus: An Informal History of Italians in the New World.* Boston: Little, Brown.

———. 1980. *The Enchanted Ground: Americans in Italy, 1760–1980.* Boston: Little, Brown.

Arciniegas, German. 1986. *America in Europe: A History of the New World in Reverse.* Translated by Gabriela Arciniegas and R. Victoria Arana. New York: Harcourt Brace Jovanovich.

Ballerini, Luigi. 1988. *Che figurato muore.* Milano: All' insegna del pesce d'oro.

Barolini, Helen, ed. 1985. *The Dream Book: An Anthology of Writings by Italian American Women.* New York: Schocken Books.

———. 1979. *Umbertina.* New York: Seaview Books.

Barzini, Luigi. 1977. *O America, When You and I Were Young.* New York: Harper and Row.

Benzoni, Gino, et al. 1987. *Le Americhe.* Milano: Electra.

Blengino, V., et al. 1986. *L'America degli italiani.* Roma: Bulzoni Editore.

Boelhower, William. 1982. *Immigrant Autobiography in the United States: Four Versions of the Italian American Self*. Verona: Essedue.

————. 1987. *Through a Glass Darkly: Ethnic Semiosis in American Literature*. New York: Oxford University Press.

Cammett, John M., ed. 1969. *The Italian American Novel*. Staten Island: American Italian Historical Association.

Caporale, Rocco. 1986. *The Italian Americans through the Generations*. Staten Island: American Italian Historical Association.

Carnevali, Emanuel. 1978. *Il primo dio*. Milano: Adelphi.

Caroli, Betty Boyd, et al., eds. 1977. *The Italian Immigrant Woman in North America*. Staten Island: American Italian Historical Association.

Child, Irwin L. 1943. *Italian or American? The Second Generation in Conflict*. New York: Russell and Russell.

Cinel, Dino. 1982. *From Italy to San Francisco: The Immigrant Experience*. Stanford: Stanford University Press.

Cordasco, Francesco, and Salvatore LaGumina. 1972. *Italians in the United States: A Bibliography of Reports, Texts, Critical Studies, and Related Material*. New York: Oriole Press.

Cordasco, Francesco, ed. 1975. *Studies in Italian American Social History: Essays in Honor of Leonard Covello*. Totowa, N.J.: Rowman and Littlefield.

————, ed. 1978. *Italian Americans: A Guide to Information Sources*. Ethnic Studies Information Guide Series. Detroit: Gale Research Co.

Covello, Leonard. 1972. *The Social Background of the Italo-American School Child*. Totowa, N.J.: Rowman and Littlefield.

Crispino, J. 1980. *The Assimilation of Ethnic Groups: The Italian Case*. Staten Island: Center for Migration Studies.

Dante Alighieri. 1970. *The Divine Comedy*. Translated with commentary by C. S. Singleton. Princeton: Princeton University Press.

DeConde, Alexander. 1971. *Half Bitter, Half Sweet: An Excursion into Italian-American History*. New York: Charles Scribner's Sons.

Di Donato, Pietro. 1939. *Christ in Concrete*. Indianapolis: Bobbs-Merrill.

di Leonardo, Micaela. 1984. *The Varieties of Ethnic Experience: Kinship, Class and Gender among California Italian-Americans*. Ithaca: Cornell University Press.

Dionisotti, Carlo. 1967. *Geografia e storia della letteratura italiana*. Torino: Giulio Einaudi.

Foerster, Robert F. 1968. *The Italian Emigration of Our Times*. New York: Russell and Russell.

Fucilla, Joseph G. 1967. *The Teaching of Italian in the United States*. New Brunswick: American Association of Teachers of Italian.

Gabriel, Daniel. 1983. *Sacco and Vanzetti: A Narrative Longpoem*. Brooklyn: Gull Books.

Gallo, Patrick J. 1974. *Ethnic Alienation: The Italian-Americans.* Madison, N.J.: Fairleigh Dickinson University Press.

Gambino, Richard. 1974. *Blood of My Blood: The Dilemma of the Italian Americans.* Garden City: Doubleday.

Gans, Herbert J. 1962. *The Urban Villagers: Group and Class in the Life of Italian Americans.* New York: Free Press.

Glazer, Nathan F., and Daniel P. Moynihan. 1970. *Beyond the Melting Pot: The Negroes, Puerto Ricans, Jews, Italians, and Irish of New York City.* Cambridge: MIT Press.

Green, Rose Basile. 1974. *The Italian-American Novel: A Document of the Interaction of Two Cultures.* Madison, N.J.: Fairleigh Dickinson University Press.

———. 1983. "Italian American Literature." In *Ethnic Perspectives in American Literature,* edited by R. DiPietro and E. Ifkovic. New York: Modern Language Association, 110–32.

Juliani, Richard N., ed. 1983. *The Family and Community Life of Italian Americans.* Staten Island: American Italian Historical Association.

Kessner, Thomas. 1977. *The Golden Door: Italian and Jewish Immigrant Mobility in New York City, 1880–1915.* New York: Oxford University Press.

La Polla, Garibaldi M. 1935. *The Grand Gennaro.* New York: Vanguard Press.

Mangione, Jerre. 1968. *A Passion for Sicilians: The World around Danilo Dolci.* New York: William Morrow.

———. 1983. *An Ethnic at Large: A Memoir of America in the Thirties and Forties.* Philadelphia: University of Pennsylvania Press.

———. [1950] 1984. *Reunion in Sicily.* New York: Columbia University Press.

Maso, Carole, 1986. *Ghost Dance.* San Francisco: North Point Press.

Massara, Giuseppe. 1984. *Americani: l'immagine letteraria degli Stati Uniti in Italia.* Palermo: Sellerio Editore.

O'Gorman, Edmondo. 1971. *The Invention of America.* Bloomington: Indiana University Press.

Orsi, Robert Anthony. 1985. *The Madonna of 115th Street: Faith and Community in Italian Harlem, 1880–1950.* New Haven: Yale University Press.

Pane, Remigio U., ed. 1983. *Italian Americans in the Professions.* Staten Island: American Italian Historical Association.

Peragallo, Olga. 1949. *Italian American Authors.* New York: Vanni.

Puzo, Mario. [1969] 1978. *The Godfather.* New York: Signet.

Rubeo, Ugo, ed. 1987. *Mal d'America: da mito a realtà.* Roma: Riuniti.

Sohn-Rethel, Alfred. 1978. *Intellectual and Manual Labor: A Critique of Epistemology.* London: Macmillan.

Soldati, Mario. 1959. *America primo amore.* Milano: Arnold Mondadori.

Todorov, Tzvetan. 1984. *The Conquest of America: The Question of The Other,* translated by Richard Howard. New York: Harper and Row.

Tomasi, Lydio, ed. 1985. *Italian Americans: New Perspectives in Italian Immigration and Ethnicity.* New York: Center for Migration Studies.

Torgovnick, Marianna De Marco. 1988. *"The Godfather* as the World's Most Typical Novel." *South Atlantic Quarterly* 87, no. 2 (Spring): 329–53.

Viscusi, Robert. 1981 *"'De vulgari eloquentia':* An Approach to the Language of Italian American Fiction." *Yale Italian Studies* 1, no. 3: 21–38.

———. 1982. "The Text in the Dust: Writing Italy across America." *Studi emigrazione* (Roma) 19, no. 65: 123–30.

———. 1983. *"Il caso della casa:* Stories of Houses in Italian America." In Juliani, *q.v.*, pp. 1–9.

———. 1983. "Professions and Faiths: Critical Choices in the Italian American Novel." In Pane, *q.v.*, pp. 41–54.

———. 1986. "Circles of the Cyclopes: Schemes of Recognition in Italian American Discourse," In L. Tomasi, *q.v.*, pp. 209–19.

red, a little white, a lot of green, on a field of pink: a controversial design for an Italian component of a multicultural canon for the United States

The white male Anglo-Saxon literary canon in the United States has been visibly dented by an emerging multicultural canon of Native American, Black, Chicano, Asian, and Euro-American writings—of women as well as men. At a 1987 conference of the Society for the Study of Multi-Ethnic Literature of the United States, a MELUS founder suggested that only Thoreau's *Walden* and Whitman's *Leaves of Grass* remain viable in a multicultural perspective.

This essay explores the possibilities of an Italian component of a multicultural canon for the United States, one that does not duplicate the themes of "Mediterranean Heritage" often found in Western Civilization courses, nor the elitist emphases of conventional history courses. In the first instance, the rhetoric is fulsome: "All our religion, almost all our law, almost all our arts, almost all that sets us above savages, has come to us from the shores of the Mediterranean."[1] This view is highly laudatory, but it omits peasants, women, and contemporary Italians, whose significance for a multicultural U.S. canon inheres in a deepening of the meaning of democracy.

Analogously, the conventional western white male view of European history regards the Italian Renaissance as a high point of human achievement. Awed by the splendors of Renaissance art, this perspective tends to denigrate southern Italians (who constituted the majority of Italian migrants to the United States) and to avoid probing questions. Today's feminist scholars ask, Was there a Renaissance for women? As Joan Kelly Scott pointed out, the Renaissance marked Italian cultural leadership of Europe, but also the beginning of modern women's subordination. As opposed to the considerable autonomy of women in the "dark" feudal ages (and of peasant women thereafter), women in the modern age have lived in a "heightened patriarchal" environment wherein love "must lead to marriage and be confined to it—for women, that is." Renaissance ideas of love ("almost exclusively a male product") expressed a new subordination of women to the interests of husbands and male-dominated kin groups.[2]

How then do we go about finding an authentic Italian component for a multicultural canon for the United States? Not by emulating the selective

---

My connotations for the chromatic design in the title are the *bandiera rossa* of international socialism, the white of popular catholicism, the green of nonviolence, and the pink of Italian feminism.

In *liberazione della donna* and this essay, I follow contemporary Italian usage in removing capitals from valenced religious and political words.

optic of Western Civilization theorists, not by fixing solely on "high culture," and not by following James Joyce, D. H. Lawrence, Ezra Pound, and others who, in their desperate search for non-Anglo-Saxon values, sometimes ended up with celebrations of the priapus and of fascism.

The search might well begin by disengaging ourselves from U.S. dominant culture and its geopolitical interests. Then considering Italy's major cultural legacy: the Franciscan tradition—with respect for all life on earth, and among humans especially the poor, the despised, and the least. Franciscan notes are found throughout Italy's peasant and current history.

In the journey to a genuinely multicultural civilization, everyone will have to pack her or his own valuables. The fundamental bottom layer of my valise will contain (1) Italian peasant folklore. This *cultura negata*, not "high" Italian civilization, determined the lives of most Italians for millenia. More democratic, more millennial, and more woman-centered than papal catholicism, this popular, often heretical, catholicism was characterized by suspicion of the established authority of church and state.[3]

For Italian Americans, this peasant legacy of autonomy was weakened as soon as the language was lost. Dominant white protestants, intent on cultural hegemony at home and empire abroad, pushed other immigrant traditions toward extinction in early twentieth-century "americanization" campaigns that became institutionalized in public education.

In light of the uncritical anticommunism, ethnocentrism, and establishment orientation of postwar education in the United States, other layers of my valise would include (2) writings of the Italian political left, including the literature of resistance to nazis and fascists, (3) literature and film of the Italian dopoguerra focusing on the "other," the third world poor and the culturally "other," (4) "unedited" judeo-christian and marxist writings of the sixties, seventies, and eighties, and literature that evokes the peasant (often "pagan") cosmology that connects the Italian subproletariat today with third world peasants.

As a balance to the banishment of utopian thinking in the United States, indispensable to my baggage would be the (5) signs of a new world civilization discernible in contemporary Italian writings of liberation theologians, independent radicals, theorists of nonviolence. And (6) feminists.

Italian themes for a U.S. multicultural canon will tap the subterranean peasant river of Italian history, and its streams and freshets in the twentieth century—represented in the writings of Antonio Gramsci, Elio Vittorini, Carlo Levi, Ignazio Silone, Pier Paolo Pasolini, Giulio Girardi, Gianni Baget-Bozzo, Primo Levi, Umberto Eco, Leonardo Sciascia, Natalia Ginsburg, Dacia Maraini, Adele Cambria, Fracesca Duranti, and Adriana Zarri.

1. Italian peasant folklore

In the legends, parables, and maxims that Italian peasant mothers taught their children for centuries, the judeo-christian gospels were interpreted within a heretical woman-centered cosmology that often put prechristian themes into the language of christianity. Teaching an ethic at once realistic, inclusive, and caring,[4] in this oral tradition[5] the mother of *Gesù* is central, universal grace embraces all human beings, morality is grounded on realism, and the family is extended to all who are hungry or hurting.

The decalogue was interpreted with a bottom optic: stealing is a sin but stealing from the poor is the worst sin. Saint Christopher was beloved because he gave a lamp to poor people engaged in smuggling. In southern Italian anarchism, "the property of the government" is "the property of the people." Believing that the legitimate proprietor of the earth is not the absentee owner but the person who cultivates it, Italian peasants occupied lands and factories after each world war of the twentieth century.

In the 1890s Sicilian women and men carried banners of the madonna and of *Gesù* in socialist demonstrations for land and bread. Precursors of what today is called liberation theology, they considered Jesus a "true socialist...but the priests do not represent him well." This peasant tradition merged with the Italian worker movement of the twentieth century and became the historical context for new left revolutionaries and feminists after 1968.[6]

2. Writings of the Italian political left and of the resistance

Acknowledged today as a major marxist theorist of the twentieth century, Antonio Gramsci was a founder of the Italian communist party, the independent third largest communist party of the world. Jailed under Mussolini's fascism, Gramsci's prison writings stress cultural as well as political revolution and the significance of recognizing regional/cultural differences in a genuine revolution. A Sardinian, he brought the subject of the different culture of southern Italy to the attention of marxists.

Gramsci encouraged the recovery of cultural heritage as indispensable to the self-confidence and *autogestione* (self-determination) necessary for authentic democracy. His concept of hegemony helps Italian and other Americans to understand the function of dominant culture as social control in modern capitalist societies. Leaving a realist as well as utopian legacy to the world left, Gramsci counseled: pessimism of the mind, optimism of the will.[7] For third world countries today, Gramsci is the theorist who forged "...the unbreakable bond between democracy and socialism, an anti-dogmatic marxism that does not have answers for everything, a marxism that must continually renew itself in the face of new problems."[8]

Underground socialism during the fascist era and the subtle resistance of women to fascist oppression are illuminated in Elio Vittorini's *In Sicily*. Italian women defied papal prohibitions of birth control and abortion and Mussolini's exhortations to lift the birthrate. Believing (as peasant women and later as feminists) that "it is my uterus and I shall manage it," they caused the Italian birthrate to fall in the fascist era, and have seen to its continued descent, exercising their right to determine their own lives.[9]

The perseveration in peasant life of the ancient woman-centered cosmology of the Mediterranean is evoked in Carlo Levi's *Cristo si 'e fermato à Eboli*. Religion for the peasant may be redundant, Levi pointed out, because "everything is, really and not symbolically, divine—the sky, the animals, Christ, and the goat." The central figure in this worldview is not *Gesù* nor the blue and white madonna of the church, but the "black madonna among the grain and the animals," a subterranean divinity cherished by third world peoples today. Neither good nor bad, she withers the grain but she also causes the flowers to bloom, and she inspires fervent devotion from Poland to Italy to Mexico.[10]

3. Literature and film of the dopoguerra focusing on the "other"

The writings of marginal Italian Jews offer a beam of light into Italy's nominally catholic society. In the eighth decade of the murderous twentieth century, the writings of Primo Levi have assured immortality. For Levi (who survived the holocaust but committed suicide in 1987), poetry may be written after Auschwitz, but the only viable poetry is that which is *impegnata* (committed). A partisan during world war II, Primo Levi wrote an important document of the resistance in his *Se questo è un uomo* (1947). Chemist as well as writer, Levi pursued the elements of the universe in the manner of a Jewish talmudic scholar. The title of Levi's *If Not Now, When?* (1982) asked a traditional Jewish prophetic question. Tormented by who was killed and who survived the holocaust, Levi enlarged the query to ask, Who is doomed, who is saved, and who are those who wait in a large gray space? Primo Levi found hope in Italy and in the new left generation of 1968 the world over, but it was hope threaded with realism: the way of commitment—religious and/or political, said Levi, is always fraught with contradiction and always sad, a sadness underlined by Levi's suicide.

The critique of the left by the left in the dopoguerra was enunciated best, perhaps, by Ignazi Silone. In the contemporary Italian political shift toward *movimentismo* instead of political parties, Silone's *Fontamara* (1934), *Bread and Wine* (1937), and *Emergency Exit* (1969) are prescient. Distrust of political parties, and of the state, is endemic in Italy today. Although Silone had helped to found the Italian communist party, he early indicated that he could not obey any party uncritically. Voicing the discontent that would remain until 1981 when the Pci broke with the soviet model of socialism, Silone is a precursor of contemporary independent radicals of Italy who leaven the large communist party (Pci) with individual moral judgment.

Combining socialism with anarchism, with Italy's liberal *risorgimento* tradition, and with Italian peasant particularism, Silone is significant for his unedited marxism—unedited in the sense of not following a party line. Insisting on decentralizing the state and demystifying left rhetoric, Silone defined socialism as the "aspiration of the poor toward social justice and equality, with the suppression of economic and political privileges." Instead of political parties, he recommended self-governing small communities, a theme that was taken up in Italy after 1968 by the new left, by feminists, and by communists.[11]

4. Unedited judeo-christianity and unedited marxism

An unedited reading of the judeo-christian gospels and of marxism, bypassing church dogma and party doctrine, is found in the work of Pier Paolo Pasolini. Filmmaker, critic, and poet, Pasolini described the Friulian peasantry of his childhood as a world of uncorrupted christianity and innocence. These were the catholic beliefs of simple people—beliefs, he said, that had "nothing to do with Rome or the glory of the Church." Similarly he criticized marxist rationalism: reason cannot, said Pasolini, be separated from feeling. Marxism was more than theory, it was, for Pasolini, "some idealism, some Catholicism, some anarchy, some humanitarianism. . . ."[12]

Criticizing the left "as a christian and a catholic," while simultaneously calling himself a "communist" and an "atheist," Pasolini engaged in the dialectical thinking that may distinguish Italians from other western political theorists. His films, particularly *The Gospel According to Saint Matthew*, pointed to the "world of the Roman shantytowns, the world of the subproletarian poor" as the end of history, "an apocalypse of the spirit" in which the destiny of the Italian subproletariat is one with peasants of the third world.

5. Signs of a new world in the writings of Italian liberation theologians, independent radicals, and theorists of nonviolence

Utopian thinking in today's Italy spans a wide arc comprising liberation theologians like Giulio Girardi and Gianni Baget-Bozzo, independent communists within the Pci like Umberto Eco, independent radicals of the left like Leonardo Sciascia. And feminists.

Utopian strains in contemporary left catholicism and liberation theology derive from Pope John XXIII, who in the early sixties described the international worker movement, colonial efforts for independence, and women's advancement as "signs of the times." Revolutionary implications of John's teaching have been analyzed by Guilio Girardi, liberation theologian whose writings are indispensable for understanding new left confrontations in Italy in 1968.

For Girardi, marxist theory is not a critique of God, but a critique of people who call themselves "religious."[13] The meaning of John's teaching, for Girardi, is that each human being shows faith in heaven by taking initiative for a new world on earth. Insisting on an *inedito* interpretation of biblical and marxist truths, Girardi voices the left catholic belief that each human being, not just the papacy, can interpret the gospels. Along with the Italian new left, he insists that marxism is important for economic liberation, but beyond marxism there will remain "the problem of the sense of life and of death, of suffering and of solitude."[14]

Girardi reflected a decade of Italian new left and feminist agitation when in the 1980s he denounced the world order of violence as grounded on the "dynamic of capitalism" yet characteristic also of "existing socialist nations." For Girardi, disarmament implies a large dismantlement endeavor: "dismantling the legitimacy of a culture of classes, dismantling violence in the family, dismantling violence in relationships of men and women, dismantling violence in majority and minority ethnic groups, dismantling violence in revolutionary culture, dismantling violence in religion itself," so that a "culture of peace, of love, and of liberty can be born."[15]

Gianni Baget-Bozzo, another Italian liberation theologian, in 1983 said that the Italian peace movement posed "the right and duty of people not to destroy the life of humanity, of not uncreating the world...the right of small nations not to become mere spaces at the disposition of the superpowers... the right of young people not to be sent to die without reason, the right of parents to protect the life that they have created with responsible parenthood."[16]

Placing marxist theory in the context of ultimate beliefs, Italian liberation theology has bonded revolutionary theory to an ethic of nonviolence. This significant development can be tracked in the history of the Italian communist party after 1968 and echoed in Umberto Eco's *The Name of the Rose*. For Italian communists this is a journey from rationalism to a sense of the void and of the sacred, and from a dogma of necessary violence to a condemnation of all justifications of killing.

Setting his novel in the franciscan era, an age that Eco parallels with 1968, the semiotician/novelist drew an analogy between the century following the death of Saint Francis and the decade of terror in Italy following 1968.[17] In the late seventies the Pci denounced the revolutionary violence of the red brigades, and in 1981 Italian communists rejected the violence inherent in leninism, condemning violence whether it is in the name of religion, patriotism, or revolution. For a majority of Italians by the 1980s, conscience, not papal or party doctrine, is the significant arbiter of moral judgment, dialectical thinking an effective mode of individual checking and balancing, and respect for differences an indispensable premise for a good society: for most Italians today both believers and unbelievers—*credenti* and *non-credenti*—will bring in the new world.

Historically the decades of the seventies and eighties in Italy may well be remembered for deepening marxism. The encounter of marxism with anarchism is suggested in the writing of Leonardo Sciascia, an Italian independent radical. Exploring the idea of "power as a criminal act," the Sicilian writer turned the 1978 kidnap and murder of Aldo Moro by the red brigades into a detective story/parable. Sciascia uncovered complicity in high places, judicial omission, police inefficiency, and the moral ambiguity of abstract concepts. Scoring the moral myopia of all major Italian parties, who insisted on not negotiating with the red brigades for the release of Aldo Moro, Sciascia pointed to the unchristian behavior of christian democrats (Dc) and the ironic behavior of communists (excluded from state governing coalitions since 1947) who joined established parties in invoking the state and refusing to negotiate for an exchange of prisoners.

Charging political parties of the right and of the left with a "stalinism" that treats humans as documents on which to write doctrine, Sciascia said that even some of the openly stalinist red brigades "traitorously" allowed compassion to determine their actions. Sciascia identified with Moro's chill before the relentless, merciless position of the government, "and all its satellites," who in defending purpose of state dismissed what all Italians who are not attached to the state know instinctively: when it is a question of saving a person's life or remaining faithful to abstract principles, one saves a life.[18]

Another Sciascia essay placed scientists in the beam of a flashlight of ethics. Adopting the case of Ettore Majorana—an Italian nuclear scientist who was thought to have committed suicide in 1938—as a vehicle for meditation on "collaborationism" in mass murder, Sciascia showed that Majorana's research by 1938 indicated that the atomic bomb could be created soon. With the contemporary Italian respect for individual moral judgment, Sciascia asked, Did the physicist design his "death" to point to the deadly use of the atomic bomb?

Sciascia's questions led him to a Carthusian monastery in Palermo where it was rumored that the American pilot who dropped the bomb on Hiroshima had come—as had Majorana. Implicit in the monk's response to Sciascia's questions is contemporary Italian respect for differences: "There are no scientists among the Carthusians."[19]

6. Italian feminists and a new world

Utopian thinking in Italy today, as suggested above, has moved beyond millennial dreams to painful ethical inquiry into means, myopias, and ends. Italy's women's movement, grounded in a peasant past and revolution and resistance in the twentieth century, placed equal rights into the 1948 constitution and the most impressive women's legislation of Europe (maybe of the world) into the Italian canon after 1968.[20] Women have been a major force in bringing about the contemporary democratic "transformation" of the Italian communist party. Today the Italian communist party considers religious belief prior to political commitment, and unlike any other communist party of the planet, considers women to be agents of social transformation. Contemporary Italian women, as independent radicals or as autonomous members of Italy's left parties, are intent on *la forza delle donne* (women's strength) to create a utopian socialism that deepens the meaning of democracy culturally and politically.

Realism and tenderness are implicit in Italian women's dialectical thinking and behavior. Natalia Ginsburg's writings, for example, are similar in spirit to Gramsci's dictum "pessimism of the mind, optimism of the will," yet there are distinctive women's notes. Her novels depict the tragic-absurd underlining of a society in rapid change, while her work in parliament (as an independent of the left) guides that change in a humane direction.[21]

In *The City and the House*, Ginsburg paints a portrait of Italian men and women living through a cultural revolution. For some men whose political commitment has weakened, political purpose is replaced by aestheticism; for some women in search of purpose, life becomes a flight from relationship to relationship. Yet, in Ginsburg's delineation, Italian society does not collapse. Strong single women keep the children amidst the ruins; cheerful women cook spaghetti and offer peasant counsel. Franciscan concern overrides conventional boundaries: a new-age male couple takes in a young pregnant woman; older women nurture abandoned children. On the contemporary Italian landscape of pain and caring, diffident fathers take joy in other people's children, find earlier rejected sons. Recording the meaning of the "immense velocity within silence" of today's Italy, Ginsburg's many marginalities (Jewish, Sicilian, a woman) enable her to describe the wreckage of the traditional patriarchal family and to illuminate possibilities in seeming chaos.[22]

Francesca Duranti's *The House on Moon Lake: A Novel* explores the inner meaning of the dissolution of traditional forms in contemporary Italy. Fabrizio, the male protagonist, regards himself as the "unhappy incarnation of all the historical defeats of the twentieth century": "rebellious women who question the rules of the game of love," "drawing room radicals" who consider him a rightist, and polluters and corrupt politicians who sully the environment. Intellectually Fabrizio veers between irony and bitterness; emotionally he suffers a "desperate childlike distress" compounded of "humiliation, a sense of injustice, impotence, rage."[23]

In her prize-winning novel, Duranti describes Fabrizio's dilemma: emotionally drawn to Fulvia, whose peasant antecedents gave her a clarity to match her "caramel, honey and ripe peach" embrace of life, yet also attracted to faustian intellectual rationalism. In the end, Fabrizio gives up Fulvia's embrace of life for Pietra, a disembodied figure whose name connotes the church. So much for some men.

Among other Italian women writers whose writings are pointers to meaning in today's Italy, are Dacia Maraini, Adele Cambria, and Adriana Zarri. Speaking out of her own religious upbringing, Maraini early criticized catholic church education for perpetuating the patriarchal ideology that sex for women is a sin, motherhood is woman's major destination in life, and a good mother sacrifices all for the family. For Maraini, patriarchal church morality protects masculine sexual interests and masculine ruling-class privileges.[24]

In her search for women's culture, Maraini has gone to prechristian sources and to subterranean history: to the Mediterranean earth mother, Greek and Roman myths and goddesses, and the behavior of uncelebrated women for millennia whose "sardonic rage" yet "tender understanding" Maraini considers "historically feminine." She contrasts these women's values with the "exaltation, fanaticism, myopia, and violence" that she found in "places of masculine revolutionary politics."[25]

Maraini's critical essays, epistolary novels, poetry, film-writing, historical plays, and new theatrical forms accompany political activism furthering feminism and nonviolence. *Dialogo di una prostituta con un cliente* is a stinging response to men of the left who early on asked, What do these women want? In *Dialogo*, Maraini reverses the traditional object of sexism: the prostitute is clothed, the client (a member of the Pci) is naked. In *Storia di Piera*, Maraini listens to a women's life with psychoanalytic insight and awareness of survivals of prechristian beliefs. Using language that aims "to explode" fantasy and reality, Maraini alludes to forbidden topics of incest, a young woman's desire to be simultaneously male and female, a girl's love for a priest.

In her recent *La bionda, la bruna, e l'asino*, Maraini reflects on the Italian women's movement, which in global perspective has launched a cultural as well as political revolution. Maraini reaffirms themes of two decades of feminist work: prostitution as a metaphor for women's condition—a commerce that conflates rules of the market and moral laws, violence as an everyday activity whose family form suggests the perversity of cruelty crossed with desire, the attraction/repulsion of fathers and daughters and mothers and sons, the unpaid work of the housewife, adultery as a search for self, old age as loss of one's body, homosexuality as chastity.[26]

Adele Cambria's plays are a major contribution to world literature of feminism/marxism. With a feminist/anarchist perspective, Cambria judges male marxists by how they behave as human beings. At *La Maddalena* (the feminist experimental theater founded by Dacia Maraini), Cambria highlighted Marx's relationship with the household governess, with whom he had an unacknowledged child. Her play about Lenin charged him with bequeathing the dubious doctrine that women's liberation is attained by women leaving the house and accepting a subordinate role in the industrial proletariat. Settling accounts with Lenin in the seventies, she blamed him for the (then) democratic centralist form of the Pci, party obtuseness about women, and the violence that "seduced a few male revolutionaries."[27] An important voice in the criticism that led to democratic changes in the Pci by the early eighties, Cambria's barbs reached Gramsci.

Examining his prison correspondence, Cambria said that Gramsci's monumental contribution to the world left had been paid for by the mental illness of his wife, by the acceptance of the female role of sacrifice of his sister-in-law, and by the equivocal behavior of another sister-in-law who was, in effect, recruited to the purposes of male society. A woman in one of Cambria's plays cries, "I want the revolution of women as one wants a lover. I want the end of the struggle, of fear, of lies. . . . I would like to dance all alone and nude on a rocky peak under the cypresses without fear of where I put my feet. I am dying tonight suffocated by desperation and the moral weight of this struggle—which is also against those few men I love."[28]

The continuing cultural revolution of left catholicism and feminism may be examined in the writings of Adriana Zarri, Italian nun and feminist, who writes a column for *Rocca*, Italy's major left catholic magazine. Close in spirit to Saint Teresa of Avila, who combined activism that skirted heresy—with contemplation, Zarri has combined activism for divorce and legal abortion with monasticism. Assaulted by the racism ("to protect the purity of the race") of the fascist anti-abortion law (that remained in the statutes until the early seventies), as well as the "ignorance of the bible, history, theology" shown by clerical defenders of prohibition of abortion, Zarri suggested the theology inherent in the feminist maxim, *Io sono mia*. For a believer, every human belongs to God, but after God, each person belongs to herself or himself.[29]

Religious reformer as well as feminist, Zarri considers the catholic church "my church" and works for the church promised by vatican council II: "poor, disarmed, respectful" giving space to "individual choice of conscience" a church that chooses "people over the sabbath." Mordant in her criticism of Pope John Paul II, Zarri said that his views lead to a "blasphemous" consolidation of church and state; his antifeminist encyclicals, said the nun, were attributable to "*massiccio virilismo*"[30] (massive male chauvinism).

Drawing an important distinction between papal and popular catholicism, Zarri describes folk beliefs as "more passionate, more lyrical, more emotional, less rigid, more visceral and chaotic, more audacious in confrontations with God." Religious beliefs of the people may be "more superstitious and pagan," but folklore beliefs have a richness, said the nun, that the church for all its splendors cannot attain. Aiming to eradicate traditional catholic dualism wherein women's sensuality is negatively tied to the earth, for Zarri, the spirit becomes visible in material manifestation.

At her farm at Molinasso where she tends rabbits and chickens, a garden of flowers and tomatoes, zucchini, and eggplant, Zarri describes herself as a hermit, an anchorite in witness against the "armed tank of curialism, authoritarianism, centralism (not democratic)" of the Roman church after vatican council II.[31] Not in flight from the world, but in witness to the joy, the hope, the harmony of the "new heavens and new worlds" promised by the gospels, the world, says Zarri, "has need of enthusiasm and commitment but also of solitude and silence in the measure that we are committed."[32]

Embodying the values of "poverty, humility, sense of dependence and of debt,"[33] Zarri is a mystic, but not one who lingers in the darkness. The void, for this nun, is a way-station for valuing "the flowers, the cats, the brooks, the plants, the clouds."[34] Recovering an ancient belief, Zarri says, "I love clear nights and the curve of the moon which is like a mouth to kiss."

Feminist, mystic, and nun, the word *immersa* connotes her belief that life is a prayer.[35] In the eternal dialectic between 'already' and 'not yet', states Adriana Zarri, the "sensation prevails of '*gia*' which renders the '*non ancora*' more hopeful."[36]

Let us imagine the possibilities of an Italian component of a multicultural canon for the United States: electoral candidates exercising dialectical imagination would announce they are simultaneously "christian" and "atheist" and "communist"; Italian Americans, educated to regard the United States as the pinnacle of democracy, would discover that Italy is the world's most hopeful experiment in self-government; U.S. writers, relaxing in the separation of art and politics, would be reminded that the only "viable poetry" is that which is "committed." Italian American catholics, whose ethnic insecurity in a protestant country has made them far churchier than their counterparts in Italy, would learn that the peasant interpretation of catholicism is more democratic and more millennial than doctrines of papal catholicism. Right-wing christians of the United States would be startled to find that Italians consider marxism not a critique of God, but of people who call themselves religious.

And U.S. feminists, impaled on rationalist marxist/feminist dilemmas, would discover that their Italian sisters are taking marxism away from the ideologues and working for a new world with feminist values at once equalitarian, nonviolent, and nurturant.

Notes

1. See David Scott Fox, *Mediterranean Heritage* (London, Henley, and Boston, 1978), 1.

2. See Joan Kelly Scott, "Did Women Have a Renaissance," in *Becoming Visible: Women in European History*, eds. Renate Bridenthal, Claudia Koonz, and Susan Stuard. (Boston, 1987, second edition), 191, 197.

3. This is a major theme of my *liberazione della donna (feminism in Italy)* (Middletown, Conn., 1986; paper edition 1988).

4. See *liberazione*, chapter 1. For the peasant tradition see bibiliography in *liberazione*. Indispensable are Salvatore Salomone-Marino, *Costumi ed usanze dei contadini di Sicilia* (Palermo, 1879); Serafino Amabile Guastella, *Le parità morali (1883),* and, above all, the multivolumed Giuseppe Pitrè library, *Biblioteca delle tradizioni popolari siciliane* (reprinted 1978).

5. See *liberazione*, preface.

6. See *liberazione*, chapter 2.

7. For Gramsci, see bibliography in *liberazione*. The two classical works are *The Modern Prince and Other Writings* (New York, 1957) and *Selections from the Prison Notebooks*, Quintin Hoare and Geoffrey Nowell Smith, eds. and trans. (New York, 1971).

8. See Jose Romas Regidor, "Gramsci a Santiago," *il manifesto*, 13 luglio 1987.

9. See bibliography in *liberazione*, especially chapter 4 on the Italian resistance.

10. See Birnbaum, "black and other madonnas," chapter 4, of book-in-progress, *Dark Wheat and Red Poppies. Folklore and socialism: Italian popular beliefs in a good society*. Carlo Levi, *Cristo si è fermato à Eboli* (first published at Rome, 1947).

11. See discussion of Silone, *liberazione*, 53.

12. See discussion of Pasolini in *liberazione*, 63, 73–75, 180–81.

13. For Giulio Girardi, the central work is *Credenti e non credenti per un mondo nuovo* (1969). For an extensive bibliography of Italian left catholicism, see *liberazione*, 332. See discussion of Girardi in *liberazione*, 68 ff.

14. Ibid. Quotation is on 70.

15. Ibid.

16. Quoted in *liberazione*, 231. See *liberazione* for bibliography of Baget-Bozzo's writings, 311.

17. See discussion in *liberazione*, 211-14.

18. See Lucia Chiavola review of Sciascia's *The Moro Affair and the Mystery of Marjorana* (New York, 1987) "Exploring a Pair of Italian Tragedies," *San Francisco Chronicle*, Books, 7 June 1987. Sciascia died in 1989.

19. Ibid.

20. See *liberazione*.

21. Ginsburg's novels offer an excellent cultural history of Italy from world war II to the present. See *La strada che va in città* (Turin, 1942); *È stato così* (Turin,

1947); *Valentino* (Turin 1957); *Ti ho sposato per alegria e altre commedie* (Turin, 1966); *The Advertisement* (1986); *Vita immaginaria* (1969–47); *Le voci della sera*, Sergio Pacifici, ed. (Turin, 1961, New York 1971); *Mai devi domandarmi* (Rome, 1970); *famiglia* (Turin, 1977). See Birnbaum, "A Patriarchal Wreckage," review of Ginsburg's *The City and the House* (New York, 1987) in *San Francisco Chronicle*, Books, 3 May, 1987.

22. Ibid.

23. See Birnbaum review of Francesca Duranti, *The House on Moon Lake: A Novel* (New York, 1987), *San Francisco Chronicle*, Books, 20 September 1987.

24. For Maraini, see *A memoria* (Milan, 1968); *Memorie di una ladra* (Milan 1972); Maraini's plays: *La famiglia normale*; *Il riscatto à teatro*; *Recitare e Venere*; *Viva l'Italia*; *La donna perfetta*; *Dialogo di una prostituta con un cliente. Suor Juana*; *Manifesto dal Carcere*; *Don Juan*; *I sogni di Clitennestra*; *Maria Stuarda*. Recent novels include *Storia di Piera* (Milan, 1980) and *Lettere à Marina* (Milan, 1981). See also discussion in *liberazione*, 113–14.

25. Ibid.

26. Dacia Maraini, *la bionda, la bruna, e l'asino*. (Rome, 1987).

27. Adele Cambria, *Marx: la moglie e la fedele governante* (Padua, 1980); *Il Lenin delle donne; dalla castrazione amorosa alla violenza terrorista* (Padua, 1981). *Amore come rivoluzione: tre sorelle per un rivoluzionario: le lettere inedite della moglie e delle cognate di Antonio Gramsci, con un testo teatrale*, "Nonostante Gramsci" (Milan, 1976).

28. "Nonostante Gramsci."

29. See Adriana Zarri, *i guardiani del sabato; riflessioni sulla chiesa italiana dopo il referendum sull'aborto* (Rome, 1981) *Nostro signore del deserto; teologia e antropologia della preghiera* (Assisi, 1978).

30. Quoted in *liberazione*, 128.

31. Adriana Zarri, *erba della mia erba. resoconto di vita* (Assisi, 1981, 1984).

32. *erba della mia erba*, 12.

33. Ibid., 149.

34. Ibid., 191.

35. Ibid., 198.

36. Ibid., 230, 241.

From Oral Tradition to Written Word:
Toward an Ethnographically Based Literary Criticism

In his essay "The Family in Southern Italy: Yesterday and Today," Leonard Moss wrote that "the novelist, who is after all an ethnographer who knows how to write, can shed great light on problems ignored by the historian" (Moss 1976, 185). If Moss's labeling of the novelist as ethnographer is valid, then we can develop some interesting approaches to literary criticism if we begin to view the role of the critic in a similar light.

More than shedding light on social problems, a culture's writers, especially its early writers, can tell us much about a storytelling tradition once a culture shifts its emphasis from oral to written channels of communication. One of the tasks of the ethnographic critic, then, is to examine this interaction of oral and written traditions.

This essay first establishes the interaction of oral and written traditions in literary study and then examines the relationship between oral and literary traditions in general before suggesting ways to create an awareness of the interaction. This approach will shed much light on the analysis of the creation and function of Italian/American literature.[1]

The Interaction between Oral and Written Poetics

Ever since it was suggested that Homer's epics were products of oral methods of composition (Parry 1932), the development of oral literature theory and research, utilizing the sciences of philology, anthropology, and literary criticism, has created an impressive body of studies (Foley 1985) that can greatly benefit the detection and description of the elements of oral tradition that find their way into writing. For the most part, the interaction between the poetics of oral and written literatures has been in one direction: that of the oral literature scholars using the developments in literary theory and criticism to illuminate texts created by oral traditions (Foley 1981, Parks 1985, Renoir 1985, and Russo 1985). Until recently (Bright 1982, Chafe 1982, Rader 1982, and Tannen 1982), there has been little if any use by literary critics of the findings put forth by scholars of oral literature.[2] The future of this interaction, I believe, will shift the direction of influence and prove especially relevant in creating both histories and criticisms of those methods of making stories that have shifted from oral to literate bases of composition and transmission.

The Use of Orality in Creating Literature

Creative writing is a genre which is necessarily written but which makes use of features associated with oral language because it depends for its effect on interpersonal involvement or the sense of identification between the writer or the characters and the reader. (Tannen 1982, 14)

After presenting a concise survey of the work done in the past twenty years in the area of orality and literacy, Deborah Tannen suggests that "strategies associated with one or the other tradition (oral or literate) can be realized in any mode" (Tannen 1982, 3). This idea has proven useful to her work on discourses and suggests an approach by which we can examine the interaction of oral and literate strategies in the creation of literature.

Tannen applied the oral/literate paradigm to her analysis of narratives told by Greek and American women about a film (Tannen 1980, 4) and found that there were differences in the narratives between the two cultures, resulting in "elaboration, or focus, or signalling load being placed on different aspects of the interaction (in the film)—on the one hand, message content, and on the other, interpersonal involvement." She attributed these differences to results she had found in earlier studies that showed Greeks were more comfortable than Americans with using formulaic language.[3] Tannen thus sets up the interaction between orality and literacy on "a continuum of relative focus on interpersonal involvement versus message content (Tannen 1980, 15)." Her way of viewing orality and literacy will prove beneficial when we begin examining written texts produced by Italian/Americans. By observing the literary interaction of characteristics of oral and written cultures, we can identify strategies that reflect tendencies to relate to oral and literate styles, remembering, of course, that any literary style is capable of evidence of either.

In *Orality and Literacy*, Walter Ong establishes the notion that writing is decontextualized and oral communication is contextualized. This attempt to separate orality and literacy has been convincingly challenged by the proponents of deconstruction. In "The Breaking of Form," Harold Bloom presents the deconstructionist notion of "intertextuality," or the relation of a poet and his or her poem to poems of the past:

> The poet's conception of himself necessarily is his poem's conception of itself, in my reading, and central to this conception is the matter of the sources of the powers of poetry.
>
> The truest sources, again necessarily, are in the powers of poems "already written," or rather, "already read." Dryden said of poets that "we have our lineal descents and clans as well as other families." (Bloom 1979, 3)

This intertextuality of poetry, I would argue, is a way of relating all creative writing to orality, for the primary sources for literature must inevitably be found in orality, especially when one considers the work of Parry and Lord on the Homeric epics. Thus, to consider literature as unrelated to orality risks leaving out a valuable way of connecting any piece of writing to its oral sources and traditions. Viewed in this light, all creative writing then is contextual.

Margaret Rader explores this idea in her essay "Context in Written Language: The Case of Imaginative Fiction." She challenges the idea that the development of writing is "always in the direction of autonomy, i.e. greater and greater context-independence" (Rader 1982, 187). By analyzing (through expansion) a case involving the use of an imaginative work of fiction, Rader demonstrates "that the conventions for reading and our experiences of many other written texts form the CONTEXT for written utterances, a context which is different from the context for spoken utterances and yet is as crucial in determining meaning" (Rader 1982, 197). Rader draws on work done by Wolfgang Iser on reader reception theory to conclude convincingly that in the case of imaginative writing the notion of context does not belong solely to the realm of oral tradition.

This notion of a context for writing is extremely important in the development of any ethnographic approach to literary scholarship, for it will be required of the ethnographic critic to present those texts (both oral and literate) against which an author takes a stance in her or his work. This aspect of context is especially interesting for first literatures that emerge out of any oral culture as it acquires literacy; once an ethnographic critic can determine this point of fusion between oral and literate cultures, it will become possible to examine whether a particular author is creating a text by transcribing an oral story (i.e., preserving an oral tradition) or by creating a literate story (i.e., creating a literary tradition). Again much of the field in this area of interaction between orality and literature has been cultivated by oral composition theorists and researchers, and awaits involvement by literary critics and historians.

Perhaps the most interesting work to those who might contemplate the examination of oral elements found in literature can be found in Robin Tolmach Lakoff's "Some of My Favorite Writers Are Literate: The Mingling of Oral and Literate Strategies in Written Communication." In many ways, Lakoff's essay is prophetic as she examines the notion of the death of literacy in today's culture. She insists that there is a great deal of evidence that literacy is losing its power as today's primary communication strategy. She also cautions those who would bemoan the loss of literacy not to equate it with a loss of culture and suggests that we must adapt to the diminishing function of literacy in our society. To illustrate the shift in today's society from a literacy based model of human communication to one based on an oral mode, Lakoff examines the interaction of oral and literate characteristics that she has found in a variety of communications media. Throughout this analysis (as she moves from fiction to magazines to cartoons and back to fiction; from styles of speaking and writing to uses of punctuation and other literary techniques to mark "orality"), Lakoff identifies oral and written styles of communication and points to attempts by contemporary authors to create literature that looks more like oral literature than written literature. If this is indeed a tendency (and I believe that Lakoff makes a strong case that it is), then it would benefit literary critics tremendously to begin getting a handle on this trend in literature, a trend she refers to as "the merging of oral and literate traditions" (Lakoff 1982, 260).

Although Lakoff's work is primarily concerned with contemporary literature, I believe that it can contribute much to the study of earlier literature, especially that literature produced by subcultures who first came to literacy by way of entering into a literate society, as did many southern Europeans, Africans, and other immigrant groups. By making a case for orality's place in writing, Lakoff not only suggests something about literacy's future but also tells us much about its past.

Another way in which oral traditions find their way into literature is through the use of dialects. Ernest Hemingway said that American literature begins with *Huckleberry Finn*, and I believe there is a case to made for examining the function of this novel—especially its use of dialect—in the establishment of an intertextuality of subsequent American narratives. Perhaps no other novel or story has done more to establish the notion of variation of voice in American literature. This is especially true for those authors whose first language is not (or was not) English, whose characters are depicted in writing as speaking a variation of standard English—this is indeed true, I would argue, in much minority and immigrant fiction, especially first-generation literature. In reacting to the prose tradition of English and American Romantics, Twain (as did Whitman earlier) did much to keep an oral tradition alive in writing. This is an area of literary history and criticism that has hardly been developed, yet it is one that is essential for establishing ethnographic approaches to the study of literature.

Elizabeth Closs Traugott provides us with an interesting and useful study of the varieties of languages in contemporary fiction. It is a study that can be of great use in developing our critical paradigm. After examing the use of dialect in a number of contemporary American narratives, Traugott suggests that when a tradition is developed for writing in a dialect "we can expect one of its characteristics to be the highlighting of the linguistic variability that is so important in the verbal repertoire of its speakers" (Traugott 1981, 33). This characteristic, Traugott says, will be different from the literary traditions produced by other cultural groups and so the study of such characteristics should "extend to the whole range of writing in English."

Examples of this use of dialect occur in early as well as contemporary Italian/American literature.[4] Authors such as Edoardo (Farfariello) Migliaccio, the *La Follia* columnist and comedian who employed "machiette" (immigrant idiom) in his writing and Pietro Di Donato (Mulas 1990) establish a strong connection between oral and literary traditions by choosing to portray characters' use of dialect.

From Homer to Home: Miles to Go

The work done with Homer by scholars of oral literature was a beginning. The academic employment of the oral tradition was kept alive through the study of classical literature such as the writing of Homer. Those who were not educated in public or private schools, such as women and immigrants who dropped out of schools, found their voices in the homes and neighborhoods. We must now move to the home, the place where the mother tongue rules, where the vernacular roosts, where language use begins and is nurtured, in order to examine the interaction of oral and written language performance. Perhaps this is where all ethnographic criticisms of literature will start. As a community, subculture, or ideolect produces its literary tradition, we must do what we can to identify its characteristics. Of course, problems will arise in isolating individual authors and specifically identifying the appropriate subculture out of which their work emerges. How do we isolate the community an American author or group of authors belongs to?

Any ethnographic approach then must take into consideration more than one's ethnicity; it must also consider the effects that interactions one has outside his or her ethnic boundaries might have on the literature one produces. It is risky business, but business that needs to be done. There are characteristics that African American women writers, for example, have in common with each other that other women writers do not share; and until we identify such characteristics, we are doomed to incomplete readings of the literature they produce. Perhaps these ethnographies will begin to emerge as critical biographies of single authors. After a number have been done on writers from the same ethnic group, comparisons can then be made to identify any emerging patterns such as theme, style, subject, etc. Then such ethnographies will be of great service to critical readers.

Toward such ethnographies we must then begin to identify oral and literate styles, structures, dictions, and other elements in a culture's or subculture's literature by first examining the role of orality and literacy in the community from which an individual writer emerges and then the subsequent communities that he or she writes in and of. It is hard work, lifelong perhaps, but work that will benefit both readers and writers.

The Italian/American Case

In light of the preceding discussion, we now have a context to examine Italian/American literature. By considering the literature produced by Americans of Italian descent as an extension of oral traditions, we can begin to examine not only what history this literature preserves but also in what manner that history is preserved. Italian Americans have a rich oral culture, one that once was passed on from generation to generation, not by diaries, not by short stories, or novels, or other literature, but primarily passed on by word of mouth. This method of carrying on tradition has moved in new directions since Italian Americans have begun to write.

Italian/American writers, such as Pietro Di Donato, John Fante, Jerre Mangione, and Mario Puzo, grew up in a primarily oral culture; many of them were the first of their families to achieve literacy. These and many of the early Italian/American writers were able to use their skills to preserve many oral stories and experiences of their culture.

All of us have heard stories from our grandparents and, had we the inclination, could retell those stories orally or in writing. In the Chicago suburb where I grew up, we had a saying that a really tough guy was one who would play "mora" for fingers. "Mora" is a game in which two opponents flash out the fingers of one hand while simultaneously yelling out the total number of fingers they think will be extended. The one who calls out the correct number scores the point. The score is kept with the fingers of the other hand.

Having never known the origins for that reference, I received an explanation through a story that my grandfather used to tell. Years later I committed this story to writing and now see it as one example of how an oral tale can be adapted to literature.[5] Grandpa used to tell the tale of the two greatest "mora" players in our town's history. The men are partners of an undefeated "mora" team. When they are asked which of the two is better, each man boasts that there is no one better than himself. Both are so confident that they agree to play against each other and score points by having the loser cut off a finger for each point lost.

This type of storytelling was an integral part of growing up Italian. The older members of my family very often answered questions with a tale. Whether it was at the dinner table, in a garden, or at a wedding reception, they'd look around, survey the audience and launch into a tale that would explain the meaning of an Italian word, why people marry, or why they left Italy.

In the towns of southern Italy, the *cantestorie*, or history singers, were the guardians of local tradition. Within the family, children learned by listening, watching, and imitating. Stories such as those my grandparents told me educated while they entertained. Perhaps my grandfather, while teaching me how to play "mora," was also telling me—through this folk-tale—not to take any game too seriously.

Similar examples can be found in much of the fiction written by Americans of Italian descent. Most recently, Josephine Gattuso Hendin portrays this *cantastoria* tradition in the interaction of a father and a daughter in her novel *The Right Thing to Do*. In dealing with a headstrong, rebellious daughter, the father (Nino) relates the story of a miracle that occurred in his Sicilian village when its people decide to grant a girl her dying wish to be buried in her father's coffin. Upon opening the father's coffin, they find that he had not decayed and call it a miracle. However, before they can place the daughter into her father's coffin, the man's body decays so that only his skeleton remains. A discussion follows concerning what would be the proper thing to do: to bury her alone or with her father. Nino uses this story to both caution his daughter about change and to release her from his rule. This use of oral tradition in writing, deftly portrayed by Hendin, echoes back to a preliterate era of immigrant culture; by capturing such stories in writing, authors such as Hendin are establishing a literary tradition built of Italian material, one that, while preserving something Italian, is also creating something American.

The Literary Folktale

In his introduction to *Mules and Men* by Zora Hurston, Robert Hemenway discusses the importance of such folktales:

> Folktales illustrate how an entire people adapted and survived in the new world experience, how they transformed what they found into a distinctive way of life. They describe the human behavior the group approves, indicated when the behavior is appropriate and suggests strategies necessary for the preservation of the group in a hostile environment. (Hemenway 1978, xxii)

Early Italian/American writers provide us with such portraits of Italians adapting to America. Books were not necessary for the first generation in southern Italy, nor were they an integral part of Italians' adaption to

American life. But for their American-born children, literacy became synonymous with "going American."

In American schools, Italian oral culture met the traditions of English literature. Children who went to school for the first time speaking only Italian discovered whole new worlds, first in the English speech and then in its literature. Some of these children, perhaps those who would have been drawn to the *cantastorie* back in Italy, fell in love with reading. Coming from homes that had few, if any, books, writers such as Fante, Di Donato, and Mangione, spent many hours in the local library, absorbing the stories they found there.

In interviews, these early Italian/American novelists tell of their introduction to the written word. In their writing, their families and communities are the basis for wonderful tales. Their books became both a bridge between oral and written cultures and a continuation of Italian storytelling traditions. In moving from an oral to a literary tradition, Italian/American writers were creating a cultural currency that enabled their culture to enter into the American cultural arena. Writers such as Pietro Di Donato and Jerre Mangione wrote primarily biographical fiction, which simultaneously celebrates the joy of their cultural traditions and relates the hardships of adjusting to a way of life where the old values and customs often clashed with those of the new land.

Di Donato's classic, *Christ in Concrete*, the story of a young boy whose father must work under dangerous conditions in a construction job and dies in an unnecessary accident on Good Friday, though noted for its realism, can be read as an expanded folktale.

Mangione's *Mount Allegro*, the story of a boy growing up in a Rochester, New York, Little Italy, offers vignettes of life in the Italian/American extended family, as American-born children struggle to reconcile their parents' Old World beliefs and uncertainty about whether or not they are "Americans":

> Those who left [Mount Allegro] for good developed strange habits and tastes. They took to drinking fruit juices at breakfast and tea with supper. They wore pyjamas to bed, drank whiskey with soda and learned to play poker....If the children had had their own way, my parents would have dropped all their Sicilian ideas and customs and behaved more like other Americans. That was my childhood dream. Yet, as much as we wanted to live an American life, we did not have the vaguest notion of how to go about it. (Mangione 1989, 208)

This excerpt is but one of the many examples that *Mount Allegro* gives us of Italians adapting to America. It contains many of our first folktales.

A second generation of Italian/American authors now in their thirties and forties has emerged, grappling with the task of rediscovering their heritage and examining it in the light of having become American. Yet the writing of many contemporary authors still contains a strong sense of the folktale. Influenced like their parents by the strong oral culture, the second generation to be born in America often grew up with few books. Although they went to school speaking English, school provided the opportunity to learn about writing as a new medium for storytelling.

There are now more than two hundred Italian/American novels that depict the immigrant struggle, second-generation conflicts between American-born children and their parents, and the third generation's search for a cultural heritage. Together these novels flesh out the dry bones of the American past chronicled in the history books. Only recently have scholars begun to address the importance of the Italian folktale in America (see Mathias and Raspa). However, it is my belief that we have been reading them for years and have yet to develop a way of looking at our literature as modern folklore.

Oral Characteristics in the Literary Tradition

In his study *Orality and Literacy*, Walter Ong identifies characteristics of oral and literate cultures. By applying a few of those characteristics to examples of Italian/American literature, we can see that early Italian/American literature is the first bridge between a primary oral culture and a newly literate culture. For the purposes of demonstration, then, I will apply a few Ong's characteristics to sample passages in order to suggest the rich possibilities such an approach can enable.

Ong has identified one characteristic of an oral culture: "The heroic tradition of primary oral culture and of early literate culture with massive oral residue, relates to the agonistic lifestyle. Oral memory works with heavy characters and the bizarre" (Ong 1982, 49). Perhaps this is why a novel such as *The Godfather* has had such a strong influence on the way Italian Americans are perceived. It works with stereotypic "heavy" characters such as Luca Brasi, the brute hit man, and Don Corleone, the patriarchal mafioso. Such characters are often found in the oral stories that get passed on from generation to generation. They become our equivalent of the homespun American folk heroes such as Mickey Finn and Paul Bunyan.

Using Ong's idea, we can suggest that Puzo's characters are closer to those of an oral tradition than to a written one. The story is more like a tall tale, which may very well explain why *The Godfather*, more mythical than literary, succeeds as a story and not as a literary masterwork. In his essay "The Making of *The Godfather*," Puzo himself admits to his attempts to create a myth: "It [*The Godfather*] has energy and I lucked out by creating a central character that was popularly accepted as genuinely mythic"(Puzo 1972, 41).

The sentence structure of oral stories, Ong tells us, is characteristically simple. These simple sentences accumulate information rather than imbed it in complex sentences filled with dependent clauses. Such structure facilitates recall. We find this simplicity throughout John Fante's work, and especially in the opening of his *Wait Until Spring, Bandini!*:

> He came along, kicking the deep snow. Here was a disgusted man. His name was Svevo Bandini, and he lived three blocks down that street. He was cold and there were holes in his shoes. That morning he had patched the holes on the inside with pieces of cardboard from a macaroni box. The macaroni in that box was not paid for. He had thought of that as he placed the cardboard inside of his shoes. (Fante 1983, 11)

Fante's style echoes an oral style by chopping up the information he presents. The tone of the novel is set with this characteristically oral style and each sentence accumulates new information. Because Fante, as a writer, is close to his oral traditions, his simple style strongly reflects that closeness.

Another characteristic of a primary oral culture is the use of repetition. Though few novels begin with traditional folktale phrases, such as "Once upon a time," many begin with the feel of a storyteller calling an audience together. This especially evidenced by the repetition of key phrases in the opening of Tina DeRosa's first novel:

> *This is my mother*, washing *strawberries*, at a sink *yellowed* by all foods, all liquids, *yellowed*. *This is my mother scalping* the *green hair* of strawberries, *scalping* them clean, leaving a pink bald spot where the *green hair* was, and the *strawberries* grow bumps under cold water, or were they already there, and nobody noticed? These are my mother's hands, skin that has touched thousands of things now touches *strawberries*, and *strawberries* are the first thing she has ever touched, but she is not noticing. (DeRosa 1980, 7; emphasis added)

Besides repetition, the use of present tense is a technique that live storytellers often employ to create a sense of things happening right before your eyes. DeRosa, a college-educated third-generation writer, employs a style that retains a closeness to the oral tradition.

From the first paragraph of Helen Barolini's chapter 1 of *Umbertina,* we get a sense of orality and of a tradition that is being passed on, one that reached the narrator by word-of-mouth, one that is passed on through writing: "She had hazel eyes, fair skin where the sun did not reach and a strong chin. In the village people said of Umbertina that she had character right from the womb. 'She'll be the man of her family,' they said" (Barolini 1982, 23). "They said"... with these words we have the sense of orality and the beginning of a story, one that is being passed along to us through the author's writing. *Umbertina* is replete with proverbs and aphorisms, the products of oral culture. Often this formulaic language is presented to the reader in Italian, an authorial choice that directly imbeds the oral tradition in a literary tradition, a move that also enables us to identify the literature as distinctly Italian/American.

Conclusion

One gets what he or she needs to write by listening. By listening to the past inside oneself, a writer stays in tune with his or her oral tradition. An African proverb says, "Ancient things remain in the ear"; undoubtedly good writers listen for them.

The Italian/American culture is one that has moved rapidly from what Ong labels as primary orality to literacy to secondary orality—the orality that occurs in the electronic media experience. This shift has played an important role in the necessity and use of the literacy that Italian Americans have achieved. But the simplicity of style, the use of dialect and of formulaic language, and exaggerated characters that we often find in the writing of first generation Italian Americans are evidence that the authors are still close to their oral traditions.

Because of these writers, we can discover how it feels to make a home in a new country, to create new ways to be American. One also sees the continuation of oral traditions in their writing. Their writing makes history come alive; it places us with the children listening at the grandparent's knee.

All literature, I would argue, in some way or another grows out of and continues to interact with an individual's and a community's uses of orality. With the development of the alphabet, orality is in a sense captured by literacy, but by no means is it erased by it. Future work requires the development of a semiotics of orality that will enable us to establish a literature's oral sources and tradition. This oral study could be developed along with William Boelhower's notion of ethnic semiosis:

> Ethnic semiosis is ultimately organized on the basis of a topological system that generates an open series of such binary isotopies as old world/new world, emigrant/immigrant, ethnic/non ethnic, presence/absence, origins/traces, dwelling/nomadism, house/road, orientation/disorientation. (Boelhower 1987, 13)

To Boelhower's series of binarisms, I would add orality/literacy. Indeed by examining the interaction of these binarisms, we can shed great light on the various literary products that emerge from any pluralistic society. A next step would be to document the evolution of the literary tradition, and for this we could benefit from the work done by Werner Sollors.

In *Beyond Ethnicity: Consent and Descent in American Culture*, Sollors compares the evolution of American ethnic writing to the evolution of American literature:

> ...we are accustomed to think of the development of American literature as "growth," as a process of increasing formal complexity from travelogues and letters..., sermons, essays and biographies to the increasingly successful mastery of poetry, prose fiction, and drama. Analogously, we may see the historical unfolding of ethnic writing as a process of growth; and again, the beginning is with immigrant and migrant letters....The literature then "grows" from nonfictional to fictional forms...; or from an autobiography to an autobiographic novel...; from folk and popular forms to high forms...; from lower to higher degrees of complexity...; and from "parochial" marginality to "universal" significance in the literary mainstream (and the American mainstream now includes more and more writers with identifiable "ethnic" backgrounds). (Sollors 1986, 241)

By examining the movement from functional literacy to creative literacy via the creation of an ethnographic criticism of literature, the literary historians and critics of the future will be better prepared to expand the canon of American literature, or at least to posit parallel canons that represent the diversity that more accurately reflects the composition of American culture.

Notes

1. This use of the slash was inspired by Anthony Julian Tamburri's examination of the hyphen in "To Hyphenate or Not to Hyphenate: What about the Italian/American Writer?" a paper delivered at the Twentieth-Century Literature Conference, 24 February 1989.

2. Though the use of the term *oral literature* is debated, especially arguing against it is Walter Ong (1982), I will use it because I feel it is the best means we have of identifying its relationship to written literature. This identification is especially important in establishing oral texts that interact with and influence writing.

3. Walter Ong associated this formulaic language with primary oral cultures. See his study *Orality and Literacy*.

4. For an excellent presentation of the Italian immigrant linguistic idiom in speech and writing, see Michael LaSorte's chapter 5, "Italglish: The Immigrant Idiom," in *La Merica: Images of Italian Greenhorn Experience*. (Philadelphia: Temple University Press, 1985).

5. This story, "Mora Amore," appears in the Prose section of Creative Works in this volume. A version of the story won second place in the 1985 National Italian/American Literary contest sponsored by Amerital-UNICO.

Works Cited

Barolini, Helen. 1982. *Umbertina*. New York: Bantam.

Bloom, Harold. 1979. "The Breaking of Form." In *Deconstruction and Criticism*, 1–37. New York: Continuum.

Boelhower, William. 1987. *Through a Glass Darkly: Ethnic Semiosis in American Literature*. New York: Oxford University Press.

Bright, William. 1982. "Poetic Structure in Oral Narrative." In *Spoken and Written Language: Exploring Orality and Literature*, edited by Deborah Tannen, 171–84. Norwood, N.J.: Ablex Publishing Co.

Chafe, Wallace L. 1982. "Integration and Involvement in Speaking, Writing, and Oral Literature." In *Spoken and Written Language: Exploring Orality and Literature*, edited by Deborah Tannen, 35–53. Norwood, N.J.: Ablex Publishing Co.

DeRosa, Tina. 1980. *Paper Fish*. Chicago: Wine Press.

Di Donato, Pietro. 1939. *Christ in Concrete*. New York: Bobbs-Merrill.

Fante, John. [1938] 1983. *Wait Until Spring, Bandini!* Santa Barbara, Calif.: Black Sparrow Press.

Foley, John Miles. 1981. "Reading the Oral Tradition Text: Aesthetics of Creation and Response." In *Oral Tradition Literature: A Festschrift for Albert Bates Lord*, edited by John Miles Foley, 262–81. Columbus O.: Slavica Publishers.
———.1985. "Tradition-dependent and -independent Features in Oral Literature: A Comparative View of the Formula." In *Comparative Research on Oral Traditions: A Memorial for Milman Parry*, edited by John Miles Foley, 185–212. Columbus, O.: Slavica Publishers.
———.1988. *The Theory of Oral Composition: History and Methodology*. Bloomington: Indiana University Press.

Hemenway, Robert E. 1978. Introduction to *Mules and Men*, by Zora Hurston. Bloomington: Indiana University Press.

Hendin, Josephine Gattuso. 1988. *The Right Thing to Do*. Boston: David R. Godine.

Lakoff, Robin Tolmach. 1982. "Some of My Favorite Writers Are Literate: The Mingling of Oral and Literate Strategies in Written Communication." In *Spoken and Written Language: Exploring Orality and Literature*, edited by Deborah Tannen, 239–60. Norwood, N.J.: Ablex Publishing Co.

Lord, Albert. 1960. *The Singer of Tales*. Cambridge: Harvard University Press.

Mangione, Jerre. 1989. *Mount Allegro*. New York: Harper and Row.

Mathias, Elizabeth, and Richard Raspa. 1985. *Italian Folktales in America: The Verbal Art of an Immigrant Woman*. Detroit: Wayne State University Press.

Moss, Leonard. 1976. "The Family in Southern Italy: Yesterday and Today." In *The United States and Italy: The First Two Hundred Years*, edited by Humbert S. Nelli. New York: The American Italian Historical Association.

Mulas, Franco. 1990. "The Ethnic Language of Pietro Di Donato's *Christ in Concrete*." In *From the Margin: Writings in Italian Americana*, edited by Anthony J. Tamburri, Paolo A. Giordano, and Fred L. Gardaphé. West Lafayette, Ind.: Purdue University Press.

Ong, Walter J. 1982. *Orality and Literacy: The Technologizing of the Word*. New York: Methuen.

Parks, Ward. 1985. "Orality and Poetics: Synchrony, Diachrony, and the Axes of Narrative Transmission." In *Comparative Research on Oral Traditions: A Memorial for Milman Parry*, edited by J. Foley, 511–32. Columbus, O.: Slavica Publishers.

Parry, Millman. 1932. "Studies in the Epic Technique of Oral Verse-Making." In *The Homeric Language as the Language of an Oral Poetry*, 43: 1–50. Vol. 2 of Harvard Studies in Classical Philology.

Puzo, Mario. 1972. *The Godfather Papers and Other Confessions*. New York: Fawcett Crest.

Rader, Margaret. 1982. "Context in Written Language: The Case of Imaginative Fiction." In *Spoken and Written Language: Exploring Orality and Literature*, edited by Deborah Tannen, 185–98. Norwood, N.J.: Ablex Publishing Co.

Renoir, Alain. 1985. "Repetition, Oral-Formulaic Style, and Affective Impact in Medieval Poetry: A Tentative Illustration." In *Comparative Research on Oral Traditions: A Memorial for Milman Parry*, edited by John Miles Foley, 533–48. Columbus, O.: Slavica Publishers.

Russo, Joseph A. 1985. "Oral Style as Performance Style in Homer's *Odyssey*: Should We Reader Homer Differently after Parry." In *Comparative Research on Oral Traditions: A Memorial for Milman Parry*, edited by John Miles Foley, 549–65. Columbus, O.: Slavica Publishers.

Sollors, Werner. 1986. *Beyond Ethnicity: Consent and Descent in American Culture*. New York: Oxford University Press.

Tannen, Deborah. 1980. "A Comparative Analysis of Oral Narrative Strategies: Athenian Greek and American English." In *The Pear Stories,* edited by Wallace Chafe. Norwood, N.J.: Ablex Publishing Co.

————. 1982. "The Oral/Literate Continuum in Discourse." In *Spoken and Written Language: Exploring Orality and Literature*, edited by Deborah Tannen, 1–16. Norwood, N.J.: Ablex Publishing Co.

Traugott, Elizabeth Closs. 1981. "The Voice of Varied Linguistic and Cultural Groups in Fiction: Some Criteria for the Use of Language Varieties in Writing." In *Writing: The Nature, Development and Teaching of Written Communication*, 111–36. Vol. 1 of *Variation in Writing: Functional and Linguistic Cultural Differences*, edited by Marcia Farr Whiteman. Hilldale, N.J.: Lawrence Erlbaum Associates Publishers.

The Ethnic Language of Pietro Di Donato's
Christ in Concrete

Pietro Di Donato's *Christ in Concrete* (1939) stands as one of the best and most powerful accounts of the Italian immigrant experience in the New World. It is the story of a full-blooded Italian bricklayer, Geremio, whose love for his homeland is reflected in his love for his devoted wife, Annunziata, their seven children, and the eighth about to be born. Geremio is an honest, hardworking man whose enduring loyalty not so much to the nation but to the particular region of his birth is manifest in his preservation of the old habits and customs. He dies on Good Friday when the building he and his *paesani* are working on collapses, burying him alive under a flood of settling concrete (hence the title of the book). After his death, and the almost immediate crippling of Luigi, Annunziata's brother, in another construction accident, the responsibility of assisting the fatherless family falls on little Paul, the oldest of the sons, who, at the age of twelve, is compelled to learn bricklaying. The novel follows this young man in his gradual growth into forced adulthood: he experiences injustice, discovers sex, and, most important, when his friend and godfather, Nazone, dies in a fall from a skyscraper, undergoes a deep religious crisis. The story ends with the death of Annunziata, apparently as a consequence of Paul's loss of faith in God. "Son," she says in a final prayer of hope for redemption, "everything in my world is for thee. For thee I desire the fullest gifts of Heaven—To thee must the good Dio bestow the world—and lasting health. He must bless thee with the flower of womankind and many-many children as yourself...and joy and peace without measure—for me— thou are the most precious...."[1]

When almost half a century ago Pietro Di Donato, a bricklayer by trade, published this first novel, many great critics praised the extraordinary talent with which he related his family's tragic story. Though quite young and burdened with the ethnic limitations of his immigrant status, Di Donato somehow possessed a wide enough vision to see beyond the confines of his immediate experience and to approach his story with objectivity and an admirable control over the emotional forces that had moved him to write it. Perhaps even more than his deep commitment to his family, himself, and his people, Di Donato's obvious fascination with the rhythms and patterns of everyday language, with the incredible triumph of communication in the face of great adversity, gives this novel its special power. Clearly it is a celebration of the gift of speech: that very faculty that so limited the immigrants in their struggle to survive in an alien culture proved ironically to be their sustaining strength, and the language they pieced together from the idioms of their Old World heritage and the strange diction of the tongue they were compelled to learn provides in these pages a metaphor of creativity as striking as that of the skycrapers they were employed to build.

It would be a great mistake to oversimplify the context in which Di Donato's characters played out their roles as urban pilgrims, for which reason a brief look at certain historical peculiarities will be useful. The situation at the turn of the century for the millions of people coming to America in search of work and bread was more complex than the simple giving and taking of two or more intermingling cultures. True, the Italian immigrants, upon reaching the American shore, felt that they had to turn to their national language in order to communicate their most immediate needs. But if we consider the high percentage of illiteracy in Italy at the beginning of the twentieth century, and the fact that most of the immigrants to the New World were from the southern regions and belonged to the working or agricultural classes, we realize that their language was far from unified, even though almost half a century had gone by since the political unification of the country. First, then, the poor immigrant had to struggle out of the linguistic limitations of the peculiar dialect of his own province, and often of his own village, before acquiring the standard speech that allowed him to communicate with his countrymen. This, of course, was not the only communicative difficulty he was faced with; the second, and surely the greater difficulty, confronted him in the marketplace or his daily work when he was forced to move into the linguistic realm of the host culture. What resulted from this intercourse was a kind of language that was neither Italian nor American—it was what could be called an American jargon, a form of hybrid speech,[2] as different and varied as the many "Little Italys" that sprang up in the large cities, each rooted in the customs and dialects of its native region.

The urban jungles[3] of America thus compelled these illiterate peasants, so lacking in self-confidence, to cling together in order to recapture some of the warmth and intimate contact they had known in their villages back home. They were lonely, and as Oscar Handlin put it, "their loneliness had more than one dimension."[4] Everything was unfamiliar to them: people, streets, building, sounds. But, more than anything, their loneliness was due to the fact that neither in the people, nor in nature, nor in the cities could they retrieve the identity they had within their families and communal life of the villages. Initially the feelings of helplessness and insecurity were partially overcome by the solidarity established among people from the same regions, provinces, or towns. The process of assimilation into the larger society was painfully slow, partly because the purpose of these immigrants, at least at first, was to earn enough money so that they could go back to their villages to build a decent house, buy some land, live an easier life. For this reason they never really thought of learning the language or trying to become Americans in the social or cultural sense. Many in fact returned to their *paese* and many more would have liked to, except that they had started a family and decided to stay, without, however, undergoing a true process of acculturation.

Di Donato's *Christ in Concrete*, more than any other Italian-American novel, presents these problems, universally valid to all immigrants, in a vivid and believable account. The American-born son of an Italian immigrant construction worker, Di Donato experienced firsthand the drama, the anxieties, and the uncertainties of immigrant life and succeeded in recapturing a strong sense of the protagonists' identity both as men and as workers striving for survival. The reader cannot help but feel the dreams and expectations of this gang of Abruzzesi immigrant masons, but above all he comes to a tragic awareness of the hopeless conditions of their lives. As a story of oppressed workers, strangers in a strange land who constantly face defeat from all sides, the book carries a highly significant historic and sociological message. God is against them, the "Job," too often extremely humanizied, is against them, and even man himself in the person of unscrupulous people like Mr. Murdin, the building contractor who brings them to their final death or crippling, is against them; yet they endure all hardships and humiliations with unshaken pride and nobility. This is ultimately what *Christ in Concrete* is about, and the author, having shared the experience, knew that in order to make his story live he had to people it with common, flesh-and-blood characters, a real gang of bricklayers engaged in the earthly but monumental difficulties of contructing a building. Who better than a bunch of uprooted laborers could have expressed the fears and uncertainties connected with the hard realities of empire-building in the New World? Only such protagonists, in all their physical strength, their loyalty to their families and to each other, and most important for the purpose of our paper, their rich, vivid, colorful everyday language. As already suggested, it is ultimately through speech, through the characters' words—and when these do not suffice, through their gestures—that we are given to partake of their bitter saga.

Certainly the fact that the author grew up and spent part of his life with this group of vocal bricklayers helped him to enlarge his sense of the dramatic, to develop his awareness of emotional effects as well as the advantages of realistic narrative and direct statement. Although the writing betrays various stylistic inconsistencies, on the whole we can say that the young author succeeded in giving us a convincingly objective view of the protagonists' world as they themselves lived and viewed it. At the same time, however, he charged it with the meaningful tensions of his own youthful feelings, without quite falling into the sentimentality that one might expect from an untutored craftsman.

Ford Madox Ford once described Hemingway's words as being like "pebbles fetched fresh from a brook. They live and shine, each in its place. So one of his pages has the effect of a brook-bottom into which you look down through the flowing water."[5] At least the first part of this metaphor could be taken easily to describe Di Donato's language in *Christ in Concrete*. For more direct support, however, we quote from Dorothy Canfield's review of the book, in which she refers specifically to Di Donato's coinage of words and more particularly perhaps to the lyrical effects of his inventive language: "Your ears are wonted to the new-minted freshness of their Italian-English metaphors and rhythms, so that to return to the correctness of our own stereotyped everyday talk is almost like leaving poetry to prose."[6] This appreciation, while a bit excessive in its flattery, is instructive mainly because it sees that Di Donato, in placing a peculiar colloquial emphasis upon the word, brought his prose to a high level of originality. It is well to bear in mind that in achieving this he was greatly aided by two very important factors: his good knowledge of the Abruzzese-Italian language he had spoken at home (from which he derived the idiom of the book) and his lifelong acquaintance with the protagonists of the story whose spontaneous dialogues provided the sparkling pebbles that his pen turned into gems.

To imagine, however, that Di Donato, in retelling the drama of his people and the tragedy that befell his family, was at the same time trying to set a new prose style in American literature would be to misunderstand both his intention and his talent. While it is true that the narrative owes much of its strength to the peculiarity of his style and language, there is nothing in these pages that pretends to literary innovation. But it might be noted that not even the vernacular American-English discovered and exploited by authors of literary importance such as Twain, Hemingway, and Faulkner resulted in a truly innovative American prose style. In their ambitious and articulate works, new words and new rhythms revealed an original expressive beauty but never actually set an authoritative standard. Their most experimental works stand today as examples of different trends in their manner of narrating, representing a more or less limited period in their literary careers, but never a final turning point, never the ultimate stage of their writing achievement or a clear point of departure for the modern American novel.

Without making any literary claims, either linguistically or stylistically, Di Donato places special emphasis on the highly figurative language of his hardworking and humble characters. His vocabulary is not what we are accustomed to define as "literary"; rather it is colloquial—the words are specific and concrete, and the images seem to be shown rather than told. The story itself seems to have forced concreteness on its author; and since he is recreating a way of life completely unfamiliar to the reader, he chooses the expedient of being as realistic as possible, thus committing himself to pictorial exactness. Events and actions are carefully described, words and expressions referring to common local customs are faithfully used and explained; and whenever the protagonists' emotions come into play, their physical manifestations are drawn with almost exaggerated detail.

Di Donato's importance as a novelist, however, rests upon his skill and inventiveness in creating and dealing with a peculiar language. Nevertheless, with extreme modesty, and on more than one occasion, he had this to say: "I was simply recording the language and the ways and the drama of my people and the tragedy of my family."[7] But it was exactly this mere recording of his people's speech, and the ethos conveyed in their tragic story, that brought him acclaim as a young artist, including the praise of having written a "small classic" on the Italian immigrant experience.

In a recent interview Di Donato once again explained his linguistic achievement in *Christ in Concrete* as follows: "I have always thought in Italian and I still do think in Italian, and then I express myself. My English words are recoinage from my Abruzzese-Vasto Italian, because I have never been influenced by the English language. I have always found it inadequate and never, never comparable or as rewarding as the Italian language, the language of my people. It is the anachronism, the irony that these people who could neither read nor write, my mother, spoke infinitely richer language than today's college professors. And that is no exaggeration because I would translate it literally. They knew just what to say."[8] No doubt there is truth in these words, which in part we accept, for we know that the only language he spoke as a child was the Abruzzese dialect of Vasto used at home by his parents and the rest of the *paesani* from the same village. It is also probable that his mother, though illiterate and having had no schooling whatever, was as intelligent and civilized as any American who had earned a college degree. But the narration in *Christ in Concrete* reveals much more than these fundamental influences. First, it shows a considerable mastery of "American-English," as the adopted language of this twenty-five-year-old bricklayer is sometimes called by second-generation Italian Americans. Second, through various verbal patterns, it manages to convey a true ethnic identity to this group of masons by preserving unaltered a variety of their cultural traits. The novel, then, is not merely the retelling of the tragic experience of an Italian immigrant family in America, but it is also a historical record of a worldview, "a monocultural worldview,"[9] narrated with conscientious fidelity from the point of view of the same protagonists who actually lived the experience.

Presumably this historical aspect is what Di Donato has in mind when he says he was simply recording his people's idiom—at times in all its vulgarity, profanity, and obscenity—but he forgets to say, perhaps deliberately, that no story, no matter how dramatic or tragic, can succeed on paper without the artist's rhetorical techniques and narrative discipline. Regardless of its stylistic inconsistencies (whether intentional or unintentional, but often pointed out by reviewers and critics as linguistic devices "to suggest the flavor of the foreign language spoken by the characters"[10]), this novel succeeds on at least two counts: besides giving to American literature a new and peculiar lyrical dimension, it convincingly documents the drama of the struggling immigrant in his failure to attain the "American Dream." Its characters, taken from the streets rather than the pages of history, leave the impression of being themselves at all times, whether in their excess of sorrow or their excess of joy, laughing or weeping, at work or in their exuberantly noisy feasts. Significantly, the only dimension that lacks expression is that of their inner moral world, which they seem to have forgotten, to have lost contact with, taken up as they are by the awesome "Job," the intensity of which often dwarfs and paralyzes them in their impossible struggle.

Throughout the novel, Di Donato uses the lively speech of his characters to achieve dramatic and rhythmic effect. By translating "the spirit of the Italian lyric conversation and colloquialism into American speech, which strikes one as quite natural,"[11] as Louis Adamic put it in his review of the book, he captures the range and intensity of feeling of his protagonists and vividly articulates their insights, passions, and expressiveness. To properly celebrate Di Donato, then, would be to praise the effectiveness of his sensitive ear and his genius for transferring his observations with a minimum of adulterations. On the simplest level he picks up not only the typical ethnic omission of articles but also the additional vowel sounds common to such speakers as Mike the "Barrel-mouth": "I don't know myself, but somebodys whose gotta bigga buncha keeds and he alla times talka from somebodys elsa!" (12). The orginality of his style, however, lies in his ability to catch such common language in its most expressive and transparent moments. The images he creates are grounded in simplicity and concreteness, but they never lack poignancy.

> "Sign nothing!" advised Katarina.
> "Yes," said the Regina, "your cross made on a thin paper will bring ruin to you and your children."
> "When you present yourself there, demand bread for your children!" said Katarina.
> Grazia sighed: "Ah, but how can a widow without the American tongue tell her needs to men whose guts do not know which way first to burst forth?"
> "Listen not to these peasants and potato-diggers, Annunziata," said Katarina. "Cart your eight hungry little children to this official post. You need not speak, for if they belong to our Christ, these men will know their duty when they look upon the faces of Geremio's children."
> "Yes, but I, this stupid Grazia who counts with fingers on nose, tell you that the full gut sees not the hungry face."
> "Nor sees God nor Christ nor Saints and company beautiful," affirmed the Regina.
> Cola raised her eyes and said: "Yes, but the wheel goes round."
> "And we 'neath it," muttered Katarina. (143)

Such imagery, as the story unfolds, becomes increasingly more colorful and idiosyncratic, highlighting not only the fictional incidents in themselves but also the particular qualities that set them off as historically unique. Indeed, the author's frequent recourse to photographic descriptions, partly taken from his own experience, gives vitality and immediacy to the protagonists' struggles. But more than his emphasis on precise physical detail, his impulse to catch the rhythms and the music of ordinary speech explains the graphic idiom he creates in the book. Lacking both a complex syntactical structure and a vast vocabulary, the language of the protagonists depends on gesture as well as a variety of cadences and intonations to impart provocative meanings to basic words:

> "'Tention, paesans!" then he quickly drank a glass of wine, wiped at his mustache and continued: "Before all the world I declare this pure love, but what a love! for the naked little angel who lies in roasted beauty under these very eyes."
> "How? How?" cried Katarina.
> "Because she is good enough to eat!"
> "Buffoon! Buffoon!" called the Regina.
> "Forward with your romance, Master Fausta!" encouraged Mike.
> "May I be split six ways if I tell not the truth; I say that I love this she-suckling with all the sincerity of my golden heart!" and thus he amorously kissed the suckling's mouth.
> "Why?" shrieked the women.
> Fausta screwed his sharp little black eyes evilly and wagged his pointed ears as the gaslight danced over his pompadour, and he hissed: "Bee-cause...love wishes to *devour*!"
> "Eeeeeeeee!" answered the women.
> "Love is a hunger!" sang Nazone operatically. "Encore! Fausta encore!"

"You men are terr-i-ble!" tittered the Lucy's fat wife.

Luigi with long knife cut into the suckling and revealed the luscious meat beneath crisp candied-like brown surface. The ohs and ahs were ecstatic, and Fausta only warming to his theory of "love" plucked a fig from the suckling's eyes and before eating it held it up and said: "Perhaps I am taken up as fool or lying one, but tell me veritably, has that creature of my wife such a fig that I may eat!" (253–54)

At times this language becomes intensely poetic and expressive, and the reader sees and feels, almost without the sense of having read, certain events and situations. Di Donato's is a language of action and movement rather than one of reflection, and because of this, his story is most meaningful when experienced as a process. Whether or not this process offers the reward of a true catharsis is perhaps debatable, for it must be said that the author fails to present a tragedy in the traditional sense of the word: his book never fully characterizes a recognizable hero. His achievement, as suggested earlier, lies elsewhere, and if his characters fail to convince us as classic types (perhaps because their individual psychologies remain unexplored), they nevertheless speak with an authenticity that gives them at least a temporary, fragmented reality—and perhaps this is all that Di Donato saw fit to reveal.

On the narrative level, the mood set at the beginning of the story through sweeping, somewhat literary images, is not sustained: "March whistled stinging snow against the brick walls and up the gaunt girders. Geremio, the foreman, swung his arms about, and gaffed the men on" (11). Such flowing, descriptive prose is soon neglected, possibly because the young writer was carried away by his eagerness to get on with his story, or possibly because he himself fell under the incantation of the powerful, all-too-human language of his protagonists' speech. In any case, mainly because of the dialogues, which are usually brief, lively, and as direct and uncomplicated as the protagonists themselves, the narrative never fails to engage us. Its apparent simplicity is at times deceptive, however, for much of the intensity of its action is artfully derived from the protagonists' feelings of homesickness, which have never been resolved.

The dialogues themselves, which are invariably fast moving and distinctively cultural and personal, occasionally seem to show the author's artistic limitations. It might be argued, however, that the seemingly too typical or too picturesque expressions of some of the dialogues, which depend on a mechanical, simplified diction, are in fact keys to the protagonists' culture and serve to preserve their Old World identity, through which their redeeming dignity is maintained. Even the frequent repetitions (which have often been regarded as a mere binding device) function as reminders of their lack of sophistication, as do the various gestures and motions accompanying their apparently artless conversations.

By general agreement, the linguistic patterns in the novel constitute the chief characteristic of Di Donato's prose. As Giovanni Sinicropi points out, they "form in their diversity one of the richest linguistic textures to be found in the twentieth-century novel."[12] This richness no doubt draws heavily on the abundance of Italianized expressions which somehow give the narrative both casualness and realism:

Geremio cautioned the men. "On your toes, boys. If he writes out slips, someone won't have big eels on the Easter table."

The Lean cursed that the padrone could take the job and all the Saints for that matter and shove it...!

Curly-headed Lazarene, the roguish, pigeon-toed scaffoldman, spat a cloud of tobacco juice and hummed to his own music... "Yes, certainly yes to your face, master padrone... and behind. This to you and all your kind!" (14)

In passages like this the author expresses himself in a colloquial street language, filled with cultural references. He is at his best when he keeps his dialogues terse, sprinkling them with homely metaphors, epithets, and innuendoes. When the book came out, Di Donato was praised for the cheerfulness and gaiety of his almost effortless, genuine, and perfect conversational style. The way he has used the English language is entirely original, whether because he thought in Italian and translated into English, as he himself claimed, or because he allowed his characters to remain as natural as if we had met them at a construction site or a wedding feast or in their squalid tenements. What distinguishes his prose, then, is its simplicity, its descriptive concreteness, and its fidelity to the idioms of speech, which place him justly in the "role of untutored sensuous artist,"[13] in Fred T. Marsh's words.

In the linear account of the story, we encounter no troubling contradictions or ambiguities, probably because Di Donato remained true to the simple but profound task he had set for himself: to disclose the essence of the drama of the poor immigrant in a hostile land. His occasional excesses, particularly in regard to character development, are not entirely without their positive effects. The protagonists are conceived as superior beings, but we get the feeling that their superiority derives from the inhuman struggle they have to face day after day in a world where prejudice plays the major role; it is their oppression that allows them to grow dramatically and to rise in our imagination above the level of ordinary men. At times, too, the intensity of emotion brings the narration close to the nature of dramatic presentation, partly because the protagonists seem so conspicuously aware of their personal drama and partly because, through dialogue, they make their situation clear to us in the way we would normally expect from a stage play.

A final comment in regard to the political tenor of the novel: while there is no evidence, at least explicitly, that Di Donato was making an ideological attack on American capitalism, there is certainly open criticism of institutions and, more specifically, condemnation of unscrupulous entrepreneurs who, blinded by easy profits and deaf to their own consciences, brought many honest immigrants and their families to ruin. Clearly Di Donato was well aware that the story itself would indirectly disclose the various injustices of capitalistic society. *Christ in Concrete*, like other novels of the immigrant experience, expresses the sobering message that the American Dream has always been reserved for those with the "right" credentials. The theme of disenchantment is made vivid by Nazone, one of the novel's tragic characters, when in desperation he asks his teenage godson to help him find work, "work that I may go to my wife and children in Abruzzi. The career of builder in this land is done. This land has become a soil that has contradicted itself." And to make the betrayal sound even more personal and ethnic, he adds: "Discovered by an Italian—named from an Italian— But oh, that I may leave this land of disillusion" (278–79).

Notes

1. Pietro Di Donato, *Christ in Concrete*, (New York: Bobbs-Merrill Co., 1939), 310–11. Numbers in parentheses throughout indicate page references from this edition.

2. Lina Unali, "Cultural and Linguistic Hybridization in Mario Puzo's *The Godfather*." (A paper read at the International Conference of the European Association for American Studies, Paris, April 1982.)

3. Rudolph Vecoli, "The Italian Americans," *Center Magazine* 7, no. 4 (July-August 1974): 31-43.

4. Oscar Handlin, *The Uprooted* (Boston: Atlantic Monthly Press, 1951, 1973), 94.

5. Quoted in the introduction to *The Hemingway Reader*, edited with introduction by Charles Poore (New York: Charles Scribner's Sons, 1953), xiv.

6. Dorothy Canfield, "A Young Bricklayer Writes," *New York Times Book Review*, 20 August 1939, 28.

7. Joseph Barbato, "A Thinking Man Whose University Was the Streets," *Italian-American Identity*, February 1977: 20-21

8. Personal interview with Pietro Di Donato, 21 June 1983.

9. William Boelhower, "The Immigrant Novel as Genre," *MELUS* 8, no. 1 (Spring 1981): 3–14.

10. Jerre Mangione, "Little Italy," *New Republic*, 30 August 1939, 110–11.

11. Louis Adamic, "Muscular Novel of Immigrant Life," *Saturday Review of Literature*, 26 August 1939, 5.

12. Giovanni Sinicropi, "*Christ in Concrete*," *Italian Americana* 3, no. 2 (Spring/Summer 1977): 175-83.

13. Fred T. Marsh, "A Find and Unusual First Novel," *New York Times Book Review*, 20 August 1939, 6.

From Southern Italian Emigrant to Reluctant American: Joseph Tusiani's *Gente Mia and Other Poems*

Quae regio in terris nostri non plena laboris?
— *Aeneid,* I, 450

In his article "The Immigrant Novel as Genre," William Boelhower makes the following macroproposition:

> An immigrant protagonist(s) representing an ethnic worldview comes to America with great expectations, and through a series of trials is led to reconsider them in terms of his final status. (Boelhower 1981, 5)

Boelhower continues that this proposition can be formulated with the following diagram:

Topos/Worldview

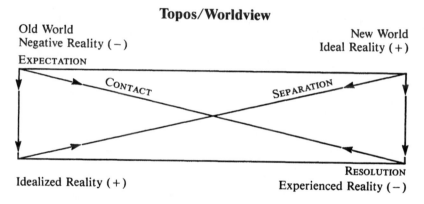

This diagram, which explains the emotional and intellectual movement of the emigrant/immigrant, is grounded by the tension created between the *Old World* and *New World*, "both as locations and as mental categories." As the emigrant begins the forced journey that takes him away from his native village/city, his family, and all that he has known (*Old World*), he leaves behind a *reality*, which, because of all the hardships endured, has acquired a negative meaning, and he sails for the *New World*, his *ideal reality*. The three major moments in this journey are, as Boelhower explains, *expectation* (dreams, possibility, opportunity), *contact* (the experiences, trials, and tribulations of the newly arrived emigrant) and *resolution* (assimilation, hyphenation, alienation). As the emigrant begins his journey his *expectation* is that his new reality will be an ideal one. With the passing of time, as his status changes from *emigrant* to that of *immigrant* and he further experiences the New World (*experienced reality*) and discovers the real America, his *separation* from the *Old World* and its customs becomes problematic and sets off an emotional response that will lead the immigrant to reverse the process and idealize the "old ways." The final *resolution* (*experienced reality*) is subsequently put into a new de-idealized context.

Joseph Tusiani's volume *Gente Mia and Other Poems* addresses, with eloquence and dignity, the southern Italian experience of immigration to the United States.[1] In these few pages (only fourteen of the compositions of *Gente Mia and Other Poems* deal with the immigration experience), Tusiani's muse inspires him to examine the major themes that are associated with immigration: the spiritually and psychologically violent act of division from one's family and native land, the dreams of the emigrant/immigrant, the prejudice he/she encounters, the process of Americanization, the question of language, the alienation and the realization, acquired through experienced reality, that the new world is not what he/she believed it was.

"Song of the Bicentennial," an intensely autobiographical poem that opens the collection of *Gente Mia and Other Poems*, examines the above-mentioned themes and, after careful reading, leaves the reader with a cynical and somber awareness of what it means to be an immigrant:

> Then who will solve this riddle of my day?
> Two languages, two lands, perhaps two souls...
> Am I a man or two strange halves of one?
> somber, indifferent light,
> setting before me with a sneer of glow,
> because there is no answer to my plight
>
> (Tusiani 1978, 7)[2]

There is no answer to the "riddle" because the immigrant is suspended between two "worlds." As separation from the Old World becomes complete, the native land acquires mythical characteristics in the mind of the immigrant:

> My long lost land was one that,
> when snows enveloped it,
> did not erase a sun that
> still in my dream was lit
>
> . . . .
> 'Twas my presepe, full of
> tu scendi dalle stelle-
> the only song and rule of
> intime cose belle. (6)

through his experienced reality, the immigrant's adopted land has lost those mythical qualities attributed to it by the old-timers back in the native village. The New World is presented as unfeeling and cold:

> But now my new-found land is
> the western world, this new,
> mysterious Atlantis
> where men like me and you,
>
> called immigrants, are silent
> when silent Night is sung
> on this Manhattan Island
> by people old and young,

> by all save those, like me
> and you, uprooted friend,
> who think of Italy-
> our lost presepe land. (6)

When reading "Song of the Bicentennial," the reader is immediately struck by three words: sunder, deracination, and uprooted:

> ...Sunder all this—you have
> erosion, desert, and abyss and night,
> yet I have ceased to be
> the man I was: the roots wherefrom I sprung
> are somewhere else instead. Deracinated—
> is this the word that somewhat hides the grief
> of one uprooted and no longer young (3)

These three powerful words evoke lucid images of the bitterness, violent separation, and displacement that for many is the final resolution of the emigration experience. Because of the dismal social and financial conditions that plagued the *mezzogiorno*, a whole generation of people was forced to look at emigration as the "lesser of all evils," even though it left the protagonists homeless in the spiritual and material definitions of the word.[3]

The history of southern Italians in the twentieth century is a history of emigration to the north of Italy, to other European countries, and to North and South America. The uprooting of individuals and generations of families, caused by powers and circumstances over which these people had no control, is a social and historical phenomenon that has been well documented.[4] It is this reality that leads the poet of *Gente mia* to contemplate the stars that dot the southern Italian sky:

> The shape—let me be wondering about
> the shape of the stars that glow,
> for something tells me that I too was born
> under the sign of one
> formed like an ocean liner going far,
> crowded with silent men called emigrants—
> my ethnic star. (4)

This deliberation of the "ethnic star," this star "formed like an ocean liner going far," is not a simple romantic notion of adventure to far off uncharted places but the contemplation of the stark reality of the southern Italian condition in the late nineteenth and the first half of the twentieth centuries, when the *contadino* had no choice but to become a nomad. It is the realization that to have a chance at a better life the *meridionale* had to leave the land of his ancestors under the most wretched of conditions. In the following passage from Tusiani's novel *Envoy from Heaven* (1965), Mother Cabrini, appearing as a fictional character, makes us aware of the dilemma of the emigrant:

No, no poet, not even a man called Dante of Florence, could ever describe what I saw in my brief stay on earth. There is some sordidness that escapes the naked eye, and there are tears that can never be mentioned. You see hundreds of people lying at the bottom of a ship, their hands resting on their few belongings, and their thoughts terrified by the uncertainty of their future. You put this entry into your diary, "Hundreds of men going to America to better their economic lot," and you think you have done your duty. But you have already sinned against them, for you have used but words, and words are not worlds. What is the real meaning of "hundreds"? You cannot add as mere ciphers hope and despair, poverty and illiteracy, homelessness and terror. You have written "men" but do they look like men to you? They look like meek and frightened lambs on their way to the slaughterhouse. And yet they are men, good, honest, simple men. Why are they there, then? Who has starved them? Who has made them so desperate as to force them to leave wives and children, and the one bit of earth they knew and loved—their little village? And then you say, "America," and you think you have described in one little word the cold of their landing in an unknown country, the humiliation of their dumb contact with men they cannot understand, the daily search for work and more work, the anxious waiting for a letter, the sleepless nights, and things of this kind. And, finally, you say "to better their economic lot!" Yes, you are right. They have sent their first money home, they have paid their debts, they have received word that their children can even go to school now. But, sir, have you seen these people live? They live in squalid cellars, they count every cent, and—shall I tell you?—they, the illiterate, the uneducated people who speak neither English nor Italian, are now capable of a pun: they say "dolor" instead of "dollar."[5]

"Dolor," terror, humiliation, are the constants of the emigration experience.

When the emigrant, after a long and wearisome crossing, arrived at Ellis Island, he/she was immediately faced with the first major obstacle of his/her new American life—a strange language. The question of language, or rather, loss of language, is of primary importance to our poet when discussing the experience of emigration. Tusiani introduces this argument in "Song of the Bicentennial" by a series of questions:

> Do I regret my origins by speaking
> this language I acquired? Do I renounce,
> by talking now in terms of only dreams,
> the sogni of my childhood? What has changed
> that I had thought unchangeable in me? (5)

Tusiani, as far as this writer knows, is the only Italian/American author who looks at the language question as a spiritual dilemma more than as a sociological problem (Tusiani 1982, 153). The answer to these questions is that something *has* changed and that every phrase, every word uttered in English separates him a little bit more from his roots:

> Now every thought I think, each word I say
> detaches me a little more from all
> I used to love— (5)

For Tusiani, when "sogni" becomes dreams, when "cielo" becomes sky, and when "mamma" is translated as mother, much more transpires than the immigrant's process of Americanization and acculturation. Tusiani, who, besides being a poet, has had a long career as a professor of Italian language and literature and as a scholar and translator of Italian classics, knows well the importance of words. Cognizant of the fact that the ideas and culture which words communicate go much deeper than the definition found in the dictionary, the poet knows that "cielo" elicits mythicized visions of the Old World and that sky will only remind the immigrant of the ghetto in the immense concrete jungle he now calls home and that when "mamma" is translated as mother a "whole world of feelings and traditions" is lost and the "disintegration of family unity becomes an altogether unpremeditated adverse effect" of immigration (Tusiani 1982, 154).

> Mother, I even wonder if I am
> the child I was, the little child you knew,
> for you did not expect your little son
> to grow apart from all that was your world.
> Yet of a sudden he was taught to say
> "Mother" for mamma, and for cielo "sky"
> That very day we lost each other... (5)

Language is something personal and individual, and loss of the Italian language is for our poet "a betrayal or denial of his original world—indeed his very origin, his very self" (Tusiani 1982, 153–54).

With the poems "The Ballad of the Coliseum" and "The Day after the Feast," the poet takes the reader away from his personal experience with immigration and examines the dreams, achievements, and disappointments of the Italian/American family and the neighborhood: "Little Italy." What historians and sociologists have so well documented in numerous studies, Tusiani conveys to the reader with the sensitivity and insight of the poetic intellect.

In "The Ballad of the Coliseum," which narrates the full history of Italian/American emigration from southern Italy to New York City, Tusiani tells the story of a simple hardworking man who would have gone to his grave unnoticed, as millions before him, were it not for the tragic and news-making circumstances of his death:[6]

> That day, he left as if in glory—
>   the father of a famous man.
> The Coliseum in the sunshine
>   boasted its half completed span—
> a lofty labyrinth of ramparts,
>   a mass of steel and wet cement
> that by no blowing wind or thunder
>   could broken be or even bent.
> Then, if no blowing wind or thunder
>   could shake or shatter it all,
> what sudden wrath of hell or heaven,
>   struck on a hardly finished wall...
> How many dead? How many injured?
>   Only one dead—our Angelo (35)

While recounting the tragic death of Angelo Lombardi, "The Ballad of the Coliseum" brings the reader inside the Italian/American family structure. The family, which is of primary importance to Italian culture, was so essential to the survival of immigrants who were shunned and looked upon as individually and culturally inferior by the dominant culture of the United States. Tusiani makes us cognizant of the forces and unity that bond this fundamental structure.

Insight into Italian/American family life is at the heart of the poem. Forced to leave his family behind in Italy and bearing the tragedy of not being able to be at his mother's side when she died:

> Another day and still another,
>   and then the first and second year...
> Time passed and then (O God!) a letter
>   in a black envelope came here.
> "Dear Angelo," it said, "Your mother
>   died of a sudden heart attack.
> She did not suffer, but kept asking
>   until the end, 'Has he come back?'" (31)

Angelo uses his savings to purchase "a blessed one way ticket / for one who soon became his bride"(32) and begins to rebuild the family:

> Many more years went by, and seven
>   boys and a girl, American born,
> calling him Papa! Papa!, made him
>   feel like a king upon a throne...
> And so our builder every evening,
>   sitting at table with his wife—
> while all enrapt his children listened—
>   counted the blessings of his life. (33-34)

We are also reminded of the important role of education in the lives of Italian/American families. Angelo works to make a better life for himself and his family. For his children the better life translates into the necessity of a college education:

> The pay is good and—let me tell you—
>   despite my age I feel much stronger,
> well, strong enough to put through college
>   (for time's a-flying) our first son.
> He'll be a lawyer—no, a doctor. (34)

But losing sight of the dream, he went "wherever a new building / was being built—uptown, downtown," and for Angelo Lombardi:

> Stone and concrete and brick and plaster
>   to him were more than trade and tool:
> they were the miracle from heaven
>   that sent his children to school. (33)

For all of his hard work and sacrifice, our protagonist's experience with immigration ends as it had started, by being violently separated from the one thing he held dear—his family. As he was not able to be at his mother's side at the time of her death, his tragic and untimely death denies him the realization of seeing his children fulfill their American reality.

"The Day after the Feast," reminiscent of Giacomo Leopardi's "La sera del dì di festa," both in its title and theme,[7] places the reader in the heart of "Little Italy"—a geographically well defined "Little Italy"—"the Belmont area of the Bronx in New York with its lady of Mount Carmel on 187th Street and its well-known market on Arthur Avenue" (Tusiani 1982, 159). On the day after the feast of Our Lady of Mount Carmel in the Bronx, the poet recalls the festivities of the previous day while life is returning to normal:

> Last night your children were the chanting throngs
> behind your statue and the parish priest,
>   and now they once again
> are what they were—unknown, hardworking men.
> Yes, you are pleased remembering this new
> procession in your honor, with a glare
>   of altar boys in red,
> a band, balloons slow-floating overhead,
> and from the sidewalks people throwing you
> signs-of-the-cross and kisses and a prayer:
>   three hours of paradise
> quite visible in all our mortal eyes.
> This morning everybody's back to work
> as if no holiday had ever been,
>   yet everybody's more
> resigned to life than ever, ever before. (24)

In describing the parade and feast that took place the previous day, the poet transports the reader into a world and culture that is not American; into a cultural extravaganza that is "part of a centuries old ritual that characterizes the faith of Southern Italians" (Tusiani 1982, 159). The religious *festa*, a mixture of pagan lore and Christian belief, is the visual manifestation of the preindustrial culture of southern Italy. A culture steeped in superstitions, belief in the supernatural and a fatalistic vision of life—*destino*.

For the Italian immigrant in the "Little Italys" of America, the *festa* is a means to recapture, albeit for a fleeting moment, the illusion of being back in "the old country" where they were understood and "unknowingly try to forget the bitterness of their deracination" (Tusiani 1982, 160). As Boelhower states in his book *Looking through a Glass Darkly: Ethnic Semiosis*, "The feast generically functions as an act of historical synthesis in which each participant feels integrated into the semiotic space of his ethnic culture" (Boelhower 1984, 116). This "act of historical synthesis" is, as I have mentioned above, a very short sequence of time, and the immigrant will soon be faced with his/her American reality as the sanitation trucks

> Roaring impassive and iconoclastic
>   . . .devour and crush
>   under metallic teeth
> the most impressive artificial wreath

along with cardboard boxes, empty plastic
bottles, confetti, in a raucous rush
   that nothing spares—not even
the remnants of a man's festive dream of heaven. (25)

and New York once again becomes

     the city where you hardly know your street. (25)

The last verses underscore the ephemeral aspect of the *festa*. The poet gives us images of objects that are not lasting, rather they are products of an American consumerist throw-away culture: artificial wreaths, plastic bottles, cardboard boxes—a consumerist culture far removed from the Italian and the Italian immigrants' frugal traditions.

Italy, in the mind of the protagonists, is recreated for a day, but the *festa* is not reality, it is just a vehicle that for a short time makes the immigrant forget that he lives in a "city where you hardly know your street."[8]

From the local ethnic level, represented in "The Day after the Feast," Tusiani shifts his focus to the national level in "Columbus Day in New York." The Columbus Day celebrations that take place in large urban centers like Chicago and New York are a statement to the Americanization of Italian Americans. Much different than the *festa* described in the "The Day after the Feast," which celebrates the day of Our Lady of Mount Carmel, Columbus Day festivities have very little to do with Italian culture and traditions and, as the poet clearly states,

Here is the epic of Columbus Day
reduced to an innocuous parade
where mayoral dreamers grin in competition,
endorsed (or almost) by the Governor,
and politicians who are neither-nor
turn on Italian smiles as cars' ignition. (10)

The poet chooses to look beyond the superficiality of the day (the politicians' smiles, the floats, the beauty queens) and sing about the true hero of the day—the unsung laborer with calloused hand who worked and died to make America what it is and who still is not recognized as "one of her children":

   . . . This is gente mia,
for I can see (is there a lump in my throat?)
dear Christopher Columbus on a float
called for all time to come Santa Maria.
   How beautiful he beams! He has the eyes
of my Grandfather, and his callous hand;
he is the immigrant of every land
unhappy in his happy paradise,
   misunderstood in all this understanding (10)

Columbus/Grandfather and the Santa Maria are the powerful symbols that synthesize the history of immigration to the United States:

Look closer! There's Grandfather, come this year
to represent Columbus on his float.

> A hero and the worthiest of note,
> he is the very one no crowd will cheer
>   tomorrow when the town goes back to work;
> but look at him today, today at last,
> in all the greatness of his humble past—
> the new Columbus conquering New York.
>   He brings the best credentials to be he—
> faith in his glance to win the fighting waves,
> dream of free people and despair of slaves
> to conquer a new land ultimately.
>   So here he is today, today at last
> riding atop his bright Santa Maria,
> the navigator of the gente mia,
> light of my future, darkness of his past,

(10–11)

The Grandfather figure is the symbol of all the immigrants that have come to this country, who through their sacrifice and suffering ("darkness of his past") made a better life possible ("light of my future"). They are for one fleeting day remembered and given their rightful place.

The pomp and gaiety of the Columbus Day festivities cannot hide a bitter truth, and the poem ends on a biting note. The recognition is temporary, "he is the one no crowd will cheer / tomorrow when the town goes back to work"; and his destiny is one that robs him of the dignity of his existence:

> the one who came to dig (for dig we must)
> for the high glory of the subway tracks
> *The immigrant who dies and yet still lacks*
> *identity with this American dust.* (10–11, emphasis added)

This poem, composed of ten quatrains, accomplishes two things: (1) it reminds America of what Italians have achieved in the new land, from its discovery by Columbus to the humble laborer;[9] and (2) it synthesizes the despair and frustration of being a misunderstood immigrant in a land of immigrants.

Conclusion

Gente Mia and Other Poems reflects on the immigrant's unique dilemma: that of being confronted with two realities, "Old World" and "New World," and feeling that he/she does not belong to either. Tusiani, in his search for an answer (or perhaps only a clearer understanding), goes beyond the scientific inquiry of the sociologist and the historian. He delves into the soul and spirituality of the immigrant as he/she quests for a unhyphenated identity, searching also for a *patria* in his/her adopted land. The answers he discovers as a result of his poetic inquiry are not pleasant. Deracination (sunder, uprootedness) and resignation are what the poet has resolved for himself and his immigrant brothers and sisters. When Tusiani declares "Civis Americanus Sum: I swore / allegiance to the Flag of Fifty Stars: / Long live

America forever more!" he does so more to remind the reader that he, as others before him, has paid the price and belongs in America, rather than convey a nationalistic message.

Through poems like "Columbus Day in New York" and "Song of the Bicentennial," Tusiani shows the reader that the American cultural milieu has absorbed the superficial and stereotypical aspects of Italian immigrant culture while never truly understanding the true character of this populace. The essence of the sacrifice and contribution of the illiterate immigrant with calloused hands has all but been forgotten.

It is up to the poet, who draws his inspiration from the injustice suffered by his people, to assure that their sacrifice will not be forgotten. By so doing the poet also arrives at a definition of his identity and that of his people:

> Now, only now for every suffered wrong
> can I discover who I am at last—
> the multitudinous Italian throng.
> I am the present for I am the past
> of those who for their future came to stay,
> humble and innocent and yet outcast. (8)

Notes

1.   Joseph Tusiani, professor of Italian and internationally known poet, translator, and scholar, was born in San Marco, Lamis (Foggia). After receiving his doctorate in English literature from the University of Naples, Tusiani emigrated to the United States where in 1948 he began his long, distinguished career.

Among Tusiani's major works we find translations of Michelangelo's poems (*The Complete Poems of Michelangelo*, 1969; Torquato Tasso's *Gerusalemme Liberata* (*Jerusalem Delivered*, 1970) and *Il mondo creato* (*Creation of the World*, 1982); Giovanni Boccaccio's *Ninfale fiesolano* (*The Nymphs of Fiesole*, 1971); and the recently completed translation of Luigi Pulci's *Morgante*.

Writing in Latin, Italian, and English, he has completed several collections of poems. In Latin we have *Melos Cordis* (1955), *Rosa Rosarum* (1984), and *In Exilio Rerum* (1985); in Italian, *Lo speco celeste* (1956) and *Odi Sacre* (1958); and in English, *Rind and All* (1962), *The Fifth Season* (1963), and *Gente Mia and Other Poems*.

Tusiani has also written a novel, *Envoy from Heaven*, and he is currently working on a trilogy using his family's history as subject matter. The first book of the trilogy, *La parola difficile*, was published in 1988 by Schiena Editore, Fasano di Puglia. This volume deals with Tusiani's emigration to the United States, seeing his father again after twenty-three years, and his life in the United States as an intellectual, a poet, and a professor. As of this writing, Tusiani has completed the other two volumes, *La parola antica* and *La parola nuova*. These volumes will appear in print in the near future.

Tusiani has received many honors for his writings and for his dedication to education. In 1956, he was the first American to win the Greenwood prize of the Poetry Society of England. In 1968, he received the Alice Fay di Castagnola Award from the Poetry Society of America and was awarded the Spirit Gold Medal from the Catholic Poetry Society of America. The honor of Cavaliere Ufficiale della Repubblica was bestowed upon him in 1973, the Leonardo Covello Educator award in 1980, and the Leone di San Marco award in 1982. In 1986, the American Association of Teachers of Italian chose Tusiani as the recipient of the first AATI Distinguished Service Award "in recognition of outstanding teaching and/or published research in the fields of Italian language, literature and civilization."

2. All further quotations from *Gente Mia and Other Poems* will be identified only by the page number.

3. Tusiani in his article "Deracination and Americanization," p. 152, refers to two inquiries on the Italian South commissioned after the Risorgimento, one by Constantino Nigra, the other by Giustino Fortunato. The inquiry by Nigra carried out immediately after annexation of the South to the new Italian state "exposed the inhuman brutality of the wealthy class as well as that of the clergy in all regions just evacuated by the Bourbons"; the inquiry by Fortunato suggested "emigration as the lesser of all evils if not the greatest of all cures. Unnatural and violent though it seemed, emigration meant only survival just as deracination meant only hope in a new springtime."

4. Cinematographers have made some of the most powerful statements on the subject. Films such as *Rocco e i suoi fratelli* (*Rocco and His Brothers*), *Tre fratelli* (*Three Brothers*), *Pane e cioccolata* (*Bread and Chocolate*) examine the emotional trauma, the sacrifice, and the tragedy that stems from immigration.

5. This excerpt is taken from Tusiani's article "Deracination and Americanization," p. 153.

6. This poem is based on a true story. Angelo Lombardi was the only casualty when a wall collapsed during the building of the New York Coliseum. Lombardi's body could not be found beneath the rubble.

7. Giacomo Leopardi (1798–1837) was born in the town of Recanati, in the Marches region of Italy. His intellectual and psychological makeup were greatly influenced by the forced isolation of his youth. His father, a tyrannical but literate man, demanded that the young Giacomo spend never-ending hours at his studies. His education included training in theology, archeology, rhetoric, astronomy, philosophy, and languages. By 1817, Leopardi had translated Horace's *Ars Poetica* and parts of the *Aeneid* and of the *Odyssey*; he had completed several original works, including two tragedies, a *History of Astronomy*, and an *Essay on the Popular Errors of the Ancients*. Most important, his extensive contact with antiquity "awakened in him a deep desire to be a poet in his own right."

This formative period also left deep psychological scars on the young Giacomo and ruined his physical health. "The seven years of mad and desperate studies," as Leopardi referred to them, left him a bitter man and his "Canti" and "Operette morali" mirror the profound anguish and loneliness he experienced in his development as a human being and as an artist. For Leopardi, the reality of adulthood never lives up to the dreams that nourish our youth, and life is a series of illusions destined to be shattered by reality.

So the reader may make his own comparison between Tusiani's "The Day after the Feast" and Leopardi's "La sera del dì di festa," the following is an English translation of Leopardi's poem done by Tusiani and published in *Italian Quarterly* 28, nos. 109–10 (Summer-Fall):136–37.

The Evening of the Holiday

Limpid, and calm, and windless is the night,
And quiet on the roofs and in the fields
The moon is resting, showing far away
Each mountain clear. Already, O my love,
All streets are hushed, and the nocturnal lamps
Through yonder windows flicker rare and dim.
You sleep, for easeful sleep now welcomes you
There in your quiet room; and not one care
Is pricking you, who do not know or think
How large a wound you opened in my breast.
You sleep; and I look out upon this sky,
Appearing now so tender to my sight,
And upon this omnipotent old Nature
That made me to this anguish. "I deny
Hope, even hope, to you," she said; "and let
Your eyes shine only with the light of tears."
This day was solemn; now you rest from all
Your merriment, and maybe in your dream
You still remember all the youths you liked,
And all who liked you. No, I dare not hope
Or even think I'm part of those your thoughts.
Meanwhile I ask myself how long to live
Remains to me, and here upon the ground
I throw myself, and shout, and fret with rage.
O days of terror in these verdant years!
Ah, from the street, not far away, I hear
The lonely singing of an artisan
Returning, late at night, to his poor home
After his pastime; and a cruel grip
Tightens my heart as I recall how things
Pass on this earth and almost leave no trace.
Gone is the festive day, soon followed by
The ordinary one, for time sweeps all
Human events away. Where is the sound,
Now, of those ancient peoples? Where is now
The clamor of our famous ancestors,
And the great empire of that Rome, the arms,
And the vast din that spread through land and seas?
Silent and peaceful, the whole world now rests,
And not a word is whispered of it all.
Still in my prime, when, warmly I desired
The festive day, and, after it was gone,
Sleepless and grieving, in my bed I turned,
If in the deep of night I heard a song
Little by little in the distance dying,
The same sad shudder used to grip my heart.

8. For a clearer understanding of the value of the *festa* in Italian/American society, see Boelhower, *Through a Glass Darkly,* 113–17.

9. Tusiani has published essays on a number of prominent immigrants in American history: Philip Mazzei, Eusebio Chino, Francis Vigo, and Antonio Ravali. Poems on Constantino Brumidi, the artist who painted the rotunda of the Capitol building in Washington, D.C., and Father Samuel Mazzuchelli, frontier priest and founder of the Sinsinawa Dominican Order, are included in *Gente Mia and Other Poems*.

Works Cited

Boelhower, William. 1981. "The Immigrant Novel as Genre." *MELUS* 8, no. 1:3–14.

———. 1984. *Through a Glass Darkly: Ethnic Semiosis*. Oxford: Oxford University Press.

Tusiani, Joseph. 1965. *Envoy from Heaven*. New York: Obolensky.

———. 1978. *Gente Mia and Other Poems*. Stone Park, Ill.: Italian Cultural Center.

———. 1982. "The Themes of Deracination and Americanization in *Gente Mia and Other Poems*." *Ethnic Groups* 4, no. 3:149–76.

Recent Italian American Literature:
The Case of John Fante

As part of our American literary heritage, the many books addressed to the Italian experience in America include a number of works whose primary origins are the period of mass immigration of Italians into the United States from 1880 to 1920. To these we may now add, at least on the sociological level, a wide range of texts that provide important insights into the exodus from Italy and the search for identity of Italians in the new land for at least three generations. As newer works appear, we note that while they remain in contact with certain aspects of the setting and themes of the earlier works, these more recent works of Italian American literature have by now taken on their own unique characteristics.

Before examining these characteristics in depth, let us consider definition of terms and literary history. In the most general sense, the phrase "recent Italian American literature" for me refers to books published after 1974. The reasons for selecting this date are twofold. First, it is the closing date for the texts included in Rose Basile Green's important survey *The Italian-American Novel: A Document of the Interaction of Two Cultures*. To date we have no follow-up work that carries us forward from her concluding "Epilogue: Projections into the 70's" to a discussion of the texts and tendencies of the literary production in the present day. And it should be noted that there is a good quantity of works to consider. At the American Italian Historical Association conference in 1969, devoted specifically to the Italian American novel, Rudolph Vecoli's count of the number of Italian American novels published by decade reveals the following: four in the 1920s; nine in the 1930s; eighteen in the 1940s; four in the 1950s; ten in the 1960s. Although I might be accused of juggling the statistics to provide the numbers for the 1970s and 1980s, I shall do so in strict accordance with literary considerations.

By expanding the possible range of texts from the Italian American novel to cover the Italian American narrative generally (a term whose use I shall maintain for the remainder of my discussion), we can include such genre as the short story, memoir, and autobiography that are so much a significant part of the canon of Italian American literature. Thus, such texts as Luigi Barzini's *O America: When You and I Were Young* (1977); Jerre Mangione's *An Ethnic at Large* (1978); Helen Barolini's *The Dream Book: An Anthology of Writings by Italian American Women* (1985); and Joe Napoli's *A Dying Cadence* (1986) gain their rightful place among texts devoted to the Italian heritage in America. The statistics would then read as follows: fifteen in the 1970s; over twenty-five in the 1980s.

The second reason for choosing post-1974 texts as those that belong to the period of recent Italian American narrative is a matter of point of view. We are at the border between protagonists of second- and third-generation

Italian Americans that introduces a new period of Italian American narrative. Writers belonging to this period may reach conclusions similar to those of the previous generation or generations but the form and content of the literary work assumes a different shape. For example, the narrator of Tina DeRosa's *Paper Fish* pays tribute to the immigrant generation and laments the leveling of the old Italian neighborhood by the wrecking ball of urban development; in this case, however, the narrator is the third-generation granddaughter of Grandma Doria and the style of the novel is stream of consciousness. In Jay Parini's *The Patch Boys*, we witness the struggle for identity on the part of Sammy Di Cantini, who grows up in an immigrant Italian family; but no less an important theme in this novel is the story of the development of the organized labor movement in the hard coal mining region of northeastern Pennsylvania. Writer Parini is a recognized poet, and his prose style reveals his love of vision and metaphor that often takes the novel beyond emphasis of theme to an appreciation of its lyric descriptions.

Robert Di Pietro and Edward Ifkovic assert in the introduction to the selection of essays presented in *Ethnic Perspectives in American Literature* that, while the definition of ethnic literature still remains a matter of much discussion, generationalism is a feature that we see often: "Whereas writers of the first generation are wont to respond to conditions in the old country and loss of an old way of life... second generation writers concern themselves with identity problems and the third generation often draws closer to the first and seeks to rediscover its roots or recover older life-styles" (Di Pietro and Ifkovic 1983, 12). As much as I agree with this concept, I believe that a line of demarcation exists even between texts from different points of view within the second generation itself. When, in the survey of contemporary Italian American novelists, Rose Basile Green discusses novels of recall, it is clear that these books go beyond the search for identity. The novel of recall is one in which "the basic impulse to search for identity precipitates the resulting self-discovery as the writer both recalls and shares the experiences of the parental home. Having survived, however, the alienation and the fragmentation of a childhood ethnically separated from that of other authors, the Italian American writer has matured with sufficient assurance to tell his experiences with honor, detachment, and objectivity" (Green 1974, 194). The best known example of such a perspective on the immigrant generation from the point of view of its own children is Jerre Mangione's *Mount Allegro*, which, through its six publications, allows us twice to see the calm and joyous recall of immigrant parents. The first four publications conclude when Gerlando as a young man just before the outbreak of World War II returns home from his visit to Italy with a newfound understanding of his family heritage on both sides of the ocean. The 1981 "final" copyright edition, in fact, includes a "finale" that reaffirms and expands the sentiments of the previous editions, but now from the perspective of a man in his seventies. The cornerstone, then, of recent Italian American narrative is the protagonist who, from the perspective of the late second generation or from that of the third generation or later, observes the immigrant parentage from beyond the struggle and search for identity. Certainly the act of looking back in time calls to mind the exodus from the Old World and the challenge of the New World; the basic feature of the Italian American narrative remains in evidence, but with the possibility now of finding anew the Old World.

To observe this tone of recent Italian American narrative more clearly, I propose to examine the two novels from the pen of the same author. John Fante published *Wait Until Spring, Bandini* in 1938 and *The Brotherhood of the Grape* in 1977. The first is an autobiographical novel, as Olga Peragallo asserts in her landmark biographical survey of Italian American authors published in 1949; and so, too, is the second, as we shall see from the comparison to follow. Separated by a period of almost forty years, Fante's two novels illustrate to us not only how the protagonist changes in his attitude toward the immigrant generation and toward his own identity, but also the changes in the narrative technique of recent Italian American literature.

The title *Wait Until Spring, Bandini* makes reference to the occupational circumstances under which Svevo Bandini must live. As a bricklayer he works only in good weather, when the mortar will not freeze, and spends much of his time awaiting its arrival. He is "Bandini, hater of snow...bah, this Colorado, the rear end of God's creation, always frozen, no place for an Italian bricklayer; ah, he was cursed with this life" (Fante 1980, 25). The anxiety of job layoffs caused by the weather or lack of work strains the relationship Svevo has with his family. He passes his leisure time drinking wine and playing cards with his Italian cronies usually at the Imperial pool hall; he is forced to spend money he has not yet earned for his wine, cigars, and groceries. The end result is that he displays too little patience and too short a temper when he is at home with the family. His wife, Maria, fares no better in this situation. Although she was born in America, the daughter of Italian immigrants, she lives in the netherland of personal identity; she can deal neither with her Italian husband nor with the American society in which they live. Reading the pages of a women's magazine, she is convinced of her "separation from the world of 'American women'" (Fante, 1980, 73). Maria's personal instability and tension with her family increases dramatically when her mother, Donna Toscana, comes to visit. The old woman rages in general against America and in particular against her daughter's vagabond of a husband. Having thrown a few coins to her grandchildren, she observes how they scramble after them: "Like animals they claw themselves to pieces, and their mother smiles her approval. Ah, poor America! Ah, America, thy children shall tear out one another's throats and die bloodthirsty beasts!... Poor, hopeless America!" (Fante 1980, 91). Donna Toscana favors Svevo even less and unabashedly says so, not saving a kind word even for her daughter: "The man you married is a brutal animal. But he married a stupid woman, and so I suppose he will never be exposed. Ah, America! Only in this corrupt land could such things happen" (Fante 1980, 93).

It is upon notice of the arrival of his mother-in-law that Svevo does his usual disappearing act, going to stay with his bachelor friend and boyhood buddy from the old country, Rocco Saccone. A central conflict in the novel occurs when Rocco gives Svevo the opportunity to earn some money for the

Christmas holidays by repairing a fireplace for the wealthy widow Effie Hildegard. The business venture turns into a love affair between Mrs. Hildegard and Svevo, and the latter subsequently moves into her large house near the mountains outside of town. The relationship, however, is one based more on curiosity and mutual differences than on mutual affection. Awed by her wealth and seeming "properness," the usually blunt and extroverted Svevo is reduced to tongue-tied obsequiousness. When she asks him to sit down, "he was so grateful that he could not speak, could only utter happy grunts at whatever she said" (Fante 1980, 176). Her naive fascination about Svevo's Italian heritage appears condescending. He is a peasant from Abruzzi and had never visited Rome, yet she wonders to herself: "So he was an Italian? Splendid. Only last year she had traveled in Italy. Beautiful. He must be so proud of his heritage....Had he ever seen the Campo Santo, the Cathedral of St. Peter's, the paintings of Michelangelo" (Fante 1980, 176).

Their cohabitation merely intensifies the differences in personal identities and socioeconomic standings. If anything, it serves for Svevo as a confirmation of who he is. When initially he senses that she wants to seduce him, he attempts to avoid the situation by leaving the house. She quickly rouses his anger and lust, though, by calling him "fool...ignorant peasant" (Fante 1980, 198). Afterwards, "he laughed the triumph of his poverty and peasantry. This Widow! She with her wealth and deep plumb warmth, slave and victim of her own challenge, sobbing in the joyful abandonment of her defeat" (Fante 1980, 199). As much as he is in awe of this wealthy college-educated woman who reads books, keeps expensive whiskey, and offers him cigarettes—instead of his usual Toscanelli stogie—they cannot know each other and are not lovers; for the two of them, "hello and goodbye...added up to the same thing. They were strangers, with passion alone to bridge the chasm of their differences" (Fante 1980, 205).

Whereas Svevo Bandini understands that he is an Italian who has become a naturalized American, his son Arturo is not at all sure about his own identity. In an important way, the title *Wait Until Spring, Bandini* applies equally, if not more so, to the son. A boy of fourteen, Arturo is an indifferent student from whom teachers and classmates alike expect nothing but problems. His saving grace is that he loves to play baseball and is good at it, but in the fierce Colorado winters he, like his father, must face a long off-season. At the most infinitesimal evidence of a break in the weather, he is ready for the ball diamond, remnants of winter snows notwithstanding. Begging the others for a game, he is told to wait: "Wait until Spring, Bandini. He argued with them about it. He won the argument. But after school, after sitting alone for an hour under the cottonwoods bordering the field, he knew they would not come, and he walked home slowly" (Fante 1980, 230). A much more urgent crisis for Arturo, however, is that of his personal identity. He pictures himself as being different, even through his enthusiasm for baseball. Like his father, he laments the winter and the poverty: "Ah, for Spring! Ah, for the crack of the bat. Wintertime,

Christmas time, rich kid time: they had high top boots and bright mufflers and fur-lined gloves" (Fante 1980, 133). On the one hand, the crux of his confusion is that he is an American but does not realize it. At the outset of the text we discover that "his name was Arturo, but he hated it and wanted to be called John. His last name was Bandini, and he wanted it to be Jones. His mother and father were Italians, but he wanted to be an American" (Fante 1980, 33). On the other hand, his infatuated daydreams of Rosa Pinelli emphasize his Italianness. He imagines declaring his love with Italian being the common bond: "I am Italian too, Rosa. Look, and my eyes are like yours. Rosa, I love you...Rosa, me and you: a couple of Italians" (Fante 1980, 116 and 118).

The climax of the novel does not offer a solution for the marital and occupational tensions of Svevo Bandini, nor does it resolve Arturo Bandini's identity crisis. But father and son come together in what seems a hopeful way. Young Arturo approaches Mrs. Hildegarde's house in search of his father to convince him to return home. Upon seeing the boy, she screams at him to get his dog off her property; finally she includes both father and son in her ranting: "You peasants...you foreigners! You're all alike, you and your dogs and all of you" (Fante 1980, 265). Reminding her that his son is an American and not a foreigner, Svevo retorts, in Italian to be sure, and calls her "Bruta animale...puttana" (Fante 1980, 265). As they start out for home together, Svevo's final words suggest happier days ahead for the Bandini family when he comments that "pretty soon we'll have spring" (Fante 1980, 266). Walking toward a patch of blue sky in the east, Arturo watches a snowflake melt on his hand. The immigrant father and his son now move toward a new understanding of each other, as symbolized by the coming of springtime. We witness, then, a rebirth that looks not only inward at these two themselves, but just as significantly at how they, as Italian Americans, stand in regard to American society at large.

The Brotherhood of the Grape continues the story of the immigrant father and his son, but in this case it is not the initiation of the son's manhood but rather the father's imminent death that brings the two together. Wait Until Spring, Bandini celebrates the discovery by the immigrants and their children of their identity as Italians in America. Brotherhood of the Grape, on the other hand, pays homage to the rediscovery of the immigrant generation on the part of the Americanized son of immigrants. In this later novel, the names of the characters change and the setting moves from a small town in the foothills of the Colorado Rockies to one in the Sierras of California, but the family is the same. Nick Molise is an expert bricklayer with the same tendencies for drinking wine, lechery, and card playing as Svevo Bandini. With wife and family he remains "impulsive, lacking patience, intolerant" (Fante 1977, 49-50). In fact, even though he is seventy-six years old and his wife, Maria, seventy-four, it is her accusations of his adultery and her demand for a divorce that bring the oldest son, Henry, home to calm them down. Henry, now fifty, working as a successful writer and living a plane ride away in Redondo Beach, returns to San Elmo at the behest of his brother, Mario. Like all the many spats between Nick and Maria through their fifty-one years of marriage, this ones resolves itself quickly, even before Henry arrives. But this homecoming provides Henry, an Italian American protagonist of the late second generation, with the chance to renew his relationship with his father and mother.

As he reflects on his childhood at home with his father, not all the memories are pleasant; he recalls with bitterness how his father did not understand his passion for books and pushed him to get a job: "There was no answer for that street-corner Dago, that low-born Abruzzian wop, the yahoo peasant ginzo, that shit-kicker, that curb crawler. What did *he* know? What had *he* read?...his ignorance, the frenzy of living under his roof, his rantings, his threats, his greed, his bullying, his gambling. Christmas without money. Graduation a suit of clothes. Debts, debts" (Fante 1977, 61).

Thirty years later Nick continues to push his son. He has the opportunity to earn fifteen hundred dollars building a stone smokehouse up in the mountains, and he wants Henry to be his helper. Such a proposition sounds absurd to the son, who is not much affected by his father's lament, a recall of his heritage extending far back to Italy: "Ten, twenty generations of stonemasons, and I'm the last, the end of the line, and nobody gives a damn, not even my own flesh and blood" (Fante 1977, 44). Henry surrenders to his father's will as he knows he must, and having finished the work, he beams with pride over their joint construction project that is his first and Nick's last: "Whatever its aesthetic flaws, the building looked indestructible... Molise and son were finished" (Fante 1977, 121).

Building the stone smokehouse together serves as the physical symbol of the bond that now unites father and son, a union that the young boy Henry and his youthful father had found impossible to accomplish. The culmination of the love and respect Henry has for his father in its most profound and spiritual sense occurs the first night they stay together in the motel before beginning the stonemason project. Henry is already in bed when Nick comes in from a card game and goes straight to bed. In the long passage that follows, Henry listens to his father's nightmarish babbling, seems to interpret it, then goes to comfort him:

> He began to moan, "Mamma mia, mamma mia." Then he was sobbing. Was this any way for a man to fall asleep, calling for his mother? It seemed he would never stop. It tore me to shreds. I knew nothing of his mother. She had been dead for over sixty years, had expired in Italy after he had left and come to America, still visiting him now in his old man's sleep, as if he felt her near in his dreams, like one lost and wandering, crying for her.
>
> I lay there tearing my hair and thinking. Stop it, Father, you are drunk and full of self-pity and you must stop it, you have no right to cry, you are my father and the right to cry belongs to my wife and children, to my mother, for it is obscene that you should cry, it humiliates me, I shall die from your grief, I cannot endure your pain, I should be spared your pain for I have enough of my own. I shall have more too, but I shall never cry before others, I shall be strong and face my last days without tears, old man. I need your life and not your death, your joy and not your dismay.

> Then I was crying too, on my feet, crossing to him. I gathered his
> limp head in my arms (as I had seen my mother do), I wiped his tears
> with a corner of the sheet, I rocked him like a child, and soon he was no
> longer crying, and I eased him gently to the pillow and he slept quietly.
> (Fante 1977, 107-8)

Nick's actual death is in a large sense anticlimactic for Henry, because
the above revelation opens a secret about who and what his father is and
why he needs to love his father as he could not do before. Throughout his
adult life, Henry has distanced himself physically and emotionally from his
family; he appears successful and assimilated in American society. That
which confuses Henry, as we see in the first paragraph of the above passage,
are the seemingly unfathomable time and distance that point back to the
roots of his own identity in Italy, symbolized by his grandmother who "had
been dead for sixty years, had expired in Italy after he [Nick] had left and
come to America." At the climax of the passage cited, and that of the novel
itself, Henry's anger converts to tears, and he embraces Nick as he "had
seen...mother do," in a gesture that serves as kind of catharsis in which the
son now understands more fully the man who is his father. This perspective
and discovery of the essence of the immigrant generation by their adult
children and grandchildren is the new perspective that is the key element of
recent Italian American narrative.

There remain, however, two other features of comparison between *Wait
Until Spring, Bandini* and *The Brotherhood of the Grape* that should not be
overlooked for possible implications upon current and future Italian American narrative. First of all, there is no doubt about the ethnic setting and
background of both novels. The self-images the characters have, and the
ways in which they deal with others, reflect mental processes that constantly
filter through a double identity: that of being both Italian and American.
An integral part of the conflict of identity young Arturo experiences manifests itself in the constant use of or reference to the use of the Italian
language in a society whose dominant language is English. We have seen
earlier his wish to be John Jones, an American (at least by name) instead of
the Italian Arturo Bandini. Svevo and his friends speak Italian when together. In fact, Arturo and his brothers use Italian, for we are told that they
understand Italian and their parents often use it (Fante 1980, 88). In *The
Brotherhood of the Grape*, however, the use and allusions to the Italian
language are sparse. We might offer several explanations for the diminishing
use of the Italian language in more recent Italian American narrative, all of
which take into consideration the interaction of the author, audience, and
protagonists of a given text. It may be the case that the author does not
know Italian, and simply to research the use of certain words or phrases in
Italian (or dialect as would be necessary in most cases) would prove shallow
and not satisfy the stylistic goals of the literary work. Another possibility is
the assumption on the part of the author that if the readers do not understand
Italian they will be distracted by its use; this might be especially true if we
ascribe to the belief that books about Italian Americans are not limited in

interest only to other Italian Americans, but belong to the broad province of those who enjoy good books. Finally, almost any text dealing with Italian Americans of the third generation and beyond has as protagonists those who have had a minimum of exposure to the Italian language, so that we would expect far fewer uses of it. Considering various combinations of these propositions, let us suggest that any use of Italian, whether we assume that the reader understands the foreign tongue or not, must be placed carefully and strategically by the writer. This is certainly the case in *The Brotherhood of the Grape.*

When Henry returns to town and is searching for his father at his favorite tavern, the following observation is a subtle indication of the passing generations: "Something else had changed: when I was a lad the patrons at the Cafè Roma spoke only Italian. Now the new breed of old cockers spoke English" (Fante 1977, 39). Of the few exchanges in Italian in this novel, one occurs at a dramatic highpoint that stands at the emotionally charged crossroads of the passing of a generation. Old Nick escapes from the hospital to join his friends for antipasto, wine, and cards at Angelo Musso's vineyard. When Henry finally finds him there, his father is in a heavy state of drunkenness and cerebral hemorrhage. As the ambulance attendants carry him away, his cronies, the brotherhood of the grape, salute him in hushed farewell, in Italian:

"Ciao, Nicola, buono fortuna."
"Addio, amico mio."
"Corragio, Nick."
"Corragioso, Nicola." (Fante 1977, 161)

Nick Molise's friends Zarlingo, Cavallaro, Antrilli, and Benedetti have lost a dear friend and Henry his father; yet the son would gladly take one of these to be his father still. Perhaps it is here that we witness the most significant, well-developed feature of *The Brotherhood of the Grape*, a feature too often overlooked in Italian American narrative. *The Brotherhood of the Grape* illustrates how an ethnic literary work steps out of the narrow confines of merely being a text written by an Italian American for other Italian Americans to read. Its central focus is on the universal problems confronted "by people in the Western Culture: relations with parents, choice of vocation, struggle to understand the basis of faith" (Newman 1980, 15). While the background of Fante's novel is Italian American, above all, Henry Molise laments the loss of his father in a universal sense: "My father lay in the hospital, a dying man, and all I felt was a tragic compassion for myself...I was scum again, proletarian scum, the son of an ill-fated mason who had struggled all his life for a bit of space on earth. Like father, like son....How could a man live without his father? How could he wake up in the morning and say to himself: my father is gone forever?" (Fante 1977, 135–36). Good Italian American narrative, like any other work of literary merit, satisfies the demands put upon it by informed readers; regardless of the narrower cultural setting from which the broad themes of an individual text emerge, such works reach high to touch those hopes, fears, desires, and concerns that unite us all in the brotherhood of man.

Therefore, critics might pay closer attention to this growing quality of universality not only in future works, but also in reviewing the many excellent works of the past decades. It is now with an excellent corpus of works to refer to that we can look to the documents of Italian American literature as texts that address the universal human condition; it is now that the literary history of the United States can take fair account of Italian American literary production; it is now as third-generation Italian Americans come of age socially, politically, and intellectually that Italian American literature can begin to have its due.

Works Cited

Di Pietro, Robert and Edward Ifkovic, eds. 1983. *Ethnic Perspectives in American Literature*. New York: Modern Language Association.

DeRosa, Tina. 1980. *Paper Fish*. Chicago: Wine Press.

Fante, John. 1977. *The Brotherhood of the Grape*. New York: Houghton Mifflin.
———. [1938] 1980. *Wait Until Spring, Bandini!* Santa Barbara, Calif.: Black Sparrow.

Green, Rose Basile. 1974. *The Italian-American Novel: A Document of the Interaction of Two Cultures*. Madison, N.J.: Fairleigh Dickinson University Press.

Newman, Katharine. 1980. "An Ethnic Scholar Views American Literature." *MELUS* 7, no. 1 (Spring).

Parini, Jay. 1986. *The Patch Boys*. New York: Henry Holt.

Peragallo, Olga. 1949. *Italian-American Authors and Their Contribution to American Literature*. New York: S. F. Vanni.

Vecoli, Rudolph J. 1969. "The Italian-American Literary Subculture: An Historical and Sociological Analysis." In *The Italian American Novel*, proceedings of the Second Annual Conference of the American Italian Historical Association, edited by John M. Cammett, 25 October 1969. Staten Island, N.Y.: American Italian Historical Association.

The Choice of Gilbert Sorrentino

T. S. Eliot, who is not one of Gilbert Sorrentino's favorite writers, said that the way for modern writers to excel is first to establish a deep awareness of the past. If no richly textured literary tradition exists in the culture of one's youth, it must be fabricated—from the past, from another culture, from whatever lies at hand. Sorrentino hybridizes his tradition out of various strands of literary modernism. He claims to have "slid out, somehow, from the oppression of the Classic European moderns" (V, 19).[1] In fact his poetry and prose are textbook modernism: the poem as "sculpted figure" (V, 7) which is Poundian; "no ideas but in things" (R, 6; V, 7, 10; SS, 24) (Williams); priority of metaphor (SS, 6-7) (Eliot, Richards); the mask (R, 16, 23), "plagiarism," wordsmithing, and lists (Joyce); the experimental mode (V, 15; R, 11-12), "indeterminacy" (V, 8), aesthetic autonomy and abstract formalism (R, 6, 22). At the same time his strongly idiosyncratic temperament, his obsession with "loss" (R, 10) and memory (R, 13), his quest for moral definition and certitude, his attack on "refinement" (SS, 5)—all give evidence of a countertendency. The desire to give the past its living record undermines his attack on ideas, analysis, meaning, and "content" (V, 11; R, 8). Sorrentino's literary work as a whole shows the strength and the danger of adopting the culture of literary modernism in its declining phases, when, through writers like Sorrentino, it was becoming postmodernism.

1

Literary modernism gave Sorrentino (1929–) a way of becoming a writer that his personal background did not make easily available. He grew up in the mixed ethnic neighborhood of Bay Ridge, Brooklyn. His paternal grandfather came from Salerno; both his paternal grandmother and father were born in Sciacca. His mother was of Irish and Welsh-Irish stock. "This is a common mixture of blood among many people of my generation and class in the large industrial cities of the North" (SS, 263–64). "Who and where were my peers?" Sorrentino asked himself when he felt literary promptings in his youth. "I lived literally, totally out of touch with anybody you might consider a writer."[2] His community in the 1930s and 1940s would have offered models worthy of imitation in certain arts, but not in literature. In one interview Sorrentino avowed that he took up writing "seriously" in 1948, when he turned nineteen; "I had no interest whatsoever in going to college" (V, 3; R, 7). The statement typifies the attitude of many Italian Americans of his generation towards higher education: professional life seemed too many jumps ahead, and it meant psychological and often geographical distance from the Italian American's strongest sociological unit, the family. Short-term needs and interests won out over higher or more remunerative goals, ultimately more satisfying because self-willed. "There's really no way out of this kind of life except by earning a lot of money, joining the army, or dying" (R, 11).

Sorrentino joined the army; but first he crossed the East River to Manhattan for a job as a clerk on Madison Avenue. Then, "by some odd occurrence (I don't know exactly how it happened) I began to read Walt Whitman. And I thought, well, I can do that too." The anecdote reveals the confidence of the young writer, but also a certain bluster and lack of sophistication in his schooling. As he continues, "I was always good in English. . . . But given the kind of working-class background that I came out of, there was literally no conception in my mind that I could become a writer, a serious writer, an artist, as it were" (V, 3). Journalism (reporting, popular magazine articles, sportswriting, etc.) was one legitimate way of becoming a writer in his situation. "So either because of that attitude on my part toward writing or because of my mother's hope for some kind of career for me when I grew up, I always thought of myself as perhaps becoming a journalist. . . . I think it was a kind of invention to cover my writing sins. If I was sitting at home scribbling something, and my mother said, what are you doing, I would say, well, I'm writing. And that would be all right because, after all, I was going to become a journalist" (V, 3). Even the word *sins* amidst the atmosphere of suspicion, however playfully chosen, calls attention to an underlying guilt that he attached to the profession of literature, to the artist.[3]

Perhaps his literary interests led Sorrentino to reconsider education. He matriculated at Brooklyn College in 1949 where he studied English and classics, left to join the Army Medical Corps in 1951, and was discharged in 1953. In that year he promised himself: "I am going to be a writer or I am going to be nothing" (R, 7). He was already composing short pieces. He now began a "vast novel" (V, 18), a work of realism written in an open idiom, a kind of urban *bildungsroman*; it was "about my old neighborhood. . . the true novel, you know the narrator growing up, Studs Lonigan, that kind of stuff," something "simply dealing with the people" (V, 13). In three years it grew to six hundred pages. Sorrentino never published it. Realist fiction was a direction he did not pursue.

In 1955 he returned to Brooklyn College "for want of something better to do. I was almost totally ignorant of my peers, but I had, as they say, glimmerings, although I knew no other writers."[4] At college, a group of individuals as "dissatisfied" as Sorrentino with the literary establishment (*Hudson Review*, *Commentary*, *Partisan Review*, etc.) was now gathering. In 1956 he founded the magazine *Neon*: "#1 was just us" (V, 23). It appeared irregularly until 1960.

Meanwhile, Sorrentino discovered new models, the cankerous prose of Wyndham Lewis, the antic disposition of Jack Kerouac. The latter figure intrigued him: "Kerouac did what we all, in these isolated pockets. . . knew *had* to be done, which was to incorporate our own experience into what we liked to think of as being serious prose," a "prose that will be accepted as, say, art" (V, 18). What is "art"? The meandering forms, sharp disjuctions, and "no precedent" tradition of the Jazz Cult (of which Lewis would hardly have approved):

> There's no precedent; that's what Kerouac really did. He said, I listen to Charlie Parker and it's valuable. I'll put that right into my story. I mean the *idea* of Charlie Parker. And we read this: it was a kind of burst of light, that we could do such a thing....Everybody was sort of scuffling around and trying to twist prose and make it do what you wanted it to do. Make it look different, by Christ! (V, 18)

Pound had said: Make it new—not quite the same as, make it look different.

In this direction Sorrentino was supported warmly by William Carlos Williams whom he met in 1956, though they had been in correspondence for several years. Williams was "for years Sorrentino's mentor,"[5] and some of Sorrentino's best essays are devoted to Williams's fiction and poetry and a defense of his work against other modernists (e.g., Eliot and even Frost, who is not considered sufficiently "American," SS, 16). The antitraditionalist stance was adopted for both prose and poetry: "Williams was the man who said in his work, no, it doesn't have to be Auden, no it doesn't have to be Roethke and it doesn't have to be Vierek and it doesn't have to be Lowell. It can be *this*" (V, 18). For Gilbert Sorrentino, however, it was not *this*, but (initially) it was Williams.[6] With the publication of *Neon* 1 "things happened so fast." He had found his models and peers, his poetics, and his audience. Though it was not without its struggles with publishers, he had begun a successful career as a poet and postmodernist novelist. He currently teaches creative writing at Stanford University.

2

Why in their first fifty years in the United States did Italian Americans fail to establish a literary culture? Why did Sorrentino have such difficulty in finding models and locating peers? By the time the sons and daughters and grandchildren of the Great Migration had attained to literary culture, they themselves were so assimilated as to have almost forgotten or repressed their origins. Even their frail memorialist tradition is sadly wanting. And, it should be noted, there are still too few memoirs, autobiographies, novels, poems, and plays by Italian Americans. Their history is often written by others not in the best position to know it—"know" in Giambattista Vico's sense, that one can most fully *know* only what one has *made*.

To return to the question: to what is due the absence of a literary tradition in Italian-American culture, an absence that left Sorrentino to shift about for six or seven years and finally to appropriate the modernist poetics of Williams and Kerouac? According to Jacob Burckhardt, one must go back to the very beginnings of the Renaissance to discover in Italy that division between high and low culture that gradually became an unbridgeable chasm in the nineteenth century. Burckhardt, the champion of Italian humanism, remarked that the most damaging criticism that could be leveled at the whole humanistic movement was that it was "anti-popular": "through it Europe became for the first time sharply divided into the cultivated and uncultivated classes. The reproach will appear groundless when we reflect that even now the fact, though clearly recognized, cannot be altered."[7] Burckhardt's *The Civilization of the Renaissance in Italy* appeared in 1860, only a generation before the Great Migration. The literary tradition of the Italian, created largely by the upper bourgeoisie, had been one of high culture. This culture became the model for Europe, though in the north of Europe the high literacy rate spread culture further down the social scale. But in southern Italy and Sicily, where literacy remained low, and where the feudal rights of the nobles, the power of foreign dynasties, and the secular authority of the Church were great, the populace did not have access to the Italian humanistic tradition. "In those miserable abodes of fear, poverty and superstition," G. M. Trevelyan wrote, "the Dark Ages were prolonged down to the end of the eighteenth century." Neither the Renaissance nor the Enlightenment penetrated deeply into these regions, and if the Napoleonic reforms did away with feudal rights, "the rule of priest and king was not so easily disposed of."[8] The victories of Garibaldi and The Thousand could not have swept away this mentality in a generation.

The reason for the absence of literary culture in Italian America is owing to its absence in the culture of its immigrant founders on their native ground. Those men and women, poor and illiterate in the main, could have had no great stake in Italy, let alone Italian humanism and literature. What might have been a great humanizing force in the life of Italian Americans had been choked off at the source. By an odd circularity, the way back for them to that culture lay through education on the northern European model: the history, art, and literature of the West which, as Toynbee remarked, Italy dominated for three long stretches of time, through Rome, through the Church, and through the Renaissance. But Italian-American writers rarely look that far back, and modern education does less and less so.

Let me stress that I am referring to the written word. Italian Americans carried the culture of their origins within them—in music, opera, design, the visual arts, dance, and the crafts. It would eventually flower also in film. One has only to go down the names in the catalogs of American orchestras beginning about 1910 to see an Italian-American contribution.[9] Literature, however, was not in the patrimony of the immigrants. Nor, too, greatest irony of all, was the example of the literary scholar, the humanist. Perhaps this is the lasting shame and tragedy of Italian civilization as its peoples embarked to the Americas.

3

The anxieties of Sorrentino's choice of peers and poetics register in his poetry. Yet it must be admitted that, in a paradoxical way, the sophisticated poetics of high modernism were well suited to Sorrentino's personality. The movement took a stance of emargination from the community. It prized, at least on one level, an impersonal art, one that distanced itself from private emotion and individual memory. These attitudes could not fail to answer to the private anguish of this talented but unmoored artist in search of a literary guild.

In one of Sorrentino's early poems, "A Fixture" (1957–58) (V, 7)—he placed it first among his selected poems—Sorrentino demarcates his private terrain. Yet he does so in an adopted language, that of Williams's "no ideas but in things":

> I've nothing to say
> to them;
>
> pride is as solid
> as summer heat.
>
> That is to say
> you can't cut it:
>
> with a knife in the kitchen
> I cut
>
> a tomato; nothing to say
> to them: let them rot
>
> and be bitten by night,
> in the country.
>
> I've nothing to say
> to them. And I won't write.

The poet turns the act of "not writing" into aggression toward "them." Such was his refusal to publish the novel "about my old neighborhood" (V, 13), a novel into which he had just poured three years of labor. His strong antipathy and curse are not only directed at "them," however, but at what they represent in himself. The themes of cutting, separation, and rejection presuppose an earlier unity. In this unity "they" are associated with the summer heat, the country, the agrarian Italian folk with their love of vines and gardens, the kitchen and female presence (the "inevitable mother" of the southern Italians[10]), and the night of the primordial past. "They" are further metonymized in the *tomato,* a totemic image in the southern Italian mind (as the potato is to the Irish and Irish American), a blood-red object that "bleeds" when cut; and in the *knife,* archetypal symbol of familial violence, but also of violence attached to the Italian-American image when Sorrentino was growing up in the thirties and forties. (Southern Italians fought—or were said to fight—with knives and guns more than fists.) All this, all of "them," are rejected so massively that elements of "them" inevitably force a return. The paradox of Sorrentino's withdrawal, his pride at being (sexually) "solid" and whole without "them," is that such unity is won at the cost of self-amputation. The castration theme issues in such words as "nothing," "solid," "heat," and the cutting, the being bitten at night (molested); even the title "A Fixture" means something attached as a semipermanent appendage, utilitarian or ornamental, its very attachment undercutting its sense of permanence. Furthermore, he has no speech and refuses to speak; yet he wishes to turn this impotence into a "triumph" (though he does not gain his true voice). "That is to say" is a kind of second start, a stutter.

   The poet cuts the tomato with a knife in the kitchen, suggesting a rejection (or worse) of kitchen/home/mother. Then he curses all of "them." "Let them rot," "be bitten by night / in the country." The persistence of the

Italian rural folkways disgusts him. A good New Yorker, Sorrentino elsewhere affects hatred of the country, but this can be seen as a deflection of
the need to nurse deeper psychic wounds. Predatory animals symbolize the
past in other poems. Here they link up with nature, night, and nightmares,
the night being associated with the country, the past, and primeval origins.
The poet projects his own fear of being "bitten" onto "them." The lines
evoke the terrifying violence of the speaker's self-hatred. Finally, "they"
cannot understand him, the poet's language; and the poet, who has the
linguistic gift denied to them, "won't write" the language that they could
understand.[11] "They" do not even inhabit the same line. The line break
before "to them," effective three times over, is the typographical enactment
of the division. The poet concludes by obsessive repetition, proving in effect
that he has "nothing" more to say except this: not writing to them, he has
written to inform *us*. He has found an audience.

Sorrentino's choice of one audience in favor of another entails the
suppression of part of his past; in the language of psychoanalysis, it is
denial. The core elements extrude in his imagery and metaphor. In "Ars
Longa" the poet is like the experienced gardener helping those tomato plants
that seem to have a will of their own. Sorrentino attempts to fuse "nature,"
culture, the immigrant, his verbal "concern," and Mallarmé ("little
chainsmoker"):

> Carefully as a man tying up tomato plants,
> they will be arranged, the words,
> they are all our concern, as that bright
> little chainsmoker knew,
>
> what is said is better than said if the
> page be impinged upon with power.

In the last line the plosive *p*'s emit what turns out to be an hubristic boast.
The alliteration attracts too much attention to itself; power here must
"impinge" from without, whereas the language should be the source of
power. In an elaborate image, memories are like the rings caused by pebbles
in a stream. Then, "we hurl pebbles" at the rings, as if trying angrily to
obliterate their forms with new rings that "argue" futilely in the water:
"words, they are neither the experience":

> nor the telling of it; a barrier of cellophane,
> to enmesh you tenderly, or fiercely,
> one is here! one there! one is in two
> or three places at ———! or is it
> yesterday, what is this, a poem?
> a group of words, a monster of the
> evening, it slouches mightily, it is in
> full possession of the land and sea

Language and poetry are associated with nature (tomato plants), hidden
memory, night (evening), and monsters. This time Sorrentino does not foist
the monstrous onto "them." Still, he avoids confrontation and thwarts
resolution. He allows this slouching monster (the word inevitably recalls

Yeats's "slouching" beast) to get away (monsters exist to be slain by heroes), to metamorphose, quite literally, into air. "'The monstrous,'" wrote Rudolph Otto, "is just the mysterious in gross form."[12] Inspiration "fills" the poet like a mysterious power:

> it fills our sail, it fills our sail,
> it fills our sail, it fills
> our sail, it fills our
> sail, it fills our sail.

Sorrentino has written that poetry affects "release" from "rootless anxiety," that it is an "excursion into a state of exhilaration" (SS, 8). This last stanza attempts sublimity, at a voyage out, at release from a tangle of memories; and Longinus said that repetition could be a way of implementing the sublime. Yet this attempt is undermined by an obsessive focus on the act, the form, and the phrase itself. We do not have sublimity but exaggeration, and the meaning is the opposite of what is stated: the power runs down. The monsters have not been exorcised. One notes in passing that repetition is a much-used feature in Sorrentino's writing.

In "The Fiction" the poet explores his artistic vocation. The fire of imaginative energy and sacrifice burns, an exotic image of pagan invocation, and one recalls the presence of the poet "chainsmoker" before the invocation of power in "Ars Longa." Yet the poet remains "lost," asking pathetically "where / did we all come from"?

> This fire moves. Upward, upward,
> smoke moved by it, forward to the
> sky. I am lost here, where
> did we all come from, I listen
> to this dear friend's history.
> Words batter at me, the wine is
> good. Words beg that I
> nod my head, monsters
> of the past are here
>
> in the room, a sudden turn and
> I will have trapped them. "What
> a time that was." Here,
> here, on my neck: to turn? God
> help me should they have that
> face, this face, what face.

Like the predatory animals, "monsters" rise from "the past," "a time that was"; exotic as they are, they seem familiar, "in the room," and must be acknowledged. In "The Uncanny," *Beyond the Pleasure Principle*, and "Medusa's Head," Freud investigated the *Unheimliche* (the "un-at-home-like"): the experience of the uncanny is characterized by sudden dread as something that is "familiar and old-established in the mind," but "which has become alienated from it" through repression, forces its way into consciousness. His examples included the *revenant*, the double, the evil eye, the Medusa, coincidences, "omnipotence of thought," and the sense of being pursued by a malignant fate or "possessed by some 'demonic power,'" all of which he traces to the "death instinct."[13] In Sorrentino's "Ars Longa," the monsters give way to the omnipotence of (the repeated) "it fills our sail." In the poem presently under discussion, the "monsters of the past" appear when defenses are worn down by wine. Once again, the "I" is ranged against "them," and with renewed omnipotence. If the monsters attack, he "will have trapped them," an ambiguous grammatical exit into the future perfect tense. The monster "on my neck" is clearly a vampire image, which links it to the feminine. Will the poet save himself by "a sudden turn" like an ambush or perhaps a different perspective? Sorrentino questions the efficacy of trapping the monsters: "to turn?" It is at least doubtful and again he seeks supernatural aid. He implores the absent "God" for help. The poem ends with a prayer that the poet have the courage to face them, whatever "they" are, with so many deceiving "faces." The past is everywhere.

One conclusion to be drawn from these poems is that Sorrentino has not been able to confront the past directly and clearly. It transforms itself into "monsters," surreal agents, and then he either castigates it or waves his magic wand to make it disappear. Toby Olson writes that, while Sorrentino's past is of central importance, the past that "we find in his work, was never real[!] in the autobiographical sense, and to think of it as such can only force it into a kind of selective realism framework."[14] All realism is selective: the point is, how representative and general is the selection of particulars. Olson accepts his formal solutions, remarking that he writes about a "historical" past "beyond redemption." This is to think that the decision to write a modernist novel instead of an autobiography solves the psychic problems that lie below generic divisions. Despite Sorrentino's protestations, his words keep pointing backward, to the "demons": "The confrontation with the demons does not necessarily lead to the creation of great art (or any art at all)," he writes, "You can write in the darkest pit and filth of yourself and come up with some dull fragments of *vers libre*, indistinguishable from that of a hundred contemporaries" (quoted in V, 54). The truth of this statement is incontrovertible. Still, Sorrentino returns frequently in his writings to private memory and the problems of the past. He attempts to solve them by a kind of leap of faith, not "explanation" but "revelation" ("God"). The lack of resolution leads to a recurrence of the problems, and recurrence only confirms them at a deeper level of repression. Sorrentino's "assimilation into Anglo-American culture," writes Maria Vittoria D'Amico, "has been so deep and radical so as not to leave much allowance for the Italian-American side."[15] One agrees, and yet the thin wedge of difference drives to the heart of the matter. The Italian-American imagery is no mere local color but at the very root of the poet's strategies and language.

4

Sorrentino composes many poems in a voice and tone that he created early in his career: bohemian, satiric, opinionated, whimsical, farouche, festooned with learning.[16] The references to Baudelaire, Mallarmé, Verlaine, Apollinaire, and Rimbaud evoke the slavish modernism of the midcentury period in American writing.[17] They do not serve him well because his special gift lies in the episodic, almost plotless novel of form. His strongest poems have a picaresque quality. In "Coast of Texas," a sequence of sixteen short lyrics, he invents a narrator by combining elements of Apollinaire's Pierrot and Jack Kerouac's Kerouac.[18] The title refers to Apollinaire's *voyage imaginaire "sur la côte du Texas"*—Baudelaire would have said *le superb Texas*—and a real journey of young soldier Sorrentino, stationed at Fort Hood, Texas. The sequence is a jagged series of false starts, fantastic concessions, unfulfilled imaginative conditions of a rapscallion. In the first poem, everything looks right for love—the blue sky, "clarity"—except for a "blank" city. Syntactical forms run headlong into one another, until we arrive at the mind's own place, marked by repetition: it "did not seem I was / In Hell / I was in Hell. O / love. That impairs my song." "Song" seems particularly reductive because the sounds do not resonate, deliberately, in this mute collage.

The narrator moves from town to town in search of a lost woman. Alone, he makes little effort to communicate with other people. His Mexicans are as real as water colors on a travel poster. His language has the informative flatness of prose as if he were telling a story that happened a while ago. But Sorrentino's rhythm is puzzling, lacking any reference to formal or spoken patterns:

> Corpus Christi
> is no place to spend Christmas
> notwithstanding those avenues
> of palms, the white houses on the green Gulf.
> The old Mexicans fish off
> stone quais, and fish off stone quais.
> I ate chili and drank rye whiskey.
> A whole novel wrote and discarded in my head.[19]
> Notwithstanding those avenues of green
> palms, Corpus Christi on the coast
> of Texas is no place to spend any time.
> Apollinaire himself avoided this blank city. (2)

The name of the city has lost its sacrificial meaning; it is not worthy of a holiday that its name celebrates. Although the beauty of the palms and white houses impress, the narrator is not charmed to sojourn. The old Mexicans fish together for food; the narrator eats alone. He drinks, writes, and is ultimately unproductive. He passes on, the city leaves him "blank," here and elsewhere in the sequence associated with the whiteness and purity of an undefiled void: "the dead / center of each o" (7). Apollinaire, his ideal poet, could not conquer this whiteness, a metaphor for the pure white *symboliste* page on which a poet leaves his ink mark. Even the "hazy coast" loses its quality as a boundary, as a logical and geographical marker: "Everyone knows Apollinaire / went mad on that hazy coast...I went mad there too" (11). Even so, the initiate knows "This is a resort town / blanco" (7), an arcane imaginative zone far removed from the workaday world.

Up and down the gulf coast the hero/narrator searches for a woman "almost unbearably / nubile" (8) and seemingly innocuous. She is a romantic Fatal Woman wearing blue jeans and sneakers. According to Mario Praz, innocence itself may be a trait of the Fatal Woman because innocence can cast a spell even more alluring (because less threatening) than experience. In no particular order, her attributes are diabolical beauty, algolagnia or sexual sadism and masochism, vampirism, a close relation between the erotic, the aesthetic, and the exotic, a Sphinx-like knowledge, and a devotion to the cult of the moon.[20] Like Pierrot, Sorrentino's speaker sings her praises by moonlight (3); he imagines her trapped in a closet (4) and haunting a "Greyhound" (an attribute of the predatory Diana) bus station (12). As elsewhere in Sorrentino's poetry, the woman is associated with air, sky, and inspiration: "All in the burning sky / she is" (6). "Waft of cloves" (15) and "a whiff of orange cunt / come out of Florida" (6) convey the exotic element combined with strong sexual desire. James Guimond comments that the language of the sequence is "appropriately obscene and sentimental" and "always precise and vivid."[21] Appropriately obscene, maybe; always precise, no. In the final poem (16) of the sequence, the masochism of walking two thousand miles is exaggerated; the woman's position is extremely awkward and hard to comprehend; kissing stockings and collar is peculiar; and why Georgia? Coleridge might have called it a poetry of fancy, not imagination:

> He would come back out
> of this butter sun, walking the
> 2000 miles. Her hip leaning
> against a tree her foot pointed in.
> Crawl through the snow and
> kiss her stockings and the collar
> of her blouse. Even through Georgia.

Sorrentino's harlequin has abased himself groveling in the snow: "He will listen to opera and Jewish / jokes, get the fuck down / in the slush and touch / her shoes." To paraphrase, the hero will do whatever it takes to win the favor of, ultimately to seduce, his lady. This odd assortment has a running thread: opera (Italian, extravagant emotion), the Jew (foreign, emarginated), sexual self-abasement, all of which connect back to his fears of the feminine peasant tradition. Her smile, "a crooked one" (11), evokes the Medusa, a version of the vampire theme. Tears, jokes, and sentimentalization represent his effort towards mitigating her power:

> Do without a hat in the wind
> off the Atlantic and weep
> into her crotch.
> He could sleep in pajamas get up
> to a job and eat lunch with
> fascists and morons, buy her
> boxes of Tampax.
> She had a crooked smile put
> his hands between her garters
> and her thighs.

Hatless in the cold, pajamas in the bed, sex on demand, lunch with fascists and morons, buying Tampax—one despairs at length of trying to find organic connections. His running together of words, grammatical patterns, and images show feverish excitement and loss of control. He is at the mercy of his compulsions. In his hero/narrator—for Sorrentino slips back and forth from relating the poem in the first and third persons—the poet has drawn one more portrait of a familiar archetype. He gives us the individual whose needs, talk, and actions have become the norm of a large subculture in Western Europe and America, the one that embodies what Christopher Lasch calls "the banality of pseudo-self-awareness."

5

References to Italian Americans are so infrequent in Sorrentino's poetry that any occurrence tends to stand out boldly. In "Country and Western" he sets the scene in South Brooklyn and looks out to the new Verrazano Narrows Bridge, named for the heroic Florentine explorer of the Atlantic coast.[22] We float again upon the vast troubled waters, their "buoys / crying," of racial memory. If the seas of memory were tranquil, the buoys would not cry:

> Getting toward the end
> of it now. Soon the buoys
> crying in Great South Bay
> and The Narrows
>
> that magnificent bridge
> dead in its autos (a dead word
>
> weeds gone, choked, no olds wops
> to eat them
>
> swiss chard, endive known
> as escarole, with oil
> and garlic, first dish
>
> a fat woman who cried easily
> and called her table by those terms
>
> first dish (second dish,
> gripping that peasant tradition
>
> dead of an overdose: of aspirin

We are "getting toward the end" of the immigrant world, of what is metonymized by the waters (crossing the ocean), the bridge, and the "weeds" (hardy nature) eaten by the impoverished newcomers used to foraging on such edibles in the Old Country. The weeds of folk medicine contrast with the killing modernity of aspirin. The prejudicial "wop" expresses a conventionalized self-hatred, masquerading as sentiment. The image of the strong-smelling garlic, "noses in which garlic smells / bad" (the line break emphasizing revulsion) retrieves memories of the immigrant past. Smell, argues Freud, is the most repressed and primitive of the senses, the most deeply associated with childhood (and with man's animalian prehistory); the indulgence of smell releases libidinal pleasure.[23] Its triple recurrence here acts like a dredge. Noses, moreover, are synecdochic condensation, the unattractive facial feature that is commonly, if erroneously, associated with southern Italian types. Fatness is another such feature. The mother figure, the "fat woman who cried easily," part symbol, part cliché, stands as the quintessential image of the immigrant past now "dead of an overdose." Later in the poem, the poet will not give the woman's real name in Italian: "Her name meant / *soldiers*." As C. K. Ogden and I. A. Richards have written: "The persistence of the primitive linguistic outlook not only throughout the whole religious world, but in the work of the profoundest thinkers, is indeed one of the most curious features of modern thought."[24] Thus, the disclosure of the name in Italian would have been to unleash uncontrollable and retributive powers, e.g., the demons. (Likewise Sorrentino suppresses the name "Verrazano," speaking only of "The Narrows" and the "magnificent bridge"— a technological wonder, not the memory of a hero). Yet Sorrentino cannot withstand her power, so he deflects it by giving not the name, but a name, in translation, in a line all to itself, and italicized (no pun): "*soldiers*." And what a name! Perhaps she was a Soldati (and one notes the past tense in "meant / *soldiers*"). But whatever the precise name in Italian, the image of soldiers bespeaks menace, power, and plurality. Thus the "fat woman" goes back to the monster on his neck. The feminine is connected with vampirism and strong, if tearful, emotion. Again, the poet sets this violent image in the midst of contrast. As if to contain the terror, he makes her one "who cried easily." We recall the "buoys / crying." The fact is that Sorrentino fears emotion whenever the subject of peasant tradition emerges; so he claims that what he dislikes is cheap sentiment and vulgarity. Actually, the human race cries easily, as Hesiod said, until it learns the art of forgetfulness.

I am not certain whether endive is known as, or could be mistaken for, escarole, but the ingredients are correct and it was always a first course. The immigrant generation that ate escarole is succeeded by the era of the automobile and drugs:

> I see her husband now
> a mild man with rimless
> glasses, her daughter
>
> with an egg
> in her milk.
> Under the shadows of that bridge
> for whom no poets will hanker.
>
> A mild-mannered man
> with rimless specs
> and a dark-blue overcoat, his Journal-American—
>
> They have all died or splintered themselves
> for this absolute air, scented
> with blood and the shit of success.
>
> That woman with her
> old and garlic savored escarole.
>
> Her name meant
> *soldiers*
>
> crossing a bridge to impress
> their inherited clutter
> on their brothers, so many pinkish faces

> noses in which garlic smells
> bad

The mild (weak) husband and daughter are secondary in the family portrait, though the conventions persist, the father with his newspaper, the daughter with milk and egg. Their options are limited; "dead or splintered," there is no possibility for organic wholeness, except the mysterious "absolute air" (from *ab solvere*, to unbind fetters, with ties to nothing) which filled the poet's sail in "Ars Longa." The return of the repressed burgeons in numerous familial images of food, smells, and cooking; the psychic wounds do not heal; they are transferred by other images of smell to present-day America, "scented / with blood and shit of success." The title of the poem connects the agrarian past with the wholly manufactured, commercialized concoction of country and western music—a far cry (in my opinion) from opera, but linked to it in the poet's mind. Country and western smacks of the very folkloristic elements that Sorrentino spurns: the foreign, the rural, the mythical, and the popular. His attempt to trivialize the immigrant tradition by putting it on the same psychic plane with the artificial (and banal) country and western music is a strong example of his rejection.

There is yet another example. As mentioned previously, this poem is one of the few to refer to the Italian-American problem. Sorrentino did not include it in his *Selected Poems, 1958–1980*.

6

Compared with his poetry, Sorrentino's fiction contains numerous references to Italian Americans. *The Sky Changes* (1966; rev. ed. 1986), his first novel, portrays an embittered couple, their son, and a driver on a car-trip from Brooklyn to San Francisco to New Mexico, ending in marital separation. Though individuals are not given names, the husband could be Italian American. At one point he wants to cook an Italian dinner and finds to his dismay that a supermarket in Jackson, Mississippi, has "no garlic, no Italian sausage, no Italian tomatoes, no tomato paste, no oregano...as he looked for these things he found himself asking the manager about each item" (SC, 47). The manager thinks he is a "strange freak, some Martian" because "nobody eats spaghetti around here....that ain't fewed." Perhaps Italian cooking represents his marginality; it is surely an example of his zest for life. Also, this is one of the novel's few comic incidents. *Steelwork* (1970) depicts a South Brooklyn neighborhood between 1935 and 1951. The subject has elements of an Italian-American novel: Carminootch (SS, 30–31), the boy Artie Salvo ("art," "safe," "saving," SS, 53–54, 146–48). There are scenes of deep pathos, for example, the closing premonitions of urban "renewal" that wiped out Italian neighborhoods everywhere. On a cold night a young boy (a dominant archetype in Sorrentino's fiction) sees where the bulldozers have torn out "a gigantic strip of grass and trees to make a highway" (S, 177). But it is hard to put one's finger on specifically Italian elements in the situation. In *Blue Pastoral* (1983), Dr. Cicarelli is an Italian dentist who can mimic the "stage 'greaseball' accent" ("*Ats*-a-nize!") which "works wonders with idiot WASPs...especially when employed at sidewalk feasts like those of Saint Anthony, San Gennaro, and Santa Rosalia, by Italo-Americans, all of whom are Ph.D.s" (BP, 7). The fake accent comes in handy when he wants to avoid eating "soggy pasta" and "eighth-rate 'food.'" Later, a black refers to the "jew-guinea-square-ass mutha-fuckin zionist conspiracy," attacking the Mafia for pushing drugs (BP, 216–17).

Aberration of Starlight (1980) is a *Rashomon*-type scenario in which four persons tell their version of events at Bud Lake, New Jersey, on a summer vacation in 1939. They are ten-year-old Billy Recco; his mother, Marie *neé* McGrath, who is divorced from Tony Recco, an Italian-born American; Tom Thebus, a divorced salesman; and her father, Tom McGrath, a vial of bitterness and resentment. After her husband left her for another woman (an Irish American named "Margie"—a successful double), Marie took her son, quit Brooklyn, and went back to live with her parents. Tom McGrath dominates the household through bullying, bribery, and pleas for sympathy and pity. The crucial scene in the parallel narratives is the dressing-down Marie gets from her father when she returns home late from a dance with Thebus (she is in her midthirties). Billy's absent father is an enigma: the Italian component is once again the suppressed conditional clause, one of the foci of hatred. Billy recalls his father coming home to a supper of "lettuce, tomatoes, and green pepper rings" (the totemic repast). In a letter to his father, Billy brags of "Tom Theboss" who "acts more like my father than you ever do" (AS, 18). The son attacks his father as "Real Dog" and "greaseball" and says that when Tom becomes his "real Father" "I will ask him to go and punch you" (AS, 19). He appears to be learning the facts of life from "Guido," a *"real* greaseball because he was born in Italy" (AS, 43). Marie hints that her marriage failed because of her husband's unabashed sexual energy and her own coldness or timidity (she refuses sex with Thebus shortly before her father's dread appearance). For her, Tony Recco (wreck?) is a "greenhorn off the boat" (an ignorant immigrant); he "bought a toupee" (from her point of view, castration fear; from his, *bella figura*) (AS, 15); he "needed someone dirty and low" (revealing jealousy and sexual repression). Dealing in psychological opposites, she imagines Tony as an "accident looking for a place to happen" (AS, 15) while Thebus, whom we learn is a genuine philanderer, is by comparison a "modern Apollo in white ducks" (AS, 64). Sorrentino lays her repression at the door of the Sisters of Charity, in particular Sister Vincent (the "conquerer"). But the Italian, the generic Tony, is associated with sexuality, the unpredictable, anarchy, liberality, and betrayal.

In 1983 Sorrentino published a brief essay on the influence of his mixed Italian and Irish cultural heritage ("Genetic Coding," SS, 262–65). His reflections on Italian national character are neither original nor accurate: Neapolitans, "extroverted" and "demonstrative"; Sicilians, "withdrawn," "proud," "convoluted." Italians supposedly "hold reality cheap," appreciate the "essential idiocy of living," and possess the "Mediterranean tragic sense of life in a pure state." On the contrary, Max Weber pointed to the Italian sense of realism and rationality (though not as broadly systematized and routinized as in the modern northern countries), for example, the business-oriented Genoese, Florentine, and Venetian, not to mention the inventor of the monastic system, Saint Benedict, and the papacy itself. No country with such a rich and varied concept of pleasure (as opposed to mere gadget-oriented "comfort") and with such natural taste in the art of living (Stendhal extolled its *promesse de bonheur*) can be said to hold reality "cheap." The "tragic sense of life" is a phrase from Unamuno on the Spanish national character, to which it applies (though Croce and a few historians, looking for a scapegoat, occasionally blame the problems of the southern Italians on Spain).

On the history of art, Sorrentino commits egregious errors: "Italian art is, generally speaking, the art of layering: one adds and adds and then adds some more, until the initial impetus, the base upon which the work rests, is almost unrecognizable" (SS, 264). His examples are Dante, Cavalcanti, Pirandello, Calvino, Fellini, and "the statues of saints in New York churches" (tepid nineteenth-century calendar religious art—why they appear in such company strains credulity). Sorrentino is reducing Italian art to ornamentalism; thus, to his untutored eye it all presents the same florid grandiosity. Actually, the opposite is true: the "base" of Italian art is classical naturalism where "nature" signifies human life seen in its universal aspect and where the artist is concerned with man's moral and intellectual potential. The "initial impetus" is not obscured in Dante and Giotto who go directly to nature; none have surpassed them in imaginative boldness, immediacy of expression, and clarity of design. Boccaccio is a paragon of an earthy realism; even Ariosto is fundamentally realist in outlook. Cavalcanti does not add and add; if anything, he subracts and subracts. As Pound said of him, "thought cuts through thought with a clear edge."[25] Calvino returns storytelling to its simplest elements. Renaissance artists from Masaccio and Piero della Francesca to Giovanni Bellini and Mantegna, from Carpaccio and Giorgione to Tintoretto and Caravaggio, all impress through dramatic intensity, profundity of subject matter, and direct human appeal; so do Leopardi and Verdi. Further, Sorrentino writes that the "hallmark" of Italian art is a "relentless investigation into the possibilities of form, a retreat from nature, a dearth of content" (SS, 264). This bespeaks Sorrentino's militant version of modernism and an antihistoricism that, in this instance, results less from ideological commitment than from ignorance. Where is "retreat from nature" and "death of content" in Leonardo, Raphael, Titian, and Tasso, or any of the above-mentioned artists? Perhaps the greatest strength of Italian art lies in its rich portrayal of that which is representative and general in human nature—a content that incidentally is not at odds with its form. Style to the Renaissance artist does not derealize; rather, form serves as the means towards realization of subject matter and the expression of the universal element, hence its abiding appeal and the main reason why Italy is the paradise of travelers. Even in the baroque period, in such artists as Bernini and Borromini, the essential form stands forth; fussy decoration does not obscure it, as in numerous vulgarizations. Ironically, Sorrentino does not mention one way in which "classical" Italian art bears a resemblance to modernism—its ability to express violence and terror. Speaking of Verdi, Mosco Carner writes, "Characters set in an atmosphere of utter gloom and writhing in a paroxysm of savage passion and suffering have never been achieved on a more impressive scale than by another great Italian realist, Dante in the *Inferno*."[26] (One should add, *The Last Judgement*.)

7

"It was your life," writes Sorrentino, "it was your knowledge of the reality of your generation that had to be written" (V, 19). That daunting sentence recalls the years of choice, 1953–56, to which we now return.

Sorrentino's earliest writings had been "very short impressionistic sketches...people I grew up with, but fictionalized, romanticized,and prettied up in a 'literary' sense. People from my own neighborhood. I had always been interested in writing about my old neighborhood, but I never quite knew how to do it" (V, 13). Not knowing "how to do it" did not mean that Sorrentino did not attempt to do so; he spent three years on the 600-page novel about his neighborhood that he refused to publish. Sorrentino set aside this writing because "it was a kind of fake omniscient look at the lives of people 'struggling to maintain their humanity.'" This mode of writing had a "terrible preciosity to it" (V, 13).

The term "preciosity" should rather be applied to the late modernist and postmodernist poetics that Sorrentino adopted, and to the mannerisms of Kerouac, perhaps the cult figure of the fifties literary scene. What Sorrentino chose was a closed idiom, a narrow range of subject matter, the eccentric over the typical, a restricted audience, and a literary culture that in the end turned from the cosmopolitanism of Eliot and Joyce to the coterie. What he rejected was an open idiom, the opportunity to draw on a vast store of private and cultural experience, the chance to communicate to the humble audience of his neighborhood (shielding himself emotionally by using inverted commas: "'struggling to maintain their humanity'") and, possibly, well beyond.

It could be argued that Sorrentino's community would never have read his books, or would have disliked the pill they would have had to swallow (more bitter than sweet, certainly, at the outset). The society of newspapers and sports magazines might not have welcomed its chronicler. The point is that without any encouragement to be an artist from his community, Sorrentino felt only the natural desire to escape and to locate a literary guild elsewhere. Even years later, in 1974, he had to put down as "precious" the only way of reaching through to a broader public and to explain his society: sketches, direct narrative, open idiom, the young individual facing an uncertain future in a large city on the eastern seaboard. Instead, his speaker is a beatnik imagining Apollinaire on the coast of Texas. In this way Italian America lost another talent. Or, rather, did not lose him because he developed into an experimental artist of note. But Italian America lost another writer who could have given a tongue to its paving stones.

Writers like Gregory Corso and Lawrence Ferlinghetti, so different from Sorrentino in one way, are like him in another. Ferlinghetti rejected the opportunity to speak for Italian America and dialectically it rejected him. He spoke instead for a small group. Who might have been the carrier of the Italian humanistic tradition subscribed to an oriental mysticism of a highly subjective coloring.

If an alternative to late modernism was available to Sorrentino and Ferlinghetti and doubtless many others, it was *history*. Elsewhere in this volume, Robert Casillo explores how certain Italian-American filmmakers, tapping into the immigrant experience, found that it possessed an inherent dramatic power capable of being transformed into works of art with wide popular appeal. To be certain, historical memory does not easily inculcate itself. For Italian Americans, the United States does not go back further than the 1890s before turning into a series of abstractions. Italy itself is mediated by numerous institutions: the strongly Americanized Catholic Church, the urban economy (opposite to the agrarian society of the immigrant founders), and schooling. Yet historical memory and imagination could have had—and can still have—a quickening influence in the minds of immigrant children and their offspring. Burckhardt's and Alfred von Martin's idea of Italian humanism as elitistic, *fons et origo*, is certainly correct. That does not mean that it must stay that way, or did. Nothing inherent in the humanist foundation and patrimony precludes it from being broadly human in its interests, more widely participatory, and more deeply rooted in mass education. Given the explicit humanist emphasis on education, such extension should mark its development. Indeed, the texts to which humanism most frequently repairs are not exclusive. Dante chose to write in the vernacular and Shakespeare appealed to the widest Elizabethan audiences. In the sophisticated technique of Virgil, style serves as a means to apprehend and communicate the universal in experience. On arriving in Latium the Trojan Ilioneus explains Aeneas' journey across "waste seas":

> no dark tempest
> drove us across the waters to your lands;
> no star, no coastline cast us off our way;
> but by design and willing minds we all
> have reached your city—exiled from a kingdom
> that once excelled all that the Sun could see
> in his long journeying from far Olympus.[27]
> (*Aeneid*, VI, 281–87)

Ilioneus asks King Latinus for some "safe shore to house our native gods" and promises in return that "our praises / will not mean little for your reputation." The archetypal experience shines through all fidelities to detail. Today the pages of Virgil lie open beside the books on nursing and engineering.

Notes

1. An earlier version of this essay appeared in Atti del Settimo Convegno Nazionale, A.I.S.N.A., *RSA*, 4–5 (1984-85), 281-303. The following is a list of abbreviations of works cited in the text and notes: AS, Sorrentino, *Aberration of Starlight* (1980; New York: Penguin Books, 1981); BP, Sorrentino, *Blue Pastoral*

(San Francisco: North Point Press, 1983); R, *Review of Contemporary Fiction*, 1 (1981); S, Sorrentino, *Steelwork* (New York: Pantheon, 1974); SC, Sorrentino, *The Sky Changes* (1966), 2d ed. rev. (San Francisco: North Point Press, 1986); SP, *Selected Poems, 1958–1980* (Santa Barbara, Calif.: Black Sparrow, 1981); SS, Sorrentino, *Something Said: Essays* (San Francisco: North Point Press, 1984); V, *Vort* 2 (Fall 1974). Hereafter abbreviations and page references are enclosed in parentheses and follow citations.

2. "*Neon, Kulchur, Etc.*," *Triquarterly*, 43 (1987): 302. "You lived in a kind of absolute vacuum" (V, 17).

3. Cf. Pope's version of the topos: "Why did I write? What sin to me unknown / Dipt my in ink, my Parents', or my own?" (*Epistle to Dr. Arbuthnot*, 125–26). Ink is the baptismal fluid cleansing the poet of his original sin. Pope also mentions the parental interdict: "I left no Calling for this idle trade, / No duty broke, no Father dis-obey'd" (129–30).

4. "*Neon, Kulchur, Etc.*," 402.

5. Jerome Kinnkowitz, *Literary Disruptions: The Making of a Post Contemporary American Fiction* (Urbana: University of Illinois Press, 1975), 165.

6. Sorrentino wrote on the jacket of his first book: "Three great literary markers are Pound, who taught me that verse is the highest of arts and gave me the sense of tradition, Williams, who showed that our language can produce it, and Creeley, who demonstrated that the attack need not be head-on." Quoted in Eric Mottram, "The Black Polar Night: The Poetry of Gilbert Sorrentino" (V, 43), which remains the best introduction to the poetry.

7. Jacob Burckhardt, *The Civilization of the Renaissance in Italy* (New York: Phaidon, 1960), 105. On cultural diffusion, see Paul Oskar Kristeller, *Renaissance Thought II: Papers on Humanism and the Arts* (New York: Harper, 1965), 69–88.

8. George Macaulay Trevelyan, *Garibaldi and The Thousand* (London: Longmans, 1909), 38, 39. Trevelyan's tone is marred by a whiggish Anglo-Saxon superciliousness, an aristocratic disdain towards an old Catholic culture in general and Sicilians in particular.

9. For example, the four De Pasquale brothers in the Philadelphia Orchestra.

10. Norman Douglas, *Old Calabria* (New York: Modern Library, 1928), 83. Douglas's travelogue is far more informed, sympathetic, and entertaining than D. H. Lawrence's *Twilight in Sicily* and *Sea and Sardinia*.

11. John O'Brien noted that in Sorrentino's *Steelwork* (about Brooklynites in his old neighborhood) and in *The Sky Changes* "there seem to me to be a lack of sympathy...toward the plight of these characters." Sorrentino responded defensively that "I don't know that there is a lack of sympathy for these people, perhaps lack of sentimentality is better." He goes on to say that "there is a great deal of sympathy." See Max Eilenberg, "A Marvellous Gift: Gilbert Sorrentino's Fiction," R, 89.

12. Rudolph Otto, *The Idea of the Holy*, John W. Harvey, trans. (London: Oxford University Press, 1923), 82.

13. Sigmund Freud, *The Standard Edition of the Complete Psychological Works,* James Strachey, gen. ed. (London: Hogarth Press and the Institute of Psycho-Analysis, 1953–74), 17:241; 18:21, 23.

14. "Sorrentino's Past," R, 52, 54. On the other hand, Sorrentino "holds a gone culture exquisitely." His paradoxes have passed unresolved into criticism of his work.

15. Maria Vittoria D'Amico, "Paradox Beyond Convention: A Note on Gilbert Sorrentino's Fiction," Atti del Settimo Convegno Nazionale, A.I.S.N.A., *RSA*, 4–5 (1984–85): 269.

16. "Extremely judgmental and sure," Olson, R, 52.

17. As Harriet Zinnes writes, "My distress is at least twofold: the enormous diminution of vision from Rimbaud to Sorrentino and then the substitution of something tinsel for art." Review of Gilbert Sorrentino, *Splendide-Hotel, Parnassus*, 3 (1972): 111.

18. And, perhaps, Eliot's Prufrock, according to James Guimond, review of *Corrosive Sublimate, Parnassus* 1 (1972): 111.

19. As Sorrentino recalls in *Splendide-Hotel* (New York: New Directions, 1973), 36; the working title of the unwritten novel had been "Blue Ray."

20. Mario Praz, *The Romantic Agony*, Angus Davidson, trans., 2d ed. (London: Oxford University Press, 1970), 207ff.

21. Guimond, op. cit. 110.

22. *Corrosive Sublimate* (Los Angeles: Black Sparrow, 1971), 32–33.

23. Sigmund Freud, *Civilization and Its Discontents*, in *Standard Edition*, 21, ch. 4, n.1.

24. C. K. Ogden and I. A. Richards, *The Meaning of Meaning: A Study of the Influence of Language Upon Thought and of the Science of Symbolism* (London: Kegan Paul, Trench, Trubner, 1923), 39.

25. Ezra Pound, *Literary Essays* (New York: New Directions, 1954), 293.

26. Mosco Carner, *Puccini: A Critical Biography*, 2d ed. (New York: Holmes and Meier, 1974), 256. The horror in Céline, Beckett, or Solzhenitsyn (when he is showing the worst effects of Stalinism) "dehumanizes"; it is nihilistic. But in Verdi and the others there is sympathy and "faith in life"; as usual Italian classicism keeps them from going off the modernist edge.

27. Virgil, *The Aeneid*, Allen Mandelbaum, trans. (New York: Bantam, 1972), 170.

Umbertina:
The Italian/American Woman's Experience

David Riesman once stated that "the Italian immigrant has to go through a gastronomically bleached and bland period before he can publicly eat garlic and spaghetti."[1] Helen Barolini's first novel, *Umbertina* (1979), deals directly with the Italian immigrant's assimilation process in the United States. She presents the lives of three women of the Longobardi family: Umbertina, the immigrant; Marguerite, Umbertina's granddaughter; and Tina, Marguerite's daughter. Each, in fact, represents a different stage of the Italian and Italian/American assimilation process to American culture. Yet Barolini's novel goes one step further than that experience to which Riesman refers in the above-cited statement; and it is thus more appropriate to change the *he* to a *she*. Indeed, as the theme of ethnic identity develops throughout the novel, there also emerges concurrently the theme of gender identity as each woman must contend with a male-oriented social structure in her struggle for personal fulfillment. In this essay, we shall see how these two apparently parallel themes are instead intertwining factors of each woman's experiences depicted in the novel.

Umbertina is a fictionalized account of the social changes and the conflicts within the Italian/American family as it grew and developed from one generation to the next—those generations Joseph Lopreato describes and analyzes in his study *Italian Americans* (1970): "peasant," "first-," "second-," and "third-generation."[2] His "peasant" family comes to life in the figure of Umbertina, a shepherd-girl from a small mountain village in Calabria, who tended goats in the burned-out hills near her birthplace until she married. After her marriage to Serafino—a marriage of convenience rather than one of love—they acquired a parcel of secularized land and gave it their best at farming. However, their attempts at making a better life for themselves were futile because of the barrenness of the land and the exorbitant taxes. It was, then, soon decided that they would go to the United States, where Serafino had spent a good part of his youth. Their subsequent move to the United States and the hardships of the trip and of their initial years in New York City are representative of those experienced by most southern Italians who made the journey during the great wave of immigration at the turn of the century. Their later years of life also correspond to the general pattern of behavior among their *paesani* in the new country: the father was considered the head of the family; the "boys" enjoyed more freedom than the "girls."

Barolini does not deal directly with the second-generation family. Instead, the members of this type of family are presented intermittently, as part of the life stories of the three women who make up the book. Yet, even here, some classic stereotypes are presented.[3] What stands out most significantly of this generation is the "apathetic individual," who tends to see things from an economic perspective and avoids the conflict of cultural duality by de-emphasizing and "de-emotionalizing" natural origin (Lopreato 1970, 42), if not at times rejecting it and proclaiming him/herself American rather than Italian.

This second-generation characteristic is portrayed in various parts of the novel by the reactions of Marguerite's parents (Carla, Umbertina's daughter, and Sam) to their daughter and granddaughter. At the beginning of Marguerite's story we learn of her parents' (especially her father's) attitude toward Italians:

> Marguerite learned that it was not nice to look too Italian and to speak bad English the way Uncle Nunzio did. Italians were not a serious people, her father would say—look at Jimmy Durante and Al Capone; Sacco and Vanzetti. Italians were buffoons, anarchists and gangsters, womanizers. "What are we, Dad, aren't we Italian?" she would ask. "We're Americans," he'd say firmly, making her wonder about all the people in the shadows who came before him. Grandmother Umbertina was exempt, even though she didn't speak good English, because she had made good. (Barolini 1979, 150; hereafter only page numbers will appear in parentheses after Barolini citations)

What Marguerite's father alludes to is the fact that Umbertina was a successful businesswoman. She had started out making sandwiches for her husband's coworkers, and, with time, opened a neighborhood "groceria [sic]" that continued to thrive. Eventually the business went completely wholesale and the entire family thus achieved social status according to the norms of social mobility in the Old Country: hard work, regular saving, and secure but gradual success (Gambino 1974, 130). But Umbertina, though successful financially, did not actually enjoy a complete sense of personal fulfillment, as we shall see later on. A similiar denial of natural origin is repeated toward the end of the novel, in a conversation between Tina and her grandfather, Sam:

> "Now let me ask you, Tina," her grandfather said, . . . "What are your plans for the future?"
> "Gramp," she said patiently, "I'm getting a Ph.D. in Italian. I want to be a scholar."
> "But why Italian?" he said in real consternation, his face frowning in bewilderment. "What will that fit you for?"
> "I can teach or write. . . ."
> "I don't understand this infatuation with Italy!" her grandfather was saying, rattling his newspaper and looking agitated. "Where will that get you? Italy has no future. What has Italy ever done for the world?"
> "Civilization, Gramp." She thought with sad resignation of this useless old argument, and of how paradoxically, non-Italians like the Jowers family were so Italophile. (397)

The significant aspect of her grandfather's reaction is his objection to his granddaughter's subject matter; he is both bewildered and agitated by her choice. Twice Tina mentions the occupation: "I want to be a scholar. . . . I can teach or write." Twice the grandfather objects to her choice of subject matter: "But why Italian? . . . What has Italy ever done for the world?" His disdain for Italian as a subject matter of study is just another way in which he denies, as in the previous passage, his Italianness.

Sam is not alone in his ethnic denial. Carla, Marguerite's mother, also engaged in the denial of her Italian ethnicity. Only with the marriage of her son to Betty Burke did she include her in-laws, whom she had not, for many years, invited into her home. Furthermore, with the excuse of tradition— since it was the same baker for her wedding—she suggested that the Italian North Side Bakery furnish the cake. But, as the author interjects, "it was not tradition, but firm assurance that the old times could never again touch her" (155). Sam and Carla had moved out of the Italian neighborhood into a much more residential and *American* one. Sam's relatives, instead, remained in the old place.

Marguerite is prototypical of Lopreato's "second-generation" (i.e., third-generation) family, which he considers to be the first "to make the big cultural break between the old society and the new" (Lopreato 1970, 74). He goes on to describe three different types of individuals who make up this group: the "rebel," the "apathetic individual," and the "in-grouper." Of the three, Marguerite best represents the "rebel," whose "impatience [and] intensity of [her] negative attitude toward the ways of the old folks" (Lopreato 1970, 76) were dominant characteristics of hers at an early age. She rebelled against middle-class malaise: the religiosity of the traditional family and her mother's middle-class civility. In fact, we read:

> At school, where all the daughters of the top Irish families went, including the mayor's daughter, she got to be known as Mad Marguerite— because she read books that no one else had heard of (Voltaire, Spengler, T. S. Eliot, Ivy Compton-Burnett) and because she defied convent ways. She wore her uniform too tight, she studied too hard, her answers were delivered in a deprecating way, and for religion class she had written a notorious answer on a test that the Virgin birth could be explained by *coitus ante portam*—"intercourse outside the door," i.e., without penetration. (152)

Indeed, we see that her defiance was not at all limited in scope: she rebelled against everything her parents' generation, as also some people of her own, considered proper and sacred. Her contempt for imposed roles is represented by her mode of dress and behavior at school. More significantly, we find a great deal of contempt for the specific role of the female, as her uniform was too tight—most *unladylike*—and her answers were offered in a deprecating manner. In addition, she studied too hard: this also was unladylike, since education was usually reserved for the male, and once having finished, he believed he would enjoy economic success. Marguerite's contempt for an imposed female role is manifested as well in her attitude toward religion. In reference to the most holy of Catholic beliefs, she describes it with what may be considered by some, a most desecrating and *vulgar* description.

Along with Marguerite's defiant efforts to break away from the Old World ways, we also see in the above-cited passage the second generation's attempt at shedding its Italianness: her parents sent her to a school "where all the daughters of the top Irish families went, including the mayor's daughter." Implied here is the belief that economic success leads to individual amelioration. Indeed, it was at this school, according to her mother, where Marguerite could meet "worthwhile girls" whom she could invite over because her family had "a nice home now" (153).

In her rebellion, Marguerite disagreed with the Old World idea that children *owed* their parents respect. She saw, to her dismay, the parent-child relationship of the Italian family set in economic terms: children *owed, paid back, bore dividends* for having done good deeds. Thus for her, the family motto could have been "Money Talks," as it was also the motto for their concept of social mobility and individual development. But Marguerite believed there was more to life than material well-being; and she turned to literature and other arts as a means of achieving some sort of personal fulfillment. Thus, her rebellion was aimed at the traditional form of education, more specifically, the overall ideological viewpoint of the parochial school, which is "person-oriented [since it] teaches children rules of behavior appropriate to the adult peer group society, and it stresses discipline." The public school, on the other hand, is "object-oriented and teaches [children] aspirations and skill for work, play, family life and community participation" (Gans 1962, 129).

With regard to her Italianness, as both a child and an adult Marguerite found herself in a "confusion of roles." And it was precisely this confusion that seemed to spark her rebellious acts. Her desire to break away from first- and second-generation (i.e., ethnic) bonds and her belief in freedom and spontaneity are evidenced by both her "quickie marriage" to Lennert Norenson "the Nordic" (as her cousin labeled him) and her later trip to England, where she strikes up an affair with a self-exiled literary type. Her subsequent marriage to Alberto, a wise and philosophical older Italian writer, and her later trips to Italy reveal, on the other hand, the extent to which she accepts her ethnicity. Yet her marriage is, at best, an ambivalent one for both personal and cultural reasons; and she is reluctant to stay in Italy for long. Thus she seems to exhibit signs of confusion indicative of the third-generation Italian. Namely, while this individual seems to be more self-confident and secure about his/her life's trajectory, there still remains some cultural residue from the previous generation.

In his study of the Italian/American family in the United States, Campisi found that there was indeed more security fostered in the third-generation individual than in the second-generation. However, he also found what he calls "conflict lags"; and because of these lags, this third-generation family many times reflects a "confused American situation" (Campisi 1948, 446). In Marguerite's case, her initial breaking away demonstrates her desire to live a life different from her parents'. Yet, she also feels a strong tie to Italy; and it is precisely her oscillation between America and Italy, between American culture and Italian culture, that perpetuates her identity confusion.

This antagonism between Americanness and Italianness is a major theme both in Marguerite's story and the novel itself. In the prologue of the novel, in fact, which takes place in her analyst's office, he interprets her dream as an expression of her "feeling of alienation...anxiety as to whether she is American, Italian, or Italo-American" (17). And she, soon after, recalling a picture of her father, describes him in a manner similar to that in which her analyst described her:

> I remember a picture of him in our album, at eighteen on his motorcycle when he had already organized the business but was still just a kid full of God knows what kind of dreams of an exciting future. I thought of him separating himself from the Italians of the North Side to make himself into a real American. He turned reactionary to do it, but he started courageously. He was caught in a terrible trap; he couldn't be either Italian like his father and mother or American like his models without feeling guilty toward one or the other side. And even now he doesn't know how to be American while accepting his Italianness because it's still painful to him. So there's conflict and bitterness. (19)

The conflict and bitterness she sees in her father is equally as strong in her: for she too was *caught in a trap*. Marguerite was an intellectually curious child of a culturally unsophisticated family, who was often chided for having her "nose in a book," something deemed ever "so impractical."[4] Throughout her life, she was constantly trying to live according to "everyone else's idea of what [her] life should be" (19). This included her parents, her husband, Alberto, and even her Italian lover. In the first case, she lay victim to her parents' shame of their Italianness which they tried not to pass on to her. In the second and third cases especially, while her Italianness was partially satisfied, she was nevertheless dependent upon them more specifically because of her gender. Consequently, she felt personally unfulfilled, that she was not her own person but rather a part of everyone else.

Tina's story may seem slightly different from the usual fourth-generation experience because she is the child of an Italian/American mother and Italian father. Yet, her father's situation notwithstanding, she does still reflect those characteristics that, according to Lopreato, the fourth-generation individual may possess.

She is introduced to us as a young American feminist of the 1960s generation, completely unidentifiable as Italian. Yet, she too struggles with the Italian/American dilemma. Like her mother, she experiences a love/hate relationship with Italy and with America. When in Italy, she is enamored of the "natural, human life": but she also realizes that as an individual, or better yet, as a woman, "it won't get [her] anyplace and that [she has] got to go back [to the United States] and plug into the system" (298).[5]

Tina's experience, however, differs greatly from that of her mother and from her great-grandmother's as well. Indeed, two major reasons come to the fore with regard to this distinction. Tina is, first of all, a member of a generation that initiated a cultural and sexual revolution, and thereby challenged an entire set of norms that trapped women, especially, of previous generations. Secondly, she is a fourth-generation Italian who was, like most members of this group, according to Lopreato, "deliberately educated in the ways of the middle-class, [according to which] education is highly valued" (86). Education is highly valued precisely because it becomes an end in itself, "used to maximize individual development of the person" (Gans 1962, 247).[6]

Tina, in fact, wants to be a "scholar who teaches for a living"; she does not want to end up both emotionally and financially dependent on marriage. Indeed, she adamantly refuses to repeat the experiences of both her mother and great-grandmother;[7] and she decides to define herself as an autonomous individual before becoming permanently involved with a man. Thus, she places her degree over her love for Jason, even at the risk of losing him, because she firmly believes that there would not exist between them a relationship "in which individuals seeking to maximize their own development as persons come together on the basis of common interests" (Gans 1962, 247). It is therefore through education that she achieves not only material well-being but also self-expression, self-fulfillment, and empathy for the behavior of others. It is precisely this last characteristic that eventually helps her understand and ultimately resolve her ethnic (if not also gender) dilemma.[8]

At the beginning of this essay, I stated that *Umbertina* can be considered a fictionalized account of the social changes and the ethnic conflicts the Italian experiences in America. Undoubtedly, this is a major theme in the novel, though not necessarily the *major* one we encounter. Early on in the novel, Barolini introduces ethnic identity as a dilemma; even earlier, however, she introduces the theme of gender identity as a dilemma. In the prologue, during Marguerite's session with her analyst, the problem of stereotyping women arises. When Marguerite tells her doctor of her occasional desire to sleep with her husband despite her wish to divorce him, he responds in the following manner:

> "Then do it, do what you feel," he said energetically.
> "But I can't! Don't you understand that if I do he'll never agree to the divorce and I haven't even gotten him to sign the separation agreement...."
> "There's a typical female wile for that. You get him to sign first and then go to bed. This is something all women understand."
> "I ... I never thought of that," she stammered, confused.
> "It's something women have always been able to do. It's a classic strategem, no?" (5)

She was, in fact, offended by his masculine arrogance, by his presumption that the female role was not only different from the male role but inferior as well. The last thing Marguerite wanted was to live on the margin of a man's existence: she wanted to be her own person, autonomous to the extent of being able to make her own decisions. But her struggle for a sense of fulfillment was impeded not only by her own lack of vision but also by the male-oriented society in which she lived.[9] It was in fact her awareness of a new feminism which induced her to seek analysis, yet her analyst proved himself to be a perpetuator of female stereotypes.

It is significant, then, that at this point in the novel Barolini deals with male chauvinism in a general context. Not just Marguerite, but all the women in the novel encounter and must confront the problem of living within a patriarchal culture. Their struggle is thus twofold: not only are they fighting against the ethnic barriers set up by the predominant culture in America—here specifically the United States—but they must also contend with gender oppression. With regard to their gender dilemma, the Italian and Italian/American women we encounter in the novel have a double-layered struggle to fight. They must, first of all, contend with the prejudices within their own ethnic group, only to deal, a second time, with similar sexist attitudes once they break the bonds of ethnicity and gain some semblance of autonomy as an individual. Thus, these women are denied a sense of personal achievement and they are relegated to a "second-class citizen" status as well.

Turning our attention back to Umbertina, we see that hers was a financial Cinderella story; not only does her immediate family but also the generations to follow benefit from her hard work and astute business sense. Nevertheless, in spite of her many victories over various economic hardships, she seemed destined to lie victim to social norms concerning the male-female relationship. In Italy, when she once interfered in the bargaining process at the market, her brother scolded her harshly even though she saved the family money and him a tongue-lashing from their father: "I'm the man, [her brother told her].... Men have to deal with these things, not women" (30–31). Indeed, however independent she may seem at times throughout her story, she most always defers to what is "customary." In fact, Barolini presents Umbertina—as was the case with many Italian women of her generation both in Italy and in the United States—as a woman conscious of her place in society, that "she was bound by men's notions of what women must be" (34).[10] When, as a young woman in Italy, it seemed she was secretly meeting Giosue (the young charcoal maker) in the hills outside her village, her father decided it was time for him to find her a husband. Once he announced Serafino's offer of marriage, she readily accepted: first, because Serafino represented something new in her life; second, because it was her father's wish that she do so.

It was Umbertina's decision that they emigrate to America, as it was also she who started the sandwich business that eventually turned into a major wholesale company. Yet, in spite of all her time and energy devoted to the family business, the future of it was in her sons' names, not in her daughters'; and the sign out front read "S. Longobardi and Sons." Thus, she adhered to family conventionality; when Serafino died, the wholesale company was at its zenith, and *he* was credited, "as was customary," with having left his family "secure, its fortune started." His obituary read: "Serafino Longobardi knew how, with his honest and untiring work, to launch his sons into business and open for them that excellent place in everyone's esteem that the Longobardi family enjoys today" (128). The irony, if not injustice to be more precise, lies in the fact that Serafino did not work in the store for most of his life; he was instead a railroad worker. When the time came for him to retire, it was Umbertina who told him he should do so. Thus, when he finally did join the family in the store, he would do "odd jobs" or roast chestnuts on the potbellied stove in bad weather.

Umbertina's incomplete sense of fulfillment—as that of any woman who compromises her position as an individual because of family conventionality or other social norms—poignantly manifests itself toward the end of her story. She realized how, as a businesswoman, she received very little, if any credit at all. She thought it indeed strange that it was Serafino's "name which triumphed and...his presence, *as a man*, which has been necessary to give her the standing from which to command" (134; emphasis added). She now realized that a woman could not be a whole person in a male-dominated society. In one way or another, in fact, the female of her generation was most always subservient to the male, whereas "increase in the freedom and family influence of the woman" began to manifest itself in the following generations (Gans 1962, 207).

That Marguerite may have lacked her own sense of direction by no means discounts the fact that she too was a victim of a male-oriented social structure. Her marriage to Lennert was a rebellious reaction to her family's insistence that "girls" should be married. That it was a "quickie marriage" to a non-Italian is also significant because it figured also as a means of an escape from her family's dominance over her life. She hoped it would bring greater possibilities in her life for self-fulfillment. Soon to be disappointed, she opted for other means. Her marriage to Alberto and the family they started left her, however, with a sense of unfulfillment, as she still yearned for professional completeness. After many attempts at various pursuits, only one seemed to have any success: *she* translating *his* poetry. Thus, life centered around him: he prospered professionally and personally, and she took care of the family.

Notwithstanding Marguerite's vague and undefined goals, Barolini poignantly demonstrates how even Alberto, consciously or not, contributed to her gender dilemma. His initial promise, "I'll make a real human being out of you," is indicative of the masculine presumption that a woman needs a man for her personal development. When she was truly depressed, he would address her as his *"bambina mia,"* telling her that she did love him and was happy but only resisted seeing it. Finally, when she insisted on divorce, his response was that she was tired of too much sun, that she should see a psychiatrist once they returned to Rome since she was still upset over the death of their son. We see, then, that Marguerite was relegated to the "homemaker role," and unhappily so.[11]

Apologetic about her work—i.e., translating Alberto's poetry—she once stated to her secret lover, Massimo, that she really wanted to be a photographer:

> "Why don't you? That's a beautiful thing to do, you know."
> "I have a family," she said. They fell silent. She tried to retrieve things. (229)

Not possessing any autonomy as an individual, Marguerite remains trapped in the traditional female role and is thus subordinate to her husband (and lover), and she is thereby unable to realize any of her desired goals. Indeed, the traditional role sometimes acts as a "brake on [the female's] aspirations and [more specifically in Marguerite's case] as an accelerator on her frustrations" (Gans 1962, 216). This is the case with Marguerite, as also with Carla and Umbertina.

These antithetical feelings Marguerite experiences with regard to her femaleness are, in a certain sense, analogous to those we have already seen concerning her Italianness. She finds herself in a confused situation, at times opting for the more traditional role while at other times wanting to break free and be her own person/woman. It is important to keep in mind that traditional roles, especially female, were passed on from one generation to the next, and among Italian immigrants it was considered "'normal' [for adolescent females] to expect and to want children when they married" (Perry 1978, 223): namely, they were expected to live our their lives as mothers and housewives, and consequently they were relegated to limited personal development as integral individuals. It is also important to remember that Marguerite's gender dilemma was complicated by the fact that she married an older, conservative Italian who was a defender of the traditional female-role, and, consequently, of a male-oriented social structure.[12] Thus, these two seemingly distinct problems of ethnicity and gender actually prove to be separate parts of a whole: the Italian/American female dilemma.

Marguerite never resolves her gender conflict. Though she remained with Alberto, she struck up an affair with a writer younger than her husband. He was to be her "bridge to a new reality." Instead, however, it was she who became his bridge to a possible literary award: she was his contact to Alberto, then editor of a literary review. She could also spread his fame by translating his prose; and she filled the sexual and emotional void between Massimo and his wife, who had, with the years, become his "domestic," serving and seconding him in everything. Thus, once again, Marguerite had become another man's woman: and when Massimo lost the award, Marguerite lost Massimo.

After the fatal car crash as she returned from their summer home during a rain storm, Marguerite's life is summed up by the last two entries in her diary. The first reinforces her ethnic dilemma:

> All those snooty, shining girls. They know who they are and where they're going. . . . I'm the only Italian name here. They're all saying they're going to be writers or doctors. . . Whoever told me I could do any of that? (310)

The second entry heightens her gender identity dilemma:

> Is this the bill for happiness? Is this paying the goddam fiddler? Now I'm pregnant and it's Massimo's child and who else but me is going to pay? Now what? Ask him to leave his wife? . . . A backroom abortion? A quick trip to Italy or Switzerland? and where would the money come from? What could I tell A.? What do women do in Italy. . . or anyplace? (312; elisions textual)

One of the implications in the first passage is that the stifling of aspirations is not necessarily unidirectional. While it is true that Marguerite is the only Italian, this impediment does not originate solely from the dominant, non-Italian culture. Someone (i.e., their parents) has told these "snooty, shining girls" that they can be doctors, lawyers, or whatever else they might aspire to be. Education for the dominant culture figures is a primary tool, if not an end in itself for individual development. The Italian American, on the other hand, did not consider education a primary source for personal well-being. This was especially true with regard to the female; an obvious inheritance from the first generation, according to whom "girls should get married" and raise a family. It is only with the third and fourth generations that education becomes a highly valued asset. Marguerite's second entry underscores the female's dilemma, which, significantly, is no longer restricted to the Italian or Italian American; here, it now concerns women in general: "What do women do in Italy...*or anyplace*? (emphasis added)" Briefly, Marguerite alone would have had to bear the burden and responsibility of her unplanned pregnancy. The illegality of abortion limits its availability and contributes to exorbitant fees, which, for her, having been primarily a homemaker and thus financially dependent on her husband, seemed virtually impossible.

Barolini's implications of female victimization become more complex at this point in the novel. Taken together, both entries sum up the problems for the Italian/American female of Marguerite's generation. Indeed, the gender dilemma is no longer limited just to the woman's right to study, opt for a professional career, and therefore decide her own destiny. Up to this point in the novel, in fact, the woman's struggle was primarily ethno-cultural and psychological: she had to fight the barriers imposed by her parents in order to escape the prison-house of ethnicity and eventually reconcile any cultural residue in her attempt at greater assimilation into the dominant culture. Now, however, an unwanted pregnancy brings to the fore the problem of physiological victimization.[13] In a male-dominated society, in which the female, as in Marguerite's case, is financially dependent upon the male, abortion—an operation that undoubtedly affects the female's life more directly than the male's—is considered illegal. Someone in Marguerite's predicament must therefore resort to an illegal, back-room abortion, which, besides being beyond her financial means, may also prove to be dangerous to her physical well-being.

Notwithstanding her lack of success in achieving some semblance of personal fulfillment, Marguerite, as victim of a patriarchal system, remained throughout intellectually curious and unwilling to bend completely to tradition. In so doing, she helped pave the way for the following generation of females, here represented by Tina.

Although Tina's situation is relatively different from her mother's and great-grandmother's, she too must confront the question of gender identity. Here, also, Barolini skillfully presents the difficulties Tina, as a woman, faces in her search for independence and personal fulfillment. Because of the emerging new feminism of the 1960s, Tina is much more aware of the inequities in all realms of the professional world. In fact, we have already seen in Marguerite's story how Tina grew increasingly more aware of her mother's plight. Specifically, Tina realizes that a woman is not a good investment, according to the professional world, because she will "quit and get married." She also understands how her father's suggestion that she could credit her career by translating his new novel would, as in Marguerite's case, make her "part of his success" and thereby deny her the opportunity of her own self-realization.

Jason, her sensitive and understanding future husband, also exhibits signs of (unconscious) male pride when he tells her she does "all the essentials so well— ... cook, make love, go with guys on trips, swim—and yet, [has a] hang-up about getting married" (360). The essentials she does so well, according to him, are in fact male-directed, especially "cook, make love, go with guys on trips," and characteristic of the traditional female role; this is precisely what Tina rejects. What is a hang-up according to Jason is, instead, for Tina, at this point in her life, freedom from the "dependency on any man who would keep her from the fullness of her own life and expectations" (337).

Barolini offers other examples in Tina's story of indoctrination into the traditional female role and of gender oppression. In a brief exchange between Tina and her grandmother, Carla, we see how the latter figures as a staunch defender of the Old World concepts of marriage as the major priority for women, and professional success, conversely, as the major priority for men:

> "Do you have any boyfriends?" her grandmother asked, standing back to appraise Tina. . . .
> "I can't bear it!" she retorted. "Is that all you want to hear about me, *nonna*?"
> "I wish you would find someone ... a beautiful girl like you. You should be able to do very well."
> "*Nonna*! Such ideas—how can you do well by marrying if you haven't got your own personal life together first? No one's rushing into marriage these days. It's much better to concentrate on one's work and have other interests."
> "That's not natural," Carla went on shaking her head. "I saw Ron Peters, who used to like your mother—he's doing so well. But she pretended she was never interested either. Now he drives a Rolls Royce, has a yacht, one son in Harvard, and a daughter in Paris." (396-97)

Significant at this point is that Carla, here a seemingly staunch defender of Old World concepts, was herself a victim of those very same prejudices. For Carla, as a young woman, once entertained ideas of finishing high school and going on to college. But because of the family business, she was pulled out of high school before she could graduate and put to work in the store. Her rewards were "charge accounts to all the stores downtown. . . , two fur coats and several Paris gowns before she was married" (135). In reality, it was not just the family business that impeded Carla's education; it was indeed also the family's strong conviction that "girls" should not go "off to sleep out of town under strange roofs. Girls should be married" (135). The notion that a woman is happy with shopping, fur coats, Paris gowns, and other material goods is indeed a masculine stereotype of the female. In the novel, the male presumption of such a notion is heightened by the fact that the offer was made to Carla by her brothers.

Barolini presents Tina's abortion not at all as a moral issue, but rather as a political statement concerning the social structure of male vis-à-vis female—namely, the power and control the former may exert over the latter. Briefly, it is an illegal, expensive, back-room operation performed by a male doctor. Once it is done, Tina thinks back to her former lover:

...that poor, sweet, easygoing Duke who would have been the last guy
in the world to bring her pain. And yet he had because he was a man,
and she, no matter what she did to her brain and willpower, was still
inhabiting a female body. Just one night that she forgot a pill, and this
was what happened. She thought about her mother's jokes about "Who
pays the fiddler? The girl pays the fiddler." (345)

In her review essay on literature dedicated to abortion over a ten-year
span, Barbara Hayler has demonstrated how many feminists argue that
opposition to abortion is only one aspect of a greater opposition to female
autonomy within a patriarchal society (Hayler 1979, 332). According to Mary
Daly, who considers such opposition as part of a larger system she calls
"gynocide," this contributes to the "domestication and deprivation of female
vitality, both physical and spiritual, [and] the 'cutting to pieces' of women's
autonomous wills" (Daly 1978, 245). More directly, she also states that the
male-oriented social structure functions "to keep women supine, objectified
and degraded—a condition ritually symbolized by the gynecologist's stirrups
and the psychiatrist's couch" (229–30). For Daly, gynecology includes the
practice of both medicine and psychiatry; accordingly, she distinguishes
between "mind-gynecologists" [psychiatrists] and "body-gynecologists" [gy-
necologists] (228). In *Umbertina*, "symbols" similar to Mary Daly's are
indeed present. One need only to think back to Marguerite's analyst for an
example of the "mind-gynecologist." However, the more forcefully described,
sociopolitical issue of the two is abortion. Barolini presents this issue to her
reader in three different doses, culminating in Tina's experience. In the last
entry of Marguerite's diary, we saw that it was the woman who was
responsible for the unwanted pregnancy; in fact, Marguerite was to pay the
consequences. The second case involves a four-month-pregnant woman who
was beaten to death by her husband because she wanted an abortion. It is
with this case that the stereotypes and injustices of a patriarchal system rise
to the surface. Angela, the woman from whom Tina asked help in procuring
an abortion, recounts:

> "She was twenty years old and already had two small children. *Naturally*
> she was viewed as the monster, while the husband, who beat her to death,
> was looked upon as acting within *his rights*. At her funeral service the
> priest said, 'She was a mother who gave two lives into the world. She
> was also a wife. In the next life she will still be a wife and mother.' "
> (340; emphasis added)

The relegation of the female exclusively to the role of wife and mother
indeed describes this twenty-year-old woman's life. A similar role had also
been imposed on Marguerite, as was apparent in her story. Also imposed
here, however, is the gender dilemma of a woman's right to self-determination. In the above-cited passage, we find that the husband was considered to
have been within his rights to kill his wife because she had decided to abort.
With this scene, Barolini also makes it clear that woman's lack of self-
determination is felt in all facets of society, even in the Church. In fact, the
priest's eulogy implies that this young woman's lack of self-determination
even extends beyond her natural life to her afterlife: "She was a mother...

[and] wife. In the next life she will still be a wife and mother." In its own way, then, the Church appears to be both highly complicit in the oppression of women and arrogant to the point of attributing its own judgment on women to God, the *father.*

Barolini reiterates this notion in Tina's visit to the male doctor who will perform her abortion. It is, in fact, with Tina's abortion that Barolini movingly describes the oppression and powerlessness the female experiences in a patriarchal society:

> She slipped off her sandals, got onto the table, and following his directions, put her feet into the steel stirrups, uselessly trying to keep her knees together.
>
> "Relax," he said, quickly forcing her knees apart and lifting her skirt up around her waist. She felt like one of the half-clothed dummies she used to see in storefronts...and she tried...to keep her feelings at dummy level.
>
> He was not a bad person; and he was quite unaware of the revulsion and anger he stirred in her as he patted and looked. By telling her to have courage he was, in his way, trying to keep her spirits up. Still, she hated him—as much as she hated the pope in his long unsullied skirts, or the fat-bellied old priests who told women they sinned, or the pigs in Parliament who daydreamed about women to fuck as they deliberated on laws that violated their bodies.
>
> No matter how cordial, the doctor was a profiteer and a butcher, and she thought of herself, legs apart, as one of those carcasses hanging in all the meat markets of Rome—revoltingly explicit with their hairy bodies intact but split up the middle....
>
> Tina thought of Mussolini hanging like a pig by his feet and his mistress hanging alongside him, her crime having been that of loving him. But even in that bad time, someone had had pity enough to pin Clara's skirt together as she hung upside-down at the gas station in Milan....
>
> Now as she lay, stiff with fear, she thought again of her mother who had willed her to life and whose death might have come because she was pregnant, just as Tina was. She was sharing with her mother for the first time the communion of motherhood. (343–44)

We see, first of all the male doctor who is seemingly cordial yet basically unsympathetic to his patient's needs during the operation; he is, according to Tina, a "profiteer and butcher" whose sole concern is not to get caught by the authorities. His exorbitant fee is largely due to the attitude of two other patriarchal groups: the "fat-bellied priests" and the "pigs in Parliament [who decided on] laws that violated [woman's bodies]." Yet, more than a violation of bodies, such an experience proves to be a violation of the entire person, i.e., body and spirit. The psychological degradation, here, is evidenced by Tina's initial feeling of intrusion as the doctor lifted her skirt, by the comparison of herself to one of the carcasses hanging in the meat markets, and by her recollection that even for Mussolini's mistress someone had had enough pity to pin her skirt together as she hung upside-down. Finally, the denial of control to women, in this specific instance, of their reproductive capabilities, and, in more general terms, of their destiny is summed up in the final sentence of the above-cited passage; for the first time, Tina "was sharing with her mother...the *communion of motherhood* (emphasis added)."

There are other examples of gender oppression that Tina confronts. Yet, in spite of these and other obstacles, she does succeed, as we have already seen in the first part of this essay, in gaining the "license to be a woman professional in a man's world" (389). At the same time, she reconciles with Jason, thereby prospering personally also.

As witness to the Italian ethnic dilemma, Barolini indeed succeeds in creating experiences similar to those reported by sociologists such as Gambino, Gans, and Lopreato. Likewise, she succeeds in portraying those experiences and difficulties of the Italian/American female, which have been recorded by Winsey, Yans-McLaughlin, and those who have contributed to the volume *The Italian Immigrant Woman in North America.* Yet, *Umbertina* is more than just a fictionalized account of those experiences. For while it is enhanced by this documentary quality, it also enjoys an unsparing true-to-life characterization of the protagonists and, thus, proves to be extremely interesting and, at times, provocative.

Finally, it is important to remember that the figure of the woman in Italian/American literature has been portrayed, for the most part, in a traditional female role by a male author. And even in those few exceptions written by women, the female has still occupied a fixed role—that of the central position in the family (Green 1978, 342). The novelty of *Umbertina* lies precisely in Barolini's treatment of women as individuals, who, at one point or another in their lives, become aware of their true plight—the duality of gender and ethnic oppression—and, especially with regard to Marguerite and Tina, attempt to free themselves from the prison-house of patriarchy.

Notes

This is a revised version of a paper presented at the Italian American Seminar of the MLA National Convention in Los Angeles (December 1982). I am grateful to Mary G. Dietz (University of Minnesota) and Peter I. Rose (Smith College) for having taken the time to read and comment upon an earlier draft. For more on the use of the slash (/) in place of the hyphen in the adjectival phrase "Italian American," see Tamburri (1989).

1. Riesman made this statement when comparing the Jewish immigrant's assimilation process to that of the Italian: "As the Italian immigrant has to go through a gastronomically bleached and bland period before he can publicly eat garlic and spaghetti, so the Jewish immigrant must also become Americanized before he can comfortably take pride in his ethnic cuisine, idiom, and gesture" (xv).

2. Both Joseph Lopreato (1970) and Paul Campisi (1948) use similar tags in distinguishing the various Italian/American generations: "peasant," "first-," and so on. The common practice among sociologists, however, is to use a slightly different set of tags. Thus, Lopreato's and Campisi's "peasant" family corresponds to the more widely used "first-generation" family; and their "first-," "second-," and "third-generation" families correspond to the more popular "second-," "third-," and "fourth-generation" families. In this essay I have opted for the more commonly used set of tags, which are also those Barolini occasionally adopts throughout her novel.

3. We can find those Italian Americans with the seemingly insignificant desire to Americanize their names—Giacomo and Benedetto soon want to be called Jake and Ben. We also encounter the more enterprising "status climber" who makes attempts at all sorts of endeavors that the previous generation cannot understand: such is the case with Paolo—soon to become Paul—who, "filled with ambitions for himself that had nothing to do with the kind of hard work and drudgery the rest of the family engaged in" and believing himself "too smart to waste his time around two-bit family stores (123–24)," suddenly finds himself without a home since he refuses to do his part in the family business.

4. We have already seen this notion expressed by her father in his conversation with Tina.

5. At other points during her story, we can find Tina comparing the two different countries, and herself as well in each place. For example: "Her sense of illimitable possibilities awaiting her could not stop at the softness and languor of Rome, beneath which, she knew, there were deadly poisons of unrest and discontent. Rome is too old, she thought; nothing matters anymore. In New York everything does. In New York she felt competitiveness throbbing in the air and became frenetic because of so much going on, because of the sense of space to fill. In Rome she was squelched by the sense of time: Everything had already been thought of and done— it was time to rest and savor" (300). To her future husband, Jason, she later described herself in the following manner: "I'm two different people, Jason. The Italian part, when I get back to Rome, likes civilized comforts: eating well, having Giovanna go out and do the shopping and prepare the *caffè-latte* for me each morning while I sleep. Here I like to get all dressed up and go shopping and have Mauro cut my hair. I dress in blankets and clogs when I'm in the States and sometimes don't comb my hair for days. I drive my grandmother in Gloversville crazy when I go see her because she says I'm a hippy. But in Rome I'm purely a sybarite" (323).

6. Also significant here is her father's educational background. While it is true that he too was very much part of the Old World, he held a university degree, and Tina initially identified intellectually with his side of her heritage.

7. Umbertina became a sort of past idol for Tina; and only after she makes a trip back to Umbertina's native village in Italy does she begin to understand truly the hardships that all her relatives who came before her, the women especially, had encountered.

8. After Tina's conversation with her grandfather, when he objected to her choice of Italian as a field of study, she demonstrates a good deal of understanding with regard to his ethnic dilemma. She thought: "What was wrong with the immigrant's children that left them so distrustful of their *italianità*? It was, she knew, the burden of the second generation, who had been forced too swiftly to tear the Old World from themselves and put on the new. They were the sons and

daughters ashamed of their illiterate, dialect-speaking forebears—the goatherds and peasants and fishermen who came over to work and survive and give these very children, the estranged ones, America. Tina was torn between compassion and indignation: She understood him, why couldn't he understand her?" (398)

9. Marguerite is a complex character in the novel; surely the most complex of all. Indeed, an analysis of her character vis-à-vis the patriarchal society in which she was raised would make for an interesting study in itself; a study that warrants more time and space than can be afforded in this essay. This notwithstanding, it should not be ignored that her lack of vision most surely stems, at least in part, from her ethnic and gender dilemma.

10. For more on the Italian peasant woman in Italy, see Chapman and Cornelison. For more on the Italian immigrant woman in America, see Winsey, Yans-McLaughlin, and Caroli.

11. Tina herself soon begins to understand how her father had led Marguerite from her own aspirations, and that he had never seen his wife as a woman: "There was never time, Tina remembered her mother saying, to live as artists, the two of them. The babies and moving absorbed Marguerite and soon her vision of herself swerved. Alberto relied on words as Marguerite did on her feelings for truth. When he told her that she should be happy with things as they were—with her successful husband, her beautiful home, her fine daughters—and not pine after what was lost or the illusion of her fulfillment, she tried to examine why her feelings mistrusted him. It was not what he had said before!" (333); and: "Tina knew her father's disappointments; she knew he had suffered from her mother's unhappiness and restlessness; *'la mamma è bambina,' 'la mamma è difficile,'* he used to write to her in college, showing how protective he had to be, and all the time he was dead wrong—her mother wasn't a child, her mother was a woman" (405). Sensitive and gentle as he may have been believed to have been, Alberto was always trying to relegate his wife to the homemaker-role.

12. Again we see that Alberto has reneged on his initial promise that they would live together as artists: "Proposing, Alberto had said that they would learn each other's language and be artists together, although it would be wise if they started a family soon." (333)

13. As we shall see in Tina's story, abortion figures as a violation of the female's body and psyche.

Works Cited

Barolini, Helen. 1979. *Umbertina*. New York: Seaview Books.

Campisi, Paul. 1948. "Ethnic Family Patterns: The Italian Family in the United States." *American Journal of Sociology* 53, no. 6 (May): 443–49.

Caroli, Betty Boyd, Robert F. Harney, and Lydio F. Tomasi, eds. 1978. *The Italian Immigrant Woman in North America*. Toronto: Multicultural History Society of Ontario.

Chapman, Charlotte Gowers. 1971. *Milocca, A Sicilian Village*. Cambridge, Mass.: Schenkan.

Cornelison, Ann. 1977. *Women of the Shadows*. New York: Vantage Books.

Daly, Mary. 1978. *Gyn/ecology: The Metaethics of Radical Feminism.* Boston: Beacon Press.

Gambino, Richard. 1974. *Blood of My Blood.* New York: Doubleday and Co.

Gans, Herbert J. 1962. *The Urban Villagers.* New York: Free Press.

Green, Rose Basile. 1978. "The Italian Immigrant Woman in American Literature." In *The Italian Immigrant Woman in North America*, edited by Betty Boyd Caroli, Robert F. Harney, and Lydio F. Tomasi. Toronto: Multicultural History Society of Ontario.

Hayler, Barbara. 1979. "Abortion." *Signs: Journal of Women in Cultural and Society* 5, no. 2: 307–23.

Lopreato, Joseph. 1970. *Italian Americans.* New York: Random House.

Perry, Harriet. 1978. "The Metonymic Definition of Female and the Concept of Honor among Italian Immigrant Families in Toronto," In *The Italian Immigrant Woman in North America*, edited by Betty Boyd Caroli, Robert F. Harney, Lydio F. Tomasi. Toronto: Multicultural History Society of Ontario.

Riesman, David. 1953. "Introduction." In *Commentary on the American Scene: Portraits of Jewish Life in America*, edited by Elliot E. Cohen. New York: Alfred A. Knopf.

Tamburri, Anthony Julian. 1989. "To Hyphenate or Not to Hyphenate: The Italian/American Writer and *Italianità.*" *Italian Journal* 3, no. 5: 37–42.

Winsey, Valentine Rossilli. 1975. "The Italian American Woman Who Arrived in the United States before World War I." In *Studies in Italian American Social History*, edited by Francesco Cordasco. New Jersey: Rowman and Littlefield.

Yans-McLaughlin, Virginia. 1977. *Family and Community: Italian Immigrants in Buffalo, 1880–1930.* Ithaca: Cornell University Press.

Robert Casillo

Moments in Italian-American Cinema:
From *Little Caesar* to Coppola and Scorsese

Return, Sicilian Muse...
> —Milton, *Lycidas*

1

What is Italian-American cinema? Strictly speaking, this definition applies to works by Italian-American directors who treat Italian-American subjects. It would thus exclude the works of Frank Capra, Vincente Minnelli, and Gregory LaCava, three Italian-Americans who enjoyed distinguished careers in Hollywood. These directors do not treat specifically ethnic subject matter nor is their ethnicity much evident in their works.

Frank Capra typifies the attitude of the first-generation ethnic artist toward his origins. In his autobiography, Capra claims that when he left Italy (Sicily) at the age of seven it disappeared from his memory.[1] Actually, instead of forgetting his past, Capra found his ethnicity troublesome through-out his long career: he feared not fitting into Hollywood society and desperately sought popular approval. Raymond Carney accounts in-sufficiently for what disturbs Vittorio Zagarrio, namely Capra's willful suppression of Italian subjects in his films. Like Gilbert Sorrentino, an Italian-American artist of a later generation, Capra refused to confront his ethnicity in his art. As Carney himself demonstrates, Capra repeatedly transfers to "American" characters and settings the unhappy circumstances of his youth: its poverty, emargination, and family catastrophe (chiefly the unexpected death of his father and the sale of the family farm, an incident reflected in many Capra films, for instance *It's A Wonderful Life* of 1946). He might have added that Capra's penchant for anachronistically populist fantasies suggests a hunger to belong to the American "mainstream." Still, Zagarrio rightly sees Capra's self-censorship as a typical response of the first-generation immigrant. Capra's films thus would stand not in an anti-thetical but complementary relation to those of Francis Ford Coppola and Martin Scorsese, whose confrontation with their ethnic origins supposedly reflects their more secure position as third- or fourth-generation Italian-Americans.[2]

Italian-American cinema in its highest form is represented by only two artists, Francis Ford Coppola and Martin Scorsese, and only a handful of brilliant films—above all *The Godfather I* and *II*, *Mean Streets*, and *Raging Bull*. Sylvester Stallone's films are exploitatively ethnic but cannot be taken seriously as art. Michael Cimino touches only obliquely on Italian-American themes in *The Year of the Dragon* (1985), while his recent aesthetic and commercial failure *The Sicilian* (1987), based on Mario Puzo's bestselling novel, treats a Sicilian subject. Although Brian De Palma's *Scarface* (1983) is based on the Howard Hawks classic of 1932, which was inspired by the life of Al Capone, its subject is the Latin-American drug traffic. More recently, De Palma directed *The Untouchables* (1987), yet another version of the agon between Al Capone and Eliot Ness. For all its hype, this work merely combines generic clichés with generic deformations, for instance Ness's implausible mounted attack on a bootlegger's convoy and the concluding slow-motion shoot-out parodying the baby carriage episode in Eisenstein's *Potemkin*. Enervated by David Mamet's tin-eared and highly literary script along with Kevin Costner's stupefying portrayal of Ness as a moralistic family man, *The Untouchables* unaccountably squanders its sole claim on our attention: Robert De Niro as Capone appears on screen for less than five minutes.

Italian-American cinema is thus a narrow though deep and important subject. Yet in order to understand the accomplishment of its major directors, one must first examine the conventional image of Italy and Italian-Americans in Hollywood films from the 1930s into the 1960s, films whose subjects are Italian-American but whose directors and leading actors are mainly of different social origin. Not only are Coppola and Scorsese aware of these earlier interpretations, they extend, develop, and criticize them in their own works.

Hollywood's earlier representation of Italians reflects the values of the predominantly Anglo-Saxon, Protestant, and middle-class core culture: hard work, discipline, punctuality, utility, economy, business probity, emotional neutrality in social contacts, and freedom from excess, for instance loud noises, gesticulation, violence, and other unseemly forms of demonstrativeness. Judged by this standard, the lower-class Italian immigrant was marked as a social outsider. On the benign side, the Italian-American was presumed to be impulsive, disorderly, undisciplined, lazy, and disturbingly addicted to sex and music (opera).[3] Much more malignantly, there emerged quite early the floridly sinister figure of the criminal or gangster. This stereotype of the Italian-American as socially dangerous probably played a role in the execution of Sacco and Vanzetti in 1927.

From the late 1920s onward, the Sons of Italy and other groups exerted pressure on Hollywood to eliminate unflattering images of Italian-Americans. In Fascist Italy, *Scarface* and *Little Caesar* were never allowed to be shown (even Fred Astaire's *Top Hat* was banned for a time for a relatively innocuous satire on an Italian), while such works as *Cry of the City*, which depicts Italian-American criminals, were dubbed so as to change these characters' ethnic identity. Martin Rome quite implausibly becomes Martin Rosky.[4] More recently, in his well-known study *Blood of My Blood*, Richard Gambino denounces the myth of "innate" Italian criminality spawned by the television series *The Untouchables* and the publicity accorded the Mafia. He complains that, "even when wholly fictional mobsters are portrayed on the screen, they must be made to be Italian-Americans," so conforming to the "long history of...Hollywood slanders."[5] Joseph Papaleo finds that in the American consciousness Italian-Americans are still associated with excess, whether of obsequiousness (the Italian waiter) or violence.[6] And yet it will be seen that Italian-Americans have been less frequently represented as gangsters than Gambino and Papaleo believe.

These protests are one-sided in another sense, for while Italian-Americans have often suffered cultural and social degradation into the 1980s, this is not the whole story. In *Orientalism*, Edward Said suggests that the foreigner absorbs not only the negative or hostile projections of the native observer but his ambivalence: the Arab's presumed sensuousness and savagery is at once condemned and secretly admired.[7] This phenomenon appears in the character of the Arab sheik as portrayed by Rudolph Valentino, a conjunction of the Arabian and Italian mystique of demonic sexuality. In at least some Hollywood films, the Italian-American gangster awakens fascination and admiration, however much his qualities are ostensibly "punished" within the films themselves. This longstanding undercurrent of admiration for the mafioso culminates in *The Godfather* films, which despite Coppola's final refusal to condone, glorify, or exonerate the Mafia, at least acknowledge that it may once have embodied admirable qualities far removed from contemporary life. Papaleo claims that *The Godfather* films "finished off" Italian-Americans in the eyes of the American public, but they are less touchy about the Mafia then formerly, just as television has recently painted a flattering image of Italian-Americans as detectives, policemen, lawyers, etc.—what Andrew Greeley protests as "positive sterotyping," hardly more truthful than the negative form. By contrast, few films criticize Italian-American life more harshly than Martin Scorsese's *Mean Streets* and *Raging Bull*.[8]

2

Up to the late 1920s, cinema gangsters were nondescript.[9] But then, one met Bennie Horovitz, Nick Scarsi, Nick Verdis, Tony Garotta, Louis Beretti, Nicky Solomon, Finger O'Dell, Louis Ricarno, Sam Vettori, Tony Camonte, Nails Nathan, Tommy Doyle, Matt Doyle, Don Quigley, Ricca Palmiera, Greener Kaufman, Maxey Campo, Joe Forgiati, and Dominic Valletti.[10] Eugene Rosow is right that these criminals are primarily Italian, usually short and dark complected and speaking in European accents and occasionally in the mother tongue. The Italian emphasis in these films was partly justified by gangland history, as in Chicago, where the Capone mob drove out the Irish under Bugs Moran. A key event in this takeover was the Saint Valentine's Day Massacre, commemorated in many films including Billy Wilder's *Some Like it Hot* (1959) and Roger Corman's *The St. Valentine's Day Massacre* (1967).

Although it refers to "wop gangs," Italian-American gangsters do not figure prominently in Josef von Sternberg's *Underworld* (1927), the first modern gangster film. Nor is it true that the first sound film to identify the gangster with the Italian-American was Mervyn Le Roy's *Little Caesar* (1931), as is often assumed. The vogue in gangster films in the early 1930s was launched by *Doorway to Hell* (1930), a romanticized version of the career of Johnny Torrio, who turned his Chicago crime kingdom over to Capone in 1925. With Lew Ayres playing Louis Ricarno, as the Torrio figure was called, *Doorway to Hell* failed largely because of the miscasting of the bland Ayres—he later played Dr. Kildare—as a criminal.[11] One cannot make this complaint against Edward G. Robinson's portrayal of Little Caesar, perhaps the definitive version of the Italian-American gangster.

Robinson had practice for this performance in playing Nick Scarsi in *The Racket* (1928)—a figure modeled, like Little Caesar, on Al Capone. Yet it has not to my knowledge been pointed out that the very idea of "Little Caesar" vilifies the Italian character. Apart from implying the objectionable shortness of some Italians, it suggests that the diminutive protagonist embodies a national megalomania contemporaneously evident in the rather short dictator Benito Mussolini. Nor have critics mentioned the connection between Italian fascism and Italian-American gangsterism in some Hollywood films—for example, in Martin Rome's (Richard Conte's) disparaging remark to the policeman Candella (Victor Mature) in *Cry of the City* (1948) that as soon as an Italian puts on a uniform he wants to make a speech. Despite Carlos Clarens's inexplicable assertion that Little Caesar (whose full name is Cesare Rico Bandello and who answers to the name Rico) does not as a character convey an ethnic background,[12] there are many indications of his *Italianità*: his accent, his pidgin English, his meal of spaghetti in a diner, and his awkward celebration of his gangland successes at the Palermo Club. But for all his impressive drive and ambition, Rico is far from being admirable or even likable. Compensating for an inferiority complex by Napoleonic ambition and lacking religious and romantic attachments, Rico sacrifices everything to an inordinate vanity symbolized by his fat cigar and flashy clothes. Because of a presumably typical Italian impulsiveness, Rico is incapable of staying on top; his downfall comes because he shoots first and asks questions afterward, whereas his Anglo-Saxon rival, Big Boy, a practitioner of more reserved "bourgeois" methods, remains invulnerable.[13] It is misleading, though, to suggest that *Little Caesar* condemns all Italians for these traits; Joe Massara (Douglas Fairbanks, Jr.), Rico's best friend, is a dancer who shuns crime for a career in entertainment, a decision that elicits Rico's latent homosexual rage and disappointment.

The other definitive portrayal of the Italian-American gangster in the early 1930s is Paul Muni as Tony Camonte in Howard Hawks's *Scarface* (completed in 1930, released in 1932). With an impressive script by Ben Hecht, *Scarface* is based on the life of Al Capone, its major inspiration apparently being the notorious incident in which Capone personally killed two of his henchmen with a baseball bat. Although this scene does not appear in *Scarface*, it figures in Nicholas Ray's *Party Girl* (1959), where Lee J. Cobb, as the mobster Rico Angelo, bludgeons a lieutenant with a billiard cue at a testimonial held ironically in the lieutenant's honor; the scene figures as well in *The St. Valentine's Day Massacre* and De Palma's *Untouchables*. Yet far more than *Little Caesar*, *Scarface* shows ambivalence towards the gangster hero. On the negative side, Hecht's story is inspired by the history of the Borgias;[14] hence its atmosphere of conspiracy and violence as well as the motif of incest between Camonte and his sister Cesca (Ann Dvorak). Hecht's approach, although more objective than crudely censorious, repeats the longstanding identification in the Anglo-Saxon mind of Italians with Renaissance duplicity. Similarly, the identification of Italians with incest confirms the horror of the native core culture towards seemingly atavistic

Old World familialism. Tony Camonte first appears as a lowbrow simian with oily hair who speaks pidgin English riddled with malapropisms; as he rises in the world of crime he becomes more professional, more "American," and more human, losing his accent and acquiring a high forehead.[15] Like Rico Bandello, Camonte likes spaghetti, which he devours voraciously—a symbol of Italian excess current in American advertising. In the original script, Camonte's mother was intended to be corrupt, gladly accepting the money that her son had stolen; she would have resembled Magdalena, the bad mother of Rico in *Little Caesar*. In the film, though, she provides food (spaghetti, naturally) and warns her daughter that her son must come to a bad end.[16] Finally, *Scarface* implicitly condemns the Italian cult of honor, since Camonte's downfall results only from his own incestuous rage over his sister's attraction to his friend Guino (excellently portrayed by George Raft).[17] As in *Little Caesar*, the impulsive Latin lacks sober middle-class methods.

Still, *Scarface* is not altogether negative in portraying Italians. Camonte's mother represents superior morality, while Camonte's nemesis among the police is Guarino; this small detail anticipates those later films in which, to avoid the suggestion of an ethnic slur, the gangster is balanced by a policeman or priest of the same ethnic origin. In *Scarface* the politicians seem little better than the gangsters; Hecht's original script has them "on the take." The main point, though, is that despite Muni's hammy performance his Camonte exerts a powerful if amoral attraction through his energy and intensity of being. These qualities are made more attractive by association with the famous sestet from *Lucia de Lammermoor* (with a revenge motif) which begins: "What restrains me in such a moment?" Camonte whistles this melody just before he murders his boss (and hence rival). In another sense, Camonte illustrates Robert Warshow's remark that the gangster embodies the great "no" to the American myth that hard work and sober habits lead to success.[18] As a "criminal disciple of Horatio Alger,"[19] Camonte's appeal lies in his rejection of slow upward mobility in favor of naked and violent acquisitiveness. Such rebellion may have had greater resonance during the Great Depression, but even today the gangster appeals to audiences cynically disillusioned with capitalism, not least through the notion that gangsters and businessmen follow the same methods.[20] It is worth noting that Al Capone considered himself not a racketeer but a businessman and that he hated the political left.[21] *Al Capone* (1976), starring Ben Gazzara, depicts Capone in his last years as riddled with syphilis and inveighing against communism.

Although without artistic merit, *Star Witness* (1931) testifies to early social conceptions of the Italian-American. The offender is the extortionist Maxey Campo (Ralph Ince), who threatens to destroy an all-American family: the solidarity of the core culture—white, Anglo-Saxon, Protestant—opposes the disruptive anarchy of the Latin. But this anxious scenario makes little sense, since not the Italian-American but the Anglo-Saxon American family has been in decline since 1900. No matter: Campo's machinations are foiled by Grandpa, a Civil War veteran and living symbol of the older America, whose testimony sends Campo to the electric chair. Grandpa's reward is a return trip to the old folks' home. So much for family solidarity.

All these films neglect the deeper causes—historical, cultural, and sociological—of ethnic crime: the gangster's behavior is a *given*. Yet these works define the representation of gangsters and other Italian-American types over the next forty years. Not only did the phallic cigar of Little Caesar become a Robinson trademark in other gangster films: it is borrowed by Lee J. Cobb in *Party Girl* and Ben Gazzara in the most recent *Al Capone*, to name a few examples. The mobster's mother comes to signify, however questionably, the perverse infantilism and clannishness of Italian-Americans. One thinks of Richard Conte's mother in *Cry of the City* and in *The Brothers Rico* (1957), and of the mother of the gangster Laranaga (Alexander Scourby) in Fritz Lang's *The Big Heat* (1954). This attribution to Italian-Americans of warped matriarchal customs—ironically during a period when some Anglo-Saxon social critics were denouncing American "Momism"—complements the frequent suggestions of the gangster's aberrant sexuality. The latent homosexuality of Little Caesar is repeated in Lang's mama's boy, Laranaga, with his fancy bathrobes, silk pajamas, and effete manservant. Camonte is incestuous; and other gangsters, such as Cobb and John Ireland (playing Cobb's lieutenant Louis Canetto) are connoisseurs of chorus girls, whom they view as so much "meat." Paradoxically, the Italian-American gangster is either too familial or else non- or anti-familial—a misconception that Coppola, in *The Godfather*, worked hard to dispel. Another feature of the gangster icon is a love of fancy clothes, confirming the popular assumption that Italian-Americans dress in vulgar style. A familiar scene in the gangster films since *Little Caesar* has been the rising gangster's visit to an expensive tailor and his emergence from the shop in a stylish (yet slightly *not* in style) new outfit. Of all mobsters, George Raft is the snappiest dresser. Finally, these films introduce a theme that persists in Coppola and Scorsese, namely the contradiction and even complementarity between Italian violence and Catholicism. In *Little Caesar* the untrustworthy driver Tony is shot on the steps of a church, while in *Cry of the City* Martin Rome is shot after having left one.

3

Italian-American critics have small reason to complain that most screen criminals are Italian-Americans. The late 1920s and early 1930s witnessed a crackdown on ethnic slurs in films and a bland homogenization of the gangster genre which began to admit of major exceptions only after World War II. The Sons of Italy were watchful of defamations as early as 1929, and, despite their failure to ban *Scarface*, they exerted enormous influence against the invidious portrayal of their brethren. To quote Carlos Clarens, "any sign of ethnic criminality was expected to disappear after the new production code went into effect in 1933, specifying in Section 1C...that 'no picture shall be produced that tends to incite bigotry or hatred among people of different races, religions, or national origins.' "[22] Hence the abundance of WASP gangsters in the films of the late 1930s. In *Marked Woman* (1937) Eduardo Ciannelli plays a criminal modeled after Lucky Luciano, then especially notorious for his involvement in the prostitution rackets; but the character's name is Johnny Vanning, probably a deliberate linguistic displacement from the name Giovanni. Although Italian-American gangsters appeared with greater frequency in films after World War II, the influence of the production code often led to the balancing of negative and favorable images in the same film, so that, as in *Cry of the City*, the criminal finds his antithesis in the policeman. In some films the portrayal of the Italian gangster was sympathetic if not wholly favorable, as in John Huston's *The Asphalt Jungle* (1951), in which the robber Ciavelli (like Nick Bianco in *Kiss of Death*) is motivated chiefly by a desire to support his impoverished family. One feels only disgust with the police when they brutally intrude upon his family grieving over his dead body. In *Johnny Allegro* (1949) George Raft is the eponymous hero of the title, a former gangster turned government agent. If Raft stands for decency and vitality, his upper-class nemesis combines snobbism, greed, and sexual impotence.

This is not to say that the films of this period are free of negative portrayals of Italian-Americans. As in Raymond Chandler's novel, the most dangerous criminal in Howard Hawks's *Big Sleep* (1946) is the mobster Lash Canino. In Otto Preminger's *Where the Sidewalk Ends* (1950), Dana Andrews plays police detective against the mobster Scalise (Gary Merrill);[23] but if Scalise is corrupt, the same goes for the Andrews character, who has committed a crime that he attempts to pin on the mobster. In Abraham Polonsky's superb *Force of Evil* (1949), the numbers game belongs to Tucker and his accomplice, Fico, who proves the more sinister and dangerous. According to Richard Gambino, in William Wyler's *Detective Story* (1951), set in a New York police station, "virtually every criminal...from ordinary thug to wealthy gangster was depicted in the crudest, most insulting stereotypes of Italian-Americans."[24] Probably the most unflattering portrayal of an Italian-American during the late 1940s is Edward G. Robinson's Johnny Rocco in John Huston's *Key Largo* (1948). An extradited gangster who seeks readmission into the United States, Rocco signifies undisciplined, exorbitant appetite, whether for money or sexual gratification. In one scene Rocco whispers obscenities into Lauren Bacall's ear. In another Humphrey Bogart asks Rocco what he wants. "I want more," says Rocco. "And what do you want when you have more?" Bogart asks. "I want more of more." Yet again the Italian-American criminal is identified with endless, aimless desire, a threat to the disciplined business mentality of the American core culture.

Two Twentieth-Century Fox productions of 1948, *Kiss of Death* and *Cry of the City*, merit close attention for their subtlety, complexity, and sympathy toward their subject matter. Each qualifies as a gangster film and *film noir*. Written by Ben Hecht and starring Victor Mature as Nick Bianco, *Kiss of Death* is one of the few films of its period to convey a plausible rather than groteque view of Italian family attitudes. A petty criminal who robs to support his family, Bianco is caught and imprisoned, whereupon his wife commits suicide and his children are confined to a Catholic orphanage. An ambitious district attorney named Di Angelo (Brian Donlevy) manipulates Bianco into becoming a stool pigeon but fails to protect him against the vengeful mob; Bianco is nearly killed. When Bianco and Di Angelo visit Bianco's daughters in the orphanage, a nun thinks that Di Angelo is the gangster, and in fact he looks and even acts like one. So in some ways the film undercuts the usual antithesis between the good Italian-American and the Italian-American criminal, just as it succeeds in making the audience sympathize with an informer. Nor is the film's most memorable criminal an Italian-American. Rather, in keeping perhaps with the production code, his name is Tommy Udo (Richard Widmark), which has no definite nationality.

Directed by Robert Siodmak and written by Richard Thorpe, *Cry of the City* is a doppelgänger narrative about two men who grew up together in the Italian ghetto of New York but chose divergent paths: one, Martin Rome, played superbly by Richard Conte, who turned to crime; the other, Lieutenant Candella, played by Victor Mature, who became a policeman and who now seeks to bring Rome to justice.[25] Colin McArthur observes that Candella sees in Rome what he might himself have, perhaps wants to become.[26] At the same time, in killing Rome, Candella rescues Rome's younger and impressionable brother from a life of crime. Curiously, Martin Rome remains something of a mama's boy, and it is interesting that his mother initially tries to shield him from the law. Presumably the Italian family opposes the state, except when, as with Candella, a rare individual succeeds in transcending purely ethnic local loyalties. One sees this parochial attitude in Rome's mockery of Candella's uniform.

Something may be made of the fact that the antagonist is named after the capital of Italy. Just before he kills his double, Candella shouts: "Stop, Rome, in the name of the law!" This statement may be taken as addressed both to Martin Rome and the city of Rome as the symbol of Italy. It implies that Italian-Americans, nursed on their "lawless" Roman tradition, must "stop" in the sense of abandoning their Italian heritage and becoming honest citizens under the Anglo-Saxon legal system. The absurdity of this cultural slur is apparent to anyone who has heard of Cicero, the canonists, and the Bologna jurists. It is also worth noting that the film is based on Henry Edward Helseth's novel *The Chair for Martin Rome*. Not only is Rome the seat of the papacy, but several popes have been named Martin, while the pope is identified not with the electric chair but with the chair or *cathedra* whence he issues offensively dogmatic pronouncements. The title is a covertly Italophobic text specifying the proper "chair" for the unregenerate Italian of the Anglo-Saxon imagination as the electric chair; his true "excommunication" is from the native American core culture.

Joseph Mankiewicz's *House of Strangers* (1949) depicts not gangsters but an Italian-American family tainted by financial malfeasance. Nonetheless, it anticipates *The Godfather* in some of its situations and themes. Gino Moretti (Edward G. Robinson), a successful banker, rules his family with an iron hand. At the dinner table he plays opera (Rossini) and browbeats his three resentful older sons. Their hatred is fueled as well by Gino's preference for Max (Richard Conte), his youngest son, a handsome and successful lawyer exempted from overt patriarchal tyranny. Like Michael Corleone, Max risks his father's displeasure by falling in love with a non-Italian woman of a higher social class—the WASPy Irene Bennett (Susan Hayward). The crisis of the film comes in two forms: the father's banking business fails through usurious practices; and Max, having been double-crossed by one of his brothers, is sent to jail for seven years for attempting to bribe a juror. Given that *House of Strangers* was directed by Joseph Mankiewicz and based on a novel by Jerome Weidman, two Jews, one suspects that the identification of Italians with illegal banking may be a projection of Jewish anxieties onto another ethnic group.[27] In any case, Gino's paternal authority collapses, and the brothers are free to express their latent hostilities against their father and his favorite son. A vengeful Conte returns from prison to a "house of strangers" and just escapes being killed. Only at the end of the film, having been saved by his upper-class fiancée, does he succeed in escaping both his familial nightmare and ethnic origins. His salvation is thus equated with his abandonment of a degrading background through an upwardly mobile marriage; this, one assumes, was also the hope of Michael Corleone in marrying Kay Adams, a New England WASP. In numerous other gangster pictures, the mark of the gangster's success is likewise marriage to a non-Italian woman with "class."

Other films of the period suggest that the Italian's ethnic traits must condemn him to social inferiority. Consider Delbert Mann's *Marty* (1955), with a script by Paddy Chayefsky, for which Ernest Borgnine, an Italian-American actor playing an Italian-American butcher, won an Academy Award for Best Actor. Many critics see this film as a highly sensitive portrayal of ethnic and lower-class life, praising its "delicate handling of a love affair between two lonely, undistinguished people."[28] Actually, the film reeks of sentimental condescension and liberal pity toward the "little people." The story concerns a thirty-four-year-old butcher who fears that no woman could ever be attracted to him; then he meets a woman (Betsy Blair) with similar doubts about herself. They fall in love, but unfortunately she is not Italian; the rest of the film treats the ultimately surmountable obstacles to their union. Italian-Americans in this film are depicted as amusingly crude but indolent, aimless, and ineffectual (see Marty's interchanges with his friend Angie). Because of their clannishness, among other defects, they seem incapable of achieving success or transcending their social origins in the approved American manner. And, once again, the hero's atypical salvation or "resuce" comes from marriage to a non-Italian girl.

Although its hero affords something of an exception to this rule, Robert Wise's *Somebody Up There Likes Me* (1958), with Paul Newman starring as the middleweight boxer Rocky Graziano, is hardly more flattering. Notwithstanding Newman's strenuously futile attempt to act like a swaggering Italian tough, Graziano emerges as a former thug who, had he not discharged his violence in the boxing ring and had he not been domesticated by a non-Italian girl (played by Pier Angeli), would have ended up as a criminal. His social milieu is desperate and crime-ridden, while his family, in contrast to the vast majority of Italian-American families, is ruled by a sadistic father. If Wise's film is a success story—the record of Graziano's triumphant career—it also implies that such success is an exception, the result of a miracle ("somebody up there likes me"), whereas most Italian-Americans are condemned to the ghetto. Nor is Graziano's success very respectable, being achieved by crude physical violence. Apart from his likability, Graziano still resembles the thugs and brutes he leaves behind.

A putative Italian savagery may also be seen in films that have nothing to do with gangsters, boxers, or ethnic settings. Dark-skinned Italian-Americans have often been cast in films and on television as Indians and Arabs, two of the traditionally demonic "enemies" of Western civilization. The first identification goes back at least to James Fenimore Cooper, whose Indians are often Italianate villains with a love of sex and violence.[29] The second begins with Rudolph Valentino and continues in many B-movies. On the other hand, Hollywood has consistently de-Italianized its Roman "epics." Apart from their large noses, the antiseptic Romans of *Ben Hur* and *Quo Vadis* have nothing identifiably Italian about them to detract from their nobility, usually speaking with a high British accent which agrees with the American fantasy of Caesar and Mark Antony as Northern European aristocrats rather than Mediterranean pagans.

At least one film of the immediate postwar period treats the Italian-American as more than a brute. Edward Dmytryk's *Christ in Concrete* (1950) focuses on the selfless devotion of an Italian-American laboring father to his family. Peter Bondanella notes that his work reveals a stylistic and substantive debt to Italian neorealism, and not surprisingly it impressed such Italian critics as Guido Aristarco and Franco Columbo. Guido Fink points out, though, that they were less interested in its artistic virtues than its thematic content. Disgusted with such works as *Cry of the City*, which portrayed the Italian-American as a criminal and primitive, they celebrated *Christ in Concrete* for its sense of the dignity of labor and the "solidarity and reciprocal impulse" of Italian-American communities. Yet if a counterweight to defamation was needed, the danger in films such as this is that a too idealistic treatment might tip the balance toward the merely "positive stereotyping."[30]

These examples are marginal to the persistent identification in the American film of the Italian-American with the gangster. This theme resurfaces in 1950 in *The Black Hand*, notable not for aesthetic quality but for its unusual attempt, however misleading, to explore the historical sources of Italian-American crime; to this extent, *The Black Hand* looks forward to *The Godfather*. Starring Gene Kelly and J. Carrol Naish, the film is inspired by New York police detective Joseph Petrosino's attempt early in this century to connect Italian-American criminal activities (the Black Hand) with Sicilian criminal organizations. Although Petrosino's murder in a Palermo street in 1909 might suggest that the connection did exist, Petrosino never succeeded in proving it.[31] The film, however, strongly implies that the Sicilian branch of the Black Hand had been the chief cause of illegal activity among Italo-Americans. Hence the disclaimer at the beginning of the film which, after praising Italians who had entered the mainstream of American culture, concludes thus: "This story deals with the hard, angry days when these new citizens began to place their stake in the American dream—when they purged the Old World Terror of the Black Hand." As Clarens remarks, the film was founded on the assumption—foolishly optimistic, as it turned out—that the Italians would achieve full respectability as citizens once they had banished a purely foreign criminal element from their midst.[32] In truth, Italian (and numerous other) criminal groups have sprung up spontaneously on American soil. In *The Black Hand* the wished-for dissociation of Italian-Americans from their bad antecedents is performed symbolically (and implausibly) by Gene Kelly as Johnny Columbo, named after the discoverer of the New World. At the film's conclusion, Columbo kills the local gang lord (Marc Lawrence) after a cathartic explosion rocks the Italian-American neighborhood. Curiously, Columbo achieves cultural exorcism by taking the law into his own hands and wielding a knife in Old World style. According to Richard Gambino, this is one of numerous works that imply that the "historical background of Italians is shameful,...that they become acceptable only as they renounce their roots," and that "Italian-Americans have a special cultural heritage of crime and thus a propensity to become criminals."[33]

The Black Hand coincided with a key development in the American consciousness of crime. The 1950s witnessed the disclosure of the power and influence of criminal organizations or syndicates, of which the Black Hand might be taken as the germ. Conducted in Washington in 1950, the Senate Crime Investigating Committee hearings suggested to many that American crime was dominated by a close-knit and far-flung association of Italian-American gangsters. This assumption, which some sociologists challenged, received further support in 1957 when the FBI apprehended many leading gangsters at an organization meeting in Apalachin, New York. Then, in 1963, Joseph Valachi assured the McClelland investigative committee of the existence of the Cosa Nostra or "our thing"—a vast network of Italian-American criminals linked by familial and other ties. So the "Mafia" became a household word.

These disclosures found their echo in films accenting not the isolated criminal or big mobster but the criminal organization, referred to as the "syndicate" and even as the Mafia (as in Phil Karlson's *Tight Spot*, 1955).[34] Not all of these associations are identified with Italian-Americans, a fact attributable perhaps to the vigilance of the Sons of Italy: the gangsters in *Hoodlum Empire* (1951), *Tight Spot*, Stuart Rosenberg's *Murder Incorporated* (1960), and the crime films of Samuel Fuller, are chiefly WASPish or nonethnic. Still, the mafioso type abounds in *Pay or Die* (1960), with Ernest Borgnine as Lieutenant Joseph Petrosino; in *Al Capone* (1959), with Rod Steiger in the title role; in Karlson's *The Brothers Rico*, where Richard Conte battles an invisibly ubiquitous syndicate run by a fellow Italian-American; in Nicholas Ray's *Party Girl* and Corman's *St. Valentine's Day Massacre*; in the character Laranaga of *The Big Heat*; and perhaps most memorably in *The Untouchables* television series, with Neville Brand (as in the film offshoot *The Scarface Mob* of 1962 and *The George Raft Story* of the preceding year) as Al Capone. Many of these films attempt to give the impression that they are based on fact, even when, as in Walter Winchell's narrations in *The Untouchables*, they are largely fabrications. In short, these films take for granted what some scholars doubt, namely the existence of a nationally united and largely Italian-American criminal organization or syndicate.[35] Yet the better gangster films of this period also show an understanding of the gangster mentality that extends beyond cliché. In *The Big Heat* the mobster Laranaga wants his children to escape the world of the syndicate and to become respectable citizens; here is anticipated the problem of Vito Corleone. The truth of this portrayal is confirmed by Columbia University sociologist Francis Ianni, who shows that many Mafia children have eschewed crime in favor of the professions.

4

What Vito Zagarrio observes of Francis Ford Coppola might also be said of Martin Scorsese. As third- or fourth-generation Italian-Americans, each is beyond the ordeal of assimilation through which their parents and grandparents suffered. Thus they are less insecure toward their ethnic past than was a director like Frank Capra, and more capable of confronting it explicitly in their films. Coppola and Scorsese do not blush to acknowledge the existence of Italian-American gangsters and other unsavory types, although they realize that these constitute but one (small) aspect of Italian-American life.

Apart from the gain in honesty, there is an advance in subtlety and understanding. Earlier Hollywood directors saw Italian-American culture from the outside; Coppola and Scorsese know it from within, with that casual mastery of detail that comes with true intimacy. Yet neither director forgets his Hollywood predecessors; they respect the American tradition of the Italian-American film, at once imitating, expanding, altering, and improving it. Nor do they traffic in cheap ethnic chauvinism or unthinking nostalgia, despite critical opinions to the contrary. If anything, they warn against the sentimentalization of ethnicity. They also register harsh criticism not only of the Mafia but of many Italian-American traits.

The Godfather I and *II* constantly echo conventions of the Hollywood gangster film. In *Scarface* and *Little Caesar*, the leading hoodlums devour spaghetti while speaking in pidgin English, heavily accented; Rico has just accomplished his first major murder. In *The Godfather II*, Vito Corleone (Robert DeNiro) eats spaghetti with the young Tessio and Clemenza, hinting in heavily accented English at the soon-to-be-achieved assassination of the extortionist Fanucci; like the earlier film, but in a richer, subtler manner, *The Godfather II* links eating and killing. As John Paul Russo shows, the paradigm for this link is Clemenza's remark after the murder of Paulie: "Leave the gun, take the cannoli."[36] Gangster films have also traditionally depicted the police and politicians as corrupt: one thinks of the police chief McCluskey (Sterling Hayden) in *The Godfather I* and Senator Geary (J. D. Spradlin) in *The Godfather II*; to the latter, Michael (Al Pacino) observes that they are "both part of the same hypocrisy." Michael's fashionable tailoring at the end of *The Godfather I*, and later his sharkskin suits, not only contrast with his early drabness as a soldier and Ivy League aspirant, but call to mind those numerous scenes in which the mobster's fancy new clothes signify his arrival as gang lord. According to Colin McArthur, the gangster film typically associates the motor car with violence.[37] To give only a few examples: in *The Godfather I*, Michael's first wife Apollonia is blown up in a car; Sonny is killed at a toll booth; and Paulie is killed after riding around for hours with Clemenza. The Senate hearings in *The Godfather II* trace to such films as *Hoodlum Empire*, while the mob summit meetings in *The Godfather I* are almost *de rigueur* for the genre.

As in *The Black Hand,* Coppola explores possible links between Italian-American crime and the Old World. This is not to say that Don Vito Corleone directly carries on a Sicilian criminal tradition, what Kay Adams denounces as "this Sicilian thing," for he and his sons are "forced" into crime by circumstance. Still, Don Vito's earliest rival, the Black Hand extortionist Fanucci, appears to represent a form of criminality carried over from the mother country. Fanucci's death at the hands of Corleone, like his histrionic, unmethodical style, suggests that he is an anachronism on American soil, what the early Italian-Americans described as a "Moustache Pete."[38] Fanucci's brilliantly orchestrated murder in *The Godfather II* also elaborates the longstanding connection between Italian music and assassination. In *Scarface,* Camonte whistles "What restrains me...?" from Donizetti and then kills his boss; the murder of Fanucci coincides with the San Gennaro Festival in Little Italy, the final shots being muffled by the band's crescendo. This operatic moment is especially satisfying since, as in the best of Fellini, the music derives not from a soundtrack but from the scene itself.[39] At the end of *The Godfather I,* Coppola juxtaposes the baptism of Michael's son with a series of murders assuring Michael's ascension to power. Some critics view this scene as celebrating sacrificial violence sanctioned by Catholic religiosity, while others (much more plausibly, in view of the film's sequel) find this conterpointing morally ironic; but in any case the parallelism of crime and Catholicism calls to mind *Little Caesar* and *Cry of the City,* in which violence occurs in close proximity to neighborhood churches.

Another major concern of the gangster film is the difficulty of Italian-Americans in transferring their allegiance from the ethnic group or family to the state. In *Cry of the City,* Lieutenant Candella prefers legality over ethnic loyalty, but Martin Rome's mother attempts at first to shield her son from the police. *The Godfather* embodies this tension in Michael Corleone, who enlists in the U.S. Army against his father's wishes and later attends his sister's wedding wearing a U.S. Army uniform. On the other hand, Michael shares Don Vito's hopes that the family will attain upper-class or bourgeois respectability; one recalls the ganglord Laranaga's desire in *The Big Heat* to save his children from the world of crime. The tragedy of *The Godfather I* is that circumstances and family loyalty prevent Michael from escaping this world. As in *House of Strangers*, the young hoodlum's hopes of rejecting his criminal origins are invested in marriage to an upper-class Anglo-Saxon woman. Yet Michael Corleone must endure his wife's constant complaint that the family remains in the crime business.

For all these continuities, decisive differences exist between the Corleone family and the representative film gangsters of the past. Little Caesar and Camonte decline because of an overwhelming vanity and lack of self-control. Loud and impulsive, each is a big spender, wearing flashy clothes and smoking big cigars as signs of power. Their problem is excessive charisma or charisma pure and simple, which keeps them (like the histrionic Fanucci) in the limelight, whereas Big Boy, the bland WASP crook in *Little Caesar*, shuns publicity and stays out of trouble. Vito and Michael Corleone typify Mafia tradition and Italian custom in their calculated remoteness, their control of events from a distance, and their freedom from histrionics. Don

Vito prefers to leave his empire to Michael not Sonny, as Sonny dresses flashily, speaks candidly and out of turn, and has an exceedingly hot head (which gets him killed). Another departure from film tradition (compare the luxurious home of Laranaga) is that the Corleone family, at least in its early days, preserves sober habits and therefore underspends. As Gambino notes, many viewers of *The Godfather I* could not believe that Don Vito lived in such unimpressive surroundings. Actually, despite the popular assumption of Italian lavishness, this portrayal agrees with Mafia and Italian habits and testifies to the sense of limit that the Don sought to bequeath to his increasingly Americanized sons.[40]

The economic and emotional sobriety of the Corleone family results partly from the fact that it stands at the center of a criminal organization which, as it gradually loses its traditional character, comes to resemble the impersonal modern corporation. However, the Corleone restraint is initially rooted in familialism, a quality that sets the Corleones apart from such radical individualists as Little Caesar and Camonte, both highly atypical examples of Italian-American behavior. In addition to their loud manners and dress, these solitary thugs are associated with homosexuality and incest. By contrast, sexual perversion has no place in the Corleone household, at least before its decline. Following his puritanical father's example, Michael Corleone is ill at ease when his sexually corrupted brother Fredo takes him to the sleazy show in Havana, and, even as his marriage is collapsing, there is no suggestion of infidelity on his part. *The Godfather* locates sexual perversion chiefly in the defamilialized world outside the Mafia and the Italian-American community, in the unmarried Jewish producer, who keeps a child star as mistress, and in the married Senator Geary, who practices sadomasochism with prostitutes. There is, though, the disturbing fact that Geary gets his kicks in a bordello run by the Corleone family. Michael's apparent assumption that prostitution is merely his line of business conforms to a once common if not typical Italian American attitude, namely the dissociation of business practice from the sphere of family values. Secure in the fidelity of her husband and his reliability as a provider, the ideal Mafia wife (such as Mama Corleone) runs her house unconcerned with what goes on in the workplace. Michael's mistake was to have married an Anglo-American woman who, incapable of separating these spheres and with some claim to a higher morality, questions the moral significance of Michael's business.

The Godfather films achieve a still more significant reversal of film tradition. As we have noted, *The Black Hand* is perhaps the first film to imply openly that Italian-Americans, in order to become respectable citizens, must purge themselves of their "criminal" Italian past. But Coppola, as John Paul Russo suggests, reverses this anti-ethnic bias. In *The Godfather I* and *II*, Sicily embodies plenitude and community, *Gemeinschaft* in the sense of tradition, custom, and extended familial relations.[41] This is most memorably conveyed in the return of the Corleone family to Sicily, where they meet their relatives and drink the wine of the native earth. For all its material advantages, America stands for *Gesellschaft* or civil society in its social atomization and merely contractual relationships, the core of which is money.

Founded on familial ties and traditional loyalties, even in crime, the Corleone family slowly succumbs to late capitalist business methods, bureaucratic organization, impersonality, and limitless acquisition. Marlon Brando is therefore wrong to claim that *The Godfather* is "about the corporate mind," that the Mafia in all its historical forms is the "best example of capitalism that we have," and that Don Vito is "like any ordinary business magnate."[42] Instead, the films dramatize the difference between Don Vito's conception of the Mafia, as an example of traditional, limited, and family-based capitalism, and its later "corporate" manifestation under Michael Corleone, who has no choice but to adopt the most modern, efficient, and defamilialized methods. Coppola's representation of the development of Italian-American crime agrees with that of scholarly observers, who find that organized crime is now interethnic and based not on tradition but corporate practice.

Admittedly Coppola romanticizes the Corleone family, especially in *The Godfather I*. Clarens complains that he is soft on Don Vito and that had he shown the sources of his wealth the illusion of Don Vito's moral superiority would vanish.[43] It also seems unlikely that Don Vito's sense of tradition or limit could have prevented him from entering the drug traffic. Yet Clarens fails to see that Coppola ironizes his own romanticism, that he has a subtle and divided consciousness toward the Mafia and his own ethnicity. The Sicilian and Little Italy episodes in *The Godfather II*, suffused photographically as if with the golden glow of nostalgia, less resemble an "objective" re-creation of an actual past than the recollection of an imaginary plenitude; they seem to represent the despairing attempt of the shattered Michael Corleone, musing in solitude on the autumnal shores of Lake Tahoe, to recapture not just an unattainable but a nonexistent ideal of paternal conduct and familial custom. Not for nothing do these episodes intrude upon the more realistic style of the contemporary narrative with their uncanny folktale elements and figures—Fanucci, the stage Italian, whose death is deserved and so brilliantly staged; the dapper thug Clemenza, who in *The Godfather I* is a sort of male godmother figure and who in the course of an evening casually introduces Vito Corleone into a life of crime by giving him a cache of stolen guns; Don Vito strolling at sunset amid the *Gemeinschaft* of Little Italy, receiving and dispensing gifts, known and honored by all members of the community; his comical chastening of the Calabrian landlord, who would drive a helpless old lady from her apartment; his self-administered killing of Don Ciccio, the murderer of his mother; and finally, the lyrical family reunion, symbolizing the perfect plenitude of contact, love, and nourishment that Russo so well describes. Coppola undoubtedly recognized the obvious ideality of these situations and images.

And yet, as Russo also suggests, if Sicily is the land of plenitude, it is also paradoxically, the origin of separation, specifically of Vito Corleone from his first family and his real name. Here is the source of that violence that divorced Don Vito from the community, pledged him to vendetta, and led him to a violent career, often against Sicilian "brethren." As if to undercut the fantasy of plenitude and presence, Coppola emphasizes the final remoteness and even inhumanity of the Godfather, whether as a person or paternal ideal. In *The Godfather I*, at the moment of his death, Don Vito transforms himself playfully into an ogre and terrifies his grandson. But still more significant is the last scene of *The Godfather II*. Having enlisted in the Army, and thus expressed an allegiance beyond the family, Michael sits alone (once more) in the dining room, waiting for a father who never appears. This scene aptly symbolizes the absence and separation that no dream of *Gemeinschaft* can ever dispel. Other Hollywood directors have sensed the conflict in the Italian-American consciousness between the Old and New Worlds, state and community, love and honor, but none has had Coppola's power of dramatization or his sympathy and understanding.

Coppola's only serious rival among Italian-American directors is Martin Scorsese, who has surpassed him as a consistent artist. Scorsese has directed three feature films on Italian-American subjects: *Who's that Knocking at My Door?* (1969); *Mean Streets* (1973) and *Raging Bull* (1980). He has also directed a forty-eight minute documentary entitled *Italian-American* (1974), consisting of interviews in which his father and mother discuss life in New York's Little Italy. These works constitute an informed, serious, and sometimes highly critical interpretation of Italian-American life, especially of the influence of the Catholic Church, the dangerous consequences of *bella figura*, and the cultural propensity to violence.

Intensely rendered though hardly original, *Who's That Knocking at My Door?* explores the crippling effect of Italian-Catholic sexual morality on male-female relations. Catholic puritanism results in immature sexuality as well as miseries of self-righteousnes, loneliness, frustration, and violence. But though Scorsese abandoned his youthful calling to the priesthood, he does not altogether reject Catholicism, for he never ceases to honor the Christian ideals of nonviolence and brotherly love.

J. R. (Harvey Keitel), the main character, is psychologically overwhelmed by the familiar Catholic distinction between woman as virgin or mother and woman as whore. He has no difficulty in fornicating with prostitutes or "broads," but he is impotent in the presence of "the girl" (Zina Bethune) he loves. Appropriately enough, J. R. and "the girl" meet in his mother's apartment, filled with icons of purity (the Madonna) yet penetrated by the profane sounds of the street. Although her angelic face, polite manners, and long blonde hair suggest absolute purity, she is willing to sleep with J. R., whom she seems to love. But for J. R., good girls do not engage in sex. Later, when the girl confesses to having been raped by her first boyfriend, a kind of double of J. R., J. R. is unreasonably disgusted to learn of her "impurity," even calling her a "broad." Still later, when he clumsily attempts a reconciliation, she rejects his offer of marriage and sends him away. This exemplar of a rigorous Catholic upbringing is more comfortable with prostitutes or his dissolute Italian-American male friends, none of whom is capable of a mature sexual relationship. The last scene finds J. R., having left the girl's apartment for the last time, once more in church. With its sadistic iconography, Catholicism figures as an antivitalistic religion, the source of sexual repression and brutality.

Scorsese deepens his investigation of Italian-American mores in *Mean Streets*, which is set in Little Italy. The main character, the pampered Charlie Civello (Harvey Keitel), dissipates his life in raucous neighborhood bars.

Interiors are infernal red, while slow motion sequences suggest the same sort of physical and moral entrapment depicted in the earlier film. The most pathetic of Charlie's riff-raff friends is his black sheep cousin, Johnny Boy, (Robert DeNiro). Foolishly and violently emulative of the "big shots," secretly envious of Charlie's popularity and easy money, Johnny Boy creates a bad impression. Without Charlie's brotherly protection, he would long ago have been cast out of this world of *bella figura*. Meanwhile, Charlie experiences a spiritual crisis. Despite residual Catholic scruples, symbolized by the purgatorial flame of the devotional candle, and amounting to a fear of the possible existence of hell, Charlie feels the pressure of his small-time mobster uncle, who as a family favor has promised him ownership of a successful restaurant. He also feels intense embarrassment because of Johnny Boy. Not only have Johnny Boy's antics irritated Charlie's uncle, he has failed to pay his debts to Michael, another of Charlie's friends. Charlie's Catholicism proves flimsy. He accepts the restaurant, and the dispossessed owner commits suicide. When Johnny Boy insults Michael, Charlie is embarrassed and outraged. Out of a reluctant sense of duty, Charlie agrees to hide Johnny Boy outside the city, yet he knows that sooner or later his cousin's fate is sealed; it is too late for Charlie to plead his cousin's case before his uncle and friends, as Johnny Boy had hoped. Michael and his hit man, played by Scorsese himself, ambush Charlie and Johnny Boy as they leave the city. Implicitly a sacrifice to Charlie's vanity, Johnny Boy is killed, while Charlie staggers away wounded and in shock.

Mean Streets contains many of Scorsese's main themes. The Madonna-whore complex surfaces in Charlie's contempt for Teresa (Amy Robinson), his lover and distant cousin. Emptied of meaning, Catholic ritual controls neither mob aggression nor the Italian-American cult of *bella figura*. Nor can Christian fraternity withstand the escalating mimetic hostility engendered by male pride and rivalry. Everyone wants to be a "big shot" by intimidation, effrontery, or physical violence. Thus for Scorsese many Italian-Americans remain suspended between an essentially egoistic paganism and true Christianity, between personal honor and charity, violence and an ideal of pacifistic humility.[44] If the truth of Catholicism lies not in such distortions as life-denying puritanism but in the imitation of Christ, few if any of Scorsese's Catholics know how to follow this lesson. For them Catholicism is a mere ornament or salve for the conscience, incapable of seriously influencing behavior. No director, not even Coppola, has gone as far as Scorsese in portraying some of the longstanding moral conflicts of Italian-American, and indeed of Italian, life, conflicts that go back probably to late Roman times. As the Italians themselves say, "*Siamo primo pagani, dopo cristiani*" ("We are pagans first, Christians second").

Scorsese further pursues these issues in *Raging Bull*, at once his finest work and by far the greatest of boxing films. *Raging Bull* marks an enormous improvement over its obvious precursor, Robert Wise's *Somebody Up There Likes Me*. Although Scorsese seems for some reason to admire this film, and has even cast Paul Newman in *The Color of Money* (1986), in *Somebody Up There Likes Me* all serious moral conflict is eliminated by Newman-Graziano's pretty-boy likability, precisely what the title announces and assures.

Newman renders Graziano's criminality as the excess of boisterous youth; all along Graziano was headed for the ghetto pantheon, minor television celebrity, and responsible domesticity. When the mob tries to make Graziano throw a fight, this urban naif preserves his innate integrity; Jake La Motta did not find the realities of the fight game so easy. The fundamental optimism and unreality of the film is most apparent in the boxing scenes, which lack the impact of real violence. In short, *Somebody Up There Likes Me* is a cloyingly upbeat "American" success story whose hero's "election" results from the fact that God "likes" him—as if God judged man by the other-directed values of personality and popularity rampant in the 1950s as today.

These banalities are absent in *Raging Bull*, which is based on the autobiography of the middleweight boxing champion Jake La Motta. This film is about the worship of violence as it infects not only La Motta but American and Italian-American culture. Seeking to defeat all possible rivals in the boxing ring, La Motta would claim for himself that violence and invulnerability that pagan religions ascribe to the gods. Thus he would achieve the ultimate *bella figura*—godlike status in the eyes of a simultaneously idolatrous and envious crowd for which all-powerful violence is the unacknowledged sign of divinity. Once again Scorsese comprehends the residual paganism in the Italian-American love of honor and revenge, values that often lead to empty rivalry and vain, crowd-pleasing displays of lethal violence. Scorsese suggests iconographically that Jake would become the living version of the sacred bull of Mediterranean patriarchy, an animal associated with divine potency, massive destruction, panic, and, as a sacrificial beast, with victimization. No less important, Scorsese understands that such false and violent arrogations of divine power oppose the highest teachings of Catholicism (and Christianity in general)—not sexual puritanism, which Scorsese recognizes as marginal to the truth of Christianity, but nonviolence, humility, and brotherly love. The chief reason that Scorsese detests the mob is that its cult of *bella figura* and violence, combined with its immense influence on certain sectors of the Italian-American community (such as boxers and fight managers), challenge the authority of Christian teaching. When the mafioso Tommy Como attempts (only half successfully) to become Jake's protector, he implicitly usurps the Church's (or Christ's) place as the rightful mediator of genuine spirituality. One cannot combine honor and vendetta, whose ultimate sign is violence and which inevitably means enslavement to the estimation of other human beings, with Christian practice; one cannot reconcile imitative rivalry with one's chosen enemies with the selfless and pacifistic imitation of the inimitable Christ. Jake La Motta is not a saint or a Christ figure, as some believe, but a parody of Christ, an example of the transcendental impulse deviated toward its meretricious earthly symbols of violence and power.

Charged by Robert DeNiro's explosive performance, *Raging Bull* is perhaps the profoundest cinematic exploration of not only Italian-American but universal violence. La Motta's personal quest for ultimate conquest through violence is self-defeating and impossible, for it arises not from genuine spiritual power or integrity but from an excessive concern for the estimation of others and by his overwhelming sense of the absence and abjection of his being; as much as he would be the conquering bull, he is also the masochistic victim, for each is an inseparable aspect of that false image of divine violence that he worships and pursues. Since nothing will appease his inner lack or satisfy his self-punishing need for more and more obstacles, La Motta receives no pleasure from winning the middleweight championship—an obvious contrast with Wise's film, where such a victory is a conventional success. In the aftermath, Jake insists upon finding more obstacles where none exist, for only vain rivalry can satisfy his contradictory impulses of conquest and self-victimization. He accuses his wife of adultery, first with his associates and then with his brother. His marriage soon breaks up and his brother rejects him, too—apt symbols of the failure of Christian values in this world. Only at the end of *Raging Bull*, after years of personal degradation, does La Motta attain some measure of peace, although he is far from fulfilling (or even comprehending) the real demands of Christianity. This conclusion is more profound and believable than that of Wise's vulgar film, in which the likable hero's fists propel him to public success and divine popularity.

5

This handful of impressive films constitutes the core of authentically Italian-American cinema. Yet during their efflorescence, the film industry has offered other interpretations of Italian-American life. Thanks largely to *The Godfather*, the gangster film revived in *The Don is Dead* (1973), *The Valachi Papers* (1971), *Honor Thy Father* (1973), and *Capone*, each registering not so much disapproval of crime as a horrified fascination with the byzantine politics of Italian-American gangs.

One may also argue that Michael Cimino's *Year of the Dragon* (1985) is more concerned with Italian-American themes than first appears. The film treats the ultimately successful effort of the policeman Charles White (Mickey Rourke) to stamp out the newly emergent criminal gangs of New York's Chinatown. A violent Vietnam War veteran of Polish origin, White loathes his own ethnic background, yet even after having changed his name to "White," as if to affirm against his self-doubts his Caucasian identity, he deflects his persistent self-hatred onto the even more emarginated Chinese. But beyond the fact that White loves a Chinese girl, what seems most curious is his insistence that the Chinese invented the Mafia, that Italian mobsters are copying Chinese predecessors; indeed, Chinese thugs are driving out the Italians. This bizarre set of displacements, among them Cimino's apparent identification with a Polish-American played by an Irish-American, suggests Cimino's uneasiness toward his own ethnicity. None of his earlier films treats an Italian-American subject.

Meanwhile, Hollywood continues to turn out versions of the familiar success story in which Italian-Americans attempt to claw themselves out of their lower-class existence. In the *Rocky* films, Sylvester Stallone far surpasses Rocky Graziano or Marciano by vindicating American honor against the Soviet heavyweight champion. It is a measure of the contemporary acceptance of the Italian-American *as* an American that Rocky, draped in the Stars and Stripes no less, has appeared on the cover of *Newsweek* magazine. Yet Stallone's shameless appeal to his own and his audience's wish-fulfillment fantasies altogether ignores the historical and social realities that disturb Scorsese and Coppola.

Stallone notwithstanding, Hollywood still sees Italian-Americans as clannish, unambitious, menial, lazy, and erratic, thus condemned to lower-class status unless some miracle intervenes or unless the core culture can enlist their normally ineffectual energies or minor virtues. To be sure, *Saturday Night Fever* (1977) is the success story of Tony Manero (John Travolta), whose love of disco dancing (note his descent from Joe Massara in *Little Caesar*) enables him to escape the ghetto. But dancing is a minor and, especially in this manifestation, lower art, being furthermore unproductive; there is no suggestion that Manero and his aimless friends might be interested in a professional or administrative career or have the opportunity to attain it. This objection is not contradicted by the obvious fact, well-known to Scorsese, that such a portrayal conforms to the social reality of many Italian-Americans (as it does to that of many Irish-, Polish-, Greek-, and Anglo-Saxon Americans). The point is that *Saturday Night Fever* lacks the social and thematic complexities of a Scorsese and is clearly based on a prejudicial social stereotype that it consciously exploits; moreover, that this stereotype is being disseminated at the very moment when many Italian-Americans have come to lose that lower- or lower-middle-class and culturally self-confining mentality that disturbed Richard Gambino and are rising to prominence in many fields. This film thus reiterates a simplistic and partly inaccurate conception of the Italian-American.

Such false and insulting assumptions are even more offensive in Stuart Rosenberg's *The Pope of Greenwich Village* (1984), a crude parody of Scorsese. Having treated the mob in *Murder Incorporated*, Rosenberg focuses with amused disgust on two Italian-American ne'er-do-wells who belong to lower Manhattan as rats to a sewer. The hero's marriage has collapsed, his WASP girlfriend is pregnant, his relationship with his cousin has homosexual undertones, and he and his cousin are in trouble with both the police and the mob after their incompetent attempt at robbery. Reminiscent of the novel *The Chair for Martin Rome*, Jewish anti-Catholicism surfaces in the mocking representation of the hero (Micky Rourke) as a pope figure, whereby Catholicism is identified with the loose morals of petty criminals. Without understanding his subject matter, Rosenberg has simply appropriated the most obvious gestures, manners, and circumstances of Scorsese's characters, his purpose being to dwell on sordid situations for their own sake.

The question remains, How to explain the emergence of Italian-American cinema? It coincides with the true "arrival" of American ethnic groups, that is, their attainment of major social, political, cultural, and economic importance. This explains the present willingness of ethnics to confront their historical condition without overwhelming embarrassment and with aesthetic detachment. Italian-Americans have enjoyed recent success not only as film directors and actors but in academics, scientific research, the law, and business. During the recent celebration of the centennial and restoration of the Statue of Liberty, two Italian-Americans played a significant role: Lee Iacocca, president of Chrysler Corporation, who led the project; and Robert DeNiro, who figured prominently in the telecast of the celebration itself. John Higham, the American historian of immigration, was widely quoted as remarking that this even symbolized the conscious recognition by American ethnics of the importance of their own past both to themselves and the nation as a whole.

And yet, important as it is, Italian-American cinema is represented in the works of only two artists and is not likely to be a long-lived phenomenon. It is rather a manifestation of what Richard Alba describes as the "twilight of ethnicity."[45] Especially apposite is Hegel's observation that the owl of Minerva flies only when the shades of night are falling; that is, reflection begins its task only when experience has lost its vividness and immediacy. Alba suggests that the current accent on ethnicity in America, far from signifying the solidarity and vitality of ethnic groups, as many assume, indicates their decline. Ethnic consciousness is largely nostalgia, a self-conscious recollection of what is passing or long past, of what was once experienced spontaneously, immediately, without self-reflection. Herein lies the key to Michael Corleone's torment in *The Godfather*. The works of Coppola and Scorsese are thus signal examples, and paramount ones aesthetically, of this twilight of ethnicity. Their aesthetic and cultural dignity is that, more than naive exercises in sentiment or nostalgia, they hold in double consciousness American-Italian life and history, its defects and virtues.

Notes

1. See Vittorio Zagarrio, "F.C.-F. C. Ovvero: *Italian-American Dream* dal film muto alle television," *Cinema & Cinema* 38 (January–March 1984) 37–38.

2. Raymond Carney, *American Vision: The Films of Frank Capra* (Cambridge: Cambridge University Press, 1986), 36–39; Zagarrio, 40. On Gilbert Sorrentino's suppression of his ethnicity in his works, see John Paul Russo, "The Poetics of Gilbert Sorrentino," *RSA* (*Rivista di studi anglo-americani*) 4–5 (1985): 281–303.

3. On the conflict between Italian values and those of the American core culture, see Robert Casillo, "Dirty Gondola: The Image of Italy in American Advertisements," *Word and Image* 1 (October–December 1985): 330–47.

4. See Guido Fink, "Orgoglio e prejiudizio: stereotipici Hollywoodiana e doppiaggio di casa nostra," *Cinema & Cinema* 38 (January–March 1984): 26–27, 29.

5. Richard Gambino, *Blood of My Blood: The Dilemma of the Italian Americans* (New York: Doubleday, 1975), 274, 277, 287, 288, 300; hereafter cited as Gambino.

6. Joseph Papaleo, "Ethnic Pictures and Ethnic Fate: The Media Image of Italian Americans," in *Ethnic Images in American Film and Television*, ed. Randall M. Miller (Philadelphia: The Back Institute, 1978), 93–94.

7. Edward Said, *Orientalism* (New York: Pantheon, 1978), passim.

8. Papaleo, "Ethnic Pictures and Ethnic Fate," 94; Richard N. Juliani, "The Image of the Italian in American Film and Television," also in *Ethnic Images in American Film and Television*, 99–100.

9. An exception is *Fair Lady* (1922) which Eugene Rosow describes as an underworld melodrama and Sicilian Black Hand revenge story; see Rosow, *Born to Lose: The Gangster Film in America* (New York: Oxford University Press, 1978), 114; hereafter cited as Rosow.

10. Rosow, 43.

11. Carlos Clarens, *Crime Movies: From Griffith to the Godfather and Beyond* (New York: W. W. Norton and Co., 1980), 54.

12. Clarens, 56.

13. See Jack Shadoian, *Dreams and Dead Ends: The American Gangster/Crime Film* (Cambridge: MIT Press, 1977), 31, 37.

14. Clarens, 85.

15. Noted by Clarens, 93.

16. See Gerald Mast, *Howard Hawks, Storyteller* (New York: Oxford University Press, 1982), 74.

17. Clarens, 98.

18. Robert Warshow, "The Gangster as Tragic Hero," in *The Immediate Experience* (New York: Doubleday, 1962), 90.

19. Colin McArthur, *Underworld USA* (New York: Viking Press, 1972), 35; hereafter cited as McArthur.

20. See Clarens, 253, discussing Roger Corman's *St. Valentine's Day Massacre*.

21. See Rosow, 88, 85.

22. Clarens, 270; see also Clarens, "The Godfather Saga," *Film Comment* 14 (January–February 1978), 21.

23. Noted by McArthur, 59.

24. Gambino, 288.

25. Noted by Guido Fink after Paul Bernard Plouffe's University of California (Berkeley) thesis, "The Tainted Adam"; see Fink, "Stereotipici Hollywoodiani," 31–32.

26. McArthur, 107.

27. According to Robert Ottoson, "the film...closely portrays the banking practices of the Giannini family (founders of the Bank of America in San Francisco). Not only were the Gianninis disturbed over this invasion of privacy, but Twentieth-Century Fox's president in New York, Spyros Skouras, took the story as a personal affront, and as a result the film received limited distribution." See Ottoson, *A Reference Guide to American Film Noir* (Metuchen, N.J.: Scarecrow Press, 1981), 85–86.

28. See *The Oxford Companion to Film*, Liz-Anne Bawden, ed. (New York: Oxford University Press, 1976), 451.

29. See for instance the character of Magua in *The Last of the Mohicans*. On the other hand, such noble Indians as Uncas in the same work and Hard Heart in *The Prairie* resemble the ancient Romans.

30. See Fink, "Orgoglio e prejiudizio," 31; Peter Bondanella, "*Christ in Concrete* di Edward Dmytryk e il neorealismo italiano," also in *Cinema & Cinema* 38 (January–March 1984): 9–16.

31. See Gambino, 274–84.

32. Quoted in Clarens, 272.

33. See Gambino, 287.

34. Clarens, 270–71.

35. See McArthur, 132; Rosow, 317–20.

36. John Paul Russo, "The Hidden Godfather: Plenitude and Absence in Francis Ford Coppola's *Godfather I* and *II*," in *Support and Struggle: Italians and Italian Americans in a Comparative Perspective*, eds. Joseph L. Tropea et. al. (Staten Island, N.Y.: American Italian Historical Association, 1986), 263–64.

37. McArthur, 30–31.

38. See Richard D. Alba, *Italian Americans: Into the Twilight of Ethnicity* (Englewood Cliffs, N.J.: Prentice Hall, 1985), 64.

39. There is in at least one instance historical link between Italian opera and Italian-American crime. Clarens notes that "grand opera and the Mafia shared the headlines in New York...when a bomb was planted at a Caruso recital at the Met, an episode reenacted in *Pay or Die* (271)."

40. Gambino, 16.

41. See Russo, passim.

42. Quoted in Gambino, 39.

43. Clarens, 286–87.

44. The discussion of *Mean Streets* in this and the preceding paragraph is based on Casillo, "Catholicism and Violence in the Films of Martin Scorsese," in *Support and Struggle: Italians and Italian-Americans in Comparative Perspective*, 284–85.

45. Alba, *Italian Americans: Into the Twilight of Ethnicity*, passim.

America through Italian/American Eyes:
Dream or Nightmare?

Historically, America has been the great dream for virtually all disenfran-
chised, oppressed peoples, and in particular for Italians. Obviously, it is
purely coincidental that the death of Lorenzo de' Medici and Christopher
Colombus's discovery of America occur in the same year. At the same time,
it is ironic and yet strangely meaningful that the death of an early, albeit
inchoate, dream of unification and national identity of Italy coincides with
the discovery of a new dream of hope. It might seem redundant to recall
that Italy was for centuries considered only "ein geograhischer Begriff,"[1]
that it was described as "più stiava che li Ebrei, più serva ch'e' Persi, più
dispersa che li Ateniesi, sanza capo, sanza ordine, battuta, spogliata, lacera,
corsa, et avessi sopportato d'ogni sorte ruina,"[2] and that the social, political,
and economic conditions of the country were, for the average citizen,
abysmal. It would be redundant were it not that for the most successful
young Italian/American filmmakers, those for whom the American Dream
would appear to have come true, it seems to have become a nightmare.[3]
This, in any case, is the way in which they tend to depict it. What the
overwhelming majority of their films shares is a sense that the American
Dream is a lie, a trick, and a deception.[4]

Is this a valid representation of the immigrant experience?[5] There can
be no hard and fast answer to this question.[6] The response will vary for each
individual, and for each individual it will be a function of past experiences,
be they lived personally, read, or learned by word of mouth. I will contend,
however, that the younger Italian/American filmmakers know primarily and
almost exclusively their Italian/American heritage; they know little or nothing of their Italian heritage. For them Italy has become either the mythical
land of loving, exuberant relatives, Dante, beautiful scenery, folklore, food,
and song, or it is entirely irrelevant. The younger Italian/American filmmakers have no firsthand experience of the social and economic conditions that
drove their forefathers to immigrate to this country, nor do they demonstrate,
for the most part, any awareness of their literary or cinematic depictions. If
any of them have read Verga, Levi, Fenoglio, and Silone, or have seen
Visconti's *La terra trema*, Germi's *Divorzio all'italiana*, De Seta's *Banditi a
Orgosolo*, the Taviani Brothers' *Padre Padrone*, Rosi's *Il bandito Giuliano*,
and Olmi's *The Tree of the Wooden Clogs*, it certainly is not apparent from
their films. Still, since it is virtually impossible for an American to understand the conditions that existed in many parts of Italy around the turn of
this century unless it is by analogy to contemporary Third World conditions,
this lacuna is understandable, albeit regrettable.

Michael Cimino depicts an incident in *The Sicilian* that would have been
instructive if it had been able to convey to an American audience the
economic plight of Sicily in the post-World-War-II years. Instead it merely

generated snickers in the audience when I saw the film. When Salvatore Giuliano announces his intention of killing the barber who had betrayed him, the barber asks the bandit to give his shoes and his watch to his son. In sociohistorical terms, this was not a symbolic, melodramatic, theatrical gesture by the barber, intended to elicit the pity of Giuliano. Rather, knowing that he was about to die, the barber left a very concrete legacy to his son. In Sicily, and in fact in much of rural Italy, including the mountains of the already industrialized Piedmont when I lived there in the fifties, shoes and clothes were passed on from father to son and from mother to daughter whenever possible. One of the most heartrending descriptions of an analogous episode occurs in Verga's short story "Rosso Malpelo", one of his many short stories describing the life of Sicilian peasants around the turn of the century, which first appeared in *Vita dei campi* in 1880. It conveys the quality of life of Italian peasants in a way that sociological studies cannot.[7] The reality depicted in this story is part of the consciousness of any socially aware Italian, thanks to the reading of the works of authors such as those mentioned above. Through their works, and in particular in Verga's short stories, the realities of life in Sicily—the hunger, the oppression, the condemnation to unrelieved misery—are presented dispassionately as the inevitable burden of fate. Individuals in this world live a life that Pasolini would have described as pre-Christian and subproletarian.[8] More recently, the films mentioned earlier in this essay have conveyed cinematically much the same reality. But this is a world that is alien to the Italian/American filmmakers. Their frame of reference when looking at America is the American dream, the great American myth they have inherited from their ancestors. When measured against that dream, the historical America must come up short. The experiences of Italian Americans in this country can be considered positive only when contrasted with what they fled. Per se, Italian Americans encountered what every immigrant confronted, and worse: hunger, discrimination, hard work when it was available, exploitation, and general alienation.

Giacosa and Puccini

The contradictory nature of the American dream has been the source of much commentary from before the genesis of the United States as a nation.[9] This contradiction received what is perhaps its earliest Italian artistic treatment in Giacomo Puccini's *Madame Butterfly* and *The Girl from the Golden West*, two works that manifested characteristics found in many of the films of the Italian/American directors. Both of these operas are concerned with the lure of America and with the often racist betrayal of that dream. Both displace the focus of the oppression from Italians in America to other locations, times, and ethnic groups following the Italian tradition—compelled by a history of foreign domination—of discussing political problems through historical analogies.[10] Both works reflect the often contradictory experiences of Puccini and of Giuseppe Giacosa, his librettoist for *La Bohème*, *Tosca*, and *Madame Butterfly* and author of the fascinating but virtually forgotten *Impressioni d'America*, which first appeared in 1892.[11] In

Madame Butterfly, perhaps Puccini's best-known opera, Pinkerton represents both the fascinating energy and appeal of America, and its betrayal of those who, like Cio-Cio-San, succumb to it. In *The Girl from the Golden West*, a work that is virtually unknown to all but the most dedicated opera fans, the situation is even more explicit. Minnie, the beautiful, pistol-packing hostess of the Polka, a mining-camp saloon in California, is the miners' Bible-quoting schoolmarm. The miners, a motley, whiskey-guzzling crowd, never quite dare threaten her virtue. They spend their time feeling homesick, worrying about their gold, preparing to lynch random strangers, and dancing with each other. Jack Rance, the sheriff, is a gambler who wants Minnie for himself. However, he loses a crooked card game against her and so must free the man she loves, the notorious Bandit Ramerrez, who tries to conceal his origins by calling himself Dick Johnson. Ramerrez is tall, handsome, dresses fashionably, "robs you like a gentleman," and says he has never killed anyone. When the miners finally capture and prepare to lynch him, Minnie, clenching a pistol between her teeth, boldly rides up at the last moment and orders, begs, and pleads with them not to hang her lover. The miners, touched by her love for the bandit, set him free, and the two lovers exit singing, "Good-bye, beloved country; good-bye my California."

The Girl from the Golden West is patently intended as a metaphor for the Italian encounter with America. Minnie, the paragon of virtue, stands for the American Dream. She is the object of desire who, in the midst of "curses and quarrels," shares the "worries and the wants" of the miners. Even though she contradicts herself often she is the promise that beckons immigrants to America. In the opera, all persons are defined in terms of their relationship to her and to the ideal she represents. But the dream is set against a dark background. In a world in which money rules, Minnie is also a commodity exploited by the bartender, Nick. And, as in American society, racism is to be found in the opera. Favorite insults are "yellow face" and "Chinese face." The miners, in their propensity for violence and excessive drinking, represent the archetypal America described by Giacosa. "Americans enjoy being drunk more than drinking.[12] . . . In the not too distant past [the Americans] must have been unrestrained and extremely violent . . . [it is therefore] comprehensible that . . . good manners be enforced by the policeman."[13] The opera's plot turns on the relationship between Ramerrez, the outsider, and Minnie. Like the immigrants described by Giacosa, Ramerrez has fatalistically accepted his destiny. Suddenly he perceives Minnie, the dream. But what can he do? If she learns the truth about him, that he is not Dick Johnson but the bandit Ramerrez, she must reject him. And yet, somehow, the miracle takes place. Even though he has merely been spared and not accepted by the miners, who represent the common man, the dream itself, Minnie, not only accepts him, she prefers him above all the others. Why Nick and the miners agree to free Ramerrez becomes clear in the last scene of the opera. In their eyes, not the least of the bandit's crimes is the "theft of [Minnie's] love." And yet, when she reminds them of her many kindnesses towards them, they are moved. Puccini would seem to be saying that each immigrant group fears the competition of the next. It is only when the former immigrants realize that a universal welcome is the basis of the

American dream that they can overcome their fear of the most recent foreigner.

The Girl of the Golden West contains the two major components of the American myth. Hope and brutality are seen in their extreme manifestations: the Golden West and the lynch mob. The happy ending of Puccini's last American opera would seem to suggest that for him the dream, the often flawed message of hope, would appear to be the predominant emotion. It is ironic that his tragedy, *Madame Butterfly*, in which the other woman dies, continues to be massively successful and popular, while *The Girl of the Golden West* is virtually forgotten. One cannot help but wonder what would have happened if Pinkerton had not married Kate, if he had instead returned to Nakasaki and married Cio-Cio-San in extremis. Would the reception of *The Girl of the Golden West* have been different if Ramerrez had really been Dick Johnson, if he had not, in other words, been Hispanic? More to the point, are Americans even now ready to accept a Caucasian, pistol-packing, female heroine who rescues a minority hero/bandit and then goes riding off into the sunset with him?

Michael Cimino

The tradition of not discussing directly the more negative aspects of the American experience for Italian Americans is emulated by Michael Cimino in *Thunderbolt and Lightfoot* (1974), *The Deer Hunter* (1978), *Heaven's Gate* (1981), *The Year of the Dragon* (1985), and *The Sicilian* (1987). Writing about Michael Cimino became something of a cottage industry from 1981 to 1986, when in the aftermath of the commercial debacle of *Heaven's Gate*, many vented the spleen generated by the commercial success of *The Deer Hunter*.[14] This notwithstanding, he continues to be an elusive target whose interviews and opinions appear far more frequently in French cinema journals than in American ones.[15] What is clear is that, given the opportunity, he is a monomaniacal perfectionist whose ego and confidence in himself as artist rank with those of that earlier Michael who was more angelic in name only.[16] His battles with his producers have been as brutally acrimonious as any between Michelangelo and his patrons, and the results have been in some ways as grandiose. Cimino is absolutely ruthless in the defense of the integrity of his projects. There is some debate as to what he might be capable of doing if forced to bend by *force majeure*. Steven Bach in *Final Cut* writes that Cimino allegedly offered to compromise rather than lose all control over the film when Bach threatened to remove the director from the production of *Heaven's Gate*.[17] According to others, including Bach, inspired by Ayn Rand's *The Fountainhead*, Cimino threatened to destroy *The Deer Hunter* (1978) rather than allow Universal Studios to shorten it from three hours to a more conventional length.[18] What is certain is that, from his earliest feature film, *Thunderbolt and Lightfoot* (1974), a work he both wrote and directed, Cimino's protagonists have seemed to be archetypal, rugged American individualists.

Thunderbolt and Lightfoot

In *Thunderbolt and Lightfoot*, Thunderbolt (Clint Eastwood) appears as a war veteran turned bank robber. He is joined by Lightfoot (Jeff Bridges), an equally iconoclastic escapee from Middle America. Their unrepentant thwarting of every law of the land is set against the majestic backdrop of wide open vistas of the American West and against the images of some of its less prepossessing inhabitants. The film offers no real explanation for the alienation of the two protagonists, nor does it appear to condemn them in any way. On the contrary, notwithstanding their ruthlessly antisocial behavior, the viewer is co-opted into rooting for them, as they wreak havoc, simply because they are *simpatici* in some odd way. The film in this sense is reminiscent of Sergio Leone's "Spaghetti" Westerns starring Clint Eastwood. There too the protagonist was not the hero in the conventional Hollywood sense. Rather, particularly in *The Good, the Bad, and the Ugly* (1968), he was an individual who followed his own code, one that was only marginally less brutal and self-serving than that of the Bad and the Ugly. In all those films, however, the criminality of the establishment so far overreached that of the individual outlaw as to make any crime committed by the latter pale in comparison. The futility and criminal stupidity of war is depicted in *The Good, the Bad, and the Ugly* in the Civil War battlefield scenes through images and terms that have few equals in film. In *Thunderbolt and Lightfoot*, these conceptual premises are suggested more by what is not said or shown than by what is, a process that will become a trademark of Cimino. How and why does a war hero who has won the Silver Star end up robbing banks with the very weapon with which he earned his medals? How and why does a boy on his way to a boarding school become a vagrant and a thief? Whence comes Lightfoot's knowledge and love of nature? A hint is offered in the scenes in which he is approached by a used-car salesman, a character who serves as the symbol for civilized America. Under the unctuous veneer of good-old-boy charm, there lies the coldly rapacious heart of a legally sanctioned thief. That Lightfoot steals the car from him thus becomes a manifestation of poetic justice of sorts. By extension, the open embrace of a life of crime by the protagonists seems preferable to the mean-spirited, cowardly, money-grubbing existences of the average citizen.

The Deer Hunter

William J. Palmer argues that the more significant films of the seventies are all at bottom concerned with the Vietnam War.[19] While Thunderbolt is a Korean war veteran, it is fairly clear, in retrospect that this film, like *M*A*S*H*, is in fact a commentary on the more recent conflict. One might thus argue that, in addition to the theological and Marxist alienations, war generates an alienation from society and that the alienated individual may well turn his war-making skills against the very society that trained him. If in *Thunderbolt and Lightfoot* we see the results of this phenomenon, in *The Deer Hunter* we are shown the causes. When it first appeared, the latter film was both acclaimed and reviled.[20] By 1979, America was ready to begin the process of historical revisionism through fiction and film, which has always characterized the popular perception of our history. Thus the Right and what might be loosely defined as Middle America perceived *The Deer Hunter* as a glorification of American values, of the heroism of the average American boy, and an indictment of all Vietnamese, enemies and allies, as subhuman monsters who should have been nuked into kingdom come. The Left, which according to Ernest Callenbach means virtually all academic film criticism in this country since 1974,[21] roundly condemned the film as being at least one or more of the following: mendacious, chauvinistic, racist, and fascist.[22] The extreme manifestation of this negative reaction to the film may well have been that of *Jump Cut*, which allegedly refused to accept a review of the film on the grounds that it does not publish positive reviews of fascist films.[23] More recently the film has been the object of more sober reappraisals that have come to recognize many of its merits. It is ironic, however, that some of the very essays that undertake to re-evaluate the film—with the significant exception of Robin Wood in *Hollywood from Vietnam to Reagan* and Michael Bliss in *Martin Scorsese and Michael Cimino*—end up damning it with faint praise.[24]

The Deer Hunter (1978) opens with images of the flames of a Carlton, Pennsylvania, foundry; analogous flames open the first Vietnam combat sequence and the sequence that depicts the fall of Saigon and the evacuation of the Americans. These images connect the three sets of victims of the American dream in the film: the Ukrainian immigrants, the American soldiers, and the South Vietnamese. All three had believed in the promises made implicitly and explicitly by this country. But these pledges are as ephemeral in their present as they were when, to the strains of the "Star-Spangled Banner," Puccini and Giacosa described the significance of the vows of Pinkerton, the "yankee vagabondo" in *Madame Butterfly*:

> He's not satisfied with life
> unless he makes his own
> the flowers of every shore...
> So I'm marrying
> in Japanese fashion
> for nine hundred and
> ninety-nine years. With the right
> to be freed every month:
> America forever!

Cio-Cio-San is an early Oriental victim of the American propensity to undertake commitments that it has no real intention of honoring. Vietnam is one of the more recent. But the American proclivity for possessing the "flowers of every shore" is not limited to those that can be found overseas. The Ukrainian community to which Michael (Robert DeNiro), Nick (Christopher Walken), Linda (Meryl Streep), Steven (John Savage), Stan (John Cazale), Axel (Chuck Aspegren), and John (George Dzundza) belong has also been victimized. Only the external trappings and rituals of their ethnic culture remain and even they are performing at best a holding action. The elegant and stately marriage of Steven and Angela degenerates into drunken chaos in the subsequent reception. The young people have been largely Americanized: Michael drives a gigantic Cadillac; Steven's fiancee is pregnant, but not by him; several of them work in the steel mill and live from paycheck to paycheck in a liquor and fatigue induced stupor. Their values are 1960s American. In an unquestioning sort of way they believe in America, in patriotism, in friendship, in doing one's duty, in getting drunk, in marriage—so long as it does not interfere too much with time out with the guys—in courage, and in manhood. Their capacity for reflection is limited and is manifested by the inarticulate way in which they express themselves whenever they attempt to convey any abstraction. Michael's obsession with "one shot" and with "this is this" are not as ridiculous as they might seem at first, they are simply rendered such by his inability to express himself. Nick's attempts at verbalization are equally inchoate. Steven cannot articulate his feelings about marrying a woman impregnated by someone other than himself. Linda escapes speaking about her feelings by talking about trivialities and by busying herself in physical activity. Angela, to the best of my recollection, says nothing throughout the film. This failure to verbalize reaches its zenith, or nadir if you prefer, in Axel, whose dialog in the film seems to be limited to "Fucking A!" They live in an environment that has been destroyed by the source of their livelihood: the steel mill. But there is in them no perception of this. They have no sense that the mill is in any way responsible for what it is doing to them and to their world. The mill is as much a part of their natural scenery as the mountains are. They do not think of themselves as cogs in the machinery, to be used or expended as profits dictate. They live before Vietnam and before the closing of the Pennsylvania (and Indiana) steel mills. To some limited extent the hunting trips represent, at least in Michael, a manifestation of his desire for a less chaotic world.

A former professor of mine once quoted an Italian saying according to which, by the time a man is twenty-five, he has made a man and killed a man. By this he meant that in order to be an adult a man must have fathered a son and been to war. If marriage is a fundamental ritual, war is another. The force of the societal and/or biological conditioning—I am not interested in debating here which is more or less responsible—that pushes young men to prove themselves by exposing themselves to privation, pain, danger, and death cannot be underestimated.[25] For Michael, Nick, and Steve, it manifests itself in their high-risk occupation. It manifests itself in Michael's reckless driving, in Nick's compulsive gambling, in Stan's concealed gun, and in the relentless drinking of all. It is the drive underlaying the hunt, a ritual that validates an individual's manhood both as provider and as potential warrior. Michael's "one shot" acquires importance in this context, not merely as an affectation, but as a manifestation of those skills that make him a better provider and a better warrior, and thus, presumably, a better man than his companions. Finally, the drive pushes them all to the supreme test, that of war itself. This drive was felt with particular intensity in American communities composed of Eastern Europeans. Their countries were overrun by the Soviets and are still, from the perspective of many of them, enslaved by the Russians and their proxies. This is particularly true of Ukranians whose oppression by Russians antecedes the advent of communism by centuries and who suffered over eight million dead as a result of Stalinist repression. Nor should we be surprised that Michael chose to join the Special Forces. Eastern European refugees, deluded by American promises of assistance in the liberation of their homelands, joined the Special Forces in droves at least until the Vietnam conflict. But modern, technological war makers do not want heroes or even warriors. They need, or think they need, accountants, logisticians, and cogs that will roll merrily off to die in accordance with the plans from higher headquarters.[26] This process of depersonalized slaughter offers the individual little sense of accomplishment, particularly if he is on the receiving end of its fury. This is true, as we have learned from Vietnam veterans of both genders, for virtually all who were involved, however marginally.

This sense of futility has extended from the war to the hearth. The earlier virile values have lost all meaning. Even before Vietnam, for Michael, there was no longer anything romantic about being a "deerslayer." As the word suggests, with the advent of modern weapons, it simply became a meaningless slaughter; it no longer represented the skills required of the heroic individual for his own survival and that of those dependent upon him. Being a "deerhunter," conversely, still had romantic connotations because it implied the emulation of the feats of an earlier model whose behavior, presumably dictated by necessity—Natti Bumpo killed for food—had established a challenge that the superior individual would overcome. This he would do while adhering to a set of rules generated by the behavior of his role model, behavior that originally was dictated by necessity: flintlocks could only fire one shot before the laborious process of muzzleloading was repeated. But after Vietnam, for Michael, being a deerhunter has become meaningless. He has accepted all the romantic/heroic challenges: he is Airborne, Special Forces, and the recipient of, among many others, that which has been called the only meaningful United States Army decoration— the Combat Infantry Badge. But he has also learned what it means to be the hunted, as the film's logo, represented by deer antlers attached to the canopy of the Army Parachute Badge, clearly indicates. Thus it should not be surprising that he refuses to kill the deer in the postwar hunt, that he rejects Cazale's macho pistol-packing posturing, and that he eschews the hero's welcome he has earned but no longer feels he deserves. All he has left are his friends. But that myth too is doomed. Steven has been rendered physically and emotionally impotent by his confrontation with death, while Nick can no longer return to the ersatz thrills furnished by life in a steel-mill town. Whether Russian roulette was ever played in Vietnam is completely irrelevant. That game of chance is intended to convey the horrifying and yet strangely intoxicating emotional intensity experienced in combat.[27] But if war was, traditionally, one of the rituals necessary for growing up, modern war can no longer fulfill that role.[28] With the destruction of the myth comes the end of externally validated meaning. Michael and his friends, however, are not intellectuals. They are incapable of undertaking an analysis of the destruction of their dreams. They are left with an emptiness and an aching void that, from their cultural perspective, can only be filled by recourse to yet another external myth: God. Thus it is that the singing of "God Bless America" at the end of the film, far from being a manifestation of neo-fascist jingoism, is in fact a prayer that expresses not only the protagonists' love for their country, but also their realization that it is in desperate need of guidance.

Heaven's Gate

The contradictions inherent in the American Dream resurface with a vengeance in *Heaven's Gate*, one of the most controversial films ever made, both because of its contents and because of its impact on extrafilmic events. Almost universally panned and even reviled in this country, the film was received enthusiastically in France.[29] The very qualities that had determined the varying and often contradictory responses to *The Deer Hunter*, virtually insured equal but opposite reactions to *Heaven's Gate*. The film was, allegedly, the greatest financial disaster in the history of American cinema. The film was also an unmitigated critical disaster in this country. Writing negative reviews of the film became a steady source of income, almost on the scale of that generated by pseudo-intellectual articles against the use of "hopefully," and culminated in Stephen Bach's eminently readable and rather self-serving *Final Cut*. Why? Granted, the film is long and it adopts many of those that I have defined elsewhere as the characteristics of the "liberated cinema."[30] But it is also highly dramatic and packed with often violent action, and in terms of its pictorial beauty, it is unquestionably on a par with any film ever made. If there ever was a filmic epic poem about the American West, this is it. The problem for critics, industry persons, and the average viewer was that Cimino did to the American West what Dante had done to Florence in particular and Italy in general: he turned over the pretty rocks and showed all the slimy, slithery ugliness that crawls around in the darkness underneath. In *Heaven's Gate*, Cimino makes explicit what had merely been implied in his earlier films. If in his earlier films he had shown the effects of the oppression and exploitation of the American working class, here he shows the concrete, violent manifestations of that oppression precisely where we least expect it—not in the teeming slums of the East, but in the wide open spaces of the West—and against rather unlikely victims—not Southern Europeans, Chinese, Indians, or Blacks, but Germanic and Slavic Europeans.

The film opens on what we are told is Harvard College in 1870.[31] The scions of the great families of America march towards the "sacred valedictory rites" of graduation from the prestigious university to the strains of "The Battle Hymn of the Republic." The Reverend Doctor (Joseph Cotten), amid much ribaldry, attempts to inject a note of seriousness, suggesting that it is the function of the privileged to educate the less fortunate masses. This however limited idealism is repeatedly deflated by the guffaws and general hilarity of the assembled students and is eventually programmatically rejected when William C. Irvine (John Hurt), the drunken, cynical "class orator" in suggestive doggerel intones an establishmentarian poesy in defense of the status quo. The rites of graduation continue with a waltz on the green and a ritualized but intense tussle among the students under the somewhat amused eyes of the belles of this ball. This would appear to be a magical moment for James Averill (Kris Kristofferson). He is clearly *primus inter pares*, but for no clearly discernible reason. He seems rather vacuous, behaves as irresponsibly as any other student, and is distinguishable from the others only because he is a better known actor and the camera focuses on him with some frequency. We do know, from his reaction to an unidentified beautiful young woman, that he is easily overwhelmed by sudden passions and that in their pursuit he will trample others underfoot, as he does when he is the first to claim a bouquet from the tree around which the students had danced and which the Class of 1871 is now defending. This opening sequence, which United Artists wanted to cut and which Cimino considered essential, serves as the first half of the frame of the film.[32] It establishes immediately that, while the privileged in America pay lip service to their obligations to those less fortunate than themselves, they are quite pleased with themselves and feel that the order of society is and should be as immutable as that of nature itself.

The film cuts abruptly to a train in the Wyoming Territory some twenty years later. An aged James, dressed in citified western clothing, is sleeping in an empty passenger compartment of a train. Out the windows of the train, we see indistinct figures huddling by the side of the tracks, and then from a reverse angle shot, we see a mass of persons riding on top of the train in scenes reminiscent of India under the British. We have been shown the privileged and the oppressed. The scene that follows shows us the mechanism that insures that the *status* remains *quo erat ante*. Suddenly, without explanation, the film cuts to a sod hovel where a man, hidden behind some hanging sheets, is butchering a cow with the assistance of his wife and child. From the actions and the tone of their voices—they are speaking a Slavic language—we know that they are terrified. There is a noise. A man's shadow darkens the sheets. The sodbuster identifies himself ("It's me, Michael") repeatedly, and repeatedly asks the unknown person to identify himself. We see the shadow of a shotgun and hear its roar. Michael goes crashing to the ground, his belly torn open. His hysterical, screaming wife comes running and tries futilely to staunch his wounds. The film cuts to Nate Champion (Christopher Walken) as he comes upon what appears to be an endless stream of immigrants. While he has not yet been identified as such, it is clear that he is a paid killer and that he is in no immediate danger of unemployment. We have been dropped into the middle of the notorious Johnson County range wars between the cattle barons and the sodbusters. But the conflict is depicted here in a manner unlike any ever shown in American movies. All the elements that we have come to recognize as characteristic of the American Western are missing. There are no "bad guys" and "good guys." There is not an individual cattle baron who has fought drought, snow, and Indians to conquer his piece of the West and wants to defend it against all comers. Nor is there the megalomaniacal land grabber who wants to become the emperor of the West. Here the cattle barons are rich, seemingly well educated, pampered Easterners and Englishmen who have acquired grazing rights by hook or by crook and plan on keeping them by any and all means including mass murder, thanks to the connivance of friendly politicians ranging from the territorial governor to the president of the United States. Frank Canton (Sam Waterston), the leader of the Stock Growers Association, wears his class privilege with an arrogance that must make any person with a spark of humanity hate him immediately. The sodbusters are hardly more admirable, even though they are occasionally amusing. They are generally violent, contentious, dirty, prudish, hypocritical, moralizing, thieving, cowardly, and self-serving. And while they may elicit our sympathy from time to time, it is only beause they are the victims of so many horrible injustices. As for the protagonists, they are hardly the epitomes of knightly virtues. The motivations of Jim Averill as county marshall are often obscure. While he does quite literally defend widows, orphans, and other assorted oppressed people, he does so only intermittently and often unsuccessfully. His counterpart, Nate Champion, the cattle barons' hired killer, is equally ambiguous. While he occasionally kills in cold blood, he rather obviously has ambivalent feelings about the immigrants and about his profession. As for the object of the sentimental interest of the male protagonists, Ella Watson (Isabelle Huppert), she is the charming, albeit filthy-mouthed madam and major attraction of the local bordello. This, of course, created problems for American viewers and critics who, by and large, are accustomed to being told for whom they should cheer.

The conflict between the Stock Growers Association and motley crew of farmers, small ranchers, and immigrants that came to be known as the Johnson County Cattle War was a relatively insignificant clash between opposing economic interests, but it has been the object of any number of American films. Cimino's version focuses on this conflict in a new and original manner. No one is spared in his indictment of materialism. The stockgrowers association, tired of having their cattle rustled by the poor and greedy immigrants, prepare a death list of 125 names, virtually the entire population of Johnson County. To implement this restoration of law and order, the cattlemen hire mercenaries at five dollars a day and fifty dollars a kill. The immigrants spend more of their time fighting among themselves, enjoying the pleasures of Ella's house of ill repute, betting on cock fights, and roller skating than in preparing to defend themselves against their enemies.[33] These are truly the poor in spirit; they are not merely *umili*, they are the *umiliati* of the world. They are reminiscent of Pasolini's pre-"Abiura dalla trilogia della vita" subproletarians.[34] They do not belong in the same world with Frank Canton, Jim Averill, Billy Irvine, and their ilk. These peasants' history of oppression, hunger, and suffering is etched on their faces. And while they are not particularly intelligent, attractive, or even brave, they have a dogged tenacity and a desperate, suicidal courage in the pursuit of their dream of property and freedom, and for this we feel some measure of sympathy and even admiration for them. This film drives home once again and with greater strength the truth of what Machiavelli said when he wrote that the rich are more dangerous to liberty than the poor because, in addition to the universal desire to acquire, they have the fear of losing their possessions. This is particularly true, he went on, because the rich can effect changes with greater force and speed. Finally, and worst of all, their bad example will tend to excite the desire for revenge, riches, and power among the poor.[35]

The final battle between the mercenaries and the peasants is a fitting *coitus interruptus* to the film. When the immigrants hear that the invaders are coming,[36] they turn on each other in abject terror. The wealthier among them are quite willing to turn the less fortunate over to the stockgrowers; they are virtually all ready to surrender Ella to their oppressors. They quarrel and they whine, but finally, confronted with the knowledge that they are about to die, they head out *en masse* against the hated enemy. Caught by surprise by this unexpectedly united front, the mercenaries circle their wagons and defend themselves. There is more visually stunning carnage in this limited engagement than in many major war films. Finally, when virtually everyone on both sides seems to be dead, just as the immigrants are about to overwhelm the invaders, the U.S. Cavalry arrives, purportedly to arrest the mercenaries and their employers, but in reality, as Jim points out, to save them. The film is almost over. Jim and Ella prepare to leave Johnson County. The white dress that Ella wears for the first time and Jim's attitude towards her suggest that, in the best Hollywood tradition, they will get married and live happily ever after. But this is not Hollywood, it is Cimino. In a last fit of anger, Canton and his thugs ambush Jim, Ella, and their friend John Bridges [sic] (Jeff Bridges). Ella and John fall immediately under a hail of bullets. Jim, deadly as always, kills Canton and routs his men. He then cradles in his arms the dead Ella, whose dress is stained with the bright crimson of her blood. Once again there is an abrupt temporal dislocation. We are now in 1903 off Newport, Rhode Island, aboard Jim's luxurious yacht. He enters a cabin. We see a sleeping woman and a picture of Jim and the beautiful young woman we had seen in the opening sequences of the film. Presumably this is the same woman. She asks for a cigarette. She seems sick or drugged. They look at each other. She scrutinizes him. He avoids her gaze and looks away.[37]

Italians, starting with Sergio Leone, have transformed the Western, if not beyond recognition, certainly beyond any return to its white hat/black hat simplistic dualisms. *Heaven's Gate*, although visually splendid, intensifies this destruction of all the myths upon which the Western, and thus good part of America's image of itself, is founded. Here Jim Averill, the knight in not-so-shining armor, is at best incapable of defending not only women, children, and the poor, but also his own woman who, far from being a virginal damsel, or even a golden hearted whore, is rather aggressively mercenary. The image of America as land of opportunity for the wretched masses from distant teeming shores is completely destroyed. What we see are images of oppression that have parallels only in Tzarist Russia and in Prussian Germany. These parallels are underlined by the fact that the peasants speak Slavic and Germanic languages and by the fur hats worn by Canton and his military advisor, Major Frank Wolcott, which are very reminiscent of those worn by Cossacks. Is this indictment of America valid? We know that American industrialists, with the connivance and often with the active cooperation of the American government, used mercenaries, the national militia, and even the U.S. Army to quell labor unrest. It should suffice to think of the Haymarket Strike of 1886, the Homestead Strike of 1892, and the Pullman Strike of 1894. One problem adduced by many critics of *Heaven's Gate* is that, while the Johnson County War did in fact take place, it did not occur exactly as described in the film. While many of the characters' names were borrowed from persons who lived in Wyoming around the end of the century, their involvement in the conflict was rather different from that described. Several, Jim Averill and Ella Watson, for example, had been hanged before the conflict ever began. What is more, the final battle did not occur as shown.[38] However, given the liberties that Hollywood Westerns have always taken with history, one cannot or should not fault Cimino on those grounds. But given that he did play fast and easy with history, one can, should, and must ask oneself what he was trying to say, or if one is intimidated by the shibboleth of the intentional fallacy, then one must ask oneself what the film does say.

The occasional speech with socialist and perhaps even communist overtones might lead us to surmise the existence of a Marxist subtext. Consider, for example, Mr. Eggleston's (Brad Dourif) Russian-accented speech to the assembled peasants: "The rich are opposed to anything that will improve conditions in this country, anything that will make it more than a cow pasture for Eastern speculators." The workers arise, take up their weapons, but in the final analysis, what they would appear to lose for the most part is their lives. Even though they might be able to defeat on the battlefield the hired thugs of the "Eastern speculators," they lose because the federal and territorial governments rescue the latter with the U.S. Cavalry. When Jim protests, the cavalry captain says, "It's the rules," meaning, obviously, not only that he must obey orders but also that the Establishment will not allow itself to be undermined, regardless of moral, ethical, or legal considerations. Again, in a narrow sense, the film is not historically correct. But in a broader sense, it is clear that the events described have occurred myriad times in this country. Thus if the message is a Marxist one, it is rather depressing: you can't win for losing. An alternative interpretation, however, is possible. In the mind of European immigrants of the period, America was a mythical land of milk and honey, a veritable heaven on earth. The 160 acres offered by the Homestead Act for fourteen dollars had to make it seem like a truly promised land of opportunity for the starving, desperate, oppressed masses of Europe. Just getting to America implied being on the very threshhold of heaven. Acquiring a piece of land and working it, they thought, would have been heaven itself. But as the film shows, the American West was no earthly paradise. Those who did not have, wanted. And those who had, even among the immigrants, were both afraid of losing what they had and at the same time wanted more. And as the film so eloquently shows, all too many Americans who had much, such as the members of the stockgrowers association, fought with all their might to keep the gates of heaven locked to the most recent arrivals. There were others, however, such as Jim Averill, who already owned a large piece of this heaven on earth and who seemingly felt a moral obligation to share with the newcomers. In order to do so, he upholds the laws and, at least in this sense, generally behaves as a responsible citizen. He too, in a sense, is at his gate of heaven. Not a material heaven, for he has much wealth, but an intangible heaven generated by his sense of justice and equity. In his struggle to pass through his gate, he is reminiscent of the rich young man who came to Jesus and asked how he could inherit eternal life. Jesus answered, "Do not murder, do not commit adultery, do not steal, do not give false testimony, do not defraud, honor your father and mother." The youth replied, "Teacher, all these things I have kept since I was a boy." Jesus looked at him and loved him. "One thing you lack," he said. "Go, sell everything you have and give to the poor and you will have treasure in heaven. Then come, follow me." At this the man's face fell. He went away sad, because he had great wealth. Jesus looked around and said to his disciples, "How hard it is for the rich to enter the kingdom of God!" The disciples were amazed at his words, but Jesus said again, "It is easier for a camel to go through the eye of a needle than for a rich man to enter the Kingdom of God."[39] As the film ends, Jim looks off with sadness (in two versions towards the setting sun and, hence, towards the West) towards that heaven that can never be his because he has been unable to give up his wealth and give of himself, and not of his things. This reading of the film lets us infer an indictment not only of Jim as individual but of all the characters. By extension, it would seem to argue that American capitalism, even at its best and most humane, continues to foster the aggressive materialism that generates bloodshed at home and abroad.

Year of the Dragon

The period following *Heaven's Gate* was not an easy one for Cimino. Many thought he would never be allowed to make another film. His faith in himself, however, never waned.[40] The high esteem in which he is held in Europe, and in France in particular, cannot but have helped him.[41] With *Year of the Dragon* (1985), Cimino could have repeated the commercial success of *The Deer Hunter*. *Year of the Dragon* has all the elements that have transformed the Clint Eastwood, Chuck Norris, Charles Bronson, and Sylvester Stallone films into box office bonanzas: a threatening, seamy, crime-ridden major metropolis; exotic, foreign, ruthless criminals; an equally exotic and foreign lust object; a criminal justice system that has not merely compromised with the forces of evil, it has totally capitulated; and a hero who is relentlessly outspoken and dogged in his unwillingness to give an inch to criminals, affirmative action, and the authorities. Martin Scorsese's *Taxi Driver* (1976) has shown how far this formula can be pushed and still be commercially successful.[42]

The opening shots of the film establish immediately the opposing forces. The exotic enemy is represented by the funeral of a Chinese crime lord at which the Chinese wear white as a sign of mourning. Among those present are the traditional bosses, seemingly rather pathetic, harmless, and often crippled old men who, as is revealed later in the film, are intended to be the analogs of their traditional Italian/American counterparts. Also present is Go Joey Tai (John Lone), the young turk of Chinatown. Slender, modern, elegant, and sleek, he is clearly meant to be reminiscent of Al Pacino in *The*

Godfather films. But something is missing. He is incapable of expressing menace on the screen. He is too pretty and too effeminate to convey more than peevish anger. He also seems to be completely without loyalties. In his climb to power, he has had his father-in-law murdered, and with one exception, he consistently betrays both his superiors and his subordinates.[43] The ineffectual and compromised authorities are represented by a stolid, obese, uniformed, and helmeted equestrian new centurion whose mirror glasses conceal his blindness to what transpires on his beat as much as they hide him from those around him. Tracy Tzu (Ariane) serves a double and rather contradictory function. On the one hand, she represents the media. As such she is aggressive, insensitive, and masculine. Her ethics do not extend beyond her professional self-interest. On the other hand, she is also meant to be the exotic lust object. The problem is that her behavior and appearance are somewhat masculine and asexual. All around them, we have the maelstrom that is Cimino's version of New York's Chinatown. A composite of various Asian cities and several American Chinatowns, it captures the feeling of "Chinatown" far better than any single city could. Into this cauldron plunges Captain Stanley White (Mickey Rourke), newly tasked with suppressing the Chinese youth gangs, while not interfering with the established arrangements between his superiors and the Triads, the Chinese criminal organizations. A rumpled mess whose appearance is an objective correlative for his disrespect for all conventions, Stanley White refuses to play the game by crooked rules. He is a policeman and he will go after all crime, regardless of arrangements, deals, or prior understandings. He is, in many ways, the epitome of the American hero. He has no antecedents (he has changed his name, even though he does not conceal that he is of Polish extraction) nor any offspring (according to his wife he deliberately avoids impregnating her). In short, he has neither past, with the exception of the experience of war (Vietnam), nor future. He lives for the moment, driven by his personal furies, completely alienated from all society. He has more in common with the other outsiders, Tracy Tzu and Joey Tai, than with his friend and colleague Louis Bukowski (Ray Barry), or his wife, Connie White (Caroline Kava). Unlike the traditional American hero, however, Stanley White never finds his moral barycenter. While he knows the history of the oppression of the Chinese in this country and appears to empathize with them, he speaks and acts in ways that can only be described as racist. That he ends up killing certain individuals who, some might argue, probably deserve it, is as accidental as it was in the case of Travis Bickle in *Taxi Driver*. Furthermore, an even larger number of completely innocent people suffer because of his monomania. Thus as character, he elicits neither the facile sympathy of the liberal Left, nor the cheers of the racist Right. The film's refusal to give us easy answers is programmatically reinforced on a filmic level, particularly by the circular shots and the scarcity of reverse angle shots, in a deliberate rejection of the Manichean characteristics of the screen.[44]

The response to *Year of the Dragon* has been ambivalent at best. When questioned about the violent reaction to the film in the Chinese American community,[45] Cimino replied that it occurred because the film was too close to the truth. He went on to add that *Year of the Dragon* was well received by younger Chinese American viewers because it shows strong Chinese on an equal footing with white people for the first time.[46] The reaction of mainland Chinese youths at Purdue University is less favorable. Many of them saw the film several times, but while they are intrigued by the depiction of the Chinese American community in the film, they feel somewhat insulted by its insinuation that the Chinese are incapable of ruling themselves and allegedly need a white person to save them from themselves.[47] Their reaction, like that of all who condemned the film because of its purported racism, foregrounds a problem that lies at the heart of the film, to wit: does the point of view of one or more protagonists reflect that of the film? Toubiana identified the problem ("On a plus parlé du racisme supposé de *Year of the Dragon* que du film, et c'est peut-être embêtant") and stated categorically: "*Year of the Dragon*, qui est le film d'un des dix plus grands cinéastes au monde actuellement est exempt des dangers idéologiques [d]ont [sic] on l'accuse à tort et à travers....Confondre ce que dit ou fait un personnage avec le point de vue du film, laisse rêveur."[48]

With *Year of the Dragon*, Cimino continued a depiction of America that, to borrow a term coined by Pasolini, might be defined as analogical.[49] As we have already noted, Cimino's films do not even attempt to be historically accurate. Rather, they would appear to be metaphors for his evolving perception of the American experience. By the time *Year of the Dragon* appeared, Cimino had already shown the effects of materialism at home and abroad (*Thunderbolt and Lightfoot, Heaven's Gate, The Deer Hunter*). He had also shown us the failure of capitalism and Marxism, the foremost contemporary materialist ideologies. With *Year of the Dragon*, he returns once again to these concerns.[50] He had already depicted the physically and spiritually destructive impact of American materialistic imperialism as it affected immigrants to the Old West in *Heaven's Gate* and their descendants in the smokestack heartland of America in *The Deer Hunter*. In *Year of the Dragon*, past and present are conflated into the experience of Chinese immigrants to this country from the 1850s to the present. The film also returns to the notion that oppression is likewise destructive to oppressors, be they willing (Joey Tai, Louis Bukowski) or unwilling (Stanley White, Tracy Tzu) participants. This is true for the protagonists of *Heaven's Gate, The Deer Hunter*, and *Year of the Dragon*. *Year of the Dragon* in addition reiterates with even greater insistence the importance of commitments, regardless of the cause. This quality, which Cimino says he had found in the figure of Christ in *Christ in Concrete*, is what distinguishes Thunderbolt (*Thunderbolt and Lightfoot*), Michael (*The Deer Hunter*), Jim Averill (*Heaven's Gate*), Stanley White (*Year of the Dragon*), and Salvatore Giuliano (*The Sicilian*) from those around them. The novelty introduced by *Year of the Dragon* is that here, for the first time, the protagonist after a traumatic, epiphanic experience—his duel to the death with Joey Tai—no longer has any second thoughts about the validity of what he is doing. While the earlier films reflected a world of meaningless materialism (*Thunderbolt and Lightfoot*) and the self-doubt and anguish that characterized post-Vietnam America (*The Deer Hunter, Heaven's Gate*), with Stanley White in *Year of the*

Dragon Cimino is depicting an aspect of America that says, in essence, "I know what is right and I will act accordingly, regardless of the consequences." This attitude created difficulties for many, even among those who most respect Cimino's work. When questioned by *Cahiers du Cinéma*, Cimino categorically denied that the final scene of the film is a criticism of Stanley White and of this seeming rebirth of interventionist if not imperialist attitudes in this country.[51] The reaction of *Cahiers du Cinéma* is to argue that Cimino does not adopt a critical posture vis-à-vis his protagonists, rather "[il] croit au discours de *chaque* personnage...sans hiérarchie de regard."[52] In this way they are able to dismiss Cimino's reading of his own film.[53] Cimino has become unconsciously, in their eyes, the interpreter of the aspirations and yearnings of America. His film is, therefore, presumably not an apology for some sort of neo-fascist racism, but a revelation of the despair underlying American attempts to recapture its sense of mission.[54] But more than that, it rediscovers what Pogo said so well many years ago: "We have found the enemy and he is us." The final battle between Stanley White and Joey Tai is a primitive *mano a mano* that not only completely negates the function of the weapons they use, but also visually abolishes all meaningful difference between them. Like two knights of old—or, to be more accurate, like two demented bulls—they charge at each other firing wildly, as indistinguishable from each other as if they were wearing armor. Stanley White, the Captain America of the film, triumphs over his triple threat nemesis, Joey Tai: a criminal, an immigrant, and not a WASP. The problem is that Stanley White himself has no more respect for the law than does Joey Tai, he also is a recent immigrant, and he too is not a WASP. Thus Stanley White's defeat of Joey Tai is also, in a sense, a destruction of himself, and his apotheosis implies, quite literally, his death as a human being. As the film ends there is a slightly blurred still frame of Stanley White and Tracy Tzu. She looks towards him submissively and adoringly as he prepares to charge off to attack more windmills, appropriately enough to the strains of Mahler's "Resurrection." Is he some sort of a savior, as Cimino seems to imply,[55] or is he the equally immortal creature from *Friday the 13th*? This would appear to be the final, paradoxical vision of America experienced by immigrants in Cimino's "trilogy": once again idealistic and energetic, still without past or future, and still mad as a hatter, it destroys family and friends in its monomaniacal determination to extirpate evil and save the world.

It is not surprising that some of the most moving depictions of the immigrant experience have been filmed by an Italian American. What is unexpected is that he focuses almost exclusively on other ethnic groups: the Ukrainians in *The Deer Hunter*, Northern and Eastern Europeans in *Heaven's Gate*, and the Chinese and the Northern Europeans in *Year of the Dragon*. Where, one cannot help but ask oneself, are the Italians? Why are they at best barely present? In *The Deer Hunter*, they are represented by Robert DeNiro and John Cazale as actors, not as protagonists. In *Heaven's Gate*, we hear a few words in dialect, offscreen, at the brothel. In *Year of the Dragon*, we find an Italian shopkeeper on Canal Street, who is being shaken down by Chinese thugs, and an Italian/American godfather, who because of his appearance and his voice cannot help but remind us of Marlon Brando as Don Vito Corleone in *The Godfather*. This godfather, however, is depicted as a pathetic and ineffectual creature by comparison to Don Vito. The answer to all these questions may be found in part in Stanley White's statement that the Mafia is not an Italian invention, that it was, in fact, originally Chinese. Cimino clearly is not here concerned in debating the history of the Mafia. Rather, he is using this device to point out a fact that has long been known by Italian Americans: organized crime in America is not only or even primarily an Italian/American phenomenon.[56] Several other Italian and Italian/American filmmakers have tried repeatedly to correct this media-abetted shibboleth and, predictably, have met with little success. Francis Ford Coppola's *The Godfather, Part II* (1974), which foregrounded the collusion between the establishment of this country and organized crime, was far less popular than *The Godfather* (1972). Sergio Leone's *Once Upon a Time in America* (1984), which depicts American Jews in a manner usually reserved for screen treatments of Italian Americans, was promptly banished from the screen. Francis Ford Coppola's brilliant and delightful *Cotton Club* (1984) goes one step farther. He shows quite clearly that the Irish, Germans, Jews, and Blacks dominated organized crime in this country before the rise to power of Lucky Luciano. Not surprisingly, this film too has been consigned to the critical trash heap. Brian De Palma's *Scarface* (1983) dramatically shows what anyone who does not live in a Trappist monastery already knows: organized crime has now become the battleground of competing Central and South American Hispanics. Cimino's films, as well as the others mentioned above, also all stress that Italian Americans are not the only ones to have immigrated to this country. Other ethnic groups, particularly Northern and Eastern Europeans, have since blended into mainstream America. Like Stanley White, they can become "real" Americans simply by changing their surnames. But this is a luxury that is denied certain Americans, such as Tracy Tzu, who, even though her ancestors had lived in America for five generations, will always be perceived as foreign. This, as Giacosa had already noted at the turn of the century, is also to an extent the continuing fate of Italian Americans.[57]

The Sicilian

As with all of Cimino's films since *The Deer Hunter*, *The Sicilian* was generally either ignored or panned by the American mass media and selectively acclaimed abroad. The review in *Variety*, which describes the film as "a botched telling of the life of postwar outlaw leader Salvatore Giuliano," is fairly typical of the American responses.[58] In France, *Cahiers du Cinéma* continued its love affair with Cimino with a lengthy two-part essay on the shooting of *The Sicilian*.[59] Once the film appeared, *Cahiers du Cinéma* published both a lengthy interview with Cimino and yet another paean to his art that admitted, grudgingly, that it was not without flaws.[60] In England, Alexander Stanbrook, having praised the film to the skies in *Films and Filming*, concludes by asking himself why the film has failed commercially and furnishes an answer that, at first blush, seems almost ludicrous: "Great movies sometimes have to wait for their audiences to grow into them."[61] As a general statement, clearly this is true. Suffice it to think of Fellini (John Simon still has not understood anything past *8½*) and Pasolini (consider the critical reaction to *Decameron*, *Canterbury Tales*, *Arabian Nights*, and *Salò* when those films appeared). It is equally true, as Robin Wood has observed that in America we are less willing to make the effort to understand a difficult American film than a difficult foreign one.[62] Failure to appreciate a film, as Robin Wood said after seeing *Heaven's Gate* for the first few times, may be a function of "passing through that period of adjustment that true innovation always demands."[63] These caveats to the contrary notwithstanding, I suspect that Cimino attempted too much in *The Sicilian* and thus created a work that is perhaps his most intellectually challenging, but that is less satisfying, in the end, than his earlier efforts.[64] As in *Year of the Dragon*, in *The Sicilian* Cimino wanted to deautomatize the response of his viewers, and thus emulated many of the practices of the counter cinema.[65] At the same time, he wanted to create an Italian mythology for American consumption.[66] He wanted Salvatore Giuliano to be a mythical hero and he also wanted it to be crystal clear who the "bad guys" were and are. The result is a film that appeals neither to the general public in search of easy stories and facile myths nor to the intellectual who wants to deconstruct the film, and by extension, society. Still, he has given us a film rich in beautiful images and resonant with intertextual references that should not be ignored. For all its problems, this film has more to say than most filmmakers' best efforts.

   The Sicilian continues to manifest the concern with class conflict that has been more or less explicit in all of Cimino's films. Here the terms of the equation are, to paraphrase that other Sicilian baron, Don Fefé Cefalù (Marcello Mastroianni) in *Divorce Italian Style*, quite mathematical. The entire film is a flashback of the presumed memories of Professor Hector Adonis (Richard Bauer) as he goes to murder Aspanu Pisciotta (John Turturro), the best friend, cousin, and murderer of Salvatore Giuliano (Christopher Lambert). The opening scenes of his flashback present somewhat lyrically, for those who do not know Sicily, the conditions that generated Salvatore Giuliano: the peasants harvest the bountiful fields of the aristocrats under the watchful eyes of their hired thugs on horseback. The aristocrats, here represented by Prince Borsa (Terence Stamp) and Duchess Camilla (Barbara Sukowa), are also accompanied by more hired thugs on horseback as they go riding. Salvatore Giuliano and Aspanu Pisciotta are taking a casket to Montelepre, when suddenly a jeep with three *Carabinieri* appears.[67] The policemen ask them for documents. A tearful Aspanu Pisciotta tries to explain that his poor dear uncle just died. Somehow the casket is knocked over. It contains not a corpse, but grain stolen by Salvatore Giuliano for the starving inhabitants of Montelepre. A policeman shoots and wounds Salvatore Giuliano; both he and Aspanu Pisciotta return fire and kill one of the policemen whose blood splatters the crucifix carved on the lid of the casket. The cousins flee pell-mell across the fields. As they come upon the line of working peasants, the latter open to let them pass. When the pursuing policemen come upon the same peasants, they close ranks and struggle to keep the jeep from passing. The two cousins arrive at the duchess's villa and steal two of her horses under her astonished and admiring eyes. The only significant element missing in the political firmament of Sicily, as seen by Cimino, is the Church, and it appears soon, as Salvatore Giuliano and Aspanu Pisciotta seek refuge in a Franciscan monastery. But this monastery is unlike those to which we have become accustomed. Here the monks, armed with clubs and guns, try, at least at first, forcibly to bar the entrance of the two cousins.[68]

For those who still have not understood the point he is trying to make, Cimino presents his theory of Sicilian politics, complete with visual aids. The notion that there are three centers of power in Sicily is graphically depicted by Salvatore Giuliano as soon as he has recovered somewhat from his wound. When a Franciscan monk asks him with whom he will ally himself, Salvatore Giuliano draws three circles in the dust. These represent Don Masino's "friends" (to the best of my recollection none of the Sicilians in the film ever use the word Mafia), Prince Borsa, and the Church. He, Giuliano, will join none of them, he says, as he draws a fourth circle. This is Giuliano, he adds. Beware, the monk tells him, you cannot survive in Sicily without the help of one of the circles. What about the people? asks Giuliano. The people, the monk says, are the sand in which you drew the circles.[69]

The Sicilian people and their suffering are at best a pretext for the film. While Cimino spends some time presenting the stars, the representatives of the three circles, we are never shown the people except in undifferentiated crowd scenes. Thus, even though we are told that the people suffer and want bread and land, we never see or feel their despair or the emotions that not only drove Salvatore Giuliano to become a bandit, but also caused him to become a hero to the people of Sicily and a threat to the local government, the Mafia, and even to the government of Italy.[70] The ability to capture on film the lives, loves, hatreds, fears, aspirations, and anguish of a people has been the hallmark of Cimino's cinema heretofore. Particularly in *Heaven's Gate* he achieved results that are comparable with those of the best Italian filmmakers. The insane, suicidal rush to battle of the immigrants in *Heaven's Gate* can be understood as the only option left to persons who have been driven over the edge by fear, hunger, despair, and hatred. All of this is established slowly (far too slowly for most American audiences and reviewers) and painstakingly. The same process occurs in *The Deer Hunter*. Virtually the entire first half of the film simply establishes the life and values of the protagonists and the milieu from which they come. Once again, many American spectators and critics considered this the weakest aspect of the film, but it is precisely the development of the protagonists as real people that makes us care for them intensely later. We cannot simply dismiss their pains, fears, and desires. In *Year of the Dragon*, the process is accelerated and abbreviated. We are told more about the suffering of the Chinese than we are shown. Still, we see enough of the life of the Chinese workers in the underground sweatshops and of the children in the youth gangs to feel some degree of empathy. In *The Sicilian*, even when Cimino does attempt to convey the desperate poverty of the people, he fails. Consider, for example, the scene discussed above, in which the barber Frisella (Trevor Ray) begs

Salvatore Giuliano for pity and then asks him to give his shoes and watch to his son "for when he is an adult." He is at best a ludicrous parody of some operatic figure. As I have already suggested, the episode itself, per se, is not implausible and could convey a concept of poverty alien to most Americans. Unfortunately, the actor, Trevor Ray, is a middle-class exponent of twentieth-century postindustrial society and as such cannot convince us that he has ever suffered the kind of hunger and poverty that might lead him to make such a gesture. The major problem of the film, in short, is that we do not believe in the tragedy of the characters. Virtually none of the alleged peasants is even vaguely convincing. While Cimino succeeded in creating some seemingly genuine peasants in *Heaven's Gate*, here he does not. When Christopher Lambert as Salvatore Giuliano tries to convey intensity, he usually merely seems obtuse. Giulia Boschi may have worked in the fields and may have lived with peasants to understand her role as Giovanna Ferra, Salvatore Giuliano's fiancée, but in the real Sicily of the late 1940s, she would have been ridden out of town on a rail.[71]

From Cimino's comments, it is clear that he was influenced to a considerable degree by Tommasi di Lampedusa's *The Leopard* and by Visconti's homonymous film, and that he did considerable research in Sicily.[72] It is equally clear that, while he was acquainted with Rosi's *Salvatore Giuliano*, he did not seek to achieve a sense of documentary realism.[73] *The Sicilian* is no more about Sicily and the bandit Giuliano than *Heaven's Gate* was about the Johnson County war and, thus, should not be evaluated as such. Cimino has said that this film, like all his films, is about the desire for America, the longing for the dream.[74] He attempts to convey this desire in the film in any number of ways: the Glenn Miller music, the ubiquitous dancing of boogie-woogie, Salvatore Giuliano's American army undershorts, and his offer to President Truman to have Sicily become the "fortysome-thingth state." Refuge in America is offered to his wife and to him as some sort of final salvation, when all else has failed. Giovanna goes when so ordered by Salvatore, but Salvatore does not. He refuses, as does the young boy who is, presumably, the heir to his mission in Sicily.

For Cimino, America is both a dream in its natural state and in its potentiality, and a nightmare in the sociopolitical reality of the country. He expresses this conflict as well as anyone in American cinema ever has. Before living in Sicily, Cimino did not or could not understand that conditions in that island were so bad for some in the past that even the most nightmarish manifestations of America were an improvement. Had he plumbed the depths of Sicilian misery as Verga did, for example, he would have truly understood that, as Don Masino says, "life is hard." The dream and miracle of America was not, as some seem to think today, that it is a land of milk and honey and easy pickings, for it never was. The miracle was and is that, although it can be as nightmarish as any place on earth, it did and does offer, at least to some extent, the opportunity of social mobility that has, historically been virtually nonexistent in most other countries. To acknowledge this reality, to depict the conditions that pushed not only Sicilians but peoples the world over to leave their homes and families would, of course, force Cimino to revise if not the source of his conflict—his perception of himself as an outsider, which is the genesis of his creative impetus—at least the metaphor he uses to convey it, that is, America as dream and nightmare. And while Cimino refused to depict the reality that was Sicily in the late 1940s, the experience of Sicily has shifted the conceptual nucleus of his work. With *The Sicilian* he has begun to acknowledge that the source of his creativity is to be found, not in external sociopolitical issues, but within himself. As Professor Adonis tells Don Masino Croce, Salvatore Giuliano has invented himself, he needs no father. Nor, in fact, do we ever see the mother of the film's Giuliano, even though historically she played a significant role in the bandit's life. Cimino's Giuliano acts driven by furies that are his alone. Sociopolitical events are purely pretexts. In this sense he is reminiscent of Howard Roark, the protagonist of Ayn Rand's *The Fountainhead*, a book that Cimino has, for some time, expressed an interest in filming.[75] Like Roark, Giuliano is a demigod of sorts, above other mortals and beyond their laws. To some degree all of Cimino's protagonists have manifested these qualities, but here they are most explicit.

Here the intimations of divinity, if we consider names and events, are so striking and so consistent, given the parallels with the Christ story, as to become impossible to ignore. Salvatore, in Italian, means saviour. Terence Stamp as Prince Borsa represents the monied class appropriately enough, given that *borsa* also means stock market. As the representative of Mammon, he must, by definition, be the antithesis and perhaps nemesis of Salvatore. Don Masino, the would-be adoptive father of Salvatore, is surnamed Croce, that is, cross. Given that the Church in the film is at the very least the accomplice of the aristocrats and the "friends," and given the crucifixion of the false priest, the appellation does not have the positive, loving, forgiving connotations it usually has. On the contrary, it would seem fairly clear that when Salvatore does not succumb to the blandishments of this devil, he, like his predecessor, will be condemned to death. The American duchess, (a postlitteram Marie Antoinette of sorts who says, if the peasants are starving, "let them eat bread") who by her own admission is no nun, cannot but remind us of a somewhat more successful Mary Magdalene. Aspanu Pisciotta, Salvatore's best friend, obviously represents Judas.

While the analogies between Cimino's Salvatore and Christ are impossible to ignore, this Salvatore has qualities that are absolutely not Christian. If anything, as Iannis Katsahnias has pointed out, he has Greek mythical qualities.[76] He is a demigod in a pagan, pre-Christian sort of way. Like all of Cimino's protagonists, he has that quality that Barzini said Sicilians call *mafioso:* he is handsome in a bold and provocative way.[77] He is, in some ways, reminiscent of Barth's *Giles Goat-Boy*, of whom the narrator says: "I was quite aware that it is the prophet who validates the prophecy, and not vice-versa—his authenticity lies not in what he says but in his manner and bearing, his every gesture, the whole embodiment of his personality."[78] The demigod, in Cimino's mythology, must pass through the crucible of death. He must not be afraid of death. At this point, what the demigod does no longer matters. Salvatore Giuliano succumbs to virtually all the temptations with which he is confronted. He is lustful, proud, and violent. He is a thief of ideas as well as of property. He has taken Silvio Ferra's message, that the people want land, and made it his own. But none of this matters because he will be, if not forgiven, certainly not forgotten. Like Christ, he dies voluntarily to insure that his myth, and perhaps his message, will be remembered both through his unborn child in America and through the boy who bids him farewell at the pier.

If there is a key to the film, it is perhaps to be found in Professor Hector Adonis, Giuliano's crippled mentor and the person through whose mind's eye we see this tale. Adonis is not, as Don Masino states at one point, a Dante specialist. He is not, in other words, concerned with an ordered, theocentric universe and a higher morality. Adonis is a Leopardi specialist. This is appropriate for, as such, he perceives nature, and presumably life, as an indifferent and often cruel stepmother. The ironically named Hector Adonis, a man who is a coward and a physically unattractive cripple, cannot but admire and even love Giuliano, because the latter possesses fully those qualities that the professor's names imply but which he lacks entirely. He loves Giuliano's daring, his dedication to his people until death, and his beauty. Thus it is Giuliano who is, in reality, both Hector and Adonis, and not the professor. Like Hector in Book VI of the *Iliad*, Giuliano leaves his wife and his—albeit as yet unborn—child and goes willingly to this death when he could have avoided his nemesis. Like Adonis, who was renowned for his beauty and was the symbol of dying and awakening vegetation, he is the object of a mystery cult: when he descends—or is thought to have descended—into Hades at the monastery, his followers lament; when he is reborn, they rejoice in the promise of his largesse. Nor is his physical death on the boat the end. He will be reborn in the memory and imagination of the people of Sicily and in Cimino's film. Thus it is that the professor recites a poem by Greek poet Constantin Cavafy, "Very Seldom," in full, by heart, to the oddly indifferent applause of his rapidly departing students:

An old man—used up, bent,
crippled by time and indulgence—
slowly walks along the narrow street.
But when he goes inside his house to hide
the shambles of his old age, his mind turns
to the share in youth that still belongs to him

His verse is now quoted by young men.
His visions come before their lively eyes.
Their healthy sensual minds,
their shapely taut bodies
stir to his perception of the beautiful.[79]

These words are spoken by Adonis, but they reflect Cimino's sentiments. It is he who with his art, the manifestation of his perception of the beautiful, stirs his audience, much as the beauty of Salvatore stirs Adonis, Don Masino, Giovanna, the Duchess, and Aspanu Pisciotta. What Cimino is presenting us with, in short, is a contemporary view of a pre-Christian world, a world that has not yet been condemned to the dualistic puritanical homophobia that determines a priori what is to be considered an object of beauty and love. Giuliano is, in our terms, completely and comfortably heterosexual. At the same time, however, he feels no self-conscious embarrassment at being the object of desire and love of the professor, of Aspanu, and perhaps most of all, of Don Masino. He belongs, in short, to the Greek pre-Christian world of Alexander, of whom he speaks with envy and a clear desire of emulation, and of Plato and his Alcibiades.

The film itself is not structured according to contemporary sensibilities and thus is difficult and even offputting to those who simply want consumer cinema.[80] Here we do not have character development or psychology. Thus, to those who expect a conventional film, it "feels flat and unexciting" and Lambert as Giuliano does not possess "the charisma...necessary to carry off the center role."[81] For them, the film also "never finds a rhythm, and is filled with many awkward transitions as well as last-ditch cutaways to flying birds, something the director would undoubtedly blame on those who succeeded him in the editing room, but are pretty sorry no matter who did them."[82] These reactions are not surprising. In *The Sicilian*, as in Greek myth, characters spring like Minerva, full blown from the mind of their creator. They are no more the free arbiters of their destinies than are characters in Greek tragedies. They must each play their individual roles, reap the rewards, and suffer the consequences. The cutaways to the flying birds are not escapism; they are explicit filmic metaphors. Giuliano, the king of the mountains, is as free of the tentacles of the three circles, the "friends," the aristocrats, and the Church as are the birds, except when he is tricked into the massacre of Portella della Ginestra.[83] During these scenes the cutaways are not to free-flying birds, but to kites. The latter may swoop and soar like the birds, but they are in fact tethered to the ground and buffeted by the wind. Even the terminology and imagery used by the characters are at the very least premodern. In explaining why Giuliano must be eliminated, Minister Trezza says, using a phrase that antedates Columbus's discovery of America, that Giuliano has sailed off the map of the earth.

The final shot of the film shows us Giuliano between a deciduous tree, symbol of Adonis, and a cross, symbol of Christ. Giuliano is the symbol of Sicily, a land where, as the professor says, leaving the bandit's funeral, "nothing ever changes." Both he and the island are caught in the transition between these two mysteries. It is a different world, one which is virtually incomprehensible from this side of the Atlantic, but it is also the world that brought Cimino beyond his obsession with America as nightmare. Seen from within by individuals who consider themselves outsiders, America, almost by definition, had to seem like a nightmare. This perception changes, however, when seen from a different perspective. It was this that Cimino discovered when he went to Sicily to film *The Sicilian:* "Une partie de la raison pour faire ce film réside dans le lien à l'Amérique, le rêve d'Amérique quand on est en-dehors de l'Amérique."[84] He now sees America from this broader perspective with the somewhat jaded eyes of contemporary Italians. America is no longer merely a place in which to have a pizzeria in New Jersey, as Salvatore Giuliano tells the duchess, it is a place to be free. And while America has riches, symbolized by Camilla, the duchess from Connecticut, Italy too has qualities that even the richest Americans desire, and for which they will emigrate to Italy. America is also not the only alternative for

Italians. Neither Salvatore Giuliano nor the boy who bids him farewell at the wharf opt to emigrate. The Italian, in other words, no longer is condemned to the status of Third World citizen who must either emigrate or starve. By extension, the Italian American is no longer a second-class citizen. In creating *The Sicilian,* Cimino has attempted to rewrite the mythological history of Italian Americans and thus free them from the bondage of an often confusing and contradictory heritage.

Notes

1. Prince Metternich, letter, 19 November 1849, *The Oxford Dictionary of Quotations* 2d ed. (London: Oxford University Press, 1966), 338.

2. Niccolò Machiavelli, *Il Principe e I discorsi* (Milano: Feltrinelli, 1971), 102.

3. I have chosen to write "Italian/American," rather than "Italian-American," Italo-American," or "Italian American," after having read an expanded version of Anthony Tamburri's discussion of signs and ethnic identity in "To Hyphenate or Not To Hyphenate: The Italian/American Writer and *Italianità,*" *Italian Journal* 3, no. 5:37–42.

4. This essay, which is part of a book-length manuscript on contemporary Italian/American filmmakers, will focus on Michael Cimino. Filmmaking is a collective enterprise; inevitably, so is film criticism. I owe more than I can say to the insightful comments and professional advice of Lorraine Lawton. I must also thank Anthony Tamburri, not merely for his encouragement as co-editor of this anthology, but for the wealth of information on the Italian/American experience that he put at my disposal with a generosity truly Italian. While purists may quibble about the quality of the video image and the aspect ration of the television screen, the advent of video cassette recorders has relieved some of the frustration which has characterized film research heretofore. All the films discussed in this essay, and many more, are currently available. For sources, see the list of Video Suppliers prepared by Lorraine Lawton. If these and similar films are not available on videotape locally, you may rent them through the mail from the following: Facets Video, 1517 W. Fullerton Ave., Chicago, IL 60614 (Ph. 1-800-331-6197, 9 a.m.–5 p.m., Mon.-Fri.) and Tammarelle's International Films, 110 Cohasset Stage Rd., Chico, CA 95926 (Ph. 916-895-3429 or 1-800-356-3577). I have had generally positive experiences with both.

5. For thought-provoking studies of certain manifestations of the Italian/American heritage in the films of Francis Ford Coppola and Martin Scorsese, see John Paul Russo, "The Hidden Godfather: Plenitude and Absence in Francis Ford Coppola's Godfather I and II," 255–81; and Robert Casillo, "Catholicism and Violence in the Films of Martin Scorsese," 283–304, in *Support and Struggle: Italians and Italian Americans in a Comparative Perspective,* Proceedings of the Seventeenth Annual Conference of the American Italian Historical Association, Joseph L. Tropea, James E. Miller, and Cheryl Beattie-Repetti, eds. (New York: American Italian Historical Association, 1986). For an Italian perspective on the Italian/American experience in film, see the *Italianamericans* issue of *Cinema & Cinema* 11, n. 38 (January–March 1984), which includes the following: Gian Piero Bruncetta, "Breve viaggio con l'emigrato cinematografico," 5–8; Peter Bondanella,

"*Christ in Concrete* di Edward Dmytryk e il neorealismo italiano," 9–16; Harry M. Geduld, *Christ in Concrete*: dal romanzo al film," 17–25; Guido Fink, "Orgoglio e pregiudizio: stereotipi hollywoodiani e doppiaggio di casa nostra," 26–35; Vito Zagarrio, "F.C.-F.C. ovvero: *Italian-American Dream* dal film muto alla televisione," 36–40; Franco Minganti, "L'eroe dai mille e tre volti: Michele, Mike, Michael Corleone," 41–48. Also useful is *Integrato Metropolitano: New York, Chicago, Torino: tre volti dell'emigrazione italiana,* Marcello Pacini, Piero Gastaldo, and Dario Arrigotti, eds. (Torino: Fondazione Giovanni Agnelli, 1982), which includes an essay on "L'immagine dell'Italiano nel cinema americano" by Gianni Rondolini and a filmography of "Gli Italiani secondo Holywood" by Gian Carlo Bertolina.

6. Daniel Aaron argues in "The Hyphenate Writer and American Letters," *Smith Alumnae Quarterly* (July 1964), 213–17, that the "hyphenated" writers are to some extent alienated from mainstream America and thus, at first, try to blur the distinctions between their other heritages and mainstream America; then they lash out at the land which treats them as illegitimate stepchildren; finally, as they become assimilated and "dehyphenated," they speak as Americans, without necessarily renouncing a "marginal perspective." In cinema Frank Capra and Vincente Minnelli might be adduced as examples of the first stage, while Francis Ford Coppola, Martin Scorsese, Michael Cimino, Brian De Palma, and Sylvester Stallone are all in transition between stages two and three.

7. Giovanni Verga, *Tutte le novelle* (Milano: Oscar Mondadori 1971), 186–99. For those who do not read Italian, this and many more of Verga's short stories can be found in Giovanni Verga, *The She-Wolf and Other Stories,* translated and introduced by Giovanni Cecchetti, 2d ed. (Berkeley: University of California Press, 1973).

8. For more information in English, see Oswald Stack, ed., *Pasolini on Pasolini* (Bloomington: Indiana University Press, 1969); and Pier Paolo Pasolini, *Heretical Empiricism,* Louise Barnett, ed., Ben Lawton and Louise Barnett, trans. (Bloomington: Indiana University Press, 1988).

9. Marc Pachter, ed., *Abroad in America: Visitors to the New Nation 1776–1914* (Washington, D.C.: National Portrait Gallery, Smithsonian Institution, 1976).

10. Suffice it to recall that Dante had to leave not just Italy but the material world when he wrote his *Divine Comedy,* while Manzoni escaped back in time with his *Betrothed*. For more information on these and other Italian authors mentioned in this essay, consult Peter Bondanella and Julia Conway Bondanella, eds., *Dictionary of Italian Literature* (Westport, Conn.: Greenwood Press, 1979), the best rapid guide to Italian literature extant in English, which includes essays on both major and minor writers and essential bibliographical references.

11. Giuseppe Giacosa, *Impressioni d'America,* 2d ed. (Milano: Cogliati, 1902).

12. Giacosa, 90.

13. Giacosa, 153.

14. What follows is at best a representative sampling: David Sterrit, *Christian Science Monitor,* 7 May 1981: 19; Richard Combs, *Monthly Film Bulletin,* October 1981: 200; Stanley Kauffman, *New Republic,* 15 May 1981: 24; John Coleman, *New Statesman,* 11 September 1981: 22; David Denby, *New York,* 11 May 1981: 64;

Archer Winsten, *New York Post,* 24 April 1981: 39; Vincent Canby, *New York Times,* 24 April 1981: C10; Joseph Gelmis, *Newsday,* 24 April 1982: (Part II) 7; Alex Keneas, *Newsday,* 24 April 1981: (Part II) 7; David Ansen, *Newsweek,* 4 May 1981: 44; Richard Corliss, *Time,* 4 May 1981: 87; Andrew Sarris, *Village Voice,* 29 April–5 May 1981: 47; Jeffrey Wells, *Films in Review* 32 (January 1981): 55–56; Colin McCulloch, letter, "The Critical Dismissal of *Heaven's Gate,*" *Cineaste* 13, no. 4 (1984): 3; Olivier Assayas, "L'Ayatollah Cimino," *Journal des Cahiers du Cinema,* 1 January 1981: XI; Olivier Assayas, "L'académie du cinéma," *Cahiers du Cinéma* 326 (July–August 1981): 18–21; Yann Lardeau, "Le cercle brisé," *Cahiers du Cinéma* 326 (July–August 1981): 54–55; Jack Kroll, "'Heaven' Can Wait," *Film Comment* 17 (January–February, 1981): 58–59; Naomi Greene, "Coppola, Cimino: The Operatics of History," *Film Quarterly* 38, no. 2 (1984/85): 28–37; Steven Bach, *Final Cut: Dreams and Disaster in the Making of* Heaven's Gate (New York: William Morrow and Co. 1985); Ann Thompson, review of *Final Cut, Film Comment* 21 (November - December 1985): 48–50; Forster Hirsch, review of *Final Cut, Cineaste,* 14, no. 4 (1986): 53–54; Robert Sklar, review of video of *Heaven's Gate, Cineaste* 14, no. 4 (1986): 29, 60.

15. Among others, see, R. Benayoun et al., "Entretien avec Michael Cimino," *Positif* 217 (April 1979): 21–29; M. Ciment and M. Henry, "Nouvel entretien avec Michael Cimino," *Positif* 246 (September 1981): 17–21; M. Chevrie, J. Narboni, and V. Ostria, "The Right Place: Entretien avec Michael Cimino," *Cahiers du Cinéma* 377 (November 1985): 9–11 + [5p]; Bill Krohn, "Un album de famille: Entretien avec Michael Cimino," *Cahiers du Cinéma* 401 (November 1987): 19–21 + [2p].

16. Kris Kristofferson on *Heaven's Gate:* "You had the feeling you were working with Michelangelo, and he was letting you paint a stroke here." In Robin Wood, *Hollywood from Vietnam to Reagan* (New York: Columbia University Press, 1986), 298.

17. Bach, 280–81.

18. Bach, 375.

19. Palmer, *The Films of the Seventies: A Social History* (Metuchen, N. J.: Scarecrow Press, 1987).

20. Given the number of articles and reviews of this film, the reader is referred to Zita Eastman, Vincent J. Aceto, and Fred Silva, eds., *Film Literature Index*, 15 vols. (Albany, N.Y.: Film and Television Documentation Center, 1973–87), which is amazingly complete and absolutely invaluable.

21. Callenbach, "Editor's Notebook," *Film Quarterly*, Fall/Winter 1974: 1.

22. J. Pilger, "Why *The Deer Hunter* Is a Lie," *New Statesman* 97 (16 March 1979): 352–53; T. Buckley, "Movies: Hollywood's War: *The Deer Hunter* Invents Cruelties to Sell Vietnam," *Harper's* 258 (April 1979): 84–88; R. C. Kranz, "*Apocalypse Now* and *The Deer Hunter:* The Lies Aren't Over," *Jump Cut* 23 (October 1980): 18–20.

23. Event reported by Frank Burke, a good friend and distinguished film scholar, who in no way can be construed to have fascist sympathies, in a conversation with the author. The evolution in *Jump Cut's* response to Cimino may be observed in John Hess, "History, Politics, Style, and Genre: *Matewan* (John Sayles, 1987) and *The Sicilian* (Michael Cimino, 1987)" *Jump Cut* (1988): 30–37, an intelligent and sensitive criticism of *The Sicilian* from a leftist perspective.

24. Nick Pease, "*The Deer Hunter* and the Demythification of the American Hero," *Literature/Film Quarterly* 7, no. 4 (1979): 254–59; John Pym, "A Bullet in the Head: Vietnam Remembered," *Sight and Sound* 48 (Spring 1979): 82–84 +; Al Auster and Leonard Quart, "Hollywood and Vietnam: The Triumph of the Will," *Cineaste* 9, no. 3 (1979): 4–9; Frank Burke, "In Defense of *The Deer Hunter* or: The Knee Jerk Is Quicker Than the Eye," *Literature/Film Quarterly* 11, no. 1 (1983): 22–27; Don Francis, "The Regeneration of America: Uses of Landscape in *The Deer Hunter*," *Literature/Film Quarterly* 11, no. 1 (1983): 16–21; Naomi Greene, "Coppola, Cimino: The Operatics of History," *Film Quarterly* 38, no. 2 (1984/85): 28–37; Judy Lee Kinney, "The Mythical Method: Fictionalizing the Vietnam War," *Wide Angle* 7, no. 4 (1985): 35–40; Wood, 270–98; Bliss, "God Bless America" (Metuchen: Scarecrow Press, 1985), 166–92.

25. For what appears to be a sociobiological argument, see the "Up Front" report on the research by anthropologist Napoleon Chagnon in "Sex and Death in the Jungle," *Discover* 9, no. 7 (July 1988): 10, which argues that tribal violence involves not only competition for food and land but also for reproductive advantage. For several diametrically opposed arguments, see the *Psychology Today* 22 (June 1988) Special Issue, which is dedicated entirely to "War and Peace: Psychology at the Summit," and in particular, Alfie Kohn, "Make Love, Not War," 34–38, which contends that studies of aggression conclude that there is no scientific basis for the belief that humans are naturally warlike. I am neither an anthropologist nor a psychologist, but as a person interested in *humanae litterae*, I can only observe that Western literature, from its inception, is concerned with young men's aspirations to become heroes through various forms of competition, including war. One explanation of this phenomenon appears in Joseph Campbell, *The Hero with a Thousand Faces* (Princeton: Princeton University Press Bollingen Series, 1972). For a historian's perspective, see John Keegan, *The Face of Battle: A Study of Agincourt, Waterloo and the Somme* (Great Britain: Jonathan Cape, 1976; rpt. New York: Penguin Books, 1985). Of particular interest is his comparison between the warfare and mountaineering of the first half of this century. He argues that the latter has become "in our time a sort of military operation, in which sport imitates war, and war of the dreariest, deadliest, most long drawn-out sort" (307).

26. See Keegan, 326–31. He goes on to argue that, given the easily predictable horrors of the modern battlefield, "the young have already made their decision. They are increasingly unwilling to serve as conscripts in armies they see as ornamental. The militant young have taken that decision a stage further: they will fight for the causes which they profess not through the mechanisms of the state and its armed power but, where necessary, against them, by clandestine and guerrilla methods" (343). Interestingly, the top mountain climbers in the 1970s and 1980s have rejected the military/technical-industrial approach characterized by endeavors such as Sir Edmund Hillary's conquest of Mt. Everest and are engaged in unaided solo ascents such as those of Wolfgang Messner.

27. "Lord Robbins, the eminent economist, describes in his autobiography how...he was brought wholly unexpectedly to realize...what an absorbing and enjoyable activity battle could be, and why in times past it had fulfilled the energies and imagination of the European upper class to the exclusion of almost all else" (Keegan, 332–33).

28. Keegan argues quite convincingly that "battle has already abolished itself" (343), because "impersonality, coercion, deliberate cruelty, all deployed on a rising scale, make the fitness of modern man to sustain the stress of battle increasingly doubtful" (331).

29. For specific reviews and articles see note 14. For a comprehensive listing of material on *Heaven's Gate* appearing in periodicals see *Film Literature Index*. One major exception to the chorus of opprobrium heaped upon *Heaven's Gate* is to be found in Michael Bliss's generally careful and intelligent analysis of the film in chapter 11, "The Beauty of Things That Fade" (193–239). Bliss also offers a detailed presentation of the odd treatment the film received from both the media and United Artists in chapter 12, "The Sabotaging of *Heaven's Gate*" (240–41). For another important corrective to the general hysteria, see Robin Wood, *Hollywood from Vietnam to Reagan*, 298–317.

30. Ben Lawton, "*Taxi Driver:* 'New Hybrid Film' or 'Liberated Cinema'?" *Italian Americana* 5 (Spring/Summer 1979): 238–48.

31. In reality these scenes were shot somewhat clandestinely at Oxford University (Bach, 329–31).

32. Bach, 274–45, 329–30.

33. Incredible and even implausible though it may seem, roller-skating might have been possible in Sweetwater since roller skates were invented in 1860.

34. Pier Paolo Pasolini, "Abiura dalla *Trilogia della vita*," in *Trilogia della vita: Il Decameron, I racconti de Canterbury, Il fiore delle mille e una notte*, Giorgio Gattei, ed. (Bologna: Cappelli, 1975), 11–13. For a partial English language translation and comments see Ben Lawton, "The Evolving Rejection of Homosexuality, the Sub-Proletariat, and the Third World in the Films of Pier Paolo Pasolini," *Italian Quarterly*, nos. 82/83 (Fall 1980/Winter 1981): 167–73.

35. Niccolò Machiavelli, Book 1, Ch 5, *Discorsi*, in *Il principe e discorsi*, Sergio Bertelli, ed. (Milano: Feltrinelli, 1971), 141.

36. Term used by Bach to describe the mercenaries led, in the film, by Frank Canton (152–53).

37. The long VHS version of the film released by MGM/UA ends on a still frame of this final evasion. Other versions end on a still frame of Jim looking towards the setting sun (Bliss, 216).

38. Bach, 142–54.

39. Mark 10: 17–25, The Bible.

40. "D'un autre coté, mon avis sur le film n'a jamais changé. . . . Je l'aime toujours, j'en suis toujours fier et je suis content d'avoir pû le faire comme je l'avais voulu. . . . Donc. . .ce fut facile de recommencer parce que je ne change jamais d'attitude à propos de mon travail ou de la direction que je prends." "The Right Place," interview by Marc Chevrie, Jean Narboni, and Vincent Ostria, translated from English by Vincent Ostria, *Cahiers du Cinéma* 377 (November 1985): 9.

41. "S'il est sans doute actuellement le meilleur cinéaste et le plus grand filmeur américain...c'est qu'il pursuit une tradition....au lieu de répéter ou de faire revenir le passé." Marc Chevrie, "Le Point de Mire," *Cahiers du Cinema* 377 (November 85): 5.

42. Scorsese's film was clearly meant as an indictment rather than a glorification of the media processes whereby raving lunatics such as Travis Bickle are transformed into heroes. For a more detailed analysis of this process see Ben Lawton, "*Taxi Driver*, 'New Hybrid Film' or 'Liberated Cinema'?" 238–48.

43. I have read no satisfactory explanation for Joey Tai's sparing the life of the old general in Thailand.

44. Cimino has stated: "Dans ce film, je voulais que le public lutte pour aimer Stanley, qu'il hésite à haïr Joey. Et ceci pas seulement émotionellement, pas seulement en fonction de la construction du scénario. Ce n'est pas seulement suggéré par la narration, mais visuellement, par la mise en scène. Vous avez sans doute remarqué que de nombreuses scènes sont filmées en un seul plan. On a l'impression qu'il y a beaucoup de plans, mais ce n'est pas le cas, c'est une alternance de gros plans et de plans éloignés dans un seul mouvement fluide. Souvent, les plans sont circulaires. Je crois qu'ainsi, le public ne réalise pas clairement les changements de point de vue ni les variations de perspective. Ce qui aide à effacer l'aspect bidimensionnel et mahichéiste de l'écran. Il n'y a pas seulement un premier plan avec les héros et un arrière-plan où des gens bavardent. On a l'impression de tourner autour d'un personnage, dans l'espace aussi bien qu'intellectuellement" ("The Right Place," 65).

45. "Asian-Americans Planning 'Dragon' Boycott Campaign," *Variety*, 14 August 1985, 3, 26; "MGM/UA Defends Anti-Asian Charges Leveled at 'Dragon,'" *Variety*, 21 August 1985, 3, 21; "Mayor of Boston Blasts 'Dragon,' Pickets Converge on Sack House," *Variety*, 28 August 1985, 3, 117; "MGM/UA Sending 'Year' Disclaimers Out to Exhibitors," *Variety*, 4 September 1985, 3, 38. The distribution of disclaimers by the studio was "startling both because it set a historical precedent (no studio, in current recollection, has ever bowed to pressure from an ethnic group by agreeing to attach a disclaimer to a movie after its release) and because few, even in the Chinese community, truly expected a major company to, essentially, agree it had made a mistake and to go to 'substantial cost'...to placate the protesters" (38).

46. "The Right Place," 64.

47. Information obtained by the author in the course of several conversations with People's Republic of China graduate students at Purdue University. There was an analogous feeling of resentment towards Bernardo Bertolucci's *The Last Emperor* predicated on the historical inaccuracies of the film and on the privileged treatment Bertolucci received when he was allowed to film in the Forbidden City where Chinese filmmakers are not allowed.

48. Serge Toubiana, *Le Journal des "Cahiers du Cinema"* 57 (December 1985): xv–xvi.

49. See Pier Paolo Pasolini, "An Epical-Religious View of the World" 18 (1965): 31–45, and "Il sentimento della storia," *Cinema nuovo* 205 (1970): 172–73.

50. "Et je crois que si l'on prend mes trois derniers films en plaçant *Heaven's Gate* en premier, *The Deer Hunter* en second et *Year of the Dragon* en troisième, on a une sorte de trilogie, un tryptique,"..."Et on peut en effet sentir une continuité entre certains thèmes" ("The Right Place," 11, 63).

51. "Non, non. Un nouveau commencement est toujours positif. Stanley a le mérite d'avoir révélé le problème. Il a rendu visible le dessous des choses....Il retrouve cette fille, Tracy, et c'est un peu l'illustration du fait que si l'on fait la guerre assez longtemps, on finit par être très proche de l'ennemi. C'est la mort de quelque chose mais aussi le début de quelque chose d'autre. C'est pourquoi j'ai utilisé la symphonie 'Résurrection' de Mahler. Il y a quelque chose de majesteux dans cette naissance de quelque chose qui renaît de la mort" ("The Right Place," 64).

52. Chevrie, "Le Point de Mire," 6.

53. "Alors, la seconde symphonie de Mahler (Résurrection) a beau planer sur les derniers plans de Stanley et Tracy réunis dans un nouvel optimisme, lorsq'un arrêt sur l'image vient figer leur élan dans une image de bonheur, quoiqu'en ait Cimino, on a du mal à prendre cela pour happy end [sic]" (Chevrie, "Le Point de Mire," 7).

54. "C'est juste une image (de l'Amérique), et l'énergie incroyable que met le film à vouloir y croire est l'énergie du désespoir" (Chevrie, 7).

55. Chevrie, 64.

56. See *An Inquiry into Organized Crime*, Luciano J. Iorizzo, ed. (The American Italian Historical Association Proceedings of the Third Annual Conference), 24 October 1970, and Frederick D. Homer, *Guns and Garlic: Myths and Realities of Organized Crime* (West Lafayette, Ind.: Purdue University Press, 1974) for two useful and thought-provoking reassessments of the Italian/American role in organized crime.

57. Chapter 7, "Gli Italiani negli Stati Uniti," 161–97.

58. T. McCarthy, "*The Sicilian*: Botched Epic Faces Better Overseas B.O. than Domestic," *Variety*, 21 October 1987, 15.

59. Bill Krohn, "Michael Cimino Tourne *The Sicilian*: Le Pacte avec le Diable," *Cahiers du Cinéma* 389 (November 1986): 35–41, and "Michel Cimino Tourne *The Sicilian (Suite)*: "L'Oiseau Noir," *Cahiers du Cinéma* 391 (January 1987): 37–45.

60. Iannis Katsahnias, "*Le Sicilien* de Michael Cimino: La colère d'Achille," *Cahiers du Cinéma* (401 (November 1987): 16–18, and Bill Krohn, "Un Album de Famille: Entretien avec Michael Cimino," *Cahiers du Cinéma* 401 (November 1987): 19–21, 62–63.

61. Stanbrook, *Films and Filming*, February 1988, 11.

62. Wood, 301.

63. Wood, 300.

64. Many of Cimino's problems in this sense are a result of his adoption of Mario Puzo's historical revisionism in his homonymous novel. John Hess summarizes the major discrepancies succinctly and discreetly (31–33). For a much harsher evaluation of the historical inaccuracies of Puzo's book, which apply equally to the film, see, Emanuele Macaluso, "I ritorni di Giuliano, *L'unità*, 3 August 1986, 13:

"I giornali ci hanno informato che Cimino ha come riferimento il nuovo libro dell'autore del 'Padrino', Puzo, che ha scritto una storia romanzata, 'Il Siciliano'', del bandito di Montelepre. Abbiamo letto il libro e francamente non vale niente. La ricostruzione segue un filo che è quello che tutti conoscono con alcune 'varianti' volte a dare il ritratto di un Giuliano forte a buono, coraggioso e generoso, amico dei poveri e nemico dei ricchi che godeva della 'devozione dell'intera popolazione dell'Isola.' Balle. Il libro è infarcito di luoghi comuni, di mediocri ovvietà; i personaggi sono colorati, caricaturali, improbabili. Puzo non conosce la storia e la geografia della Sicilia, gli usi e i costumi, il linguaggio e le abitudini dei siciliani. Il libro è una paccotaglia per il grosso pubblico americano."

65. For a comparative taxonomy of conventional and counter cinemas, see Peter Wollen, "Counter Cinema: Vent D'Est," *Afterimage* (Autumn 1972): 6–16.

66. This is Christophe Lambert's understanding of his role as told to Saverio Lodato, "Ciak! A Montelepre si gira Robin Hood," *L'unità*, 3 August 1986, 13.

67. *Carabinieri*, the Italian national paramilitary police, is concerned with the suppression of banditry, terrorism, drug traffic, and organized crime, among other tasks. In Italian films it is often the object of humor for the alleged illiteracy and lack of intelligence of its members. See Lina Wertmüller, *A Joke of Destiny* (1985).

68. The implication that friars are involved in organized crime in Sicily is not without historical foundation. Luigi Barzini in *The Italians* dedicates a page to the "good friars of Mazzarino...who were recently arrested and tried for having acted as messengers between the Mafia and its intended victims" (265).

69. Here and elsewhere when I report the dialog of characters in the film without quotation marks I am recreating an approximation of their speech.

70. "King of the Bandits: Sicily's 'Robin Hood' Is a Murderer, a Poet and a Politician," *Life*, 23 February 1948, 63–64. This romantic report on Giuliano includes several anecdotes, among them the story of his encounter with the Duchess of Pratoameno who, at least in part, must have inspired the Duchess of Camilla character. Also included are the first published photograph of Giuliano, who was easily as handsome as Lambert, and one of Giuliano's cartoons advocating secession from Italy and unification with the United States.

71. Krohn, "L'Oiseau Noir," 42–43.

72. Krohn, "Un Album de Famille," 19–20, 62.

73. Krohn, "Un Album de Famille," 21.

74. Krohn, "Un Album de Famille," 20.

75. Bach, 91.

76. Katsahnias, 16–18.

77. Barzini, 264.

78. John Barth, *Giles Goat-Boy* (Greenwich, Conn.: Fawcett Publications, 1966) xxviii–xxix.

79. Edmund Keeley, *Cavafy's Alexandria: Study of a Myth in Progress* (Cambridge: Harvard University Press, 1976), 62.

80. Pasolini, "Il cinema impopolare," *Nuovi argomenti* 20 (October/December 1970): 166–76. Reprinted in Pier Paolo Pasolini, *Empirismo eretico* (Milano: Garzanti, 1972), 273–80. Available in English in Pier Paolo Pasolini, *Heretical Empiricism*, Louise Barnett, ed., Ben Lawton and Louise Barnett, trans. (Bloomington: Indiana University Press, 1988).

81. McCarthy, 15.

82. McCarthy, 15.

83. Here, as elsewhere, Cimino follows Puzo's historical revisionism in order to maintain the illusion that Giuliano was a Robin Hood of sorts, rather than the leader of a right-wing death squad. This legend is also being perpetuated in Sicily by one of Giuliano's last living relatives who makes a living selling postcards, ceramics, and "perfino un amaro digestivo dedicati a Giuliano." For more information see, Saverio Lodato, "Ciak! A Montelepre si gira Robin Hood, *L'unità*, 3 August 1986, 13. In reality, Giuliano was both tool and victim of those very circles of power which he eschews in the film. Not only was he responsible, as he himself acknowledged, for the 1 May 1947 massacre of Portella della Ginestra, he also attacked and killed leftist politicians and labor organizers to affect the forthcoming elections. Notwithstanding, or perhaps because of, his successes—the Popular Front received only 26 of 2,948 votes cast, while the Christian Democratic Party received 1,539 votes—the powers-that-were decided to eliminate him before he revealed the identity of his backers. For more details, see Emanuele Macaluso, "I ritorni di Giuliano, *L'unità* 13.

84. Krohn, 21.

Select Bibliography

When people discuss a book on Italian Americans, more likely than not it is a sociological/historical study full of the statistics and the historical places of immigration. Rarely does a discussion on Italian Americans center around a novel, a poem, a play, or a film that deals with the immigration experience or what it means to be Italian American. From the memoirs of Pascal D'Angelo to the novels of Pietro Di Donato and Mario Puzo through the poetry of Joseph Tusiani and Phyllis Capello, many first-, second-, and third-generation Italian/American artists have documented extensively throughout this century the Italian/American experience in biographies, novels, poems, plays, and, lately, the cinema.

In the following bibliography, we do not presume to include every written work that deals with the Italian/American experience, but we wish to introduce you to some of the best work on the subject. For other bibliographical references, we suggest you consult the extensive bibliography included in Rose Basile Green's *The Italian-American Novel: A Document of the Interaction of Two Cultures* (Madison, N.J.: Fairleigh Dickinson University Press, 1974) and Helen Barolini's *Dream Book: An Anthology of Writings by Italian American Women* (New York: Schocken Books, 1985). In addition, the Works Cited sections following some essays in the Critical Essays part of this volume offer useful information.

Narrative Works

Ainsworth, Catherine H. 1976. *Italian-American Folktales.* London: Clyde Press.

Altavilla, Corrado. 1938. *Gente Lontana.* Milan: Medici Domus.

Ardizzone, Tony. 1978. *In the Name of the Father.* New York: Doubleday and Co.

———. 1986a. *Heart of the Order.* New York: Henry Holt and Co.

———. 1986b. *The Evening News* (short stories). Athens: University of Georgia Press.

Arleo, Joseph. 1970. *The Grand Street Collector.* New York: Walker and Co.

Arrighi, Antonio A. 1971. *The Story of Antonio, the Galley Slave.* New York: Fleming H. Revell Co.

Barolini, Helen. [1979] 1982. *Umbertina.* New York: Bantam Books.

———. 1986. *Love in the Middle Ages.* New York: William Morrow and Co.

Benasutti, Marion. 1966. *No Steady Job for Papa.* New York: Vanguard Press.

Bonetti, Edward. 1957. *The Wine Cellar* (short fiction). New York: Viking Press.

Bryant, Dorothy Calvetti. 1978. *Miss Giardino.* Berkeley, Calif.: Ata Books.

Buranelli, Prosper. 1930. *You Gotta Be Rough.* Garden City, N.Y.: Doubleday, Doran and Co.

————. 1931. *Big Nick*. Garden City, N.Y.: Doubleday, Doran and Co.

————. 1940. *News Reel Murder*. New York: Wilfred Funf.

Calitri, Charles. 1952. *Rickey*. New York: Charles Scribner's Sons.

————. 1958. *Strike Heaven on the Face*. New York: Crown Publishers.

————1962. *Father*. New York: Crown Publishers.

Canzoneri, Robert. 1965. *I Do So Politely*. Boston: Houghton Mifflin Co.

————. 1969. *Men with Little Hammers*. New York: Dial Press.

————. 1970. *Barbed Wire and Other Stories*. New York: Dial Press.

Cautela, Giuseppe. 1925. *Moon Harvest*. New York: Lincoln MacVeagh, Dial Press.

Cenedella, Robert. 1963. *A Little to the East*. New York: G. P. Putnam's Sons.

Ciambelli, Bernardino. 1893a. *I drammi dell'emigrazione, sequito ai misteri*. New York: Frugone and Balletto.

————. 1893b. *I misteri di Mulberry*. New York: Frugone and Balletto.

————. 1895. *I misteri della polizia il delitto di Water Street*. New York: Frugone and Balletto.

————. 1899. *I misteri di Bleeker Street*. New York: Frugone and Balletto.

————. 1915. *I sotterranei di NY*. New York: Società Libreria Italiana.

————. 1919. *La trovatella di Mulberry Street: ovvero la stella dei cinque punti*. New York: Società Libreria Italiana.

Corsel, Ralph. 1968. *Up There the Stars*. New York: Citadel Press.

Covello, Leonard, and Guido D'Agostino. 1958. *The Heart Is the Teacher* (memoirs). New York: McGraw-Hill.

D'Agostino, Guido. 1940. *Olives on the Apple Tree*. New York: Doubleday, Doran and Co.

————. 1942. *Hills beyond Manhattan*. New York: Doubleday, Doran and Co.

————. 1947. *My Enemy the World*. New York: Dial Press.

————. 1952. *The Barking of a Lonely Fox*. New York: McGraw-Hill.

D'Angelo, Lou. 1971. *What the Ancients Said*. Garden City, N.Y.: Doubleday and Co.

————. 1981. *A Circle of Friends*. Garden City, N.Y.: Doubleday and Co.

D'Angelo, Pascal. 1924. *Son of Italy* (memoirs). New York: Macmillan Co.

De Capite, Michael. 1943. *Maria*. New York: John Day Co.

————. 1944. *No Bright Banner*. New York: John Day Co.

————. 1948. *The Bennett Place*. New York: John Day Co.

De Capite, Raymond. 1960. *The Coming of Fabrizze*. New York: David McKay Co.

————. 1961. *A Lost King*. New York: David McKay Co.

De Lillo, Don. 1971. *Americana*. Boston: Houghton Mifflin Co.

————. 1972. *End Zone*. Boston: Houghton Mifflin Co.

DeRosa, Tina. 1980. *Paper Fish*. Chicago: Wine Press.

Di Donato, Pietro. 1939. *Christ in Concrete*. Indianapolis: Bobbs-Merrill Co.

————. 1959. *This Woman*. New York: Ballantine Books.

————. 1960. *Three Circles of Light*. New York: Julian Messner.

————. 1970. *Naked Author* (short stories). New York: Phaedra.

Difranco, Anthony. 1984. *The Streets of Paradise*. New York: Bantam Books.

Ets, Marie Hall. 1970. *Rosa: The Life of an Italian Immigrant*. Minneapolis: University of Minnesota Press.

Fante, John. 1940. *Dago Red* (short stories). New York: Viking Press.

————. [1939] 1982a. *Ask the Dust*. Santa Barbara, Calif.: Black Sparrow Press.

————. 1982b. *Dreams from Bunker Hill*. Santa Barbara, Calif.: Black Sparrow Press.

————. [1938, 1980] 1983. *Wait Until Spring, Bandini*. Santa Barbara, Calif.: Black Sparrow Press.

————. 1985a. *Nineteen Thirty-Three Was a Bad Year*. Santa Barbara, Calif.: Black Sparrow.

————. 1985b. *The Road to Los Angeles*. Santa Barbara, Calif.: Black Sparrow.

————. 1985c. *The Wine of Youth*. Santa Barbara, Calif.: Black Sparrow.

————. 1986. *West of Rome*. Santa Barbara, Calif.: Black Sparrow.

————. [1977] 1988. *The Brotherhood of the Grape*. Santa Barbara, Calif.: Black Sparrow Press.

————. [1952] 1988. *Full of Life*. 2d ed. Santa Barbara, Calif.: Black Sparrow Press.

Ficarra, Bernard J. 1953. *I Zappatori*. Boston: Christopher Publishing House.

Forgione, Louis. 1924. *Reamer Lou*. New York: E. P. Dutton and Co.

————. 1928a. *The Men of Silence*. New York: E. P. Dutton and Co.

————. 1928b. *The River Between*. New York: E. P. Dutton and Co.

Fumento, Rocco. 1954a. *Devil by the Tail*. New York: Alfred A. Knopf.

————. 1954b. *Tree of Dark Reflection*. New York: McGraw-Hill.

Gambino, Richard. 1981. *Bread and Roses*. New York: Avon Books.

Giardina, Anthony. 1987. *A Boy's Pretension*. New York: Simon and Schuster.

Guido de Vries, Rachel. 1986. *Tender Warriors*. Ithaca, N.Y.: Firebrand Books.

Hendin, Josephine Gattuso. 1988. *The Right Thing to Do*. Boston: David R. Godine, Publisher.

Higham, John. 1959. *Strangers in the Land*. New Brunswick, N.J.: Rutgers University Press.

Ianuzzi, John Nicholas. 1970. *Part 35*. New York: Richard W. Baron Publishing Co.

———. 1972. *Sicilian Defense*. New York: Richard W. Baron Publishing Co.

Lapolla, Garibaldi Marto. 1931. *The Fire in the Flesh*. New York: Vanguard Press.

———. 1932. *Miss Rollins in Love*. New York: Vanguard Press.

———. 1935. *The Grand Gennaro*. New York: Vanguard Press.

Laxalt, Robert. 1964. *A Man in the Wheatfield*. New York: Harper and Row, Publishers.

Longo, Lucas. 1968. *The Family on Vendetta Street*. New York: Doubleday and Co.

McHale, Tom. 1970. *Principato*. New York: Viking Press.

Madalena, Lawrence. 1959. *Confetti for Gino*. New York: Doubleday and Co.

Maggio, Joe. 1972. *Company Man*. New York: G. P. Putnam's Sons.

Mancini, Anthony. 1982. *The Miracle of Pelham Bay Park*. New York: E. P. Dutton.

Mangione, Jerre. 1948. *The Ship and the Flame*. New York: A. A. Wyn.

———. 1950. *Reunion in Sicily*. Boston: Houghton Mifflin Co.

———. 1965. *Night Search*. New York: Crown Publishing Co.

———. 1969. *America Is Also Italian*. New York: G. P. Putnam's Sons.

———. [1973, 1978] 1983. *An Ethnic at Large: A Memoir of America in the Thirties and Forties*. Philadelphia: University of Pennsylvania Press.

———. [1942, 1981] 1989. *Mount Allegro* (memoirs). Boston: Harper and Row.

Marchiello, Maurice R. 1969. *Crossing the Tracks*. New York: Vantage Press.

Marrotta, Kenny. 1985. *A Piece of Earth*. New York: William Morrow and Co.

Maso, Carole. 1986. *Ghost Dance*. San Francisco: North Point Press.

Mathias, Elizabeth, and Richard Raspa. 1985. *Italian Folktales in America*. Detroit: Wayne State University Press.

Mays, Lucinda. 1979. *The Other Shore*. New York: Atheneum Publishers.

Mazzuchelli, Samuel. 1967. *The Memoirs of Father Samuel Mazzuchelli, O.P.* Chicago: Priory Press.

Miller, Sidney. 1941. *Home Is Here*. New York: Macmillan Co.

Mirabelli, Eugene. 1972. *No Resting Place*. New York: Viking Press.

Moroso, John A. 1923. *Stumbling Hard*. New York: Macaulay.

Morreale, Ben. 1973. *A Few Virtuous Men*. Montreal: Tundra Books.

———. 1977. *Monday, Tuesday, Never Come Sunday*. Montreal: Tundra Books.

———. 1979. "The Prince of Racalmuto." *Italian Americana* 5, no. 1: 47–54.

Napoli, Joseph. 1986. *A Dying Cadence* (memoirs). West Bethesda, Md.: Marna Press.

Pagano, Jo. 1940. *The Paesanos*. Boston: Atlantic Monthly Press, Little, Brown and Co.

———. 1943. *Golden Wedding*. New York: Random House.

————. 1947. *The Condemned.* New York: Prentice Hall.

Panella, Vincent. 1979. *The Other Side: Growing Up Italian in America* (memoirs). Garden City, N.Y.: Doubleday.

Panetta, George. 1944. *We Ride a White Donkey.* New York: Harcourt, Brace and Co.

————. 1947. *Jimmy Potts Gets a Haircut.* New York: Doubleday.

————. 1957. *Viva Madison Avenue!* New York: Harcourt, Brace and Co.

————. 1966. *The Sea Beach Express.* New York: Harper and Row.

Panunzio, Constantine M. [1921] 1924. *The Soul of an Immigrant* (memoirs). New York: Macmillan Co.

————. 1971. *Immigration Crossroads.* Englewood, N.J.: Jerome S. Ozer.

Papaleo, Joseph. 1967. *All the Comforts.* Boston: Little, Brown and Co.

————. 1970. *Out of Place.* Boston: Little, Brown and Co.

Parini, Jay. 1986. *The Patch Boys.* New York: Henry Holt and Co.

Pasinetti, P. M. 1965. *The Smile on the Face of the Lion.* New York: Random House.

————. 1970. *From the Academy Bridge.* New York: Random House.

Pellegrini, Angelo. 1956. *Americans by Choice* (memoirs). New York: Macmillan Co.

————. 1986. *American Dream: An Immigrant's Quest* (memoirs). Berkeley, Calif.: North Point Press.

Piazza, Ben. 1964. *The Exact and Very Strange Truth.* New York: Farrar.

Pollini, Francis. 1961. *Night.* New York: G. P. Putnam's Sons.

————. 1965a. *Excursion.* New York: G. P. Putnam's Sons.

————. 1965b. *Glover.* New York: G. P. Putnam's Sons.

————. 1967. *The Crown.* New York: G. P. Putnam's Sons.

————. 1968. *Pretty Maids All in a Row.* New York: Delacorte Press and Dell Publishing Co.

Puzo, Mario. 1955. *The Dark Arena.* New York: Random House.

————. 1964. *The Fortunate Pilgrim.* New York: Atheneum Publishers.

————. 1969. *The Godfather.* New York: G. P. Putnam's Sons.

————. 1979. *Fools Die.* New York: New American Library.

————. 1984. *The Sicilian.* New York: Linden Press.

Rimanelli, Giose. 1957. *Original Sin.* New York: Random House.

————, ed. 1966. *Modern Canadian Stories* (short fiction). Toronto: Ryerson Press.

————. 1971. "Benedetta in Guysterland" (unpublished novel).

————. 1984. *Day of the Lion.* New York: Random House.

Ruddy, Anna C. [1908] 1975. *The Heart of the Stranger.* New York: Arno Press.

Scammacca, Nat. 1979. *Due mondi*. Trapani, Italy: Editrice Antigruppo Siciliano and Cross-Cultural Communications.

———. 1986. *Bye Bye America: Memories of a Sicilian American* (memoirs). English language edition. Trapani, Italy: Editrice Antigruppo Siciliano and Cross-Cultural Communications.

———. 1989. *Sikano L'Americano*. Trapani, Italy: Editrice Antigruppo Siciliano and Cross-Cultural Communications.

Seeca, Pasquale. 1927. *Il presidente Scoppetta*. N.p.

Segale, Sister Blandina. [1912] 1948. *At the End of the Santa Fe Trail*. Milwaukee: Bruce Publishers.

Siciliano, Vincent. 1970. *Unless They Kill Me First*. New York: Hawthorn Books.

Sorrentino, Gilbert. 1969. *Mulligan Stew*. New York: Grove Press.

———. 1980. *Aberration of Starlight*. New York: Random House.

———. 1981. *Crystal Vision*. San Francisco: North Point Press.

———. 1983. *Blue Pastoral*. San Francisco: North Point Press.

———. 1985. *Odd Number*. San Francisco: North Point Press.

———. 1986. *The Sky Changes*. San Francisco: North Point Press.

Sorrentino, Joseph. 1971. *Up from Never*. New York: Prentice Hall.

Tomasi, Mari. 1940. *Deep Grow the Roots*. Philadelphia: J. B. Lippincott Co.

———. 1949. *Like Lesser Gods*. Milwaukee: Bruce Publishing Co.

Tusiani, Joseph. 1965. *Envoy from Heaven*. New York: Obolensky.

———. 1988. *La parola difficile*. Fasano di Puglia: Schena Editore.

Valerio, Anthony. 1982. *The Mediterranean Runs through Brooklyn*. New York: H. B. Davis.

———. 1986. *Valentino and the Great Italians*. New York: Freundlich Books.

Valenti, Angelo. 1975. *Golden Gate*. Salem, N.H.: Ayer Co., Publishers.

Vannucci, Lynn. 1987. *Coyote*. Toronto: Bantam Books.

Ventura, Luigi Donato. 1913. *Peppino*. New York: William R. Jenkins Co.

Vergara, Joseph. 1968. *Love and Pasta*. New York: Harper and Row, Publishers.

Viertel, Joseph. 1962. *To Love and Corrupt*. New York: Random House.

Villa, Sihio. 1923. *The Unbidden Guest*. New York: Macmillan Co.

Vivante, Arturo. [1958] 1967. *The French Girls of Killini* (short stories). Boston: Little, Brown and Co.

———. 1959. *A Goodly Babe*. Boston: Little, Brown and Co.

———. [1959, 1966] 1969. *Doctor Giovanni*. Boston: Little, Brown and Co.

Poetry

Ciardi, John. 1979. *For Instance*. New York: W. W. Norton and Co.

———. 1984. *Selected Poems*. Fayetteville: University of Arkansas Press.

———. 1985. *The Birds of Pompeii*. Fayetteville: University of Arkansas Press.

Carnevali, Emanuel. 1978. *Il primo Dio* (poetry and prose essays). Milan: Adelphi.

Citino, David. 1980. *Last Rites and Other Poems*. Columbus: Ohio State University Press.

———. 1985. *The Appassionata Doctrines*. Cleveland: Cleveland State Poetry Center.

———. 1986. *The Gift of Fire*. Fayetteville: University of Arkansas Press.

Clements, Arthur L. 1987. *Common Blessings*. Franklin Lakes, N.J.: Lincoln Springs Press.

Corso, Gregory Nunzio. 1970. *Elegiac Feelings American*. New York: New Directions.

———. 1974. *Earth Egg*. New York: Unmuzzled Ox Press.

———. n.d. *Gasoline, the Vestal Lady on Brattle*. San Francisco: City Lights Books.

De Iuliis, Celestino. 1981. *Love's Sinning Song*. Toronto: Canadian Center for Italian Culture and Education.

Di Cicco, Pier Giorgio. 1979. *The Tough Romance*. Toronto: McClelland and Stewart.

Di Prima, Diane. 1971. *Revolutionary Letters*. San Francisco, Calif.: City Lights Books.

———. 1977. *Selected Poems: Nineteen Fifty-Six to Nineteen Seventy-Six*. Berkeley, Calif.: North Atlantic Books.

———. 1978. *Loba*. Berkeley, Calif.: Wingbow Press.

Ferlinghetti, Lawrence. 1958. *Coney Island of the Mind*. New York: New Directions.

———. 1979. *Landscapes of Living and Dying*. New York: New Directions.

———. 1981. *Endless Life: The Selected Poems*. New York: New Directions.

———. 1984. *Over All the Obscene Boundaries: European Poems in Transitions*. New York: New Directions.

Gabriel, Daniel. 1983. *Sacco and Vanzetti: A Narrative Longpoem*. Brooklyn, N.Y.: Gull Books.

Gilbert, Sandra. 1979. *In The Fourth World: Poems*. Foreword by Richard Eberhart. Tuscaloosa: University of Alabama Press.

———. 1984. *Emily's Bread: Poems*. New York: W. W. Norton and Co.

Gillan, Maria M. 1981. *Flowers from the Tree of Night*. Seattle: Chantry Press.

———. 1985. *Winter Light*. Seattle: Chantry Press.

———. 1989. *The Weather of Old Seasons*. Merrick N.Y.: Cross-Cultural Communications.

Gioseffi, Daniela. 1979. *Eggs in the Lake*. Brockport, N.Y.: BOA Editions.

Giovanitti, Arturo. 1975. *The Collected Poems of Arturo Giovanitti*. Salem, N.H.: Ayer Co., Publishers.

Green, Rose Basile. 1974. *Primo Vino*. New York: A. S. Barnes and Co.

————. n.d. *To Reason Why.* Cranbury, N.J.: Associated University Presses.

Mariani, Paul. 1979. *Timing Devices: Poems.* Boston: David R. Godine, Publisher.

————. 1982. *Crossing Cocytus and Other Poems.* New York: Grove Press.

————. 1985. *Prime Mover.* New York: Grove Press.

Paolucci, Anne. 1981. *Riding the Mast Where It Swings.* 2d ed. Bergenfield, N.J.: Griffon House Publications.

————. n.d. *Poems Written for Sbek's Mummies, Marie Menken & Other Important Persons, Places and Things.* Bergenfield, N.J.: Griffon House Publications.

Parini, Jay. 1988. *Town Life: Poems.* New York: Henry Holt and Co.

Pucelli, Rodolfo. 1949. *Sonetti biografici di italo-americani.* Milan: N.p.

Scalapino, Leslie. 1979. *This Eating & Walking at the Same Time Is Associated Alright.* Bolinas, Calif.: Tombouctou.

————. 1982. *Considering How Exaggerated Music Is.* San Francisco: North Point Press.

————. 1985. *That They Were at the Beach.* San Francisco: North Point Press.

————. 1988. *Way.* San Francisco: North Point Press.

Scammacca, Nat. 1985. *Schammachanat.* Trappani: Editrice Antigruppo Siciliano and Cross-Cultural Communications.

Sorrentino, Gilbert. 1976. *A Dozen Oranges.* Santa Barbara, Calif.: Black Sparrow Press.

————. 1978. *The Orangery.* Austin: University of Texas Press.

————. 1981. *Selected Poems: Nineteen Fifty-Eight to Nineteen Eighty.* Santa Rosa, Calif.: Black Sparrow Press.

Stefanile, Felix. 1970. *A Fig Tree in America.* New Rochelle, N.Y.: Elizabeth Press.

————. 1976. *East River Nocturne.* New Rochelle, N.Y.: Elizabeth Press.

————. 1982. *In That Far Country.* West Lafayette, Ind.: Sparrow Press.

Tusiani, Joseph. 1962. *Rind and All: Fifty Poems.* New York: Monastine Press.

————. 1964. *The Fifth Season: Poems.* New York: Obolensky.

————. 1978. *Gente Mia and Other Poems.* Stone Park, Ill.: Italian Cultural Center.

Critical Studies

Ahearn, Carol Bonomo. 1986a. "Kenny Marotta: Exploring the Roots of a Writer," *Fra Noi* 25 (June): 47.

————. 1986b. "Interview: Helen Barolini" *Fra Noi* 25 (September): 51.

Aleandri, Emelise. 1983. "Italian-American Theatre." In *Ethnic Theatre in the United States,* edited by Maxine Schwartz Seller, 237–58. Westport, Conn.: Greenwood Press.

Alfonsi, Ferdinando, ed. 1985. *Poeti italo-americani/ Italo-American Poets: Antologia bilingue/ A Bilingual Anthology.* Catanzaro, Italy: Antonio Carello Editore.

————. 1989. *Dictionary of Italian-American Poets.* New York: Peter Lang.

Arcudi, Bruno. 1979. "*Gente Mia and Other Poems.*" *Italian Americana* 5, no. 1: 116–18.

Aaron, Daniel. 1984–85. "The Hyphenate American Writer." *Rivista di studi anglo-americani* (nos. 3–5): 11–28.

Ballerini, Luigi, and Fredi Chiappelli. 1985. "Contributi espressive della scritture e parlate Americo-Italiane." In *Atti dei convegni Lincei.* Rome: Accademia Nazionale dei Lincei.

Barolini, Helen. 1985a. "The Case of Mari Tomasi." In *Italians and Irish in America,* proceedings of the Sixteenth Annual Conference of the American Italian Historical Association, edited by Francis X. Femminella, 1977–86. Staten Island, N.Y.: American Italian Historical Association.

————, ed. 1985b. *The Dream Book: An Anthology of Writings by Italian American Women.* New York: Schocken Books.

————. 1986. "Becoming a Literary Person Out of Context," *Massachusetts Review* 27, no. 2: 262–74.

Bergin, Thomas G. 1987–88 "Giose Rimanelli: A Cousin to the Knight of La Mancha?" *Misure critiche* 12–13, nos. 65–69: 11–13.

Bernardi, Adria. 1990. *Houses with Names: The Italian Immigrants of Highwood, Illinois.* Champaign: University of Illinois Press.

Bevilacqua, Winifred Farrant. 1984–85. "*Rosa, The Life of an Italian Immigrant.*" *Rivista di studi anglo-americani* 3, nos. 4–5: 545–56.

Bloom, James D. 1986. Review of *The Patch Boys,* by Jay Parini. *New York Times Book Review* (21 December): 18.

Boelhower, William. 1981. "The Immigrant Novel as Genre." *MELUS* 8, no. 1 (Spring): 3–14.

————. 1982a. *Immigrant Autobiography in the United States: Four Versions of the Italian American Self.* Verona: Essedue Edizioni.

————. 1982b. "The Brave New World of Immigrant Autobiography." *MELUS* 9, no. 2: 5–23.

————. 1984–85. "Describing the Italian American Self." *Rivista di studi anglo-americani* 3, nos. 4–5: 533–44.

————. [1984] 1987. *Through a Glass Darkly: Ethnic Semiosis in American Litera-ture.* Venice, Italy: Edizioni Helvetia; republished by Oxford University Press.

Bona, Mary Jo. 1987. "Broken Images, Broken Lives: Carmolina's Journey in Tina DeRosa's *Paper Fish.*" *MELUS* 14, nos. 3–4: 87–106.

————. 1990. "Mari Tomasi's *Like Lesser Gods* and the Making of an Ethnic *Bildungsroman.*" *Voices in Italian Americana* 1, no. 1: 15–34.

Bondanella, Peter. 1984–85. "Edward Dmytryk's *Christ in Concrete* and Italian Neorealism." *Rivista di studi anglo-americani* 3, nos. 4–5: 227–40.

Brown, Carole. 1979. "From Saracen to Iggy: The Novels of Ben Morreale." *Italian Americana* 5, no. 2: 205–21.

Cateura, Linda. 1986. *Growing Up Italian.* New York: William Morrow and Co.

Cammett, John M., ed. 1969. *The Italian American Novel.,* proceedings of the Second Annual American Italian Historical Association Conference. Staten Island, N.Y.: American Italian Historical Association.

Cipolla, Gaetano. 1977. "Francesca Cabrini: 'Figura Matris' in a Contemporary Novel." *Italian Americana* 3, no. 2: 162–73.

Cocchi, Raffaele. 1984–85. "Gregory Corso: Poetic Vision and Memory as a Child of Italian Origin on the Streets and Roads of America." *Rivista di studi anglo-americani* 3, nos. 4–5: 343–52.

Coles, Nicholas. 1987. "Mantraps: Men at Work in Pietro Di Donato's *Christ in Concrete* and Thomas Bell's *Out of this Furnace." MELUS* 14, nos. 3–4: 23–32.

Cordasco, Francesco, and Salvatore LaGumina. 1972. *Italians in the United States: A Bibliography of Reports, Texts, Critical Studies, and Related Materials.* New York: Oriole Editions.

Correa-Zoli, Y. 1980 "The Language of Italian Americans." In *Language in the U.S.A.,* edited by C. A. Ferguson and S. Brice Heath, 239–56. Cambridge: Cambridge University Press.

Cortes, Carlos E. 1987. "Italian Americans in Film: From Immigrants to Icons." *MELUS* 14, nos. 3–4: 107–26.

D'Amico, Maria Vittoria. 1984–85. "Paradox beyond Convention: Gilbert Sorrentino's Fiction." *Rivista di studi anglo-americani* 3, nos. 4–5: 269–80.

di Biagi, Flaminio. 1987. "Italian American Writers: Notes for a Wider Categorization." *MELUS* 14, nos. 3–4: 141–52.

Di Pietro, Robert. 1976. "Language as a Marker of Italian Ethnicity." *Studi emigrazione* 42 (June): 203–17.

———. 1986. "Language, Culture and the Expression of Ethnicity among Italian Americans." In *Support and Struggle: Italians and Italian Americans in a Comparative Perspective,* proceedings of the Seventeenth Annual Conference of the American Italian Historical Association, edited by Joseph L. Tropea, James E. Miller, and Cheryl Beattie-Repetti, 249–54. Staten Island: American Italian Historical Association.

Di Scipio, Giuseppe Carlo. 1985. "Italian-American Playwrights on the Rise." *Journal of Popular Culture* 19, no. 3: 103–8.

Esposito, Michael D. 1980a. "The Travail of Pietro Di Donato." *MELUS* 7, no. 2: 47–60.

———. 1980b. "Pietro Di Donato Re-evaluated." *Italian Americana* 6, no. 2: 179–92.

———. 1986. "The Evolution of Pietro Di Donato's Perceptions of Italian Americans." In *The Italian-Americans through the Generations,* proceedings of the Fifteenth Annual Conference of the American Italian Historical Association, edited by Rocco Caporale, 176–84. Staten Island, N.Y.: American Italian Historical Association.

Estavan, Lawrence. 1976. *The Italian Theatre in San Francisco*. San Bernardino, Calif.: Borgo Press.

Ferraro, Thomas J. 1989. "Blood in the Marketplace: The Business of Family in the *Godfather* Narratives." In *The Invention of Ethnicity*, edited by Werner Sollors, 176–207. New York: Oxford University Press.

Fratti, Mario. 1976. "Italian-American Playwrights." *La parola del popolo* (September–October): 281–83.

Gambino, Richard. 1975. *Blood of My Blood: The Dilemma of the Italian Americans*. New York: Doubleday and Co.

Gardaphé, Fred L. 1985. "An Interview with Tina DeRosa." *Fra Noi* 24 (May): 23.

———. 1986a. "Morreale Uncovers His Sicilian Roots." *Fra Noi* 25 (April): 41.

———. 1986b. "Lawrence Ferlinghetti: Ageless Radical Fights for Politics and Poetry." *Fra Noi* 25 (May): 45.

———. 1986c. "Family at the Root of Ardizzone's Fiction." *Fra Noi* 25 (October): 47.

———. 1987a. "Parini's *Patch Boys* Mines Italian American Heritage." *Fra Noi* 26 (April): 37.

———. 1987b. "Italian American Fiction: A Third Generation Renaissance." *MELUS* 14, nos. 3–4: 69–86.

———. 1987–88. "Giose Rimanelli: New Directions of a Literary Missionary." *Misure critiche* 12–13, nos. 65–67: 235–43.

———, ed. 1989. *Italian American Ways: Recipes and Traditions*. New York: Harper and Row.

Geduld, Harry M. 1984–85. "*Christ in Concrete*: Fiction into Film." *Rivista di studi anglo americani* 3, nos. 4–5: 241–56.

Giordano, Fedora. 1984. "An Archetypal World: Images of Italy in the Poetry of John Ciardi." *Rivista di studi anglo-americani* 3, nos. 4–5: 305–14.

Green, Rose Basile. 1974. *The Italian-American Novel: A Document of the Interaction of Two Cultures*. Madison, N.J.: Fairleigh Dickinson University Press.

———. 1976. "The Italian-American Novel: An Ethnic Component of a More Representative American Literature." *La parola del popolo* (September–October): 329–35.

———. 1983. "Italian-American Literature." In *Ethnic Perspective in American Literature: Selected Essays on the European Contribution*, edited by Robert J. Di Pietro and Edward Ifkovic, 110–32. New York: Modern Language Association.

Holte, James Craig. 1978. "Benjamin Franklin and Italian-American Narratives." *MELUS* 5, no. 4: 99–102.

———. 1982a. "Private Lives and Public Faces: Ethnic American Autobiography." *Ethnic Groups* 4, nos. 1–2: 61–83.

———. 1982b. "The Representative Voice: Autobiography and the Ethnic Experience." *MELUS* 9, no. 2: 25–46.

———. 1988. *The Ethnic I: A Sourcebook for Ethnic American Autobiography.* New York: Greenwood Press.

Kirschenbaum, Blossom. 1987. "Diane di Prima: Extending *La Famiglia.*" *MELUS* 14, nos. 3–4: 53–68.

Lawton, Ben. 1979. "*Taxi Driver:* 'New Hybrid Film' or 'Liberated Cinema'?" *Italian Americana* 5, no. 2 (Spring-Summer): 238–48.

Losito, Leonardo A. 1984–85. "An Approach to Italian-American Poetry." *Rivista di studi anglo-americani* 3, nos. 4–5: 365–83.

Mangione, Jerre. [1965] 1968. *A Passion for Sicilians: The World around Danilo Dolci.* New Brunswick, N.J.: Transaction Books.

———. 1981. "A Double Life: The Fate of the Urban Ethnic." In *Literature and the Urban Experience,* edited by Michael C. Jaye and Ann Chalmers Watts, 169–83. New Brunswick, N.J.: Rutgers University Press.

———. [1972] 1983a. *The Dream and the Deal: The Federal Writers' Project 1935–1943.* Philadelphia: University of Pennsylvania Press.

———. [1973, 1978] 1983b. *An Ethnic at Large: A Memoir of America in the Thirties and Forties.* Philadelphia: University of Pennsylvania Press.

———. [1950] 1984. *Reunion in Sicily.* New York: Columbia University Press.

———. 1984–85. "My Experience as an Italian American Writer." *Rivista di studi anglo-americani* 3, nos. 4–5: 67–86.

———. 1986. "Comments." In *Contemporary Novelists,* 4th ed., edited by D. L. Kirkpatrick, 570–72. New York: St. Martin's Press.

Mathias, Elizabeth, and Richard Raspa. 1985. *Italian Folktales in America.* Detroit: Wayne State University Press.

Meckel, Richard A. 1987. "The Not So Fundamental Sociology of Garibaldi Marto Lapolla." *MELUS* 14, nos. 3–4: 127–40.

Mignone, Mario. 1976. "Il teatro di Mario Fratti." *La parola del popolo* (September-October): 283–89.

Minganti, Franco. 1984–85. "The Hero with a Thousand and Three Faces: Michele, Mike, Michael Coreleone." *Rivista di studi anglo-americani* 3, nos. 4–5: 257–68.

Monguio, Luis. 1987–88. "Giose Rimanelli: The American Writer." *Misure critiche.* 12–13, nos. 65–67: 159–61.

Morreale, Ben. 1981. "Jerre Mangione: The Sicilian Sources." *Italian Americana* 7, no. 1: 5–18.

———. 1986. "Mangione and the Yearning for Home." *Fra Noi* 25 (November): 41.

Mulas, Francesco. 1985. "Interview: Jerre Mangione." *MELUS* 12, no. 4: 73–84.

———. 1984–85. "Prolepsis in Mario Puzo's *The Godfather.*" *Rivista di studi anglo-americani* 3, nos. 4–5: 353–64.

Nepaulsingh, Colbert I. "Rimanelli nelle rime: Life and Fiction, Life and Life." *Misure critiche* 12–13, nos. 65–67: 230–34.

Oliver, Lawrence J. 1987a. " 'Great Equalizer' or 'Cruel Stepmother'? Image of the School in Italian-American Literature." *Journal of Ethnic Studies* 15, no. 2: 113–30.

———. 1987b. "The Re-visioning of New York's Little Italys: From Hotels to Puzo. *MELUS* 14, nos. 3–4: 5–22.

Patti, Samuel J. 1986. "Autobiography: The Root of the Italian-American Narrative." *Annali d'italianistica* 4: 242–48.

Peragallo, Olga. 1949. *Italian American Authors and Their Contribution to American Literature.* New York: S. F. Vanni.

Rimanelli, Giose, ed., 1976. *Italian Literature: Roots and Branches.* New Haven, Conn.: Yale University Press.

Russo, John Paul. 1984–85. "The Poetics of Gilbert Sorrentino," *Rivista di studi anglo-americani* 3, nos. 4–5: 281–303.

Reilly, John M. 1985. "Literary Versions of Ethnic History from Upstate New York." In *Upstate Literature: Essays in Memory of Thomas F. O'Donnell,* edited by Frank Bergmann, 183–200. Syracuse, N.Y.: Syracuse University Press.

Sartori, Daniela Carpi. 1985. "Emanuel Carnevali and Guido Gozzano." *Rivista di studi anglo-americani* 3, nos. 4–5: 315–28.

Sinicropi, Giovanni. 1977. "*Christ in Concrete.*" *Italian Americana* 3, no. 2: 177–83.

Stefanile, Felix. 1990. "Poets and Emulation: Dana Gioia and Jay Parini." *Voices in Italian Americana* 1, no. 1: 35–50.

Stern, Kenneth. 1987–88. "Fiction and Indeterminacy: In Honor of Giose Rimanelli." *Misure critiche.* 12–13, nos. 65–67: 223–29.

Tamburri, Anthony Julian. 1989. "To Hyphenate or Not To Hyphenate: The Italian/ American Writer and *Italianità,*" *Italian Journal* 3, no. 5: 37–42.

Tanelli, Orazio. 1986. "Orizzonti poetici italo-americani." *La follia di New York* (March–April): 22–23.

Torgovnick, Marianna De Marco. 1988. "*The Godfather* as the World's Most Typical Novel." *South Atlantic Quarterly* 87, no. 2: 329–53.

Traldi, Alberto. 1976. "La tematica dell'emigrazione nella narrativa italo-americana." *Comunità* 30: 245–72.

Trovato, Mario. 1976. "Vittorio Nardi: poeta italo-americano." *La parola del popolo* (September–October): 340–41.

Tusiani, Joseph. 1982. "The Themes of Deracination and Americanization in *Gente Mia and Other Poems.*" *Ethnic Groups* 4, no. 3: 149–76.

———. 1986. "Garibaldi in American Poetry." In *The Italian Americans through the Generations,* proceedings of the Fifteenth Annual Conference of the American Italian Historical Association, edited by Rocco Caporale, 64–75. Staten Island, N.Y.: American Italian Historical Association.

Vecoli, Rudolph J. 1969. "The Italian-American Literary Subculture: An Historical and Sociological Analysis." *The Italian American Novel,* proceedings of the

Second Annual Conference of the American Italian Historical Assocation, edited by John M. Cammett. Staten Island, N.Y.: America Historical Association.

—————. 1984–85. "The Search for an Italian American Identity." *Rivista di studi anglo-americani* 3, nos. 4–5: 29–66.

Viscusi, Robert. 1981. "'*De vulgari eloquentia*': An Approach to the Language of Italian American Fiction." *Yale Italian Studies* 1 (Winter): 21–38.

—————. 1982. "The Text in the Dust: Writing Italy across America." *Studi emigrazione* 19, no. 65: 123–30.

—————. 1983a. "*Il caso della casa:* Stories of Houses in Italian America." In *The Family and Community Life of Italian Americans,* proceedings of the Thirteenth Annual Conference of the American Italian Historical Association, edited by Richard J. Juliani, 1–10. Staten Island, N.Y.: American Italian Historical Association.

—————. 1983b. "Professions and Faiths: Critical Choices in the Italian American Novel." In *Italian American in the Professions,* proceedings of the Twelfth Annual Conference of the American Italian Historical Association, edited by Remigio Pane, 41–54. Staten Island, N.Y.: American Italian Historical Association.

—————. 1986a. "Circles of the Cyclopes: Schemes of Recognition in Italian American Discourse." In *Italian Americans: New Perspectives in Italian Immigration and Ethnicity,* edited by Lydio Tomasi, 209–19. New York: Center for Migration Studies.

—————. 1986b. " 'The Semiology of Semen': Questioning the Father." In *The Italian Americans through the Generations,* proceedings of the Fifteenth Annual Conference of the American Italian Historical Association, edited by Rocco Caporale, 185–95. Staten Island, N.Y.: American Italian Historical Association.

—————. 1990. "Breaking the Silence: Strategic Imperatives for Italian American Culture." *Voices in Italian Americana* 1, no. 1: 1–13.

Von Heune-Greenberg, Dorthee. 1987. "Interview: Pietro Di Donato." *MELUS* 14, nos. 3–4: 33–52.

Journals

Italian Americana. Carol Bonomo Ahearn, University of Rhode Island, Continuing Education, 199 Promenade Street, Providence, RI 02903.

la bella figura. Rose Romano, ed. P.O. Box 411223, San Francisco, CA. 94141–1223.

Voices in Italian Americana. Anthony Julian Tamburri, Paolo A. Giordano, and Fred L. Gardaphé, eds. Department of Foreign Languages and Literatures, Stanley Coulter Hall, Purdue University, West Lafayette, IN 47907.

Paolo A. Giordano
Fred L. Gardaphé
Anthony Julian Tamburri

Select Filmography and Bibliography of Film Directors

The information that follows is intended primarily to make the films of the current generation of Italian/American directors more easily accessible to the individual viewer.

Thanks to the ever greater availability of films of all kinds on videotape, it is now possible even for those who do not reside in major urban centers to view the works of directors great—and not so great—at very reasonable prices. Under the Video Suppliers section of this Filmography, we have listed names and addresses of distributors of the movies available on videotape. We have not included information concerning the distributors of these works on 16mm film because it is available elsewhere and usually is of interest to institutions such as universities and museums. Furthermore, 16mm films tend to be prohibitively expensive for the individual.

We have included a bibliography of books and book chapters concerning Italian/American directors, but we have not included articles because they are so numerous that to do so would require an additional volume. If you are interested in further information, consult the essays on Italian/American cinema in this anthology and *Film Literature Index,* 15 vols., edited by Zita Eastman, Vincent J. Aceto, and Fred Silva. (Albany, N.Y.: Film and Television Documentation Center, 1973–79).

Select Filmography

In this filmography, an asterisk (*) indicates the film was not available for general distribution at the time of publication of this volume.

Cimino, Michael. 1974. *Thunderbolt and Lightfoot*. 20th CFV—MGM/UA.
> ———. 1978. *The Deer Hunter*. MCA—Swank.
> ———. 1980. *Heaven's Gate*. MGM/UA.
> ———. 1985. *Year of the Dragon*. MGM/UA.
> ———. 1987. *The Sicilian*. Vestron.

Coppola, Francis Ford. 1962. *Bellboy and the Playgirls*. Sony.
> ———. 1962. *Tonight for Sure*. *.
> ———. 1963. *Dementia 13*. Crown/V Yesteryear.
> ———. 1967. *You're a Big Boy Now*. Warner.
> ———. 1968. *Finian's Rainbow*. Warner.
> ———. 1969. *The Rain People*. Warner.
> ———. 1972. *The Godfather*. Paramount.
> ———. 1974. *The Conversation*. Paramount.
> ———. 1974. *The Godfather II*. Paramount.
> ———. 1979. *Apocalypse Now*. Paramount.
> ———. 1981. *The Godfather: The Complete Epic*. Paramount.

———. 1982. *One from the Heart*. RCA/Col.

———. 1983. *Outsiders*. Warner.

———. 1983. *Rumble Fish*. MCA.

———. 1985. *Cotton Club*. Embassy.

———. 1985. *Rip Van Winkle* [Faerie Tale Theatre]. CBS/Fox.

———. 1986. *Peggy Sue Got Married*. CBS/Fox.

———. 1987. *Gardens of Stone*. CBS/Fox.

———. 1988. *Tucker*. Paramount.

———. 1989. *New York Stories*. Touchstone.

De Palma, Brian. 1968. *Greetings*. Vidmark.

———. 1970. *Hi Mom!* *.

———. 1973. *Sisters*. Warner.

———. 1974. *Phantom of the Paradise*. Key.

———. 1976. *Carrie*. CBS/Fox.

———. 1976. *Obsession*. RCA/Col.

———. 1978. *The Fury*. CBS/Fox.

———. 1979. *Home Movies*. Vestron.

———. 1980. *Dressed to Kill*. Warner.

———. 1981. *Blowout*. Warner.

———. 1983. *Scarface*. MCA.

———. 1984. *Body Double*. RCA/Col.

———. 1986. *Wise Guys*. CBS/Fox.

———. 1987. *The Untouchables*. Paramount.

———. 1989. *Casualties of War*. Columbia.

Scorsese, Martin. 1969. *Who's That Knocking at My Door?*.

———. 1972. *Boxcar Bertha*. Vestron.

———. 1973. *Mean Streets*. Warner.

———. 1974. *Alice Doesn't Live Here Anymore*. Warner—Swank.

———. 1976. *Taxi Driver*. RCA/Col—Swank.

———. 1977. *New York, New York*. CBS/Fox.

———. 1978. *The Last Waltz*. CBS/Fox.

———. 1980. *Raging Bull*. CBS/Fox.

———. 1982. *The King of Comedy*. RCA/Col.

———. 1985. *After Hours*. Warner.

———. 1986. *The Color of Money*. Touchstone.

———. 1988. *The Last Temptation of Christ*. MCA.

———. 1989. *New York Stories*. Touchstone.

Short Films

———. 1963. *What's a Nice Girl Like You Doing in a Place Like This?*. 9 min. GPS.

———. 1964. *It's Not Just You, Murray!*. 15 min. *.

———. 1967. *The Big Shave*. 6 min. GPS.

———. 1970. *Street Scenes*. 75 min. *.

———. 1974. *Italianamerican*. 48 min. *.

———. 1978. *American Boy: A Profile of Steven Prince*. 55 min. *.

———. 1987. *Bad*. With Michael Jackson. 24 min. *.

Stallone, Sylvester. 1978. *Paradise Alley*. MCA.

———. 1979. *Rocky II*. CBS/Fox.

———. 1982. *Rocky III*. CBS/Fox.

———. 1983. *Staying Alive*. Paramount.

———. 1985. *Rocky IV*. CBS/Fox.

Video Suppliers

Most of the major films listed above are available from better quality video stores. If you cannot find a particular title in your local video store, you may be able to buy or rent it from either of the two major distributors of foreign films, classics, and other hard-to-find movies:

Facets Video. 1517 W. Fullerton Ave., Chicago, IL 60614. Ph. (800) 331-6197, 9 a.m.–5 p.m., Mon.–Fri.

Tamarelle's International Films. 110 Cohasset Stage Rd., Chico, CA 95926. Ph. (800) 356-3577 or (916) 895-3429.

Both organizations have essentially the same titles and charge approximately the same for purchase or rental of the films. Purchase prices usually drop dramatically after a film has been available on video for a few months.

If all else fails, you may have to contact the distributors of the films on video directly. Thanks to Mark Andrews and Von's Videos, West Lafayette, IN 47906, for their help in compiling the following coded list of distributors and manufacturers.

APP.   Applause Productions, 85D Longview Rd., Port Washington, NY 11050-3099. Ph. (516) 883-7460.

AWA.   Award Films, 525 N. Laurel Ave., Los Angeles, CA 90048. Ph. (213) 462-5997.

BAK.   Baker and Taylor Video, 7000 N. Austin Ave., Niles, IL 60648. Ph. (800) 323-0626 or (312) 561-2500.

BEL.   Bel Canto. See Paramount Home Video.

BLA.   Blackhawk Films/Video, 1235 W. Fifth St., POB 3990, Davenport, IA 52802. Ph. (319) 323-9736.

BUD.   Budget Video, 4590 N. Highland Ave., #108, Los Angeles, CA 90028. Ph. (800) 621-0849 or (213) 466-0121.

CAB.   Cable Films, POB 7171, Country Club Station, Kansas City, MO 64113. Ph. (913) 362-2804.

CBS.   CBS/Fox Video, 1211 Avenue of the Americas, Second Floor, New York, NY 10036. Ph. (800) 742-1200 or (212) 819-3200.

CGP.   Cinema Group Pictures. See Palisades Entertainment.

CHA.   Charter Entertainment, 1901 Avenue of the Stars, Los Angeles, CA 90067. Ph. (213) 556-7467.

CIC.   CIC, 1111 Finch Ave. W., Suite 454, Toronto, Ontario M3J2E5.

CND.   Condor Video, 5730 Buckingham Parkway, Culver City, CA 90230. Ph. (213) 216-7900.

CNT.   Continental Video. See Palisades Entertainment.

COM.　　Commtron, 1501 50th St., Suite 300, West Des Moines, IA 50265. Ph. (800) 247-8032 or (515) 224-1784.

COR.　　Corinth Films, 34 Gansevoort St., New York, NY 10014. Ph. (800) 221-4720 or (212) 463–0305.

CRI.　　Criterion, 2139 Manning Ave., Los Angeles, CA 90025. Ph. (800) 443-2001 or (213) 475-3524.

CRV.　　Crown Video, 225 Park Ave. S., New York, NY 10003. Ph. (212) 254-1600.

CTR.　　Children's Treasures, 1901 Avenue of the Stars, Los Angeles, CA 90067. Ph. (213) 556-7438.

CVD.　　Coast Video Distributing, Inc., 500 N. Ventu Park Rd., Newbury Park, CA 91320. Ph. (805) 499-5827.

EHE.　　Embassy Entertainment (c/o Nelson Entertainment), 335 N. Maple Dr., Suite 350, Beverly Hills, CA 90210. Ph. (213) 285-6000.

EUR.　　Euro-American Home Video, 4818 Yuma St., NW, Washington, DC 20016. Ph. (202) 363-8835.

FAC.　　Facets Multimedia, Inc., 1517 W. Fullerton Ave., Chicago, IL 60614. Ph. (800) 331-6197 or (312) 281-9075.

FCL.　　Film Classics, 7313 Varna Ave., North Hollywood, CA 91605. Ph. (818) 764-0319.

FHE.　　Family Home Entertainment, 500 N. Ventu Park Rd., Newbury Park, CA 91320. Ph. (800) 423-7455 or (805) 499-5827.

FRI.　　Fries Home Video, 6922 Hollywood Blvd., Los Angeles, CA 90028. Ph. (213) 466-2266.

GLV.　　German Language Video Center, 7625 Pendleton Pike, Indianapolis, IN 46226. Ph. (317) 547-1257.

GPS.　　Glenn Photo Supply (GPS), 6924 Canby Ave., #103, Reseda, CA 91335. Ph. (213) 981-5506.

HBO.　　HBO Video, Inc., 1370 Avenue of the Americas, New York, NY 10019. Ph. (800) 648-7650 or (212) 977-8990.

HHT.　　Hollywood Home Theatre, 1540 N. Highland Ave., Suite 110, Hollywood, CA 90028. Ph. (800) 621-0849, Ext. 176, or (213) 466-0121.

IHV.　　International Home Video, 431 N. Figueroa St., Wilmington, CA 90744. Ph. (213) 513-1149.

IVE.　　International Video Entertainment, 500 N. Ventu Park Rd., POB 2520, Newbury Park, CA 91320. Ph. (800) 423-7455 or (805) 499-5827.

JLT.　　JLT Films, Inc., 480 Central Ave., Northfield, IL 60093. Ph. (312) 441-9440.

KEY.　　Key Video (c/o CBS/Fox Home Video), 1211 Avenue of the Americas, Second Floor, New York, NY 10036. Ph. (212) 819-3200.

KIN.	Kino International Corp., 333 W. 39th St., Suite 503, New York, NY 10018. Ph. (212) 629-6880.
KUL.	Kultur International Films, Ltd., 121 Highway 36, West Long Branch, NJ 07764. Ph. (800) 458-5887 or (201) 229-2343.
LGT.	Lightning Video, POB 4000, Stamford, CT 06907. Ph. (203) 967-9200.
LHV.	Lorimar Home Video, 17942 Cowan Ave., Irvine, CA 92714. Ph. (800) 624-2694 or (714) 474-0355.
MAD.	Madera Cinevideo, 620 E. Yosemite Ave., Madera, CA 93638. Ph. (209) 661-6000.
MAG.	Magnum Entertainment, 9301 Wilshire Blvd., Suite 602, Beverly Hills, CA 90212. Ph. (213) 278-9981.
MAR.	Mark V. International, Inc., 19770 Bahama St., North Ridge, CA 91324. Ph. (800) 433-9753 or (818) 407-3800.
MCA.	MCA Home Video, 70 Universal City Plaza, Universal City, CA 91608. Ph. (818) 777-4300 or (818) 508-4315. Also, 445 Park Avenue, New York, NY 10022. Ph. (212) 759-7500.
MED.	Media Home Entertainment, 5730 Buckingham Pkwy., Culver City, CA 90230. Ph. (213) 216-7900.
MGM/CBS Video.	Same Information as MGM/UA.
MGM.	MGM/UA Entertainment, 10000 Washington Blvd., Culver City, CA 90232-2728. Ph. (213) 280-6000. Also, 1350 Avenue of the Americas, New York, NY 10019. Ph. (212) 408-0500.
MON.	Monterey Home Video, POB 2648, Malibu, CA 90265. Ph. (213) 457-5595.
MPI.	MPI Home Video, 15825 Rob Roy Dr., Oak Forest, IL 60452. Ph. (800) 323-0442 or (312) 687-7881.
MSD.	M. S. Distributing, 1050 Arthur Ave., Elk Grove Village, IL 60007. Ph. (312) 364-2888.
PAL.	Palisades Entertainment, 1875 Century Park E., Los Angeles, CA 90067. Ph. (800) 821-3427 or (213) 785-3100. Also, 2320 Cottner, Los Angeles, CA 90064. Ph. (213) 477-3427.
PAR.	Paramount Home Video, 5555 Melrose Ave., Hollywood, CA 90038. Ph. (213) 468-5000.
PAV.	Pacific Arts Video, 50 N. La Cienega Blvd., Suite 210, Beverly Hills, CA 90211. Ph. (213) 657-2233.
PLA.	Playhouse Video, 1211 Avenue of the Americas, New York, NY 10036. Ph. (212) 819-3200.
PRH.	Program Hunters, 11669 Santa Monica Blvd., #106, Los Angeles, CA 90025. Ph (213) 477-3088.

PRI.	Prism Entertainment Corp., 1888 Century Park E., Suite 1000, Los Angeles, CA 90067. Ph. (213) 277-3270.
RCA.	RCA/Columbia Pictures Home Entertainment, 3500 W. Olive Ave., Burbank, CA 91505. Ph. (800) 722-2748 or (818) 953-7900.
REP.	Republic Pictures Home Video, 12636 Beatrice St., Los Angeles, CA 90066–0930. Ph. (213) 306-4040.
RIZ.	Rizzoli International Publications, Inc., 597 Fifth Ave., New York, NY 10017. Ph. (800) 433-1238 or (212) 223-0100.
SHO.	Showcase Productions, Inc., 6910 Hayvenhurst Ave., Suite 100, Van Nuys, CA 91406. Ph. (818) 785-7977.
SON.	Sony Video Software, 1700 Broadway, New York, NY 10019. Ph. (800) 832-2422 or (212) 698-4947.
SVR.	Swank Video Rentals, 201 S. Jefferson Ave., St. Louis, MO 63103. Ph. (800) 325-3344 or call collect (314) 534-6300.
THV.	Touchstone Home Video (c/o Disney Home Video), 500 S. Buena Vista St., Burbank, CA 91506. Ph. (818) 840-1875.
TWC.	Twentieth-Century Fox Video, 9440 Santa Monica Blvd., Beverly Hills, CA 90210. Ph. (800) 356-7667.
TWE.	Trans World Entertainment, 6464 Sunset Blvd., Suite 1100, Hollywood, CA 90028. Ph. (800) 521-0107 or (213) 461-0467.
UAV.	United American Video Corp., POB 7563, Charlotte, NC 28217. Ph. (704) 394-8796.
UEI.	United Entertainment, Inc., 4111 S. Darlington St., Suite 600, Tulsa, OK 74135. Ph. (918) 622-6460.
UVI.	Unicorn Video, 20822 Dearborn St., Chatsworth, CA 91311. Ph. (800) 528-4336 or (818) 407-1333.
VAC.	Video Action, 708 W. First St., Los Angeles, CA 90012. Ph. (800) 422-2241 or (213) 687-8262. Also, 237 Ogden Ave., Jersey City, NJ 07307. Ph. (800) 323-2955 or (201) 792-3833.
VAI.	Video Artists International, Inc., POB 153, Ansonia Station, New York, NY 10023. Ph. (800) 338-2566 or (212) 799-7798.
VAM.	Vid-America, Inc., 231 E. 55th St., New York, NY 10022. Ph. (212) 355-1600.
VCP.	Video City Productions, 22704 Ventura Blvd., Suite 339, Woodland Hills, CA 91364. Ph. (800) 367-4865 or (818) 710-9653.
VDI.	Video Dimensions, 530 W. 23rd St., New York, NY 10011. Ph. (212) 529-6135.
VEN.	Vidmark Enterprises, 2901 Ocean Blvd., Suite 213, Santa Monica, CA 90291. Ph. (800) 351-7070 or (213) 399-8877.
VES.	Vestron Video, POB 4000, Stamford, CT 06907. Ph. (203) 967-9200.
VGE.	Video Gems, 731 N. La Brea Ave., POB 38188, Los Angeles, CA 90038. Ph. (213) 938-2385.

VHV.   Vista Home Video, 645 Madison Ave., New York, NY 10022.
              Ph. (212) 582-0500.

VLO.   Video Latino, 431 N. Figueroa St., Wilmington, CA 90744.
              Ph. (213) 513-1149.

VYE.   Video Yesteryear, Box C, Sandy Hook, CT 06482.
              Ph. (800) 243-0987 or (203) 426-2574.

WAX.   Wax Works/Video Works, Inc., 325 E. Third St., Owensboro, KY
              42301. Ph. (800) 626-1918 or (502) 926-0008. Also, 4011 Winchester
              Rd., Memphis, TN 38118. Ph. (800) 423-0880 or (901) 366-4088.

WHV.   Warner Home Video, Inc., 4000 Warner Blvd., Burbank, CA 91505-
              4253. Ph. (800) 323-4767 or (818) 954-6000.

WVP.   World Video Pictures, Inc., 12401 Wilshire Blvd., Suite 102, Los
              Angeles, CA 90025. Ph. (213) 820-6100.

Select Bibliography

Bach, Steven. 1985. *Final Cut: Dreams and Disaster in the Making of "Heaven's Gate."* New York: William Morrow and Co.

Baker, Fred. 1973. "Francis Ford Coppola on the Director." In *Movie People,* edited by Christopher Morgan, 66–88. New York: Lancer Books.

Bliss, Michael. 1983. *Brian De Palma.* Metuchen, N.J.: Scarecrow Press.
———. 1985. *Martin Scorsese and Michael Cimino.* Metuchen, N.J.: Scarecrow Press.

Coppola, Eleanor. 1979. *Notes: Eleanor Coppola.* New York: Simon and Schuster.

Crispin, A. C. 1985. *Sylvester.* New York: Warner Publishers.
———. 1987. *Sylvester Stallone.* New York: St. Martin's Press.

Daly, Marsha. 1984. *Sylvester Stallone: An Illustrated Life.* New York: St. Martin's Press.

Dworkin, Susan. 1984. *Double De Palma: A Film Study with Brian De Palma.* New York: Newmarket.

Gelmis, Joseph. 1970. "Francis Ford Coppola." In *The Film Director as Superstar,* edited by Joseph Gelmis, 177–90. Garden City, N.Y.: Doubleday.

Green, Carl, and William R. Sanford. 1987. *Sylvester Stallone.* Mankato, Minn.: Crestwood House.

Johnson, Robert K. 1977. *Francis Ford Coppola.* Boston: Twayne Publishers.

Kael, Pauline. 1973. "Alchemy." In *Deeper into Movies,* edited by Pauline Kael, 420–26. Boston: Atlantic-Little, Brown.

Kauffmann, Stanley. 1975. *Living Images.* New York: Harper and Row, Publishers.

Kelly, Mary Pat. 1980. *Martin Scorsese: The First Decade.* Pleasantville, N.Y.: Redgrave Publishing Co.

Kolker, Robert P. 1980. *A Cinema of Loneliness: Penn, Kubrick, Coppola, Scorsese, Altman.* New York: Oxford University Press.

————. 1983. *The Altering Eye: Contemporary International Cinema.* New York: Oxford University Press.

————. 1988. *A Cinema of Loneliness: Penn, Kubrick, Scorsese, Spielberg, Altman.* New York: Oxford University Press. [N.B.: The 1988 revised edition no longer includes the essay on Coppola.]

Madsen, Axel. 1975. "Bogdanovich and Coppola." In *The New Hollywood,* edited by Peter Lehman, 108–16. New York: Thomas Y. Crowell.

Mast, Gerald. 1986. "The New American Auteurs." In *A Short History of the Movies,* 4th ed., edited by Gerald Mast, 484–95. New York: Macmillan.

Monaco, James. 1979. *American Film Now.* New York: New American Library.

Palmer, William J. 1987. *The Films of the Seventies.* Metuchen, N.J.: Scarecrow Press.

Pechter, William S. 1973. "Keeping Up with the Corleones." In *Films 72–73,* edited by David Denby, 4–9. Indianapolis: Bobbs-Merrill.

Robin, Jeff. N.d. *Stallone!* Forthcoming.

Sarris, Andrew. 1986. *The American Cinema: Directors and Directions,* 1929–68. Chicago: University of Chicago Press.

Solomon, Stanley J. 1976. *Beyond Formula: American Film Genres.* New York: Harcourt Brace Jovanovich.

Sylbert, Paul. 1974. *Final Cut.* Scranton, Pa.: Seabury Press.

Weinberg, Herman G. 1972. *The Complete Greed.* New York: Arno Press.

Weiss, Marion. 1987. *Martin Scorsese: A Guide to References and Resources.* Boston: G. K. Hall and Co.

Wood, Robin. 1986. *Hollywood from Vietnam to Reagan.* New York: Columbia University Press.

Lorraine Lawton

Contributors

Tony Ardizzone teaches creative writing and American literature at Indiana University. He is author of two novels, *In the Name of the Father* and *Heart of the Order,* and a collection of short stories, *The Evening News,* which received the Flannery O'Connor Award for Short Fiction. He has also been awarded the Virginia Prize for Fiction, the Lawrence Foundation Award, and two fellowships from the National Endowment for the Arts.

Helen Barolini, who has taught with the Trinity College program in Italy and at Pace University, has written the novels *Umbertina* and *Love in the Middle Ages,* and edited *The Dream Book: An Anthology of Writings by Italian American Women* (1985, paperback 1987), which received an American Book Award. Her most recently published work, *Festa,* is a collection of recipes and recollections. Forthcoming is her translation of Antonio Barolini's *Croton Elegies.* She is a winner of a National Endowment for the Arts grant.

Adria Bernardi has worked as a journalist in Chicago and Memphis. A graduate of Carleton College, she has studied Italian literature at the University of Chicago. Her first book, *Houses with Names: The Italian Immigrants of Highwood, Illinois* (1990), an oral history and series of essays, is based on interviews with elderly Italian immigrants from her grandparents' community.

Lucia Chiavola Birnbaum, who holds a doctorate in United States and European history, is an affiliated scholar of the Institute for Research on Women and Gender at Stanford University. Her *liberazione della donna: feminism in Italy* (1986, paperback 1988) won an American Book Award from the Before Columbus Foundation. Her book-in-progress is entitled *Dark Wheat and Red Poppies: Folklore and Italian Socialism, a Study in Popular Beliefs.*

Phyllis Capello's work has appeared in *Little Magazine, Mothering,* the *New York Quarterly,* and *Pulp.* She has also contributed to numerous anthologies, among which are *The Wind in Our Sails* (1982), *Mother/Poet* (1986), and *The Dream Book: An Anthology of Writings by Italian American Women.* She is currently working on two novels, *The Priest's Daughter* and *Our Lady's Field,* and a collection of poetry, *Everything Shifts to This Center.*

Peter Carravetta, an associate professor of Italian at Queens College of the City University of New York, is coeditor of the anthology *Postmoderno e letteratura* (Milano 1984) and author of a collection of critical studies, *Prefaces to the Diaphora: Rhetorics, Allegory, and the Interpretation of Postmodernity.* Founding editor of the journal *differentia: Review of Italian Thought,* he has published poetry in Italian and English as well as scholarly papers and essays on a variety of topics. Carravetta is the recipient of a Fulbright Fellowship for research at the University of Rome in 1990.

Robert Casillo, a professor of English at the University of Miami, is author of *The Genealogy of Demons: Anti-Semitism, Fascism, and the Myths of Ezra Pound.* He has written numerous articles on a variety of subjects, including Pound, Ruskin, Hemingway, Solzhenitsyn, Stendhal, Mme. de Stael, Italy, and Italian Americans. He is now completing two books: one on Ruskin and Pound, the other on Ruskin and Lewis Mumford.

Diana Cavallo, who teaches at the University of Pennsylvania, is currently at work on a novel, *Juniper Street Sketches.* She is author of *A Bridge of Leaves* (fiction) and *The Lower East Side: A Portrait in Time* (nonfiction), and has been anthologized in *The Dream Book: An Anthology of Writings by Italian American Women.* Formerly a director of the Westside Writers Workshop in New York City, a Fulbright Teaching Fellow, and a lecturer for the United States Information Service in Italy, she is listed in various *Who's Who* publications.

Arthur L. Clements teaches modern and Renaissance literature and creative writing at the State University of New York at Binghamton. In addition to his poetry, fiction, and essays appearing in numerous journals and anthologies, he has had published an edition of *John Donne's Poetry;* two critical books, *The Mystical Poetry of Thomas Traherne* and *Poetry of Contemplation: John Donne, George Herbert, Henry Vaughan, and the Modern Period;* and a book of poems, *Common Blessings,* which was awarded the 1988 American Literary Translators Association Award for translation into Italian and publication in a bilingual edition, *Benedizioni comuni.*

Celestino De Iuliis, dramatist, poet, and translator, has taught Italian in both the United States and Canada. His translations of Dario Fo, Luigi Pirandello, Michel Tremblay, and Jean Barbeau have been performed in Canada and Italy. His first book of verse, *Love's Sinning Song,* appeared in 1981. Presently preparing for the production of an original play, *I Love You, Mary Brown,* he is also well into his first novel, *Gazebo.*

Tina DeRosa's first book, *Paper Fish,* a novel, was published in 1980 with a grant from the National Endowment for the Arts. Her second book, *John Baptist Scalabrini, Father to the Migrants* (1987), is a biography of the founder of the Missionary Order of Saint Charles. She is currently working on a third book.

Diane di Prima, a second-generation American of Italian descent, was born in Brooklyn, New York. While living in Manhattan, she cofounded the New York Poets Theatre; founded the Poets Press, which published many new writers at the time; and became known as the most important woman writer of the Beat movement. For the past twenty years, she has been living in northern California. From 1980 to 1986, she taught hermetic and esoteric traditions in poetry at New College of California. She is one of the cofounders and teachers of the San Francisco Institute of Magical and Healing Arts. A new edition of her collected poems, *Pieces of a Song,* is forthcoming. Di Prima is the author of twenty-nine published books of poetry and prose, translated into over twenty languages. She is currently at work on *Not Quite Buffalo Stew,* a satire of California life; *Recollections of My Life as a Woman,* a memoir; and a book on Shelley as magician/poet.

Lawrence Ferlinghetti, who was born in New York in 1919, obtained an A.B. from the University of North Carolina, served in the Navy during World War II, and then received an M.A. in literature from Columbia University. In 1947 he moved to Paris where he earned a Doctorat de l'Université from the Sorbonne. In 1951 he returned to San Francisco, where in 1953 he and Peter D. Martin founded City Lights, the first all-paperback bookstore in the country. Under the City Lights imprint, Ferlinghetti began the Pocket Poets series, bringing out work by Antonin Artaud, Kenneth Rexroth, and William Carlos Williams, as well as many exciting new writers, such as Gregory Corso, Allen Ginsberg, Jack Kerouac, and Frank O'Hara. City Lights published Ferlinghetti's first book of poems, *Pictures from a Gone World* (1955). His other books of poetry include *A Coney Island of the Mind, Landscapes of Living and Dying, A Trip to Italy and France,* and *Endless Life: The Selected Poems (1955–1980).* Ferlinghetti has also written two collections of plays, *Routines* and *Unfair Arguments after Existence,* and two works of fiction, *Her* and *Mexican Night.* In 1968 he was honored with the Premio Internazionale di Poesie Etna-Taormina, Italy.

Jonathan Galassi was born in Seattle, Washington, in 1949. He has worked as a book editor since 1973 and is currently editor-in-chief of Farrar, Straus and Giroux in New York City. His publications include *Morning Run: Poems* (1988) and two volumes of translations from the work of Eugenio Montale, *Otherwise: Last and First Poems* (1984) and *The Second Life of Art: Selected Essays* (1982). He is currently preparing a translation of Montale's major poetry.

Kenneth Gangemi is Swedish on his mother's side. He was born in 1937, grew up in Scarsdale, New York, and graduated from Rensselaer Polytechnic Institute with a degree in engineering. He later attended San Francisco State College and Stanford University. He has published one collection of poetry, *Lydia* (1970), and four works of fiction: *Olt* (1969), *Corroboree* (1977), *The Volcanoes from Puebla* (1979) and *The Interceptor Pilot* (1980). He lives in New York City.

Fred L. Gardaphé is an associate professor of English at Columbia College in Chicago. His play, *Vinegar and Oil,* was produced in Chicago in 1987. He has published short fiction in many journals and reviews. With Anthony Julian Tamburri and Paolo A. Giordano, he is cofounder of *Voices in Italian Americana: A Literary and Cultural Review (VIA)* and is review editor of that journal as well. His articles on Italian/American literature have appeared in *MELUS, Misure critiche,* and other journals and newspapers. His latest essay, "My House Is Not Your House: Jerre Mangione and Italian/American Autobiography," will appear in *American Lives,* a forthcoming volume.

Sandra (Mortola) Gilbert, a professor of English at the University of California at Davis, has published four collections of poetry, including most recently *Blood Pressure* (1988). With Susan Gubar, she is coauthor of *The Madwoman in the Attic: The Woman Writer and the Nineteenth-Century Literary Imagination* (1979) and *No Man's Land: The Place of the Woman Writer in the Twentieth Century*—volume 1, *The War of the Words* (1988), and volume 2, *Sexchanges* (1989). In addition, she has published *Acts of Attention: The Poems of D. H. Lawrence* (1972) and with Gubar has coedited *Shakespeare's Sisters: Feminist Essays on Women Poets* (1979) and *The Norton Anthology of Literature by Women* (1985).

Maria Mazziotti Gillan, director of the Poetry Center at Passaic County College and editor of *Footwork: The Paterson Literary Review,* has won an American Literary Translator's Award (1987) and two New Jersey State Council on the Arts Fellowships in Poetry (1980 and 1985). Her books include *Winter Light* (1985), *Luce d'inverno* (bilingual, 1988), and *The Weather of Old Seasons* (1989). In addition, her work was published in *The Dream Book: An Anthology of Writings by Italian American Women*.

Dana Gioia, who was born in Los Angeles in 1950, works as an executive for a major American corporation and lives outside New York City. He received B.A. and M.B.A. degrees from Stanford University. His poems, essays, and translations have appeared in many magazines, including the *Hudson Review,* the *Nation,* the *New Yorker,* the *Paris Review,* and *Poetry.* With William Jay Smith, he coedited *Poems from Italy,* a comprehensive bilingual anthology of Italian poetry from the Middle Ages to the present. *Daily Horoscope,* his widely noted first collection of poems, appeared in 1986, and a collection of his literary essays and reviews will appear next year. In 1984 Gioia was chosen by *Esquire* for their first register of "Men and Women under 40 Who Are Changing the Nation."

Paolo A. Giordano, a professor of Italian at Loyola University (Chicago) and director and academic dean of that university's Rome campus, was born in Bordighera, Italy, and emigrated to this country in 1957. He has studied at Middlebury College, the University of Florence, and Indiana University, where he received his Ph.D. in Italian studies with a minor in art history. He is cofounder and coeditor of the journals *Italiana* and *Voices in Italian Americana: A Literary and Cultural Review (VIA).* He is currently working on a translation of the Renaissance comedy *Il barro.*

Daniela Gioseffi is one of a very few Italian/American women to be widely published by established presses as a poet and writer of fiction. Her poems have appeared in anthologies alongside the work of Emily Dickinson and Muriel Rukeyser, as well as in such magazines as *Antaeus, Choice,* the *Nation,* and the *Paris Review.* Her book of poems, *Eggs in the Lake,* and her novel, *The Great American Belly,* were praised in the United States and abroad. Her poetry and plays have received awards from the New York State Council on the Arts. Her sixth book, *Women on War: Global Voices for Survival,* won the 1990 American Book Award. She has published literary criticism in leading periodicals and is a member of the National Book Critics Circle. In 1990 her work was aired on National Public Radio as winner of the PEN Syndicated Fiction Award.

Salvatore La Puma received the Flannery O'Connor Award for Short Fiction in 1987 and an American Book Award in 1988 for his collection of stories, *The Boys of Bensonhurst.* Individual stories by him have appeared in the *Antioch Review,* the *Boston Review,* the *Kenyon Review,* the *Southern Review,* and *ZYZZYVA.* His novel, *A Time for Wedding Cake,* is forthcoming in January 1991.

Ben Lawton, an associate professor of Italian and film at Purdue University, was a founder of the university's recurring film conferences and was frequent editor of its *Film Studies Annuals.* He has written widely on Italian and Italian/American film and literature as well as edited *Literary and Socio-Political Trends in Italian Cinema.* The translator of Pier Paolo Pasolini's *Heretical Empiricism,* he cofounded Purdue's Conference on Romance Languages, Literatures, and Film and the *Romance Languages Annual.* He is currently working on a book on Italian/American filmmakers.

Lorraine Lawton teaches Italian and French at Purdue University. Her research includes women's studies as well as modernist and postmodernist theoretical trends and their impact on Italian, French, and American literature and cinema. The winner of several awards for her studies of nineteenth- and twentieth-century authors, she initiated the Department of Foreign Languages and Literatures Graduate Student Colloquia at Purdue. She is currently developing a cultural exchange program between Italian and American women writers, scholars, and filmmakers.

Jerre Mangione, author of ten books of fiction and nonfiction, was born in Rochester, New York, and grew up among scores of Sicilian relatives. His first book, *Mount Allegro,* recently reissued in paperback by its sixth American publisher, is the story of that experience. Other major works include *Reunion in Sicily, An Ethnic at Large,* and *A Passion for Sicilians.* His two novels are *The Ship and the Flame* and *Night Search.* One reviewer described *Night Search* as a "philosophical thriller."

Kenny Marotta, who teaches in the University of Virginia Young Writers Workshop, has held writing residencies at the University of Idaho and the University of Pittsburgh at Johnstown. Born in Boston and raised in Saint Louis, he now lives in Charlottesville, Virginia. He has published a novel, *A Piece of Earth* (1985), and several stories in the *Virginia Quarterly Review* and the *Western Humanities Review.* Recently he has completed a collection of related short stories and a novella.

Jerome Mazzaro teaches at the State University of New York at Buffalo. Born in Detroit, Michigan, the son of immigrant parents, he was educated in public schools and earned degrees from Wayne State University (A.B. 1954, Ph.D. 1963) and the University of Iowa (M.A. 1956). His publications include three books of poetry, *Changing the Windows* (1966), *The Caves of Love* (1985), and *Rubbings* (1985), as well as critical studies and a highly praised verse translation of Juvenal's *Satires* (1965). In 1964 he was awarded a Guggenheim Fellowship, and in 1979–80 he served as Hadley Fellow at Bennington College.

Ben Morreale was born in the United States but spent a good part of his childhood in Racalmuto, Sicily. He attended Brooklyn College and the Sorbonne in Paris, where he lived for seven years and from where he often returned to Sicily. His short stories have appeared in the *Antioch Review, Encounter,* and the *Paris Review.* He has published three novels with Sicily as a theme: *The Seventh Saracen, A Few Virtuous Men, Monday, Tuesday. . . Never Come Sunday.*

Franco Mulas is a tenured researcher in the English Department at the University of Sassari in Sardinia, Italy. Published widely on both English and American literature, he has translated into Italian, with a critical introduction, Robert Frost's "A Masque of Reason" and "A Masque of Mercy." In 1986 Mulas was awarded a NATO Fellowship for research on the relationship between Italian/American writers and American literary journals from 1900 to 1945. He conducted his research at the University of Chicago where he was a visiting scholar. Currently he is at work on a book entitled *The Italian Landscape in Hemingway's Novels.*

Adeodato Piazza Nicolai, poet and translator, was born in Vigo di Cadore, Italy, in 1944 and emigrated to the United States in 1959. Educated at Wabash College in Indiana and the University of Chicago, his work has appeared both in Italian and American literary publications. He is author of three volumes of poetry: *La visita di Rebecca* (1979), *I due volti di Janus* (poems and translations, 1980), and *La doppia finzione* (1988). Prof. Glauco Cambon presented a selection of Nicolai's dialect poetry in the Fall 1987 issue of *Forum italicum.*

Joseph Papaleo, chairman of the writing program at Sarah Lawrence College, has held guest professorships in Italy. He studied at Sarah Lawrence (B.A.), the University of Florence, Italy (Diploma), and Columbia University (M.A.). He is the author of two novels, *All the Comforts* and *Out of Place;* a book of poems, *Picasso at Ninety-One;* and numerous short stories appearing in, among others, *Attenzione,* the *Dial, Epoch, Harper's,* the *New Yorker,* the *Paris Review,* and *Penthouse.* He has translated Eugenio Montale's poetry and Dario Fo's theater. Papaleo has received grants from the Guggenheim Foundation and the New York State Creative Arts Public Service Award and has won the Ramapo Poetry Award.

Jay Parini is a professor of English at Middlebury College in Vermont. He has published numerous articles and books, including three novels, *The Love Run, Patch Boys,* and *The Last Station;* three books of poetry, *Singing in Time, Anthracite Country,* and *Town Life;* and a biography, *Theodore Roethke: An American Romantic.*

Samuel J. Patti, an independent scholar who lives in Pittsburgh, Pennsylvania, teaches part time and owns and operates La Prima Espresso Company. He has done graduate studies in Italian at the University of Pittsburgh and the University of Pennsylvania, where his dissertation on Italian/American literature is in progress. For two years he served as lecturer in Italian at the University of Virginia. Patti's articles include "Bloomfield: An Italian Working-Class Neighborhood," coauthored with William Simons and George Herman, and "Autobiography: The Root of the Italian-American Narrative."

Diane Raptosh, who is a visiting assistant professor of English at the College of Idaho, has published her poetry in *la bella figura,* the *Kansas Quarterly,* the *Malahat Review,* the *Michigan Quarterly Review,* and the *Mid-American Review.* In addition, her work appears in a variety of anthologies including *Idaho's Poetry: A Centennial Anthology* and *Anthology of Magazine Verse and Yearbook of American Poetry* (1988).

Vilma Ricci, an active community worker and businesswoman, was born in Toronto and has been involved in the Italian Canadian literary scene for over twenty years. As translator and researcher, she collaborated on the publication of *Italian Canadian Voices: An Anthology of Poetry and Prose* and has written or edited various articles, memoirs, and histories on the Italian immigrant experience in Canada. Her first publication, *Quebec Avenue and Other Stories,* appeared in 1985. At present she is working on *Cairo,* a collection of poems described as midlife juvenilia.

Giose Rimanelli, a professor of Italian and comparative literature at the State University of New York at Albany, was born in Casacalenda (Molise), Italy, in 1925 and is an American citizen. He is the author of several books, among which are the novels *The Day of the Lion* and *Original Sin.*

Lisa Ruffolo, who has taught fiction writing at the University of Wisconsin at Madison and Edgewood College, is currently a principal in The Software Resource, a firm specializing in writing computer-user manuals. In addition to her recently published first collection of short fiction, *Holidays,* her short fiction has appeared in the *Beloit Fiction Journal, Mademoiselle,* and the *Short Story Review.*

John Paul Russo is a professor of English at the University of Miami in Florida. He received his doctorate from Harvard University and has been awarded a Rockefeller

Fellowship and two Fulbright Fellowships to Italy. His publications include *Alexander Pope: Tradition and Identity, I. A. Richards: His Life and Work,* and essays in the history of criticism. The city of Gela presented him with a gold medal for his contribution to cultural relations between Italy and the United States. He has been visiting professor at the universities of Rome and Genoa.

Felix Stefanile, a professor emeritus of English at Purdue University, was born in 1920. His poems, essays, and translations from Italian poetry have been published widely, and he is the author of nine volumes of poetry and poetry in translation. He and his wife, Selma, are the editors and publishers of one of the oldest poetry presses in the United States, Sparrow Press, established in 1954.

Anthony Julian Tamburri teaches Italian at Purdue University. His research interests focus chiefly on Italian studies in the nineteenth and twentieth centuries, including literary theory, the avant-garde, literature, and the arts. He has written *Of Saltimbanchi and Incendiari: Aldo Palazzeschi and Avant-Gardism in Italy* (1990) and has another book forthcoming, *Per una lettura retrospettiva. Prose giovanili di Aldo Palazzeschi.* In addition, he is cofounding coeditor of *Voices in Italian Americana: A Literary and Cultural Review (VIA)* and cofounder of Purdue's Conference on Romance Languages, Literatures, and Films and the *Romance Languages Annual.*

Joseph Tusiani came to the United States in 1947. An internationally known poet and translator of Italian classics, his major translations include the *Complete Poems of Michelangelo,* Tasso's *Jerusalem Delivered* and *Creation of the World.* Writing in Italian, Latin, and English, he is the author of three collections of verse, *Rind and All, The Fifth Season,* and *Gente Mia and Other Poems.* Among his many awards, Tusiani was the first American to win the Greenwood Prize of the Poetry Society of England, and he also received the Alice Fay di Castagnola Award from the Poetry Society of America. Most recently he has published the first of three volumes of a prose autobiography, *La parola difficile.*

Robert Viscusi is executive officer of the Wolfe Institute for the Humanities at Brooklyn College of the City University of New York. He is the author of *Max Beerbohm, Or the Dandy Dante: Rereading with Mirrors* and has edited the volume *Victorian Learning for Browning Institute Studies.* His work in literary theory, nineteenth- and twentieth-century British literature, Anglo/Italian literary relations, and Italian/American writing has been widely published.

Ralph Fasanella was born to Italian immigrant parents in New York City on Labor Day in 1914. His father was an iceman, his mother a buttonhole maker. At age nine the child dropped out of school to work with his father, and at fourteen his formal education ended when he "graduated" from a Catholic reform school. Later he fought against fascism in Spain, was a candidate for the New York City Council, and worked as a laborer and CIO organizer in the 1930s and 1940s. Toward the end of World War II, he began to sketch and then to paint, first in gouache, later in oil. His early response to the canvas was unrestrained, passionate, and emotional, and those early paintings exhibited a stunning sense of movement and dynamism. Fasanella's later work is more focused, structured, and complex. The subtle gestures of his figures speak of the passion and pain and vitality of the American industrial working class. Since the early seventies, Fasanella has received critical acclaim and widespread recognition. His paintings have been exhibited throughout this country and in Europe. His work has been the subject of documentaries by the British Broadcasting Corporation, the Public Broadcasting System, and the Columbia Broadcasting System.

Index

The following index records names, titles of written and visual texts, and other items found in both our introductory material and in the section of critical essays. We would like to thank Sarah Hill for her indispensable assistance in the compilation of this index.